Financial Accounting Theory

– An Accounting Quality Approach

Emmeli Runesson Niuosha Samani Jan Marton

Studentlitteratur

Studentlitteratur publishes digitally as well as in print formats. Studentlitteratur's printed matter is sustainably produced, both as regards paper and the printing process.

Art. No 39652
ISBN 978-91-44-12059-1
1st edition
1:1

studentlitteratur.se
Studentlitteratur AB, Lund

Cover design: Jens Martin/Signalera
Cover illustration: Jag_cz/Shutterstock

Design: Jesper Sjöstrand/Metamorf Design
Images: Shutterstock

Printed by Interak, Poland 2018

CONTENTS

Part III Accounting quality in capital markets research

Part IV Accounting quality, managerial incentives and governance mechanisms

Part V Accounting quality and financial statement items

LETTER TO THE READER

Dear reader,

As a reader of this book, you are in a fortunate position. You are about to enter the exciting world of accounting theory! But why accounting theory? Would it not be better to focus on more technical aspects of the accounting process, such as bookkeeping or how to prepare financial statements in practice? The simple answer is a resounding "no."

We take accounting theory to mean the overarching ideas and key conceptual structures that form the basis of financial accounting. Knowledge of these, we believe, will aid you in the understanding of why accounting standards are designed the way they are, why firms' financial statements look the way they do, and what the consequences of this are. This in turn facilitates your future work as a preparer, auditor or analyst of financial statements, or even as a researcher or standard-setter.

Purpose When we set out to write this book, we wanted to convey the idea that financial accounting is about closing information gaps and increasing the level of transparency between firms and their stakeholders. In presenting the theories that have been the most influential in the field of financial accounting over the years, we therefore reflect on how they relate to the widely accepted objective in financial accounting—to be *useful* and meet the information needs of capital market users. Accounting that helps fulfill this objective is considered to be of **high quality**.

We intentionally keep references to theories *contextual*. Instead of isolating and discussing one theory at a time, we refer to relevant theoretical arguments and beliefs in the context of capital markets, accounting quality and user needs. That is, we structure the text around the quest for high-quality financial statements. We also emphasize empirical research, because we believe that findings therein clearly illustrate the theoretical foundations and academic views on the role of (high-quality) accounting.

In introducing the reader to prominent theories and research in the field of financial accounting, we respond to calls for more *research-based education*. Some references in this book are now considered old, even "classics," and they are found in every other book on financial accounting theory. Other references are to newer studies. These may one day become classics, or they simply illustrate current streams of literature. We want you, the reader, to be familiar with both types of studies in order to better understand how knowledge about financial accounting has been and is being developed.

The reader This book is intended for you who are studying accounting at a Master's level or an advanced Bachelor's level. A general understanding of financial accounting and bookkeeping, as well as familiarity with accounting standards, is assumed. Prior knowledge of accounting and the logic of balance sheets, income statements and financial reports in general allows the reader to fully digest and appreciate the complexity of the issues discussed in the text. Although this book is not directly based on any particular regulatory regime, International Financial Reporting Standards serve as the main basis for discussion.

Using the book The chapters are designed to be read in chronological order rather than function as stand-alone units. In each chapter, key learning objectives are provided before the main text, whereas key words and a summary appear at the end.

There are many theories, ideas or hypotheses in the financial accounting literature. They come with labels such as agency theory, legitimacy theory, signaling theory and the efficient market hypothesis. These are applicable and can have explanatory power in different contexts and they all have something unique to say about accounting as an economic or social phenomenon. However, we believe that by organizing a textbook based on the above categorizations, the text will come out highly fragmented. Instead, we present accounting in a context, as a process and a product, with different actors—researchers, standard-setters, preparers and users of financial reporting—all of whom are interested in the qualities and *quality* of this process and product. The quality of accounting, including the effectiveness of accounting as a tool for communication (or obfuscation), is the common denominator. Having said that, the theories and hypotheses mentioned above are an integral part of the study of said process and product, meaning we refer to the theories and hypotheses whenever they are relevant to the discussion at hand.

A few typographical features are used throughout the text to help you recognize what type of content is covered: **Boldface words** indicate key terms one should pay special attention to. They relate to the learning outcomes and tend to be subject-specific, such as **accruals quality** or the **efficient market hypothesis**. Meanwhile, *italics* are simply used for emphasis.

Text boxes provide in-depth material that aid readers in understanding more complex issues. Certain examples, citations and technical explanations are found here.

Now, all that is left to do is wish you a pleasant journey into the world of financial accounting. Happy reading!

Gothenburg, August 2018

Emmeli Runesson, Niuosha Samani and *Jan Marton*

Part I

Accounting fundamentals, accounting theory and the information environment

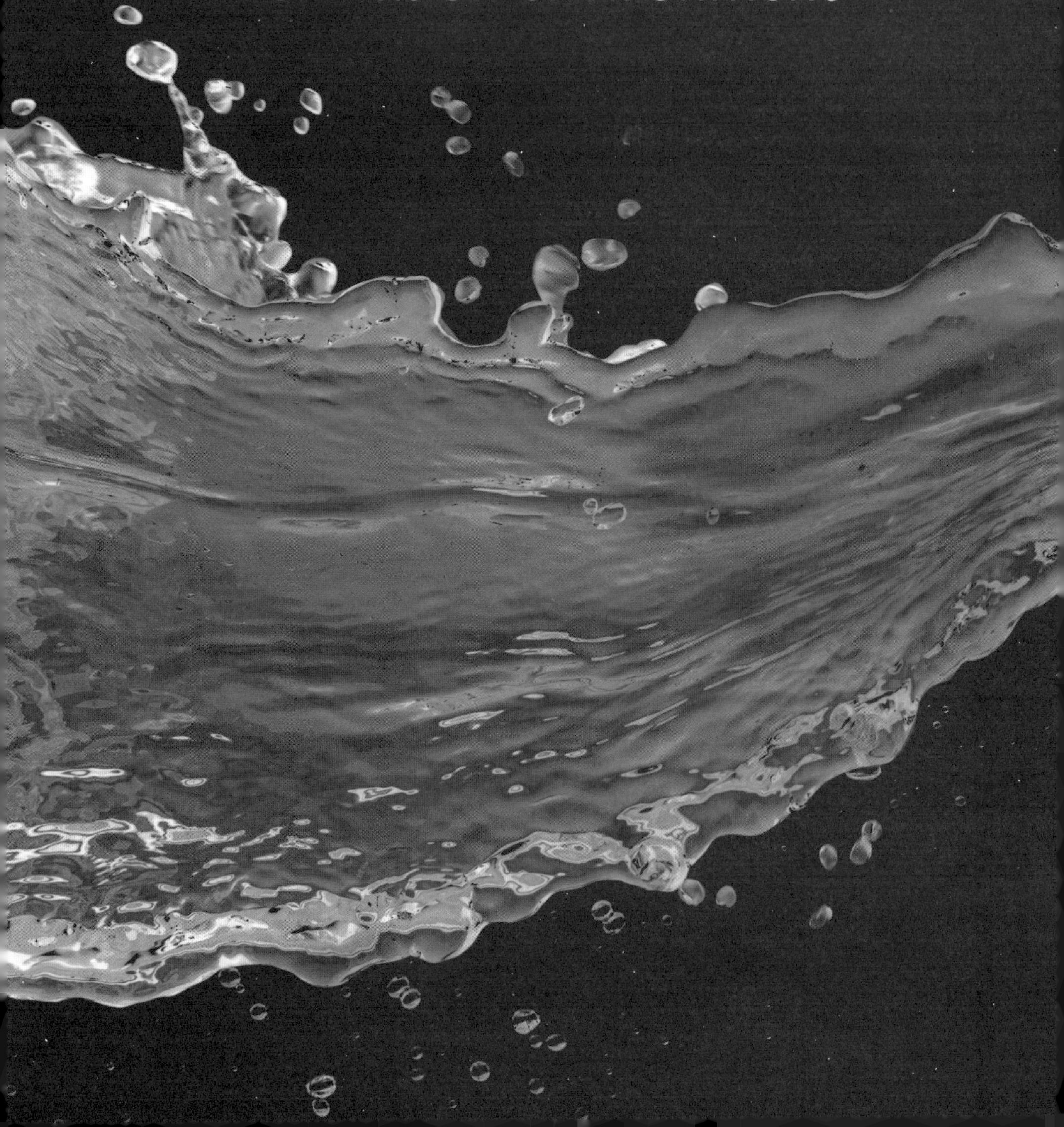

The first part of the book, particularly Chapter 1, introduces the key concepts, ideas and theories used in the field of financial accounting. By highlighting the financial reporting context, which encompasses the roles of financial reporting and the actors involved, we seek to show the significance of accounting quality in relation to the theories employed. Accounting quality is a key concept in the subject of accounting, for in being a measure of the informativeness and usefulness of the information, it affects the decision-making of capital market participants and the effectiveness of firm contracts. Much research is explicitly or implicitly referring to the quality of the accounts when assessing the role and effectiveness of financial reports. Consequently, it is relevant to consider the **determinants** of accounting quality, including the standard-setting regime, the quality of enforcement and monitoring mechanisms, as well as the incentives of management. We suggest that accounting quality may be viewed as the common denominator of the theories that have primarily influenced the field.

In Chapter 2 we introduce some well-established definitions of what a theory is and assert that there are few actual **accounting theories** and far from one unified theory of accounting. There are, however, commonly employed theories and hypotheses used in the field of financial accounting. These are briefly reviewed and may be used as a springboard for discussions on a variety of topics covered in this book. Most of these are **positive** – as opposed to **normative**. The latter take value positions and, by using logical reasoning, aim to prescribe how something should be accounted for and why. The former, on the other hand, aim to explain and predict outcomes based on empirical observations and draw conclusions from statistical associations. While the existence of conceptually based accounting standards seems to imply that accounting theory is fundamentally normative, the development of normative theories is not independent of positive theories. Although the objectives of accounting may be determined using a normative approach, positive theories aid in examining the consequences of defined objectives or the effectiveness of policies implemented to achieve these. So, if the objective of standard-setting bodies such as the IASB is to achieve high-quality accounting via enhanced transparency and comparability of financial statements, research employing a positive approach is needed to examine how transparency and comparability are achieved, as well the consequences of corresponding policies and practices.

We define high-quality accounting as **useful** accounting and present several perspectives one may use for understanding usefulness. The **capital market**

perspective holds a central position in such a discussion. Both historically and today, capital providers are considered the main, **intended users** of financial reports. Intended users, including investors and creditors, require high-quality information to support them in their decision-making. Given that the intended users are capital market users, the prominent use of market-based theories in accounting is not surprising. In Chapter 3, we explore the notion of efficient markets and the implications of this for financial accounting. We also consider the situation in which one group of market participants knows more than another group; that is, when there is information asymmetry. Information asymmetry has major consequences for capital markets and leads to inefficiencies. The role played by accounting information in overcoming potential informational inefficiencies is discussed in the last sections of Part I.

CHAPTER 1

Introduction

Learning outcomes

Upon completion of this chapter, you will:

- Have gained insight into the context of financial accounting and the link between the different actors that affect, or are affected by, the financial reporting process.
- Understand the role of capital markets for the shaping, evaluation and theorization of financial accounting.
- Have an understanding of some of the underlying concepts and ideas presented in this book.

ACCOUNTING CAN BE TRACED BACK to ancient civilizations. Largely coinciding with the abandonment of hunter-gatherer cultures, its emergence was driven by the need to keep records of more complex human transactions. The ever greater level of complexity of exchanges was made possible by improved record-keeping in turn helped foster further exchanges. What thus took place was a coevolutionary process of transactions and the recording of those transactions. Whereas the development of more advanced civilizations has been attributed to the creation of a collective awareness enabled by writing in general, it becomes apparent that the development of complex economic interaction and cooperation is likely to have been enabled through systematic keeping of accounts. Complex human societies therefore owe much of their qualities and wealth to the institutionalized memory and opportunities for exchange created by accounting.[1]

Adopting a European perspective, increased trade in the 13th to 16th centuries, the development of credit and organizations through which capital could be put to use (joint ventures and partnerships rather than limited liability firms at that time) helped fuel the need for accounts to keep track of the movement and use of capital. Initially, accounting was primarily meant for the owner of the enterprise himself, who simultaneously served as the manager. Profits were often estimated or recognized at the end of a project. With *going*

1 See discussion in Basu and Waymire (2006)

concerns being less common, accruals were of little or no use. With the separation of capital providers from the actors conducting business, the need for accounting increased.

Double-entry bookkeeping was born during the Italian Renaissance and the first records encountered date back as early as the 13th century. Structured methods of accounting enabled investors to see how their money was actually being put to use and helped ensure that it was not squandered. In 1494, *Summa de Arithmetica, Geometria, Proportioni et Proportionalita* (Summary of arithmetic, geometry, proportions and proportionality) was published by the friar Luca Pacioli (see Text Box 1.1). First and foremost, it was a work of mathematics, but it also contained *Particularis de computis et Scripturis* (Particulars of Reckonings and Their Recording), which was about double-entry bookkeeping (see also Text Box 1.2). This was the first accounting publication ever, consistent with the printing technology having been used for less than a hundred years at the time and only for a few years in Venice, where *Summa* was printed.

Text Box 1.1 **Pacioli's Particulars of Reckonings and Their Recording**

An extract from *Complete translation of Pacioli (Geijsbeek et al., 1914) / Section Nine–Treatise XI. / Particulars of Reckonings and Their Recording. / Chapter 1. Things that are necessary to the good merchant and the method of keeping a ledger with its journal, in Venice and elsewhere.*

In order that the subjects of His Illustrious Highness, the most honorable and magnanimous Duke of Urbino (D. U. D. S.–Docis Urbini Domini Serenissimi), may have all the rules that a good merchant needs, I decided to compile, in addition to the subjects already treated in this work, a special treatise which is much needed. I have compiled it for this purpose only, i.e., that they (the subjects) may whenever necessary find in it everything with regard to accounts and their keeping. And thereby I wish to give them enough rules to enable them to keep all their accounts and books in an orderly way. For, as we know, there are three things needed by any one who wishes to carry on business carefully. The most important of these is cash or any equivalent, according to that saying, *Unum aliquid necessarium est substantia*. Without this, business can hardly be carried on.

It has happened that many without capital of their own but whose credit was good, carried on big transactions and by means of their credit, which they faithfully kept, became very wealthy. We became acquainted with many of these throughout Italy. In the great republics nothing was considered superior to the word of the good merchant, and oaths were taken on the word of a good merchant. On this confidence rested the faith they had in the trustworthiness of an upright merchant. And this is not strange, because, according to the Christian religion, we are saved by faith, and without it it is impossible to please God.

The second thing necessary in business is to be a good bookkeeper and ready mathematician. To become such we have given above (in the foregoing sections of the book) the rules and canons necessary to each transaction, so that any diligent reader can understand it all by himself. If one has not understood this first part well, it will be useless for him to read the following.

The third and last thing is to arrange all the transactions in such a systematic way that one may understand each one of them at a glance, i.e., by the debit (*debito*–owed to) and credit (*credito*–owed by) method. This is very essential to merchants, because, without making the entries systematically it would be impossible to conduct their business, for they would have no rest and their minds would always be troubled. For this purpose

I have written this treatise, in which, step by step, the method is given of making all sorts of entries. Although one cannot write out every essential detail for all cases, nevertheless a careful mind will be able, from what is given, to make the application to any particular case.

This treatise will adopt the system used in Venice, which is certainly to be recommended above all the others, for by means of this, one can find his way in any other. We shall divide this treatise in two principal parts. The one we shall call the Inventory, and the other, Disposition (arrangement). We shall talk first of the one and then of the other, according to the order contained in the accompanying Table of Contents, from which the reader may take what he needs in his special case.

He who wants to know how to keep a ledger and its journal in due order must pay strict attention to what I shall say. To understand the procedure well, we will take the case of one who is just starting in business, and tell how he must proceed in keeping his accounts and books so that at a glance he may find each thing in its place. For, if he does not put each thing in its own place, he will find himself in great trouble and confusion as to all his affairs, according to the familiar saying, *Ubi non est ordo, ibi est confusio* (Where there is no order, there is confusion). In order to give a perfect model to every merchant, we will divide the whole system, as we have said, in two principal parts, and we will arrange these so clearly that one can get good results from them.

During the Age of Discovery (15th to 18th centuries in Europe), a common type of business venture was trade voyages by sea. Seeking funding via joint-stock companies, which allowed multiple shareholders to own stock jointly and thus share the investment risks, became increasingly popular and these companies partially came to replace trade guilds and medieval partnerships. Buying stock in a particular voyage was not uncommon, but as there was not necessarily enough cash at the end of the voyage, stockholders were instead paid with stocks in future voyages (a precursor to the modern stock dividend). The accumulation of such stocks eventually called for the issuance of permanent stock in all future voyages. This in turn led to the need for the periodic recognition of profit and loss, as well as a balance sheet. The importance and prevalence of non-current assets also expanded in this setting, as did inventories, and this had an impact on the relevance of keeping track of values of non-monetary assets.

With the advent of industrialization in the 19th century, the need for financing on a large scale increased substantially, leading to an increased distance between capital providers and management. Further, the operations of manufacturing firms do not have an obvious end, so the need for periodical reporting increased. As a consequence, the use of accruals increased, and with that, the complexity of the accounting system. It is not a coincidence that auditing firms and professional accounting organizations started appearing in the latter half of the 19th century.

Much of the need for financial accounting is related to the separation of capital providers from management. In this book, our choice to focus on capital providers and the role of financial accounting in relation to these users of corporate reports is believed to be justified by reference to history and how financial accounting came about and developed historically.

Text Box 1.2 **Double-entry bookkeeping**

It may come as a surprise to many that the concept of zero is relatively modern, and negative numbers were even considered fictitious and suspicious as late as in 16th century Europe! Some mathematicians could accept negative numbers in theory, but considered them nonsense in practice. Although negative numbers were likely accepted in the field of commerce before that of mathematics, Pacioli, being a mathematician, was thought to fully reject negative numbers and actively sought to avoid them. Whereas the balance sheet equation A = L + E (Assets = Liabilities + Equity) might have been expressed as A – L = E, this would have necessitated minus signs and, indeed, negative numbers (Peters and Emery, 1978). This is believed to have played a significant role in the development of double-entry bookkeeping. The inherent duality in bookkeeping, caused by the fact that any transaction requires at least two parties (a recipient and a contributor, if you will), could not be solved by subtraction as we think of the term. The recording of debits and credits—the essence of double-entry bookkeeping—was introduced as a workaround in the absence of negative numbers.

1.1 Perspectives on useful accounting—a utilitarian view

We started this chapter by very briefly recounting how financial accounting came about historically; as business transactions became more complex and businesses grew in importance and influence, reliable statements of profits and losses became essential. Not least in the age of industrialization, external capital providers needed information about the financial health of the entrepreneurial endeavors they had funded. It follows that to speak of accounting theory without exploring **accounting quality** is to overlook what permeates any serious attempt to discern, decide and describe the purpose of accounting and how it should be shaped.

"Accounting quality" is sometimes used in certain specific applications, such as when one is interested in the quality of earnings or the quality of corporate disclosures, but this use for the term is too narrow. Ultimately, quality is what standard-setters are concerned with when designing financial accounting standards, it is what theorists are concerned with when attempting to explain the purpose of accounting or what affects accounting outcomes and it is what empirical researchers attempt to evaluate when studying associations between accounting outcomes and a wide range of economic factors.

The question of how to distinguish "good" from "bad" accounting may seem deceptively simple. However, in order for *quality* to mean anything, one must have an idea of what distinguishes high quality from low quality. We take the perspective that accounting should be **utilitarian**; that is, it should be useful. Thus, we say that:

High quality = Usefulness

This definition requires us to identify the **intended user**. Below, we present some of the most common user perspectives. It is worthwhile noting that they need not be mutually exclusive; meaning that different perspectives do not necessarily require distinct accounting treatments for the financial statements to be useful. Meanwhile, it is unlikely that a single set of financial statements can meet *all* user needs.

1.1.1 Economic (capital market) perspective

The capital market or economic perspective is the most dominant among researchers as well as standard-setters. Central to this perspective is the idea that accounting has economic consequences—for all capital market participants as well as the economy as a whole. Capital markets can serve the individual firm and its capital providers, both of which seek to gain from engaging in economic transactions with each other (a microeconomic perspective). In order for capital markets to function efficiently and for there to be efficient capital allocation, information is needed. Financial accounting constitutes an important source of information in this context. Efficient capital allocation is not only beneficial for the firm and individual investors, but also has implications for the economy on an aggregate level (a macroeconomic perspective).

As pointed out below, accounting may be seen as a communication device and as such it constitutes a transfer of information (a transaction) between economic actors. Now, take a moment to consider basic economic theory. Although overly simplistic, neoclassical economics models portray markets as being perfect and assume **zero transaction costs**. If there are no transaction costs, accounting is not needed, since all actors in such a market already have all of the available information. This assumption clearly has to be relaxed in order to even begin considering the usefulness of accounting. Instead, **information asymmetry** between market participants is introduced as a potential obstacle to successful economic exchanges. Overcoming this asymmetry is indeed one of the main objectives of accounting, and the meaning of "useful" accounting may then be deduced from this:

> Useful (and consequently high-quality) accounting is that which provides users with such information to let them make informed decisions with respect to the decision models they employ.

Such a definition, naturally, is of little use in and of itself since both a user and a decision model must be specified. For example, we may specify that the user is a capital provider and that the decisions concern buying, holding or selling stock, controlling and monitoring management or, alternatively, giving or withdrawing credit. We think of this as a **capital market perspective** on accounting. When individual firms and investors are in focus, we adopt a **microeconomic perspective**.

Due to the role of external investors and creditors in the development of accounting, it is not strange that the objective of financial reporting is often stated in terms of its usefulness to these parties. However, a distinction between the investor and the creditor may be necessary, as their information needs differ slightly (see Text Box 1.3).

Investors as users Investors are interested in the value created by the firm as this value represents the return available to investors. Much emphasis is placed on *future earnings*, as these represent the primary accounting measure of the value added in operations. However, investors only have information about a firm's *current* (and historic) earnings. Therefore, the quality of earnings can be stated as the degree to which current (reported) earnings serve as an indicator of future earnings (Penman, 2010, p. 607). Apart from deciding whether to buy, hold or sell shares, investors—via the board of directors—require high-quality earnings

Text Box 1.3 **Investors versus creditors**

It may appear that the equity investor is "more important" than the creditor when discussing the roles of accounting in relation to capital providers. The median debt-to-equity ratio for Swedish firms listed on the Stockholm Stock Exchange as of 2014 was 38%, so this is perhaps understandable, but a key reason why investors may be considered *the* main users of firms' financial reports is that they are often smaller and have a smaller stake in the firm individually, making them more vulnerable to misrepresentation in the publicly available information. Meanwhile, a typical creditor, such as a bank, may have large positions in an individual firm and is thus less likely to be able to diversify away the risk posed by its lending decisions. As a result, it is more likely to demand and receive inside information that is not easily accessible to individual investors. This is believed to hold even in spite of a large number of institutional investors with large holdings. An additional reason why equity investors are seen as important is that they are the ones with decision-making power in the firm. They are the ones appointing management and they may also replace management should they want to (through the board of directors).

numbers that reflect the underlying performance of the firm in order to evaluate the managerial abilities of the executives and compensate them accordingly. More specifically, high-quality earnings play a key role in enhancing the efficiency of the monitoring performed by boards by providing reliable information on past decisions by managers. Here, as opposed to above, what are emphasized are *past earnings*.

Assuming a certain accounting treatment leads to a given earnings number, one might ask whether this end product is of high quality and whether the process through which the number was produced is of high quality. In research, one therefore attempts to create *proxies* for high-quality earnings. When one reads about the persistence of earnings, the incidence of abnormal accruals or the value relevance of earnings, what is implicitly alluded to is the quality of the financial statements and/or the system used to produce them (we return to these measures in Chapter 7) and their usefulness for shareholders.

Notably, however, accounting quality is not only about earnings. Another main concern from a capital market perspective is what should be included in the financial reports as supplementary disclosures. Potential disclosures may be of a quantitative kind, reflecting financial data not deemed appropriate to include in the primary financial statements or other non-financial but quantifiable data, such as information on employees. Disclosures may also be of a more qualitative kind and may therefore be referred to as "narrative" reports, such as management's discussion and analysis (MD&A). As we discover in coming chapters, disclosures can have a real economic effect on capital markets by reducing information asymmetries.

Creditors as users Creditors focus on somewhat different aspects of the information set compared to investors. For them, liquidity and the ability of a firm to pay back its debts are of central importance. Accordingly, the financial statements should be transparent with respect to the firm's ability to do just that. The balance sheet, showing the assets that in the event of delinquency could be liquidated, as well as the debt burden in the form of liabilities and their urgency to be repaid, is naturally of special interest. Current earnings and the shareholders' equity are generally secondary in importance to creditors. Having said that, earnings are obviously relevant in evaluating the prospects of the firm, while the firm's equity (in the form of accumulated earnings and other shareholder capital injections into the firm) constitutes funds that may be used toward debt repayment.

Regulated balance sheets, on which assets are sorted according to liquidity and liabilities are sorted based on whether they are current or non-current, reflect times in which a creditor perspective was adopted to a much larger degree. In order to make the balance sheet fully consistent with the investor's point of view, *strategic* or *analytical* balance sheets might be created by reformulating them so that assets and liabilities are instead sorted based on whether they derive from operating or financing activities. Exactly how the financial statements are shaped may be thought of as a point to reflect upon in relation to accounting quality, given that it is costly for users to process and interpret the information (i.e., reformulate financial statements).

As an example of how the presentation of information can have consequences for the perceived accounting quality, one may consider whether creditors concerned with debt covenant violations may be affected by whether certain liabilities are formally recognized on the balance sheet or simply mentioned in the supplementary disclosures.

From a creditor perspective, high-quality accounting represents the debt portion of a firm's balance sheet in a way that is faithful to the underlying economics. This entails correctly labeling liabilities as liabilities (where "correctly" is open to debate). What constitutes a liability may at first seem obvious, but throughout the history of standard-setting, definitions have changed, as have recognition requirements. For example, the IASB's definition of liabilities was recently changed (in March 2018). Furthermore, the distinction between a liability, a provision and a contingent liability is subject to judgment, while the distinction between liabilities and equity may be controversial (with some instruments including features of both). Even when definitions are clear in theory, the application of those definitions can cause practical difficulties for preparers, thereby reducing the usefulness of the financial statements to the reader.

The majority of accounting theories adopting a capital market perspective are interested in what makes accounting useful to capital providers, either with the aim of *prescribing* how the accounting should be designed in order to be useful for lending, investment or monitoring activities, or with the purpose of describing *what actually determines* accounting outcomes and their usefulness for capital market users. What is considered useful may then also vary depending on the above activities.

So far we have assumed the perspective of individual actors in capital markets. Meanwhile, from a **macroeconomic perspective**, good accounting could be said to be that which helps achieve the greatest allocational efficiency in an economy and, ultimately, the highest economic growth. Information asymmetry constitutes an obstacle for achieving these objectives, just as it constitutes an obstacle for individual investors and creditors.

Capital allocation occurs via capital markets, so in that sense, the two perspectives mentioned so far are closely entwined. However, accounting may have more "direct" effects on economic growth. Some claim recent economic crises, such as the one originating in the US subprime mortgage market in 2007, were—if not caused—exacerbated by current accounting policies. For example, there has been a debate about the role of fair value accounting and mark-to-market valuation approaches in creating financial bubbles.[2]

Another example of how different accounting treatments may have macroeconomic effects is by considering loan loss provisioning in banks. For example, when banks make provisions for losses on delinquent loans, different accounting rules may result in more or less timely provisions. If a rule or standard delays provisions by having high requirements on the verifiability of a potential loss, then signals concerning upcoming losses may be given to the market too late. If many banks collectively delay their provisions, deferring expenses to bad times, this will have a potentially pro-cyclical effect on the economy (Perez et al., 2008). This is because such behavior is bound to prevent healthy restrictions on lending when the economy is still running at full throttle, thereby exacerbating economic downturns. Some would say that delayed recognition of losses in banks was yet another contributor to the economic crisis in 2007 and onwards (Marton and Runesson, 2017).

From a macroeconomic perspective, useful accounting is that which aids the economy on an aggregate level to achieve its objectives of growth and prosperity.

1.1.2 Social (stakeholder) perspective

Although standard-setters and mainstream accounting research adopt an economic perspective when it comes to determining the usefulness of accounting, there are alternative views one might consider. For example, from the perspective of some stakeholders, "true" earnings should also reflect social or environmental costs. According to this view, a firm's operations do not only affect the firm's financiers, or even its employees. There are wider consequences of doing business, and these should be taken into account when considering good accounting. For example, a firm's activities may have a social or environmental impact imposing costs on society not borne by the firm's owners (i.e., there are *externalities*). In economics, externalities are any benefits or costs borne by parties other than those controlling them. As a consequence, certain goods or services may be over- or under-produced, since actual costs and benefits may be under- or overestimated by a producer of such goods or services. Whenever there are significant externalities, the markets in question suffer from inefficiencies. To the extent that certain costs are not reflected in reported earnings, they constitute "hidden" costs from the point of view of other stakeholders (or, indeed, society). It could be claimed that such earnings are *not* "true" or representative of central underlying value creation and that reported earnings should reflect these costs in order to be useful for various stakeholders. At the very least, it may be desirable to have high-quality disclosures regarding the social and environmental impact of a firm's operations. For example, *integrated reporting*, which combines financial accounting with sustainability reporting, is likely to represent higher-quality accounting from a social perspective.

2 Although fair value accounting has practical implementation problems, it includes theoretical advantages; to suggest that historical cost accounting is the remedy is thus claimed by some to be based on faulty reasoning (see Laux and Leuz, 2009).

1.1.3 Taxation perspective

High-quality accounting takes on yet another meaning if tax authorities are the intended users. Because tax authorities do not make decisions where the outcomes are contingent on the future performance of the firm, the interest does not lie in the ability of earnings to predict future value added *per se*. Instead, tax authorities are interested in historic earnings reflecting performance in a fiscal year. High-quality earnings from a taxation perspective imply that earnings have been determined in accordance with tax regulation, so that the tax authorities, on the basis of financial statements (or tax returns), can determine the amount of tax owed by the firm for a given year. The extent to which earnings reflect underlying value creation is of secondary importance.[3]

Frequently, there is little correspondence between accounting quality from a capital market perspective and a taxation perspective. The objectives of capital market users are related to value creation (investors) or financial stability (creditors), as discussed above. Tax authorities, on the other hand, are concerned with firms following tax regulation. Tax regulation, in turn, is determined by the political system and based on political objectives. For example, politicians may want to support investments in tangible assets by allowing faster depreciation (and tax deductions) of such assets, even though the tax depreciation does not correspond to useful life. This is the case in Sweden and many other industrialized countries.

Because of the different objectives, many accounting standard frameworks are explicitly not intended for tax purposes. Such is the case of both **International Financial Reporting Standards (IFRS)** and **US Generally Accepted Accounting Principles (GAAP)**. Individual countries may still base their tax reporting on IFRS, but this is unusual.

1.2 Financial accounting in a capital market context

One assumption we made from the start is that the **preparer** of financial reports is a firm. Even though we focus on accounting for firms (business entities), we still recognize that the discussion may to some extent be relevant for other entities (e.g., the public sector).

As always, it is important to contextualize the phenomena one is attempting to learn more about. In this case, we need to consider which factors (**determinants**) affect the financial reporting process, what is the ultimate outcome (**consequences**) of this process and what constitutes high-quality accounting (see Figure 1.1). We return to these three ideas—the definitions, determinants and consequences—of accounting quality throughout this book.

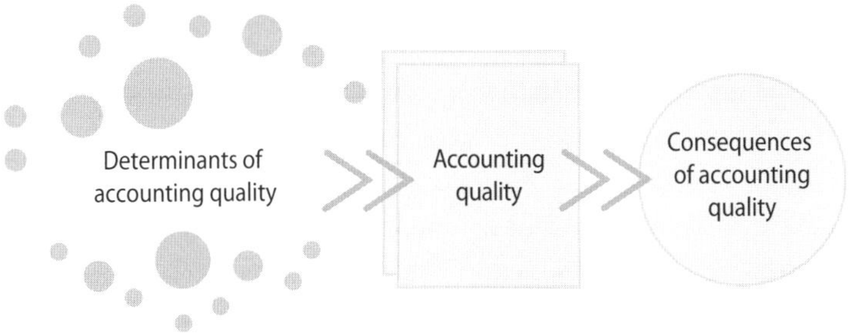

Figure 1.1
Accounting quality and its determinants and consequences in a capital market context

3 Of course, the observant reader notes that current or past performance are dependent on predictions of the future, assuming the present value of an asset is a function of discounted future cash flows.

First, we consider the consequences, as this sets the stage for all that follows; this involves defining the user. Second, we look at what quality actually *is*; here, we consider the definitions and measures of both standard-setters and researchers. Finally, we consider different determinants of (what can explain) accounting quality. Whereas we in the previous section defined accounting quality loosely as *usefulness*, we now turn to the consequences and determinants of accounting quality. Throughout this discussion, we home in on what usefulness might actually mean in the given context.

1.2.1 Consequences of high-quality accounting

As we saw in the previous section, there are many potential perspectives one can adopt concerning usefulness. Consequently, there are many potential users of financial accounting. Because different users (e.g., investors, debtholders, boards of directors, governments and tax authorities) have different objectives and therefore different information needs, the meaning of accounting quality varies depending on the user. We adopt the view that capital providers are the main, or intended, users and that high-quality accounting must primarily be discussed in relation to this group. We believe this to be consistent not only with the view held by the world's largest standard-setters, the **International Accounting Standards Board (IASB)** and the **US Financial Accounting Standards Board (FASB)**, but also with how accounting has evolved over time. Having said that, the IASB and the FASB argue that because these users require information that is detailed, relevant and reliable to support them in their decision-making, such information should also satisfy other users' needs for information.

Capital providers may be classified as either equity-owners or debtholders (or a combination of the two). Examples are individual shareholders, institutional investors (e.g., pension funds), banks and bond-holders. Even though they are not actual capital providers, analysts and other financial intermediaries acting in capital markets are also included in this group of users.

The consequences of high-quality accounting are largely thought to be better functioning capital markets. This follows from reduced information asymmetry, more efficient capital allocation as well as better monitoring of firm management. Whether and in which scenarios this applies has occupied much of accounting literature, as we shall see in later chapters.

1.2.2 Determinants of high-quality accounting

We have argued that accounting information is of high quality if it is useful for decision-making in capital markets. However, what determines accounting output and thereby the usefulness of financial accounting?

Determinants of accounting quality can be found both inside and outside the firm. The nature of the underlying economic transactions and conditions, managerial and firm-level incentives and the effectiveness of the board of directors and auditors in monitoring management and the financial reporting process are the primary **firm-specific factors** that determine accounting quality. National or supranational regulatory bodies and enforcement agencies, as well as the broader institutional, legal and even cultural setting are the primary **institutional factors**.

The main factors studied in the literature are:

Firm-specific factors:

- Underlying economic transactions and conditions
- Incentives
- Monitoring mechanisms

Institutional factors:

- Regulation
- Enforcement
- Other institutional features

These are described briefly below.

Underlying economic transactions and conditions

In essence, financial statements provide information about a firm's economic **events** (i.e., transactions, which are normally reflected in the income statement) and **states** (i.e., existing conditions, which are normally reflected in the balance sheet). The usefulness of financial statements may be thought of as the outcome of two successful processes. First, there has to be a strong link between the financial statements and the underlying economic events and states. In the jargon of standard-setters, they should be **faithfully represented**. Second, the financial statements should be **relevant** for the decision-making of users. If financial statements faithfully represent what they purport to represent, but the information is irrelevant and has no valuation implications, it cannot be useful.

Truly capturing the underlying economic transactions and conditions is not straightforward, as these are not directly observable. The transactions may be complex and may be completed over long periods. In measuring them, management must make estimates and this requires expertise. A thorough understanding of the firm's operations and its business environment is necessary. Managers are given discretion in choosing accounting methods that reflect the underlying economic states and events and must make professional judgments. In an ideal scenario, managers thus make accurate estimations and valuations and make hitherto private information public. However, financial statements are prone to include more or less material errors that may ultimately lead to lower-quality information. These errors can be either intentional or unintentional.

Unintentional errors arise due to the inherent complexity in some transactions. The difficulty in capturing underlying economics can lead to errors in financial statement items, in spite of management's best intentions. This may be referred to as the innate **measurement uncertainty**.

Meanwhile, intentional errors occur when managers use their discretionary power over accounting choices in order to influence the way in which economic transactions are reflected in the financial statements. They may, for example, use discretion opportunistically to inflate earnings and thus increase their bonuses. Manipulation of this sort is referred to as **earnings management** and takes on various forms. Ultimately, this leads to information asymmetry between the firm and the capital market, since management knows more about the underlying economics compared to the capital providers.

Incentives

Evidence from research in accounting shows that managerial incentives constitute a major determinant of accounting outcomes. Given that accounting standards provide room for managers to exercise their judgment, managerial incentives matter and affect strategic decisions and choices related to accounting methods. Managers whose interests are aligned with the interests of shareholders desire greater transparency and will choose accounting methods that convey private information about the firm's underlying economic transactions and conditions. In contrast, managers whose interests are not aligned in such a way may instead have incentives to make accounting choices that lead to private gain to the detriment of shareholders. Depending on the extent to which managers are opportunistic and the interests are aligned, the incentives will lead to varying outcomes. It is worth noting here that although there are in other words both positive and negative incentives, the term "incentives" is often used in the accounting literature in a negative sense. Therefore, there is a desire to curb managerial incentives.

Although one mostly considers management's incentives, accounting outcomes also depend on *firm-level* incentives. Firm-level incentives capture the forces and pressures from outside the firm and may loosely be divided into *capital market* and *legitimization* incentives. Capital market incentives are stronger the greater the presumed demand for information by capital providers. Firms have incentives to provide higher-quality accounting if they fear negative consequences of information asymmetry. Expected future growth opportunities, external financing needs, globalization and complexity of operations may all constitute incentives to disclose high-quality information and reduce the information asymmetry that is detrimental to firm value. Meanwhile, legitimization incentives originate from pressures from stakeholders and various institutions to obtain, maintain or regain **corporate legitimacy**. Examples include pressure from society to display corporate social responsibility or pressure to present financial statements that conform to certain norms and traditions (institutions).

Monitoring mechanisms

Building on what was just said, various monitoring mechanisms are introduced in firms in order to keep an eye on management and prevent opportunistic behavior, such as rent-extraction (i.e., using the firm's resources at the expense of owners; examples include shirking and the illegitimate use of the corporate jet). There are a number of mechanisms that fall into this category. First, shareholders holding a relatively large number of shares in a firm (so-called *large* owners) can exercise their power vis-à-vis managers and thus act as monitors.

Second, absent large owners, contractual arrangements (such as compensation contracts) that aim to align the interests of managers and shareholders are considered optimal in terms of incentivizing managers to make decisions that are in line with shareholder interests. However, contractual arrangements are not perfect; they may even create new incentives for managers to make opportunistic accounting choices. An obvious example would be when managers make accounting choices that inflate the current earnings in order to increase their bonuses (another type of rent-extracting behavior). Another example is when managers make accounting choices to avoid debt covenant violations (which can be costly to the firm and thus to managers). Third, the board of directors and high-quality auditors are considered important for a number of reasons. They may have a direct effect on managerial incentives by acting as deterrents, while also enforcing internal control mechanisms and ensuring the efficiency of incentive contracts. This has an overall positive effect on the quality of financial reports.

Regulation

Regulation can take different forms. Although accounting standards are the fundamental building blocks of high-quality accounting, corporate governance regulation, industry-specific regulation and legislation are all forms of regulation and thus elements of the institutional environmental.

Different sets of accounting standards focus on somewhat different aspects and vary with respect to how comprehensive and theoretically coherent they are. IFRS, which are developed by the IASB, and US GAAP, which are developed by the FASB, focus on capital markets and are generally perceived as comprehensive. They also attempt to develop theoretically coherent conceptual frameworks while considering the cost-effectiveness of different accounting methods. While the standard-setters are criticized for having a focus that is too narrow or not doing enough to ensure high-quality accounting, there is steady development. Accounting standards, and the conceptual frameworks, have never been as theoretically or conceptually coherent as they are today. The conceptual frameworks provide specific guidelines on qualitative characteristics that reports should possess, such as *relevance* and *faithful representation*, and individual standards should contribute to the achievement of these objectives. It is widely believed that relevant and faithfully represented reports are of high quality and useful for making decisions.

How standards are formulated will affect the outcome of the financial reporting process. One concrete dimension along which standards can vary is the extent to which they are principles-based. A principles-based accounting framework requires substantial judgment by preparers because they have fewer bright-line rules. An extreme example of a principles-based framework would be one expressing some general principle(s)—for instance that financial statements should be relevant and faithfully represent the underlying economics—and leaves it to the firm to decide what this means (i.e, not provide any additional guidance in the form of standards, guidelines or examples). The opposite of a principles-based approach is a rules-based approach, where little or no judgment is required by preparers—either due to overly detailed rules or due to very simplistic rules with few or no underlying principles. As we see in later chapters, IFRS are considered more principles-based than US GAAP or other local GAAP.

Enforcement and other institutional features

The legal environment, enforcement structures and other institutional features of countries are also important factors that affect the financial reporting process and thus accounting quality. Some countries are more shareholder-oriented, with legal systems that to a larger degree reflect the interest of shareholders. Countries offering strong shareholder protection are usually characterized by large equity markets, where the main source of capital comes from equity invested by external shareholders. Other countries might have other strong stakeholders, such as creditors and unions, which have shaped their legal systems in a way that reflects the interests of these other groups. Shareholder protection, therefore, is not the primary focus and is only weakly implemented, with a lower level of transparency being an expected outcome.

The importance of country-level enforcement has received increased interest in research in recent years. The enforcement of compliance with accounting standards and other regulation is recognized as important for the quality of financial reporting. Many argue that the benefits of applying high-quality accounting standards cannot be achieved without having proper enforcement mechanisms in place.

The above discussion allows us to be more specific in our references to determinants and consequences. Figure 1.2 provides more detail. It shows the fundamental idea that a firm engages in economic transactions (also events or flows), thus creating certain conditions (also states or stocks). These transactions and conditions will be reflected more or less effectively in the financial statements (or more broadly, in the financial reports) through the financial reporting process. The financial reports are then communicated to the intended users of such statements—capital providers or capital markets.

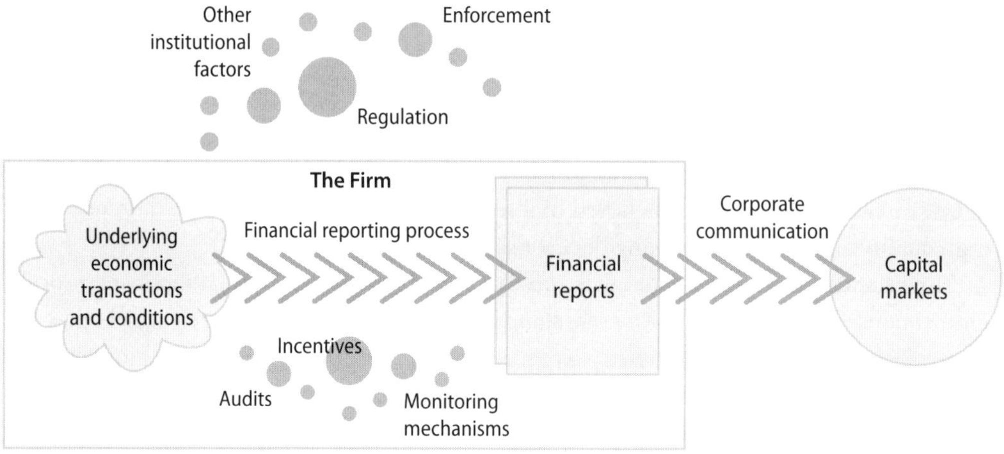

Figure 1.2 Financial reporting in a context

1.2.3 Information uncertainty

When discussing accounting quality and the usefulness of accounting, we believe that the concept of **information uncertainty** deserves special attention. In general, the quality and thereby usefulness of accounting is strongly associated with the uncertainty found in the different parts of the reporting process. Accounting is more than a collection of economic facts and figures or raw data; it is organized and *processed* data that constitute *information*. To be meaningful, information needs to be communicated and interpreted. As such, accounting requires a producer or transmitter, as well as a user or receiver. Given this context, there are two reasons for uncertainty in accounting.

First, the economic states and events to be depicted could be innately uncertain. For example, measurement of all items in the balance sheet—with the exception of cash—is based on the occurrence of uncertain future events. In other words, managers of reporting firms (preparers of financial statements) have incomplete information concerning future events that must be predicted in order to prepare the financial statements. Therefore, forecasts based on professional judgment are necessary. This constitutes **measurement uncertainty**. This is especially high for items where measurement involves substantial estimation complexity, such as goodwill, infrequently traded financial instruments and provisions. The economic context will also have an effect. For example, goodwill is more easily estimated in some industries compared to others, and the measurement of financial instruments is affected by the volatility of financial markets, meaning that they are more easily measured in times of financial stability.

Second, there is information asymmetry between preparers and users of financial statements. The users, for reasons that should be apparent, know less than preparers about the underlying economics and about which measurement is particularly uncertain! To the extent that financial reporting affects the relative wealth of these two parties, there could also be incentives for preparers to intentionally bias financial statements. This type of uncertainty does not affect preparers, but represents an additional source of uncertainty from the user's perspective. Monitoring and enforcement can reduce the ability of preparers to bias measurement, thus reducing uncertainty from a user perspective. This is especially relevant in settings where managers have incentives to, for example, manage earnings. Supplemental disclosures also represent a way to mitigate negative effects of high-judgment accounting standards and contribute to the reduction of uncertainty from a user perspective. Firms can communicate the bases for their estimates of future events, thus enabling users to form their own opinions regarding the probability of these events occurring and regarding the reasonableness of the estimates. Examples from IFRS include requirements to disclose assumptions used in fair value measurement and in goodwill impairment testing. In sum, the level of uncertainty is higher for users than for preparers, as the former are affected by both innate uncertainty and by the effects of information asymmetry. This is shown in Figure 1.3, where the information uncertainty (IU) that users face constitutes the *sum* of information asymmetry (IA) and measurement uncertainty (MU). Whatever the cause of the uncertainty highlighted above, there is evidence in the literature that a negative effect of uncertainty is poorly functioning financial markets, which ultimately dampens growth and reduces investments in value-creating businesses (which could potentially generate future jobs and profits).

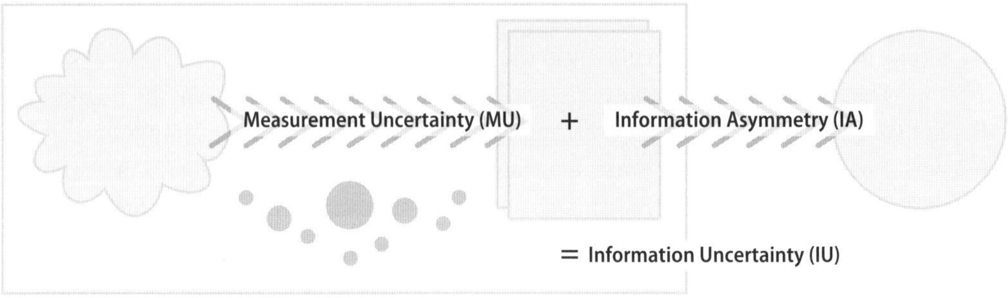

Figure 1.3 Information uncertainty

Several recent events have led to an increase in information uncertainty in the context described above. Some events represent shocks to accounting systems and to financial markets, pointing to deep-seated problems with financial reporting as we know it. For example, in the wake of the financial crisis in 2007–2008, problems with financial reporting in banks were identified and in connection with the IT bubble in 2000–2002, financial reporting issues in many IT- and growth firms became visible. Such shocks have arguably made users more wary of making certain investment decisions, which we may attribute to a higher perceived level of uncertainty about judgments made by preparers in the financial reporting process. Other events, which represent gradual changes in the business environment, include the globalization of financial markets and an increased focus on areas of reporting where there is little regulation or established practice, such as sustainability reporting.

As regards *globalization* of financial markets, the result is an increase in the average geographic distance between preparers and users. The likelihood of users having prior knowledge of, or experience with, preparers consequently decreases, which in turn increases uncertainty. In addition, achieving consistent application and enforcement of accounting standards becomes increasingly difficult, as more and more countries become involved in the globalization of accounting standards. Firms' familiarity with national existing practice is not sufficient or even desirable when attempting to achieve global consistency in the application of the standards.

The move, internationally, to IFRS has largely meant a move to more principles-based accounting standards, as IFRS are typically considered more principles-based than most pre-existing local standards they replace (see above). In addition, IFRS tend to become increasingly principles-based over time, with more recent standards being more principles-based than older ones. Overall quality implications of IFRS seem to be largely favorable according to international research, as the standards seem to promote greater transparency and a greater focus on the needs of capital market participants. Of course, studies on aggregate effects will be noisy and do not take into account specific features of the standards, such as indeed their principles-based nature and which, if any, possibly adverse consequences may follow from this. For example, do IFRS promote higher-quality information through an increased emphasis on the value of making managers' private information public (via their judgments), or do they cause a higher level of uncertainty in financial statements? Such questions have fueled a debate in Europe (including Sweden) regarding the use of fair value and accounting for business combinations, where some argue that the uncertainty level is too high for certain financial statement items.

Both the increasing use of IFRS and the globalization of financial markets have resulted in increased amounts of disclosure by firms. Recent developments include more voluminous annual reports, extensive web sites and more communication carried out by firms overall. However, rather than providing more substantial data, the apparent information being disseminated is believed to be increasingly focused on story-telling. More information, in combination with questions concerning the relevance and usefulness of the information, has generated a debate about the quality of accounting disclosures.

1.3 The broader information environment

As mentioned above, other users of corporate reports have objectives that are not fully shared with shareholders and as such, they may wish that the reporting process also takes into account non-financial events and states affecting the firm. These include social and environmental considerations. A growing demand for this is evidenced by more and more firms engaging in **corporate social responsibility (CSR) reporting** or **sustainability reporting**. Some firms combine sustainability reports with their financial reports, a phenomenon known as **integrated reporting**. The presence of well-organized unions has forced managers to provide information on employee conditions, while the emergence of many non-governmental organizations (NGOs) has raised awareness regarding the interests and values of various environmental groups. Although the pressure from social and environmental groups has contributed to corporate social and environmental disclosures in annual reports, the information provided is only partly regulated (see Text Box 1.4) and subject to substantial managerial discretion. Opportunistically demonstrating an overly positive picture of the firm is recognized as a form of **impression management** (of which earnings management can be one form).

The need for introducing mandatory CSR requirements in corporate reports and strengthening regulation in this area is very much debated. The main problem of standardizing these reports is the diversity in the underlying corporate practice. It is also argued that the voluntary nature of CSR is critical for motivating firms to follow "best practice," since managers see CSR as an opportunity for establishing a competitive advantage. At this point in time, it is difficult to evaluate the quality of CRS or sustainability reporting, since the objectives of such reporting are not clearly stated or widely acknowledged, and there is no authoritative definition of quality in this context. This constitutes a limitation on research, but also, most definitely, a call to arms and room for theorizing and influencing policy.

We mention this aspect of the information environment mainly because we believe that investors are also concerned about this issue—if for no other reason than that it may have value implications (however difficult these are to estimate). A bad reputation with customers, caused by poor environmental performance or poor working conditions, will have economic implications and lead to financial setbacks. Although we make occasional references to this field, we do not discuss this in depth in this book.

Text Box 1.4 **EU Directive on Non-Financial Information**

In December 2014, the European Commission adopted a directive (2014/95/EU) obliging large (exceeding 500 employees) public companies to provide non-financial disclosures relating to environmental and social impact starting in 2018. The main aim of this directive is to increase the transparency of sustainability topics in large corporations within the EU. Following this regulation, a large number of firms in member states are required to include information on five sustainability topics: environmental protection; social responsibility and treatment of employees; respect for human rights; anti-corruption and bribery; and diversity on company boards. The introduction of the EU directive concerning non-financial information is the very first attempt, at least within the EU, to provide standardized reports on CSR matters. The evidence on the application of this regulation on firms, however, has yet to be provided. In particular, it should be of interest to examine the role of this regulatory change in improving the quality of disclosures of non-financial information in annual reports.

1.4 Accounting, reporting and disclosures—Getting the terminology in order

For the purpose of this book, we believe it is useful to have clear definitions of the terms we use in the text and also an idea of how they relate to each other. Hence, we now proceed with a discussion of the terminology.

Accounting is often thought of as only having to do with bookkeeping and measurement. However, accounting is much more, as it is also about *communication*. In relation to the discussion above: having low measurement uncertainty but high information asymmetry due to poor communication will lead to high information uncertainty. Disclosures provide a tool for decreasing information asymmetry and we therefore devote significant space both to measurement and disclosures in this text. However, we limit ourselves to disclosures between the firm and the outside world, rather than on internal communication. In this sense, our focus is on **financial accounting**. We contrast this with **management accounting**, which is concerned with the intraorganizational use of financial data for strategic decision-making. In other words, while management accounting is concerned with information that assists managers in their decision-making within the organization, financial accounting is concerned with the production of financial reports for the benefit of outsiders. Having made this distinction, we often just use the term *accounting* when referring to *financial accounting*.

Thus, we also introduce the closely related term **financial reporting**, which refers to the process of producing **financial reports**. Financial reports contain all manners of financial information, not least of which are the **financial statements**. The financial statements constitute **regulated** aspects of firms' financial reporting. These may, in turn, be divided into **primary financial statements** (including the balance sheet, income statement, statement of changes in shareholders' equity and cash flow statement) and notes to the (primary) financial statements. The notes are referred to in different frameworks simply as notes, **supplementary disclosures**, or **footnote disclosures**.

Meanwhile, a firm makes many other **voluntary disclosures**. These are, by definition, unregulated and may be provided in a firm's financial reports alongside the financial statements (including in the form of notes), but also via corporate web sites, press releases, social media or other channels. Sustainability reporting belongs in part to the voluntary disclosure category, but more regulation is gradually being introduced. Figure 1.4 provides a broader picture of the firm's information environment.[4]

In most cases, we view accounting as a broad term encompassing *measurement* and *disclosure*. That is, disclosure is a subset of accounting. However, accounting may also be viewed as a subset of disclosure to the extent that the focus is also on disclosures not related to accounting. Non-financial disclosures—especially if they are also non-quantitative—are often thought of as not being related to accounting (e.g., employee statistics, market and product data, or disclosures of corporate strategies), but that line is hard to draw, as the accounting literature focuses on a very wide range of corporate disclosures (e.g., management forecasts, the chief executive officer's (CEO's) letter to shareholders and sustainability disclosures). In sum, when we (or academic papers) speak of disclosure in more general terms, both accounting data and non-accounting data are implied. The financial reports are an example of accounting data, with financial statements and earnings numbers constituting a subset of these.

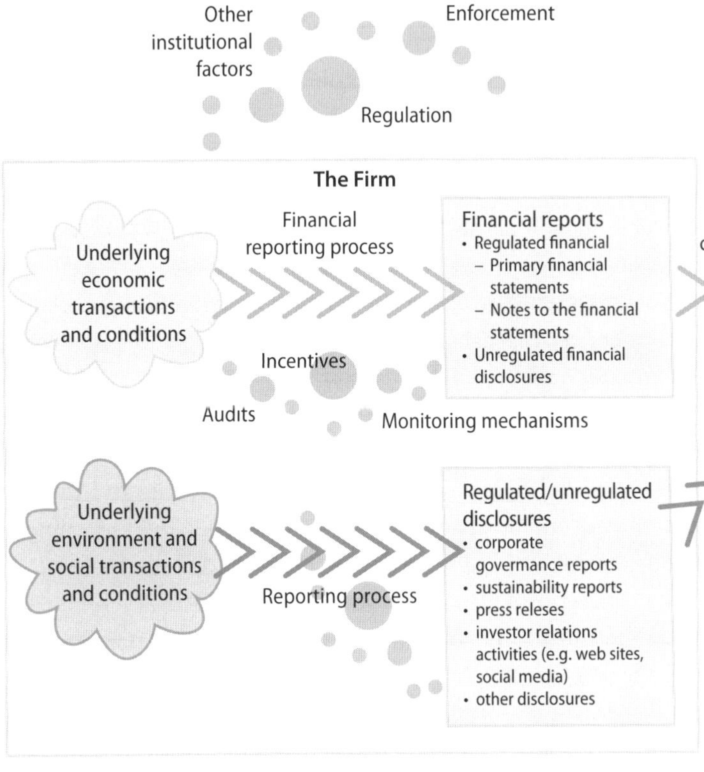

Figure 1.4 The broader information environment

4 Although not shown in the figure, information about the firm may be disseminated via other non-corporate sources, for example via analysts or print media. We do not discuss this further in the book.

Finally, and throughout this text, we often alternate between the terms "financial accounting," "financial reporting," "financial reports" and "financial statements." Although a distinction between the terms can provide more specific information in certain contexts, we sometimes use the terms interchangeably.

1.5 Financial accounting theory

So far, we have made few explicit references to theory. **Financial accounting theory** is, in fact, a broad term and may refer to a number of ideas and theories employed in the field. What we have done up until now is to provide the context in which the theories are used.

One set of theories in financial accounting are *descriptive*. They seek to describe, explain and predict various phenomena, including the determinants and consequences of financial accounting. For example, we have said that financial reports are produced by firm management, management follows regulation in the form of accounting standards and this process and the outcome are affected by a number of factors, such as incentives management may have, enforcement of the regulation and various other types of monitoring activities. Most descriptive theories used when studying these phenomena come from other fields, such as economics, finance and organizational studies. Examples include agency theory and institutional theory.

Until a little over half a century ago, theory was more concerned about *what should be* rather than about *what is*, and empirical work was essentially non-existent. As we shall see in the next chapter, theory in accounting was *prescriptive* rather than descriptive. Prescriptive theories are much more specific to accounting, and they differ from "typical" scientific theories found in the natural sciences. Specifically, they do not lend themselves easily to formulations of testable hypotheses, they often contain value statements and they imply the existence of *objectives*. In this book, we highlight *usefulness* as one of the key objectives of financial accounting. To the extent that accounting standard-setters attempt to achieve conceptual or theoretical coherence, we treat standards and standard-setters' conceptual frameworks as forming a part of accounting theory and study these in order to better understand the objectives.[5] When we look at empirical research mainly based on *descriptive* theories, our knowledge of *prescriptive* theory helps us evaluate accounting quality and gives meaning to our work (see Figure 1.5).

Scientific theories in a number of fields can be used to describe, explain and predict the determinants and consequences of financial accounting, and thus quality. Prescriptive theories in accounting provide objectives (e.g., usefulness) for financial accounting, in relation to which one may evaluate determinants and consequences.

We further note that much of the empirical research does not make explicit references to any theory. This is explained by the fact that this research is largely *paradigmatic*. That is, the literature exists within an established paradigm. A **paradigm** is literally a (typical) pattern or a model, and a *research* paradigm refers to a particular world view or perspective on which the theoretical and empirical work is based. Because the view or perspective is widely

5 Even though *accounting* is broader than *financial accounting*, we henceforth use the terms "financial accounting theory" and "accounting theory" interchangeably.

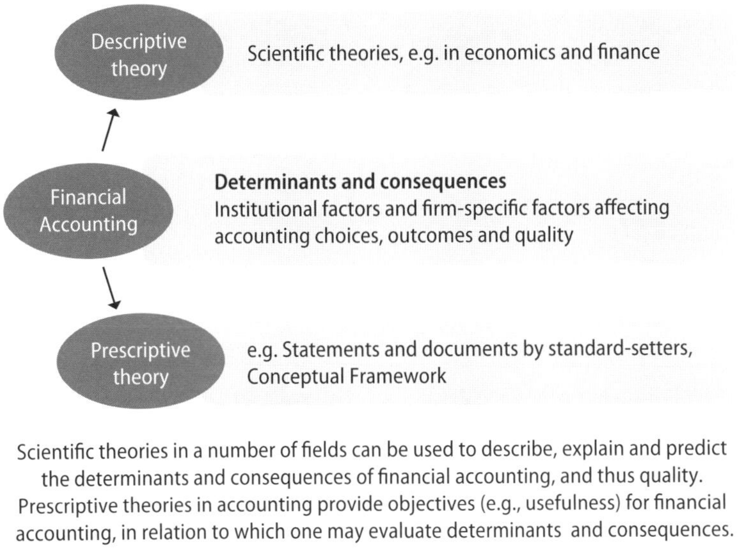

Figure 1.5
Theory in a capital market context

accepted, there is little need to state explicitly what it is or the underlying assumptions. Rather than attempting to revolutionize the field, or question the validity of overarching theories, each study seeks to make an **incremental contribution** by providing more insights in relation to the given theories or beliefs within the paradigm.

1.6 Organization and contents of the book

The organization of the book follows the basic structure already presented in Figures 1.2 and 1.4. Below, we present a summary of the different parts of the book, followed by the intended learning outcomes.

Part I In order to develop theory, it is important to first define the objectives of financial accounting, which in turn requires that the intended *user* of financial statements is identified. We point out that a capital market perspective holds a central position in discussions regarding accounting quality (i.e, the focus is on capital market users). The theories we concentrate on are the ones seen as dominant in the field and they largely coincide with the capital market perspective. Key concepts are discussed, such as theory, the usefulness of accounting, information asymmetry and the valuation and stewardship roles of accounting.

Part II This part provides a brief history of financial accounting regulation and thus some of the related theoretical developments. The meaning of accounting quality is explored from a standard-setting perspective. An overview of the IASB's Conceptual Framework is provided, along with the ideas that helped shape it. The objectives of financial accounting are here revisited, and the qualitative characteristics that financial statements should possess are discussed. The two primary qualitative characteristics of *relevance* and *faithful representation* are highlighted, where the former defines quality in terms of the relation between financial statements and the users, while the latter defines quality in terms of the relation between financial statements and economic transactions and conditions.

Part III This part explores the ways in which researchers have discussed and measured accounting quality, not least in relation to the objectives set out by standard-setters (e.g., the qualitative characteristics). The notion of the usefulness of accounting is central in this context, as the *consequences* of accounting for capital markets is in focus. Earnings quality and disclosure quality, being the main components of accounting quality, are explained and operationalized. A large number of empirical studies are cited here, but we also keep coming back to the underlying (economic) theories that motivate research in this area.

In Parts IV and V of the book, we turn to factors believed to affect the quality of financial accounting, the so-called *determinants* of accounting quality.

Part IV Whenever accounting standards provide room for managers to exercise their judgment in making accounting choices and estimates, incentives can potentially play an important role in determining the quality of the information provided. Our focus here is thus on managerial incentives and on the theories that predict managerial behavior. Potentially suboptimal choices by management, as well as lack of compliance with standards, may be reduced by means of internal monitoring and control mechanisms, high-quality audits and country-level enforcement. Regardless of which framework or standards a firm follows, the institutional environment in which a firm is domiciled or operates matters. That is why the second half of this part of the book turns to these accounting quality determinants.

Part V This part of the book examines one particular aspect of accounting regulation—standard-setting. We provide extensive examples of current regulation, individual accounting items and the debate surrounding these. Theoretical, conceptual or other issues are raised due to their important effect on financial reporting outcomes and thus accounting quality.

The usefulness of financial statements depends on factors such as which framework is used (e.g., IFRS, Swedish GAAP or US GAAP), which individual accounting policies are permitted and how much judgment is permissible.

Concluding chapter The book ends with a concluding chapter that summarizes research in financial accounting and provides reflections on possible future research activities in the field.

Learning outcomes of the book By reading this book, you will gain insight into the following:

- The context of financial accounting for capital markets, including the determinants and consequences of accounting quality.
- Different theories used in the field of financial accounting and related empirical work.
- Definitions of quality in financial accounting and how accounting quality contributes to the achievement of user objectives.
- How accounting quality is affected by regulation, enforcement, other institutional factors and preparer incentives.
- The issues that arise in different financial reporting areas and current treatment in accounting standards.
- Seminal and contemporary research in financial accounting (both theoretical and empirical).

CHAPTER 2

Theoretical underpinnings

Learning outcomes

Upon completion of this chapter, you will:

- Have an understanding of the different views on theory that exist in the subject of accounting.
- Be familiar with the main theories and hypotheses used in the field of financial accounting.
- Recognize the importance of accounting quality in theoretical and empirical accounting research.

> It should be emphasized at the outset that accounting is carried out to accomplish objectives and is therefore tinged with purpose. Moreover, as a profession accounting must be placed in a setting which takes account of the additional social purposes that society expects a profession to fulfill. [...] The realization that accounting is directly related to a vital, changing social order should encourage meaningful research directed toward the place of accounting in this order [Devine (1960) in "Research methodology and accounting theory formation" in *The Accounting Review*, p. 391].

THEORY IS A SOMEWHAT SLIPPERY CONCEPT in the accounting discipline. Is accounting even a science, or is it rather an art? It has been claimed that accounting as a university subject has become exceedingly practice- and job-oriented, provoking the question of whether it should have the status of an academic discipline as opposed to solely a vocation (Demski, 2007). Being a language of business and a communication device, accounting can also be seen as multidisciplinary: it serves as a tool in the realms of management and finance, it dabbles in legal lingo as it concerns itself with rules and regulations, but it is also explained using the laws of economics. Can accounting—as a profession, and as a practice of measuring and communicating—be studied in the same manner as a natural science? Can theories in accounting be evaluated using the same standards? Answering these questions satisfactorily requires a longer and more philosophically oriented discussion than we provide here. It also requires a far more detailed exposition on the philosophy of science. Nevertheless, a brief introduction to key concepts should help the reader understand some of the complexities associated with theorization in accounting.

We begin by asking ourselves what a **scientific theory** actually is. This requires us to decide on how we acquire knowledge. In philosophy, **epistemology** or the *theory of knowledge* is concerned with the nature and source of human knowledge. Two basic epistemological views that are relevant to our particular discussion, are those of **rationalism** and **empiricism**. This distinction was apparent already in ancient Greece to the great thinkers of early Western philosophy (and the forefathers of modern science). Whereas Socrates and Plato may be labeled rationalists, believing that knowledge is obtained through *reason* alone, Aristotle may be classified as an empiricist, arguing that knowledge is obtained through *experience* and *observation*. Socrates' valued student, Plato, believed that a world of ideal forms (which we may call "models") existed. These forms are abstract objects or perfect patterns (paradigms) of which objects we experience in the physical world are mere imperfect copies. His theory of forms illustrates the rationalist view that truth can be achieved by reasoning alone. Accordingly, what we perceive with our five senses can never truly tell us what is real.[1] To understand why, an example might help. Imagine that you have seen an equilateral triangle. What you have actually observed, however, is only a more or less precise representation of such a triangle. Any drawing or illustration, even using advanced computer technology, can only be an attempt to create such a triangular shape. Thus, we cannot build our knowledge based on empirical observations. However, Plato's student, Aristotle, leaned much more toward empiricism. Empiricism has the advantage of allowing a researcher or philosopher to be wrong, as one does not generate theories built on reasoning. Our theories change as we make new observations. Empiricism thus challenges rationalism and emphasizes the role of experience and external evidence. More modern examples of (British) empiricists include Thomas Hobbes, David Hume and John Locke, while examples of (Continental) rationalists include René Descartes, Baruch Spinoza and Gottfried Leibniz.

One reason we are interested in epistemology is that it is intimately related to methodology. Based on one's view of how knowledge is obtained, a different methodology is adopted. **Deduction** is based on there being postulates, premises or assumptions that are held to be true. Based on these as well as logical reasoning, one may arrive at a given theory. It is common to think of deduction as going from the general to the specific. For example, if the premise is that all mammals have hair on their bodies and cats are mammals, then valid deductive reasoning (logic) will lead us to conclude that all cats have hair on their bodies. For this reason, deductive reasoning is often associated with rationalism. The use of **inductive** methods, however, emphasizes observations of actual phenomena or practices as a source

1 Another branch of philosophy is **metaphysics**, of which *ontology* in turn is a central branch that is concerned with the nature of being and reality. A commonly discussed dichotomy in this context is *realism* versus *nominalism*. Whereas realism holds that there are actual, real entities behind *universals* (i.e., general ideas), nominalism rejects the existence of universals and states that there are only individual instances of the "thing" a universal is said to describe. Whereas the *term* "cat" exists, there is no underlying, abstract universal cat. The distinction is less trivial than it may sound, but we do not delve deeper into these philosophical issues here. It is sufficient to conclude that Plato's ideal forms represent universals in **platonic realism**. Furthermore, translating the distinction between realism and nominalism to accounting, the question is whether accounting items exist merely as terms, or actually represent some underlying real economic events and transactions.

of knowledge. As such, it is an empirical approach. One uses examples or specifics to make inferences about the general. We may observe one hairy cat, then another and then fifty more, and if all cats we observe have hair on their bodies, we may start to feel comfortable concluding that cats indeed have hair on their bodies. We can arrive at this conclusion through *inductive logic.*[2]

This brings us to the concept of **positivism**. Positivism (a term developed in the 19th century by French sociologist, Auguste Comte) posits that scientific knowledge is the only authentic knowledge. Positivists are empiricists (and realists, see footnote above) who are concerned with the development of general laws and predictions through empirical observation and inductive logic. The role of a positivist science is to *describe*, *explain* and *predict* by identifying causal relationships. Further, science should be value-free, and the logic underpinning natural science can be applied in social science as well. One branch of positivism is logical positivism (now defunct), which emphasized the notion of *verificiationism* (that statements must be empirically verifiable to be meaningful). In the 20th century, **post-positivism** (also referred to as post-empiricism) appeared as a marriage between empiricism—that the origin of all knowledge is experienced via empirical observations—and the belief that careful principles of logic and scientific methods are uniquely helpful in terms of generating scientific knowledge.[3]

One of the most well-known critics of logical positivism, and heralded by some to be one of the greatest philosophers of the 20th century, is Karl Popper. Similar to Plato in the past, present-day Popper was more of an idealistic thinker who saw an absolute theoretical truth as the ultimate goal and desire for science—although not necessarily obtainable (Flyvbjerg, 2001). A self-named "critical rationlist", he was opposed to classical empiricism and its purely inductive approach. This does not mean he did not believe in the value of making empirical observations—quite the opposite. The distinction between science and non-science was central to his argumentation, and what made a theory scientific was its ability to be *falsified*. **Falsificationism**, which has been highly influential in the development of empirical sciences, stands in contrast to the idea that scientific theories are *corroborated* or accepted. Popper was opposed to the positivist view that scientists should (must) use induction to *prove* or *verify* theories. He argued that almost any theory could be supported by an inductive approach. Scientists should instead make "bold hypotheses" or "risky" predictions that could be false, and use rigorous methods, including the use of empirical data, to test them.

Thomas Kuhn, another influential thinker we think is useful to mention, is famous for his contribution to scientific progress and development by introducing the idea of **paradigm shifts**. According to Kuhn, scientific models and examples (i.e., paradigms) are constantly competing, which ultimately leads to the revolution of science (i.e., a paradigm shift). The notable contribution of Kuhn's argument is related to the interpretation of reality, which

---

2 Of course, some specimens are furrier than others while some may appear completely hairless, potentially confounding our results—this constitutes a common criticism of said approach.

3 In contrast to positivism, post-positivism accepts that theorists have a direct impact on their research. Therefore, social values and norms are recognized under this paradigm and normative purposes are considered relevant to scientific methods. Causal relationships are seen as important by post-positivists, but the full separation between subject and object claimed by positivists is seen as an unrealistic assumption.

changes when one paradigm overthrows another. The idea of competing theories is something many researchers today are familiar with. It is not possible to find a comprehensive theory able to fully reflect reality. Kuhn's main work, *The Structure of Scientific Revolutions*, has not been without critics and many other philosophers see his work as a description of the history and development of science, as well as lacking explanations for the reasons behind this process (see Ryan et al., 2002, Chapter 1). Nevertheless, his work has been broadly adopted in the social sciences and is for instance used to explain paradigms and paradigm shifts in economics and political science.

In accounting, one may also observe such paradigm shifts. Prior to the 1960s, accounting as an academic discipline mostly concerned itself with making statements about what accounting *should* be. As computing power grew, access to data increased and research came to focus more on what accounting *is*. This is perhaps the most prominent example of a paradigm shift in accounting. In the following sections, we look more closely at how accounting research has developed, and how the perception of valid theorizing has changed, over the past 50–70 years.

2.1 Accounting theory: Definitions and concepts

The word "theory" is often used in layman terms to refer to a belief, conjecture or hypothesis. This can be misleading, as most scholars would agree that a *scientific* theory should constitute a well-researched and rigorous explanation of the studied phenomenon and not dabble in speculation. A theory itself is not a hypothesis, but opens up for the formulation of empirically testable hypotheses, which may be used to challenge or refute the validity of the theory by means of scientific methods.

The first distinguishing feature of *theory* (as opposed to *practice*) is that the former is concerned with general explanations or abstract contemplations of a given phenomenon, based on certain assumptions and conditions. Two reasonable and helpful layman definitions of *theory* are provided by the *American Heritage Dictionary of the English Language* (5th ed.):

> A set of statements or principles devised to explain a group of facts or phenomena, especially one that has been repeatedly tested or is widely accepted and can be used to make predictions about natural phenomena.
>
> The branch of a science or art consisting of its explanatory statements, accepted principles, and methods of analysis, as opposed to practice.

Collins English Dictionary broadens the definition of the term *theory* further and suggests that a theory can be "a system of rules, procedures, and assumptions used to produce a result," in which case the rules and procedures themselves have a theory status. If a theory is characterized by a set of principles, explanations and/or methods, we might all feel confident that we know some accounting theory. Knowing a set of Generally Accepted Accounting Principles (GAAP) or bookkeeping laws means having read or heard theory in accounting. However, this definition should be viewed with skepticism from an academic perspective, as accounting conventions may potentially be rather arbitrary.

In this book, we adopt a rather broad view that accounting theory should have at least one of the following aims or functions:

1. To describe and explain *how* something *is* accounted for and/or *why* something is accounted for in a certain way
2. To prescribe, using logical reasoning, *how* and/or *why* something *should* be accounted for in a certain way.

The resulting theory is **descriptive** or **positive** if consistent with the first point, and **prescriptive** or **normative** if consistent with the second point. We believe this to be consistent with the way theory has been discussed in the accounting literature (and social science in general). However, allowing a theory to be purely prescriptive is likely to be objectionable from a natural science point of view. In the natural sciences, theory should be based on the accumulation of evidence (e.g., through the testing of hypotheses). By contrast, a prescriptive theory is not necessarily falsifiable in the typical sense; however, it may be criticized or *refuted* on the basis of any potential lack of inherent logic or consistency with *given principles, premises or assumptions* (including those that are value-based). Frequently, one settles for a normative theory to be useful and practicable. One main difference between normative and positive theories is that rather than adopting value positions, positive theories aim to explain and predict outcomes or estimate statistical relationships without interventions based on individual judgments. That is, they are *value-free*. It should be highlighted however, that positive research is not to be equated with classical positivism—instead, Popperian falsificationism is usually embraced.

In many ways, normative theories remind us of the accounting norms themselves. To distinguish normative theories from GAAP, however, one should apply a stringent argumentation, whereas GAAP may merely constitute a set of rules. As will be seen later, we identify one particular part of GAAP as representing an attempt at developing accounting theory (albeit non-scientific or at least non-academic), and this is the Conceptual Framework associated with and accompanying certain accounting regulations, notably those of the IASB and the FASB in the US. Although historically suffering from arbitrariness, having emerged in an *ad hoc* fashion and often as an urgent response to some market event, the regulatory frameworks are becoming increasingly stringent, not least because of the emphasis placed on the importance of an internally consistent Conceptual Framework.

Since normative (prescriptive) theories concern what *should* be done, while positive (descriptive) theories concern what *is*, it is tempting to associate the former with deduction and the latter with induction. As a result of deduction and induction almost invariably being linked together, however, both positive and normative theories may be arrived at deductively or inductively. This is consistent with the idea that normative and positive theories do not exist in isolation, but may benefit from one another. As clearly discussed by Friedman (1953), policy conclusions from normative theories rest on predictions concerning the consequences of a given policy:

> Normative economics and the art of economics, on the other hand, cannot be independent of positive economics. Any policy conclusion necessarily rests on a prediction about the consequences of doing one thing rather than another, a prediction that must be based—implicitly or explicitly—on positive economics. (p.5)

2.2 The normative–positive divide

Even though it may seem obvious that normative and positive research could happily coexist and be incrementally useful when used in synthesis, this dichotomy has long constituted a sharp demarcation line in the accounting community. A similar divide exists in the field of economics, where "objective" positive research is said to focus on facts and causal relationships, while "subjective" normative research makes value judgments to determine the desirability of economic events. One source of dispute is the claim that one approach is more *scientific* than the other. Although the reader will note that research cited in this book is primarily empirical and may be classified as positive or descriptive, we do not wish to advocate one rather than the other. Our focus on positive research is merely a reflection of the state of affairs in the subject of accounting, and of what is considered *mainstream* research in the field.

Whereas the first few decades of the last century saw inductive, empirical (positive) approaches to the development of accounting thought, deductive reasoning and associated normative research became more popular in the post-World War II era, and experienced something of a "golden age" in the 1960s (see discussion and further references in Edwards et al., 2013). However, this would not last, and normative theorists struggled to maintain a foothold as positive research expanded. One explanation for the trend was that US business schools' doctoral programs changed in response to criticism that (accounting) research was not sufficiently scientific (Zeff, 1989). It also, clearly, coincided with the expansion of financial databases and trends in finance and economics toward more computerized methods of data analysis (Dyckman and Zeff, 2015). Accounting theory became based on neoclassical economics and a shift to capital market theory came about (Ravenscroft and Williams, 2009).

As hinted at above, the happy co-mingling of positive and normative research did not prove tenable. The exposition of capital market research in accounting (pioneered by, Ball and Brown, 1968; Beaver, 1968) and, in particular, *positive accounting theory (PAT)* (Watts and Zimmerman, 1978; Watts and Zimmerman, 1979; Watts and Zimmerman, 1986) marked the definite beginning of a new era, and the end of another (Edwards et al., 2013). Before embarking on the criticism, it was in all fairness a partially reasonable response to the frequently *ad hoc* inductive or otherwise opinion-driven studies that dominated accounting research in the middle of the 20th century. Positive research in general, and PAT in particular, was an attempt to introduce rigor into the field and enhance the scientific status of accounting in academia. PAT—which, in essence, is concerned with describing and explaining accounting choice—declares value judgments (prescriptive statements) to be inappropriate and less scientific than descriptive, or positive work. Accounting research should be concerned with what *is*, and not about what *ought to be*.[4]

Criticism of Ross Watts' and Jerold Zimmerman's positive accounting theory is direct and unequivocal in such papers as written by Chambers (1993) and Sterling (1990). One rarely sees critique of this kind between scholars within a research paradigm (most individuals probably think it imprudent to quarrel for fear of professional backlashes), but the disagreements

4 Paradoxically, as pointed out by Sterling (1990), this very tenet is normative in nature, and thus contradicts itself.

between positive and normative scholars have been intense and bordered on feuds. Robert Sterling, a torchbearer for normative research, makes it clear that accounting research should (also) be concerned with *what accounting ought to be*—in direct contrast to PAT. His review of Watts' and Zimmerman's 1986 book, *Positive Accounting Theory*, is scathing and to the point. In his estimation, PAT makes "every effort to make `normative' the eighth deadly sin" (Sterling, 1990, p. 114).

> [I]nstead of trying to determine how to improve the present state of accounting we are told to try to determine the present state of accounting. (p 98)

The perceived folly of this is clear. Rather than using positive research (empirical findings) to make normative statements, accounting theory must—according to PAT—remain value-free in order to be scientific. Studying accounting practice as well as providing explanations for observed practice and predicting unobserved phenomena, is scientific. Suggesting how to improve practice, however, is *not*.

To highlight the absurdity of this point of view, Sterling (1990) draws parallels to cartography, and points to the "[well-known mistake in economics and science] of confusing the map with the territory". If financial statements are the map, the underlying economic events and transactions are the actual territory, and PAT advocates seem enamored with the map, or even make the fatal mistake of trying to traverse the *map* rather than the *territory*. Even worse than "confusing the accounting map (financial statements) with the accounting territory (economic goods), PAT *fails to recognize* (or at least acknowledge) the existence of an accounting territory" (emphasis added). In other words, by focusing solely on the financial statements and on the practice behind their preparation, the underlying economics are omitted from the analysis. The focus has thus shifted from *accounting* to the *accountants*. Sterling (1990) summarizes:

> Although [PAT] purports to be a study of accounting, it is in fact a study of accountants (and other people who select accounting methods). It should be abundantly obvious that accountant is to accounting as biologist is to biology, cartographer is to cartography, ... , zoologist is to zoology, and that distinguishing the practitioner from the subject matter in all these disciplines is as crucial as it is obvious. (p. 131)

This is not to say that it is always inappropriate or irrelevant to study practitioners' behavior. In fact, as argued by Watts and Zimmerman (1990, p. 147) (as part of their responds to criticism), "[t]here would be no accounting without accountants, managers, or preparers of the numbers." However, PAT is not a behavioral theory, because it does not seek to explain how accountants behave. The core assumption—and another source of criticism—is that people are **utility maximizers**. In arguing for the scientific qualities of PAT, the authors cite Karl Popper (see above), but the very same assumption of utility maximization is heavily criticized by Popper (1959) for being non-falsifiable (and thus non-scientific). Sterling (1990) explains:

> Since *all* behaviour is explained by utility maximization — the fireman will be said to have maximized his utility by his heroic charge into the inferno to save the child and by his cowardly refusal to enter the inferno — it in fact explains *no* behaviour. In that respect, it is similar to explanations that invoke fate, destiny, God's will, and the like. Since fate may be invoked to explain why x occurred (when it occurred) and also invoked to explain why x did not occur (when it did not occur), it explains both x and not-x and therefore explains neither. For the same reasons, utility maximization is not an acceptable explanation. Undoubtedly it has some truth to it and therefore it would probably be worthwhile to define it more precisely, that is, delimit the term so it could be used to explain some behaviour by preventing it from explaining all behaviour. (p. 103)

Because PAT starts with the assumption of utility maximization, it is problematic that it also *concludes* with the "major empirical finding" that managers are utility-maximizers and that this will affect their accounting choices. Apparently, what we learn from the theory is that we should be wary of opportunistic accounting practitioners. Sterling (1990) makes this point in near exasperation, expressing his wish for PAT to at least give some recommendations as to what can be done about this. If the initial assumption is that managers will engage in earnings management, then a useful theory would presumably say something about how accounting practice—and thus accounting—may be improved. By presenting an urgent problem, then prohibiting us from solving it by requiring descriptives only, science is stunted (Sterling, 1990). Sterling uses medical science as an example of how detrimental this is—if we identify the smallpox virus but are limited to describing the virus, disallowing prescriptions to be vaccinated, the virus would only spread—granted, giving us more material for descriptive research, but severely limiting the research agenda (and hindering improvement in people's health and welfare).

This brings us to the next point. However attractive the notion is that accounting researchers should be objective, accounting is a social science, a branch of humanities. It is a profession and a practice, involving professionalism and judgments.[5] Accounting practice is not *discovered*, it is *agreed upon*. In philosophy, one may speak of the social construction (see, e.g. Searle, 1995; Berger and Luckmann, 1966) of reality. Social reality is created (and language creates reality, rather than merely reflecting it). We need not delve deeper into this philosophical standpoint, but conclude that accounting is created by humans to serve a purpose. Devine (1960) wrote:

> It is a trite commonplace that accounting is a service activity, and only a few eccentrics would hold the view that society should subsidize accountants for accounting's sake or for the esthetic value of the product. In fact, it is argued that accounting not only should be useful to the group that pays the bill but should also have its procedures appraised by reference to some quantitative scale of social usefulness. Accounting is tinged by the public interest! (p. 397)

The "first order of business" must therefore be to decide on the exact purpose of accounting.

5 This can also be used as an argument in defense of PAT and its (implicit) focus on *accountants* and accounting *choices*.

It is not obvious who decides this. Even general-purpose statements will be limited in some ways, favoring some stakeholders rather than others. The past fifty years have witnessed a clear capital market-orientation in research; whether this will remain the case in the future is beyond our capacity to say. Having decided on a purpose, however, provides a framework that enables us to "investigate and conduct research in terms of carefully constructed objectives" (Devine, 1960, p. 399). Such research may permit or even require a range of empirical and deductive approaches.

Perhaps fortunately, recent research, despite being empirical, makes implicit if not explicit suggestions about what can be done, given the evidence provided. For example, if an empirical study compares two accounting methods, and these have different implications for capital markets, then one may be assumed to be superior to another. What is "good" and "bad" is thus implied, if not stated in prescriptive terms. As stated by Watts and Zimmerman (1990, p. 148), "A positive theory differs from a normative theory, though a positive theory can have normative implications once an objective function is specified."

This brings us to an important point: we perceive *a large portion of* accounting research, whether normative or positive, to ultimately be concerned with ways of improving accounting practice (and the quality of outcomes). Individual scholars may disagree with this, but as pointed out by Edwards et al. (2013), the most renowned normative thinkers "all sought to improve its quality and usefulness based on normative thinking informed by observations concerning the interconnection between accounting and commerce." Meanwhile, many empirical researchers today are eager to inform standard-setters and other authoritative financial bodies, highlighting how their key contribution is to regulation (and the improvement of accounting quality). It is a only a pity that communication between the two "camps" falters. As pointed out by Hopwood (2007):

> On the one hand, we have those who can research the consequences of accounting, be it with a capital market or behavioral emphasis. Such researchers currently represent the mainstream of accounting research. On the other hand, however, are those who have a thorough understanding of accounting itself and can reflect on its internal logics and the possibilities for these to change. Such researchers tended to be more in vogue from the 1930s until the period in the 1960s that witnessed the intellectual developments we have just discussed. In an ideal world, researchers having such obviously complementary interests and skills would communicate and collaborate, but that has very rarely happened. We tend to have one emphasis or the other despite the fact that both are needed.

Finally, and to conclude, "better" can only be understood in terms of objectives that are specified *a priori* by value judgments—such as improved decision-making and resource allocation. While the objectives of accounting may be determined normatively through a political system, normative statements and theories can tell us how to best achieve this objective, not least when informed by positive theories on the consequences of actual policies and resulting practice.

2.3 A summary of theories and hypotheses in the field of financial accounting

In light of the above, and probably to the fervent accounting scholar's disappointment, it is perhaps surprising to find that there are few actual *accounting theories*. Perhaps less surprisingly, there is no unified "Theory of Accounting." Instead, most of the theories we speak of in financial accounting are adopted from other disciplines—primarily microeconomics, finance, and management studies that apply sociology. Below, we briefly describe the core elements of commonly employed theories, assumptions and hypotheses in the field of financial accounting. We also touch briefly upon the contexts in which they have been used and how they relate to accounting quality. The purpose is to provide concise reference material to facilitate the reading of subsequent chapters. Since the theories and ideas are interlinked, there is no obvious starting point. An overview and introduction to key terminology therefore facilitates the presentation of each successive topic.

All of the theories below are predominantly descriptive. They have been used to explain the *role* (and thus consequences) of financial reporting and explore *determinants* of financial accounting outcomes. Whereas the first four sections primarily provide a market or economic perspective to the study of accounting, the last two adopt a broader perspective by considering a wider range of stakeholders and the interactions between organizations and society. With respect to normative theory, we acknowledge the debate in the literature, making references to it whenever appropriate, and further refer to standard-setters' work as an example of current accounting thought.

2.3.1 Efficient market hypothesis (EMH)

The **efficient market hypothesis (EMH)** is an extension of microeconomic price theory that essentially predicts that security *prices fully incorporate all available information in the market*. Under market efficiency, it is impossible to consistently gain abnormal or excess returns (i.e., returns that exceed the market's) given a set of information that is available to market participants *and* given the same accepted level of risk.

Fama (1970), a pioneer in developing the EMH, distinguishes between different categories of EMH tests based on the nature of information. *Strong form* efficiency means that share prices reflect *all* information—public *and* private (i.e., insider); *semi-strong form* efficiency assumes prices reflect all information *publicly known*; and *weak form* efficiency implies that the current share price incorporates all historical data, meaning that past security prices cannot be used to predict current or future prices. Each one of these forms of efficiency subsumes the previous, meaning that if markets are efficient in the semi-strong form, the assumptions of weak form efficiency also hold. Among these types of efficiency, the *semi-strong* form is most often accepted and assumed, although in some situations it appears as if not even weak form efficiency holds. Meanwhile, *strong form* efficiency is not considered realistic as it denies the possibility that corporate insiders could use private information to earn excess returns on their investments at the expense of outsiders.

There are primarily two ways of testing the validity of the EMH: 1) Is it possible to consistently gain abnormal returns at a given risk level? That is, is it possible to beat the market more often than not without investing in assets that have above-market risk? 2) Are stock market prices correct (which should be roughly true if prices reflect all the available information)?[6] However, it is notoriously difficult to carry out tests based on the above questions.

In order to test the EMH based on the first question, one must ensure that the measurement of returns is **risk-adjusted**; that is, higher returns are naturally required for riskier assets, and this must be accounted for. Simply put, one must estimate expected returns in order to calculate abnormal returns. This requires some form of asset pricing model. At around the same time as the birth of the EMH, finance researchers were developing the Capital Asset Pricing Model (CAPM). CAPM predicts that:

$$\text{expected rate of return on a security} = \text{risk-free rate} + \underbrace{\beta \times \text{market portfolio's risk}}_{\text{Risk premium for stock}}$$

where β ("beta") is the volatility or variation in the price of a stock compared to the market, where values of "1" indicate equal volatility, values above "1" indicate higher volatility and values below "1" indicate lower volatility. Note that by definition, the market as a whole always has a β of "1." All in all, the expected rate of return on a security should only rise above the risk-free rate and the average market returns to the extent that the underlying instrument is considered more *volatile*. The problem is that evidence of *inefficiencies* may be a result of errors in the pricing model used. If it is incomplete, it will not accurately account for all the risk factors that affect the price. Tests of the EMH thus become *joint tests* of the accuracy of the asset pricing model and of market efficiency, which clearly presents researchers with a conundrum! In fact, in a much-cited paper (Fama and French, 1992), Fama himself shows that expected returns behave as if risk is not only due to volatility in the instrument, but also due to the firm's size and B/M (book-to-market) ratio[7]. Evidence indicated that more volatile stocks had *not* outperformed the market during the long test window.

In order to test the EMH based on the second question, one must identify clearly mispriced stock. This is more difficult than it sounds. What about stock market "bubbles" and crashes that seem to occur at regular intervals? Are these not obvious indications that markets are inefficient? Advocates of the EMH would deny this. It is often difficult to rule out the possibility that the information set or perceived risk levels changed, which would be rational explanations for changes in security prices and consistent with market efficiency. After all, unexpected events will and should affect market prices when markets are efficient. More importantly, for a "bubble" to indicate inefficiency, it is not sufficient to simply point to extreme price changes after the fact. With 20/20 hindsight, mispricing may seem obvious.

6 See https://www.youtube.com/watch?v=bM9bYOBuKF4 for a very insightful debate between Eugene Fama and Richard Thaler.

7 Because of the lack of theoretical explanations for this, they were surprised that the work was even published (see interview with Euguene Fama: https://www.youtube.com/watch?v=nS6HAzOEJgM). However, the so-called Fama-French 3-factor model has become enormously popular among academics.

However, unless a "bubble" is identified *before the fact* and the *end* can be predicted, it is doubtful that it disproves efficiency.

The EMH is a model and as with all models, it is necessarily an incomplete representation of the real world. For example, the EMH-CAPM framework relies on some strict assumptions, such as that investors are rational, have the same set of information and have homogeneous expectations (and thus interpret information uniformly). It assumes perfect markets, meaning that there are no transaction costs, no costs of contracting and no information processing costs (Modigliani and Miller, 1958).

Although there are examples of when the EMH does not hold, consistent evidence against it is surprisingly difficult to come by, which means that in both research and practice, the EMH is to be viewed a useful null hypothesis. Fama says (and Richard Thaler, a behavioral researcher, agrees): "I don't know any investors who shouldn't behave as if markets are efficient."[8]

The EMH and CAPM greatly influenced the accounting literature beginning in the late 1960s. Especially the work by Ball and Brown (1968) and Beaver (1968) had a major influence on future empirical research in accounting. This body of research emphasized the role of financial accounting in providing information to the security market. Adopting an **information perspective**, one tried to find a significant relationship between accounting information and stock price—if the price changes upon the release of information, presumably that information is **value-relevant**. Whereas normative researchers in the past worried that earnings numbers were meaningless, especially in the absence of *uniform* measures (see Chapter 4), positive research showed that earnings were indeed useful. Because the EMH implies that accounting information is *not* the sole source of information (Watts and Zimmerman, 1986), investors and financial analysts compete to obtain information from various sources that may or may not be based on accounting. Essentially, because there are other sources of information, the earnings number will be evaluated by investors using these other sources, and they will make sense of the earnings number no matter how it has been calculated, thus preventing it from being meaningless. Nor are managers able to make up fictitious earnings numbers, as this would be discovered by the market.

One important possible implication of the EMH for accounting is that accounting choices adopted by firms do *not* affect their share prices in the market under the condition that detailed information of these accounting choices are provided. The idea is that accounting choices by firms do not directly affect future cash flows and are thus irrelevant to firm value. As long as sufficient information about accounting procedures and policies are disclosed, investors are able to "see through" the accounting choices, and predict the ultimate future cash flows and returns.

Over the past few decades, criticism toward the EMH has flourished. Research in behavioral finance—and perhaps to a lesser degree in accounting—have pointed to investors' lack of rationality and not least to the costs of processing information, which prevents prices from quickly converging to some "fundamental" or "intrinsic" value.

Furthermore, it is important to note that the EMH makes no distinction between which

8 See interview with Richard Thaler and Euguene Fama: https://www.youtube.com/watch?v=bM9bYOBuKF4

type or quality of information or which format of presentation is preferable (we shall see in later chapters that this assumption is debated in recent accounting literature). The EMH assumes that as soon as the information is "out there," it is used by investors and stock prices adjust correspondingly. In reality, information-processing costs may have to be taken into account, as these can slow down price adjustments, thereby making markets less efficient. As a consequence, strategies used or examined by firms, investors and researchers that exploit nuances in language, readability and legibility of texts and understandability and visibility of disclosures (especially supplementary disclosures compared to formally recognized line items) may make sense.

We return to the EMH as we devote an entire chapter (Chapter 3) to market efficiency and information asymmetry. For now, it is sufficient to conclude that the EMH has had a significant impact on finance research as well as on accounting research ever since its emergence about half a century ago.

2.3.2 Theory of asymmetric information

Strong form efficiency assumes that prices reflect *all*, public and private, information. However, this form of the hypothesis is generally rejected based on evidence that individuals with private information (e.g., corporate insiders) can benefit from trading based on private information. This brings us to another set of important theories in the accounting literature: theories on asymmetrical information.

Whenever transacting parties in a market are not privy to the same information, markets have been shown to become inefficient. In the extreme case, when one party has no information at all, the market may in fact break down altogether. The most well-known theories on asymmetric information were developed independently by George Akerlof, Michael Spence and Joseph Stiglitz, all of whom received the Nobel Memorial Prize in Economic Sciences in 2001 for their contributions to the field. Akerlof's and Spence's ideas are presented subsequently.

In his seminal article, Akerlof (1970) describes what may happen to a market under extreme information asymmetry—the seller has all the information about the product and the buyer has none. Taking the example of the used-car market, if low-quality cars ("lemons") cannot be distinguished from high-quality cars, sellers of low-quality cars will be encouraged to enter while sellers of high-quality cars will opt out of the market. The reasoning behind this is derived from distributional assumptions concerning the price and quantity of cars in the market. If one assumes that the quality of cars is normally distributed from 0 to 1, where 0 represents the lowest quality and 1 represents the highest quality, then the average car will have a quality of 0.5. Buyers, who have no information on which to base their market valuation of a given car, will assume that the quality of the car is 0.5 and be willing to pay (set the market price) accordingly. However, sellers of cars that are of higher quality than 0.5 will be unwilling to transact, knowing that their cars are undervalued at the market price. Buyers, in turn, know that only low-quality cars, whose value is equal to or below the market price, will be available for sale, which leads to a new, lower equilibrium price being set. In fact, at any price, high-quality cars will be undervalued (since they are better than the average car). This will force more sellers out of the market, causing buyers to demand an even larger discount on the price, pushing down the market value of every car even further. A downward spiral is created until only cars worth close to nil will be up for sale (see Text Box 2.1). Although both buyers and sellers could benefit from transacting, the fact that they cannot agree on a price in the absence of information means that the market breaks down. Where capital markets are concerned, this has wider implications as those requiring capital cannot obtain it at what they deem a fair price, leading to a suboptimal allocation of resources in the economy. When shares are offered at a discount, there is an increase in what firms must sacrifice in order to gain access to capital (i.e., the cost of capital increases).

One proposed solution to the information asymmetry problem that is relevant in a capital market setting is the one offered by Michael Spence in his seminal paper from 1973. The original theory uses the labor market as an example to illustrate the strategy known as **signaling**. In brief, the idea is that information asymmetry in the labor market means that employers cannot distinguish between productive and less productive workers. Employers are thus unwilling to offer more than the unconditional (average) wage to any job applicant. A potential employee who considers him- or herself more productive (of higher quality) would want to *signal* this in order to be paid a higher wage. Instead of actually raising the productivity of the worker, *education* may be used as a **signal** to future employers that the individual is capable of obtaining a degree. Because it is costly—an investment is needed in terms of both money and effort—education serves as a potentially effective signal of productivity to employers.

Text Box 2.1 **The distribution of used cars when there is information asymmetry: The "lemon" problem**

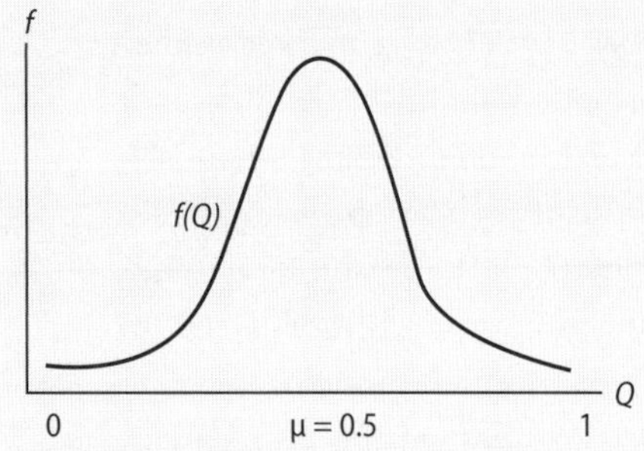

Assumption:
- The quality of cars available on the market is normally distributed at the outset
- Sellers know the quality of cars on the market, while buyers do not

In the absence of information, the market collapses.

No equilibrium price much greater than zero can be reached because buyers know that sellers have an information advantage (i.e. there is information asymmetry) and a price cannot be agreed upon

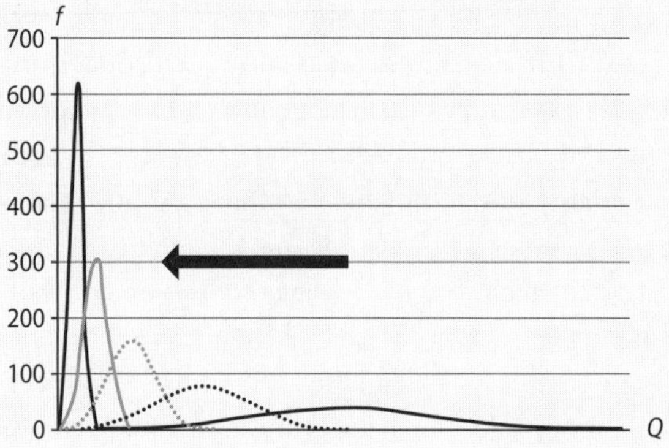

Signaling theory has been used in the accounting literature to explain why disclosures are made. The underlying premise is that if disclosures may be considered effective signals, they will help investors distinguish between high- and low-quality firms and thus reduce information asymmetry.

2.3.3 The nature of the firm and agency theory

In introductory microeconomic textbooks, the **neoclassical theory of the firm** makes several simplified assumptions regarding the firm, including that the owner and the entrepreneur (manager) is the same individual, that there is no uncertainty in the world and no transaction costs and that there is only one product and production function, all of which make the one goal of profit-maximization attainable. This is not to be considered particularly realistic, but in many applications it may serve as a useful point of departure or benchmark, as one introduces more complex scenarios. In reality, firms typically do not just have one product or production function. They tend to operate on many different product and geographical markets. Also, maximizing profits is not necessarily what the firm does. Rather, firms may aim for profit-*satisficing*, which is equivalent to making "good enough" profits. Managerial individual motives and incentives and the sheer size and complexity of the structure of firms have been raised as explanations for why profit maximization is not achieved. However, by allowing the firm to have varying objectives, the task of predicting firm behavior and strategies becomes very difficult.

The **nexus of contracts** view of the firm (e.g., Coase, 1937) sees the firm as a collection of formal and informal contracts between different individuals and attempts to explain why these contracts come about and how they affect the firm. The modern theory of the firm does not treat the firm as a decision-maker in its own right; rather, the decisions are made by the various contracting parties (managers, shareholders, employees, debtholders, regulatory bodies, boards of directors, suppliers or customers). By looking at the firm as a series of contracts, the firm's boundaries become an object of study. Where does a firm "end" and where does the market take over? What should be done in-house and what should be outsourced?

Consider a market composed only of individuals who specialize in doing one thing and trade whatever they cannot do themselves. Many market transactions between these otherwise independent actors become necessary, including finding a suitable party with which to do the transaction, negotiating the contract terms, arranging for the transaction to take place and monitoring the quality of whatever is being purchased. With **zero transaction costs**, this will be a highly efficient setup. But what happens if one allows for the possibility of **non-zero transaction costs**? After all, carrying out all of the above tasks takes time and it is not effortless. Transaction costs are likely to exist and be higher the greater the frequency of the underlying transaction, the more specific the traded asset (assets that can only be used in a particular line of production are going to be more difficult to purchase in the market because any seller will want to be compensated greatly for the required specialization and the risk associated with having only one buyer) and the greater the uncertainty surrounding the transaction. Uncertainty here is driven by behavioral uncertainty due to **opportunism**

Text Box 2.2 **Transaction-cost economics**

Transaction cost theory was pioneered by Ronald Coase and his student Oliver E. Williamson, both of whom received the Nobel Memorial Prize in Economic Sciences (Coase in 1991 and Williamson in 2009) for their proposals on transaction cost theory. In a much-cited paper "Transaction-cost economics: The governance of contractual relations," Williamson (1979) focuses on how firms minimize their transactions costs—referred by him as how firms "economize" on transaction costs. In order to answer this question, he compares contracts that vary by the degree of complexity and duration. In many cases and for many contracts, *specific* investment in human and physical capital is needed and the inherent complexity of these types of contracts generally leads to greater transaction costs. To moderate transaction costs in such contracts, Williamson introduces the importance of *governance structures*. According to Williamson (1979, p.246):

> Governance structures, however, are properly regarded as part of the optimization problem. For some transactions, a shift from one structure to another may permit a simultaneous reduction in both the expense of writing a complex contract (which economizes on bounded rationality) and the expense of executing it effectively in an adaptive, sequential way (by attenuating opportunism).

Opportunism is seen as a central concept in studying transaction costs. A combination of suitable governance structures may limit opportunism and, therefore, contribute to the optimization of transaction costs.

by transacting parties, lack of communication or simply by other changes no one is able to foresee (Text Box 2.2). Apart from transaction costs, another cost associated with the market is that contracts will by necessity be incomplete, due to the **bounded rationality** of the contracting parties. Everything cannot be foreseen or included in the contract. The assumption of opportunism and bounded rationality are central to transaction cost economics; transaction costs increase the harder it is to achieve complete contracts and the more opportunism there is. These interact with each other since, if contracts were complete, there would be no room for opportunism.

If it becomes too costly to transact, the market is abandoned. But since not everything can be done by any one individual, he/she organizes production in a firm, which functions as a nexus of contracts. It is cheaper to negotiate contracts within the boundaries of the firm, which in practice is run as a "benign dictatorship"[9]. For example, the manager negotiates with the employee that he or she should carry out a job for a fixed amount. Because of the hundreds of small tasks that need to be carried out, it is cheaper to settle everything within an employment contract. Although the contract by its nature will be incomplete, with few details concerning what the employee should do, it is nevertheless an efficient solution. Implicit, social contracts exist within the firm, which both parties have incentives to adhere to—simply because it is costly to interact with the market for every single transaction. Then why does the firm not

9 *The Economist*, July 29, 2017, p. 54

grow indefinitely, becoming a monopoly? Primarily two reasons exist: first, organizational costs increase disproportionately when the complexity and size of the firm increases; second, efficiency losses in the production are predicted as a result of increased firm size. This may be summarized as there being *diminishing returns to management* (Coase, 1937).

A central assumption of microeconomic theory is that individuals act to maximize their own utility. What the nexus of contracts view implies is that whether a firm profit maximizes is dependent on whether this is consistent with the manager's own utility maximization. When the manager is also the owner, profit maximization and utility maximization are more likely to go hand in hand. However, as soon as a firm grows, the owner and the manager tend to be different individuals. Meanwhile, the underlying reason for designing contracts is the allocation of decision rights to the best-informed party. However, the delegation of tasks by one party (the **principal**) to another (the **agent**) can be problematic, given the assumption that contracting parties are self-interested and seek to maximize their own utility. Managers may, for example, find utility in job security that comes from taking low risk (leading to lower profits), in enjoying non-pecuniary perquisites that are costly to the firm or in making decisions that are suboptimal in the long run but beneficial in the short run as this increases bonuses (neglecting to make investments in order to reduce costs and raise earnings upon which variable pay is based).

Agency theory is concerned with resolving problems due to conflicts of interests between these parties (so-called **agency problems**). The first explicit proposals of agency theory were made in the early 1970s by Stephen Ross in the field of economics and Barry Mitnick in the field of political science.[10] Agency theory *of the firm*, meanwhile, was developed by Jensen and Meckling and their paper from 1976 has by now received more citations than almost any other paper in business research. Under the nexus of contracts view of firms, principal-agent relationships, and thus principal-agent problems, are inherent to firms.

The separation of ownership from control (Berle and Means, 1932) is the primary source of agency conflicts between managers and shareholders. Whereas the decisions are made by managers, the ultimate costs or benefits of these decisions are borne by investors. The managers of a corporation may have personal goals that compete with the owners' goal of maximizing shareholder wealth. Assuming imperfect labor and capital markets, managers are predicted to maximize their own utility, as other stakeholders do, which implies that corporate resources will not completely be used for increasing shareholder value.

Principals anticipate that agents will undertake self-serving activities that could be detrimental to their economic welfare. In order to alleviate the negative consequences of this problem, agency theory describes the need for monitoring and contracting in order to restrict the agent's potentially opportunistic actions. Costly monitoring activities—such as recruiting a board of directors to oversee management or auditing financial statements—and contractual arrangements—such as compensation contracts that are linked to firm performance—are supposed to be present in firms in order to resolve the agency problems, since the absence of any contractual mechanism or monitoring system can have much more costly consequences for principals.

10 See Mitnick's own account: http://www.pitt.edu/~mitnick/agencytheory/agencytheoryoriginrev11806r.htm

Monitoring in the shape of financial reporting and auditing can help offer guarantees that an agent's consumption of benefits is limited. Accounting information thus plays an important role in mitigating agency costs. Accounting is used in shaping the contracts that aim to mitigate agency costs. For example, as a main solution to agency problems, compensation contracts are suggested to be useful in aligning the interests of managers and shareholders. Compensation contracts, such as bonus plans, are often written using accounting numbers. Furthermore, debt contracts frequently include restrictions that are defined under debt covenants conditional on certain accounting numbers. Contracting parties are also interested in the auditing process that provides *assurance* on the accounting information provided by firms. The use of accounting information as the main basis for evaluating the performance of the agent implies that the quality of accounting information is critical for these contracts to be efficient.

2.3.4 Positive accounting theory (PAT)

As we saw above, Watts and Zimmerman proposed the **positive accounting theory** (PAT) (see. e.g., Watts and Zimmerman, 1978; Watts and Zimmerman, 1986; Watts and Zimmerman, 1990), which is perhaps one of the most well-recognized theories in the accounting literature. Instead of providing specific solutions or prescriptions for accounting practice, positive accounting theory promotes a positive approach in accounting research. This approach received considerable criticism for not being unique, and more resembling a methodological approach (i.e., positivism) rather than a theoretical approach. In defending the choice of the term "positive accounting theory," Watts and Zimmerman (1990, p. 148) state that:

> Positive accounting research existed long before the publication of our 1978 and 1979 papers. We applied the label "positive" to a set of existing research studies. The prime reason we attached this adjective in "Towards a Positive Theory of the Determination of Accounting Standards" was to emphasize that accounting theory's role is to provide explanations and predictions for accounting practice.

However, this is contentious in itself, as it precludes the normative role of accounting theory. Be that as it may, what else does PAT entail? It focuses on utility-maximizing actors, the sources of incentives, and the effect of incentives on accounting practice.

One implication of the EMH is that accounting is not the sole source of information about the firm—which was a widely held belief in the 1960s before the EMH gained ground in accounting research. Watts and Zimmerman (1986) point to two consequences of this for researchers. First, it led them to examine whether accounting numbers convey useful information to capital markets (see comments on the EMH and the information perspective above). This research, which studied the association between accounting earnings and prices, took the EMH to be valid. That is, there was no test of the EMH in this context. Second, it opened up for the test of the EMH against a competing hypothesis—one suggesting that investors are misled by opportunistic accounting choices made by firms. That investors would be misled is not controversial if accounting is the sole source of information about the firm. However, since the EMH implies that accounting competes with other sources of information (such as the media, financial analysts or any expert opinions), it would seem less likely that investors are "fooled." Indeed, the EMH and CAPM predict that accounting choice has *no effect on value* (see previous section), since—in the absence of taxes and tax effects—accounting choices have no cash flow effects. The crucial point here is that all investors know about the accounting methods used, so that they will see through, for example, opportunistic income shifting. So-called "no-effect" hypotheses in accounting provided no room for predicting and explaining why certain accounting choices are favored as compared to others. For example, why do some firms choose straight-line and others accelerated depreciation methods? Watts and Zimmerman (1990) assert that to predict and explain *accounting choices*, accounting researchers must relax the assumption of zero information and contracting costs (e.g., Jensen and Meckling, 1976). Recognition of these costs is necessary for predicting and explaining accounting choices[11], which came to be the focus of subsequent positive research. The view adopted in PAT is that accounting choices define contracts, affect contracting costs and, therefore, have economic consequences. PAT opens up for the possibility that managerial incentives to choose accounting methods depend on the costs and benefits of contracts. For example, accounting earnings are frequently used in executive compensation contracts (e.g., bonus plans). This suggests that the accounting choices made by management have a direct effect on the wealth of managers and are therefore potentially opportunistic. This is referred to as the **management compensation hypothesis**. The **debt hypothesis** and **political cost hypothesis** are other hypotheses associated with PAT. The former focuses on the use of accounting numbers in debt covenants and on managerial incentives to increase earnings (and thereby equity) to avoid covenant violations, while the latter explains the adoption of accounting methods to lower earnings resulting from political attention and lobbying. All of these hypotheses can be grouped together using the term **accounting choice theory** (Watts, 1992).

In explaining the relationship between accounting choices and contracting costs, two competing perspectives are considered. On the one hand, the *efficiency perspective* suggests that accounting procedures are chosen cost-effectively in order to increase firm value. Meanwhile, the *opportunistic perspective* refers to managers' *ex post* choice of different accounting procedures, based on the underlying features of the contracts. This latter perspective is explained by managerial incentives to maximize their own utility at the expense of other stakeholders, a key assumption of agency theory. We elaborate upon these two opposing perspectives and the implications of these in accounting choice research in Chapter 8.

2.3.5 Institutional theory

One prominent theoretical perspective in organizational (management) studies is **institutional theory** (e.g. Meyer and Rowan, 1977; DiMaggio and Powell, 1983; Zucker, 1987). It makes the organization its own unit of analysis, rather than a mere aggregation of

11 In the extreme case of zero transaction costs, there is no need for accounting. As soon as a piece of information is known to *one*, it is known to *everyone*.

individuals with varying incentives, and emphasizes the role of factors other than economic rationality in determining organizational actions. The institutional setting, including cultural values, industry tradition or standards, regulation and environmental norms, helps explain organizational behavior. The organization responds to the above factors in order to achieve *legitimization* rather than economic *optimization*.

DiMaggio and Powell (1983) explain the main factors of institutionalization through different mechanisms of institutional isomorphic change. **Isomorphism** is derived from the Greek words *isos*, meaning "same, equal," and *morphe*, meaning "shape, form." In other words, it can be understood as a process of being shaped or formed to become like or equal to something else. Isomorphic change may be a result of **coercive**, **mimetic** or **normative** forces.

Coercive isomorphism refers to change brought on by force induced by authorities. Examples of coercive forces on the development of accounting practice include domestic laws and EU directives, enforcement agencies, such as the SEC, and corporate governance legislation, such as the Sarbanes-Oxley (SOX) Act of 2002 with its focus on internal control mechanisms in US firms. Politicians and corporate lobbyists, acting directly or through these bodies, constitute more examples.

Mimetic isomorphism refers to when uncertainty drives organizations to try to legitimize themselves by imitating other successful organizations (peers). Disclosures of corporate social responsibility can frequently illustrate how firms mimic or emulate the behavior of other firms that are successful at communicating "green" strategies with stakeholders. Copying disclosures of larger (legitimized) firms is another example of observed behavior. Text Box 2.3 shows a small Spanish firm emulating a larger Spanish firm in the disclosure of its main sources of judgment and estimation uncertainty (required by IAS 1).

Text Box 2.3 **Institutional forces shaping disclosure decisions**

The following illustrates how a small company emulates a larger company in the same country, possibly for legitimization reasons. The disclosure in question is discretionary and relates to critical assumptions and estimates in the financial statements (Note 1 in most annual reports).

NOTE 5. RESPONSIBILITY FOR THE INFORMATION AND ESTIMATES MADE

The information contained in these financial statements is the responsibility of the Directors of the Parent Company.

In drawing up the accompanying consolidated financial statements, estimates have occasionally been used by the Management of the Group to quantify certain assets, liabilities, income, expenses and commitments recorded therein. These estimates basically refer to:

- The measurement of assets and goodwill to determine whether there are impairment losses (Note 3.d).
- The assumptions used for the actuarial calculation of pension and redundancy liabilities and commitments (Note 19).
- The useful life of the property, plant and equipment and intangible assets (Note 8 and 9).

- The assumptions used to calculate the fair value of financial instruments (Note 17).
- The probability of occurrence and the amount of liabilities for an indeterminate amount of contingent liabilities.
- The recoverability of deferred tax assets based on estimates of future results.

2.2 RESPONSIBILITY FOR THE INFORMATION AND USE OF ESTIMATES

The information in these financial statements is the responsibility of the Board of Directors, who expressly state that all the principles and methods provided for in IFRSs have been applied.

In preparing the accompanying consolidated financial statements estimates were occasionally made the senior executives of the Group in order to quantify certain of the assets, liabilities, income, expenses and commitments reported therein. These estimates relate basically to the following:

- The measurement of assets and goodwill to ascertain whether there are any impairment losses thereon (see Note 3-e).
- The assumptions used in the actuarial calculation of the pension liabilities and commitments and collective redundancy procedures (see Note 16).
- The useful life of the property, plant and equipment and intangible assets (see Notes 3-a and 3-d).
- The methods used to measure the fair value of the financial instruments (see Notes 3-g and 19).
- The power supplied to customers not read by meters.
- Certain electricity system aggregates, including those corresponding to other utilities such as output, customer billings, power consumed, incentives for the distribution activity, etc. that make it possible to estimate the overall settlements in the electricity system and which could affect the amounts of the assets, liabilities, income and expenses related with the electricity system business and, in particular, the shortfall in revenue from regulated activities in Spain.
- The interpretation of certain legislation concerning the regulation of the electricity industry the definitive economic effects of which will be ultimately determined by the decisions taken by the agencies competent for the settlement thereof, since said decisions had not yet been taken at the date of preparation of these consolidated financial statements.
- The probability of the occurrence and the amount of liabilities which are uncertain as to their amount or contingent liabilities (see Note 3-m).
- The future facility closure and land restoration costs (see Notes 3.a and16.3).
- The results for tax purposes of the various Group companies that will be reported to the tax authorities in the future that served as the basis for recognising the various income tax-related balances in the accompanying consolidated financial statements (see Note 3-o).

Normative isomorphism is change due to pressure to conform to professional practice and standards, including industry norms. Looking at Text Box 2.3, an alternative or complementary explanation for the similarity of the texts could be that they share auditors and that the audit firm's template determines the outcome. Several institutions could represent different forces simultaneously. For example, accounting standards are an extension of EU law and could possibly be seen as a coercive force. Because there are few sanctions levied on European firms that do *not* comply, however, it could be more appropriate to view standards as a normative force generated as a result of a collaboration between independent professionals.

In general, some researchers in financial accounting have adopted an institutional perspective in attempting to explain accounting choices and estimates at the firm level. For example, in the airline industry, it is common to estimate the expected useful life of an aircraft to be 20 years. Institutional theory would suggest that firms are not primarily concerned with the accuracy of this number, but seek to legitimize their decisions by conforming to accepted industry practice and benchmarks (which illustrative examples provided in accounting standards may have helped create), following guidance and advice from the "Big 4" audit firms, copying large and/or successful peers and complying with regulatory restrictions. As such, outcomes tend to be the result of a combination of institutional forces. These considerations are relevant when evaluating accounting quality, since the financial reporting process risks being a product of institutional forces rather than being geared toward reflecting the firm's underlying economics.

Sometimes, changing a firm's formal structure in order to achieve legitimacy may seem undesirable. Changes may, for example, be costly in that they reduce organizational efficiency or flexibility, or they may be in conflict with the firm's ideological beliefs. A firm might then **decouple** its formal policies from its actual practice. Rather than isomorphic adaptation, the firm responds to institutional pressures by making *apparent* changes to its behavior or structure (Meyer and Rowan, 1977). A loose implementation of IFRS may be an example of how firms comply superficially, but make little effort to undertake substantial changes. A consistent application of IFRS may be obstructed by the fact that firms keep adhering to old practices and views even after they have officially adopted a new framework or set of standards. Rather than *de facto* (actual) harmonization of accounting standards, only *de jure* (formal) harmonization is achieved. Disclosure practices, in particular, have been shown to be associated with factors that would have influenced firms *before* IFRS adoption, such as the legal origin of the firm. By decoupling, a firm minimizes costs while (potentially) establishing or maintaining legitimacy.

2.3.6 Legitimacy theory

Legitimacy theory posits that organizational actions are shaped in a social context and are therefore affected by society's expectations (similar to institutional theory)(Guthrie and Parker, 1989; Lindblom 1983). Corporate disclosures, in particular, constitute a response to contextual factors—such as economic, social and political factors—provided in order to justify corporate actions. Through voluntary disclosure, organizations ensure, or perhaps pretend, that they meet social expectations. Lack of action by a firm in accordance with these expectations may have damaging consequences for its reputation. Furthermore, achieving legitimacy requires continuous actions in response to new expectations. Lindblom (1983) explains that the "legitimacy gap" is not constant over time; instead, it fluctuates as expectations of the public change. Resistance by firms to respond to public expectations increases the legitimacy gap and leads to larger conflicts. In attempting to explain accounting choices and accounting quality, legitimacy concerns have been used to explain both high- and poor-quality accounts.

Legitimacy theory in accounting is primarily used in a corporate social responsibility

(CSR) context. CSR reports mainly address public concerns regarding social and environmental matters and have become more and more focused on sustainability issues. The large number of voluntary sustainability disclosures could arguably best be explained by attempts to legitimize businesses. The extent and nature of sustainability disclosures change with the level and nature of expectations. At a time when firms undertake actions that may raise social or environmental concerns, firms may provide additional disclosures to explain and legitimize those actions. Legitimization may be desirable from a broader societal perspective, a consumer perspective or even an owner's perspective. The ethical considerations of investors, as well as their concerns over the costs of a firm's failure to achieve legitimacy, may drive them to also demand high-quality sustainability disclosures (we return briefly to CSR reporting and disclosure quality in Chapter 6).

One way of approaching legitimacy is to consider and contrast the institutional perspective with the **strategic perspective** (Beelitz and Merkl-Davies, 2012; Suchman, 1995). Whereas the former views legitimacy as something bestowed upon the organization by external parties (outsiders "looking in"), the latter views legitimacy as something that management is in control of and actively works for (insiders "looking out"). Management strategically demonstrates to external parties that "organisational practices are congruent with society's norms, values, and beliefs" (Beelitz and Merkl-Davies, 2012). Furthermore, from an institutional perspective, legitimacy is achieved through isomorphism, while from a strategic perspective, it is achieved through *substantive management*, including organizational change and the adoption of "violated values." If carrying out actual change is undesirable, decoupling (see previous section) may be performed according to the institutional perspective, or *symbolic management*, according to the strategic perspective. In their analysis of "CEO-speak" (the language of corporate leadership) following a legitimacy-threatening incident at a nuclear power plant, Beelitz and Merkl-Davies (2012) show examples of symbolic management. Two possible strategies are elaborated upon: By using excuses, apologies and justifications, a firm may attempt to reestablish legitimacy through words. Alternatively, a firm constructs a "firewall" between the negative event and the rest of the organization by admitting to the problems but emphasizing their limited nature (Beelitz and Merkl-Davies, 2012). Symbolic management and decoupling may be viewed as different forms of **impression management**.

We have now discussed a number of theories in accounting that have their roots in economic theory. Other theories applied in accounting research include social constructivism and critical theory. Different theories have different domains of applicability and focus on different research questions. Economic theory is useful for studying economic effects of accounting standards (for example in relation to capital market users), while social constructivism tends to focus on how concepts and understandings of the world are created in social interaction. Research applying critical theory, meanwhile, often focuses on how accounting is used to construct or maintain power structures in society. In this book, we focus on research based on economic theory as we focus on economic phenomena. A reason for this is the dominant role of economics-based research in financial accounting. In addition, it agrees with the view adopted by global standard-setters such as the IASB and the FASB.

2.4 Accounting quality and accounting theory

As discussed in Chapter 1 and clarified here, financial accounting literature contains references to a number of primarily descriptive theories, most of which have their roots in economics or other fields of social science. Hence, "accounting theory" is an umbrella term that does not actually refer to a single theory of accounting, but rather to a group of theories that have influenced the field. Whether they complement or compete with one another, the validity of these theories may be evaluated based on their ability to accurately describe a given (accounting) phenomenon.

But what would a prescriptive theory in accounting look like? As stated earlier in this chapter, a viable prescriptive theory would say something about desirable accounting practice based on given postulates, premises or assumptions. There are no widely cited theories of the sort, although normative statements are found in both standard-setting and research. Standards *are* norms, which explains their normative nature, while researchers often present positive research followed by implications for standard-setting, where the prescription is often implicit.

At this stage, we propose a **metatheory of financial accounting** that links the other theories together based on the concept of **accounting quality**. We argue that accounting quality is what standard-setters strive for, what capital markets desire, what firms must take a stance toward and what researchers in the field are concerned with. In other words, *accounting quality* is a key concept in the subject of accounting as it affects the ability of financial statement users to make capital allocation decisions and has implications for the effectiveness of contracts. It is affected by the standard-setting regime, the quality of enforcement and monitoring mechanisms as well as the incentives of management. This has been acknowledged by accounting scholars in their studies of standard implementation effects, managerial incentives and contracting implications of accounting choices. In describing how accounting quality affects, or is affected by, their chosen subject matter, researchers seek to prescribe ways in which accounting quality may be enhanced. The structure of this book follows this logic, as was explained in the introductory chapter.

A metatheory of financial accounting based on accounting quality includes both descriptive and prescriptive elements:

- *Descriptive (metatheoretical) statement no. 1:* Theories used in financial accounting are ultimately concerned with accounting quality.
- *Descriptive statement no. 2:* Standards, enforcement, auditors, internal monitoring and incentives determine accounting quality (see Part IV and V of the book).
- *Descriptive statement no. 3:* Accounting quality affects capital markets via the cost of capital and user perceptions of the firm (see Part III).
- *Prescriptive statement no. 1:* Accounting quality is achieved through faithfully represented and relevant—and therefore useful—financial reports (see Part II).
- *Prescriptive statement no. 2:* Accounting standards should allow more/less judgment in the preparation of financial reports in order to achieve higher-quality accounting (see Part V).

The main assumption underlying the prescriptive elements is that the objective of accounting is to be *useful*. Whereas "high quality" could be specified in terms of how faithfully represented (reliable), relevant, timely and understandable the information is, *usefulness* highlights the common view that accounting is utilitarian, represents a form of communication and constitutes a transaction *between different parties*: preparers and users. In Chapter 1, we look at different possible perspectives on useful accounting (and thus accounting quality), but ultimately focus on the capital markets perspective. In Chapter 3, we elaborate further on capital markets and the theories closely tied to this perspective.

2.5 Conclusions

Influenced by the dominant scientific paradigm in social science, the accounting discipline has adopted a post-positivistic scientific approach, where predictions and causal relationships are considered important for generating scientific knowledge while acknowledging the influence of normative values and objectives. Mainstream accounting research has largely adopted this view and attempts to explain and predict accounting practice by allowing for the direction of some pre-defined normative objectives—such as *better* accounting quality!

The concept of accounting quality is central in accounting research, and theories that have been used in the financial accounting discipline directly or indirectly deal with the main objective of accounting—being useful and thus of high quality.

Here, we summarize the main takeaways from the theories we introduced in this chapter:

1. There is typically information asymmetry between the firm (insiders) and capital providers (outsiders). Accounting in general and financial reporting in particular is meant to reduce this information gap. Questions asked include whether accounting provides information, and thus reduces information asymmetry. Primarily, these questions use theories on asymmetric information and agency theory.
2. The determinants of accounting output is of interest to accounting researchers. Questions asked include: What determines which information a firm releases? What drives accounting choices within a firm? What affects a firm's accounting policies? These questions are answered using theories on asymmetric information (signaling theory), agency theory, positive accounting theory, institutional theory and legitimacy theory.
3. Accounting quality as a concept may be incorporated into all of these theories. Quality matters for how effective financial reports are at reducing information asymmetries, market inefficiencies and agency problems. The quality will be affected by incentives and pressures to disclose, as explored through, for example, signaling, institutional or legitimacy theory.

Theories we have not yet touched upon are those that relate to *regulation*. In one sense, regulation can explain disclosure from an institutional perspective, although one no longer deals with *voluntary* disclosure *choices*, but rather *compliance* with mandatory disclosure requirements. Most of the time, economic theory is adopted in the context of accounting regulation. The main question here is: Do external non-market forces—more specifically, regulatory bodies—need to demand that information be released, or do firms do this adequately on their own accord? Although we do not refer to explicit theories on regulation, we devote a large part of the book to standard-setting and enforcement of standards, starting with the rationales for regulation in Chapter 4. Finally, other common queries made by researchers as well as regulators include: "Is this standard effective in promoting high-quality reporting?" "Which accounting policy should be promoted and which choices should be permitted?" Throughout, we thus refer implicitly and explicitly to the accounting quality effects of regulation and enforcement.

CHAPTER 3

A capital market perspective and the roles of accounting

Learning outcomes

Upon completion of this chapter, you will gain insight into key concepts relating to capital markets, such as:

- Market efficiency and its implications for accounting.
- Information asymmetry between the firm and capital markets.
- Principal-agent theory.
- The valuation and stewardship roles of accounting, as well as possible trade-offs between the two.

SO FAR, WE HAVE EXPLORED THE IDEA that high-quality accounting is accounting that is useful, and that the concept of usefulness is only relevant if one specifies an intended user. Although it is possible to think of various potential users and thus uses of accounting, we have advanced the idea that *capital market providers* are the primary, or intended, users of financial accounting. We now consider some key ideas and concepts relating to capital markets and the role of accounting in this context. More specifically, we:

- explore the notion of efficient capital markets and its implications for accounting,
- recognize the existence and effects of information asymmetries (which result from the fact that capital providers and firm management comprise different individuals) on accounting choices, and
- elaborate on the roles of accounting in closing information gaps between the firm and the market.

3.1 The efficient market hypothesis (EMH)

In the previous chapter, we introduced the Efficient Market Hypothesis (EMH), which in very simple terms states that:

Stock prices fully reflect all available information.

As pointed out by Fama (1970), this is "obviously an extreme null hypothesis [and] we do not expect it to be literally true"—not least because the term "all available information" is impossibly broad. It follows that in order to test this hypothesis, it is useful to categorize different subsets of information for which the statement is possibly true. Fama (1970) proposes three forms, and three related tests, of efficiency: *weak form* tests, *semi-strong form* tests and *strong form* tests. **Weak form** tests focus on whether prices fully reflect past security prices. The information set thus consists of historical prices (returns). **Semi-strong form** tests are concerned with whether prices fully reflect "other obviously publicly available information." **Strong form** tests focus on the possibility that prices fully reflect information to which some group of individuals has monopolistic access (insider information). Rejecting the null hypothesis of efficient capital markets has largely been unsuccessful when considering the weak and semi-strong form. Meanwhile, strong form efficiency is an approximation to the general statement that "prices fully reflect *all* available information" and, as stated above, it is thus too extreme to be viable. Instead, tests have focused on different groups in the investment community that may have access to special information and for which the statement may be true—such as average investors, professional investors and corporate insiders. Even when considering professional mutual fund managers, the model or hypothesis has been incredibly resistant to outright rejection.

The EMH in its "purest" form (i.e., under strong form efficiency) relies on some rather extreme assumptions of perfect markets. These include that there is a large number of buyers and sellers, products are homogeneous, participants are price-takers (no individual can affect price), there is perfect information (meaning information about prices is transparent and known by all participants), there are zero transaction costs, sellers are profit-maximizers and buyers are rational. However, these are not strictly required assumptions. Fama (1970) points out that these market conditions— such as that information is freely available to all market participants and there are no transaction costs in trading—are *sufficient but not necessary* conditions for market efficiency. In other words, they are possible but not necessary sources of inefficiency. This is good news for the EMH, since these conditions do not fully hold in real world markets; instead, the extent to which they do not hold, and the effect of this on price formation, is the "major goal of empirical work in this area" (p. 388).

Although several of the assumptions are questionable, a stock market is in some respects as good a representation of a perfect market as they come. For example, few people would dispute the first assumption, that many stock markets, especially in the US, are characterized by a large number of buyers and sellers. One thus speaks of stock markets as having high **liquidity**, which is a measure of how easy it is to make a quick trade at a given price. A liquid market allows assets to be traded at stable prices, because buyers and sellers agree on the price and must not wait long to find a party who values the asset at the same level as they do. This may, for example, be contrasted with markets for antiquities, which are not particularly liquid.

Meanwhile, given a variety of information sources that are not freely available and the existence of differences in how much information is possessed by different market participants, it would seem as if the assumptions of zero transaction costs and **perfect information** are unrealistic. Generally speaking, the greater the transaction costs, the less efficient the market. In a world where all existing information (including private information in firms) is available to everybody at no cost, prices will indeed adjust immediately upon the release (creation) of new information. By contrast, in the "real" world, obtaining information is not without cost, even when there are several sources of "free" information. Information-processing costs constitute a type of transaction cost that reduces market efficiency. That is, even when obtaining information does not involve monetary transactions, the reading and analysis of an annual report requires both time and effort (as well as a relatively advanced prior understanding of accounting, also obtained at a potentially substantial cost). This reduces the speed at which prices adjust. Hence, investors face a trade-off when assessing the information from different sources: they must decide how much they are willing to pay (in terms of both time and money) and how much information they need to acquire. With respect to the perfect information assumption, however, we note that the EMH does not require every individual to possess every single piece of available information—it is enough that market participants possess the information collectively. The assumption is that informed traders—to the benefit of uninformed traders—will trade on the market until an equilibrium price that reflects all available information is reached.

As for **investor rationality**, even taking information-processing costs into account, the assumption is that investors understand and use the information they possess in a homogeneous and rational manner, with profit-maximization in mind. Research in the field of behavioral finance has attempted to show that markets are not efficient due to the existence of **behavioral biases** among investors. Perhaps you know someone who buys and sells shares based on a "gut feeling" or perhaps you yourself act on a whim sometimes. This, however, does not necessarily make markets inefficient (either). The EMH does not require all participants to act rationally at all times, only that investors act rationally on average.

We do not seek to prove the realism of the above assumptions, nor do we systematically go through the general evidence that either supports or rejects market efficiency. For a more detailed exposition of the EMH, please refer to the finance literature. In the next two sections, however, we consider *some* of the evidence of market efficiency and the implications for accounting of each form of efficiency, along with observed empirical deviances from market efficiency in the weak and semi-strong forms (and consequently of the strong form). In general, as pointed out in Chapter 2, because tests of the EMH are joint tests of the market model used to calculate expected returns (a proxy for the market equilibrium) and the EMH (referred to as the *joint hypothesis problem*), the "evidence" has received considerable criticism. Brenner (1979) shows that "different market models lead to different conclusions" concerning the EMH, which is why researchers should not rely solely on one model. Further, documented deviances from efficiency—or **anomalies**—are of interest to us because they have been the focus of much *accounting* literature. Three streams of research are of particular interest here: that which documents a *Post-Earnings Announcement Drift (PEAD)*, that which investigates the effects of *fundamental analysis* and that which concerns *accruals anomalies* (see Richardson et al., 2010, for a detailed exposition). Whereas we return to the accruals anomaly in Chapter 7, we consider the former two in more depth below. Note that as much as these anomalies point to weakness in the EMH, "it takes a theory to beat a theory," as noted by Fama[1], "and these

1 See https://www.youtube.com/watch?v=bM9bYOBuKF4

anomalies are not theories." It behooves future researchers to try to develop working theories that can serve as adequate counter-theories to the EMH. The *adaptive market hypothesis* and the *incomplete revelations hypothesis* are two such attempts. We briefly present these at the end of this section.

3.1.1 Weak form efficiency

Weak form efficiency means that you cannot study past or current stock prices in order to predict future prices, since price changes are independent. This is implied by the **random walk** theory, which models stock price changes as stochastic (random) processes.[2] Much research points to markets being at least weak form efficient. However, traders who perform **technical analysis**, which is based on the study of time-series patterns or *trends* in the stock price, believe that the EMH in its weak form does *not* hold. If markets are not weak form efficient, investors can make abnormal returns by basing their investing patterns on statements such as "the stock market tends to do better on Fridays than on Mondays" or "the stock market goes down in October each year." **Momentum trading** is based on predictable price movements and the belief that if a share price has been going up (down) for a certain period of time, it will continue to do so for any particular length of time. That is, a momentum trader buys stock that has performed well in the *past* and sells stock that has performed poorly in the *past*). A highly cited finance paper by Jegadeesh and Titman (1993) shows that momentum trading generates abnormal returns.

The accounting literature has seen a considerable amount of effort put into describing and explaining a phenomenon known as **post-earnings announcement drift (PEAD)**, in which a firm's stock price continues to drift upwards upon good earnings news and downwards upon bad earnings news. That is, the market does not respond immediately to the release of new information, and today's prices are *not* independent from yesterday's or tomorrow's. In theory, PEAD allows investors to make (anomalous) abnormal returns if they trade based on the expected movement in stock price—a drift that could take place over days, weeks or even months. This constitutes evidence that markets are not even weak form efficient.

PEAD was introduced in the literature several decades ago, foundational papers (as presented by Richardson et al., 2010) being Foster et al. (1984), Bernard and Thomas (1989) and Bernard and Thomas (1990). Even Ball and Brown (1968) showed evidence of PEAD, but it was not recognized as such at the time (the authors' purpose was different). Those who question the EMH and seek to explain why PEAD would occur commonly base their arguments on theories in the growing field of behavioral finance. The **cognitive biases** and **limited attention** of investors are seen as credible explanations (e.g., Hirshleifer et al., 2012). That is, markets fail to be fully efficient because investors cannot process available information quickly enough for prices to reflect that information at all times. Understanding the implications of current earnings for future earnings is necessary in order to calculate a

2 More specifically, stock returns over time represent a one-dimensional random walk that may be described using a **Markov chain**; that is, the probability of transitioning to any particular state only depends on the current state (and not on any previous states).

market value based on expected future earnings or cash flow streams, and these implications may not be immediately or fully obvious. The EMH does not model how information is analyzed and whether or not information is easy to interpret. In practice, however, this becomes an issue. Therefore, investors and analysts can *create private information* through the *analysis of public information*. Evidence consistent with this is found in studies that show investor sophistication and the size of trades to be associated with abnormal returns from PEAD (Bartov et al., 2000b; Battalio and Mendenhall, 2005; Shivakumar, 2006). Investor sophistication, believed to be captured by institutional ownership, leads to a lower PEAD (and lower abnormal returns), while small trades, which are typically carried out by small (and less sophisticated) investors, lead to a higher PEAD (and higher abnormal returns). DellaVigna and Pollet (2009) present compelling evidence that Friday earnings announcements are followed by greater drifts, consistent with investors' limited attention at the end of the week. However, since investor sophistication has not been found to explain the accrual anomaly (see Chapter 7), the validity of such an explanation may be questioned. Even if the trading behavior of small or unsophisticated investors is the cause of the drift, it is noteworthy that sophisticated investors do not fully exploit this opportunity to make abnormal returns, *immediately eliminating* the drift (Richardson et al., 2010). More research is therefore called for in this area—as there is no consensus on what explains the drift.

The very existence of PEAD is disputed by many scholars, as it contradicts the EMH. Findings are instead explained in terms of *risk* and/or *transaction costs*. A risk-based explanation states that abnormal returns following an earnings announcement are miscalculated since CAPM, or a derivation thereof, is misspecified (the *joint hypothesis problem*). That is, abnormal returns occur due to incomplete risk adjustment and not due to an actual delayed price response. Meanwhile, the transaction cost explanation is based on the idea that even if investors are rational and act correctly based on information given to them, accessing and interpreting the information is likely to be costly. Because it is costly to obtain and act on information instantaneously, there *are* inefficiencies and possibly a slight drift. However, whether it is actually possible to exploit these inefficiencies in order to earn abnormal returns is highly questionable, since the costs themselves eat away at the profit. The observed price drift has also decreased over the years, a likely explanation being greater trading efficiency and IT-related developments (including algorithmic and high-frequency trading, HFT). Information-processing costs have dropped, partly because machines can pick up information more quickly and partly because digital information can be disseminated more quickly.

In sum, if markets are *not* weakly efficient, the trading strategies described in this section can generate abnormal returns. That is, a successful approach to trading would be to study current price trends. Prices are most likely not accurate, because they are predictable and do not fully reflect available information. However, if markets are weak form efficient, future returns cannot be predicted using information in current and historical returns, and more effort is required on behalf of the investor in order to earn abnormal returns. For example, as long as the market is not also semi-strong form efficient, one strategy is to scrutinize current public information in the form of financial statements or past earnings announcements (see below).

3.1.2 Semi-strong form efficiency

Many investors use financial information to determine the intrinsic value of a firm. The **intrinsic value** is the "true" or underlying value. Current and past events can give signals about the future, and depending on the expected future potential of the firm, a decision will be made to buy, hold or sell equity. For investors interested in carrying out a **fundamental analysis** of the firm—in which the aim is to determine a firm's intrinsic value—the financial statements come in handy (see, e.g., Penman, 2012). But is an investor who carries out fundamental analysis able to "beat the market"? The short answer is that if markets are at least semi-strong efficient, it should not be possible to earn abnormal profits by studying publicly available information. After all, the market price already incorporates that information. On the contrary, traders who perform fundamental analysis of firms and their financial statements tend to believe that the EMH in its semi-strong form does *not* hold.

Under semi-strong efficiency, it is sufficient that a small number of **sophisticated** or **informed investors** or analysts are able to assimilate the information and trade on it for prices to (instantly) reflect available information. Security prices, which quickly adjust to the new information, will in other words provide accurate signals concerning the underlying value of the instrument. As a result, other market participants—so-called naïve investors—are **price-protected**. Sometimes you hear stories about how monkeys can make a reasonable return on the stock market. This is because the monkeys are price-protected and benefit from the activities of the informed investors.

What about existing evidence of some investors always outperforming the market? Surely they know something that the rest of us do not? The fact is that it is notoriously difficult to beat the market *consistently*, with only a limited number of sophisticated investors being able to achieve long-run abnormal profits. Furthermore, even though the existence of extremely skilled investors or fund managers seems to point to market inefficiencies, proving this is difficult. As Fama points out "for every winning active investor, there's gotta be a losing active investor ('cause the passive investors are out of the game): it's not a hypothesis, it's arithmetic!"[3] Active investment is what is known as a zero-sum game. Many investors will, for reasons of pure probability, beat the market by chance, even in a completely efficient market (just like the monkeys). The question is whether they can *predictably* earn abnormal returns.

In the 1930s, two professors at Columbia Business School, Benjamin Graham and David Dodd, wrote a book on **value investing** (essentially fundamental security analysis). This came to be updated multiple times over the entire 20th century and what came about was a Graham-Dodd "following" consisting of investors who believed in the value of performing fundamental security analysis. Warren Buffet is one of the most well-known advocates of this approach to investing. As much as Buffet challenges the notion that markets are efficient and points to the existence of nonsensical prices, he does not deny the difficulty for a "normal" investor to make abnormal returns. Many fundamental analysts will point out that it is better for non-professional investors looking for a share in the stock market to simply buy

3 See "The Arithmetic of Active Management" by Nobel laureate William Sharpe 1991.

index funds (and look for the lowest fees). Considering that they are price-protected, this is the best deal for them. Likewise, the average institutional fund manager or large portfolio manager should relax any efforts to actually outperform the market—since it is not logically possible for these actors as a whole to "beat themselves" (Graham, 1976). Does assuming that markets are at least semi-strong form efficient mean that investors should stop carrying out fundamental analysis? What would happen if sophisticated investors stopped gathering information altogether? Paradoxically, if everyone believed the market was efficient, it would cease to be so! See Text Box 3.1 for more on this line of reasoning.

If markets are semi-strong form efficient, investors cannot consistently make abnormal returns by studying financial statements. However, the role of financial statements is still to provide the investment community with information that may assist in the process of price formation. It is not the only source of information about the firm, but an important one. It is reasonable to believe that if firms neglected to produce financial reports, the source of reliable information would decrease, causing investors to rely on indirect sources and verbal communication, in turn potentially raising the noise-to-signal ratio in the market. More

Text Box 3.1 **On the impossibility of market efficiency**

If investors believed markets to be efficient and neglected to search for information, stock prices would to a greater extent be affected by the noise introduced by too many non-informed decisions. This would lead to *in*efficiency.

Grossman and Stiglitz (1980) argue that completely efficient markets are impossible:

> If competitive equilibrium is defined as a situation in which prices are such that all arbitrage profits are eliminated, is it possible that a competitive economy always be in equilibrium? Clearly not, for then those who arbitrage make no (private) return from their (privately) costly activity. Hence the assumptions that all markets, including that for information, are always in equilibrium and always perfectly arbitraged are inconsistent when arbitrage is costly.

Instead, they propose a model "in which there is an equilibrium degree of disequilibrium." In this model,

> prices reflect the information of informed individuals (arbitrageurs) but only partially, so that those who expend resources to obtain information do receive compensation.

The above is consistent with a view that market efficiency is a *process*, not a *state*. For markets to move toward efficiency, it is necessary that investors search for undervalued and overvalued stock and that there is a possibility for them to outperform the market. When investors find incorrectly valued stock, they buy and sell based on others' mistakes and mispricing, offering prices that better reflect a firm's actual future performance and thus contributing to making the market efficient. Should prices become "too" accurate, the search will stop, once again reducing efficiency.

Markets thus need to move constantly in and out of (partial) efficiency and some level of inefficiency must always remain.

inside information from a firm leads investors to have more confidence in using available information in the securities market and improves their predictions of firms' future returns.

The creation of semi-strong form efficient capital markets is encouraged by regulators. For listed firms, for example, the release of information is heavily regulated. Information must be made available to all market participants simultaneously, so that it is not partially public. This makes it more likely that prices respond immediately when information is released, but do not respond *before* the release of information. In fact, substantial evidence seems to support the semi-strong (and, by implication, weak) form of efficiency in (at least the largest) stock markets.

Having said that, we finish by referring to an accounting study looking at the use of fundamental analysis (Ou and Penman, 1989). The authors start by acknowledging that a great deal of research to date has looked at how prices reflect earnings information. Those studies assume that markets are largely efficient and as such, prices correctly reveal fundamental firm values. By contrast, Ou and Penman (1989) do not assume market efficiency—rather, they question it. The aim of the study is to assess whether financial statement analysis reveals information that is not reflected in prices. That is, if an accounting attribute is not captured by security prices, it does not have to mean that it is not value-relevant. It simply means that the market has failed to perceive it as value-relevant (you can read more about value relevance in Chapter 7). By looking at a summary value measure from financial statements composed of many financial descriptors or future earnings indicators, the authors seek to predict future stock returns. By taking long positions in stocks with attributes that on average predict negative future earnings changes and short positions in stocks with attributes that on average predict positive future earnings changes, they present a successful investment strategy.[4] What they find is that financial statement analysis captures fundamentals, or intrinsic values, that are in fact not reflected in prices.

3.1.3 Strong form efficiency

If markets are characterized by strong efficiency, *all* information is reflected in stock prices. This implies that the public release of private information should have no impact on stock returns, because prices already incorporate that information. The implications for financial accounting is that carefully prepared financial statements would be redundant (see, for instance, Fields et al., 2001). Also, absent any tax effects, *accounting choices do not matter* because any value-relevant information management has access to is already incorporated into the prices. That is, neither opportunistic accounting choices, nor choices that convey private information, have an effect on value.

As pointed out above, this is not regarded as descriptive of actual stock markets. After all, people inside the firm, for example managers, have access to information about the firm's activities that is not likely to be known to outside market participants without actual disclosures. Therefore, accounting choices *do* matter and it is likely that insiders could benefit from trading on private information, whether it involves selling shares before bad news are

4 Essentially, going long means to buy while going short means to sell.

released or buying stock prior to the release of positive earnings numbers. In most countries, insider trading laws prevent insiders from trading based on private information, consistent with regulators believing markets not to exhibit strong efficiency.

3.2 Alternative hypotheses

The most prominent argument against even the possibility of efficient markets is that investors are irrational and exhibit behavioral biases. Pioneers in this area include psychologists Amos Tversky and David Kahneman (see, for instance, Kahneman and Tversky, 1979), for which the Nobel Memorial Prize in Economic Sciences was awarded in 2002). Their work, which focused on human cognitive biases, included studies on the heuristics employed when making judgments under uncertainty as well as decision-making in relation to risky prospects (see, for instance, Tversky and Kahneman, 1974; Kahneman and Tversky, 1973; Kahneman and Tversky, 1979; Tversky and Kahneman, 1992). Their influence on behavioral economics has been substantial, specifically through their demonstration of the behavioral bias known as loss aversion. **Loss aversion** implies that people prefer *not losing* any given amount over *gaining* that same amount. On average, this leads to poor financial decisions. Other behavioral biases include overconfidence, overreaction and herding (doing what everybody else is doing). Such phenomena are of interest in the field of financial accounting, for example in relation to investor responses to earnings announcements or other disclosures.

Another prominent researcher in the field is Richard Thaler, a disciple of Kahneman and, incidentally, also a Nobel laureate (as of 2017). His research, for which he was awarded the Nobel Memorial Prize, focuses on limited rationality, social preferences and lack of self-control.[5] In his book *Misbehaving: The Making of Behavioral Economics*, Thaler points to the stock market crash of 1987 as one piece of evidence against investor rationality. On that October day, now known as "Black Monday," the value of the Dow Jones Industrial Average (DJIA) dropped by nearly 23%. For markets to exhibit efficiency, prices should ideally change quickly upon the release of new information, but prices should not be *too* volatile. Nor should prices change in the absence of news. The fact that this seemed to be the case in the 1987 crash indicates that the price, at least at one point in time, must have been incorrect, for surely the underlying value of the DJIA's collective assets did not suddenly drop by a quarter over the weekend leading up to the Black Monday.[6]

Overall, **behavioral economists** attempt to explain economic decision-making by considering the effect of human psychology, emotions and cognition. We do not elaborate on the findings in this field, but conclude that there is compelling evidence that investors make investment decisions based on apparently non-rational considerations. In concrete terms,

5 www.nobelprize.org/nobel_prizes/economic-sciences/laureates/2017/press.html

6 World markets have seen plenty of "bubbles" in their history, some of the most famous examples include Holland's "tulip mania" in the 17th century, England's South Sea Bubble in the 18th century (see next chapter) and the US stock market crashes of 1929 and 1987. Can markets be efficient given that they at times seem so erratic? Can the EMH explain market crashes and "bubbles"? In accordance with the EMH this is not mispricing. According to this hypothesis, a steep rise in prices, followed by an equally steep fall, is simply a reflection of changed perceptions regarding the underlying value. That is, the EMH predicts that the valuation at any point in time is the best estimate, based on the information available, of the actual value. Thus, there can *be no bubbles* (or mispricing) under the EMH.

this could mean not carrying out analyses of intrinsic or fundamental values, but making choices based on heuristics (i.e., shortcuts and rules of thumb), emotional cues or erroneous assumptions. For example, investors trade based on fear or the belief that if stock prices are rising, they will continue to do so. Such behavior constitutes a self-reinforcing mechanism, making prices increase even further, until a potential "pricing bubble" is created. Momentum trading is in fact one of the more troublesome pieces of "evidence" against the EMH. Prices set this way point away from rationality, because they do not reflect information about underlying values. Whereas it would seem that a lack of rationality would simply cause prices to change *ad hoc*, thereby adding noise to prices but not actually making the market inefficient, one key assumption concerning behavioral biases is that they are predictable. Here, lack of rationality thus results in predictable prices, which goes against the EMH. As long as everyone believes in price increases, the bubble will continue to inflate as nobody wants to be "left behind" (this is an example of herding behavior, a type of behavioral bias). Other behavioral biases result from *limited attention* (also mentioned above in relation to PEAD). Hirshleifer and Teoh (2003) show that investors' limited attention has an impact on their decision-making, and that this has implications for the *presentation* of financial information. The idea that investors do not consider all available data brings us to another hypothesis: the **Incomplete Revelation Hypothesis**, which posits that information that is more costly to extract from public data is less completely revealed by market prices (Bloomfield, 2002). This is explained by the fact that information extraction is costly, and the benefits of trading on a piece of information must exceed the cost of analyzing it.

The question then is whether the existence of behavioral biases must mean that markets cannot be efficient? Those defending the EMH are most likely to view irrationality as having a negligible impact on prices, as market forces would ensure that prices return to rational levels (Lo, 2005). Alternatively, the **Adaptive Markets Hypothesis (AMH)** (Lo, 2004, 2005) is an attempt to reconcile behavioral economics with the EMH. It draws on evolutionary biology and the laws of natural selection to predict the behavior of markets. By allowing market forces and preferences to interact, a more dynamic economy, driven by competition and the notion of the "survival of the richest," is modeled. It further draws on the work by Simon (1955), another Nobel Laureate, which describes humans as having **bounded rationality**. The idea of a **homo economicus** who always makes rational and optimal choices was discarded in favor of the concept of **satisficing**. Optimization is costly, so humans make choices that are *sufficient* rather than optimal. Lo (2005) adds an evolutionary perspective to this by suggesting that people arrive at their satisfactory decisions via trial and error and natural selection. They develop heuristics for solving various problems, but these are adapted to a given environment. Change the environment, and previous decisions seem suboptimal. He points out that:

> rather than labeling such behavior irrational, we should recognize that suboptimal behavior is likely when we take heuristics out of their evolutionary context. A more accurate term for such behavior might be "maladaptive" (Lo, 2005, p.11).

All in all, the AMH shows that persistent evidence in support of the EMH need not be at odds with equally persistent evidence of investors' lack of rationality:

> In efficient markets, investors do not make mistakes, nor is there any learning and adaptation because the market environment is stationary and always in equilibrium. In the AMH framework, mistakes occur frequently, but individuals are capable of learning from mistakes and adapting their behavior accordingly. However, [...] adaptation does not occur independently of market forces but is driven by competition, that is, the push for survival. (Lo, 2005, p.11).

Overall, this is largely consistent with the statement that market efficiency is a process, not a state (see above).

Through this brief overview, we have not attempted to provide a comprehensive picture of the concept of efficient markets. However, we hope to have provided a few insights into relevant research in economics and finance helping the reader to understand the context surrounding the financial accounting literature.

3.3 Information asymmetry and the roles of accounting

> With complete and perfect markets, there is no substantive role for financial disclosures and thus no demand for accounting or accounting regulation. However, in our world of imperfect and incomplete markets, the demand for accounting and accounting regulation implies that accounting disclosures and accounting-based contracts are efficient ways of addressing market imperfections. (Fields et al., 2001)

As we saw in the previous two chapters, **information asymmetry** refers to the idea that one type of participant in the market knows more than another type of participant.

In this section, we focus specifically on information differences existing between the firm (management) and the equity market (investors),[7] and the idea that accounting may reduce these differences.[8] We recall from above that if markets are at least semi-strong efficient, prices reflect all publicly available information. Unless they are strong form efficient, however, they do *not* reflect private information. If a firm (its management) has more information than investors, there is information asymmetry.

We present an overview of the two most common problems associated with information asymmetry in a management/equity market setting. For each, we consider the role of information and accounting in addressing these. We present two widely accepted objectives of accounting—the **valuation role** of accounting and the **stewardship (contracting) role** of accounting (Watts and Zimmerman, 1986). The valuation role refers to the use of accounting

---

7 It is also possible to consider information asymmetry *within* a firm or *within* a market. We have touched upon potential information gaps between different participants *within* the market, as we have spoken of informed and uninformed investors, but we do not explore topics related to intraorganizational communication (or lack thereof).

8 Information asymmetry between the firm and debt markets is also possible. However, we focus on equity markets, as this is consistent with the general focus in the literature.

for security pricing, while the stewardship role refers to the use of accounting in contractual relations between owners and managers of firms.

The literature concerned with the consequences and determinants of earnings quality and disclosure quality, as well as with measures of these, originates in the valuation and stewardship roles of accounting.

3.3.1 The valuation role of accounting: An *ex ante* perspective

The **valuation** or **information** role forms the basis for a well-established research area in the financial accounting literature (see Kothari, 2001, for a comprehensive review of the literature on capital market effects of accounting). The effectiveness of this role is investigated in research, as seen by, for example, attempts to measure market responses to various financial reporting items and studies on the usefulness of accounting numbers for valuation. It may be useful to think of this role as being an *ex ante* role, or taking a "pre-transaction" perspective, because one of the key concepts here is *adverse selection* (see below) and the influence of accounting on decision-making is in relation to buying and selling shares (transacting).

Essentially, whenever there is information asymmetry between buyers and sellers of securities, capital markets are believed not to function well. Whenever a firm's management (seller) has more information about the firm than potential investors (buyers), investors will have difficulties distinguishing "good" firms (with good prospects) from "bad" firms (with poor prospects). If buyers expect a firm to be average and are therefore willing to pay the average price, they will underpay for "good" firms and "overpay" for bad firms. This can lead to **adverse selection**, a phenomenon implying that the sellers offering the worst deal self-select into the market and are therefore systematically overrepresented. Meanwhile, the sellers of "good" stock opt out. The mechanism behind this effect was first identified in the insurance industry, where it is used to refer to the fact that *buyers* of insurance self-select into the insurance market based on their perceived need for a policy. That is, people who are more likely to be involved in traffic accidents want more car insurance, those who are sick want health insurance, and so on. Insurance companies have a difficult time distinguishing between high- and low-risk customers. They often use crude measures, such as age, meaning that young people pay more for car insurance, even if a particular young individual may drive very carefully. Still, the risk of self-selection raises insurance premiums for all buyers of insurance. This, in turn, raises the probability that low-risk buyers opt out of the market, since the insurance policy becomes too expensive in relation to their perceived probability of economic loss, which results in even higher premiums. In the complete absence of information, markets may even break down entirely and trading cease altogether (see *Akerlof's lemon problem* in the previous chapter, section 2.3.2). Translating this into a capital market setting, the result of adverse selection is that investors are "stuck with" bad investment options and must demand a large compensation for this in terms of a higher required return. In order to ensure that firm shares do not have to be sold at a discount, managers have incentives to enhance transparency and choose a higher degree of disclosure of firm-specific information (Healy and Palepu, 2001; Verrecchia, 2001). **Signaling theory** suggests that "good" firms can distinguish themselves from "bad" firms and thus avoid adverse selection and reduce the problem of asymmetrical information (Verrecchia, 1983; Dye, 1985). However, in order for a signal to be potent, it must be difficult for a low-quality signaler to send a high-quality signal. One may ask whether disclosures in the form of financial reports are costly enough to be effective signals. Some finance researchers argue that dividends and stock repurchases are more costly and therefore more effective signals than accounting disclosures. For example, the payment of dividends is commonly viewed as an indication of positive future prospects (although one could also argue that the payment of dividends indicates a distribution of excess cash due to a *lack* of future profitable investment opportunities). Since a distribution of cash is costly unless you have cash to spare and need not risk future transaction costs associated with seeking future external financing, it is considered a credible "good news" signal. Meanwhile, disclosures can be costly because in conveying private information to the market regarding the firm, management might be giving away proprietary information that competitors could then use to their advantage (see Darrough and Stoughton, 1990, for a formal modeling of this trade-off). For example, Gelb (2000) shows that accounting disclosures can be costly, at least in competitive industries where proprietary costs are potentially high. Clarkson et al. (1994) test this empirically and find that disclosures of favorable forecasts by "good news" firms are comparatively less probable in highly competitive industries (in which the cost of revealing proprietary information is greater). This is consistent with **proprietary cost theory**, which suggests that the release of firm-specific and potentially sensitive information entails (indirect) costs that impose a constraint on the amount of disclosures a firm is willing to make. More specifically, these costs are measured as reduced future cash inflows as a result of, for example, reduced consumer demand, labor and supplier contract renegotiation costs, or legal action taken against the firm.

The above reasoning implies that disclosures of favorable news in financial reports may be viewed as credible signals of a firm's performance.[9] Financial reporting of high quality is a potentially effective way of reducing information asymmetries and aiding investors in the estimation of firm value. Conversely, information asymmetry between buyers and sellers makes markets less efficient, where mispricing and adverse selection represent potential outcomes.

3.3.2 The stewardship role of accounting: An *ex post* perspective

In this section, we see that *ex post*, or "post-transaction" investors who have acquired shares—and need to ensure that their investment is protected—face additional problems in the presence of information asymmetry. Given the separation of ownership from control, decisions are made by managers, but the ultimate costs or benefits of those decisions are borne by the investors or owners (Berle and Means, 1932). This implies that corporate resources may not be used entirely for increasing shareholder value, but may instead be used for the benefit of corporate insiders (i.e., managers) (Demsetz and Lehn, 1985). **Agency theory** proposes that the manager (agent) has interests that are in conflict with those of the investor (principal), and given the limited transparency between the agent and the

9 Of course, given the existence of managerial incentives to manipulate said signals, regulation and enforcement are introduced to ensure that credible signals are provided through compliance with specific disclosure requirements.

principal, the agent will have incentives and opportunities to act in a self-interested way to the detriment of the principal (Jensen and Meckling, 1976). Such agency conflicts may create problems of **moral hazard**, which is a result of *unobservable* individual actions being taken by the parties that do not incur the full cost of taking the risk of investing. Managers may decrease shareholder value by making investment decisions that are not beneficial to shareholders or fail to play an active role, thus not paying the consequences for the risks of their decision-making.

This leads to a demand for monitoring and other activities (Jensen and Meckling, 1976) that align the interests of the agents and principals. Such activities, or *governance mechanisms*, are based on contracts between said parties. Information enhances the efficiency of the contracts by decreasing the uncertainty in contractual conditions and plays a key role when designing, negotiating and evaluating the contracts. In sum, high-quality accounting information facilitates efficient contracting and monitoring activities. This is labeled the **stewardship** or **contracting** role of accounting.

An example of a commonly employed contract is executive compensation contracts, designed to give shareholders signals about managers' unobservable actions. Accounting performance-based compensation plans—where managerial pay may be linked to a firm's accounting earnings—are examples of such contracts. The underlying idea is that because both owners and managers become better off when firm performance is high, their interests are aligned. Compensation contracts are more efficient when accounting is of high quality and faithfully represents firm performance. Ironically, accounting quality, and specifically earnings quality, may be reduced by the very fact that accounting earnings are used to measure performance. Opportunistic managers wanting to improve the apparent performance of the firm could make accounting choices that are not reflective of the underlying economics. Alternative measures that are commonly used in compensation contracts include market-based performance measures, such as stock returns. These measures are less likely to be influenced by managers and their accounting choices. Their weakness, however, is that—even though they are objective—they are often noisy measures of managerial performance, since stock prices may reflect economy-wide events or trends that are outside the control of managers. We discuss the use of performance measures in compensation contracts in detail in Chapter 8. For now, we conclude that not even a well-designed compensation package is likely to resolve all conflicts of interest and agency problems. Therefore, additional governance mechanisms should be implemented.

One such mechanism is the board of directors, which carries out both advisory and monitoring functions. High-quality financial reports are important means of communication from management to independent directors and thus necessary for an efficient monitoring of managerial performance. Although the board of directors typically also has access to internal reports, public disclosures and financial information have the advantage of being subject to various regulations, enforcement and audits. Hence, they constitute a comparatively credible source of information for the boards in their decision-making.

An additional concern from a stewardship perspective is that different capital providers may have different interests in the firm (see Text Box 3.2).

Text Box 3.2 **The stewardship role of accounting for debt contracts**

The stewardship role of accounting is not only important in contracts designed to mitigate agency conflicts between managers and shareholders. Accounting also plays an important role in enhancing transparency and reducing uncertainty when designing and evaluating debt contracts. Debt contracts often include formal terms and conditions that are defined under debt covenants. These debt covenants, in turn, are frequently based on accounting information, such as the total level of debt-to-equity in the balance sheet.

The use of accounting information in defining the underlying restricting conditions in debt covenants may affect management's accounting choices.

Additional agency problems may arise when firms have both equity and debt, due to the different interests of shareholders and debtholders. For example, shareholders, who are residual recipients of earnings, tend to favor riskier investments in the hope of obtaining greater returns. Debtholders, who do not benefit from higher returns and suffer if returns are too low, tend to prefer less risky investments. This makes designing efficient contracts more complex.

3.3.3 The trade-off between the valuation and the stewardship roles of accounting

Before proceeding, we want to emphasize what is pointed out by Glover (2012):

> Valuation and stewardship are inherently interwoven. One needs to assess stewardship to value the firm, and value creation is a natural focus of stewardship assessment when shareholders are making the assessment. (p.371)

Having said that, it is worth highlighting some fundamental differences in the two roles of accounting described here.

In developing accounting standards, the IASB and the FASB aim to ensure a high degree of transparency and comparability of financial statements. This, in turn, should contribute to the efficient functioning of security markets. The explicit focus has mostly been on the valuation role of accounting, and thus on improving capital allocation decisions, reducing the cost of equity capital for firms and increasing cross-border investment. Explicit reference to the stewardship role of accounting (i.e., the impact of accounting information on the efficiency of contractual relationships) has been more limited. However, the stewardship role of accounting, which is relevant in the context of performance evaluation and managerial assessment, also has important implications for well-functioning capital markets. In the 2010 update to the Conceptual Framework, the IASB gave more prominence to the stewardship role of accounting, making it an explicit objective for firms to provide users of financial statements with information that can help them assess management's stewardship (Whittington, 2008b).

Whereas the valuation role of accounting has a greater *future orientation*, as investors aim to estimate values based on predictions of future firm performance, the stewardship role focuses on providing *historical feedback* to investors as they evaluate managerial performance. This distinction is important to consider when evaluating the usefulness of the information, since this will be dependent on the perspective taken. Indeed, accounting that is useful for valuation purposes might not be equally useful for stewardship purposes. For example, fair value accounting may be advantageous from a valuation perspective, since fair values are generally considered more contemporary and informative of current market conditions, and thus more value-relevant. The stewardship role of accounting, meanwhile, implies that accounting measures should first and foremost be *reliable* measures that are less influenced by managerial judgments. In this respect, accounting measures that are less volatile and more historically oriented may be more useful. The fact that the two fundamental roles of accounting are not aligned, causing a trade-off to exist between the roles, constitutes a potential dilemma for standard-setters. If one type of information allows investors to evaluate managerial performance but produces imprecise estimates of firm value, then an obvious question becomes: Where should the focus lie?

Historically, global standard-setters such as the IASB and the FASB have placed greater weight on the valuation role of accounting, although evidence from the literature, as well as needs in the current business environment, point to the significance of accounting information in contracting and stewardship decisions. Zimmerman (2015) argues that in today's business environment, the stewardship role of accounting becomes (increasingly) important due to the increased complexity of firms and the potential conflicts of interests caused by this added complexity. As he points out, "the valuation role remains important, but there is little to value unless the conflicts of interest are first mitigated" (p. 485).

3.4 Conclusions

Whether markets are fully or partially efficient has implications for financial accounting. Whereas strong form efficiency precludes the need for producing public financial disclosures, the other forms of efficiency rely to a greater extent on disclosures being made.[10] The semi-strong and strong form of efficiency further implies that the manner in which the information is presented is of little or no consequence to firm valuation. The model only makes a distinction between information that is available and information that is not. No distinction is made between *how* the information is made available; for example, if it is included in the balance sheet or if it is disclosed in the supplementary notes. Further, strong form efficiency suggests that there are no information processing costs and that private information is easily conveyed through price. This means that (opportunistic) accounting choices cannot be used to mislead investors.

Evidence supporting and rejecting the EMH is abundant, but there is no general consensus on this matter. Importantly, different markets can be efficient to different extents and the "scale" is not binary. A real-world market is neither entirely inefficient nor entirely

10 Note that although our focus is on regulated financial reports (including voluntary disclosures within these), disclosures are also made via corporate web sites, management announcements, conference calls or other investor relations activities involving financial institutions, analysts or other intermediaries.

efficient. Nevertheless, many studies seek to refute the EMH and some counter-arguments and counter-hypotheses have been advanced.

Given the existence of information asymmetries between investors and managements of firms, the roles of accounting are largely concerned with reducing these asymmetries. Accounting can help both in the process of deciding whether to buy, hold or sell equity (the valuation role) and in evaluating and monitoring managerial performance (the stewardship role). Overall, the relevance of capital markets and capital market users for the discussion of the role, qualit*ies* and qualit*y* of accounting cannot be overstated.

Part II
Accounting quality and regulation

The first determinant of accounting output (and quality) we consider is **regulation.** In this part of the book, we provide rationales for regulation and give examples of accounting regulation, including how it has developed in a select group of countries (Chapter 4). Regulation can take different forms, but in this book we focus on regulation through accounting standards. The two most important accounting standard-setters are the FASB and the IASB. Both of these have developed conceptual frameworks (separately and jointly) that form the conceptual foundation for accounting standards and thus financial reporting. In doing so, they have in essence contributed to the development of normative accounting theory. The IASB's current Conceptual Framework, including key concepts that help define accounting quality from the point of view of standard-setters, is covered in Chapter 5.

CHAPTER 4

Regulation of accounting

Learning outcomes

Upon completion of this chapter, you will gain insight into:

- The economic rationales for accounting regulation (i.e., the economic efficiency perspective on regulation).
- Factors explaining forms of regulation, consequences for the profession and how all of these aspects may be linked to the intended user and other contextual factors.
- The development of regulation and accounting in the Anglo-American world and, consequently, the background of international standard-setting as it is known today.
- The trade-off between principles- and rules-based accounting standards.

THE WORD "REGULATION" HAS DIFFERENT CONNOTATIONS for different people and in different contexts. Regulation may lead us to think of bureaucracy, red-tape and lack of flexibility. It can also be a source of comfort and reassurance, as laws and rules help bring order to society. Whatever our view, regulation permeates our everyday lives. Whether we are taking a university course, downloading a smartphone app, making an online purchase or riding a bike through the city, there will be regulation governing what is acceptable or required behavior by the parties involved in any given activity.

In practice, it is not so much a question of *whether or not* there should be regulation, but rather *how much* and *how* one should regulate. Economists tend to focus on regulation of commodity markets, not least in the utilities and transportation sectors, but also in the financial sector. References are often made to the regulation and *de*regulation of the railroad industry, airline industry, telecommunications and banking sector; in all these cases, "regulation" tends to refer to the process of introducing more regulation while "deregulation" refers to the process of partially removing regulation. A deregulated industry, however, does not imply that there are no longer any regulatory requirements in the industry. All markets are subject to regulation. In this chapter, we consider regulation of financial markets, and especially regulation of corporate information dissemination (i.e., financial accounting).

4.1 Economic rationales for and against regulation

Having reached the conclusion in previous chapters that information is useful when making decisions, could information dissemination not be left to the market? That is, could one not let market mechanisms ensure that an optimal level of information is provided? After all, firms provide information to shareholders and other interest groups beyond what is required by standard-setters and governments. Firms partly do this to avoid information asymmetry problems that are detrimental to the firm and its management, but also as a response to political and social pressure, both from individuals, special interest groups and non-governmental organizations (NGOs). For example, as illustrated by Akerlof (1970), in a setting of information asymmetry, firms with high-quality products have incentives to voluntarily disclose information to buyers (see Chapter 2). Meanwhile, firms performing poorly are compelled to explain their weak results, environmentally questionable activities or unfavorable working conditions throughout the supply chain for legitimacy reasons. That is, information asymmetry theories describing adverse selection, moral hazard and signaling, as well as institutional theory and legitimacy theory, have all been used to explain voluntary disclosures.

Below, we present some of the rationales for regulation that exist in spite of available market solutions. There are plenty of economic theory-based rationales for regulation in the literature. One way or another, they rely on the existence of market failure. **Market failure** implies that there is inefficient allocation of goods and services and that one party could become better off without any other party becoming worse off as a result.

Market failures, for the purpose of our discussion, may be categorized into four types: asymmetric information, public goods, externalities and market power. We consider each one below.

4.1.1 Asymmetric information

As we have seen previously, under assumptions of asymmetric (also *incomplete*) information, markets break down or fail. They become inefficient. Consequently, investors lack the ability to distinguish between good and bad investments. To ensure that investors obtain the information they need, financial statements need to be regulated. One reason for asymmetric information existing in the first place is that management and ownership are separated, and the reason it is not eliminated is due to managerial opportunism. If managers are profit-satisficers rather than profit-maximizers, withholding information from the principal could be in the agent's (i.e., management's) interest. Thus, when left to the complete discretion of managers, disclosures risk suffering from low quality (consistent with agency theory).

Indeed, it has been shown repeatedly that without enforceable restrictions on corporate or managerial activities, as well as mandated disclosure requirements, undesirable aspects of a firm's business are likely to be kept at least partially in the dark. While managers have incentives to disclose some voluntary information, there may be potential net benefits of disclosing opportunistically or withholding certain facts. Now, one could argue that a market-based solution to incomplete information would be to let users define their information needs in a *contract*. In the case of investors and creditors, they would do this in exchange for providing capital to the firm. However, the contract-based solution is likely to be inefficient, as it would be costly for individual investors and creditors to determine what information is needed, enter into said contracts, and verify the reliability of the information. Disclosures must be believable to the user, and regulation is seen as an efficient way of increasing the believability of information that may otherwise be selectively published and depend on managerial incentives. Hence, the negative consequences of information asymmetry are likely to prevail without regulation. In addition, comparability over time and across firms is an important quality aspect of accounting (see next chapter), as this contributes to the reduction of information asymmetry and uncertainty. Regulation is likely to create more consistent output (and therefore higher comparability) compared to a solution based on individual contracts.

4.1.2 Public goods and externalities

Another rationale for regulation is that accounting may be viewed as a public good. In economics, a **public good** is one where individuals who pay for said good cannot stop non-payers from enjoying and benefiting from it (i.e., it is non-excludable) and where one individual's usage of it does not reduce another individual's ability to benefit from it (i.e., it is non-rivalrous). Future potential shareholders are perhaps the primary beneficiaries, but also society as a whole to the extent that there are wider wealth effects of a well-functioning financial market. These wider effects are considered *externalities*—a type of market failure. **Externalities** are costs or benefits borne by an external part rather than by the party whose activities generate them. A polluting firm may cause losses for a farmer as his crops become contaminated, but this cost is not included in the accounts of the polluting firm. This would constitute a *negative* externality. Since the firm in this scenario does not bear the full costs of production, the costs are furthermore not reflected in the price of its goods. This leads to an *overproduction* of such goods. Meanwhile, the market for accounting information perhaps suffers mostly from *positive* externalities, meaning that those receiving the benefits of the information do not bear the cost of preparing and disseminating it. The users, and the economy as a whole, are believed to benefit from the production of accounting information, but the cost is only borne by the firms producing the information. This can potentially lead to an *underproduction* of accounting as firms attempt to minimize their costs—at least in the absence of regulation.

In some instances, instead of ensuring the availability of a product or service, regulators could be interested in *limiting* the availability of the provided output. Most people consider it a good thing that, for example, the Swedish National Food Agency (*Livsmedelsverket*) and the US Food and Drug Administration (FDA) regulate and monitor the manufacturing and distribution of a wide range of goods that could potentially be harmful to the public. Firms may have profit incentives to maximize sales, while governments, the public and even consumers may want to restrict the use of certain products. Cigarettes, alcohol and recreational drugs are prime examples where countries continuously debate the appropriate level of regulation that should accompany their sale. In some cases, the manufacturing and sale of these products are banned altogether.

As far as accounting is concerned, surely *too much* information cannot be considered harmful? It may, however, be viewed as a source of inefficiency. When firms compete to signal their high quality, they provide more disclosures in order to avoid undervaluation. *Overproduction* of information is a problem because shareholder wealth and firm resources are used inefficiently. Regulation of disclosure is a solution if it results in less competition and less wasted resources. This reduces redundant disclosures while, simultaneously, forcing non-disclosers to disclose. In sum, regulation in the form of accounting standards, along with enforcement, can help ensure that firms provide the desirable amount of information—given that accounting is a public good and given the presence of externalities.

4.1.3 Market power

In determining what should be regulated and the extent of regulation, governments need to strike a fine balance. Few people are likely to enjoy a situation where the state decides in detail what should be allowed to be produced and consumed in the country (Eastern Europeans and Cubans have had first-hand experience of this not too long ago). Liberals tend to believe that grown-up citizens should be free to make their own choices, whether good or bad. This, of course, ignores the possibility of externalities. In general, the most prominent rationales for regulation based on economic theory all share a common denominator—and that is that the consumer needs protection. This is especially the case in markets that are **naturally monopolistic**. A natural monopoly is a market where there are large benefits to operating at a large scale (i.e., there are **economies of scale**). To keep costs down, it is optimal to have just one firm in the market. There are high barriers to entry into such a market (meaning it is difficult for new firms to enter and be competitive) because unless operating at a large scale, it is difficult or impossible to be profitable. Once a firm with first-mover advantage has cleared out the competition and operates alone, however, it has incentives to raise prices and earn exorbitant profits. Such a market would likely be subject to regulation. By fixing the price at a lower level, regulators can force the firm to produce a higher output at a lower price.[1] But how can the above arguments about monopolies be applied to an accounting context? If management has monopoly control of corporate information (i.e., private, firm-specific information), then the above could be relevant to consider.[2] Especially when management needs to make critical accounting choices or estimates about highly firm-specific events and conditions, mandatory disclosures about these can reduce information uncertainty for investors.

---

1 **Capture theory**, however, suggests that over time, regulators in many industries have been "captured" by the industries they regulate, so that instead of protecting consumers from paying too much (monopoly prices), regulators start protecting the firms from competitors (Stigler, 1971; Peltzman, 1976). Lobbyists are pointed out as major culprits here. All in all, the theory weakens the pro-regulation argument.

2 Under the strong form of EMH, there are other sources of information so that investors are not systematically misled by managers. Monopoly control of information is thus not considered a significant threat.

To sum up, perhaps the shortest answer carrying some merit in relation to the question "Why regulate?" is that it is necessary in order to achieve the intended objectives of accounting (i.e., it is necessary to ensure that accounting is useful). A slightly longer answer involves looking at the actual causes of capital market breakdowns, such as the existence of externalities or information asymmetry. Empirical research in financial accounting has long strived to inform regulators of the effects of accounting standards, thus providing positive (empirical) evidence as the basis of normative statements. One problem with suggesting regulation as a remedy to alleged market failures is that government (or supragovernment) regulation is also costly, and possibly no less costly than private contract solutions. Watts and Zimmerman (1986) point out that a thorough cost-benefit analysis would be necessary to determine whether regulation is superior to the alternative of leaving information dissemination up to the market. There are potential inefficiencies caused by regulation too—regulation can upset the free-market price equilibrium, so that a suboptimal amount of a given good is provided. Furthermore, economists believe that economic growth to a large extent depends on risk-taking in firms. Costs are compounded to the extent that regulation makes firms more bureaucratic and risk-averse.

It is also important that the above discussion does not constitute a comprehensive list of reasons to regulate. There are, for example, also political motivations for regulation, including regulation of accounting. To the extent that accounting affects the distribution of wealth in the economy, there could be ideological reasons for regulating this distribution. An obvious example is when accounting is used for taxation purposes. The tax system is clearly linked to the political system, and in such settings accounting regulation will affect the amount of tax paid by different firms. It is difficult to see how a free market development of accounting could serve as a basis for a tax system.

In practice, as much as regulatory developments may be based in theory—economic or otherwise—political pressure to regulate is undoubtedly strong. It is interesting to observe that increases in regulation of financial reporting tend to come as a direct response to accounting scandals and financial crises. Accounting regulation has been introduced and shaped in attempts to overcome reductions of public confidence in the capital markets and in financial reporting. For example, in the US, the stock market crash of 1929 and the subsequent Great Depression led to the creation of the Securities and Exchange Commission (SEC) through the Securities Act of 1934. More recent major changes in the accounting and governance regulations in the US are related to several noteworthy accounting scandals at the beginning of the 21st century, as well the financial crisis in 2007–2008. In particular, the effectiveness of corporate governance regarding monitoring of the financial reporting process was highly criticized. These failures ultimately led to the introduction of new regulations, such as the Sarbanes-Oxley Act of 2002 (SOX) in the US, which enforced several reforms with respect to the corporate governance structure of firms, and the Dodd-Frank Bill on financial reforms in 2010. In Europe, particularly after several corporate scandals in the UK in the late 1980s, a great deal of attention was devoted to the corporate governance of firms. This led to the creation of a series of guidelines and requirements for "good" corporate governance (e.g., Cadbury, 1992), which were subsequently adopted by EU member states under the EU's codes of good governance.

4.2 Determinants of accounting regulation and its outcomes

Once there is agreement for the need of regulation, the question is *how* this should be done. Though it may seem obvious that regulation should be done by states, accounting has seen different forms of regulation. These include regulation by states, by private standard-setters and by practice. The state regulates through legislation, while private standard-setters regulate through standards or recommendations. Initially, accounting emerged as a practice, where accountants tended to follow some type of *accepted practice*. In some senses, practice may constitute a form of "soft" regulation, but for the purpose of our discussion, we do not consider them *regulation*.

Accounting systems—including regulation of accounting—have developed in different ways in different countries. This is believed to be due to differences in the way capital markets have developed, what the perceived objective of accounting has been and what the legal systems have looked like. Meanwhile, increased economic globalization in the last few decades has resulted in increased global accounting harmonization.

In his model of international differences in accounting, Nobes (1992) presents factors explaining said differences, as well as the dimensions along which accounting systems may vary:

- **The financing system and the tax system** are the two primary factors explaining differences in accounting systems. Financing can either be dominated by equity financing through stock markets or by credit financing through banks. The main characteristic of the tax system of interest is whether there is a link between financial reporting and taxation. In other words, the most important explanatory factors are related to who the user is—in other words, equity investors, creditors and/or tax authorities.
- **Forms of regulation and the role of the profession** constitute dimensions along which accounting systems vary. Regulation is either done through state legislation or through private standard-setting. Countries with private standard-setting tend to have a large and influential accounting profession, meaning that the regulatory structure and the role of the profession go hand-in-hand. These, in turn, are closely tied to the user (see above).

In addition to the explanatory factors and dimensions proposed by Nobes, we present two dimensions we refer to as *principles- versus rules-based approach to regulation* and *enforceability and enforcement*:

- **Principles-based versus rules-based regulation** differ in that rules-based accounting standards are usually thought of as containing detailed rules on how to handle a certain accounting situation, whereas principles-based standards outline the general principles that should be followed. Principles should reflect some underlying economics, or the fundamental situation of the firm, and the approach to a greater extent relies upon preparer judgment in order for the objective of regulation to be achieved. We return to the comparison between principles-based and rules-based regulation in more depth in the last section of this chapter.

- **Enforceability** and therefore, enforcement, of accounting regulation differs primarily between different forms of regulation. Enforcement may be strong or weak. It may be carried out by courts or by specialized enforcement agencies. Courts commonly enforce tax regulation, but also other state-backed regulations, while specialized authorities usually oversee capital markets (e.g., the SEC in the US). It is also possible to have different forms of "self-regulation," where the accounting profession is responsible for the enforcement of regulation. If "regulation" is determined by a set of "accepted practices"—which are not formally written down but established through the experience of accountants and auditors—enforcement becomes particularly challenging, if not impossible.

Different forms of regulation involve different advantages and disadvantages. State regulation has the advantage of being clearly enforceable through the court system (see above). A disadvantage is that state regulation takes a long time to change, as legislative changes in most countries are slow processes. Private standard-setters, and practice, are quicker to adapt to changed circumstances, but the feasibility of (successful) enforcement of this type of regulation is less evident. Another distinction between the modes of regulation is that states take political considerations into account while private standard-setters tend to be apolitical and focus on economic and accounting expertise. Therefore, states tend to be more suitable decision-makers when accounting regulation aims to address political objectives (e.g., when accounting is used for taxation), while private standard-setters are more suitable when regulation is used to meet economic objectives (e.g., when accounting is used in capital markets). Which type of regulation is appropriate depends on the context and the intended user of accounting.

Based on the above classifications, Nobes (1992) identifies two main groups of countries: the Anglo-American group and the Continental group (see Table 4.1). Even though accounting is becoming internationally harmonized, the historical differences between the two groups of countries still remain today. Using the classification model presented in Nobes (1992), it is possible to identify both the explanatory factors for differences in accounting systems as well as some basic differences in the systems *per se*.

The Anglo-American group consists of the US, the UK, Canada and Australia, among others. This group is characterized by a long history of active equity markets. For the small investor in such markets—with no direct access to management—financial reporting represents a very important source of information. Especially in the US, the protection of small investors has been a clear policy objective in accounting regulation. Furthermore, these countries have no, or only a weak, link between financial reporting and taxation. Therefore, financial reporting can develop for the needs of equity markets without consideration of tax issues, producing a strong accounting profession.

The Continental group consists of most of Europe besides the UK, with important countries in this group being Germany and France. In this group, owners tend to be large, long-term, and connected through corporate networks. In such a setting, financial reporting is less important, as these owners have direct access to management. An important source of finance is bank lending. Compared to stock market investors, banks are less dependent on financial reporting (as they can demand additional information from the firm in exchange for granting a loan) and have different information needs in the financial reporting they do receive. Furthermore, these countries traditionally have a link between financial reporting and taxation, so tax issues must be considered in preparing the accounts.

Table 4.1 Characteristics of Nobes' two groups of countries

	Anglo-American group	Continental group
Financing	Equity investors	Creditors, banks
Link between financial reporting and taxation	Weak	Strong
Form of regulation	Private-sector standard-setting	State legislation
Role of profession	Large	Small

In other words, the groups differ with respect to which user is in focus. Anglo-American countries focus on equity investors as users, while Continental countries focus on well-informed large owners, banks and tax authorities. This affects the accounting systems, as well as the regulation of accounting. When equity investors are in focus, economic arguments are used in the design of accounting standards. Therefore, it is logical to have economic experts, in the form of private bodies, serving as standard-setters. This is the basis for standard-setting in both the UK and the US—even though governments are backing up the standards to an increasing degree, as a need for stronger enforcement has been identified. Still, standards are issued by private bodies of experts. With such standards, a high degree of economic expertise among preparers is also likely to be required. As a result, the accounting profession is large and important in Anglo-American countries, having influence both in the production of standards and in their interpretation among preparers. Meanwhile, in Continental countries, the link between financial reporting and taxation adds a political dimension to accounting regulation. Therefore, regulation is performed by the state, via legislation. Such regulation has a high involvement of legal rather than economic experts. It is also consistent with a smaller accounting profession.

Consistent with the above, Nobes (1992) describes different characteristics of the accounting systems *per se*. Equity investors are interested in the economic performance of the firm (as it relates to equity values), which suggests that accounting for such investors should attempt to convey the underlying economics of the firm. Nobes (1992) calls this characteristic a focus on "fairness." Creditors, on the other hand, have an asymmetric economic exposure to the firm (they risk substantial losses if the firm is doing unexpectedly poorly, but no additional gains if the firm is doing unexpectedly well). Therefore, they have preferred conservative accounting. When there is a link between financial accounting and taxation, firms prefer conservative accounting, simply because it tends to delay tax payments. The term used by Nobes (1992) to denote conservatism is "prudence." Thus, in the terminology of Nobes (1992), Anglo-American countries tend to focus on fairness, while Continental countries focus on prudence.

In this book, we focus on accounting as it has developed in the Anglo-American group of countries. The reasons for this focus is that the Anglo-American view of accounting dominates US and international standard-setting, and most international research on financial accounting studies settings where this view has been adopted. Therefore, anyone who is interested in learning about IFRS and the IASB will find it enlightening to study the background of accounting regulation in the Anglo-American group of countries.

4.3 A brief history of Anglo-American accounting regulation

In the following sections, we go through the development of accounting in the UK and the US. Diversified ownership and highly developed equity markets are believed to lead to a greater demand for high-quality accounting information and a stronger accounting profession, and the UK and the US exemplify these relationships well. We then proceed to discuss differences between Anglo-American and Continental countries and conclude with a discussion on the current harmonization of accounting.

In the introductory chapter, we emphasized that whereas the purposes of accounting in the early days was to keep records to be used by the owner himself and the lenders (and possibly also as a basis for tax), accounting practice and regulation developed substantially when individual shareholdings became prevalent and businesses grew through trade and the industrial revolution. As stated in an earlier section, regulation tends to develop retroactively in response to market failures or discontent regarding the *status quo*—this applies to accounting regulation as well. To see the historical, social and economic context in which accounting and accounting regulation has developed is instrumental to one's understanding of the subject. However, this subject deserves a whole book in itself and we do not make any claims to provide an in-depth analysis of events and causes of these events. We merely give an overview and a background, highlighting some of the developments that have inspired our thinking today.

4.3.1 The UK

As was alluded to in Chapter 1, increased economic activity in Europe during the 16th to 18th centuries may to a large extent be attributed to the expansionist patterns prevailing in Europe at the time. The South Sea Company is one of the better known joint-stock companies from that time. Although it attracted considerable amounts of capital under the pretext that there were profits to be made from trade with South America, its main purpose was to arrange and manage loans to the government (decades of warfare had left England debt-ridden) and thus serve as an alternative to the role played by the monopolistic Bank of England at the time. What was hoped for was arguably not so much dividends stemming from profitable trade, but rather a rising share price in itself (Hoppit, 2002). A speculative frenzy led to a sevenfold increase in the firm's share price over a six-month period in 1720. The realization that came upon investors only a few months later, that there was little substance behind the valuation, led to the collapse of the share price and what amounted to the bursting of the bubble. The South Sea Bubble, as it became known, however, was not a solitary event (for example, the East India Company also doubled its share price that year), but it came to symbolize the financial turmoil that led the British parliament to issue the Bubble Act of 1719. In fact, some scholars point to evidence that the Bubble Act was a direct product of the South Sea Company itself—drawn up to eliminate competition for funds from non-chartered firms at a time when capital was scarce (Harris, 1994). This is especially convincing considering how the act predated the full-scale bursting of the bubble. Either way, the act meant a temporary end for the joint stock company as the act stated that only royally chartered companies could issue public shares. Stock trading was more limited and subdued in subsequent decades—a period that has been referred to as the Age of Stagnation.

Even so, stock trades did take place and it was around this time that the London Stock Exchange was formed. Its roots go back to the late 1600s and the London coffee houses. Stock dealers convening at the Royal Exchange had been forced out due to their rowdiness and the coffee houses provided new venues. Jonathan's Coffee House in Change Alley is the most well-known and the location from which the earliest evidence of organized trading in marketable securities in London originates. From there, one Mr Castaing issued a periodic list of stock and commodity prices as early as 1698. After a fire destroyed most coffee houses in the area in 1748, "New Jonathan's" was set up in a new location by some 150 stock brokers in 1773—and would promptly be renamed "The Stock Exchange." However, many other stock exchanges coexisted with this exchange and fraud was common. Although an entrance fee was charged, it was not until 1801 that it instead became the first regulated stock exchange with annual subscription fees.[3] Meanwhile, the earliest accounting firms in the country date back to this time.

The startup of new corporations in the UK was highly restricted under the Bubble Act.[4] British nervousness following the South Sea Bubble further meant that corporations were only permitted if shareholders had unlimited liability. Another precaution against calamity was the requirement that balance sheets were drawn up periodically. Lack of disclosure was what had allowed investors to be misled in the previous shipping bubble (including the South Sea company). Whereas independence is a concept well-known in the accounting world today, with the very specific meaning that auditors should not have any other business transactions with the firm they audit, at that time it was *required* that the auditor owned shares in the firm. This was a way of ensuring shareholder control over the firm's management (in early recognition of potential agency conflicts).

With the advent of the 19th century, the industrial revolution was at full throttle. The Bubble Act, which is believed to have slowed the British economy, was repealed in 1825. But with economic growth and technological development going hand in hand with various corporate scandals (not least in relation to a speculative frenzy in railway shares), the

3 http://www.londonstockexchange.com

4 This may be contrasted with the US, where incorporation via registration was sufficient from 1811.

government saw the need for new regulation. The first-ever Companies Acts was followed by many more, along with several Bankruptcy Acts, a Chartered Companies Act, a Limited Liability Act and various liquidation acts, among many others.[5] Still, no income statements were required and the content and the form of the balance sheet were left unregulated. In fact, the Joint Stock Companies Act of 1856 even took a step backward in making the balance sheet and the audit voluntary. Apparently, it was believed by many that private contracts should govern what information was provided, since it was up to the shareholders and creditors to decide with whom they did business (Day, 2000).

Although the 19th century was buzzing with industrial and financial activity, accountants were still rare at the time. The exact number of accountants in Britain in the time period of 1850–70 has been disputed, with numbers varying from less than a hundred to a few thousand (see discussion in Walker and Lee, 1999). By the 1870s, several "societies" of accountants had been established in the large cities of England and in 1880, a national accounting body was created, the **Institute of Chartered Accountants in England and Wales (ICAEW)**, which exists to this day. Records of practicing accountants became more reliable with the formation of the ICAEW, which reports some 16,000 accountants in 1881 (Edwards and Walker, 2007). It is worth noting that the roots of several of today's national accounting bodies can also be traced back to the end of the 1800s.

No general theory of accounting governed the work of these bodies at the time and very little or nothing was achieved in the area of principles (Day, 2000). In the first decade of the 1900s, compulsory filing of annual balance sheets was reintroduced but reporting practice was still of low quality by later standards. The lack of consolidation of group accounts and the ability to hide results using subsidiaries was a major cause for concern. The Companies Act of 1929, which mandated income statements, and the Companies Act of 1948, which covered group accounting, remedied some of these problems. Meanwhile, between 1942 and 1969, the ICAEW issued an authoritative series of *Recommendations on Accounting Principles*. "Until then ... the least progressive of the professional bodies, [this came about] more by evolution than by deliberate policy" (Day, 2000, with reference to Zeff (1971)). Several accounting scandals in the 1960s and 1970s signaled once and for all the state of financial reporting in the country and led the institute to eventually release its *Statement of Intent on Accounting Standards in the 1970s*. In 1970, the ICAEW established the Accounting Standards Steering Committee (ASSC), which would later be renamed the Accounting Standards Committee (ASC), as its membership expanded and included the six major accountancy bodies in the country. The role of the committee was to develop and communicate standards for financial reporting and it issued 34 Statements of Standard Accounting Practice (SSAP) between 1971 and 1990. The ICAEW was also active in the development of international accounting practice. Together with fifteen other professional accounting bodies in the UK and eight other countries, the ICAEW helped establish the **International Accounting Standards Committee (IASC)** in 1973. The founding of the IASC—the forerunner of the IASB—in London underlines the impact of the UK on international standard-setting in accounting.

In 1975 the ASSC published *The Corporate Report*, which was a discussion paper inquiring

5 http://www.icaew.com

into the role and scope of financial reports and their intended users and usefulness. As such, it is considered a foundational document. Among the major problems facing the standards was a lack of enforcement, their ambiguous relationship with company law, the lack of a conceptual framework and coherence between standards, as well as the fact that funding for the ASC came from the accountancy profession, which meant that its lack of independence constituted a potential threat to objectivity. In 1990 the government stepped in, establishing the **Financial Reporting Council (FRC)** and its two subsidiary bodies, one of which was the **Accounting Standards Board (ASB)**, which took over standard-setting after 1990. Today, the FRC is funded by the government as well as by the accounting profession and the financial community. As of 2012, following a number of reforms and restructurings, it is responsible for standard-setting in the country.

To summarize, the UK financial reporting environment has developed in response to the needs of investors in financial markets. The link to taxation is relatively weak. This suggests an economic perspective on the development of accounting standards and, consequently, that regulation has been developed by the accounting profession and by private standard-setters. In the last few decades, the government has increased its role, at least as an enforcer of standards. Internationalization has also had a large impact. As a member of the EU, the UK implemented IFRS for listed firms in 2005, meaning that FRC standard-setting is now focused on non-listed firms. It is currently unclear what will happen to accounting regulation after "Brexit" in 2019.

In relation to the size of its economy, the UK has among the largest number of accounting professionals in the world (Nobes, 1992), and the profession is experienced in standard-setting. Today, London can be seen as the "capital of international accounting" as the IASB is based there, and the "Big Four" accounting firms (Deloitte, EY, KPMG, PwC) have their global IFRS expertise in London. While the Big Four are currently headquartered in the US, much of their origins stem from the UK.

4.3.2 The US

Trade between the UK and the US granted New York a special position, transforming it into the leading US port.[6] The New York Stock Exchange (NYSE) was established in 1792, its roots incidentally also going back to a coffee house (in lower Manhattan). Although trading ebbed and flowed, it grew considerably during the 1800s, with investments in railroads and oil ventures being particularly noteworthy. During this time, the need for accounts and audits started to grow and the American Association of Public Accountants (AAPA) was formed in 1887. Financed by the government, it came into being as a response to calls for regulation to protect citizens and individual investors from the frequently harsh business environment created by growing power elites and corporations of a monopolistic nature. This can be seen as a significant period for a profession that had been unregulated for thousands of years. One objective of the AAPA was to shape accounting and one of the earliest recommendations from the group was that the items on the balance sheets should be ordered based on liquidity

6 http://www.fundinguniverse.com/company-histories/new-york-stock-exchange-inc-history

(a clear creditor perspective). In 1917, the American Institute of Accountants (AIA) replaced the AAPA (and introduced stricter admission requirements for members).[7]

It may be noted that whereas British regulation came about as a call for disclosure, US regulation was more concerned with **uniformity**. An event that has been said to be important in the development of accounting principles in the US was the publication of a memorandum labeled *Uniform Accounts* in 1917, concerning the accounting for interest expenses. Although published by the AIA at the request of the Federal Trade Commission (FTC), the document appeared in the *Federal Reserve Bulletin* after having been approved by the Federal Reserve Board (FRB), the main governing body of the US central banking system (Zeff, 1984; Chatfield and Vangermeersch, 2014). This was presumably a result of the AIA's desire to establish credibility with the FRB, which was very concerned with the creditworthiness of banks.

In the 1920s and 1930s the influence of the stock exchanges grew, and stock ownership increased two-, three- and fourfold over the next decades. This meant that stockholders rather than creditors became the primary users of financial statements. The number of shares listed on NYSE expanded greatly at this time, from a little over 50 million shares in 1900 to over 1 billion in 1930 (see Figure 4.1).[8] Trading volume has risen exponentially ever since the turn of the last century (note logarithmic values in the two bottom graphs).

The 1929 crash of the New York Stock Exchange (NYSE) was partially blamed on accountants and poor accounting. However, the exchange itself was not exactly a "role model" in that it did not require regular financial statements until 1899 and *audited* statements were still not required by 1929. This lax regulatory setting would rapidly change in the few years following the 1933 inauguration of F. Roosevelt as US president. Securities regulation took the form of, among others, the Truth-in-Securities Act and the Securities Exchange Act. In 1934, the **Securities and Exchange Commission (SEC)** was set up by Congress to administer said acts and monitor firms' compliance. The NYSE had started requiring independent audits of statements by listed companies in 1933.

The SEC would let the actual creation of accounting principles be led by the private accounting profession rather than formulate principles itself. It was made explicit that financial statements needed to be prepared in accordance with accepted principles. The AIA (the main representative of the profession) founded the Committee on Accounting Procedure (CAP), which published numerous bulletins.

Meanwhile, the American Association of University Instructors in Accounting was an independent body established to support *research* within the field of accounting and thus develop better accounting methods. Originally formed in 1916, the organization became the **American Accounting Association (AAA)** in 1935.

In 1936, after further controversies regarding AIA membership requirements and a split and remerger with one dissentious group, the American Institute of Public Accountants (AIPA) came into existence. "Certified" was added to the name in 1957, and with that **the American Institute of Certified Public Accountants (AICPA)** appeared as we now know it.

7 https://www.aicpa.org/about/missionandhistory/history-of-the-aicpa.html
8 http://www.nyxdata.com/nysedata/

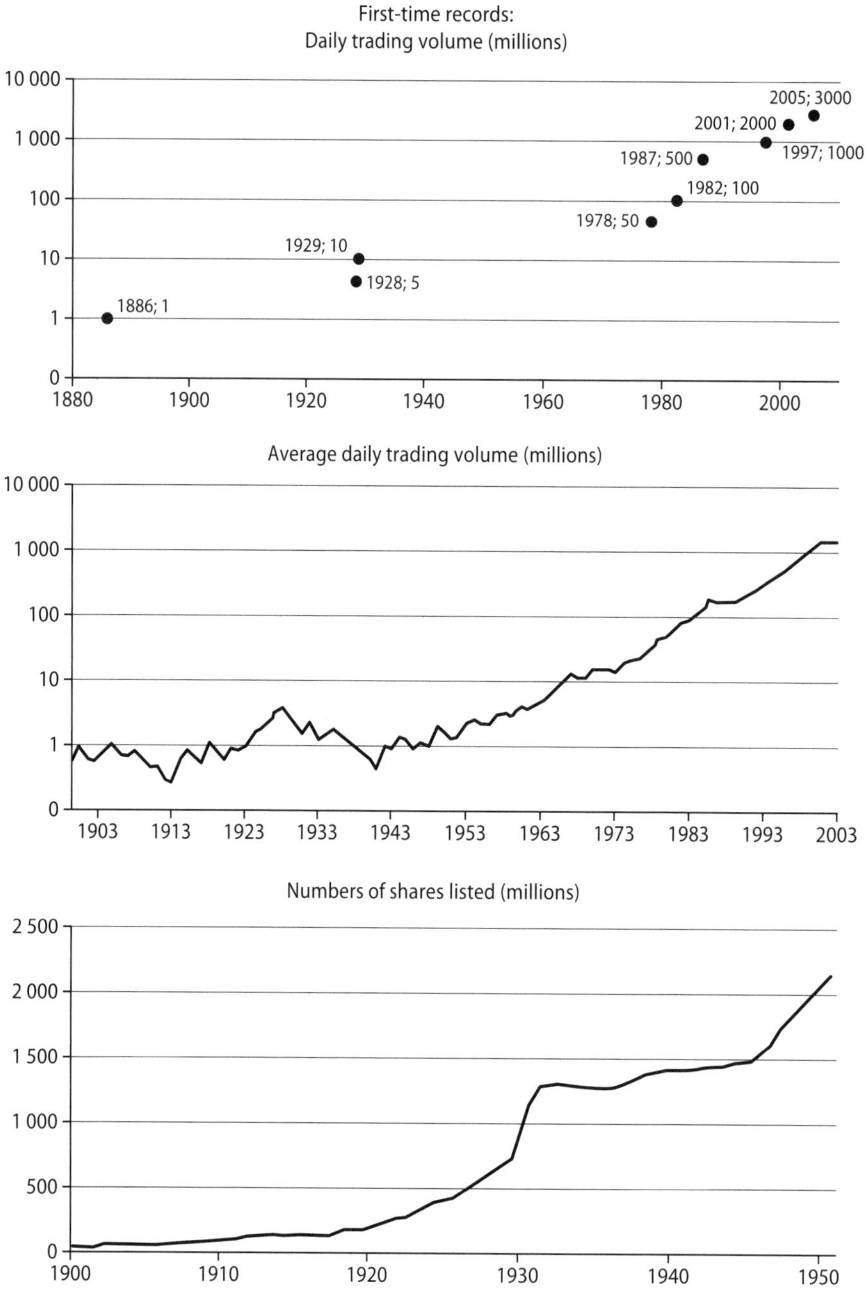

Figure 4.1 Number of shares listed and trading volume at the New York Stock Exchange between selected dates

A professional body, it is involved in regulatory and audit activities and oversees the US CPA (Certified Public Accountant) examination.

The new middle class of the post-war era bought stocks and the number of shares grew exponentially during the second half of the last century (see Figure 4.1). More emphasis was placed on shareholders and information dissemination, and with this came a shift in focus from the balance sheet to the income statement. Around the 1950s, however, many different reporting alternatives made interpreting earnings figures difficult. That there was no "correct" figure puzzled many investors. The definition of earnings as operating earnings (by the AIA) with a focus on recurrent earnings rather than extraordinary earnings further puzzled some investors. Although a sound earnings capacity measure in theory, it would lead to earnings management and to the classification of losses as extraordinary and gains as recurrent. Notably, the debate over which earnings measure to use still rages to this day (cf. discussion on net income and other comprehensive income in Chapter 15).

Consistency also became increasingly important as comparisons between firms became relevant. The lack of comparability (also due to price level fluctuations at the time) provoked reactions and criticism toward the CAP. The AAA expressed a need for *comparability* in the 1957 issuance of Accounting and Reporting Standards. It should be noted that uniformity, which was called for in 1917 by the FRB and in 1936 by the AAA, does not automatically lead to comparability. Uniform treatment of transactions of different underlying economics would lead to surface comparability rather than true comparability (cf. section 4.5).

Eventually, in 1959, the CAP was replaced by the Accounting Principles Board (APB) as a response to the expressed lack of rigor in the reporting to date. APB, consisting of practitioners, academics, business people and government officials, was to create generally accepted accounting principles in a written format and deal with current controversial issues. The Accounting Research Division (ARD) of the APB would provide the Board with a solid base for their conclusions. In his *Report on the Accounting Research Activities of the American Institute of Certified Public Accountants*, the chairman of the APB writes that the research staff should preferably hold both the CPA title and have a PhD (Powell, 1961). Meanwhile, the AAA has not been directly involved in standard-setting since the 1960s, but has taken on more of a consulting role, representing views and research in the academic community.

The development of accounting principles by the APB was deemed too slow by both the profession and the SEC. This led to the AICPA and the AAA calling for an investigation on how best to go about setting accounting standards. Thus, in 1973 the **Financial Accounting Standards Board (FASB)**, the **Financial Accounting Foundation (FAF)** and the **Financial Accounting Standards Advisory Council (FASAC)** were formed (replacing the APB). Whereas the foundation elects trustees who in turn fund, select and oversee the operations of the Board, and the council shares views and advice with the Board based on contact with practitioners, the Board itself develops the standards and principles. AICPA thus largely had to surrender this role, although it still has influence over standard-setting. Due process was introduced at this time as well. The SEC has endorsed the FASB as being authoritative on accounting standard-setting matters and enforces those standards. In 1984, the **Emerging Issues Task Force (EITF)** was formed to support the FASB. In addition, the FASB has a staff of more than 100 employees to support its activities.

There were several objectives with the creation of the FASB, including:

- **Independence** – The members of the FASB not only represent the audit profession, but also preparers, users and academics. Board members must sever ties with their former employers and are employed full-time by the FASB. The trustees of the FAF are intended to "shield" board members from political pressure. The intention is to allow the FASB to develop conceptually rigorous standards without too much political influence.
- **Transparency** – The development of new standards is intended to be transparent and responsive to stakeholder viewpoints, thereby increasing the legitimacy of standards. There is a due process, where stakeholders can comment at several stages of development (see Text Box 4.1). All the FASB meetings are open to the public. FASAC provides practice-oriented comments.
- **Conceptual rigor** – Before the the FASB, standard-setting was seen as being too *ad hoc*. One of the first things the FASB did was to create a Conceptual Framework (see Chapter 5).
- **Resources** – The FASB has enough resources to develop high-quality standards. The EITF handles smaller issues requiring a quick resolution, so that the FASB can focus on larger projects. The support staff provides help in the development of standards and gathers background material. Adequate resources promote independence and support conceptual rigor of standards.

Text Box 4.1 **The due process of the FASB and the IASB**

The FASB's guiding principle is that a new standard is issued when a cost-benefit analysis reveals that the expected benefits of a change exceed the cost of that change. After a financial reporting issue has been identified, a project is added to the Board's technical agenda based on certain criteria, such as whether there exists the possibility of actually reaching a solution that is politically acceptable. The various related issues are determined, after which follows an **Exposure Draft (ED)** of a standard, sometimes preceded by a **Discussion Paper (DP)**. Both the DP and the ED are intended to allow for various stakeholders to give their input by way of Comment Letters. A public roundtable meeting often follows the ED, after which the Board considers necessary revisions to the ED before an Accounting Standards Update is issued, containing the changes to the Accounting Standards Codification.[9] The IASB has been heavily inspired by the FASB's due process, and has a very similar standard-setting process.

Today, US GAAP constitute one of two sets of standards with global influence. Its influence is direct, in that firms in the world's largest economy must comply with the framework, as well as indirect, through its impact on IFRS. Hence, its complexity has been carried into IFRS (as discussed in section 4.4). In addition, the Big Four accounting firms are all headquartered in the US. Through its strong accounting profession and relatively long history of advanced

9 http://www.fasb.org

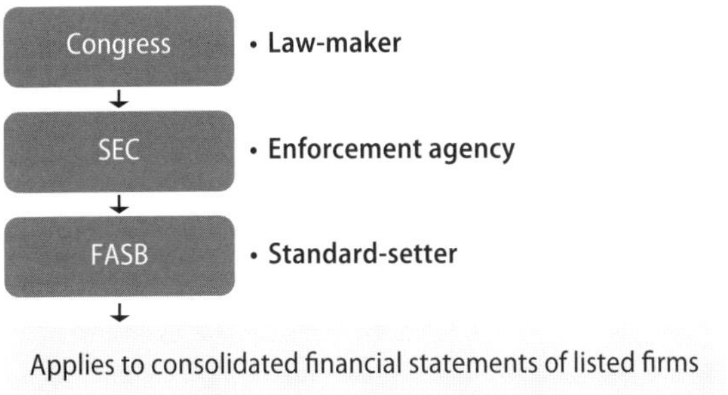

Figure 4.2 US regulatory structure

accounting standard-setting, the US inarguably has an influence on the rest of the world in terms of how to conceptually address accounting issues.

Structural aspects of US standard-setting have also influenced structures elsewhere. The IASB has more or less copied the structure of the FASB (see section 4.4 d). The overall structure of US accounting regulation and enforcement (shown in Figure 4.2) combines positive aspects of both government and private-sector standard-setting. Congress has passed laws and set up the SEC as a government agency. This ensures legitimacy and strong enforcement of standards. Meanwhile, the FASB, as a private standard-setter with economic and accounting expertise, assures the development of economically rigorous and conceptually consistent standards. Finally, the accounting standards only apply to the consolidated financial statements of listed firms. This structure was subsequently copied by the EU in the introduction of IFRS.

We finish this section by concluding that the US financial accounting system has clearly developed based on the needs of financial markets, especially equity markets. The tax system, meanwhile, has developed separately from the financial reporting system. The federal regulation of accounting only applies to listed firms, while unlisted firms are regulated by states. States also have a central role in auditing, as they certify auditors. Notably, unlisted firms are not required to prepare public financial statements and are consequently not subject to audits. In other words, US GAAP are not only *intended to be useful* for listed firms, they are *only* intended for such firms. When US GAAP—in all their complexity—influences IFRS, it is worthwhile remembering the intended target groups of the original regulation.

4.4 Harmonization

As pointed out above, UK and US developments have greatly influenced the way we view accounting today. In fact, the IASB's Conceptual Framework is all but derived from the FASB's corresponding documentation. This is not surprising, as the IASB is focused on useful information for equity investors, in agreement with the Anglo-American view. As stock markets have gained importance in Continental countries, the influence of IFRS has grown. This influence is further strengthened by the drive for global harmonization of accounting—the topic of discussion over the next few pages.

The context in many Continental countries has partially changed in recent decades, as the importance and activity of stock markets have increased. This has led to financial reporting more adapted to equity market needs. Meanwhile, an increased level of globalization with more cross-border investing has in turn fueled the need for an international **harmonization of accounting**. Both of these developments have in turn been driven by factors such as deregulation of financial markets, technological development and new derivative financial products (enabling more effective management of, for instance, currency risk).

This development has had a fundamental effect on listed firms in Continental countries for two reasons. First, listed firms in general are the ones most affected by harmonization trends. Second, as Anglo-American accounting is focused on the needs of equity markets, harmonization has meant that Continental countries are moving closer to Anglo-American accounting. For unlisted firms, the effect is much smaller. For such firms, traditional accounting is still used in many Continental countries.

It should be noted that harmonization of accounting is not an objective in itself. Rather, it is a means for accounting standard setters to achieve the main objective of accounting—usefulness—in a world of globalized and increasingly important equity markets.

Early attempts at accounting harmonization were initiated globally by the UN and regionally by the EU already in the 1970s. Further, the International Accounting Standards Committee (IASC) created in 1973 by the accounting profession in a number of countries had an idea of developing accounting standards that could be used worldwide. However, it was not until the advent of global equity markets in the 1990s that harmonization started to develop quickly. By the late 1990s, there was a discussion about whether US GAAP or IAS (the predecessor to IFRS) would be useful as global standards.

In 2001 the IASC was transformed into the IASB. The new organization was heavily influenced by the FASB in how to meet the objectives of an independent expert body and gain stakeholder legitimacy. The **IFRS Foundation** has trustees who appoint the board members of the IASB. The IFRS Foundation functions as an umbrella to protect the independence of the board members. The members of the IASB are diverse accounting experts, coming from accounting firms, preparers, users and universities. Their independence is further strengthened in that they must sever all ties with their former employer. Like the FASB, the IASB strives to increase the legitimacy of issued standards through structured stakeholder input in the standard-setting process. This is done by the **IFRS Advisory Council** (similar to FASAC in the FASB), which provides current input from practice. Further, there is a due process where all stakeholders can comment at several stages of the process. The IASB is also—like the FASB—supported by an entity that handles current issues (**IFRS Interpretations Committee**, similar to EITF) and a substantial support staff.

Currently, IFRS are a *de facto* global standard for listed firms, even though US GAAP are used in the world's largest equity markets (NYSE and Nasdaq). The use of IFRS in the US has been discussed over the last decades, especially in the early 2000s. Following an agreement in 2002, the FASB and the IASB also collaborated in the production of many standards, through the so-called "Norwalk Agreement" (the FASB is located in Norwalk, Connecticut). Although a transition to IFRS now seems unlikely to occur in any foreseeable future, it is fair to say that the US has exercised great influence over IFRS. Many aspects of the IASB and IFRS are modeled on the FASB and US GAAP. As seen above, the organizational structure and due process are similar. The conceptual frameworks in IFRS and US GAAP are also similar. Further, many of the actual standards exhibit great similarities, either based on explicit cooperation, or based on the IASB being inspired by US GAAP in its standard-setting. There are several reasons for this. Most saliently, the US (the FASB) has developed a set of accounting standards that are both comprehensive and adapted to the needs of equity markets (which the world was looking for). The FASB has the world's largest resources dedicated to accounting standard-setting and long experience and expertise in developing the type of standards that are in demand. Also, the SEC is a significant contributor to the legitimacy of the standards. If standards are acceptable to the SEC, they should be acceptable to other securities regulators. From a user perspective, the US equity markets (by far the largest in the world) are important sources of finance for large firms from other countries. So, reporting in accordance with the needs of those markets is helpful for firms from other countries in achieving legitimacy as well as producing decision-useful financial reports.

The overall structure of US regulation also inspired the structure of EU regulation. The EU (previously the EC) has worked toward harmonization of accounting regulation since the 1970s. There are two separate processes for harmonization in the EU: 1) comprehensive harmonization through **directives**, and 2) harmonization of consolidated financial statements of listed firms through **regulations**. The first directive aimed at harmonization of accounting (the so-called 4th directive) was issued in 1978. It required member states to integrate the directive into their own legislation and apply it to most limited liability companies. Although some level of harmonization was achieved, it was far from a complete success (Flower, 1994).

In 2002, the EU adopted the IFRS/IAS regulation, which required full implementation of IFRS for the consolidated financial statements of all listed firms from 2005. This was a substantial step toward real harmonization for all listed firms. A regulation becomes law directly and does not require integration into the laws of member states. With the IFRS/IAS regulation, the EU adopted a system similar to that in the US, where governments enforce standards but the standards are developed by a private standard-setter. An overview of the structure is provided in Figure 4.3. The similarities between the structures depicted in Figures 4.2 and 4.3 are easy to detect.

Finally, even if the IFRS/IAS regulation has had substantial harmonizing effects, there is literature pointing out that it is far from complete (Kvaal and Nobes, 2012; Nobes, 2013). International differences in IFRS practice suggest that institutional settings, forms of regulation and enforcement have considerable effects on the implementation of IFRS.

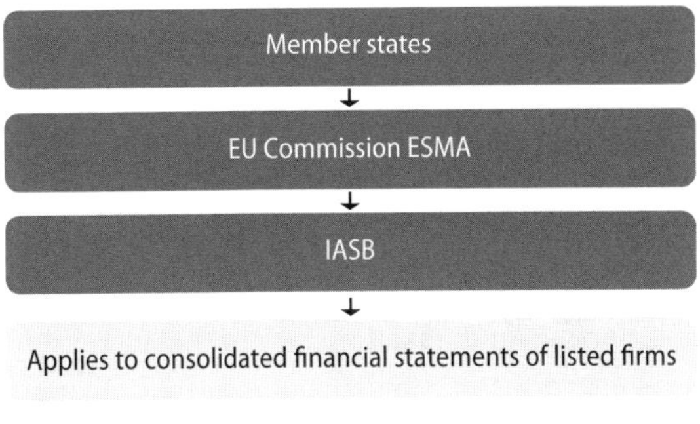

Figure 4.3 EU regulatory structure

4.4.1 Accounting regulation in Sweden

Sweden is an example of a country traditionally belonging to the Continental group of countries, but which has been heavily influenced by Anglo-American accounting over the course of the last four decades. In the 1920s, there was considerable activity on the Stockholm Stock Exchange. A Swedish company—Kreuger & Toll—was the most heavily traded on the NYSE in the late 1920s. In 1932, the company went bankrupt and this had a large impact on the Swedish economy. Ownership of large firms was restructured in the 1930s and networks of firms with banks at the center were created. These networks had substantial cross-ownership and finance was provided by the banks. As a result, the Stockholm Stock Exchange became largely inactive. From 1930 to 1980, conservative accounting was preferred by the banks. In addition, the strong link between financial reporting and taxation provided a strong incentive for firms to be conservative (since it allows for postponement of taxes). The large owners had direct access to management, so there was limited need for sophisticated financial accounting (Text Box 4.2).

From the 1920s and for many decades onwards, accounting was regulated solely through laws. In the 1960s, the Swedish audit profession, through its organization **FAR**, started issuing accounting recommendations. In the 1970s, the Swedish government set up **Bokföringsnämnden (BFN)** (the Swedish Accounting Standards Board) as the primary standard-setter in Sweden. Even though BFN is a government agency, it has some characteristics of private expert-based standard-setters.

Starting in 1980, the Stockholm Stock Exchange began coming back to life. A higher activity on the stock market and an increasing international investor presence in Sweden was driving the need for more equity-oriented financial reporting. In 1989, the Swedish accounting profession and Swedish industry formed **Redovisningsrådet (RR)** (the Swedish Financial Accounting Standards Council, SFASC). It issued standards applicable to listed firms. Its stock market focus put its standards close to IAS. In fact, there was a gradual migration toward IAS between 1990 and 2004 to such a degree that almost all of the IAS (issued by the IASC) was eventually adopted by RR. The standards, however, had more of the character of being recommendations, meaning that a failure to act in accordance with the original IAS was not always strongly sanctioned. The dual standard-setting of BFN and RR started a path toward different requirements for listed and unlisted firms.

Following the EU adoption of IFRS in January 2005, all listed firms in Sweden had to comply with IFRS when preparing their consolidated financial statements. As a consequence, the IASB (through the EU) started having a direct, rather than only an indirect, effect on Swedish accounting regulation. Following requirements in the EU, IFRS/IAS regulation enforcement has been strengthened. Specifically, since 2007, **Finansinspektionen (FI)** (the Swedish Financial Supervisory Authority, SFSA) is responsible for enforcing accounting standards in listed firms.

Traditionally, Sweden had one set of accounting regulation for all purposes; in other words, the same rules applied to both large and listed as well as small and owner-operated firms, and they applied to both financial reporting and taxation. With the increasing sophistication and complexity of regulation for listed firms, Sweden saw a need for having

Text Box 4.2 **Ownership structure in Swedish firms**

There are major differences between the Swedish equity market and the Anglo-Saxon markets with respect to ownership structure. In Sweden, ownership of firms is typically concentrated, meaning that the majority of a firm's shares is held by one or a few large shareholders. Furthermore, there are different classes of shares (class A and class B). Such a dual-class share system gives owners so-called excess control through the possibility of having a proportionally larger number of votes than they do shares or share capital. In light of this concentrated ownership, the need for higher transparency and good firm governance may seem redundant (as large shareholders are able to promote their own interests in firms). However, it is also important to ensure that the interests of individual investors (i.e., small shareholders) are protected. Hence, there are several accounting and governance regulations meant to enhance the transparency and the scrutiny of the Swedish stock market. Given the ownership structure, there was much resistance to IFRS, with its focus on small, uninformed investors (cf. Carrington et al., 2015).

different rules for different types of firms. While standard-setting for listed Swedish firms has become integrated into a global and EU framework, regulation for unlisted firms remains Swedish. BFN has issued different recommendations for different types of firms. While many limited liability companies follow the so-called **K3** regulation (a Swedish version of IFRS for small and medium-sized entities, SMEs), small limited liability companies, partnerships and sole proprietorships follow regulation that is very much tax-oriented (**K2** and **K1** regulation). Having said that, Sweden still maintains a strong link between financial reporting and taxation in legal entities, even if there is no such link with regard to consolidated financial statements.

4.5 Principles-based and rules-based approaches to regulation

In this final section, we continue the comparison of different types of accounting regulation by considering regulation from the point of view of *how it is written*. Here we refer to the conception that regulation can take the form of general principles and guidelines or detailed rules. The relative merits of principles and rules were especially discussed in the accounting literature in the 2000s, in relation to the discussion regarding IFRS adoption in the US. Since various reporting scandals took place in the early 2000s (e.g., Enron and Worldcom), the SEC came to question the effectiveness of US GAAP as a prevention tool for accounting manipulation and speculated that bright-line rules, believed to characterize US GAAP, may create loopholes for manipulation rather than prevent it. Principles-based accounting standards—which were believed to describe IFRS and allegedly focus on the underlying economics—may be preferable in this regard.

But what *is* a principle? Let us use the German highway system, the *Autobahn*, to illustrate this idea. Many sections of the *Autobahn* have no official speed limit (i.e., no rules governing how fast cars can travel). There is an underlying principle, however, which is that one should drive at a speed that may be considered appropriate considering congestion levels, visibility, surface conditions and so forth. Driver discretion is required here (as drivers can be held responsible for reckless behavior should they cause an accident). Meanwhile, an example of a principle in accounting is that the depreciation rate for a tangible, fixed asset should reflect the useful life of that asset. A (simplistic) alternative would be to require a bright-line rule: for example, five years of depreciation for all tangible assets. Higher-level principles are found in standard-setters' conceptual frameworks, including that financial statements should be relevant and faithfully represent underlying economics. The role of standards is to provide additional guidance on how to achieve relevance and faithful representation, but if accounting regulation were perfectly principles-based, there would be no need for standards. They would be redundant since the principle that financial statements should be relevant and faithfully represent underlying economics has, in theory, already been stated.

Whether it is beneficial to have principles-based advisory speed limits on the Autobahn rather than rules (hard speed limits) can of course be debated. Most reasons provided are likely political ("keep voters happy" or "keep car manufacturers happy"). But there is also an efficiency reason, as rules and enforcement impose direct costs as well as indirect costs—the indirect costs coming from loss of efficiency when traveling more slowly than conditions require. Analogous to this, having bright-line accounting rules would take away the need for preparer judgment and—at least in theory—reduce the influence of incentives on measurement by reducing the need for estimates. However, such rules risk decreasing the faithful representation and the relevance of the reported numbers (reducing efficiency and imposing indirect costs). In the depreciation example, if five-year depreciation is required, assets used for several decades might be depreciated over the same length of time as assets used only for a few years. In other words, the drawback includes a potentially inaccurate representation of the underlying economics when rules are too simplistic, or increased costs of preparation when standards are too comprehensive or complex. Principles-based standards entail more flexibility compared to rules-based standards, and this flexibility in accounting procedures is expected by some to lead to a more informative signal about underlying economic events (Dye and Verrecchia, 1995).

Assuming principles help ensure that financial statements reflect the underlying economics of events and states, one might question the necessity of rules. Perhaps a partial explanation is that accounting standards have been created reactively rather than proactively, as may be seen from history. Accounting scandals hardly began with Enron or Worldcom. The South Sea Company is but one example from the past. The Watergate investigations in the US led to disputes over the accounting profession, the FASB and even the SEC. Notably, different regulatory solutions have been proposed at different times. For example, after the Watergate scandal in 1972, uniform accounting (with a focus on stricter rules) was again called for. This stands in contrast with the reactions following the demise of Enron, where it appeared as if principles rather than rules could have helped prevent what happened. Meanwhile, the negative consequences of increased discretion (or flexibility), such as potentially increased room for opportunistic choices and estimates, have been one of the main concerns in the literature (Agoglia et al., 2011).

As mentioned, one may associate US GAAP with rules rather than principles. The view that "US GAAP are rules-based while IFRS are principles-based" is so widespread these days that it has almost achieved mythical status. Perhaps this may be ascribed to the fact that US GAAP comprise a staggering 17,000 pages. The IFRS are comparatively small in scope (but nevertheless consist of nearly 4,000 pages). It is true that US GAAP contain more rules than IFRS, if for no other reason than its sheer scope and the fact that it is older (giving it more time to develop rules). However, the idea of principles was seen early in the Anglo-American world. For example, in 1936, the AAA in the US published *A Tentative Statement of Accounting Principles Underlying Corporate Financial Statements*. Admittedly, apart from "tentative" being removed in later versions (1941), "principles" was considered an overly ambitious term, wherefore it was decided that it would be replaced by "concepts and standards" in 1948.

In all fairness, attempts were made in the US during the first half of the 20th century to develop principles, but there was no wide acceptance of any one approach. The AAA eventually (in 1966) published **A Statement of Basic Accounting Theory (ASOBAT)**, which was distinctly user-oriented, thereby setting a clear objective for accounting. Consistent with our discussion in Chapter 2, having an objective was believed to be a prerequisite for principles to be useful. This, of course, is not unproblematic, since users are diverse. A more pragmatic solution is presumably to demand the fulfillment of certain criteria, known today as *qualitative characteristics* (see Chapter 5). It was also suggested that diverse user needs be met by presenting multiple performance measures (both historical and current cost should be given alongside one another).

However, the fact remains that desirable principles were pondered upon early on. It has also wisely been pointed out that many or most rules are based on some underlying principle, while many principles that are difficult and require discretion are commonly illustrated with examples and detailed guidance that take on the status of rules for preparers as well as auditors (Nelson, 2003; Bennett et al., 2006; Benston et al., 2006). In other words, rules are derived from principles—and neither rules nor principles exist in isolation. Moreover, by no means is it possible to say that IFRS lack rules. Regardless of which accounting framework is adhered to, all accruals-based accounting methods require financial statement preparers to use their discretion and judgment in making estimations and valuations (Fields et al., 2001).

Having said that, we believe the distinction between US GAAP and IFRS based on how principles-based or rules-based they are still holds some merit. It is also valid to relate the discussion of rules and principles to the model presented by Nobes (1992) (cf. section 4.4). Anglo-American countries have a focus on "fairness," meaning the objective of financial statements is to reflect underlying economics. In order to enable this, it must be possible to adapt financial reporting to the unique situation of the reporting firm. US GAAP and IFRS have two distinct approaches for achieving adaptability. US GAAP tend to define reporting requirements for each specific economic situation, resulting in detailed rules. IFRS provide principles that allow for adoption in the individual case. The result is that US GAAP are more objective and IFRS are more subjective. One reason for the demand for objectivity in US GAAP is that the risk of litigation is high in the US. Having more detailed rules reduces uncertainty and may thereby decrease litigation risk for both firms and their auditors. Meanwhile, in countries with a link between financial reporting and taxation, principles-based accounting is difficult. Tax rules must limit preparer flexibility and must be enforceable in tax courts. Therefore, accounting in Continental countries has traditionally been rules-based as well—although in a less complex way than in US GAAP.

It is important to note that the objective of principles-based standards is that management should evaluate the firm's unique economic situation and apply the principles to that situation. If done correctly, similar economic events are accounted for in a similar way, and dissimilar events in a dissimilar way. What is problematic is if similar events are accounted for in different ways, or if different events are accounted for in similar ways. See Gordon and Gallery (2012) for a discussion on this issue.

The dichotomy between rules and principles is fundamental in relation to quality, and it is an issue we return to throughout this book. In Part V—when we go through different accounting items—we see examples of how accounting standards may be more or less principles-based. Overall, some research indicates that principles-based standards do not work well when preparers have strong incentives and that they require stronger enforcement compared to rules-based standards.

4.6 Conclusions

Economic theory predicts that when markets fail, inefficiencies may result. Regulation is suggested as a solution to this problem, and this is also believed to be applicable in the case of financial accounting. Underproduction of corporate information is especially problematic, provided that accounting is a public good contributing to well-functioning capital markets and society as a whole. When a cost-benefit analysis shows that it is relatively costly for managers to disclose firm activities, they may choose to withhold information in the absence of regulation.

Regulation is likely to develop in accordance with investor needs (via capital markets) or state needs (via the taxation system) and take on different forms accordingly. The regulatory role of the state versus private actors will vary depending on the main user of accounting, as will the way in which regulation is written (e.g., whether it is principles- or rules-based). With respect to the latter point, we emphasize that the distinction between principles-based and rules-based standards is not a clear binary distinction, especially not when applied to specific frameworks. All influential standards have some rules that are derived from some principles, which means that the difference between US GAAP and IFRS is a matter of degree and should not be overstated.

Primarily two groups of countries exist when it comes to accounting regulation: the Anglo-American group and the Continental group. The former is characterized by equity financing, no link between financial reporting and taxation, private-sector standard-setting and an influential accounting profession, while the latter is characterized by bank financing, a link between financial reporting and taxation, regulation through state legislation and a relatively small accounting profession. Our focus on the Anglo-American group stems from the fact that our view of accounting today is becoming more and more Anglified in tandem with the growth of international capital markets. Harmonization of accounting implies drawing closer to the Anglo-American views, with international accounting standards being developed drawing heavily on regulation developed in the UK and the US.

CHAPTER 5

Conceptual frameworks of accounting

Learning outcomes

Upon completion of this chapter, you will gain insight into:

- The contribution of the world's most influential standard-setters to accounting theory through the development of a Conceptual Framework for financial accounting.
- The meaning and implied definition of accounting quality as conveyed through the Conceptual Framework.
- The various qualitative characteristics useful financial statements should possess, including the trade-off between the two primary (fundamental) characteristics: relevance and faithful representation.
- The notion that in spite of widespread talk of principles in accounting, no explicit principles exist in the Conceptual Framework, but have now been subsumed by the qualitative characteristics.

AS POINTED OUT in Part I, the extent to which financial reporting is useful may act as a measure of what constitutes good or high-quality accounting. So far, however, little reference has been made to exact criteria that can make the financial statements useful.

Although their work is far from complete or perfect, those who have come the farthest in the attempt to formulate such criteria are the world's two most influential standard-setting bodies, the FASB and the IASB.

The FASB developed a **Conceptual Framework** in the 1970s. The IASC (the IASB's predecessor) published its version in 1989. The *Framework*, as it was called, was heavily inspired by the FASB's Conceptual Framework. In 2010, the FASB and IASB jointly revised parts of their previous frameworks. In 2018, the IASB issued a complete new Conceptual Framework, which is no longer identical with the FASB version. In this chapter and throughout this textbook, we refer to the IASB Conceptual Framework (henceforth CF), unless otherwise noted.

Through the CF, the Boards have in essence contributed to normative accounting theory.

It contains a declaration of the objective of financial reporting, the basic elements of financial statements and the characteristics that make them useful (and fulfill the objective), and it provides definitions of core concepts and principles governing the preparation of financial reports. Among other things, the purpose of such a document is to assist standard-setters in the standard-setting process, promote harmonization of accounting standards and practice, assist preparers of financial statements in applying standards as well as handling scenarios not yet covered by a specific standard, thus serving as a foundation upon which auditors are able to evaluate financial statements.

However, the road toward a new, and more complete, framework has been far from straight. The difficulty of developing a coherent framework—and ultimately theory—of accounting, can make even the development of a CF seem futile. Many scholars, professionals and other interested parties have also been critical of the work of the standard-setting bodies. In fact, some rather point to the organizations' *lack* of achievement, their flailing attempts at coherence and the abundance of inconsistent and theoretically devoid documents produced over the past century. We neither defend nor denounce such views, but rather wish to present the standard-setters' efforts to-date. Although much work remains, we believe that regulators and the accountancy profession have come a significant way over the past decades.

Sometimes conceptual stringency has given way to pragmatic solutions, and prevailing beliefs and theories have affected the development of the standards. For example, the view of the manager as an agent and the shareholder as a principal with misaligned interests may on the one hand have caused standard-setters to view management with unwarranted skepticism, leading them to formulate rules that prioritize reliability over relevance of the financial statements. On the other hand, perhaps a healthy dose of skepticism has been exercised, given the severe consequences of past bubbles and scandals due to lacking or misleading disclosures. Perhaps it is worth promoting reliability of the information even if it occurs at the risk of losing some of its relevance. These are difficult issues that standard-setters, researchers and firms battle with continuously. Furthermore, pragmatism is closely tied to cost-benefit analyses. *Perfect* accounting is definitely too costly in relation to the benefits generated.

We now examine some of the key points in the CF more closely, starting with the standard-setters' view on the objective and primary users of financial reports and moving on to the qualitative characteristics of financial reports. Finally, some general principles of accounting (that are implied but not explicit in the CF) are discussed. Recently, the IASB issued a new Conceptual Framework. Whenever this has bearing on the discussion at hand, we will refer to some of the points raised in relation to the development of a new framework. Note that not all parts of the CF are covered in this chapter. Issues that deal with measurement, recognition, disclosure and entities are instead covered in Part V. All chapters of the CF—including where we discuss them in this book—are listed in Table 5.1.

Table 5.1 Chapter guide to the CF and this book

Chapter in Conceptual Framework	Chapter in this book
Chapter 1: The objective of financial reporting	Chapter 5
Chapter 2: Qualitative characteristics of useful reporting	Chapter 5
Chapter 3: The reporting entity	Chapter 14
Chapter 4: Elements of financial statements	Chapter 10
Chapter 5: Recognition and derecognition	Chapter 10
Chapter 6: Measurement	Chapter 10
Chapter 7: Presentation and disclosure	Chapter 15
Chapter 8: Capital and capital maintenance	Not directly addressed

5.1 Intended users and objectives of financial reporting

We have thus far argued that fulfilling the needs of capital markets is the main objective of accounting and financial reporting. We have done this based on the historical development of accounting and accounting institutions. Let us now look at what the IASB and the FASB have to say on the matter. In the CF, the intended objective of financial reporting is formulated as follows:

> The objective of general purpose financial reporting is to provide financial information about the reporting entity that is useful to existing and potential investors, lenders and other creditors in making decisions about providing resources to the entity. Those decisions involve decisions about:
>
> i buying, selling or holding equity and debt instruments;
> ii providing or settling loans and other forms of credit; or
> iii exercising rights to vote on, or otherwise influence, management's actions that affect the use of the entity's economic resources. (1.2)
>
> To make the assessments [...], existing and potential investors, lenders and other creditors need information about:
>
> i the economic resources of the entity, claims against the entity and changes in those resources and claims; and
> ii how efficiently and effectively the entity's management and governing boards have discharged their responsibilities to use the entity's economic resources. (1.4)

In these sentences, the Boards have effectively conveyed the valuation and stewardship roles of accounting. That is, accounting should be useful for the decision-making of investors and creditors regarding buying, selling or holding a firm's equity or debt instruments, but also for determining management's performance.

In the Basis for Conclusions (BC) to the actual framework, one can read:

> The 2006 Discussion Paper that led to Chapter 1 stated that the objective of financial reporting should focus on resource allocation decisions. Although most respondents to the 2006 Discussion Paper agreed that providing useful information for decision making was the appropriate objective, they said that investors, lenders and other creditors make other decisions that are aided by financial reporting information in addition to resource allocation decisions. For example, shareholders who vote on whether to retain directors or replace them, and on how members of management should be remunerated for their services, need information on which to base their decisions. Shareholders' decision-making process may include evaluating how management of the entity performed against management in competing entities in similar circumstances. (BC1.28)

It is pointed out in the CF that equity investors and creditors may have different information needs, but in the writing of standards, the objective is to satisfy the needs of both types of users. Further, the CF points out that other users may find financial statements useful, but that these other users are not considered in the development of accounting standards.

> Other parties, such as regulators and members of the public other than investors, lenders, and other creditors, also may find general purpose financial reports useful. However, those reports are not primarily directed to these other groups. (1.10)

Some may object to this, but it is not too far-fetched to assume that if the quality of the information is such that if it is adequate for investors, the needs of other users will most likely also be met. Of course, there are other *types* of information that due to their nature are not of immediate interest to the investor but may serve the interests of the public. The most salient example is information about the potential environmental impact of a firm's operations. One need not question the importance of such information, but may still be able to conclude that this lies outside the domain of *financial* reporting. That is, useful information that is not of a financial character may still be communicated by the firm and even be required through other regulatory bodies, but this is outside the scope of financial reporting. To the extent that the information *is* of a financial character and/or affects firm value, it *will* be useful to the investor and is therefore encompassed by the objectives of financial reports.

The next question, then, is what type of information the intended users need. Financial statements provide information about an entity's resources, claims against the entity and changes in resources and claims. In accounting, resources are referred to as assets, while claims are referred to as liabilities and equity, all of which are reflected on a balance sheet. Meanwhile, changes in resources and claims result in revenues and expenses, which are shown in the income statement. This is all very well, but it still has no meaning unless one knows what assets, liabilities, equity, income, expenses and "useful" are. These words in turn need to be defined as they are abstract terms with no immediate representation in the real world. Say the words "cat" or "house" and an image is conjured up of these items (admittedly, slightly different images may come to mind depending on one's disposition toward them and because of the existing varieties and subcategories). A consensus, therefore, needs to be reached in order for an artificial "truth" to take form with respect to assets, liabilities, equity, and so on.

The very first paragraph of the first chapter of the CF reads:

> The objective of general purpose financial reporting forms the foundation of the *Conceptual Framework*. Other aspects of the *Conceptual Framework*—the qualitative characteristics of, and the cost constraint on, useful financial information, a reporting entity concept, elements of financial statements, recognition and derecognition, measurement, presentation and disclosure—flow logically from the objective. (1.1, italics in original)

This wording may suggest that once an objective is established, all the rest follows automatically. Obviously, things are not that simple. However, the "other aspects" referred to in the CF should be logically derived from the intended objective. The IASB and the FASB have clarified that their aim is for accounting to have predictive value for the outside capital provider, as evidenced, for instance, in the focus on making decisions about providing resources to the entity. As for what actually makes the information useful—this requires more work. The years that the CF has been in the making, the hundreds of commentaries received following the publication of discussion papers on a CF and the debate surrounding the CF is evidence that accounting stirs up emotions and that what is "right" and "wrong" is highly debatable.[1] Various principles and qualitative characteristics are at the center of this discussion. Before one can determine the usefulness and thereby the quality of any given firm's financial statements, one needs to specify in greater detail which **principles** the statements should be based on and which qualitative characteristics constitute usefulness.

5.2 Qualitative characteristics

The CF defines a number of so-called "qualitative characteristics." These are characteristics that—if exhibited in financial statements—make the statements useful. This may therefore be viewed as the standard-setters' definition of accounting quality.

> To a large extent, financial reports are based on estimates, judgements and models rather than exact depictions. The *Conceptual Framework* establishes the concepts that underlie those estimates, judgements and models. The concepts are the goal towards which the Board and preparers of financial reports strive. As with most goals, the *Conceptual Framework's* vision of ideal financial reporting is unlikely to be achieved in full, at least not in the short term, because it takes time to understand, accept and implement new ways of analysing transactions and other events. Nevertheless, establishing a goal towards which to strive is essential if financial reporting is to evolve so as to improve its usefulness. (1.11, italics in original)

As noted in the previous chapter, accounting regulation in the Anglo-American world was more often than not developed as a response to some problem, scandal or other triggering

1 A "cat" is not just a cat but can be a ragdoll or a Burmese, long-haired or short-haired, skinny or fat.

event. It came about in a *reactive* rather than a *proactive* manner. In Germany, Sweden and many other Continental countries, the situation was the same, but the tax authorities and the governments made the demands, rather than the market. In the US, **qualitative characteristics** of financial reporting were first introduced in the ASOBAT (see previous chapter). There, they were first known as "objectives" and encompassed the terms *relevance*, *understandability*, *verifiability*, *neutrality*, *timeliness*, *comparability* and *completeness*. Along with these, several other required "features" of accounting existed, later known as "fundamentals" by the FASB: *accounting entity*, *going concern*, *accrual*, *judgment*, *substance over form*, *materiality*, etc. There were also measurement principles: conservatism, emphasis on income, application of judgment, how to value assets and liabilities upon recognition, when to recognize revenue (upon sale) and the matching principle. However, the logic behind these features and the stated objectives was not clear. The ASOBAT was largely descriptive, but in cases when it was prescriptive, the reasoning was not presented. It was a start, however, as it was the precursor to today's Conceptual Framework.

The APB (Accounting Principles Board, see previous chapter) was criticized for the non-practical approach in its statements (not least in the ASOBAT). At the time, a conclusion was drawn that it is more appropriate to speak of *standards* rather than principles. Principles were seen as not particularly effective because of the way accounting, being a social science, is bound to be a set of conventions rather than universal truths. The aforementioned standards were solutions rather than truths and were thus a reflection of pragmatism. When the FASB was formed and thus replaced the APB, its role was to develop *standards*. In reality, however, the FASB did not abandon the idea of principles or objectives. For example, the Conceptual Framework, which consisted of a number of Statements of Financial Accounting Concepts (SFACs), was one way of promoting the idea of underlying principles. The cynical observer will say that to this day, no consensus has been reached on what a *principle* or accounting *fundamental* is, meaning that there can be no consistent or coherent theory of accounting(!).

We return to some of the principles below. Meanwhile, we now consider the qualitative characteristics laid out in the CF. Financial reports possessing these characteristics are deemed useful and are therefore of high quality. A distinction is made between **fundamental characteristics** and **enhancing characteristics**. The two fundamental qualities are **relevance** and **faithful representation**. An inherent characteristic of relevance is that the information item is **material** and that it has either **predictive** or **confirmatory** value (or both). This means that based on the financial statements, it should be possible to make forecasts about the future (of interest to equity investors and creditor) or confirm previously made forecasts. Meanwhile, **completeness**, **neutrality** and being **free from error** are aspects of, and thus constitute, faithful representation. A somewhat simplified picture of how these concepts relate to users and underlying economics is to look at faithful representation as defining the ability of financial reports to accurately capture the underlying economics, whereas relevance relates to how financial reports are perceived by users. More specifically, accounting is relevant if somebody can use it as a basis for making decisions. These links are illustrated in Figure 5.1.

The remaining characteristics, **comparability**, **verifiability**, **understandability** and **timeliness**, are considered enhancing—and thus not strictly necessary—characteristics.

Figure 5.1 The link between economic events and conditions, financial reports and users

The enhancing qualitative characteristics either relate to one of the two fundamental qualitative characteristics or are contextual. Comparability and verifiability relate to faithful representation and understandability relates to relevance. Meanwhile, timeliness has to do with when financial statements are made public. The boards reject the idea that such a classification is arbitrary (BC2.10) by arguing that unless financial reports possess the two fundamental characteristics, they cannot be useful, regardless of how comparable, verifiable, timely or understandable they are. They may, however, be useful even if they lack those enhancing characteristics. Hence, there is a qualitative and real distinction between the two sets of characteristics. This set of qualitative characteristics is shown in Figure 5.2. Although the qualitative characteristics from previous frameworks were similar, one of the major changes that made it into the 2010 (and, subsequently, the 2018) version is the classification of the characteristics as fundamental and enhancing. We now go through the characteristics one by one.

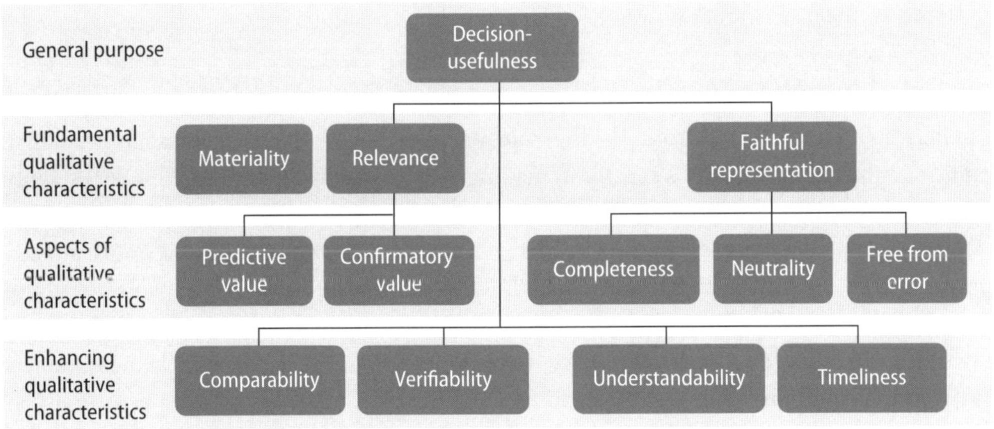

Figure 5.2 The qualitative characteristics (CF, 2018)

5.2.1 Relevance

The first fundamental qualitative characteristic is **relevance**. The argument is that if the information is not relevant, it cannot be useful. One layman definition of relevance is "having a bearing on or connection with the matter at hand." Provided with the objective of financial statements, it should be apparent that relevance essentially indicates that information has bearing on the decision-making process of capital providers. Relevant information is described as follows in the CF:

> Relevant financial information is capable of making a difference in the decisions made by users. Information may be capable of making a difference in a decision even if some users choose not to take advantage of it or are already aware of it from other sources. Financial information is capable of making a difference in decisions if it has predictive value, confirmatory value or both. Financial information has predictive value if it can be used as an input to processes employed by users to predict future outcomes. Financial information need not be a prediction or forecast to have predictive value. Financial information with predictive value is employed by users in making their own predictions. Financial information has confirmatory value if it provides feedback about (confirms or changes) previous evaluations. The predictive value and confirmatory value of financial information are interrelated. Information that has predictive value often also has confirmatory value. For example, revenue information for the current year, which can be used as the basis for predicting revenues in future years, can also be compared with revenue predictions for the current year that were made in past years. The results of those comparisons can help a user to correct and improve the processes that were used to make those previous predictions. (2.6–2.10)

As noted above, the concept of relevance is operationalized as financial statements having a predictive and confirmatory role. The two roles are interrelated. If information has predictive and/or confirmatory value, it is capable of making a difference in the decisions made by equity investors and creditors. The CF further states that "information may be capable of making a difference in a decision even if some users choose not to take advantage of it or are already aware of it from other sources." This, and the introduction of the term "capable" (see also BC2.13–BC2.14 to the CF) in the definition, should clear up a common misunderstanding regarding the concept of relevance: that relevant information necessarily brings about a revision in capital providers' estimates of future outcomes, otherwise it does not qualify as information at all, much less decision-relevant ditto.

Let us consider this a bit further. Recall the EMH (see Chapters 2 and 3), which suggests that when new, value-relevant information enters the market, it has an effect on price. To test the EMH, one therefore studies the market's reaction to such information. However, if one instead wanted to test whether accounting earnings are relevant, *assuming* that the EMH holds, one cannot simply watch whether there is a market reaction. The idea in the CF is that as long as the information is *capable* of bringing about a revision, it may be considered relevant, even if it does not actually bring about a revision. This is a reasonable modification, since the provision of a certain information item via other sources would otherwise be claimed to render the disclosure irrelevant and therefore unsuitable for inclusion. This is one reason why the CF points to *confirmatory* value, where accounting information can be relevant if it confirms information from other sources (e.g., as implied in previously made forecasts).

This argument extends to general-purpose statements in general. In the Basis for Conclusions, the Boards acknowledge that some constituents believe that with advances in technology, financial reports as we know them today may not be necessary. Large amounts of data can be gathered online via databases and processed using, for example, eXtensible Business Reporting Language (XBRL) or some other "Big Data" analysis tool. The Boards, however, believe that general-purpose financial reports are "the most efficient and effective way to meet the information needs of a variety of users," not least because they do not require extensive technical skills. One can imagine a future in which information is provided in its entirety via other sources in advance of the publication of financial reports, but that the value of these reports is in their ability to aggregate and provide a clear overview of summary measures that have also been audited.

For information to be relevant, it also needs to be material. A piece of information is **material** if its omission from the financial statements may influence the economic decisions of the users of the statements. Materiality can be related to the size or type of an accounting item.

The problem arising, despite these concise and carefully formulated definitions, is that they possibly generate as many new questions as they answer. In operationalizing the definition, which decision models are used, which information is actually relevant and how should the information be translated into inputs for the decision models? Preparers of financial statements must exercise judgment in determining relevance and materiality. Meanwhile, actual ways of measuring relevance have been explored in the accounting literature and, as we shall see later, one operationalization of the concept is found in studies on the value relevance of book values and earnings. As mentioned briefly in previous chapters, this is concerned with the way market values covary with or respond to changes in reported accounting numbers, which is explained further in Chapter 7.

5.2.2 Faithful representation

The other fundamental qualitative characteristic is **faithful representation**. The CF says the following in explaining faithful representation:

> Financial reports represent economic phenomena in words and numbers. To be useful, financial information must not only represent relevant phenomena, but it must also faithfully represent the phenomena that it purports to represent. [...] To be a perfectly faithful representation, a depiction would have three characteristics. It would be complete, neutral and free from error. Of course, perfection is seldom, if ever, achievable. The Board's objective is to maximize those qualities to the extent possible. (2.12–2.13)

The term faithful representation was present in the earlier version of the CF but acquired a new meaning in the 2010 version (which is maintained in the 2018 version). There was no formal definition of what faithful representation entailed; instead, examples of what might constitute faithfully represented information were provided. Meanwhile, one of the principal qualitative characteristics was **reliability**, with faithful representation being one aspect of reliability. In the current CF, faithful representation has instead replaced reliability. The IASB explains the reason for the change (BC2.25–BC2.26):

> The comments of respondents to numerous proposed standards indicated a lack of a common understanding of the term *reliability*. Some focused on *verifiability* or *free from material error* to the virtual exclusion of faithful representation. Others focused more on faithful representation, perhaps combined with neutrality. Some apparently think that reliability refers primarily to precision.
>
> Because attempts to explain what reliability was intended to mean in this context have proved unsuccessful, the Board sought a different term that would more clearly convey the intended meaning. The term *faithful representation*, the faithful depiction in financial reports of economic phenomena, was the result of that search. That term encompasses the main characteristics that the previous frameworks included as aspects of reliability.

Thus, completeness and neutrality, which used to be aspects of reliability, and the "free from error" criterion, which was part of the definition of reliability, have all been subsumed by faithful representation. Reliability as a concept has been abandoned altogether. As for "verifiability" not being a formal requirement, the Boards conclude that (BC2.62):

> Some respondents pointed out that including verifiability as an aspect of faithful representation could result in excluding information that is not readily verifiable. Those respondents recognised that many forward-looking estimates that are very important in providing relevant information (for example, expected cash flows, useful lives and salvage values) cannot be directly verified. However, excluding information about those estimates would make the financial reports much less useful. The Board agreed and repositioned verifiability as an enhancing qualitative characteristic, very desirable but not necessarily required.

Whereas relevance has been measured empirically in terms of value relevance, measuring or capturing representational faithfulness remains somewhat elusive (CF BC2.50 and BC2.51). The reason for this is that an empirical measure of faithful representation requires an operationalization of underlying economics that is independent of the financial statements. Possibly, this could be done in certain circumstances for individual financial statement items (see, for example, Marton and Runesson, 2017) regarding loan loss provisions in banks), even if it is not obtainable for summary measures such as earnings or equity. The background for this difficulty is that the very reason for having financial statements is that we cannot directly observe underlying economics.

Finally, we point out one of the greatest challenges where faithful representation is concerned: managerial discretion. Faithfully represented information is complete, neutral and free from error. Unintentional measurement errors could cause information to not be faithfully represented, but intentional biases would exacerbate the situation by making the information non-neutral and potentially incomplete as well. By being selective in terms of what is included and reported, completeness suffers and the resulting information could be misleading to investors.

5.2.3 Trade-off between relevance and faithful representation

The CF points out that useful information must be both relevant and faithfully represented. It is not enough that one of the two fundamental qualitative characteristics is fulfilled. Meanwhile, there is sometimes a conflict between the two concepts. Some potentially relevant information could be difficult to represent faithfully, simply because there is too much uncertainty in the measurement. The trade-off between the two fundamental qualitative characteristics, relevance and faithful representation, or (as it is mostly referred to in the accounting literature) the **trade-off between relevance and reliability**, constitutes one of the main issues in developing accounting theory.

Meeting both the relevance and the reliability criteria can be difficult, meaning that sometimes one must prioritize one quality at the expense of another.

One example is the recognition and measurement of internally generated intangible assets (cf. Chapter 11). Whereas recognizing intangible assets in the balance sheet is relevant for investors' decisions in valuing the firm, the underlying problem is that measuring these assets reliably is difficult. Not only is it difficult to determine the asset's ability to generate future cash flows as this depends on the successful implementation of firm strategies, the business environment and macroeconomic events, it is also inherently difficult to reliably estimate the cost of developing an asset that has no physical form or presence. Yet, by allowing these complexities to determine that such assets should not be recognized because they cannot be faithfully represented potentially reduces the relevance of the information provided. In other words, one may prefer information that is not entirely faithfully represented if it still carries relevance. Here, one may think of *time* as being a determinant of quality. If one instead puts more time and effort into trying to collect and present data that is complete and free from error—thus making it more faithfully represented—the information may end up being less relevant to users by the time it is actually made public. In the extreme case, one may wait to present the estimated value until *after* all the cash flows related to the asset have already been recorded, in which case there may be no uncertainty regarding the value at all. However, by then the relevance of the information is highly questionable!

Another situation in which one must consider the trade-off between relevance and faithful representation is in the conflicting roles of accounting. The stewardship role of accounting places more focus on the importance of having financial statements that are of high quality in contracting relationships, whereas the valuation role of accounting places more focus on the quality of the financial statements in a valuation setting. In the former case, faithful representation is often considered more important than relevance. That the information should be faithfully represented is absolutely necessary if management compensation contracts are to be based on accounting performance measures—which is often the case when shareholders want to align management's interests with their own. This, in turn, has consequences for how standards are developed. Those who believe faithful representation should be prioritized over relevance tend to support historical cost as a basis for measurement, while those who favor relevance are more open to fair value accounting. Historic cost and fair value are two opposite bases for valuation (see Chapter 10), with fair value being criticized not least in relation to the stewardship role of accounting. Giving managers too much discretion in estimating the fair value of assets may give them an opportunity to manipulate accounting measures and thereby receive a higher compensation. In other words, although accounting numbers must be relevant in order to inform investors regarding managerial performance, the risk of managers using their discretion to manipulate earnings measures is costly, as it would counteract the role of accounting as a means to reduce agency conflicts.

We return to the trade-off between relevance and faithful representation in Part V as we discuss individual accounting items.

5.2.4 Comparability

We now consider the additional qualitative characteristics that *enhance* the usefulness of financial reports.

The stance taken in the CF is that **comparability** enhances the usefulness of reports, but is not an absolute prerequisite for usefulness. The term refers to comparability *between firms* as well as *over time* in a given firm (see Figure 5.3). Both types of comparability are important in making accounting useful for investors and creditors and are thus consistent with the aim of financial reporting throughout history: to allow investors and creditors to make informed choices regarding the best investment and lending opportunities. Any decision to provide an entity with capital necessarily involves a trade-off in which the investor or creditor must place their capital with the knowledge that they would forgo returns from elsewhere. Investing in securities involves relative valuation, where the expected risk-adjusted return of one security is compared to the expected return from alternative securities. When comparing equity securities, it is advantageous if the financial statements of the issuing firms are comparable.

One may contrast *comparability* with the old concept of *uniformity*. Uniformity sounds desirable as it allows for comparisons between entities. The IASB, however, is unambiguous that comparability does *not* mean uniformity. "For information to be comparable, like

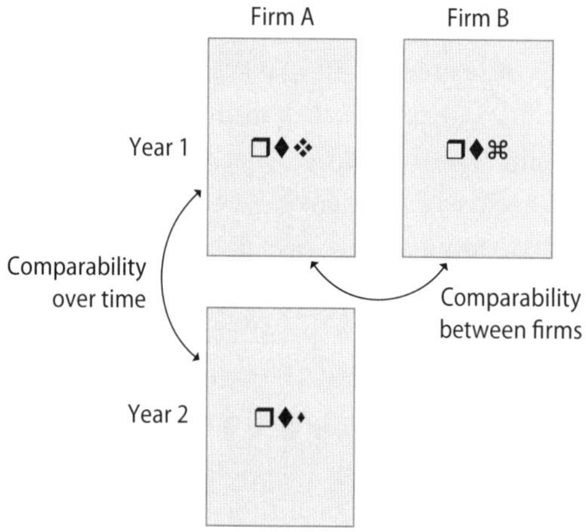

Figure 5.3
Comparability over time and between firms

Figure 5.4 True or surface comparability?

things must look alike and different things must look different. Comparability of financial information is not enhanced by making unlike things look alike any more than it is enhanced by making like things look different" (2.27). In contrast, *uniformity* implies that unlike things indeed may look alike. If all firms use a depreciation rate of five years for their machinery and equipment, uniform accounting has been achieved. However, it will be detrimental to comparability (and usefulness) if the actual useful life of the assets varies between three and ten years. This is in a way reflective of the idea behind faithful representation. Faithfully represented information can only really be achieved if management uses its private information to convey the actual or underlying economics of the firm. If all firms present their information according to this criterion, *like things will look alike and different things will look different*. If one enforces an accounting rule that disregards the underlying economics or restricts estimations of the value of an asset to only verifiable inputs, comparability could suffer. One might achieve "surface comparability"—that is, apparent similarities where there are none, such as what would be brought on by uniformity—but not actual comparability (cf. Chapter 4). Figure 5.4 illustrates the concept of uniformity or surface comparability. In one of the cases, the representation may be considered "better" than in the other, better reflecting the underlying reality.

Furthermore, the CF points out that the term *consistency* is related to comparability, but that they are not the same. Rather, consistency in the application of accounting standards is a tool for achieving the objective of comparability.

Comparability and consistency are related to harmonization of accounting (see section 4.4). Harmonization entails an increase in comparability between firms in different countries. Now, with IFRS being used in many countries around the world, *de jure* harmonization has largely been achieved. That means that accounting standards have been harmonized. In order to achieve *de facto* harmonization, however, the standards must also be consistently implemented. *De facto* harmonization refers to comparability in actual financial statements between firms in different countries. Consistent application may be difficult to achieve with principles-based accounting standards, such as IFRS (see also section 4.5), but the alternative might be surface comparability brought about via constraining rules.

5.2.5 Verifiability

Verifiability can refer to the availability of objective evidence as a basis for the measurement of financial statement items (e.g., an invoice). However, the definition in the CF is broader, in that an estimate can be viewed as verifiable if different people would reach a consensus about it. Accordingly, estimates are (indirectly) verifiable even if there is no (direct) verification document available. As noted in the above discussion on faithful representation, making verifiability a fundamental qualitative characteristic is seen as inappropriate. Still, as it is highly desirable, it is included as an enhancing qualitative characteristic.

An additional reason for having verifiability as an enhancing rather than a fundamental qualitative characteristic is that verifiability is at odds with completeness (which is an aspect of faithful representation). Not all events and conditions are verifiable, even if they are important from a completeness perspective.

5.2.6 Timeliness

The enhancing characteristic of **timeliness** is mentioned by standard-setters mostly in passing and has attracted little attention.

Information is timely if it is made available to decision-makers at such a time as to be capable of influencing their decisions. "Generally, the older the information is, the less useful it is" (2.33). Even though the IASB and the FASB have previously included a timeliness criterion from slightly different angles (the former stating it as a constraint on relevance and the latter referring to it as an aspect of relevance), there was little substantive difference in the implications. As it stands today, timeliness is considered an enhancing characteristic, as relevance and faithful representation do not directly depend on it.

5.2.7 Understandability

Understandability refers to the requirement that the information presented in financial reports, by being "clear" and "concise," should be understandable to users who have "reasonable knowledge of business and economic activities and who review and analyze the information diligently" (2.36). This, however, does not preclude the possibility that even such users may require help from advisers or experts. This is very interesting in the context of the efficient market hypothesis (see section 3.1) and the availability of information—if available information is not understandable, what are the consequences? Or if it is understandable to only a select few, are other investors price-protected in the sense that the market will remain efficient despite interpretation difficulties experienced by some parties? As we discuss research on readability and presentation format in Part III, we consider the role of understandability in practice.

There is a trade-off between understandability and completeness. Omitting information because it is difficult might make the report more accessible, clearer and more understandable, but the fact that there is information missing may also mislead users.

5.3 Principles excluded from the Conceptual Framework

Perhaps paradoxically, the term *principles* is not used in any part of the Conceptual Framework. As important as it might seem that principles govern the preparation of high-quality financial reports, and despite the fact that IFRS are often referred to as "principles-based" standards, there is no section termed principles in the Conceptual Framework. The explanation for this is that the principles of the Conceptual Framework have been subsumed by the qualitative characteristics. That is, if financial statements possess said qualitative characteristics, they will indirectly reflect the underlying principles that were traditionally explicit. Two of the most glaring omissions are the principles that historically were commonly referred to and which concern measurement issues in financial statements. They are the *matching* principle and *prudence* (conservatism in American English). Two additional concepts that have been commonly referred to in accounting are **substance over form** and **true and fair view**. These concepts have similarities to faithful representation, but the Boards have chosen not to use them in the CF. All of these concepts are discussed below and their relationships with the qualitative characteristics are explained.

5.3.1 Matching principle

The **matching principle** states that expenses should be matched to the revenues they help generate. More specifically, expenses should be recognized in, or allocated to, the period in which revenues are recognized. This is one of the core features of accrual accounting and is a principle that relates to the measurement of performance in the income statement.

The reason why the matching principle is no longer an explicit principle is because the theoretical basis for it is inconsistent with the Boards' increasing balance sheet focus. Having a **balance sheet focus** means that measurement originates in the value of assets and liabilities. Items in the income statement are *a function of changes in the balance sheet*, where income is defined as *increases* in assets or *decreases* in liabilities, while expenses are defined as *decreases* in assets or *increases* in liabilities (see more in Chapter 10). For example, if an expense arises immediately upon the purchase of some basic resource used in the production, this will be associated with a decrease in cash or cash equivalent (an asset) or an increase in accounts payable (a liability).

The balance sheet focus leaves no room for the matching principle to dictate when an expense should be recorded. Instead of viewing an expense as a function of a decrease in assets or an increase in liabilities, when matching is applied expenses are matched to revenues and recognized accordingly.

Nevertheless, one could argue that the matching principle is implied in the concept of faithful representation. If financial statements (especially the income statement) actually reflect the economic phenomena that they purport to reflect, a good depiction of performance should be provided. Arguably, such a depiction involves the use of appropriate accruals and a matching of revenues and expenses.

The matching principle is more directly discernible in some specific accounting standards, for example IFRS 15 *Revenue from Contracts with Customers* (see Chapter 13). According to this standard, revenue is recognized as the firm is performing its obligations to the customer, i.e. as it incurs expenses.

5.3.2 Prudence

The **prudence (conservatism)** principle states that it is better to understate than to overstate the value of assets, while the reverse is true for liabilities. Applying the mechanics of double-entry bookkeeping, this results in a deferral of profits to later periods. Prudence is an asymmetric principle (assets and liabilities are treated differently) and, as such, is in disagreement with the neutrality criterion forming a part of faithful representation.

Historically, two motivations have been given for the prudence principle. First, since management of most firms is believed to be inherently optimistic regarding their own business, prudence in accounting is an effective means of obtaining neutrality in financial statements. According to this view, neutrality is the objective, but prudence is a means for achieving this by neutralizing an overly optimistic management.

The second motivation for the prudence principle is based on the assumption that it is better to be positively rather than negatively surprised. Prudence leads to "bad news" being reported earlier than "good news." Thus, a financial statement user looking at financial statements at a certain point in time is more likely to be positively than negatively surprised by events that have already occurred but are not yet reported. That is because "bad news events" that have occurred are more likely to have been reflected in financial statements than "good news events."

The effect of prudence on the relevance of financial statements would depend on the user. It is by no means evident that equity investors, who want to make a neutral forecast regarding future performance, are helped by non-neutral financial statements. Meanwhile, creditors, with their asymmetric exposure, may find this useful. Furthermore, research has shown that prudence enhances quality in contractual settings. For example, Watts (2003) shows that asymmetric recognition of losses and gains is beneficial for the stewardship function of accounting. Asymmetric recognition means that the requirements for recognizing gains are higher than for recognizing losses, which leads to conservatism in accounting. The reason such conservatism is useful is that it helps prevent managerial opportunism in a principal-agent setting. Meanwhile, note that conservatism is not necessarily beneficial from a valuation perspective, and that the difference between the valuation and stewardship perspectives is one possible explanation for the higher level of conservatism in Continental compared to Anglo-American countries (cf. Chapter 4).

Interestingly, the IASC included prudence in the 1989 version of its CF, but it was removed in the 2010 update. The motivation for the removal was that prudence is inconsistent with neutrality (which, by the way, was also included in the CF from 1989). The removal has been heavily criticized, and the IASB reinstated prudence in the 2018 Conceptual Framework. The new motivation for inclusion is based on a somewhat convoluted discussion in the Basis for Conclusion about being prudent in measurement, while still being neutral in the outcome. What the IASB wants is for preparers to exercise "caution" and that the reintroduction of an explicit prudence principle would reduce the effect of managerial optimism as well as confusion concerning the reporting objectives. However, the history of the term in many jurisdictions has too many connotations to the old meaning of prudence—as being an objective in itself. That prudence should contribute to neutrality or reduce confusion thus seems counterintuitive. Additionally, the use of the term "cautious prudence" may be perceived as tautological (just as "incautious prudence" is a contradiction in terms). A suggested solution is to simply focus on the importance of exercising caution when making judgments under conditions of uncertainty—thus omitting the "prudence" label—as it seems reasonable that by exercising caution, faithful representation is more likely to be achieved. Overall, the impression is that the IASB is giving in to stakeholder pressure, but that they do not actually want prudence in the CF.

Meanwhile, individual standards within IFRS clearly reflect the prudence principle. For example, IAS 36 *Impairment of Assets* requires write-downs for impaired assets, but there is no corresponding standard for increases in the value of assets when warranted. IAS 37 *Provisions, Contingent Liabilities and Contingent Assets* requires provisions for liabilities with a probability of occurrence of 50% or higher, while assets must be near certain in order to be recognized. It is clear that the IASB takes the view that there are greater risks in the recognition of assets than of liabilities. This view is very much consistent with the prudence principle.

Future research might consider what the actual quality effects of prudence are, since the theoretical arguments for striving for prudence are somewhat conflicting—even when one accepts neutrality as the end objective and prudence only as a means of achieving this.

5.3.3 Substance over form

Substance over form refers to the idea that financial statements should reflect the economic substance rather than the legal form of events and conditions. The IASB points out that including this principle in the CF would be redundant, as it is already covered by faithful representation (BC2.32). That is, if one faithfully represents underlying economic phenomena, the substance and not the form is indeed captured. However, to avoid misunderstandings, this is made more explicit in the 2018 Conceptual Framework (BC2.33).

Individual standards also reflect the idea of substance over form. A clear example is IFRS

16 *Leases* (see Chapter 11), where lease agreements are accounted for in accordance with their economic substance rather than their legal form.

5.3.4 True and fair view

The criterion that financial statements should provide a true and fair view originally comes from accounting in the UK (it also has a Swedish equivalent: *rättvisande bild*). It was later implemented in the 4th and 7th EU directives on company law. There is no statutory definition of what constitutes a **true and fair view**, but it refers to the quality of truthfully reflecting underlying economic phenomena by being "accurate and comprehensive to within acceptable limits" (a cost-benefit analysis is probably necessary to determine what these limits are).[2] It is an abstract concept that has been subject to national interpretations based on local accounting standards and, in turn, current (local) practice. In the UK, *a true and fair view* was linked to an *override* possibility. This meant that if the application of an accounting standard resulted in financial statements that did not provide a true and fair view, firms *should* deviate from standards. In the EU version, this was interpreted differently in different countries, so that the override possibility only existed in some countries. Even though IFRS do have an override possibility (IAS 1 *Presentation of Financial Statements*, paragraphs 19–24), it is more restrictive than the traditional UK version. IAS 1 refers to "extremely rare circumstances" and the override is rarely used in practice. IFRS are similar to US GAAP in this regard, as US GAAP have an override possibility but it is rarely applied.

Much discussion concerning *true and fair* has followed the replacement of local standards by IFRS. Some parties seem to have been worried that this principle has been abandoned by the Boards, not least with the omission of *prudence* in the 2010 version of the CF (which is believed by many to contribute to a true and fair view of the underlying economics). However, the IASB itself points out that if the qualitative characteristics are met, financial statements do give a true and fair view (BC2.70). In that way, *true and fair*, just like *substance over form*, may be seen as redundant. Given that *true and fair* has been interpreted in different ways in practice, the qualitative characteristics have more precise definitions and would seem better able to define and thus encourage high-quality accounting.

5.4 Conclusions

The world's most influential standard-setters have developed a comprehensive Conceptual Framework for financial accounting. In formulating criteria for financial statements, based on a number of underlying concepts, they have contributed to normative accounting theory. More specifically, they have set out objectives, defined intended users and proposed a number of qualitative characteristics financial statements should possess, thus attempting to create a coherent financial reporting framework. The reasoning behind the choices (found in the Basis for Conclusions) is based on attempts to create theoretically consistent standards,

2 "Legal opinion obtained by Accounting Standards Committee on true and fair view, with particular reference to the role of accounting standards," Hoffman and Arden, 1983. Available at https://www.frc.org.uk

although constraints are (perhaps inevitably) introduced by cost-benefit analyses and the need for pragmatism.

The standard-setters agree that useful financial statements are *relevant* and *faithfully represent* that which they purport to represent. We note that, sometimes, fully achieving these two qualities is not possible due to the potential trade-off between them.

Part III

Accounting quality in capital markets research

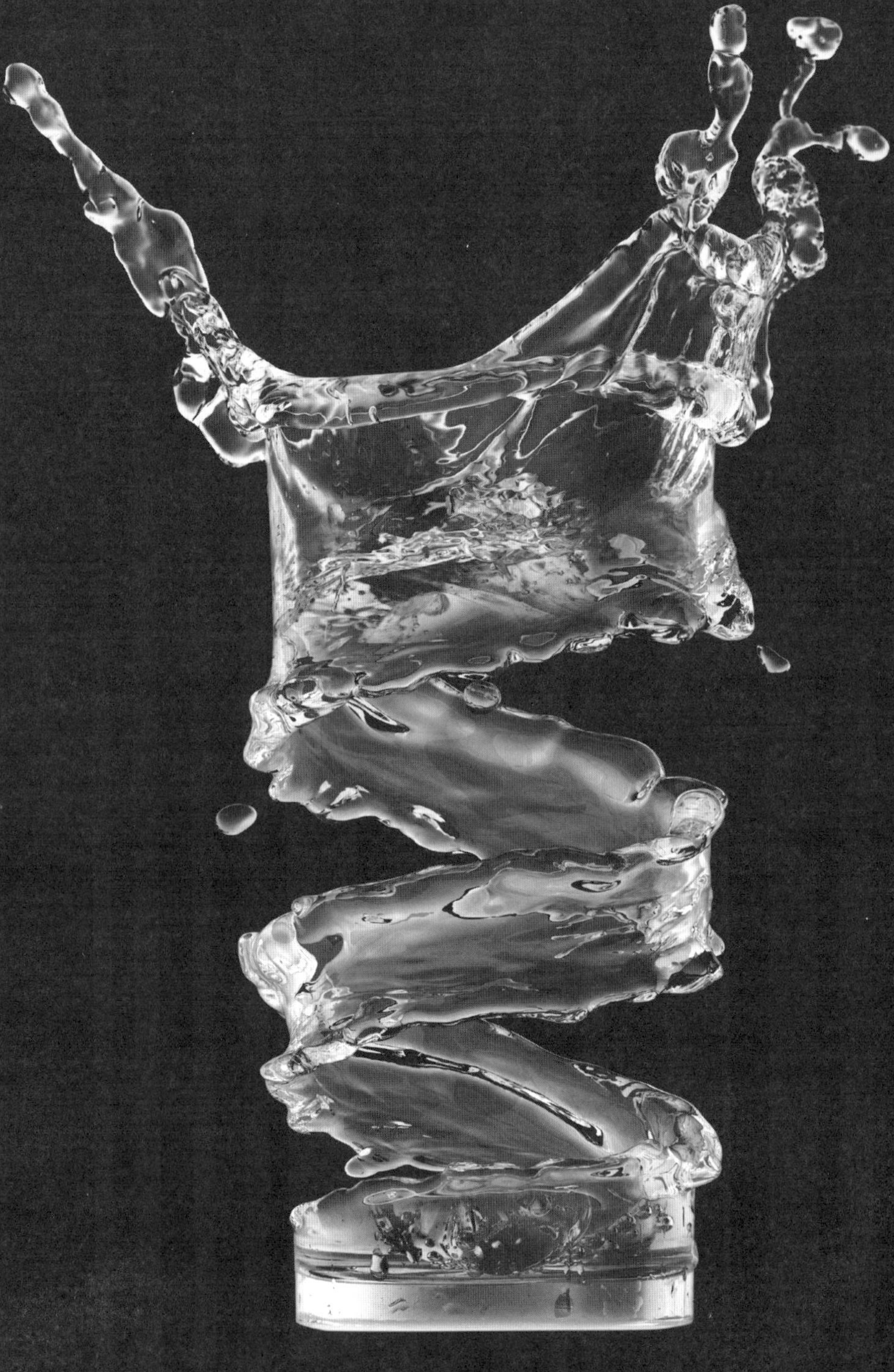

Having identified capital providers as the most important users of financial reporting, we have said that financial accounting plays two principal roles for investors—a valuation role and a stewardship role. Whereas creditors are interested in the value of the firm's assets, investors are interested in the value of the firm's equity. As owners of the firm, investors are also concerned with how well the firm is managed, wanting to ensure that they enjoy the highest possible profits or yields from the firm's operations. Being **residual claimants** means that their pay-off will vary in direct proportion to how successfully the firm generates profits, while creditors are paid the same amount regardless of profitability (provided, of course, that the firm does not default on its loans).

Reiterating what was argued in the introduction to this book, the quality of the information provided—accounting quality—must therefore be considered important. This is true whether one takes a creditor perspective or an investor perspective, and regardless of whether one considers the valuation or the stewardship role of accounting. The concept of accounting quality, and the effect of the demand for high-quality accounting on the development of accounting theory, has so far permeated this text and will continue to do so throughout. In the previous chapter, we considered accounting quality as defined by standard-setters. In this part of the book, we examine how accounting quality has been operationalized in the empirical accounting literature and study some of the evidence on how accounting quality affects users of financial reporting.

So far, we have treated the term **accounting quality** in a rather abstract manner, albeit using references to standard-setting terms such as "relevance" and "faithful representation" as being fundamental qualitative characteristics. However, having more and higher-quality disclosure and the effect of that on information uncertainty and asymmetry has been the focus of a large body of empirical research. The word "disclosure" may be defined both broadly and narrowly. In a broad sense, disclosures include all information provided by the firm to the market, for example information in the primary financial statements, the rest of the annual report and press releases. In a narrow sense, the term refers to the supplementary, often textual, information that is provided in addition to the primary financial statements (i.e., the footnote disclosures). In research, the broad definition is often used, while in a context of standard-setting, the narrow definition is used. Furthermore, looking at the accounting literature, the reader may note that **accounting quality** is taken to mostly mean **earnings quality**. We adopt a broader perspective by stating that accounting quality encompasses all aspects of the financial reporting process. In fact, earnings quality may be viewed as a subset of **disclosure quality**, which in turn is a subset of accounting quality. Because earnings releases are a part of the larger disclosure environment, earnings quality is but one aspect of disclosure quality. However, due to the significance of the earnings concept and the large amount of space generally dedicated to earnings quality in the accounting literature, we treat it separately from disclosures of a more general character.

Earnings numbers, and thus quality, may be affected by a firm's financial reporting practices. This, in turn, is determined by the overall framework or accounting standards adopted by the firm, but also by individual accounting methods and policies used, managerial incentives, as well as mechanisms and institutions put in place to enforce the rules and monitor the financial reporting processes.

Whereas we return to the **determinants** of accounting quality in later parts of the book, we now turn to some of the proposed definitions, measures and operationalizations of disclosure quality and earnings quality in academic research.[1]

Building on some of the material laid out in Chapter 3, we provide evidence on the effects of disclosures on users, discuss different types of disclosures and explain reasons for disclosure in accordance with a number of theories (Chapter 6). Finally, we present measures of disclosure quality in general (Chapter 6) and earnings quality in particular (Chapter 7).

---

1 Most empirical research in financial accounting is based on statistical inference and analysis. Students interested in research on financial accounting topics will find it advantageous to be familiar with at least some basic statistical concepts, such as **variables**, **linear regression models**, **coefficients** and **significance levels**. This book does not assume knowledge of statistics, but we do occasionally provide more in-depth technical explanations of some topics (see text boxes), allowing those seeking a further understanding to be introduced to some of the methodological considerations inherent in the research at hand.

CHAPTER 6

Disclosures and disclosure quality

Learning outcomes

Upon completion of this chapter, you will have gained insight into:

- The different ways in which disclosure quality affects the capital market and firms' cost of capital, and how these effects have been operationalized and measured.
- Different *types* of disclosure that have been considered in the accounting literature, including mandatory and voluntary, financial and non-financial disclosures.
- The determinants of disclosures and which theories have been used for predicting disclosure practices.
- Various *measures* of disclosure and what they say about the current interpretation of quality in the empirical accounting literature.

THE FIRST COMPONENT OF ACCOUNTING QUALITY we address is **disclosure quality**. We first examine the effects of making disclosures. Much of this research is concerned with disclosures in general, with no distinction being made between different types of disclosures or the quality of the information. When developing theoretical models, in particular, researchers often rely on (simplistic) assumptions about the firm's information environment in order to illustrate certain features. By contrast, empirical studies require actual operationalizations of disclosures and their economic consequences. That is, researchers need measurable variables and at least partially quantifiable data. We therefore proceed with different types of disclosure and measures of disclosure quality.

6.1 Effect of disclosures on capital markets

As explained in an earlier chapter, lack of information between market participants can reduce market efficiency or even cause the market to break down completely. Accounting research has therefore long focused on how higher transparency and higher quality of financial reports may help overcome these potential threats.

We now look at some of the evidence that disclosures indeed do have capital market effects.

6.1.1 Effects on market liquidity, trading volume and analysts

If there is information asymmetry, less informed traders may be hesitant to make investment decisions, such as selling or buying stock, because they are uncertain whether they will receive or pay a fair price. Disclosures have been shown to reduce this uncertainty and make more investors willing to participate in the capital market and make trades (Diamond and Verrecchia, 1991; Kim and Verrecchia, 1994).

This will increase market **liquidity**. High market liquidity is in turn associated with greater market efficiency. Liquidity helps make markets efficient, but greater efficiency also increases liquidity. Sometimes disclosures are made voluntarily, because firms presumably know that it is beneficial for them to be transparent, but regulatory measures can also help improve liquidity, as documented in a study of disclosure regulation brought on by the US SEC (Bushee and Leuz, 2005).

Two concepts closely related to liquidity are **trading volume** and **bid-ask spreads**. Both measures are believed to reflect adverse selection and information asymmetry. A high level of liquidity means an investor need not fear being unable to exchange its stock for cash at any given point in time. Low liquidity means that the risk of holding a particular inventory increases, that the cost of processing orders increases and that the risk of having to trade with more informed investors increases. Trading volume reflects liquidity to the extent that it captures investors' willingness to trade. Meanwhile, the bid-ask spread is the difference between the bid price and the ask price (see Example 6.1). A buyer will pay the ask price, while the seller will receive the bid price. The bid and the ask price will always differ, with the ask price being the higher of the two.

Example 6.1 **Bid-ask spread**

For example, a security may be quoted as EUR 5.67 / 5.73. Investor B wants to buy and must pay EUR 5.73 (the ask price). Investor S wants to sell but only receives EUR 5.67 (the bid price). The difference (EUR 0.06) is the bid-ask spread, or simply the spread.

In this example, what happened to the 6 euro cents that made up the difference? These go to the market maker (broker), who sets the bid-ask spread to cover the costs of illiquidity. Lower liquidity therefore means greater spreads, the exact size of which will be determined by the price level, the number of market makers (brokers) and price volatility. A high price level, few market makers and high volatility will increase transaction or liquidity costs. One can also think of low liquidity as the result of spreads growing (reverse causality), which occurs if there is a low trading volume or a price cannot easily be settled on.

Normally, when information is released, one expects greater trading volumes and liquidity as investors respond to the information. However, the relationship between disclosures and liquidity need not be altogether straightforward. For example, Kim and Verrecchia (1994) suggest that around earnings announcements, information asymmetry may *increase between investors* due to certain traders being more able than others to benefit from the announcement and make sophisticated judgments regarding the firm's performance. This would lead to lower liquidity and higher bid-ask spreads following the release of earnings information.

It should be fairly clear that all firms desire high liquidity for their stock. Without investor willingness to trade or invest, a firm's funds could quickly run dry. This could force management to give up on expansion plans or even scale back on operations, which in the end would be highly detrimental to the value of the firm.

There is also a believed link between information asymmetry and the actions of equity analysts. It has been shown that by increasing disclosure, firms can attract a larger **analyst following** (Lang and Lundholm, 1996). This is explained by disclosures making information acquisition less costly, thus increasing analyst supply. Furthermore, more information from companies means a greater demand for analysts from investors as well as companies, since there is more information to process. This suggests that analysts are information *transmitters* or information intermediaries. It also implies that information processing is costly and far from immediate, and that having more analysts makes firm communication (and markets) more efficient. If analysts had been information *emitters*, or providers, their information would compete with firm disclosures and the relation between analyst following and disclosure level would be negative. In other words, as disclosures increase, analyst numbers would decrease. One could of course debate the direction of causality for the observed association (see Text Box 6.1). Could it be that more analysts means that there is added pressure to disclose?

Text Box 6.1 **Causality in accounting research**

Tests using *lead* and *lag* variables may be used for testing the direction of causation between a set of variables. Assume a variable Y that for one observation (firm) takes on value 10 at time *t–1*, 20 at time *t* and 30 at time *t+1*. Then its lag variable, Y^{lag}, will take on value 10 at time *t* and 20 at time *t+1*, while its lead variable, Y^{lead}, would take the value of 20 at time *t–1* and 30 at time *t*.

time	Y	Y^{lag}	Y^{lead}
$t-1$	10	.	20
t	20	10	30
$t+1$	30	20	.

If some variable X is correlated with Y^{lead} (which thus contain future values of Y) and not just Y, then one may infer that X influences Y and not the other way around. Conversely, if X is correlated with Y^{lag} (which contains the past values of Y), then one may infer that Y instead influences X. Lang and Lundholm (1996) used this approach to attempt to tease out whether disclosures indeed affect analyst behavior or whether the reverse is true. The direction of causation appears to be that disclosures first and foremost affect analysts.

It has also been found that a greater level of disclosure improves analyst **forecast accuracy** (Hope, 2003b; Lang and Lundholm, 1996) and reduces **forecast dispersion** (Lang and Lundholm, 1996), that is, how accurate their estimates of future earnings are and the level of disagreement among estimates. This constitutes further evidence of reduced information asymmetry as a result of disclosures. It seems natural that accuracy should increase with more information (unless the disclosures are deliberately misleading), but what about forecast dispersion? Dispersion is often used as a measure of information uncertainty, and if disclosures reduce information uncertainty, dispersion is likewise reduced. The assumption is that analysts differ in their private information (i.e., the information they have prior to public disclosure), initially leading to uncertainty regarding firm value and diverse forecasts, but that forecasts converge as information is made public, or shared, by the firm. Could dispersion increase with disclosure? This is possible and indicates that analysts use different forecasting models that place different weights on different types of information (there are non-homogeneous beliefs).

Furthermore, a negative association has been found between disclosure informativeness, as measured by its timeliness, and **forecast volatility**. That is, the more informative the disclosure, the less volatile the forecasts. This is explained using the idea that higher-quality and more timely disclosures reduce surprises and therefore extreme forecast revisions (Lang and Lundholm, 1996).

6.1.2 Effects on firms' cost of capital

Information asymmetry—either between investors and the firm or between different types of investors—has been shown theoretically as well as empirically to have an adverse impact on a firm's cost of capital; conversely, disclosure is believed to reduce the cost of capital. The **cost of capital** is an important concept in accounting as well as in finance. The cost of capital is just what the term suggests—the cost of obtaining and using capital. With borrowed capital, we refer to *debt* cost of capital, and with equity capital we speak of *equity* cost of capital. This is the interest yield demanded on borrowed capital or the returns required on invested equity capital. Putting it somewhat differently, the cost of capital is the equivalent *and* the opposite of the required rate of return set up by investors or the interest rate demanded by creditors. The cost of capital will be different for different securities because different capital providers accept different levels of risk.

In essence, investors perceive an **information risk** in the absence of information. This risk raises investors' required return on their investments (and thus the cost of capital for the firm). Underlying this belief is the assumption that information risk is **non-diversifiable**. By non-diversifiable risk, one refers to volatility that cannot be reduced by adding another equity instrument to one's investment portfolio. The systematic risk inherent to the market is a non-diversifiable risk. The opposite is diversifiable risk, or non-systematic risk, which is security-specific (see more in Text Box 6.2). If one holds a large enough portfolio of different investments, their security-specific risks may in theory be eliminated as, being random, they would cancel each other out on an aggregate level.

Theoretical research supporting a negative association between disclosure level and cost of equity capital has followed two related streams. The first says that greater disclosure enhances stock market liquidity, which reduces the cost of equity capital either through reduced transaction costs (lower bid-ask spreads) or increased demand for a firm's securities (greater trading volume). This stream of research includes work by Glosten and Milgrom (1985), Amihud and Mendelson (1986) and Diamond and Verrecchia (1991).

The second stream of research, which includes studies by Barry and Brown (1985), Handa and Linn (1993), Easley and O'Hara (2004) and Lambert et al. (2007), suggests that greater disclosure reduces the **estimation risk** arising from investors' estimates of the parameters of an asset's return or payoff distribution.

Text Box 6.2 **More on the cost of capital**

Because the cost of capital is difficult to capture or measure (as it is a perceived, required return by investors), operationalizations of the cost of capital usually require proxies. **Proxies** are used by researchers as substitutes for the actual phenomenon when the phenomenon to be measured is abstract in nature or difficult to measure for other reasons. For example, as proxies for the cost of capital, researchers have used liquidity, bid-ask spreads and trading volume—concepts presented above. Another proxy is **extreme share price volatility**. This may be deemed an appropriate proxy to the extent that sudden price movements reflect surprises and reactions to the release of generally untimely or delayed private information. Excessive price fluctuations may further reflect investor irrationality, fears and disagreements in the absence of complete information. Although the above proxies do not measure the actual cost a firm incurs when obtaining capital, they represent a form of market inefficiency associated with higher costs of capital.

Additionally, the **implied cost of capital** can be derived from a valuation model. A commonly used model is the Capital Asset Pricing Model (CAPM). The difficulty of measuring cost of capital as a researcher is noted by Botosan (1997)—traditional models in corporate finance that estimate cost of capital, such as the CAPM, leave no room for information to play a role, or display a weak correlation with market volatility (and thus become difficult to justify as being accurate or reliable). Be that as it may, the formula for the investors' required rate of return, as it is defined by CAPM, can be estimated as:

$$r_i = r_f + \underbrace{\beta_i \times \underbrace{(r_m - r_f)}_{\text{Market portfolio's risk premium}}}_{\text{Risk premium for stock}}$$

where r_f is the risk-free interest rate, β_i is the systematic risk on security i and r_m is the return on the market portfolio. The basic idea is that the return investors demand on security i is equal to the risk-free rate (such as the one that could be gained by owning government bonds) plus a market premium. A diversified investment strategy means that investors can diversify away idiosyncratic or non-systematic risk, but the systematic market risk cannot be diversified away. The market premium is captured by the volatility of the stock (i.e., β_i) times the market portfolio's risk premium. A β greater than 1 indicates volatility above the market and a β lower than 1 indicates volatility below the market. So, the market premium will be higher than the market portfolio's risk premium if the stock in question is very risky, and vice versa if the stock is not that risky. Estimation of β may be undertaken by observing past volatilities (i.e, using time-series data to statistically calculate β).

In attempting to explain stock returns, various extensions have been made to the CAPM, essentially replacing the original model. These so-called **multi-factor asset pricing models** take factors other than market volatility into account according to the following general setup:

$$r_i = r_f + \beta_i^{F1} \times [\text{Risk premium for } F1] + \beta_i^{F2} \times [\text{Risk premium for } F2] + \ldots + \beta_i^{Fk} \times [\text{Risk premium for } Fk]$$

Possibly the best-known of these is the **Fama-French three-factor model**, which includes two additional risk factors: a firm's market value of equity (firm size) and book-to-market ratio. That is, stock returns depend systematically on the risk-free rate and market returns, but also on firm-specific characteristics. Converting the Fama-French (or CAPM) specification to a regression model, one can calculate the different beta factor coefficients based on cross-sectional (across firms) or historical time-series data. Using the calculated coefficient values, one can then estimate the expected return for a given stock *i* or portfolio of stocks. Fama and French (1992) showed that firm size and book-to-market ratio indeed explained cross-sectional variations in returns for their sample of firms. However, providing theoretical reasons for these empirical findings is not an easy task!

In their paper, Easley and O'Hara (2004) conclude that information indeed affects a firm's cost of capital. It does so via a separate "information risk" factor in their asymmetric information asset-pricing model. By changing the information structure (e.g., through accounting standards or financial analyst coverage), a firm would thus be able to influence its cost of capital. They point to the apparent paradox of information being central to the Efficient Market Hypothesis (EMH, see Chapter 3), but that information is not included in any of the commonly used asset-pricing models. That is, CAPM and multi-factor models (which are extensions of CAPM and include additional factors other than market risk) do not incorporate *information risk* as a separate factor. Generically, such a model would have the following structure:

$$r_i = rf + \text{Risk premium from factors 1 through k} + \underbrace{\text{Information risk}}_{\text{A separate risk factor}}$$

It may be questionable whether information risk is indeed non-diversifiable, as it would appear unique to the firm. In fact, Lambert et al. (2007) dispute the claim by Easley and O'Hara (2004) that information quality represents a unique risk factor arising from information asymmetry. Using theoretical modeling, they show that increased disclosure about a firm's future cash flows reduces the assessed variance of said cash flows, but this is diversifiable. That is, the information effect disappears when the number of traders grows sufficiently large (see also Hughes et al., 2007). They agree, however, that information quality can affect the cost of capital in another way. The disclosure affects the assessed covariances of a firm's cash flows with the cash flows of *other* firms. This constitutes an estimation risk that is *not* diversifiable (i.e., it does not disappear in large economies). However, the information effect should not be treated as a unique risk factor in CAPM since it is "fully captured by an appropriately specified forward-looking beta and the marketwide premium for risk" (p. 411). Another "indirect" effect of better information is that it reduces expropriation of funds by firm managers for their own benefits; that is, agency costs may be reduced and this has real cash flow effects from the investor's point of view. Furthermore, Lambert et al. (2007, p. 389) point out that:

> [Studies such as Diamond and Verrecchia (1991), Baiman and Verrecchia (1996) and Easley and O'Hara (2004)] analyze settings with a single firm (or settings where cash flows across firms are uncorrelated). Thus, it is unclear whether the effects demonstrated in these studies survive the forces of diversification and extend to more general multisecurity settings. We emphasize, however, that we do not dispute the possible role of market liquidity for firms' cost of capital, as several empirical studies suggest (e.g., Amihud and Mendelson [1986], Chordia, Roll, and Subrahmanyam [2001], Easley, Hvidkjaer, and O'Hara [2002], Pastor and Stambaugh [2003]). Our paper focuses on an alternative, and possibly more direct, explanation as to how information quality influences nondiversifiable risks [related to the covariance of cash flows].

Many empirical research papers could arguably be accused of oversimplifying the evidence on the relationship between information asymmetry and the cost of capital. Some do not recognize the underlying controversy of many of the findings, while others cite findings on the wrong grounds; that is, the underlying assumptions are overlooked. This is made apparent in several papers that refer to the above "debate," such as Bhattacharya et al. (2013), Christensen et al. (2010), Kim and Park (2009), Francis et al. (2008) and Core et al. (2008).

Nevertheless, during the 1990s and 2000s, many empirical studies showed that the cost of capital could be reduced through disclosures (Coller and Yohn, 1997; Sengupta, 1998; Kothari et al., 2009). A commonly cited study by Botosan (1997) is able to establish a correlation between cost of capital and disclosure after controlling for firm beta and size, but only for firms with a low analyst following. This is explained in terms of the annual report (which is used to measure disclosure) carrying higher weight for small firms and their analysts. Botosan and Plumlee (2002) extend this study by looking at a larger timespan and multiple industries and find that while disclosures in the annual report reduce the cost of capital, more timely disclosures (such as quarterly reports) *increase* the cost of capital. This last finding seems counterintuitive but may be explained by the fact that their chosen cost of capital measure is stock price volatility. Whereas high volatility may reflect market inefficiencies, it may be caused by frantic trading in the short run—in turn a sign of investors having a short-term focus rather than of the released information being lacking. Meanwhile, no relation is found between the cost of capital and investor relations. It is concluded that the disclosure *type* matters (i.e., annual reports, interim reports, unregulated disclosures on websites) and that when studying one particular disclosure outlet, one must simultaneously control for other disclosure outlets. Furthermore, it matters how the cost of capital is measured.

Finally, with respect to the cost of capital, whereas most of the literature looks at the cost of *equity* capital, Sengupta (1998) concludes that disclosure quality can help lower a firm's cost of *debt* financing. A higher cost of debt capital for non-disclosing firms is attributed to worries that the firm's management is withholding adverse information. If creditors fear default risk, they will demand higher risk premiums. Just like in the case above, negative suspicions of the firm can be costly to the firm—more costly than actually disclosing undesirable outcomes. The importance of disclosures for the cost of debt is found to be higher for firms with high stock returns volatility, possibly due to leverage and profitability in such cases being less informative regarding default risk.

Although the above relationships have not been labeled using any particular theory, they may be thought of as "theories of information asymmetry." Ultimately, they may be linked to adverse selection and the effect of information asymmetry in the market as presented by Akerlof (1970) and the desirability of *signaling* for reducing information asymmetry. The focus in the accounting literature is, thereby, on the *reduction* of information asymmetry (i.e., signaling via *disclosures*).

6.1.3 Effects of "bad news" disclosures

In the above discussion, we have implicitly equated "disclosure" with "amount of disclosure." In general, more disclosure means greater transparency and positive market effects. However, the actual content of the information that is revealed—whether it may be classified as "good news" or "bad news"—could potentially have differential effects.

Examples of such bad news could obviously be bad performance, but also certain types of disclosures that, by construction, are "negative": for example, risk-factor disclosures and disclosures regarding the effectiveness of internal control systems. If disclosures about firm risk reveal unknown (new) risks, it is expected that this could increase rather than reduce information uncertainty. If disclosures, on the other hand, help investors better understand previously known risks, a reduction in uncertainty would follow (Kravet and Muslu, 2013). Evidence has been presented that is consistent with the first prediction, that risk-factor disclosures under US GAAP *increases* information uncertainty, as reflected in increased stock return volatility, *increased* trading volume (cf. Botosan and Plumlee, 2002) and more dispersed forecast revisions.

As for research on disclosures concerning the effectiveness of internal control systems—which are required by the SOX Act of 2002—could these also *increase* information uncertainty? They are meant to highlight potential weaknesses that could result in errors in the financial statements. According to findings by Hammersley et al. (2008), the market reacts negatively to disclosures of internal control weaknesses, and this is especially pronounced in the case of *material* weaknesses and when disclosures are vague. Management's assurance that effective controls are in place despite weaknesses and, to a lesser extent, having a Big Four auditor moderate the negative reaction. Similar results were shown by Beneish et al. (2008). There is, however, also evidence that a firm that has problems with its internal control systems might be better off disclosing those deficiencies (Kim and Park, 2009). If the firm successfully reduces investors' information uncertainty, as measured by lower volatility in stock returns and lower dispersion in analysts' earnings forecasts, there is less negative market response. This is especially the case if the reported deficiencies are non-material but have been suspected by investors.

All of this should affect whether it is desirable to make a disclosure. We have seen, so far, that disclosures can reduce information asymmetry, ultimately reducing information uncertainty. What is proposed here, however, is that certain disclosures, in spite of reducing information asymmetry, do *not* reduce information uncertainty. Gordon et al. (2017) propose that in the case of the above-mentioned disclosures, an increase in *measurement* uncertainty offsets the decrease in information asymmetry, leading to higher information uncertainty. A possible implication of this is that firms should want to withhold high-uncertainty information as long as possible in order not to suffer reductions in the share price. The negative effect of risk-factor disclosures and "bad news" disclosures in general are also discussed in the context of proprietary costs (see, for instance, Abraham and Shrives, 2014). If firms foresee a reduction in future cash flows, this is clearly a cost that would be included in the cost-benefit analysis of potential disclosers and that may explain the unwillingness of firms to be transparent.

6.1.4 Effects on corporate governance

In the previous section, we explained how high-quality disclosures are important in decreasing information uncertainty, typically by reducing information asymmetry and adverse selection. Apart from affecting the cost of capital and thus firm valuation, disclosure policies and disclosure quality are believed to affect the severity of agency problems, which arise when managerial actions are unobservable to the principal and when self-interested managers do not pay for the consequences of their decision-making.

As we saw briefly in Chapter 3, and as we discuss more in Chapter 8, agency theorists have long focused on the necessity of efficient governance and contracting mechanisms. In particular, efficient contracts that align the interests of management and shareholders are said to be a solution to the agency problem. However, with efficient contracting and governance mechanisms being able to reduce agency problems, is there still a need for high transparency and more disclosures?

The answer is a resounding "yes!" Disclosures play an important role in the communication between the firm and its investors and their representatives on the board. A large body of empirical research—particularly after corporate governance and accounting scandals at the beginning of the 2000s—has focused on the role of financial reporting and disclosure in addressing agency problems and enhancing transparency between managements and boards (see, Armstrong et al., 2010). For example, high-quality disclosures can assist boards in the development of efficient compensation contracts that align the interests of executives and shareholders. The idea is that these contracts are inevitably incomplete and need to be processed and monitored using supplementary information. Continuous monitoring can help counteract pernicious effects of management retaining residual control rights (even in the presence of an independent board of directors), which enable them to expropriate funds from shareholders through excessive pay (Goergen and Renneboog, 2011).

Bushman et al. (2004) argue that timely financial reporting assists the board of directors in carrying out their monitoring and advisory responsibilities. They also note that timely recognition of "bad news" as compared to "good news" is more valued by boards of directors since the former is the main source of information conflicts between managements and board. That is, while managers may have incentives to disclose "good news" about the firm, they are less likely to voluntarily deliver "bad news" in a timely manner. Timely recognition and disclosure of "bad news" (indicating conservative accounting) has been shown to enhance the monitoring ability of boards. The effect of greater transparency as a result of the adoption of internationally recognized accounting standards (i.e., IFRS and US GAAP) has also been investigated. Ozkan et al. (2012) and Wu and Zhang (2009) find that improved transparency had a positive effect on firms' internal performance evaluation and on the efficiency of compensation contracts (as measured by higher pay-performance sensitivity). We will return to the efficiency of compensation contracts in Chapter 8.

6.2 Voluntary disclosures

The regulated financial statements—balance sheet, income statement, statement of changes in equity, cash flow statement and supplementary notes—are arguably the most important parts of corporate reports and of the firm's information dissemination as a whole. While we treat these mandatory elements and the related standards in a separate part of the book (Part V), we now turn to three types of voluntary or less regulated disclosures that deserve special attention: sustainability disclosures, the CEO's letter to shareholders and management's discussion and analysis. What these have in common is that they are highly discretionary (see Text Box 6.3 for a commentary on additional voluntary sources).

6.2.1 Management's discussion and analysis

In the US, Management's Discussion and Analysis (MD&A) is a formal section (Item 7) of Form 10-K required by the SEC.[1] This means that it is actually *not* voluntary for firms using US GAAP

In one of Microsoft's 10-K reports, the purpose of the section is expressed as follows:

> The following Management's Discussion and Analysis ("MD&A") is intended to help the reader understand the results of operations and financial condition of Microsoft Corporation. MD&A is provided as a supplement to, and should be read in conjunction with, our consolidated financial statements and the accompanying Notes to Financial Statements. (Microsoft, 10-K report 2014)

In IFRS, there is no requirement to have an MD&A section, but one nevertheless finds a similar discussion in most annual reports.[2] For example, in the 2014 annual report from Siemens AG, a section labeled Combined Management Report runs from page 171 to 247, in which they, among other things, discuss the firm's business and economic environment,

---

1 Form 10-K, or simply the 10-K, is the annual filing required by the SEC for firms listed on US stock exchanges. The equivalent required quarterly filing is known as Form 10-Q.

2 It is mandatory in some countries in the EU.

Text Box 6.3 **Note on other sources of corporate communication**

Throughout this book, we have maintained our focus on corporate reports. Although voluntary disclosures are indeed made in these reports, we further acknowledge that other aspects of corporate communication are also considered important by both firms and users. For example, investor relations websites, press releases, social media outlets and other public channels may be used for conveying key pieces of information to the markets. One may therefore be interested in the quality of such information as well, not least because of how those other forms of information may complement, confirm, crowd out, or otherwise interact with information disseminated via more "traditional" channels (i.e., the "books").

Due to the increasing use of the Internet as a source of communication between insiders (i.e., management) and outsiders (i.e., investors, analysts, press, etc.), recent research has examined the informativeness and effectiveness of Internet-based channels of communications. Kirk and Vincent (2014) find that managers are more likely to invest in establishing internal professional investor relations (IR) in larger and younger firms, as well as in better performing and growing firms. The authors argue that especially in firms that face greater uncertainty about future earnings and cash-flows, IR is used to reduce the uncertainty. The textual attributes (i.e., tone and readability) of different sources of corporate communication have also been the focus of recent research. For instance, Lundholm et al. (2014) show that the annual filings and earnings press releases of foreign firms listed on US stock exchanges are more readable and contain more numbers. This implies that clearer and more informative disclosures are used by foreign firms to reduce investors' information disadvantage or psychological distance. Generally, the evidence from research points to the importance of clearer and more concrete corporate communication in different media, especially in firms facing uncertainty in their information environment.

sustainability issues, the results of operations and their overall financial position, as well as expected developments and associated material opportunities and risks.

Studies having examined the MD&A are quite numerous. There is evidence that firms consider the MD&A a component of their overall disclosure package and that the quality of the disclosures varies, just as the quality of other disclosure outlets varies with factors such as expected firm performance, changes in senior management, firm size, listing status and the extent of disclosure through alternative channels (Clarkson et al., 1999). The content is further determined by the information efficiency of stock prices; that is, firms tend to make more forward-looking statements in the MD&A section when their stock prices are poorer reflections of future earnings potential (Muslu et al., 2015). The quality of MD&A as rated by the SEC is further associated with higher accuracy and lower dispersion of analysts' earnings forecasts (Barron et al., 1999). Not only content but textual *tone* has been shown to be important in the MD&A, with short-window market reactions being observed in response to changes in tone (Feldman et al., 2010). The tone in the forward-looking statements appears to have validity and predictive ability based on the positive correlation found between tone and current performance, as well as between tone and future performance (Li, 2010).

The SEC issued interpretive guidance in 2003, in which it emphasizes the importance of the MD&A and highlights the areas that are in particular need of improvement:

> We believe that management's most important responsibilities include communicating with investors in a clear and straightforward manner. MD&A is a critical component of that communication. The Commission has long sought through its rules, enforcement actions and interpretive processes to elicit MD&A that not only meets technical disclosure requirements but generally is informative and transparent. We believe and expect that when companies follow the guidance in this release, the overall quality of their MD&A will improve. (SEC, 2003)
>
> [...] This guidance is intended to elicit more meaningful disclosure in MD&A in a number of areas, including the overall presentation and focus of MD&A, with general emphasis on the discussion and analysis of known trends, demands, commitments, events and uncertainties, and specific guidance on disclosures about liquidity, capital resources and critical accounting estimates.

Clearly, this conveys the belief that the MD&A section can be a timely and useful source of information to investors and not least sell-side analysts, something that has also received support in research (see, for instance, Clarkson et al., 1999; Barron et al., 1999). Nevertheless, improvements have been called for, given the amount of standardized and generic disclosures provided.

6.2.2 The CEO's letter to the shareholders

In the CEO's letter to the shareholders (or simply the CEO letter), the chief executive officer gives his or her view on the events of the year and the firm's future outlook. The letter constitutes a voluntary narrative disclosure that is not audited or regulated in any accounting standard. Perhaps primarily due to their discretionary nature, the relevance and usefulness of CEO letters has been questioned. Early papers looking at whether the content of CEO letters could help predict future performance showed some evidence of their usefulness (see, for instance, Fisher and Hu, 1988; McConnell et al., 1986; Swales Jr., 1988), but these results need to be complemented by more recent studies. Although some claim that the CEO letter is the part of the annual report investors are most likely to read, it is widely believed not to contain any substantive information that would help investors in their decision-making. Either way, research has documented the role of the CEO letter as being to convey the organizational identity, strategy or future outlook (Amernic and Craig, 2007; Zachary et al., 2011); legitimize corporate actions or attempt to change stakeholders' views of the firm (Tengblad and Ohlsson, 2010; Weber, 2010; Prasad and Mir, 2002; Geppert and Lawrence, 2008; Hyland, 1998) and explain corporate performance (Hooghiemstra, 2010; Clatworthy and Jones, 2006; Clapham and Schwenk, 1991; Salancik and Meindl, 1984; Bettman and Weitz, 1983). Overall, Segars and Kohut (2001) point to the CEO letter as a strategic communication tool.

The language of the CEO letter may also be analyzed in order to understand executive leadership styles or CEO personality traits (Amernic and Craig, 2007; Amernic and Craig, 2011). That is, by analyzing the "tone at the top" or "corporate speak" (see Thomas, 1997, in Segars and Kohut, 2001) by using written narratives, speeches and other forms of communication, a CEO's managerial style may be gauged. This technique has drawn inspiration from the field of political science, in which, for example, speeches of politicians are analyzed in a similar fashion. Ideally, deficiencies in leadership may thus be detected. An example of how this has been studied in a corporate governance setting is with respect to destructive narcissism, which leads to poor strategic decisions, as evidenced by overpayment for mergers and acquisitions (Chatterjee and Hambrick, 2007). Another example of research on CEO speak is a study focusing on CEO communication following a nuclear power plant incident (Beelitz and Merkl-Davies, 2012). The authors conclude that the discourse used by CEOs represents a strategic tool for restoring legitimacy. Rather than communicating to increase transparency and accountability, CEOs manage stakeholder impressions by signaling change while maintaining the *status quo*.

The idea of CEO letters being used to communicate corporate values, explain performance and activities and influence investor or public opinion of the firm may be extended to any narrative corporate disclosure. Whether this communication is indicative of actual underlying economic events and states, or mostly used as an impression management tool, will likely vary across firms, meaning that one cannot rule out either explanation for how disclosure choices are made. One may classify disclosures in terms of whether they are biased or non-biased and opportunistic or non-opportunistic, particularly when information is provided voluntarily. Opportunistic disclosures refer to texts that are deliberately misleading, while biased disclosures may arise from unintentional estimation errors or misjudgment. An example of a biased disclosure that is not necessarily opportunistic is genuinely optimistic forecasts of a firm's future performance or prospects.

Based on these dimensions, three combinations (with different implications) are possible in practice (see Table 6.1). In brief, biased and opportunistic disclosures are misleading, as are biased and non-opportunistic disclosures. Bias and opportunism thus reduce the quality of the disclosures. Meanwhile, non-biased, non-opportunistic disclosures are (if relevant) likely to provide useful information and are therefore of high quality.

Table 6.1 Bias versus opportunism in disclosures

	Biased	Non-biased
Opportunistic	Deliberately misleading disclosures. Monitoring and regulation would help.	N/A (Opportunistic disclosures are in all likelihood biased)
Non-opportunistic	Misleading disclosure as a result of estimation difficulties. Monitoring and regulation would not necessarily help.	Informative disclosure that are potentially useful for decision-making.

6.2.3 Sustainability disclosures

Due to the existence of a wide range of firm stakeholders, it is possible to imagine many types of information being sought after by these actors. Disclosures of the firm's environmental and social conditions, sometimes provided in separate **sustainability** or **corporate social responsibility (CSR)** reports, are examples of non-financial information that may be relevant for the decision-making of shareholders and other stakeholders. Perhaps certain customers, employees or not-for-profit organizations have a special interest in this for moral or ideological reasons; however, one need not limit the analysis of non-financial disclosures, such as sustainability disclosures, to a narrow setting involving only such users. Those who provide capital to firms are primarily interested in obtaining a good return on their investments, but profitability is dependent on a firm's ability to successfully operate in its community in the long run. The legitimacy of the business is therefore likely to be essential to a firm's economic performance. Just as the term *sustainability* may refer to environmental, social *and* economic sustainability, the *interaction* between environmental, social and economic goals is what determines a firm's future. In this section, we use the term sustainability reporting (disclosures) to primarily refer to reports (disclosures) of environmental and social aspects of a firm's business, consistent with how the term is most frequently used in the literature.

When speaking of measuring the quality of non-financial disclosures, one criticism may be that the objectives of these disclosures are less clear. We have seen above that the purpose of financial disclosures is to provide information to investors that can serve as useful inputs in their decision models and reduce information asymmetries that create inefficiencies in the capital markets. By contrast, the benefit of providing disclosures regarding toxic waste levels to a non-governmental organization (NGO) may not be entirely clear. This makes it difficult to determine whether the provided information is of high, sufficient or inferior quality. However, if we maintain a capital market perspective, the objective of non-financial disclosures is the same as for financial disclosures, and they may be judged by the same measure. If investors "buy future earnings," non-financial sustainability disclosures should help investors in terms of quantifying environmental or social costs and benefits.[3] In contrast to mandated financial disclosures, these non-financial disclosures relate to activities that may never have direct cash flow effects for the firm. An example is the non-quantifiable effects of today's polluting businesses on tomorrow's environment. These are externalities in the economic sense of the word and, by definition, externalities are costs and benefits incurred by a different party than the one producing them. To the extent that all investors—present and future—agree that these will remain externalities and will not have to be paid for by the firm, they may therefore be ignored by these users. If customers or other actors in the firm's environment, however, decide to punish a firm for not taking due responsibility for its actions, there could very well be economic effects—real cash flow effects—via, for example, a reduction in that firm's sales. In the long run, a poor reputation or image can send an otherwise profitable firm into bankruptcy. At the very least, negative public opinion can reduce shareholder value.

Regulation of sustainability reporting

Non-financial disclosures are largely discretionary, meaning that managers to a significant extent can decide how much and what to disclose. Information on measures of pollution levels is rarely mandatory, while fees, fines and liabilities for environmental damages are hard to estimate. Therefore, firm size and industry, regulatory influences, capital market pressures,

3 Many firm activities that have an impact on the environment need to be disclosed in the financial reports. A firm may be required to quantify, estimate and account for certain costs in the form of current expenses, provisions or contingencies (e.g., environmental clean-up costs). This will be the case if there are expected direct cash flow effects for the firm.

litigation risk due to lacking information and socio-political pressures contribute in varying degrees to explaining disclosure outcomes (Barth et al., 1997; Brammer and Pavelin, 2008).

In other words, the level and nature—and thereby quality—of sustainability disclosures are dependent on a number of factors. While the definition of quality is not spelled out by any of the global standard-setters for financial reporting, the independent international organization **Global Reporting Initiative (GRI)** has over the last two decades promoted sustainability reporting and issues **Sustainability Reporting Standards** with the aim of increasing reporting quality (see Text Box 6.4). We do not draw conclusions about the success of these, but acknowledge criticism stating that the focus of the guidelines is toward quantity rather than quality, and that firms' reporting practices often lean toward impression management.

Text Box 6.4 **Definition of sustainability reporting according to the Global Reporting Initiative**

The Global Reporting Initiative spells out the meaning of sustainability reporting on its website:[4]

> A sustainability report is a report published by a company or organization about the economic, environmental and social impacts caused by its everyday activities. A sustainability report also presents the organization's values and governance model, and demonstrates the link between its strategy and its commitment to a sustainable global economy.
>
> Sustainability reporting can help organizations to measure, understand and communicate their economic, environmental, social and governance performance, and then set goals, and manage change more effectively. A sustainability report is the key platform for communicating sustainability performance and impacts—whether positive or negative.
>
> Sustainability reporting can be considered as synonymous with other terms for non-financial reporting; triple bottom line reporting, corporate social responsibility (CSR) reporting, and more. It is also an intrinsic element of integrated reporting; a more recent development that combines the analysis of financial and non-financial performance.

A relevant question to ask is whether stricter regulation in this area would increase disclosure quality. Frost (2007) suggests that voluntary provisions of this type of non-financial disclosures may be inadequate in securing a higher level of disclosure and that this is an area that would indeed benefit from stricter regulations. This is based on evidence from an Australian setting, showing that disclosures about environmental performance increased following mandatory environmental reporting guidelines. Meanwhile, although many have hoped that IFRS will bring about harmonization in reporting practices, not least in the EU, we may continue to see differences in how IFRS firms make environmental disclosures—

4 https://www.globalreporting.org/information/sustainability-reporting/Pages/default.aspx

even when these disclosures are regulated in different standards. The impact of firm size and the institutional environment (country) may be expected to be significant. Barbu et al. (2014) conclude that IFRS is not applied consistently and that the persistence of reporting traditions influences environmental disclosures.

As for mandatory environmental disclosures under US GAAP, disclosure practices in a sample of firms subject to environmental sanctions have been examined by Peters and Romi (2013). Specifically, the authors seek to find the factors that lead to non-compliance with environmental sanction disclosures. They argue that whereas such disclosures are mandatory and required by the SEC, the lack of consistency in disclosures among firms subject to environmental sanctions requires more investigation. Relative to studies that have examined the determinants of "voluntary" disclosures, the determinants of non-compliance with mandatory disclosures have been explored to a lesser degree. The underlying factors that affect compliance or non-compliance are partly explained using incentive theories (i.e., those used in explaining voluntary disclosure practices) or in terms of cost-benefit analyses. The authors also consider legitimacy theory in order to understand whether socio-political factors play a role in this respect. They find that strategic disclosure decisions are explained by proprietary costs as well as corporate reputation concerns. They also conclude that non-compliance with sanction disclosures is rampant and that the current regulatory system is therefore not effective.

Finally, some firms recognize that the public view is likely to view the disclosures in question as highly discretionary and manipulable. This seems clear from the fact that firms voluntarily provide independent assurance on their sustainability reports (i.e,. voluntary audits). Although independent assurance is a costly process, the benefits of providing assurance may outweigh the costs. Such benefits may be explained using capital markets-based disclosure theories related to information asymmetry and adverse selection concerns. Another reason for providing assurance is motivated by socio-political or stakeholder-oriented theories. This is supported by findings that firms in sectors exposed to higher social and environmental risks (including mining and utilities) are also more likely to provide assurance on their sustainability reports (Simnett et al., 2009).

We do not investigate sustainability disclosures (or their quality) from a wider stakeholder perspective here. However, because of dynamic or long-term effects on a firm's ability to generate income, the environmental and social impact of a firm's activities is of potential interest to financial investors and creditors. Consequently, there are many studies that have investigated different aspects of **environmental disclosures** in relation to capital markets. Determinants of these disclosures have likewise received attention, with a variety of explanations being provided for differences in disclosure quality. In the next two sections, therefore, we scrutinize the evidence on determinants and consequences a little further.

Determinants of sustainability disclosures

In the accounting literature, the reasons for complying with GRI standards or making voluntary sustainability disclosures may be outlined in accordance with two prominent perspectives:

- Socio-political perspective
- Economic perspective

The first perspective encompasses **socio-political theories**. These may be used in order to explain why social, environmental but also economic information is provided. They suggest that a firm's disclosures will be a function of what is perceived as desirable or proper in a certain setting, given existing social or political norms and value systems. Socio-political theories include legitimacy theory, stakeholder theory and political economy theory. The second perspective is economics-based and centers on how information is provided mainly in order to reduce information asymmetries in the market. Consistent with the economics-based view, greater firm risk, dispersed ownership and dependence on external financing are factors that are positively associated with disclosure level (Cormier and Magnan, 1999). Disclosures are made, however, after considering trade-offs between capital market benefits of disclosures and potential proprietary costs.

Empirical research has sought to establish which—if any—type of relation exists between environmental disclosure and environmental performance. Overall, the evidence is mixed, with many early studies essentially finding no association (Fekrat et al., 1996; Freedman and Wasley, 1990; Wiseman, 1982; Ingram and Frazier, 1980), some finding a negative association between disclosure and environmental performance (Patten, 2002; Cormier and Magnan, 1999) and others finding a positive association (Al-Tuwaijri et al., 2004). From a socio-political perspective, legitimization motives predict a negative association—that is, less disclosure with *increased* performance or more disclosure the poorer the performance. This is because there is social and political pressure on environmentally poor performers to legitimize their business. Meanwhile, economics-based theories predict a positive association, as "good" performers want to distinguish themselves from "bad" performers by disclosing more. Observed inconsistencies between studies may be attributed to the fact that the above-mentioned theories pull in different directions, and more sophisticated research designs are needed in order to tease out the effect of each opposing force. Small samples, failure to control for firm size and industry and other methodological shortcomings have been presented as culprits of incorrect inferences (Patten, 2002; Al-Tuwaijri et al., 2004). For example, there is evidence that environmental disclosures are higher in environmentally sensitive industries (i.e., oil exploration, paper, chemical and allied products, petroleum refining, or metals) and in firms with worse environmental performance. Interestingly, however, the negative association between performance and disclosure is less pronounced in environmentally sensitive industries—presumably because they already face significant pressure to disclose. Poor environmental performance in less environmentally sensitive industries is, by contrast, more strongly associated with increased disclosure levels. Given the level of toxic release levels, firms in these industries may feel greater pressure to explain their environmental performance due to higher expectations for these firms to be environmentally clean. There is also evidence that the use of less specific (non-monetary) environmental disclosures is more prevalent for poorly performing firms in non-environmentally sensitive industries (Cho and Patten, 2007). This is explained by the fact there is a relatively greater need to explain poor environmental performance in these industries, and a greater instance of non-monetary disclosures is viewed as a tool for legitimizing corporate actions. Meanwhile, the use of non-monetary disclosures is not seen as an effective legitimization tool in environmentally sensitive industries; instead, more specific (monetary) disclosures are found to increase with poor performance in these industries.

In addition to environmental performance, *economic* performance can also play a role in disclosure decisions, confounding results if such performance is not controlled for. Firms with high economic performance may disclose potentially "negative" environmental information to raise their credibility in the long run (Cormier and Magnan, 1999), while those with low economic performance disclose less, since the benefits of disclosing are outweighed by potential costs (e.g., reputational, political, contracting, or proprietary costs). For example, the disclosure of certain environmental liabilities in a poorly performing firm may threaten its reputation and thus affect its future financing abilities and operations. Moreover, competitors may take advantage of a situation in which a firm is ill-equipped to effectively respond to stakeholders' pressures and actions.

Furthermore, even as socio-political theories argue that the amount and specificity of social and environmental disclosures will increase over time and in response to external pressure (Clarkson et al., 2008; Walden and Schwartz, 1997), there is evidence of disclosure levels actually decreasing for legitimacy reasons (De Villiers and Van Staden, 2006). Whereas an increase in disclosure may be a way of addressing community concerns in relation to particular issues at a certain point in time, a decrease in disclosure may, conversely, be the result of reduced public attention to those issues. By providing less—or less specific—information, a firm may be able to avoid unwanted scrutiny and, from the firm's perspective, avoid raising unnecessary concerns. The presentation of mitigating facts about sensitive operations or a reluctance to reveal sensitive information may be explained using legitimacy theory. If a firm believes a previously strong stakeholder group now has less power, it may see benefits of providing less information to the extent that attention can be diverted from issues the firm believes are threatening to its image. In other words, a firm may not be able to avoid certain sensitive topics to the extent that they are trending, but as soon as they *can* be avoided without raising suspicions, the firm may wish to deflect attention from them.

The relationship between environmental disclosures and environmental performance not only concerns disclosure *level*, but also disclosure *content*, and further controversies exist in this area. To the extent that disclosures are made, legitimacy theory predicts that *positive* disclosures are used for mitigating negative effects of poor performance. Consistent with this, unfavorable media attention (capturing social pressure) has been shown to be associated with "soft" disclosures (unverifiable claims of environmental commitment) (Clarkson et al., 2008) and positive information designed to present the firm in a good light (Deegan et al., 2002). Also, in a sample of firms that have been successfully prosecuted for environmental wrong-doings, *favorable* environmental disclosures increased *and* outweighed unfavorable information. Given the firms' current circumstances, this is interpreted as clear signs of impression management and attempts to mislead investors (Deegan and Rankin, 1996). Similarly, the language and the tone of US corporate environmental disclosure is found to exhibit more "optimism" and "uncertainty" when the environmental performance is bad (Cho et al., 2010). This is consistent with verbal tone being used as a way to either conceal information concerning firm performance or influence the perception of a firm.

Capital market effects of sustainability disclosures

If users did not care about social and environmental disclosures, it would be of little interest for firms to make them and there would be little reason for researchers to investigate them. The underlying assumption of socio-political theories as well as economics-based theories of disclosures is that firms make decisions based on how their actions will be perceived by shareholders and/or other stakeholders. The premise that information can serve as a regulatory tool—an approach through which states hope to influence firm behavior by ensuring that information relating to their activities are made public—only works if investors really care about firms being good corporate citizens (Freedman and Patten, 2004). As stated above, given the assumption that investors want to earn high returns on their investment, they will be interested in environmental and social aspects of firms' activities to the extent that these have cash flow effects. The underlying assumption is fairly reasonable given that the purpose of entering the stock market—as opposed to giving money to charity or engaging in not-for-profit business ventures—is essentially always financially motivated. In the extreme case, they are interested in profit maximization, but even individual investors who would consider trade-offs between profit, on the one hand, and environmental and social responsibility, on the other, will be interested in the economic implications of the environmental and social aspects of a firm's activities.

Based on the evidence, however, it has been difficult to determine stock market effects of these types of disclosures. Consistent with the view that investors are potentially concerned with future cash flow effects of environmental and social activities within a firm, Stevens (1984) shows that firms that disclosed higher estimated future pollution costs had a lower stock return compared to firms that disclosed lower future environmental costs. Conversely, there is some evidence that while investors punish bad pollution performers (as captured by a toxic emissions measure), firms can mitigate this effect through complementary disclosures (Freedman and Patten, 2004). This implies that if there are market-based incentives to reduce emission levels following mandatory requirements to provide information on toxic releases, regulators must heed (opportunistic) environmental disclosures used for offseting negative market consequences.

Many other studies see no significant relationship between social and environmental disclosure and financial market performance (stock returns) (see Murray et al., 2006, and earlier literature cited therein). A plausible explanation for mixed results in prior literature, as suggested by Al-Tuwaijri et al. (2004), is that there are interactions among environmental performance, environmental disclosure and economic performance, as all of these are based on management's (unobservable) strategies. Hence, a more complete picture of environmental activities together with environmental disclosures is needed in order to provide evidence on capital market effects of such disclosures.

6.3 Determinants of disclosure

We started this chapter by discussing the *effects* of disclosure on capital markets. You may recall from Chapter 1 the *determinants* of accounting outcomes in general. Making references to theory where appropriate, we now turn to some of the most prominent determinants in the disclosure (quality) literature: regulation (standards) and incentives. We categorize the incentives as *firm-level* incentives to disclose and *managerial* incentives to disclose. Note that the firm-level (especially capital markets-derived) incentives may be loosely tied to the valuation role of accounting, whereas the managerial incentives may be tied to the stewardship role of accounting. Also, both voluntary disclosures and compliance with mandatory disclosure requirements are implied.

6.3.1 Firm-level incentives

Firm-level incentives may be divided loosely into those that are capital markets-derived and those that are not. The first group may also be thought of as asset pricing- or valuation-related and derived from theories on adverse selection. The second group can hold any number of incentives, but we limit the discussion to legitimization-derived incentives, as these are often of interest to capital markets as well. For this reason, we do not wish to overly emphasize the distinction between capital markets-derived and non-capital markets-derived incentives.

Capital markets incentives

As pointed out by Ball et al. (2003), capital market forces are an important determinant of disclosure, and they become more so as the amount of publicly traded equity, grows. Many empirical studies have identified determinants of disclosure that may be explained using capital markets-based incentives (see uses in, for instance, Barth et al., 2008b; Bushee and Leuz, 2005; Lang and Lundholm, 1993; Leuz and Schrand, 2009; Leuz and Verrecchia, 2000; Nagar et al., 2003; Webb et al., 2008). Equity-market pressures on required returns and earnings targets can have both positive and negative consequences for disclosure quality. To the extent that managers believe that information asymmetry is detrimental to firm value, managers will make disclosures to overcome information differences. In reality, incentives to disclose appear to be conditioned on a number of factors, such as performance, financing needs and firm size. We go through these next.

Performance One generally predicts a positive relationship between performance and disclosure. For good news firms, economic theories predict that concerns about adverse selection should lead to more disclosures or higher transparency (including a higher level of readability). For bad news firms, the reverse is true (Webb et al., 2008; Leuz and Verrecchia, 2000). That is, good news firms want to highlight their good performance while bad news firms want to hide their bad performance. Sometimes performance refers to financial ditto, but the reasoning may also be extended to a greater disclosure framework, covering, for example, environmental performance. In particular, if investors punish bad environmental performers (which has been shown to be the case), it is perhaps not surprising that firms try to hide environmentally sensitive data from the stock market. However, if investors *suspect* that there *is* bad news, a firm could be better off disclosing it; that is, the effect of the bad news announcement can be mitigated if the firm is forthcoming about it, thus reducing information uncertainty.

Further, it may be noted that low-performing firms may for fear of legal repercussions (legal liability reasons) be induced to disclose certain negative information, which suggests a negative relationship between disclosure and performance. Consequently, the predictions are not conclusive, and empirical studies show mixed results (see discussion and references in Lang and Lundholm, 1993). Performance is commonly measured as abnormal returns, unexpected earnings or return on assets (Lang and Lundholm, 1993; Leuz and Schrand, 2009; Webb et al., 2008).

Financing needs Firms with greater financing needs are believed to have incentives to increase disclosure in order to reduce information asymmetries between management and capital providers. Ultimately, in so doing, they expect to obtain cheaper financing (Bushee and Leuz, 2005). Proxies for financing needs in research commonly include leverage, capital intensity, debt issues and equity issues.[5] Another, slightly different proxy for financing needs is growth or growth potential, such as the percentage growth in sales (Leuz and Schrand, 2009), the assumption being that a firm going through an expansive phase will need more external financing.

The provided hypotheses regarding the positive relation between disclosure and security issuance originate in adverse selection and information asymmetry reduction—more disclosure removes the potentially negative signal about firm value (possibly due to the equity offering itself) and increases the number of willing investors and, as a result, the equilibrium price (Lang and Lundholm, 1993).

Globalization and complexity of operations Firms with geographically dispersed operations or a diversified product portfolio will need to be more transparent in order to overcome information barriers due to high complexity. Because investors are more familiar with firms to which they enjoy geographical proximity, globally active firms will disclose more to overcome *home bias*—the tendency of investors to concentrate their portfolios on firms in their home country (e.g., Kang et al., 1997; Ke et al., 2010). Studies have shown that investors value foreign earnings less than domestic earnings, possibly due to lacking disclosures (Thomas, 1999; Callen et al., 2005). Furthermore, Duru and Reeb (2002) find analysts' forecast accuracy to be lower for more globalized firms, which indicates added

5 Examples of how these variables may be measured are worth mentioning. Leverage can simply be total liabilities over total assets, interest-bearing or long-term debt over total assets or a debt-equity ratio measured as long-term debt over market value of equity plus book value of preferred shares and long-term debt (Lang and Lundholm, 1993; Leuz and Schrand, 2009; Webb et al., 2008). Meanwhile, capital intensity may be measured as long-term assets divided by total assets (Leuz and Verrecchia, 2000), debt issue as the annual percentage increase of liabilities or long-term debt and equity issue as the percentage increase of common stock (Barth et al., 2008).

complexity with multinational operations. More disclosure is needed to overcome these "barriers." Webb et al. (2008) study the interaction between globalization and the legal environment on disclosures and conclude that not only does globalization increase the disclosure level, but this is particularly the case in weak legal environments. This is because accounting quality is generally lower in such jurisdictions and because investor trust is often lower (since protection of rights is weaker). So, while disclosure is of lower quality in general for firms in weak legal environments (see more in Chapter 9), the effect of globalization on disclosure practices is more pronounced in such regimes. Studies using globalization as a variable affecting disclosure use foreign exchange listings, foreign subsidiaries and the foreign sales ratio as proxies.

Ownership structure Just as there is greater information asymmetry between the market and highly globalized firms, there are greater information barriers when ownership is dispersed. When there are many shareholders with individual small holdings, firms have incentives to be more transparent in order to minimize information asymmetry. That is, disclosure levels rise with this type of ownership structure. Meanwhile, higher ownership concentration is suggested by Leuz and Verrecchia (2000) to indicate the presence of insiders who have comparatively more extensive access to private information about the firm. This reduces the firm's need to make public disclosures. The most common empirical proxy for ownership concentration is the proportion of widely held shares, also known as free float (Leuz and Verrecchia, 2000). This measures the percentage of shares not owned by management, other parties closely affiliated with the firm or majority shareholders.

Proprietary costs Finally, a constraint on disclosure is introduced by the existence of *proprietary costs*. As we saw briefly in Chapter 3, proprietary costs are costs incurred by firms when revealing proprietary (firm-specific and potentially sensitive) information. These costs are indirect, as they represent a reduction in future cash flows due to, for example, potential regulatory actions following disclosures, competitors benefiting from the information, or customers shying away from the firm's products. The existence of proprietary costs is expected to be associated with a lower level and quality of disclosure. In other words, if there is any possibility that outsiders use the disclosed information in a way that leads to further costs to the firm (and those costs exceed the benefits of disclosure), there would little incentive to disclose. We mention this under the capital markets incentive heading, since proprietary cost theory is often offered as an alternative to economic theory and adverse selection as an explanation for disclosure.

Legitimization incentives

Especially where environmental disclosures are concerned, legitimacy theory and institutional theory predict that firms respond to pressures from a variety of stakeholders and institutions, and make disclosures in order to gain or maintain legitimacy (see section 6.2.3). Whether firms disclose more or less tends to be dependent on performance (environmental or economic), but evidence on the relation has often been weak or mixed. In general, poor performance is usually predicted to lead to *more* disclosure as management attempts to *explain* and *justify* past events.

6.3.2 Managerial incentives

Incentives to disclose that originate with the manager are typically *agency-based* or *contractual*. The alleged inclination among managers to want to maximize their own rather than the owners' profits places a constraint on the willingness or tendency to disclose. Meanwhile, various contracts and control mechanisms are put in place to induce managers to be transparent. For example, a well-designed compensation contract, which aligns the interests of managers and shareholders, can motivate managers to be more transparent and provide more relevant, firm-specific disclosures.

Since we devote an entire chapter to managerial incentives (Chapter 8) and accounting choice (one aspect of which is disclosure choice), it is here sufficient to point out that opportunism in managers, contractual efficiency and the strength of monitoring all affect the ability of managers to make discretionary disclosure choices.

6.3.3 Regulation

Regulation has a large impact on firms' disclosure outcomes. Accounting standards, audit standards, corporate governance standards and industry-specific regulation are all part of the regulatory framework. Here, we present some of the findings in the literature relating to disclosure quality under different accounting standards. While we consider individual accounting items in Part V of the book, there is a considerable amount of research on GAAP and their aggregate quality effects. For example, the introduction of mandatory IFRS adoption in the EU has lent itself to many such studies. The burning question is whether a shift to IFRS is favorable for users (capital markets). In the US, there was talk about adopting IFRS as well (see Chapter 4) and academics were quick to help provide evidence of the adoption effect in Europe in the mid-2000s.[6] All in all, after more than a decade's worth of research (see also Text Box 6.5), there is broad, general consensus in the literature about the following:

- **Finding I: IFRS has higher accounting quality than most local GAAP**.
  Explanations include:
  - IFRS encourages more decision-relevant financial reporting
  - There is better enforcement of these better standards than of local standards
  - There is a greater commitment to transparency under IFRS

- **The implications of this are:**
  - Cost of capital should be lower for IFRS firms
  - There is less uncertainty regarding future cash flows in these firms
  - Stocks in these firms enjoy greater liquidity (due to transparency and internationalization)

6 Of course, one must understand and remember that comparing IFRS to European local GAAP is very different from comparing IFRS to US GAAP. The US standards are already considered to be of high quality, to the extent that a quality improvement when switching from German or Swedish GAAP to IFRS cannot be used to infer that the same improvement would come about for an equivalent US firm.

- **Finding II: IFRS and US GAAP firms have a lower cost of capital compared to local GAAP firms.** For example,
  - Greater commitment to transparency reduces the cost of capital (Leuz and Verrecchia, 2000)
  - Improved information content of annual earnings announcements occurs after mandatory IFRS adoption, where information content is measured in terms of trading volume and return volatility (Landsman et al., 2012)
  - Improved liquidity occurs after mandatory IFRS adoption—although this is (at least partly) an enforcement effect (Barth and Israeli, 2013; Christensen et al., 2013a)

Text Box 6.5 **Disclosures, cost of capital and accounting standards: Some empirical evidence**

Many comparisons have been made between local GAAP, US GAAP and IFRS with respect to differences in cost of capital. A brief summary of findings are shown here.

Daske and Gebhardt (2006) find that disclosure quality significantly increased for both voluntary and mandatory adopters of IFRS in Germany, Austria and Switzerland. However, self-selection issues exist, which means that when firms *choose* (select) a certain behavior, in this case to report according to IFRS, one cannot separate the effect of the *higher ambition* of these firms from the effect of the standards themselves. Mandatory adopters experience an improvement as well, however, which is more convincing evidence of the benefits of IFRS. The quality scores come from "financial report 'beauty contests' hosted by various business journals ... and conducted by leading academic scholars." (p.462) The authors claim a strength of their study is that their measure relies on actual perceptions of the actual reports (rather than quantitative indices, see section 6.4).

It has also been shown that analyst forecast accuracy is positively associated with IFRS compliance as measured by a disclosure index of selected standards, suggesting IFRS disclosure requirements reduce information asymmetry (Hodgdon et al., 2008). Moreover, analysts' forecast accuracy is observed to increase upon switching from local GAAP to IFRS, as is the number of foreign analysts (Tan et al., 2011).

Another study looking at the capital market consequences of IFRS was conducted by Daske et al. (2008). The results are not ascribed to disclosure quality or earnings quality specifically, but one may assume that one of the two, or both, have improved under IFRS. Findings show a reduction in the (implied) cost of capital and an increase in market liquidity for firms that have voluntarily switched to IFRS. More importantly, the same applies to firms that have been *required* to adopt IFRS. The improvements, however, are restricted to firms operating in an environment having strict legal enforcement, suggesting that incentives play a role.

It may also be relevant to consider a firm's intentions when shifting to a new set of standards. Could a firm affect investor perceptions by signaling a *commitment* to increased or improved disclosures? A "commitment" implies disclosure decisions are made *ex ante* (i.e., before the fact) and might not fully capture actual disclosure behavior. One study, however, finds that German firms that announced that they would henceforth adopt US GAAP rather than German GAAP experienced reduced bid-ask spreads and increased trading volume (Leuz and Verrecchia, 2000). This is consistent with US GAAP—being considered a more transparent framework than German GAAP—having a beneficial effect on cost of capital by reducing investor uncertainty regarding the reported numbers. It should be pointed out that this is not a GAAP comparison paper *per se*, but it indicates that investors perceive US GAAP to be of higher quality than German GAAP.

6.4 Disclosure quality metrics

In this final section, we take a closer look at how researchers have measured disclosures in practice; that is, how they have operationalized disclosure quality in empirical studies. Operationalizations can be exceedingly difficult. Some researchers explicitly suggest that the conceptual framework(s) of the IASB and the FASB should be used to define quality, meaning that high-quality disclosures are those that are relevant, reliable (faithfully represented), understandable and comparable. What this means in practice, however, is not clear. How do you measure understandability? How do you measure comparability? What about relevance and faithful representation? In fact, the empirical accounting literature does not normally make explicit claims to having directly measured any of these qualities, but it is often implied in the various proxies for disclosure quality that have been developed.

Studies looking at *voluntary* disclosures have perhaps been the most creative in this context. The reason voluntary disclosures are so attractive to measure is that they exhibit greater variability than *mandatory* disclosures. Commonly employed disclosure metrics (discussed below) are:

- Analysts' rankings
- Index-based measures
- Textual attributes (e.g., readability, specificity, tone)
- Earnings quality

6.4.1 Analysts' rankings

One measure of disclosure quality is to use **analysts' ratings of reporting quality**. Early American studies make references to the Financial Analysts Federation (FAF), the Association for Investment Management and Research (AIMR), the Center for International Financial Analysis and Research (CIFAR) and S&P (see, for instance, Lang and Lundholm, 1993; Lundholm and Myers, 2002). These provide disclosure scores based on analyst ratings. Annual report "beauty contests" or awards are examples of analyst-based disclosure scores.

The advantage of using these measures is that they are objective from the researcher's point of view; that is, there is no bias caused by the views or interests of the person conducting the study. However, since the scores often relate to analysts' *perceptions* regarding the quality and informativeness of the information provided by firms, they are inevitably subjective and somewhat "indirect" measures of quality.

6.4.2 Index-based measures

A potentially more direct and indeed transparent way of measuring disclosure quality is for the researcher to use checklists of what constitutes high quality in a particular setting, and then construct an index that quantifies quality (see Table 6.2), while giving a detailed account of how this was done. The quantitative index created by Botosan (1997) serves well as an example here, with variations of it appearing in several subsequent studies (see Cheng and Courtenay, 2006; Francis et al., 2008; Jiang et al., 2011; Luo et al., 2006; Webb et al.,

Table 6.2 Disclosure index by Botosan (1997).

	Extract of major elements of DSCORE
I.	**Background Information:**
	Statement of corporate goals or objectives
	Competitive environment
	Principle products
II.	**Ten- or Five-Year Summary of Historical Results:**
	Return-on-assets or sufficient information to compute return-on-assets (i.e., net income, tax rate, interest expense and total assets)
	Asset turnover or sufficient information to compute asset turnover (i.e., sales and total assets)
	Net profit margin or sufficient information to compute net profit margin (i.e., net income, tax rate, interest expense and sales)
III.	**Key Non-Financial Statistics:**
	Number of employees
	Market share
	Growth in units sold
IV.	**Projected Information:**
	Forecasted market share
	Cash flow forecast
	Sales forecast
V.	**Management Discussion and Analysis:**
	Change in sales
	Change in operating income
	Change in capital expenditures or R&D

2008.). Because quantity tends to be equated with quality in this context, and little attention is paid to the clarity or informativeness of the disclosure item, criticism may be directed at this approach.

Disclosure quantity versus quality

There is likely a rather strong link between the quality and the quantity of disclosure, but the appropriateness is perhaps especially questionable in view of the IASB's and the FASB's *Disclosure Initiative* (discussed in more detail in section 15.4.1). The assumption that "more is better" seems precarious, not least in light of concerns that corporate investors and other users of firms' financial reports are faced with information overload. Disclosures, in order to be useful, should not only convey relevant information to users, but they also need to be efficient. Even though today's disclosures may be substantial, they may also be exceedingly complex to process. We therefore consider complexity in the next section.

The distinction between the *quality* and *quantity* of disclosure is an important one. Accounting regulation changes have been blamed for a sudden and extensive increase in the amount of public disclosures required from firms, resulting in **information overload.**

Regulators tend to issue more and more requirements but never remove previously issued requirements. This contributes to a build-up of rules (and explains the view that US GAAP, if for no other reason than being older than IFRS, is rules-based). The result is annual reports that are poorly organized and abound with duplicate disclosures, boilerplate disclosures or otherwise irrelevant disclosures that appear to be included simply because they existed on an auditor's checklist. The use of so-called **boilerplate disclosures** (i.e., the automatic incorporation of standardized text passages by firms) has made financial reports overflow with pages, making annual reports cluttered and sometimes described as being used as "dumping grounds."

Both the IASB and the FASB have taken steps to address this issue through the Disclosure Initiative. Ideally, firms should *communicate* rather than just comply. Better—not more—information is desired. Too often, it is difficult to sift out relevant firm-specific disclosures from less informative, generic disclosures. That is, actual, relevant data is being drowned out by general references to accounting policies and standard requirements (see Text Box 6.6 for examples).

Overall, equating quantity with quality has been questioned—not just because quantifications can be arbitrary, but because more information does not always result in transparency.

Text Box 6.6 **Generic disclosure examples**

Below we provide two examples of firm disclosures regarding the areas that are particularly affected by management's judgment and where there is a high level of estimation uncertainty. Almost any annual report could serve as an example of the general, non-specific nature of this type of disclosure. The similarities between the texts below, and their similarity to what you find in the actual accounting standard, should be evident.

From AG Group's Annual Report 2012
Estimates and discretionary assessments are evaluated continuously and based on historical experience and other factors, including expectations of future events that are regarded as reasonable under the current circumstances. The Group prepares estimates and makes assumptions concerning the future. The accounting estimates that are made as a result of this will rarely coincide in full with the final outcome. Estimates and assumptions/prerequisites that represent a significant risk of major changes in the book value of assets and liabilities during the next financial year are discussed below. [...]

Retirement benefits—The present value of the retirement benefit obligations depends on a number of factors that are determined on an actuarial basis using a number of assumptions. This includes assumptions related to the discount rate, wage inflation, adjustment of retirement benefits, expected return on plan assets, and demographic factors such as disability and mortality. These assumptions are based on observable market prices and historical developments in the Group and society as a whole. Changes in assumptions will affect the projected retirement benefit obligations and retirement benefit expense.

From Terna Group's *Integrated* Report, 2014 (396 pages in total)
Preparation of the Consolidated Financial Statements requires the use by the management of estimates and assumptions that affect the carrying amounts of assets and liabilities and related disclosures, in addition to contingent assets and liabilities at the reporting date. The estimates and associated assumptions are based on previous experience and various factors that are believed to be reasonable under the circumstances, and were applied to measure carrying amounts of assets and liabilities that are not readily apparent from other objective sources. Actual results may differ from these estimates. The estimates and underlying assumptions are reviewed periodically and the effects of any changes are recognised in the income statement for the year, if they relate solely to that period. In the case that the review affects both current and future years, the change is recorded in the year in which the estimate is reviewed as well as in the relative future years. The critical areas for key estimates and assumptions used by management in applying the IFRSs endorsed by the European Commission that could have significant effects on the Separate Financial Statements or that could give rise to risks that would entail significant adjustments to the carrying amount of assets and liabilities in subsequent years are summarised below. [...]

Employee benefits: The liability for employee benefits paid upon or following termination of employment in relation to defined benefit plans or other long-term benefits is recognised net of any plan assets and is measured on the basis of actuarial assumptions, estimating the amount of future benefits that employees have vested at the reporting date. The actuarial valuations used to quantify employee benefits (of all plans except termination benefits) were made on the basis of the "vested benefits" method by means of the "Projected Unit Credit" (PUC) criterion. These valuations are based on economic and demographic assumptions: discounting rate (used to determine the present value of the obligation, determined considering the return of high quality bond securities in line with the duration of the group of workers measured), inflation rate, rate at which future salary levels increase, increase rate of average health reimbursement, increase rate of electrical consumer goods prices and demographic techniques, such as, for example, mortality and invalidity, retirement, resignation, advances and family members.

In sum, the first paragraph is found in similar wording in almost every single IFRS annual report, and the second paragraph essentially just conveys *ex ante* expectations concerning the accounting issue in that particular area.

6.4.3 Textual attributes

Textual attributes have become more and more popular in research on disclosures, because of increased computing power and data availability in recent years. Digitalization and IT advances, leading to "big data" developments, have driven computerized analyses of texts and narrative disclosures. However, studies of some textual attributes have been around for a long time. For example, the complexity of financial reporting is commonly examined in terms of the **readability** of financial reports and the readability measures used were developed as far back as in the 1960s (or earlier). In theory, the readability of financial reports is important, provided that information content is lost when corporate texts are too voluminous or complex to read. Criticism of the validity of various readability measures, especially in a financial reporting context, has likely deterred some researchers, but they are definitely still being used. Examples of readability measures include the Gunning-Fog Index and the Flesch–Kincaid reading grade level. The formulas used for calculating these rely on factors such as word length, number of syllables and sentence length. The **management obfuscation hypothesis** (Courtis, 1986) predicts that self-interested managers opportunistically choose to *obfuscate* information (i.e., hide information) by making disclosures difficult to read. More generally, this hypothesis is consistent with impression management (i.e., the act of opportunistically portraying firm activities or performance in a biased manner in order to influence stakeholder impressions of the firm).

Standard-setters as well as researchers have shown interest in the readability, presentation format, and placement of information in corporate reports. For example, in 1999, the SEC launched the **Plain English** handbook to encourage the preparation of corporate disclosure documents that are "visually inviting," "logically organized," and "understandable on the first reading."[7] This entails having short sentences, bullet lists, and descriptive headers; avoiding legal and highly technical terms, boilerplates, and repetitions.

Related research on presentation issues challenges the EMH, in which any direct implication of the presentation of information is disregarded. In providing an alternative view to EMH, Bloomfield (2002) presents the Incomplete Revelation Hypothesis (IRH), which focuses on the cost and difficulty of processing information (see also Chapter 3). Difficulties in processing information produce noise in trading and therefore result in prices that are less effective in reflecting information completely. Li (2008) argues that if information can be more or less costly to process, managers may have incentives to "strategically" make disclosures of bad news less transparent (and thus costlier to process). Consistent with the management obfuscation hypothesis, he finds that annual reports of firms with lower or less persistent earnings are more difficult to read. Laksmana et al. (2012) examine the disclosure quality of executive compensation contracts and investigate weather the readability of CEO compensation disclosure changes with the extent and mix of compensation plans. The main finding here is that when CEO pay exceeds the benchmark pay, disclosures are more difficult to read. This is also consistent with the management obfuscation hypothesis.

Another qualitative feature of disclosures that has recently received increasing attention is disclosure **tone**. The tone, or sentiment, of texts is observed using either manual or computerized content analysis. An example of the latter is to use dictionary-based software applications that quantify different aspects of tone, including certainty, optimism, aggression, ambivalence and satisfaction. This is done because textual tone is believed to convey relevant information to capital market participants.

Feldman et al. (2010) study the tone change in the MD&A section of US reports and weather it provides any additional information about stock prices beyond what is captured by preliminary earnings surprises, accruals and operating cash flows. The results suggest that disclosures and the tone change of MD&A are informative and value relevant, as they affect future stock prices. Studies have also shown that qualitative attributes of *analysts'* reports, such as detail and tone, provide capital market participants with relevant information regarding earnings forecasts and stock trade recommendations (Twedt and Rees, 2012).

7 See https://www.sec.gov/pdf/handbook.pdf

Further, Merkley (2014) examines how earnings performance relates to firms' narrative R&D disclosure decisions in relation to detail, tone and readability. He finds that managers adjust R&D disclosures based on earnings performance to provide relevant information rather than to obfuscate performance. For example, poorer performance does not lead to less readable reports, and the changes in tone are consistent with the changes in performance. There is also evidence that analysts find high-quality, narrative R&D disclosures useful, since such disclosures are associated with lower forecast dispersion and higher forecast accuracy.

The *joint* effect of tone and readability has also been examined. Tan et al. (2014) find that when readability is low, positive language sentiment or a positive tone in financial disclosures has a positive effect on less sophisticated investors and their perception of earnings. Finally, the tone of disclosures may also be used strategically by management (see, for instance, García Osma and Guillamón, 2008; Cho et al., 2010), with an overly positive verbal tone of disclosure being used as an impression management tool.

Recently, research has sought to examine the *specificity* level of disclosures, which is consistent with the Disclosure Initiative and standard-setters' emphasis on the need for relevant, firm-*specific* disclosures. Hope et al. (2016) focus on the level of detail of firms' risk-factor disclosures and measure this using a computing algorithm (Named Entity Recognition, NER) that takes into account the number of named locations and organizations, quantitative disclosures in terms of percentages and dollar amounts, as well as times and dates. The economic consequences of more detailed risk-factor disclosures include positive market reactions, a greater trading volume, and lower analyst forecast dispersion. This is consistent with such disclosures being more informative for investors.

As mentioned above, computerized text analysis is an emerging area of research in many disciplines, including accounting and finance. This coincides with the rapid increase in available data in recent years, as well as improved tools for processing and analyzing it. Table 6.3 summarizes some of the commonly used measures, some of which are based on state-of-the-art technologies using artificial intelligence and other methods that ensure relatively high levels of objectivity (for a more extensive review of papers using text analysis in accounting and finance, see Loughran and McDonald, 2016)).

Table 6.3 Summary of measures used in textual analysis

Concept	Common measures	A selection of references
Complexity	The length or volume of text, measured as the number of words in textual sections of annual reports or using the file size of the report (applicable when file formats are standardized, such as in SEC filings).	Lang and Stice-Lawrence (2015); Geppert and Lawrence (2008); Filzen and Peterson (2015)
Readability	The average sentence length and the number of syllables in words. The Gunning Fog (1952) index, calculated as 0.4 *(average number of words per sentence + percent of words in excess of two syllables)	Lehavy et al. (2011); Courtis (1995); Courtis (1986); Laksmana et al. (2012); Li (2008)

Concept	Common measures	A selection of references
Boilerplates	The incorporation of standardized text passages. Boilerplates may be measured as the extent to which an annual report contains standardized phrases—meaning 4-word phrases (tetragrams) that appear frequently in documents in a firm's home country	Lang and Stice-Lawrence (2015); Abraham and Shrives (2014); Campbell et al. (2014)
Specificity	Level of detail and firm-specific information as captured by the prevalence of specific entity names, including names of locations, people, organizations, dollar amounts, percentages, dates, or times. These may be identified using the Stanford Named Entity Recognizer (NER) tool	Hope et al. (2016)
Stickiness	Disclosures that do not change over time. These can be measured as the number of sentences that include at least one 8-word phrase that is repeated from the same firm's prior year report	Brown and Tucker (2011)
Latent Dirichlet Allocation (LDA)	A Bayesian computational linguistic that identifies the latent topics in a large corpus of documents. LDA uses the probability of words co-occurring within documents to identify sets of topics and their associated words and is conceptually similar to factor analysis	(Huang et al., 2014; Li, 2010)

6.5 Conclusions

While information asymmetry can harm capital market functions, disclosures can help raise market liquidity and lower the cost of capital, thereby promoting an efficient allocation of resources in an economy. Positive market consequences of disclosure have been explained in terms of lower information risk (which is a non-diversifiable, separate risk factor). This, in turn, comes about as a result of reduced estimation risk, reduced transaction costs or an increased demand for a firm's securities. Further, disclosures lead to more accurate and more certain forecasts of future firm performance and thus constitute a good basis for investment decisions. In sum, these results indicate that high-quality corporate disclosures generate benefits for investors, as they reduce information asymmetries and information risk. Especially firms that perform well are likely to perceive such benefits of disclosure, incentivizing managers to disclose, while firms with low financial performance may opt for less than full disclosure. Firms perceiving high proprietary costs of disclosure are similarly unwilling to disclose.

In understanding the determinants and consequences of disclosure decisions, it is important to consider both regulated (mandatory) and unregulated (voluntary) information. Regulated disclosures appear in the primary financial statements as numbers or text (i.e., quantitative or qualitative disclosures). Unregulated disclosures tend to be qualitative or narrative and are used by firms to explain or comment on past performance, or discuss future prospects. Such disclosures, being highly discretionary, may be useful if they convey management's private information, or misleading if they are used opportunistically to manage stakeholder (including investor and creditor) impressions of the firm. In sum, one may classify the disclosures as either:

- providing incrementally useful information and analysis of performance in an attempt to reduce information asymmetry
- managing impressions, not least for legitimization reasons
- communicating *retrospective sense-making*, consisting of explanations of *why* things happened the way they did (especially when performance is poor)

The CEO's letter to shareholders is one potential communication channel, as is management's discussion and analysis. Whereas MD&A is unregulated in IFRS, it is mandated by the US SEC, albeit still discretionary in format. Another largely unregulated area (but with an increasing amount of guidelines) is sustainability reporting. The nature and quality of these have been widely researched and explained using, *inter alia*, socio-political theories and economic theories.

Existing evidence from financial accounting research shows that qualitative features of disclosure carry relevant information to investors and analysts or may otherwise affect these parties. This means that when striving to enhance the quality of disclosures, only focusing on compliance with disclosure requirements or on the amount of voluntary disclosure provided may have the reverse effect. A check-the-box mentality can lead to boilerplate disclosures and information overload. The main issue today with respect to transparency is not how to get firms to increase disclosure quantity, but how to encourage firms to increase disclosure quality. Hence, the current project by the FASB and the IASB, in which the aim is to enhance the usefulness of financial information while limiting the extent of boilerplates, is timely. When measuring disclosure quality, researchers have consequently gone beyond "quantity" and explored various textual attributes of disclosures.

CHAPTER 7
Earnings quality

Learning outcomes

Upon completion of this chapter, you will have gained insight into:

- Why earnings quality is such an important feature of financial reporting.
- Different earnings quality measures, including both *properties* of the earnings number itself and external indicators of earnings quality.
- Various accruals models and value relevance models.

INVESTORS BUY FUTURE EARNINGS. It is largely believed that the single best indicator of future earnings is *current* earnings. The ability of investors to predict future performance is thus dependent on the quality of the reported earnings number. But what *is* high-quality earnings? As has been hinted at previously, there is no such thing as *true* earnings. Earnings cannot be directly observed. In fact, it should be clear to anyone doing accounting that an earnings number is made up of different components, all of which are subject to more or less judgment, meaning that earnings are always a function of their specific context. That is, depending on who the user is, and what exactly he or she is attempting to estimate or predict, the number in focus will vary (as will what determines whether it is a useful number). There are many potential earnings numbers—earnings before interest, taxes, depreciation, amortization (EBITDA), earnings before interest and taxes (EBIT), earnings before minority interests, earnings after minority interests, net income excluding other comprehensive income and comprehensive income, to name a few.[1] Even if there was no uncertainty in the measures or there was no leeway to manage earnings, the best that can be said for earnings is that they reflect some consensus among standard-setters. Whether earnings are "true" or misstated must then be evaluated based on a given framework. Since we have stressed that

1 Whereas some users focus on the "bottom-line" number (net income), others believe operating income (e.g., EBIT, EBITDA) is the better indicator of value creation (and therefore more relevant).

usefulness is a sign of quality, it is reasonable to allow ourselves to speak of—if not true earnings—earnings that are of higher quality *given our objective* with regard to informing capital providers of the economic performance of the firm.[2]

That is, similarly to how we define accounting quality in terms of the extent to which financial reporting supports the decision models used, earnings quality can be thought of as the extent to which users are provided with information about a firm's performance that is relevant for decision-making (Dechow et al., 2010). In Chapter 6, we see that higher disclosure quality reduces information asymmetry between the capital market and the firm and therefore has positive consequences for users (as well as the firm itself). These findings can be extended to a specific type of disclosure—the earnings number.

The quality of the earnings number is important and, consequently, so is the quality of the process leading to that number. Earnings, just as disclosures, will depend on the accounting standards followed (e.g., Swedish GAAP or IFRS). It will also depend on the individual policies chosen. Many standards provide firms with the option to choose among alternative methods. For example, in accounting for the value of tangible assets, a firm might choose between the historical cost model or the revaluation model, and then it should choose an appropriate depreciation method. Apart from discrete choices, judgments also have to be made. Having chosen a depreciation method, managers must apply their judgment in assessing the remaining useful life of the asset in order to know the depreciation schedule. We here point out that all of these factors contribute to the final earnings number and its quality. Some factors might be argued to raise the quality *ex ante*; that is, regardless of your subsequent choices, earnings generated under IFRS may be argued to better fulfill investor needs. Other factors might only raise the quality in certain situations, *ex post*; that is, whether higher quality is achieved will depend on whether the choice was appropriate for that particular transaction and on the quality of the judgment made in that particular case.

All in all, we might say that earnings quality will vary along the following dimensions or according to the following hierarchy:

- Accounting standard followed
- Accounting policy or method chosen (given the above point)
- Judgments made (given the above two points)

Unintentional errors and poor choices, along with intentional manipulation of earnings, can lead to lower quality. In Part IV and V of this book, we delve deeper into the different choices available to preparers of financial reports, looking at concrete examples of how earnings quality is affected on an item-by-item basis. The impact of accounting standards on quality, as well as the effect of incentives, enforcement and monitoring on earnings quality, is considered.

Similar to the case of disclosure quality, measuring earnings quality is not trivial. Although one would ideally like to capture the extent to which earnings are relevant,

2 If, for example, tax authorities are the main users of the earnings number, then it should potentially reflect other income and expenses, thereby altering what is considered high-quality earnings.

faithfully represented, comparable and so forth, direct measures of these characteristics do not exist. Therefore, proxies have to be used. We now turn to the different ways of measuring earnings quality, classifying common proxies into two categories (see also Dechow et al., 2010, on which this classification is loosely based):

- **Properties of earnings**: This chiefly refers to how an earnings number behaves in relation to itself (over time) or to other closely related accounting measures, such as cash flows or balance sheet items. Common examples of these are earnings persistence, smoothness of earnings, asymmetric timeliness of earnings, abnormal accruals and earnings exhibiting target-beating behavior.
- **External indicators of earnings quality**

Rather than focusing on the earnings numbers themselves, one may gauge the quality of earnings by looking at market indicators and intermediaries' evaluation of earnings, where intermediaries are actors outside of management communicating firm information to investors. *Value relevance* relates accounting estimates of earnings or changes in earnings to market measures (of earnings or equity). Different types of earnings-returns and equity-price models are thus used here. Meanwhile, *intermediaries' evaluation of earnings* refer to, for example, audit opinions, internal audit reports on the existence of internal control procedures and analysts' reports.

This chapter is devoted to going through each one of these proxies for earnings quality.

7.1 Earnings properties

Before considering the properties of earnings and the reasons for why they may represent a firm's earnings quality, it is helpful to first reflect on the two key components of earnings: *accruals* and *cash flows*. In the long run, earnings and levered free cash flows from operations (OCF)[3] will be equal to each other. In the short run, however, they differ by accruals:

Earnings = OCF + Accruals

Note that operating cash flows are those that are related to core, value-creating activities as opposed to financing activities, which represent transactions with capital providers.[4] Meanwhile, accruals are adjustments to the accounts for earned revenues and incurred expenses that have not yet had any cash flow effects or, alternatively, unearned revenues and deferred (prepaid) expenses that show up in the cash flow statement but should not yet affect income. Accruals, as defined here, also capture investments in, or liquidations of, operating items, thus representing all changes in (net) operating assets.

Since cash flows represent actual transactions involving highly liquid assets, they are

3 We define free cash flows from operations as the net cash flow coming from sales and other operating activities, *less* cash flows invested in operations. Although it is not important for the argument here, in order to be technically correct, the free cash flows considered must be "levered", meaning net interest payments (to creditors) after tax are deducted.

4 Financing cash flows other than net interest payments are ignored because they have no effect on earnings, even though they lead to the recording of accruals (e.g., changes in financial debt).

often considered "objective," whereas accruals require management to estimate the value of non-cash-related items and are therefore thought of as "subjective." Why, then, should investors be interested in accruals and why, indeed, should accountants record accruals?

The simple answer is that cash flows are often a poor measure of value creation. Barth et al. (1999) assert that

> [t]he basic premise of accrual accounting is that earnings, which is cash flows from operations plus accruals, is a better indicator of future earnings, dividends, and cash flows than current and past cash flows.

As further pointed out by Dechow (1994) in a well-cited article:

> Two important accounting principles that guide the production of earnings are the revenue recognition principle and the matching principle.[5] The revenue recognition principle requires revenues to be recognized when a firm has performed all, or a substantial portion, of services to be provided and cash receipt is reasonably certain. The matching principle requires cash outlays associated directly with revenues to be expensed in the period in which the firm recognizes the revenue. By having such principles, the accrual process is hypothesized to mitigate timing and matching problems inherent in cash flows so that earnings more closely reflects firm performance. (Dechow, 1994, p. 4)

Cash flow measures mix activities that add value in current periods with investments in, and liquidation of, assets—which in the best case are associated with value creation in earlier or future periods. In her paper, Dechow (1994) explores conditions in which accruals are more useful than in others in terms of their contribution to the ability of earnings to measure firm performance (as captured by stock returns). She concludes, among other things, that the longer the firm's operating cycle and the shorter the performance measurement interval, the more inadequate cash flow measures are. This follows from the fact that timing and matching problems are more severe in these cases. Think of an operating cycle as being the average amount of time elapsing between the cash outflow needed in the production of a product and the cash inflow generated from the sale of that product (see Example 7.1).

Example 7.1 **Earnings and cash flows**

We can exemplify the net income and cash flow effects in two firms that differ with respect to operating cycle. Note: the same example could have illustrated differences in measurement interval. Assume that for a complete operating cycle, expenses are 100, revenues are 110 and that net income is thus 10 and the return on the investment is 10% (assuming investment is 100).

In Firm A, one records income on an annual basis and the operating cycle is two years (Firm A), which means that a cash flow-based performance measure will likely

5 Note that even though the matching principle is not an explicit principle in the IASB's most recent Conceptual Framework, it is an underlying principle of accrual accounting (cf. Chapter 4).

differ greatly from an earnings-based measure. In the income statement, no expenses or revenues will have been recorded in the first period, consistent with the matching and revenue recognition principles. A negative cash flow, however, will have been recorded. In the following period, when the sale of the product takes place, expenses and revenues will be recorded, along with a positive cash flow from that sale. If credit sales rather than cash sales take place, then the recording of cash flows will be even more arbitrary.

One may contrast this with a scenario in which a firm's operating cycle is very short (Firm B). For example, assume one records income on an annual basis and the operating cycle is *half* a year in Firm B. Additionally, the operating cycles line up neatly with the fiscal year. Then a cash flow-based performance measure will likely correspond closely to an earnings-based measure, as two full operating cycles have been completed and both cash flows and earnings will capture this.

Scenario A

	Period 1	*Period 2*
Cash in		110
Cash out	–100	
Net cash flow	**–100**	**110**
Revenues		110
Expenses		–100
Net income	**0**	**10**

Scenario B

	Period 1	*Period 2*
Cash in	220	220
Cash out	–200	-200
Net cash flow	**20**	**20**
Revenues	220	220
Expenses	–200	-200
Net income	**20**	**20**

In the table, Scenario A shows half a completed operating cycle per period, while Scenario B shows two completed operating cycles per period. Cash flows differ largely from income in the first scenario and are very volatile. They are not good representations of value creation. In the second scenario, cash flows and accruals-based income measures are equivalent.

Does the above unequivocally support the use of accruals in making earnings more useful in the decision models of investors? The short answer is "yes"; after all, accruals is what makes accounting *accounting* and not *cash counting*. But because accruals are subject to much discretion (as stated above, they are "subjective"), unintentional measurement errors as well as intentional biases will cause their quality to vary. Meanwhile, cash flows are by no means useless, and the cash flow statement should not be underestimated as a tool for discovering biases in accruals (see, for instance, Ohlson and Aier, 2009) or any high-quality textbook on *Financial Statement Analysis*). As we now proceed with various earnings properties, we see how one may capture variations in the quality of accruals and, in turn, the quality of earnings.

7.1.1 Earnings persistence

Earnings persistence is a measure of how earnings from one year are carried forward into the next; that is, it is a measure of how sustainable earnings are or, in yet other terms, to what extent they are recurring (see Text Box 7.1). It is argued that persistence indicates high

Text Box 7.1 **Technical explanation of earnings persistence**

The measurement of persistence may be expressed in a regression model (Freeman et al., 1982):

$$Earnings_t = \alpha + \gamma\, Earnings_{t-1} + \varepsilon_t$$

where γ measures persistence, *α* is an intercept and ε is simply a random error term. In other words, persistence is the slope coefficient from a regression of current earnings (*t*) on lagged earnings (*t*–1). The model represents an autoregressive process, which means that the dependent variable (current earnings) depends linearly on previous values of itself (past earnings), plus a random term.

quality in that firms with more persistent earnings have a more sustainable cash flow stream, which makes them more useful for discounted cash flow-based equity valuation models commonly used by investors.

Furthermore, a study by Sloan (1996), in which earnings are broken down into accruals and cash flows, sheds light on the difference in persistence between the two components, with cash flows being more persistent than accruals. Operating and short-term accruals are in turn less persistent than financial and long-term accruals, respectively. Low persistence of accruals is thought to be explained by measurement difficulties as well as performance-related explanations, such as growth.

The consequences of persistence have been studied with respect to equity markets. Sloan (1996) shows that the difference in persistence between accruals and cash flows is not fully understood by the market, causing high-accruals firms to be relatively overvalued compared to low-accruals firms. More specifically, securities are assigned to different portfolios based on the magnitude of accruals in earnings. A hedge portfolio strategy that takes long positions in low-accruals portfolios and short positions in high-accruals portfolios (and takes riskiness into account) yields significantly positive abnormal returns.[6] This has been referred to as the **accruals anomaly** in the literature (see Chapter 3 for a closer description of capital market anomalies) and is evidence of the existence of market inefficiencies. Although abnormal returns have been reduced over the years, they still remain even after accounting for risk and transaction costs (unlike the post-earnings announcement drift anomaly, of which there is less evidence).

Because of the maintained assumption that persistence of earnings is useful for equity valuation, persistence is considered an earnings quality proxy. The problem with this metric, however, is that it depends on fundamental performance and type of firm. Furthermore, type

6 *Hedging* is a common term in finance and is nothing but a type of insurance against loss. Hedging a portfolio means that the investor offsets the positions in that portfolio with investments that are inversely related to the original investments. Different type of *derivative instruments* normally fulfill this criterion, including options, swaps and futures. Taking a *long position* in an instrument simply means buying or owning it. Taking a *short position*, meanwhile, is more complex, involves more risk and is done when the price of a security is expected to drop. It involves borrowing the instrument from a broker (at a fee, of course), selling it, buying it back after the price has gone down (thus profiting from the difference in price) and returning it to the broker.

of industry, product type, competition, capital intensity and firm size may affect persistence and thus add noise to the measure. Additionally, persistence is not immune to earnings management devices; that is, it may be created artificially (at least in the short run).

Persistence of earnings is not specified as an explicit quality criterion by the IASB. However, to the extent that persistent earnings are more relevant to investors, persistence will be an indicator of earnings quality. If investors can more easily predict future earnings and thus make better investment decisions, persistent earnings are also more useful earnings.

7.1.2 Earnings smoothness

Another feature of earnings that has been considered a quality indicator is earnings **smoothness**. In general, smooth earnings are the result of applying accrual accounting to improve decision usefulness. The use of accruals is meant to ensure that accounting better captures the creation of value, by shifting the recognition of revenues and expenses to periods in which services and goods are indeed received or provided, rather than allowing cash payments and receipts to determine the apparent value of operations. Because of the accruals component, earnings are in their nature smoother than cash flows. Smooth earnings sound desirable, since they reflect the smoothing effect of the accruals function. However, smooth*ing* tends to imply undesirable, unwarranted or abnormal smoothness brought about artificially. Hence, earnings smoothing has negative connotations.

Earnings smoothing may seem highly reminiscent of the earnings persistence concept. After all, smooth earnings should in general be more persistent. What sets them apart, however, is that while we defined persistence in terms of how earnings behave over time, smoothing has to do with how earnings relate to an external benchmark. While smoothing and persistence will commonly be correlated, the difference between the two is revealed through their empirical constructs. More specifically, smoothing is typically measured as the ratio of cash flow variability (variance) to earnings variability (variance):

$$\frac{\text{var(CF)}}{\text{var}(Earnings)} \qquad (7.1)$$

Since cash flows are the part of earnings that do not involve accruals, they are considered a useful reference point. Whenever earnings variability differs from cash flow variability, accruals must have been used; a high ratio indicates a high level of smoothing accruals.

There is somewhat mixed evidence of whether smoothing really constitutes a good measure of earnings quality (or rather the lack of it). For example, research has shown value relevance to be decreasing in the magnitude of income smoothing, whereas stock returns have been shown to increase with smoothing. Since a high value relevance of earnings and high stock returns are both considered "a good thing," and they relate to smoothing in opposite ways, this may be used to point to the difficulties in knowing the nature of the smoothing. By referring to the "nature" of earnings smoothing, one is implying that, just like when persistence is concerned, different smoothing levels may be justified depending on the context. It has been suggested that smoothing may be categorized as being *natural*, *real* or *artificial* (Lapointe-Antunes et al., 2006). "Natural" reflects smooth income-generation in certain industries and businesses. At one end of the spectrum, one finds cash-only businesses (with no prepaid [i.e., accrued] expenses and no accrued [i.e., deferred] income); at the other end of the spectrum, one finds, for instance, real estate and construction businesses. "Real" reflects smoothness achieved through operating decisions and the timing of these. Finally, "artificial" is an accounting device. Artificial smoothing may originate in classification changes or timing alterations (classificatory or inter-temporal). Whether income smoothing is perceived as a good or bad thing thus depends on the nature of the smoothing (see also Text Box 7.2).

Text Box 7.2 **Smoothing in the banking industries—good or bad?**

By timing the provisions for credit losses, banks have been shown to smooth earnings (Ahmed et al., 1999; Fonseca and González, 2008; Liu and Ryan, 2006). Normally, this would be taken as a sign of low earnings quality. This is likely to be true if users of financial statements are equity investors. Because earnings volatility may be an indicator of high risk, firms may be motivated to hide part of operating and cash flow volatility by smoothing income. Provided that individual investors have diversification possibilities, artificial smoothing is thus not desirable (e.g., Dechow et al., 2010). Meanwhile, governments have no diversification possibilities and asymmetric exposure to the performance of banks, as they may have to cover losses to protect taxpayers and secure the systemic role of banks. They may therefore benefit from income smoothing if this is the outcome of timelier recognition of losses. According to Laeven and Majnoni (2003), banks tend to make provisions too late, when in economic downturns, instead of when faced with favorable conditions. Beatty and Liao (2011) show that later recognition of credit losses has a real economic effect, in that it leads to more procyclical lending practices by banks. By contrast, smoothing can promote counter-cyclicality and help reduce risk-taking behavior as banks build reserves in good times and reverse them in bad times (Bushman and Williams, 2012; Wall and Koch, 2000). The findings by Gebhardt and Novotny-Farkas (2011), that smoothing decreases after IFRS adoption, may then be interpreted as a decrease rather than an increase in earnings quality.

7.1.3 Abnormal accruals

So far, we have discussed the role of accruals and their relation to cash flows in the context of persistence and smoothing. In so doing, we have treated all accruals equally (with the exception of the reference to "artificial smoothing"). However, researchers have for many decades attempted to distinguish between high-quality accruals and low-quality accruals. Whereas the former reflect fundamental performance and are referred to as normal accruals, low-quality or **abnormal accruals** are accruals that do *not* reflect performance, either due to measurement errors or intentional distortions. Since they are not informative concerning the underlying economics of the firm in a given period, they reduce earnings quality. Penman (2012) defines high-quality earnings as those that do not **reverse**. Using income-*increasing* accruals to boost profits in one period *must* result in income-*decreasing* accruals in future periods. That is the nature of accrual accounting—earnings cannot be inflated forever, simply shifted between periods. The question is simply how long it takes before "reality" catches up with opportunistic managers.

How, then, does one tell whether a firm's accruals are reasonable or normal? Different *regression* models aiming to gauge accruals quality exist in the empirical literature. They share a couple of common features:

- the dependent variable captures total and actual accruals in the firm at a given time.
- the independent variables represent accounting items that should affect the size of the total accruals.
- the unexplained variation in actual accruals is captured by the regression model's error terms (or the residuals). The size or variance of the errors is the measure of the abnormal accruals.

We present the most prevalent of these models below.

In the Jones (1991) model, total accruals are modeled as being a function of the change in revenues and property, plant and equipment (PP&E), see Text Box 7.3. More specifically, variations in total accruals explained by variations in these two factors—changes in revenues and PP&E—are believed to capture normal or **non-discretionary** accruals, whereas variations in total accruals that cannot be explained by variations in these two factors must be due to the use of **discretionary** accruals.[7] The intuition behind this is that revenues are thought to capture the underlying economic environment of the firm, or actual performance, while PP&E controls for non-discretionary depreciation expenses found in total accruals. Total accruals, meanwhile, reflect items such as depreciation and amortization expenses and changes in working capital (such as increases or decreases in inventory or accounts payable). If a firm experiences an increase in its total accruals but no corresponding increase in the change in revenues or its PP&E, this must be due to discretionary accruals.

In the so-called *modified* Jones model (Dechow et al., 1995), total accruals are also a function of the change in revenues and PP&E, but revenues in this model are adjusted for the growth in credit sales (Text Box 7.3). Dechow et al. (1995) argue that given that exercising discretion in the recognition of credit sales is easier compared to cash sales, the modified Jones model should be more successful at detecting earnings management than the original model.

Text Box 7.3 **Technical explanation of the Jones model and the modified Jones model**

The Jones (1991) model may be stated as:

$$TA = \alpha + \beta_1 \Delta Rev + \beta_2 \text{ PPE} + \varepsilon, \qquad (7.2)$$

where *TA* is total accruals, ΔRev is sales growth and *PPE* is property, plant and equipment. Meanwhile, the expanded model by Dechow et al. (1995) (the modified Jones model) is stated as:

7 The original meaning of the word "discretionary" does not actually imply anything "bad," but reflects the use of discretion or judgment. However, "discretionary" is often used to mean "opportunistic" in the literature. Unless explicitly stated, we use "discretionary" and "opportunistic" interchangeably to reflect the vocabulary of the literature cited.

$$TA = \alpha + \beta_1 (\Delta Rev - \Delta Rec) + \beta_2 \text{PPE} + \varepsilon, \tag{7.3}$$

so that the latter excludes growth in credit sales (ΔRec) in years identified as manipulation years. In both cases, abnormal accruals are the residuals (ε) estimated from each model. That is, all accruals *not* explained by the listed factors must not be normal but rather distortions (i.e., discretionary accruals).

As pointed out in Dechow et al. (2010), equation (7.3) lowers the chances of identifying abnormal accruals as normal (i.e., making Type II errors in hypothesis testing), but both models suffer from another potential error in that they identify some accruals as abnormal when they are in fact normal (i.e., Type I error in hypothesis testing). This is evidenced by the fact that the residuals tend to be positively correlated with total accruals and earnings performance.

Another model, proposed by Dechow and Dichev (2002), only focuses on short-term accruals and thus the change in working capital. The authors theorize that the change in working capital is a function of cash flows in the previous period, cash flows in the current period and cash flows in the immediate future period. Expressed in a simpler way, the change in working capital is equal to the sum of operating cash flows (Text Box 7.4). This appears entirely reasonable, considering that working capital is a current item that should be transformed into cash flows within one period (normally defined as 12 months).

Text Box 7.4 **Technical explanation of the Dechow and Dichev model**

The actual regression equation is formulated as:

$$\Delta WC = b_0 + b_1 CFO_{t-1} + b_2 CFO_t + b_3 CFO_{t+1} + \varepsilon_t, \tag{7.4}$$

It thus focuses on the matching function of accruals to cash flows, operationalized as the change in working capital, ΔWC, and cash flow from operations, CFO, respectively. More specifically, CFO_{t-1} represents deferred income and accrued expenses and CFO_{t+1} represents accrued income and deferred (prepaid) expenses.

Abnormal accruals are measured in this model as the standard deviation (or absolute size) of the residuals, $\sigma(\varepsilon)$. A higher standard deviation means lower accrual quality, the reasoning being that it is when the accruals not captured by the model vary considerably that one may suspect errors (i.e., when the residuals have a high standard deviation).

A weakness of this definition of abnormal accruals is that the standard deviation of the residuals is partly driven by the natural variability in accruals, meaning that underlying volatility in earnings leads to lower-quality earnings by design.

The ability of this model to explain variations in accruals is higher than that of the Jones models, suggesting that it constitutes an improvement to the modeling of earnings quality using abnormal accruals measures. It is found that larger abnormal accruals, as defined by Dechow and Dichev (2002), are correlated with less persistent earnings, longer operating cycles, larger accruals and greater volatility in earnings, accruals and cash flows. Firms with larger abnormal accruals are also smaller and more likely to report a loss. This supports the claim that the model by Dechow and Dichev (2002) captures some aspect of earnings quality. An obvious and important limitation, however, is that the model does not capture accrual distortions caused by long-term accruals. For instance, PP&E or goodwill impairments are not reflected in the model. In order to improve upon the above-mentioned models, McNichols (2002) combines the Jones (1991) model with the Dechow and Dichev (2002) model. The model by McNichols (2002) states that the change in working capital is a function not only of total operating cash flows, but also of sales growth and property, plant and equipment (Text Box 7.5).

This is by no means an exhaustive list of models that have been used in the literature, but is an attempt to introduce the reader to some of the most influential ones.

Text Box 7.5 **Technical explanation of the McNichols model**

The regression model suggested by McNichols (2002) is:

$$\Delta WC_t = b_0 + b_1 CFO_{t-1} + b_2 CFO_t + b_3\ CFO_{t+1} + b_4 \Delta Sales_t + b_5 PPE_t + \varepsilon_t \tag{7.5}$$

In an empirical application, Francis et al. (2005) use the McNichols (2002) model and further break down the variation of the residuals (σ(ε)) into "innate estimation errors" and "discretionary estimation errors." That is, some of the variation can be explained by fundamental performance (product cycle, sales, etc); in other words, innate estimation errors. Only the remainder of the variation is considered strictly discretionary. This reduces potential overstatement of abnormal accruals. The decomposition by Francis et al. (2005) looks as follows:

$$\begin{aligned}\sigma(\varepsilon)_t = \gamma_0 + \gamma_1 Size_t + \gamma_2 \sigma(CFO)_t + \gamma_3 \sigma(Sales)_t \\ + \gamma_4 OperCycle_t + \gamma_5 NegEarn_t + v_t,\end{aligned} \tag{7.6}$$

where "the predicted value of σ(ε) represents the quality of the accruals system to capture the firm's fundamental performance and the residual v represents discretionary accrual quality" (Dechow et al., 2010, p.360). In the above model, factors that reflect the firm's fundamental performance include firm size *Size*, as measured by the firm's total assets; volatility in cash flow from operations (σ(*CFO*)) and volatility in sales (σ(*Sales*)), the length of the firm's operating cycle (*OperCycle*); and incidence of negative earnings realizations (*NegEarn*).

Finally, an important feature of these models is that they are often estimated at the industry-level, meaning that what is considered "normal" and "abnormal" is determined by industry standards. However, the coefficient estimates are then assumed constant within an industry, and large residuals for a given firm may therefore be due to inappropriate industry classification and not due to errors or earnings management. In some industries, many firm observations may lie far from the regression line, meaning that the model has a poor fit and large residuals in general. This is a concern for industries that, for example, experience large growth. In these cases, one is likely to overestimate the abnormal accruals.

What evidence, then, is there that these models actually capture earnings quality? By looking at the association between accruals quality and other variables one expects to be correlated with accruals quality, one may infer that a given model has some validity. For example, using the modified Jones model, Heninger (2001) shows that auditor litigation is more frequent in cases where firms have income-increasing (positive) abnormal accruals, which the author takes to mean that auditors are being held accountable for low earnings quality and should therefore pay attention to income-increasing abnormal accruals. The estimation of abnormal accruals was done using a number of different accruals models in a study showing consistent results in relation to earnings persistence. Whereas Sloan (1996) showed that accruals were mispriced due to investors overestimating their persistence, Xie (2001) shows that consistent with their discretionary nature, abnormal accruals are even less persistent and suffer from more severe market mispricing. However, one study that directly tests the ability of various accruals models to detect earnings management (as indicated by qualified audit opinions) shows that only two of the four are successful (Bartov et al., 2000a). Notably, a positive association between abnormal accruals and the likelihood of, for example, receiving a qualified audit opinion need not mean that the accruals model is valid. Butler et al. (2004), in contrast to several previous studies, find no evidence that firms with non-clean audit opinions manage earnings more than firms with clean opinions. They point to the misspecification problem of several of the common accruals models and that financial distress-related accruals will tend to be classified as abnormal, thus questioning the results by Bartov et al. (2000a). The literature is constantly evaluating and re-evaluating the various accruals models.

Accruals quality and the capital market In research in general, as well as in this book in particular, the effect of accruals quality on the market is of interest. As we saw in Chapter 6, much empirical research supports the idea that disclosure quality reduces the cost of capital of firms. Studies looking at earnings quality and the cost of capital are based on the same line of argument. Francis et al. (2005, p.324) write:

> [O]ur broad-sample evidence supports the view that the capital market consequences of differences in accruals quality arise because accruals quality proxies for information risk, a risk factor that cannot be diversified away in equilibrium (Easley and O'Hara, 2004; O'Hara, 2003; Leuz and Verrecchia, 2004). In contrast to other firm characteristics that have been shown by prior research to empirically predict cross-sectional differences in costs of capital, notably size and the book-to-market ratio, accruals quality maps into a theoretically grounded cost of capital determinant: information risk.

As stated, Francis et al. (2005) (FLOS) motivate their empirical study based on the theoretical modeling by Easley and O'Hara (2004). For reasons laid out in Chapter 6, however, these types of empirical findings have been questioned.

> Whether accounting quality in general, and accruals quality (AQ) in particular, affects the cost of capital is an important subject for researchers and practitioners. While the intuition of many people is that information matters for the capital markets, there is no well-accepted theory that proves that information risk is not diversifiable. In light of recent research, the theoretical case for information effects on the cost of capital has grown weaker. Lambert et al. (2007) show that the information effect in Easley and O'Hara (2004) is diversifiable. They also seem to nuance Leuz and Verrecchia (2005) in the sense that information risk does not affect expected returns directly but may affect them indirectly through a link with beta.

> On the other hand, in contrast to the theory literature, a variety of existing empirical work, including FLOS (2004, 2005), presents almost unanimous evidence that accounting quality matters for expected returns. Accordingly, it seems important that theoretical and empirical researchers come to more agreement on these issues before they are considered closed. (Core et al., 2008, p. 20)

Core et al. (2008, p.21) further point out that "the consequences of AQ may well be manifested in other risk factors even though AQ itself is not a separate risk factor." Remember that in "Lambert et al.'s (2007) model [... accounting information affects] the cost of capital by influencing investors' assessments of the covariance of firm cash flows with those of the market, and therefore by affecting firm beta." In determining the effect of accounting on the cost of capital, researchers are encouraged to explore the underlying factors that determine accruals quality, disclosure quality and information risk.

7.1.4 Earnings timeliness

Another important property of earnings is argued to be their *timeliness*. Timeliness of financial reporting, which is considered an enhancing characteristic of financial reporting according to the Conceptual Framework, is said to be important since timely information generally conveys more decision-relevant information (see also Text Box 7.2). Actual timeliness has to do with how quickly information is provided about some underlying economic event, but since this is not observable, one has to invent a proxy for this event. **Earnings timeliness** in research reflects the extent to which current earnings capture the information impounded in current stock returns (see Text Box 7.6). The underlying assumption, of course, is that the stock market is (reasonably) efficient and therefore useful to benchmark against. But if the market is assumed to be efficient, why be interested in timely accounting earnings in the first place? Why can market participants not simply rely on stock returns? Bushman et al. (2004) suggest that accounting information is necessary in identifying the *source* of changes in a firm's stock price. Note that while accounting information comes as a result of choices that are under the control of management, stock prices may vary, sometimes considerably, depending on market conditions. Hence, market participants may use accounting information in order to distinguish events that are under the control of management from events that are uncontrollable and affected by economy-wide conditions (such as the recent financial crisis in 2007–2008).

Is there a downside to timeliness? One may want to consider what would happen if accounting earnings were *perfectly* timely and thus reflected *all* the information underlying stock prices. Would this maximize earnings relevance? Or would earnings instead become completely *irrelevant* since they are identical to stock returns and may thus be considered superfluous? One thing that is certain is that such earnings would be partly speculative as they take into account value changes following from unverifiable, future events. Incorporating a large amount of speculation into the earnings number would likely be undesirable. Investors need accounting to verify the information set underlying the stock price changes.

Different components of earnings have varying levels of timeliness due to prudence (or conservatism) in financial reporting (read more about *prudence* in Part II). The conservative basis in accounting is defined by Basu (1997) as a higher degree of verification connected to the recording of gains compared to the recording of losses. For example, unrealized losses—which constitute bad news—are recognized when they take place, whereas gains from increases in values—which constitute good news—are not recognized until they are realized. Given that several accounting standards are defined based on conservative principles (e.g., IAS 36 *Impairment of Assets* and IAS 37 *Provisions, Contingent Liabilities and Contingent Assets*), it is expected that the recognition of bad news tends to be more timely than the recognition of good news. Conservatism is seen as advantageous by standard-setters to the extent that relatively more timely recognition of bad news alleviates information asymmetry problems and restricts undue optimism by managers. The reason why this latter assumption is reasonable is that managers have significant incentives to hide or distort bad news, while they are likely to be naturally inclined to disclose good news in a more timely manner. Therefore, high timeliness of earnings, and particularly conservative financial reports, can contribute to a more transparent information environment.

Text Box 7.6 **Technical explanation of the Basu model**

The model developed by Basu (1997) is broadly used in the accounting literature for measuring the extent of timeliness and conservatism in accounting earnings.

$$\Delta EARN_t = b_0 + b_1 NEG_t + b_2 RET_t + b_3 NEG_t \times RET_t + \varepsilon_t, \tag{7.7}$$

In the above model, $\Delta EARN_t$ is changes in earnings per share scaled by prior year-end price. NEG_t is a dummy variable equal to one for firms with negative returns and zero otherwise. RET_t is annual stock returns. The variable of interest is $NEG_t \times RET_t$ and its coefficient b_3. While b_2 measures the responsiveness of earnings to stock returns in the positive returns sample, b_3 measures the difference in responsiveness of earnings to stock returns between the positive and negative returns samples. Basu (1997) finds that earnings are about four and half times more sensitive to negative returns than they are to positive returns. That is, earnings are more timely in reflecting "bad news" than "good news."

7.1.5 Target beating

Finally, we recognize *earnings that just meet or beat a target* as a type of property of earnings that has been used as a warning sign of low-quality earnings. Earnings targets can either be targets set by the firm itself or by external parties, such as analysts. Evidence suggests that whenever such targets are *just* met, this may be attributed to target beating behavior achieved by using manipulation of accruals. A universal earnings target is simply to achieve a positive net income. Because it is that much more preferable to report a small profit than a small loss, the observed "kink" in the distribution of earnings around zero (see Figure 7.1) has suggested to researchers that firms manage their earnings out of the red (i.e., they deliberately avoid negative bottom line numbers).

While, according to a study by Dechow et al. (2003), *small but positive profits* cannot

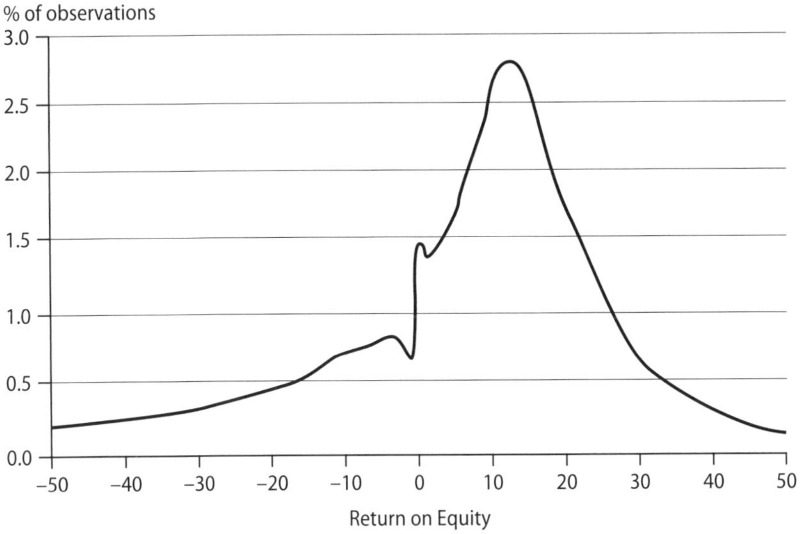

Figure 7.1 Kinky earnings. This figure shows net income at the fiscal year end, scaled by the market value of equity at the beginning of the year. The "kink" in the frequency diagram points to an end-of-fiscal-year effect, as such a distribution cannot be found for the first, second and third quarters of the year. Source: Jacob and Jorgensen (2007)

be linked to discretionary accruals, other studies find small profits to be more common in fourth-quarter reporting when pressures to beat targets are the highest (Jacob and Jorgensen, 2007) and in the absence of high-effort audits (measured as fewer audit hours) (see Caramanis and Lennox, 2008).

Even though target beating behavior may be observed on an aggregate level, when looking at a large sample of firms, it is difficult to detect low earnings quality—brought on by target beating—in individual cases. A firm could have a near-zero result for completely legitimate reasons. Of course, the same applies to the other measures discussed here (earnings persistence, earnings timeliness, etc.). Interestingly, consistent target beating has been shown to be linked to a *higher* stock valuation (Bhojraj et al., 2009), which suggests that the market is not concerned with target beating or that it is evidence of earnings management. Rather, investors behave as if they are pleased when firms just beat their targets. In sum, although there is evidence that small profits may indicate lower-quality accounting, target beating is a noisy measure of earnings quality.

Text Box 7.7 **Earnings quality and accounting standards**

Changes in earnings quality and the incidence of earnings management before and after IFRS adoption have been popular topics for research over the past decade. Papers include those studying effects of voluntary as well as mandatory adoption of IFRS—worldwide (e.g., Jeanjean and Stolowy, 2008; Goodwin et al., 2008; Daske et al., 2008) and in the European Union (e.g., Callao and Jarne, 2010; Aharony et al., 2010; Chen et al., 2010; Cormier et al., 2009; Barth et al., 2008; Paananen and Lin, 2009)

Evidence shows that income smoothing using discretionary accruals is lower for firms that follow IFRS or US GAAP compared to firms using other local GAAP, as well as for firms with a generally higher level of disclosure (Lapointe-Antunes et al., 2006). The choice of accounting standard has more impact on earnings quality than the disclosure level *per se*. Also, investors place less value on discretionary accruals when firms disclose more or report according to IFRS or US GAAP, which suggests that these firms are more transparent and, consequently, earnings smoothing is more easily detected. Meanwhile, earnings management, as defined by the reporting of a greater proportion of small profits to small losses, is found to increase or remain unaffected by mandatory adoption of IFRS in Australia, France and the UK (Jeanjean and Stolowy, 2008). Increased earnings smoothing and less timely recognition of losses are also found to be features of the post-adoption period in Chen et al. (2010) and Ahmed et al. (2013). However, they show that earnings management toward a target decreases (Chen et al., 2010) or is unaffected (Ahmed et al., 2013). Whereas discretionary accruals are found by Chen et al. (2010) to decrease after EU adoption of IFRS, Ahmed et al. (2013) observe more aggressive accruals.

A well-cited paper on the voluntary adoption of IFRS, which also uses several of the same quality indicators, is Barth et al. (2008b). The quality measures used include earnings management using accruals and timely loss recognition. They find that quality improves in the post-adoption period, although the financial reporting standards *per se* cannot be proven to be the reason; rather, incentives that adopting firms may have could drive results. To at least partially control for this, variables such as growth, leverage and financing needs are introduced. The hypothesis that the improvement is in fact associated with a switch to IFRS is based on the idea that principles-based standards, which characterize IFRS, promote higher-quality reporting. Half of their measures support their hypothesis, where one aspect of earnings management is the frequency with which a firm reports a small positive net income and another is earnings smoothing. Another highly cited paper provides evidence from Germany and concludes that voluntary adoption of IFRS is not associated with less earnings management (Tendeloo and Vanstraelen, 2005).

7.1.6 Which firms have higher earnings quality?

Empirical research on earnings quality has shown that certain firm characteristics can help predict whether a firm will have higher or lower quality. A couple of examples are provided here:

- *Firm growth* and high investment levels may lead to lower earnings quality due to lower persistence in fast-growing earnings and due to higher measurement errors (in accruals). The proxies that are used for measuring firm growth are sales growth or net operating asset growth (see Nissim and Penman, 2001).
- There is mixed evidence with respect to *firm size* (measured as the logarithm of total sales, total assets, total revenue, or the market capitalization). Large firms are generally believed to have better internal controls over financial reporting (Ball and Foster, 1982), thus producing higher quality earnings. However, large firms are also believed to have an incentive to bias earnings downward or smooth earnings in order to avoid political costs (Moses, 1987). That is, firms with monopolistic tendencies risk legal action if they are "too" profitable.

- *Leverage*, which indicates the extent to which firms are debt-financed, is also found to be associated with earnings quality, albeit mostly in a negative direction. For example, highly levered firms may manipulate earnings through income increasing abnormal accruals to avoid violating debt covenants (Labelle, 1990; Daley and Vigeland, 1983).
- *Firm performance* and especially *weak* firm performance, as measured by lower financial ratios or a higher incidence of losses, is found to be associated with lower earnings quality (Balsam et al., 1995). This is simply because poorly performing firms have more incentives to engage in various forms of earnings management to show more positive prospects.

The above firm-specific determinants of earning quality are almost always present as control variables in earnings quality models. A considerable number of other determinants of earnings quality are related to managerial incentives (or mechanisms to limit them) and therefore mainly discussed in Chapter 8 on incentives (see also Text box 7.7).

7.2 External indicators of earnings quality

Below, we examine a number of common external indicators of earnings quality. These require information outside of financial statements, such as equity market data or analyst report data.

7.2.1 Value relevance

A firm's equity represents the net present value of discounted future cash flows to equity-holders. Whereas the per-share *book* value of equity is an accounting measure of this amount, the stock price (i.e., market value of equity per share) is the equivalent *market* measure. Earnings, in turn, measure changes in the book value, whereas stock returns measure changes in the market value. Being different measures of the same thing, it is desirable for them to correlate. In measuring the quality of earnings, in the literature it has therefore been of interest to observe whether and how movements in stock prices or price derivatives (such as stock returns) *covary* with accounting numbers. A high correlation between book values and market measures is referred to as earnings or book values having (high) **value relevance**.

It is important to realize that although earnings are derived from changes in the book value of equity and the two measures should covary, the book value need not approximate the market value in order to be useful. Certainly, market values are typically (much) higher than book values. The simple explanation for this is that accounting conservatism and restrictive asset and revenue recognition criteria prevent certain values from appearing in the books. By contrast, investors incorporate expectations about future earnings in their valuation of a firm and its equity. If book values are close to market values, it typically means that there are few growth opportunities in a particular firm. Alternatively, book values will approach market values if liberal (the opposite of conservative) accounting or fair values have been used (see more on bases for measurement in Chapter 10). If current earnings and thus book values reflected future growth, the accounts would likely be too speculative and lose their ability to serve as “anchors” for investors (see discussion in Penman, 2012). Remember, investors attempt to gauge the intrinsic, or underlying, value of firms and book values may help them in this work. Meanwhile, the *market* value of equity reflects investors’ average perception of the intrinsic value of equity, but it is not the same as the underlying value itself.

As soon as market data became more readily accessible in the 1960s due to growing digitalized databases, accounting and finance researchers initiated more widespread investigations into the potential uses of accounting data, and specifically earnings, in the market. At the time, there were doubts as to whether accounting was useful or relevant *at all* for market participants, given that it competes with other sources of information. In an era of normative, policy-oriented research, it was argued that given all the choices that went into establishing the earnings components, the final earnings number is really nothing more than the sum of “two apples and three pears” (Watts and Zimmerman, 1986). That is, it is useless. There was little empirical data at the time to prove or disprove these claims. However, this soon changed as price data started to become available to US researchers in the 1960s. As shown in the seminal papers by Ball and Brown (1968) and Beaver (1968) in accounting, and Fama et al. (1969) in finance, earnings announcements *do* produce market reactions, albeit with greater or smaller delays. What we now take for granted was considered important findings, such as when the aforementioned studies showed that earnings announcements indeed caused various market responses. Since then, studies on investor responsiveness to earnings releases have been too numerous to count (see, for example, Harris et al., 1994; Easton and Harris, 1991; Easton et al., 1992; Ohlson and Penman, 1992; Collins et al., 1997; Hung, 2001; Barth et al., 2008; Aharony et al., 2010).

Throughout the 1990s, the relationship between earnings and market returns was a popular topic of study for financial accounting researchers and the term *value relevance* was coined. The analytical work by Ohlson (1995) and Feltham and Ohlson (1995) constituted an important catalyst and laid the foundation (partly after the fact) for the empirical research that came at this time. They helped formalize the relationship between market values and earnings through a model specification that lent itself to empirical testing using linear regression techniques (see Text Box 7.8).

Value relevance studies come in various forms, with three categories having been identified by Holthausen and Watts (2001):

- **Relative association** studies: These compare equivalent accounting numbers produced using different methods or GAAP with respect to a given market measure, in order to determine which accounting system is more value relevant, typically based on the statistical fit of the model (e.g., using R-squared).
- **Incremental association** studies: These are more concerned with long-term relationships between accounting numbers and market values (prices or returns). If the regression parameters representing a given item are different from zero or some specified value based on theory, the accounting measure is correlated with the market measure and value relevance is consequently high. These are also referred to as *long-window* studies.

- **Marginal information content** studies: These are set up as **event studies** or **short-windowed studies**, where the event in question is the release of some accounting number. Value relevance is deemed high if there is a significant market reaction to the information release, as this would indicate a high information content in the disclosure.

Whereas the first two focus on the *contemporaneous* association between market values and accounting numbers, the third looks at the *response* of one to the other (meaning that they are measured sequentially). The above setups have been popular whenever it has been of interest to compare different standards, such as the effect of IFRS adoption (e.g., Aharony et al., 2010; Barth et al., 2008), in order to estimate the market effect of changes to individual standards (Davis-Friday et al., 1999; Amir, 1993; Barth et al., 1992; Choi et al., 1997) (see Text Box 7.10) or to evaluate the relevance of different income measures (Dhaliwal et al., 1999; Biddle and Choi, 2006). In all of the above types of studies, the inference is that the higher the value relevance, the higher the usefulness of the accounting numbers. Even so, does value relevance imply quality?

Text Box 7.8 **The Ohlson model**

One of the most influential papers in financial accounting is bound to be *Earnings, book values and dividends in equity valuation* (Ohlson, 1995). Ohlson relates market value to current and future earnings, book values and dividends and shows how these are *linearly* interrelated. Some of the assumptions made are related to the nature of accounting. One is that the **clean surplus relation** holds. This means that any changes to a firm's book value not attributable to dividend payments (broadly defined as all transactions with owners) must pass through the income statement.

The clean surplus relation may be expressed mathematically as:

$$y_t - y_{t-1} = x_t - d_t \tag{7.8}$$

where y_t and y_{t-1} are book value of equity in the current and previous periods, respectively, x_t is current earnings and d_t is current dividends. The equation thus reads: the change in book value between the current and previous period is equal to current earnings less current dividends.

In deriving a model of firm valuation, *abnormal* (also *residual* or *excess*) earnings are used. Abnormal earnings are those exceeding shareholders' required return on their investment and may be written mathematically as:

$$x_t^e = x_t - (r - 1)y_{t-1} \tag{7.9}$$

where x_t^e are abnormal earnings in the current period and $(r - 1)$ is the required rate of return (in the model, investors are risk-neutral and the required return in question is the *risk-free rate*). That is, actual current earnings less the required return on the beginning-of-year book value of equity gives abnormal earnings. This is easy to remember if one thinks of book value of equity as the investment made by shareholders. Note that abnormal earnings can take on both positive and negative values.

Another assumption is that firm value may be expressed using the dividend discount model (commonly used for asset valuation in the field of finance), as follows:

$$P_t = \sum_{\tau=1}^{\infty} \frac{d_{t+\tau}}{r^{\tau}} \tag{7.10}$$

That is, the value (price) of a firm (its equity) is equal to the sum of all discounted expected future dividends (and r is the cost of capital). Using this and the above equations and assumptions, it can be shown that the market value of a firm's equity can be expressed in terms of the current book value of equity plus discounted expected future abnormal earnings (rather than dividends):

$$\begin{aligned} y_t - y_{t-1} &= x_t - d_t \Rightarrow \\ x_t &= y_t - y_{t-1} + d_t \end{aligned} \tag{7.11}$$

Plugging the above into the excess earnings equation, we have that:

$$\begin{aligned} x_t^e &= y_t - y_{t-1} + d_t - (r-1)y_{t-1} \Rightarrow \\ x_t^e &= y_t - y_{t-1} + d_t - ry_{t-1} + y_{t-1} \Rightarrow \\ x_t^e &= y_t + d_t - ry_{t-1} \Rightarrow \\ d_t &= x_t^e - y_t + ry_{t-1} \end{aligned} \tag{7.12}$$

Plugging the above into the dividend discount equation, we have that:

$$P_t = \underbrace{y_t}_{\text{book value of equity}} + \underbrace{\sum_{\tau=1} \frac{x_{t+\tau}^e}{r^{\tau}}}_{\text{premium over book value}} \tag{7.13}$$

(provided that the expected future discounted value of the book value of equity approaches zero at an infinitely distant horizon, $y_{t+\tau}/r^{\tau} \rightarrow 0$ as $\tau \rightarrow \infty$). This is referred to as the **residual income model** (or excess earnings model).

It is pointed out that it was shown early on by Edwards and Bell (1961) and Peasnell (1981, 1982) (see Ohlson, 1995) that the clean surplus relation leads to this result. The importance of this result cannot be overemphasized, as it clarifies the role of accounting numbers in a valuation setting and ensures that one does not need to predict future dividends to arrive at firm value, only future excess earnings. This is an attractive notion in light of the notion that dividends represent *distribution* of value, while excess earnings may be said to capture actual value *creation*. Value is not created unless returns exceed the required. The above model shows this intuitively: the market value of equity is equal to the book value of equity plus all excess earnings. An investor is willing to pay a premium, which is more than the book value of equity, only if future excess earnings are expected to be made. This has influenced much of the thinking in the subject of *financial statement analysis* (see for example Penman, 2012).

The actual contribution of the Ohlson (1995) paper comes in the next step, which, using the residual income model, provides a conceptual basis for empirical value relevance studies. This requires another assumption that is related to the behavior of excess earnings over time.

The assumption is that expected future excess earnings are a *linear function* of current excess earnings, other value-relevant information and some random factor. More specifically, the excess earnings should follow an autoregressive process, meaning that each value of excess earnings is linearly dependent on its previous values plus some random term. Under this assumption, one may show that expected future excess earnings may be replaced by an expression involving only current excess earnings. Value is expressed as:

$$P_t = y_t + \alpha_1 x_t^e + \alpha_2 v_t \tag{7.14}$$

where a_n are constants and v_t is other information. If indeed excess earnings follow an autoregressive process, then x_t^e already incorporates v_t, meaning that this term equals zero and drops out of the equation. The conclusion is that value is determined by current book value plus current excess earnings.

Finally, the assumption is made that dividends affect current book value but not current earnings. That is, dividends may be *paid out of* current earnings but do not affect calculations of current earnings. Current book value, however, is reduced by the amount of the dividend. Dividend irrelevancy, according to Modigliani and Miller (1958); Miller and Modigliani (1961), applies (i.e., one dollar of dividend today reduces market value by one dollar or, in other words, the reduction of book value by one dollar reduces the market value by the same amount). However, the total amount that investors receive is unaffected, since one adds the dividend payment to the market value of their equity holdings. Meanwhile, future earnings are affected negatively by dividend payments (since there is less equity in the firm left that may generate earnings). Note that while the book value and thus future earnings are affected by dividend payments, excess earnings are *un*affected—precisely the property that makes the measure so useful in the analysis.

A numerical example of this should convince the reader:

$$x_t^e = x_t - y_{t-1} r$$

Before any dividends, assume:

$$x_t^e = 24 - 200 \times 0.10 = 4$$

That is, the actual earnings are 24, the beginning-of-year book value is 200 and the required return *r* is 10%. The actual return is 24/200 = 12%. Assume a dividend of 40 is paid out of book value. Firms do not give up positive net present value (NPV) investment to pay dividends. This would indeed destroy value. Dividends are paid out of zero NPV assets (e.g., cash), which would have earned only *r* (10%).

$$x_t^e = 20 - 160 \cdot 0.10 = 4$$

Earnings in year *t* drops by 10% *times* 40 = 4 (and not by 12% × 40) because 40 of assets have been removed from the firm. That is, the book value drops by the amount of the dividend, but expected abnormal earnings are unaffected. Correspondingly, a valuation based on abnormal earnings also falls dollar for dollar. The above discussion relates to the key feature of the model—that neither current dividend nor future dividend policies affect expected excess earnings.

The impact of the Ohlson model on empirical research may be seen in the plethora of value relevance studies in the 1990s that benefited from theoretical justifications of the relevance of accounting numbers for equity valuation. For related model developments, see also Feltham and Ohlson (1995) and Penman and Sougiannis (1998).

How good a measure of accounting quality is value relevance? First, the contemporaneous association studies may seem a bit paradoxical. If the market's valuation is used as a benchmark against which one evaluates the accounting numbers, then it seems as if the market has little use for those numbers, thus rendering earnings irrelevant. That is, if market values *precede* book values and are good reflections of underlying or *intrinsic* economic values, how can book values or earnings be useful? Here, one might of course point to the corroboratory role of accounting. However, one should not interpret contemporaneous association studies so strictly. Market values need not precede book values. The question may simply be whether market returns respond to earnings over a time period, as the test does not preclude the issuance of interim numbers or other sources informing the market.

Event studies (marginal association studies) are perhaps the most straightforward to interpret, because if one assumes market efficiency in the semi-strong form, then an accounting event should bring about a response in the market if the information release is considered reliable and relevant. There is no paradox here since the cause and effect is fairly clear—accounting values *precede* market values. The main objection here would be the following: Could information not be relevant without a price revision taking place? Going back to the influential standard-setters' definition of relevance, one would answer "yes" to that question (see Chapter 5).

In attempting to empirically model relevance but also reliability (more recently "faithful representation"), value relevance has been widely used (see Text Box 7.9). This brings us to the second point of criticism. Although making normative suggestions based on positive research is often desirable, it is necessary to consider the specific context from which the findings originate; policy implications cannot be directly inferred from any observed statistical associations. Some researchers are more critical than others in this respect, with some highlighting that investors are not even the sole users of financial information, which is why one should not jump to conclusions regarding the desirability of a given accounting measure subjected to a value relevance study (see discussions in, for example, Beaver and Demski, 1974; Holthausen and Watts, 2001; Kothari, 2001). It is especially interesting to note that because market values reflect the net present value of cumulative future earnings, an accounting system achieving a near perfect value relevance "score" would likely have strayed from the widely accepted revenue recognition principle (see Lee, 1999). Thus, there may be a non-linear relationship between value relevance and quality, meaning that a perfect correlation between book values and market values is suboptimal. Barth et al. (2001a), meanwhile, defend the value relevance literature in arguing that it has helped operationalize difficult and abstract concepts advocated by standard-setters, such as relevance and reliability, and that although there *are* other users of accounting, this does not reduce the possible contributions of findings on value relevance in the context of equity markets.

The main criticism against value relevance studies, and which has probably made it lose its popularity over the years, is that the earnings-returns relationship is a noisy measure that fails to distinguish the accounting system from fundamental performance or other institutional factors (Dechow et al., 2010; Holthausen and Watts, 2001). It is especially problematic in studies doing country comparisons. That is, it may not be the quality of the accounts that differs between firms. Instead, the market response will vary between countries due to the fact that the return-generating process is different in different countries. If one compares the value relevance of different accounting regimes in different countries, one should assume that the markets are similar with respect to their efficiency. Variations in the ability of different markets to capture and reflect fundamental value will make it almost impossible to draw conclusions in heterogeneous macroeconomic settings or institutional environments. That is, you may not capture *earnings* at all, only *response* tendencies. Also, because stock prices reflect so many other factors than accounting data, the models may be misspecified and lead to incorrect inferences if the omitted factors (variables) are correlated systematically with the firm's earnings-generating process.[8] Overall, firms that score high on value relevance also score high on other earnings quality measures, suggesting that value relevance still *is* an acceptable—though flawed—proxy for quality. For example, consistent with accruals and cash flows having different levels of persistence and forecasting abilities regarding future (abnormal) earnings, the two earnings components also have different valuation implications (i.e., different earnings-returns relationships) (Barth et al., 1999). In general, all earnings quality measures discussed in this chapter have strengths and weaknesses, and the best approach is: 1) to consider their appropriateness in a given research setting, and 2) to use several measures and compare and contrast the results. Conclusions are more robust if the measures all converge on the same findings.

Text Box 7.9 **Technical explanation of value relevance models**

A standard price model may be expressed as follows:

$$P_{it} = \alpha_0 + \alpha_1 EPS_{it} + \alpha_2 BPS_{it} + \varepsilon_{it} \tag{7.15}$$

where *P* is the price three months after the fiscal year-end, *EPS* and *BPS* are earnings per share and book value per share at the fiscal year-end and ε is a random disturbance term.

Meanwhile, a simple return model may be written as:

$$RET_{it} = \alpha_0 + \alpha_1 EPS_{it} + \varepsilon_{it} \tag{7.16}$$

8 One *could* argue that market efficiency is not required at all and that a value relevance setup could instead be used for *testing* market efficiency as one observes market responses to accounting information. But this is problematic for another reason, and that is that it is difficult to distinguish market inefficiency from information lacking relevance, representational faithfulness or news content.

where *RET* is stock market returns (capital gain plus dividends) over a given period ending at the fiscal year end (or a few months later) and *EPS* is earnings per share for the fiscal year. Both variables are deflated by beginning-of-period price (i.e., at the start of the fiscal year).

These models allow for somewhat different inferences. The price model focuses on firm value at a given point in time and is thus interested in what is contained in that value at that time, whereas return models reflect price changes over a time period and thus focus on increases or decreases in value.

Easton and Harris (1991) use a combined model of both earnings levels and earnings changes and show that these measures act complementarily in explaining raw returns. They go back to the modeling by Feltham and Ohlson (1995) and show that earnings deflated by beginning-of-period price is associated with returns, and changes in earnings are similarly associated with returns.

$$RET_{it} = \alpha_0 + \alpha_1 EPS_{it} + \alpha_2 \Delta EPS_{it} + \varepsilon_{it} \tag{7.17}$$

While current earnings is an approximation of expected earnings, changes in earnings is a suggested proxy for *unexpected* earnings. Since returns measure changes in expectations regarding future cash flows, the change variable intuitively seems to be a better predictor variable for returns (Ohlson and Shroff, 1992). However, Easton and Harris (1991) clearly show the complementarity of levels and changes in earnings in the return regression. One of the points made in the more theoretical paper by Ohlson and Shroff (1992) is that when both returns and earnings levels are unpredictable (the unpredictability of the former being the consequence of market efficiency), earnings levels are superior to earnings changes in explaining returns.

What is the actual measure of earnings quality here? One can look at the earnings response coefficient (ERC), represented by a_1 and a_2. The higher the correlation between the independent variable and the dependent variable, the higher the coefficient. Also, *R*-squared, which measures the overall fit of a regression model—that is, how well variations in the independent variables explain variations in the dependent variable—may be used as a quality measure. Importantly, the use of equity markets and price variations in response to earnings as indications of earnings quality should be applied with care when speaking of earnings quality for other decision-makers.

Caveats There is evidence that earnings response coefficients are correlated with the firm's information environment in broader terms and that earnings response coefficients are potentially inflated. Biased coefficients arise when one fails to take into account important factors that could affect the association between earnings and returns (i.e., studies may suffer from *correlated omitted variables bias*). Hence, economic development controls and other attributes of the information environment would complement the earnings figure, making it more useful.

Finally, what does decreasing value relevance over time in a given setting, as documented by Brown et al. (1999), infer with regard to the quality of accounting? Perhaps very little. While varying institutional environments can cause noise and even bias in the models, business models that change over time can likewise produce misleading results. If intangible assets become more common in firms and their importance for firm value grows in relation to other assets, market values will deviate more from book values to the extent that conservative accounting rules prevent firms from recognizing the intangible assets in their balance sheets (see conclusions by Srivastava, 2014) and Collins et al., 1997)). Consequently, GAAP measures will reflect intrinsic values (underlying economics) to a lesser extent than the stock market potentially will. Whether or not decreasing value relevance is a problem depends on the willingness of standard-setters and users to accept varying degrees of reliability in the accounts. It is, in other words, yet another example of the trade-off between faithful representation and relevance when considering quality. Studies on effects of accounting standards are discussed in Text Box 7.10.

Text Box 7.10 **Value relevance and IFRS**

There have been quite a number of studies evaluating the accounting quality effects of IFRS adoption that have investigated the particular effect on value relevance. We have gathered some of the most cited below.

One study looking at value relevance before and after IFRS adoption was conducted by Aharony et al. (2010). They conclude that IFRS adoption is most beneficial when local GAAP deviate from or are less compatible with IFRS. That is, firms in these countries benefit the most from switching to IFRS. A comparability index is devised for the purpose of their study. They find that there is greater incremental value relevance of the studied accounting items under local GAAP (prior to IFRS adoption) for firms operating in countries where the standards were more compatible with IFRS, suggesting that IFRS improves value relevance. This is based on evidence from value relevance tests pre- and post-adoption in 14 different countries. The items in focus are goodwill, R&D and revaluation of PP&E. The authors decompose both a price model and a return model to observe the coefficients of the individual accounting items (chosen *a priori* since they are thought to differ most significantly between IFRS and local standards).

Horton et al. (2013) and Capkun et al. (2008) find that earnings reconciliation adjustments between various domestic GAAP in Europe and IFRS are value relevant, indicating that IFRS earnings carry incremental information to the market. Equity reconciliation adjustments are not incrementally value relevant, however, perhaps reflecting the fact that equity numbers do not differ considerably between IFRS and other GAAP. Meanwhile, using a French sample, Cormier et al. (2009) find that adjustments of equity upon IFRS adoption are value relevant. In looking at the quality effects of voluntary IFRS adoption, value relevance (measured as R-squared) was also examined by Barth et al. (2008b) and found to increase when going from domestic GAAP to IFRS.

7.2.2 Intermediaries' evaluation of earnings

We now look at the final category of earnings quality indicators. Here, the most prominent ones are analysts' reports, internal and external audit reports and statements by enforcers such as the SEC. While analysts' reports reveal analysts' forecasting ability and thus, potentially and indirectly, the usefulness of earnings in a given firm, the issuance by the SEC of an *Accounting and Auditing Enforcement Release* (AAER) typically indicates serious negligence or downright fraudulent behavior. By looking at whether a firm has been subject to SEC investigations, financial statement users may successfully identify firms with low-quality earnings. Researchers, in particular, may avoid the problem of over-identifying abnormal accruals (Dechow et al., 2010). An AAER sample, on the other hand, is characterized by quite extreme observations and one may therefore miss lowearnings- quality firms that have escaped SEC scrutiny. Clearly, non-US firms are further excluded from the sample.

In addition to investigations imposed by institutional enforcements, the internal control of the firm may trigger restatements. Several studies have shown that there is a positive and significant association between the quality of internal controls in firms and various proxies for earnings quality (e.g., Doyle et al., 2007). Hence, as an indirect measure of low earnings quality, previous studies have considered weaknesses in internal control systems as indicators of a greater possibility for earnings misstatement. In Chapter 9, we discuss in detail the *effects* of control and enforcement mechanisms on enhancing the quality of financial reports.

As pointed out in Chapter 6, analysts' forecast errors and dispersion are often used as proxies for information uncertainty. Higher information uncertainty tends to follow from low disclosure quality in general (or from "bad news" disclosures) and from low earnings quality in particular. Examples of studies that have used analyst forecast errors and forecast dispersion as measures of financial reporting quality include De Franco et al. (2011), who look at financial statement comparability, In-Mu et al. (2010), who look at the effect of ownership structure on reporting quality and analyst forecasting activities, Kang et al. (2012), who study the effect of removing US GAAP reconciliation statements for foreign IFRS filers in the US, and Christensen et al. (2013b), who examine the interaction between discretionary and non-discretionary accruals in a stewardship (contracting) setting. What these studies have in common is their use of analyst forecasts to draw conclusions regarding reporting quality, and not least earnings quality, in the sample firms.

7.3 Conclusions

Earnings is an abstract term, a man-made construction. What is "true" can therefore not be discovered, but must be decided upon. What should be reflected in the estimations of (changes in) asset and liability values depends on the reporting objective. From a capital market perspective, "true" earnings are those that reflect the underlying economic value added to the firm. This is what investors want to predict and know in order to make informed investment decisions as well as to successfully monitor management.

The quality of earnings is assessed by looking at the properties of earnings—such as earnings persistence, smoothness of earnings, timeliness of earnings and accruals quality—as well as the value relevance of earnings, and intermediaries' evaluation of earnings. Studies focusing on properties of earnings take into account the variation of earnings over time, how quickly information is provided about some underlying economic event, and the extent of discretionary or abnormal accruals. Value relevance studies focus on the relationship between book values and market values. However, one should note that what is interesting is not the *magnitude* of the difference between these two; what matters is how they *covary*. In brief, earnings should be associated with market returns in order to be value relevant.

While the above measures have been broadly used by accounting researchers, one needs to remember that the models used for measuring earnings quality make several assumptions and that they can only provide *indications* of earnings quality (or a lack of it). The quality of earnings is very much dependent on the underlying *innate* factors of the business or operating environment, and measures used in research suffer from various methodological shortcomings. For example, the variation in earnings or the size of abnormal accruals may reflect the underlying complexity of the firm's operations rather than any discretionary behavior. Researchers should therefore consider and present multiple measures of earnings quality before drawing conclusions.

Part IV

Accounting quality, managerial incentives and governance mechanisms

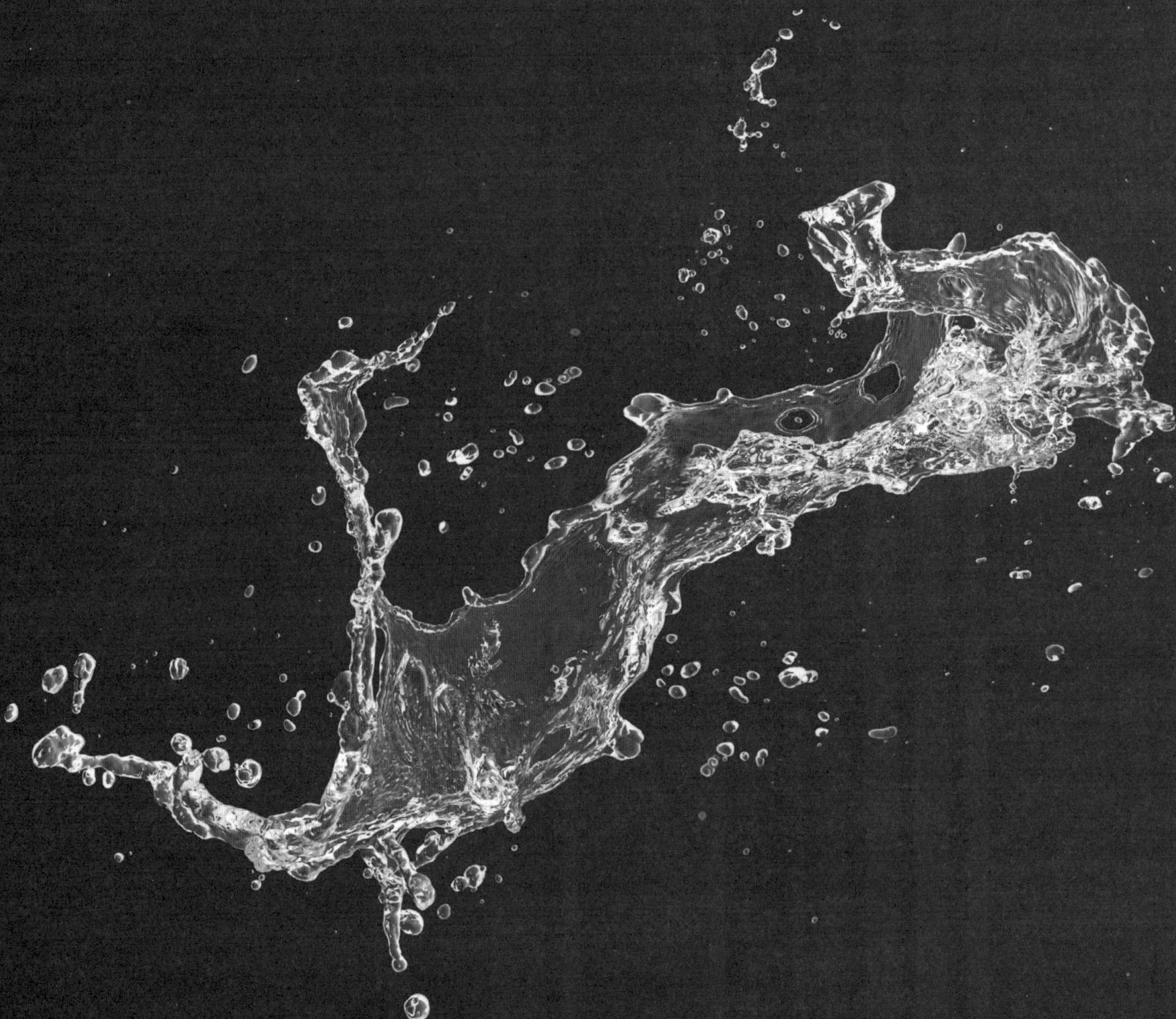

If accounting quality had been determined solely by the quality of accounting standards, things would have been simpler: you, as students, would not have had to read as much about accounting quality, accountants would have more straightforward job descriptions and regulatory bodies could optimize how standards were written. But, such is not the world we live in, and perhaps it would also have been less interesting!

High-quality accounting standards are the first step toward high-quality accounting, but these alone do not ensure high-quality accounting. Standards are applied and interpreted by individuals with certain interests and incentives, and this ultimately has a significant impact on outcomes. Owners of firms delegate the responsibility of running operations to managers, because they are best suited for the task; however, they are also bounded by their own interests, which are not necessarily aligned with the interests of shareholders. This, together with information asymmetries between management and owners, may have major consequences. Previously, we discussed how adverse selection and moral hazard can lead to inefficiencies in the securities market, where moral hazard refers to incentive (or hidden action) problems when managers' actions are unobservable to shareholders. The incentive problem and the mechanisms—specifically contracting and monitoring mechanisms—that can help resolve or reduce it are the focus in this part of the book.

In Chapter 8, we discuss the importance of so-called **optimal** contracts that align the interests of managers and shareholders. More importantly, we focus on the role of accounting information as an **integral** component of optimal contracts. Accounting numbers that are used effectively can convey relevant information about the performance of managers and thus enhance contract efficiency. Whether accounting **is** effective is dependent on how managers use their discretion over the reported numbers. The possibility of **ex-post** opportunism—that is, managers using their discretion opportunistically in order to manipulate earnings and gain more benefits—must be considered. **Accounting choice** occupies a large body of research in the accounting literature, some of which we present here.

The possibility that managers retain residual control over the contracts—and the accounting numbers that are used as part of these contracts—necessitates additional monitoring mechanisms in firms. Monitoring mechanisms come in different guises and they may complement or substitute each other. Perhaps the most-recognized monitoring agent in a firm is a high-quality, external auditor. We tend to consider financial reports to be of higher quality when reviewed by external auditors. Hence, their independence, ethical conduct and effort matter in ensuring the quality of the accounts. Moreover, the board of directors is responsible for monitoring management and, not least, the financial reporting process. This may be done by the board as a whole or inside an audit committee. Large owners, who have a large share of their wealth invested in a given firm, can also be efficient monitors and ensure higher-quality earnings through their exertion of power over management. All in all, continuous and efficient monitoring, as well as country-level (non-firm-specific) enforcement mechanisms, are needed to make sure accounting standards are followed and that their objective—to enhance the quality of accounting information—is achieved. This is explored further in Chapter 9.

CHAPTER 8

Incentives

Learning outcomes

Upon completion of this chapter, you will have gained insight into:

- The role of contracts in mitigating the incentive problem brought on by the separation of ownership and control.
- The role of accounting in facilitating the creation of efficient contracts.
- The role of incentives in shaping accounting choices.

NEARLY ALL HUMAN ACTIONS AND EFFORTS are motivated either by the expectation of a reward or by the fear of punishment. Positive reinforcement in the form of greater wealth, reciprocated emotions, financial security, fame or simply the good feeling some people experience upon achieving major accomplishments constitute common **incentives**. Incentives to work hard, to study, to win in a competition, or to invest or save money can push people to try to achieve goals they would not otherwise have tried to achieve. In economics, as well as in other disciplines, individuals' incentive structures have long been a critical topic of research. Jensen (1994, p. 41) states that:

> Indeed, the issue of incentives goes to the heart of what it means to maximize or optimize, indeed to the very core of what it means to choose. Rational individuals always choose the option that makes them better off as they see it. This is, by definition, what we mean by purposeful action—the attempt to accomplish some end. And it is the difference in (expected) well-offness between taking one action as opposed to another, that provides incentives and results in choice.

In economic terms, one might say that incentives stem from the desire to achieve a higher expected utility. Some scholars question the underlying premise of incentives in economic theories, suggesting that the assumption of rational self-interest is simplistic and wrong (e.g.,

Brennan, 1994). In response to this, Jensen (1994) clarifies that having no incentives implies that alternative courses of action and choices must result in the same degree of utility as viewed by an individual. Indeed, it seems unrealistic that alternative choices would lead to more or less the same outcomes or that an individual would be indifferent to the outcomes. Assuming that choices—and thus incentives—matter, the main issue is not *whether* to incentivize, but rather *how* to incentivize individuals. In the context of control and ownership of a firm, shareholders must learn how to give the manager incentives to select and implement actions that increase shareholder wealth.

The role of incentives received much attention from early economists who viewed the corporation as a nexus of contracts (Coase, 1937). As we saw in Chapter 2, the *nexus of contracts* view of the firm defines the firm as a collection of contracts between different individuals, such as managers and shareholders. The delegation of tasks by one party (the *principal*) to another (the *agent*) can be problematic under primarily two conditions:

1. The principal does not have access to complete information regarding the firm's investment opportunities and managerial actions, and
2. the goals of the agent and the principal diverge as each follows his or her own interests (i.e., there are conflicts of interests).

Under the assumption that all parties wish to maximize their own utility, the above can lead to moral hazard or the **hidden action problem**—a particular type of **incentive problem** (see, for instance, Lambert, 2001).

In Chapter 3, we discussed information asymmetry and how adverse selection and moral hazard can lead to inefficiencies and failures in the securities market. Much of what we observe in this context originates in the incentive problem, which in turn stems from one of the fundamental features of modern corporations—the separation of ownership from control. In this chapter, we focus on the conflict of interest between managers and investors, how a lack of information exacerbates the incentive problem and the role of contracts and accounting (as an integral part of the contracts) in mitigating this problem. Further, we discuss the role of managerial incentives in determining accounting choices.

8.1 Agency theory and optimal contracts

Information asymmetry and conflicts of interests between contract holders are two of the underlying assumptions of theories on incentive problems. A much-cited theory in this context is *agency theory* (introduced in Chapter 2). In the principal-agent framework, decisions are made by managers (agents), but the ultimate costs or benefits of such decisions are borne by shareholders (principals). This means that owing to the conflicts of interests between the agent and the principal, and the hidden actions of the agent, corporate resources may not be used fully to increase shareholder value; instead, corporate resources may be expropriated and used to the benefit of managers at the expense of shareholders.

The question is how the incentive problem can be reduced. Agency theory describes the need for efficient **control mechanisms** or **governance mechanisms** in order to monitor and discipline the agent. Fama (1980) considered the forces of the labor market and the competition from other firms to be an effective way of disciplining managers. This is because the signals provided by an efficient capital market regarding the values of firms' securities can influence the managerial labor market and, thereby, impel managers to act in accordance with the interest of the firm's security holders. It is likely that managers who are concerned with their reputation in the labor market will reduce their shirking, as any shirking will be known in the market. However, empirical evidence has shown that although the incentive problem is reduced with the help of market forces, it does not disappear completely. Furthermore, managers have risk preferences that depend on their career concerns. Holmström (1999) observes that managers' concern for their future career may negatively influence their incentives to take on risky projects that are in the interest of shareholders. As market forces fail to protect the manager against high risks, they are suboptimal for eliminating incentive problems. Even assuming that the market can impose pressure on managers and that we accept the reputation concerns of managers, the elimination of undesirable actions, particularly in the short run, seems highly unlikely. A demand for additional control mechanisms thus remains.

Agency theorists have consequently emphasized the importance of additional governance mechanisms (Fama and Jensen, 1983; Jensen and Meckling, 1976). Although introducing and structuring these is not costless, shareholders bear these costs since the lack of such mechanisms would lead to more costly consequences. In today's businesses, particularly in large corporations with large numbers of shareholders, several governance mechanisms, such as the board of directors and auditors, are nearly always present. In many countries, these mechanisms are also subject to regulatory requirements.

The most recognized solution to the incentive problem (also considered the first best solution) is for shareholders to directly monitor managers and oversee their actions. This has a particular appeal to large owners holding a considerable share of a firm's capital. However, in large (multi-national) corporations with many (small) shareholders, direct monitoring by the owners is not likely to be attainable or practical. **Monitoring mechanisms** (of a more indirect kind) must therefore be used. The board of directors, which represents the shareholders and whose main responsibility is to monitor managers, is one such mechanism. However, the board often achieves limited monitoring performance due to information asymmetry between the board and management.

In the absence of efficient direct monitoring, shareholders may consider designing contracts that give managers incentives to select and implement actions that are in the interest of shareholders (thus achieving alignment of interests).

Optimal contracts, which align the interests of managers with those of shareholders, are often considered the most efficient alternative to direct monitoring by the owners and the board of directors. Such optimal contracts can take the form of so-called **incentive contracts** that tie the manager's pay to firm performance (see Text Box 8.1). Jensen and Murphy (1990) provide a model showing that by linking managerial pay to firm performance—that is, by increasing the **pay-performance relation**—an optimal contract is designed where the agent's expected utility is tied to the principal's objectives.[1] Using firm performance in the evaluation of managerial performance provides incentives for managers to take appropriate actions (i.e., actions that are aligned with the interests of shareholders). An important question, however, is which measures of firm performance are relevant for the performance evaluation of managers?

Text Box 8.1 **Pay-performance relation**

Executive compensation plans consist of several components, including a base salary, an annual bonus, share options and restricted stocks. The base salary and annual bonuses are defined as *cash compensation* and options and restricted stocks are common forms of *equity-based compensation*. Jensen and Murphy (1990) look at the sensitivity of pay of top-level executives in the US and firm performance. They define the *pay-performance sensitivity* as the association between a dollar change in CEO wealth (i.e., increased pay) and a dollar change in shareholder wealth (i.e., increased performance measured by the change in value-weighted return). Higher sensitivity implies closer alignment of interests between the CEO and shareholders, which is the underlying aim of optimal contracts. They estimated the pay-performance sensitivity for CEO total pay, CEO cash compensation and CEO equity-based compensation.

$$\Delta(Pay)_t = a + b\Delta(Shareholder\ Wealth)_t$$

In the above equation, *b* is the coefficient indicating the pay-performance sensitivity. An interesting finding of their analysis is that while this coefficient appears to be positive and statistically significant, the magnitude of the coefficient is small. A small magnitude indicates that the economic significance of the estimated coefficient is low, especially for CEO cash compensation. Specifically, they find that on average, CEO total pay changes $3.25 for every $1000 change in shareholder wealth and CEO cash compensation changes by only about 30 cent per $1000 change in shareholder wealth. They argue that the lack of strong pay-performance sensitivity for CEO pay is puzzling and inconsistent with the implications of optimal contracting models. They suggest that political forces and restrictions are the cause of inefficient compensation contracts.

Later evidence, however, suggests that the pay-performance sensitivity may have increased since the study of Jensen and Murphy in the early 1980s. For example, Hall and Liebman (1998) document that the pay-performance sensitivity experiences an increase in the years of their sample (1992–1994). Perry and Zenner (2001) further document that bonus and total compensation payouts are increasingly sensitive to stock returns after 1993. They suggest that some firms have reduced salaries in response to regulatory changes that involve higher transparency require-

1 Bushman and Smith (2001) explain how the pay-performance relation in optimal contracts ties the agent's expected utility to the principal's objectives. Note that the agent's expected utility is a function of two main factors: 1) the benefits from the provided compensation; and 2) the cost of providing effort and risk aversion. However, the latter factors, effort and risk aversion, are unobservable, which results in a "second best" contract. This means that the principal needs to balance the trade-off between providing incentives for managers to increase shareholder wealth and compensate the agent for bearing risk imposed by the contract. The principal's expected utility is directly related to firm performance, which in turn depends on managerial ability and effort. Therefore, the classic models are designed based on *observable* and *enforceable* performance measures to align the incentives of the risk-averse agent with those of the principal.

ments and pressure from institutional investors. This sudden change could also be explained by a dramatic increase in the use of stock options or restricted stock in executive compensation packages (see Chapter 13 regarding accounting for share-based compensation plans).

For a performance measure to be useful in creating optimal contracts, it must be *informative* of managerial actions. It should not only be precise and free from error and bias, but also filter out any components that are beyond the control of the manager. Below, we discuss and compare accounting-based performance measures and market-based performance measures commonly used in compensation contracts.

8.1.1 Accounting-based performance measures in compensation contracts

Accounting-based performance measures, such as net income, are believed to be relevant measures in designing compensation contracts, given that such measures are directly affected by managers' decisions and performance. Accordingly, profit-sharing and bonus plans, in which managers are given a share of firm accounting performance, are common types of compensation contracts.

Holmström (1979) provides a model that can be related to the role of accounting information in compensation contracts. According to his **informativeness principle**, any additional information that provides informative signal about the agent's actions and efforts and allows for a more accurate judgment of his or her performance, is useful for improving the efficiency of compensation contracts. Thus, information should be relevant, precise and understandable with respect to *achievable* results—results that should not be beyond the control of managers. The model implies that the quality of accounting information, in particular accounting earnings, is important for the efficiency of contracts. A less noisy and more accurate net income figure is better able to reflect managerial performance thus more likely to be used in determining compensation contracts.

In describing the desirable qualitative characteristics of accounting information, we learned that there is a trade-off between the two fundamental qualities of relevance and faithful representation. For example, a piece of information perceived by market participants as being relevant is not necessarily free from error. It is important to note that the trade-off between relevant and faithfully represented information should not only be considered with respect to the valuation role of accounting, but also with respect to the stewardship (or contracting) role of accounting, in which the main aim is to evaluate managerial performance. In contracts—and not least in compensation contracts—such a trade-off has important implications. That is, an increased ability of net income to capture the current performance of managers may be at the expense of the precision and faithful representation of net income. The challenge is thus to obtain an accounting performance measure representing the best possible trade-off between these two principle characteristics in the accounting framework.

At the core of this challenge lies the quality of accruals (see Chapter 7). The main problem with accruals is that they are subject to both unintentional errors and deliberate bias, causing net income to be a noisy measure of managerial performance in compensation contracts.

This problem with accruals becomes critical especially when firms have weak internal control systems. The discretionary nature of accruals means that they are dependent on managerial judgment and discretion. Hence, poor corporate governance (covered in Chapter 9) gives opportunistic managers opportunities to misuse accruals in reporting earnings for their own benefit. By overestimating earnings, they may increase compensation levels at the cost of shareholders (e.g., causing future devaluations). Owing to these potential problems, there is a need for supplementary controls and monitoring of accounting processes whenever accounting-based measures are used. Another way of increasing the informativeness of accounting earnings is to increase accompanying disclosures. In particular, full disclosure, whether voluntary or mandated, can increase pay-performance sensitivity by enabling the firm's compensation committee to better evaluate managerial effort and use the appropriate performance measure in developing the compensation contracts.

Although high-quality accounting performance measures should reflect managerial effort and performance, some factors limit their usefulness in compensation contracts. One especially salient reason for why earnings may not reflect managerial performance is that earnings are conservative in their nature, and as such managerial effort may be captured with delay. For example, while most R&D expenditures are recognized in the current period, the realization of benefits from such expenditures is often assessed in future periods due to conservative accounting principles. Therefore, using accounting-based compensation plans, such as bonus plans, may not be motivational and fully informative of managerial effort in firms that are more future-oriented (e.g., firms with a large focus on R&D).

A related question arising in this context is which accounting treatments and policies are able to provide better bases for compensation contracts. For example, one may want to consider the effect of fair value accounting, which has become more frequently used with the widespread adoption of IFRS, on the efficiency of said contracts. Fair value accounting is said to be less conservative and more value relevant compared to historical cost accounting. The proponents of fair value accounting have emphasized its role in enhancing the transparency and comparability of accounts (see Barlev and Haddad, 2003), which can have a direct implication for the efficiency of contracts. Fair value-based reports may also enhance the stewardship role by directing managers toward the value of shareholders' equity. However, there are also some drawbacks of using the fair value with respect to the stewardship role of accounting. Penman (2007) notes that managers should be rewarded for adding value (earnings) and not based on (arbitrary) changes in market prices. Earnings volatility due to fair value accounting can lead to noisy measurement of managerial performance and therefore be less attractive to managers. Furthermore, fair value accounting increases the need for managers to exercise judgment and make estimates, which exposes shareholders to greater risks of expropriation.

8.1.2 Market-based performance measures in compensation contracts

An alternative and sometimes preferred performance measure in compensation contracts is stock price. This is a **market-based** or **share-based performance measure**, which may be contrasted with the accounting-based performance measures discussed thus far. Stock options and restricted stocks, as common types of equity-based compensation plans, are important and popular in large and growing firms. Share price carries information about the firm's market valuation and as such, it is a relevant performance measure from a shareholder point of view. Furthermore, share-based compensation can incentivize managers to undertake risky projects and increase the long-term value of the firm. The efficiency of compensation contracts using accounting-based and market-based performance measures has been widely examined in empirical accounting research. One may compare and contrast accounting-based measures with market-based measures, as well as compare different measures of the same type with one another.

The main benefit of using share price in compensation contracts is that unlike net income, share price can also reflect expected future benefits; that is, it is not deflated by conservative accounting policies. This implies that firms relying on future revenues to support current operations may prefer to use share price as a main driver of compensation contracts (see above comment concerning R&D-intense firms). In addition, compared to net income, share price is less likely to be subject to direct manipulation and managerial bias. It has been shown that executives are more likely to receive share-based compensation as the complexity of firms increases (e.g., Bushman et al., 2004). It is argued that in firms with more complex operations, the incremental informativeness of earnings on managerial effort diminishes and it is more difficult to assess the manager's action. Furthermore, greater business complexity demands greater managerial discretion, which opens up more possibilities for opportunistic earnings management. Similarly, in firms with large investment (growth) opportunities, management actions are considered particularly difficult to monitor, causing such firms to link executive pay to market-based performance to a greater extent than others (Smith Jr and Watts, 1992). In such firms, market-based performance indicators are preferred to accounting-based indicators, since stock price and market returns are believed to better reflect the economic consequences of management's actions (Baber et al., 1996).

Share price also carries some disadvantages when it comes to contract efficiency, one of the main problems being related to its volatility—especially when executives are paid with stock options. Whereas regular investors can diversify their portfolio, executives who receive equity-based pay may have disproportionately large holdings of shares in their own firms. This increased risk exposure can make them unwilling to take on additional risk in the form of risky projects with potentially high yields. In the best of worlds, stock options may induce risk-averse CEOs to take larger risks than they would otherwise—which should be in the shareholders' interest. However, uncontrollable, economy-wide events (such as the financial crisis in 2007–2008 and the boom that preceded it) can also cause executives who are granted a large number of options to take *excessive* risks in an attempt to "turn the tide" or in the belief that positive trends will continue. This would *not* be in the interest of shareholders. Another danger of basing pay on market prices is that managers may be overly focused on changes in short-term share prices at the expense of long-term shareholder value. Major corporate accounting scandals such as Enron and Worldcom are believed to have been exacerbated by incentives to raise share prices by managers who were granted a large number of options.

The above problems have generated much debate regarding the current state of compensation plans for executives, particularly stock option plans. Therefore, although accounting performance measures may be less able to address the risk-aversion of managers and bring more short-termism, as compared to share-based performance measures, researchers point to the potential usefulness of the former for enhancing the efficiency of compensation contracts, especially for filtering out noise inherent to other performance measures, such as stock price (see Bushman and Smith, 2001) (see also Text Box 8.2).

Text Box 8.2 **Research on performance measures**

The key to an efficient compensation contract is using proper performance measures. Therefore, a large number of studies have examined the usefulness of various accounting or share-based performance measures and compared them.

Lambert and Larcker (1987) explicitly focus on the informativeness principle (see Holmström, 1979)) and compare the relative weight placed on accounting- and market-based performance measures in compensation contracts. They find that firms place relatively more weight on market performance in three situations:

> (i) the variance of the accounting measure of performance is high relative to the variance of the market measure of performance, (ii) the firm is experiencing high growth rates in assets and sales, and (iii) the value of the manager's personal holdings of his firm's stock is low. (p. 86)

Boschen et al. (2003) argue that unexpectedly good accounting performance is not rewarded in the long run, since the observed positive impact on executive compensation in early periods is followed by *lower* future compensation. By contrast, unexpected increases in the price of the firm's stock, however, is followed by positive long run effects on executive pay. One possible explanation for the lack of a positive and persistent link between accounting performance and CEO compensation over time is said to be related to accounting choices (by CEOs) that inflate the current earnings but result in lower future earnings. That is, upward earnings management, for example through aggressively accelerating the recognition of revenues, distorts the *long-term* compensation responses to accounting performance.

Nagar et al. (2003) provide evidence on how stock price-based incentives in the form of share-based compensation and share ownership mitigate agency problems. They predict that managers are reluctant to publicly disseminate the information demanded by investors unless providing such information is also beneficial for managers. Accordingly, they find that the extent of a firm's disclosure, measured by management's earnings forecasts and analysts' ratings of firm disclosure, increases when managers are granted more shares and options. This is because managers who receive share-based compensation are motivated to provide more disclosures, since their wealth is partly dependent on share price, which in turn increases with the quality of the information environment (i.e., the issuance of high-quality disclosures).

The general quality of standards under IFRS for the purpose of contracting has received much attention over the past ten years. In one such paper by Ozkan et al. (2012), the contractual implication of the mandatory transition to IFRS by European firms is examined. They provide some evidence of an increased use of accounting performance measures in compensation contracts after the adoption of IFRS, which indicates that higher quality as well as higher comparability of accounting earnings after the adoption of IFRS is valued by compensation committees, as this may facilitate compensation contracting. Contradictory evidence is, however, provided by Banghøj et al. (2018) and Voulgaris et al. (2014), who suggest that a larger reliance on fair value accounting in IFRS leads to more volatile earnings that fail to screen out market-related noise (i.e., that are outside of management's control), in turn reducing the use of accounting-based performance measures in compensation contracts.

To sum up, the use of accounting-based measures may be preferred to market-based measures due to the fact that the latter is more affected by factors outside the manager's control. Furthermore, since accounting-based measures are less volatile, they prevent excessive risk-taking by managers. On the other hand, accounting numbers may be subject to manipulation or arbitrary accounting treatments, simply because they are under the manager's control. As such, they may be less value-relevant and fail to capture future cash flows. Furthermore, it has been argued that certain types of firms may find it more relevant to rely on market-based measures, such as those operating in high-tech industries with a substantial portion of R&D activities. By contrast, in firms with shorter business cycles and more short-term-oriented business strategies, the use of net income or other accounting performance measures may be preferred. In the next section, as we look at accounting choice, we further explore the implications of accounting quality for the use of accounting-based performance measures in contractual settings.

8.2 Incentives and accounting choice

Accounting choice is a large research field in accounting and touches upon the *raison d'être* of accounting, as both determinants and consequences of managerial choices are investigated. In a well-cited review paper, Fields et al. (2001, p. 256) define **accounting choice** as:

> An accounting choice is any decision whose primary purpose is to influence (either in form or substance) the output of the accounting system in a particular way, including not only financial statements published in accordance with GAAP, but also tax returns and regulatory filings.

The above definition is broad enough to include the accounting choices related to certain accounting items (e.g., expensing versus capitalizing R&D expenditures), as well as *real* investment or operation decisions that may ultimately affect accounting numbers (i.e., they have economic consequences).

The authors also state that (p. 256):

> Research on accounting choice addresses the fundamental question of whether accounting matters. With complete and perfect markets, there is no substantive role for financial disclosures and thus no demand for accounting or accounting regulation. However, in our world of imperfect and incomplete markets, the demand for accounting and accounting regulation implies that accounting disclosures and accounting-based contracts are efficient ways of addressing market imperfections.

Accounting choices may be non-opportunistic and reflect managers' attempts to make the numbers reflect underlying economic events and states. However, the types of accounting choices that have perhaps received the most attention are those related to various external pressures to achieve a certain accounting outcome. Those accounting choices are commonly referred to as **opportunistic accounting choices** and are detrimental to shareholders as they, for instance, serve to maximize managers' utility. Opportunistic choices of accounting procedures are also referred to as **earnings management**. Although some definitions of earnings management do not preclude the possibility that earnings may be managed in a "positive way," we adhere to the less neutral definition that implies opportunism. Healy and Wahlen (1999, p. 368) propose the following definition:

> Earnings management occurs when managers use judgment in financial reporting and in structuring transactions to alter financial reports to either mislead some stakeholders about the underlying economic performance of the company or to influence contractual outcomes that depend on reported accounting numbers.

As is clear from the definition, earnings management (as is the case with all opportunistic accounting choices) may be tied to actual operating decisions or to management of accruals. For example, a "real" (operating) decision may be to delay R&D investments in order to avoid expenses in the current period, while a related accounting choice may be to capitalize doubtful R&D expenditures in order to, as above, avoid expenses in the current period. As seen in Chapter 7, accounting earnings can be decomposed into cash flows from operations and accruals. Accruals can be further decomposed into two parts: non-discretionary accruals and discretionary accruals (Jones, 1991; Healy, 1985). Whereas non-discretionary accruals vary among firms for "natural" reasons due to underlying differences in firm operations, discretionary accruals are the ones influenced by managerial incentives and thus of interest when studying earnings management. This type of earnings management is referred to as **accruals-based earnings management**. The manipulation of real operating activities, motivated by managers' incentive to reach certain reporting goals and mislead some stakeholders, is recognized as **real earnings management** (Roychowdhury, 2006). Although the accounting literature has mostly been concerned with accounting choices and accruals-based earnings management, more recently the research in this area is concerned with both types and whether they complement or substitute each other (see, for instance, Cohen and Zarowin, 2010; Cohen et al., 2008; Achleitner et al., 2014). A distinctive feature of real earnings management is that it may have direct negative effects on cash flow in future periods and therefore real effects on firm value. For example, managers may opportunistically reduce R&D expenditures in order to increase current period earnings. However, an aggressive cut in discretionary expenditures, such as R&D, may lead to future devaluations in firms.

When considering earnings management via the accruals system, it is important to recognize that accounting choices do not alter the underlying value of the firm—the exception being when there are *actual* cash flow effects. Two situations in which there *are* cash flow effects are when there are income tax implications (this affects both managers and owners) and when there are wealth transfers between managers and the firm's stakeholders.

The latter refers to when accounting choices—being an integral part of contracts—affect the value of the firm and the relative wealth of various parties. In Holthausen and Leftwich (1983), the predictions of accounting choices with economic consequences are mainly linked to contracting and monitoring costs associated with firms' contractual agreements, such as management compensation.[2] In other words, since accounting numbers are used in compensation contracts, the choice of accounting techniques may affect the value of the firm and the wealth of managers and shareholders. Depending on the structure of compensation contracts, *ex post* opportunistic accounting choices may be made by managers to increase their own wealth. The implicit assumption of successful earnings management is therefore that compensation committees or other external parties are unable to fully understand or unravel the effect of the earnings management (Fields et al., 2001). Given that there is information asymmetry and markets are imperfect (there *are* transaction, contracting and information processing costs), opportunistic accounting choices become a problem.

In the next few sections, we look at different incentives for making (opportunistic) accounting choices, specifically those originating from contractual relationships, political processes and market forces. In doing so, we build on what we said in Chapter 1 with respect to incentives as an important *determinant* of accounting quality.

8.2.1 Compensation contracts

So far we have discussed how optimal contracts may help address the incentive problem. That is, the purpose of contracts between shareholders and managers is to solve agency conflicts by aligning the interests of the contracting parties. Primarily, one seeks to reduce managerial shirking and other actions preventing utility-maximization for owners. As mentioned before, to reach this aim, contracts should be supplemented with performance measures that reflect managerial performance. While the contracts may induce managers to make business decisions maximizing firm value (in which case they are successful), they may also, ironically, give managers incentives for making choices that are opportunistic. This is especially important to consider when accounting-based compensation contracts are employed.

A large body of accounting research has examined the effect of executive compensation plans and the incentives provided by those plans on certain accounting choices. This effect, also known under the **compensation hypothesis** (Watts and Zimmerman, 1986), predicts that managers make income-increasing or income-decreasing accounting choices depending on the costs or benefits of their compensation contracts. Fields et al. (2001) argue that:

> managers whose incentives are consistent with those of the firms' owners may exercise accounting choices to convey private information to investors; other managers may use discretion opportunistically, possibly inflating earnings to increase their compensation. (p. 257)

2 Contracting costs refer to the costs of negotiating and designing contracts, while monitoring costs are the costs of evaluating the terms and the performance of managers under contracts.

This means that in explaining the relationship between accounting choices and contracts, there are two competing perspectives:

- Efficiency perspective
- Opportunistic perspective

The former suggests that discretionary accounting choices lead to efficient contracts, while the latter suggests that managers take advantage of the flexibility in accounting choices after knowing the nature of the contract, thereby reducing its efficiency. In other words, while performance-based compensation plans may potentially mitigate conflicts of interest, the same contracts may encourage managers to manipulate the accounting information for their own benefit and thus increase their pay. Indeed, given that the performance measures used for evaluating managers are also under the direct control of the managers, one faces a difficult dilemma. While accruals may be helpful in creating an earnings number that reflects underlying value creation, those accruals are inherently discretionary and may be manipulated. As "accounting is an integral part of contracts that define the firm" (Watts and Zimmerman, 1978, p. 180), it is essential to ensure that managers choose accounting methods that lead to efficient contracts. Whereas flexibility is needed in order to enhance the efficiency of contracts and motivate managers to act in the best interests of shareholders, "[c]ontracts that use accounting numbers are not effective in aligning managers' and contracting parties' interests if managers have complete discretion over the reported accounting numbers" (Watts and Zimmerman, 1990, p. 135). By managing accruals opportunistically, managers may choose accounting methods that transfer wealth to themselves at the expense of another party. This may, for example, be done using questionable depreciation rates for long-lived assets, avoiding goodwill write-offs or over- or undervaluing inventory at the end of the fiscal year.

Generally, the existence of bonus plans is more likely to lead to income-increasing accruals in earlier periods, since these lead to higher accounting earnings and therefore an increased amount of earnings-based bonuses in those periods. When the accruals reverse (remember, one cannot increase earnings indefinitely, see Chapter 7), contracts or perhaps even the executive might have been replaced. Furthermore, as the correlation between accounting-based performance measures and compensation becomes stronger through contracts, the likelihood of finding an association between income-increasing accruals and executive compensation increases. Healy (1985) examines the relationship between accruals and CEO bonus plans and provides evidence that bonus plans lead managers to engage in income-increasing as well as income-decreasing procedures. Healy argues that a problem in previous studies examining the relationship between bonus schemes and accounting choices is the assumption that managers always wish to *increase* income. Incentives to use income-increasing accruals are explained by the use of short-term bonuses when the firm is expected to reach or exceed a specific level of earnings (i.e., a target). However, in cases where earnings are low and it is unlikely that managers reach the earnings target (even by using income-increasing accruals), managers have incentives to reduce the level of earnings even further in order to increase the probability and the extent of bonuses in coming years. This strategy is known as "taking a bath," which explains management incentives to use income-decreasing accruals to reduce current-year earnings and increase the probability of future benefits.

The ability to manipulate accruals is dependent on accounting standards and on which accounting methods are permissible. While flexibility in choosing methods and making judgments (given a chosen method) may allow managers to convey private information regarding future cash flows, they may also result in opportunistic accounting choices, especially when there are incentive-distorting compensation contracts. One accounting area involving extensive managerial judgment is goodwill accounting. CEO compensation structures are considered an important factor explaining goodwill recognition choices under IFRS 3 *Business Combinations*. Detzen and Zülch (2012) find that with increasing cash bonus intensity, managers recognize more goodwill in relation to other intangible assets, which suggests that, on average, goodwill is recognized in excess of its economic determinants. The incentive to over-allocate the purchase price to goodwill is due to that goodwill is not amortized but rather written off at the discretion of management. Having more goodwill is thus likely to increase post-acquisition bonuses. However, the authors also show that this relationship is not linear; instead, the relationship appears only for CEOs receiving cash bonuses without caps. Hence, they suggest that introducing caps in bonus plans and therefore limiting CEO bonuses to a given percentage of their base salary may be optimal and help avoid increased impairment risk in the future. Similarly, Shalev et al. (2013) find that CEOs whose compensation packages rely more on earnings-based bonuses are more likely to over-allocate the purchase price to goodwill. However, they find that the over-allocation to goodwill decreases when other performance measures, such as earnings growth, are used in bonus plans.

8.2.2 Debt contracts

Although managerial incentives and accounting outcomes have mostly been studied with respect to compensation contracts, empirical research has also provided evidence on other types of contracts. In particular, the contractual relationships between debtholders and managers and how these affect accounting choices have received attention in the accounting literature. Debt contracts usually contain accounting-based covenants and the conditions specified in these covenants may influence the accounting choices of managers. This is often known simply as the **debt hypothesis**.

Prior accounting research has mainly studied whether managers change accounting methods to *avoid* covenant violations. In a survey study, Graham et al. (2005) assess the impact of debt contracts on accounting choices and find that in firms identified as being close to a violation of a contract, accounting choices are more likely to be made to avoid such a violation (Jha, 2013; Franz et al., 2014). The costs associated with violating debt covenants depend on the extent of debt in firms. Indebtedness is generally believed to lead to lower earnings quality, as the risks and costs of violating debt contracts are higher for highly indebted firms, which in turn makes them more likely to manage earnings (Peasnell et al., 2000; DeFond and Jiambalvo, 1994; Franz et al., 2014).

8.2.3 Political and regulatory forces

A commonly cited source of managerial incentives is the *political process*. Various types of legislation and regulation, including industry-specific regulation, tax regulation and anti-monopoly laws, are examples of political forces affecting corporate decision-making and, more specifically, accounting. As mentioned by Watts and Zimmerman (1978, p. 223), "to the extent that a given firm is subject to potential wealth transfers in the political process, its manager is hypothesized to adopt accounting procedures that reduce the transfer." Firms that do not respond appropriately to political pressures face **political costs**, which may induce them to make opportunistic accounting choices in order to avoid such costs (the *political cost hypothesis*).

Ball et al. (2003), who studied the properties of accounting income in four East Asian countries, emphasize the role of incentives in addition to accounting standards in determining income properties (and thus accounting quality). Given that the examined countries adopted high-quality standards inspired by US GAAP and IAS, one might expect high-quality financial statements. However, the authors emphasize the role of political pressure in shaping incentives:

> Political forces include the extent of involvement of governments in codifying and enforcing accounting standards, taxes, and political incentives to reduce the volatility of reported income (i.e. to avoid large profits and large losses). These [...] political variables profoundly affect financial reporting practice. (p. 236)

Ball et al. (2003) argue that political (and market) forces vary across countries and can help explain national differences in accounting quality. This is important to take into account when considering the possibility of achieving worldwide harmonization of accounting. The political process is closely tied to the institutional environment, which we focus more on in the next chapter.

As for industry-specific regulation, quite a large stream of literature looks at the effect of the Basel Accord and other frameworks on accounting choices in banks and financial institutions. More specifically, many studies examine capital management and earnings management before and after changes to minimum capital requirements (capital-adequacy ratios) (see, for instance, Moyer, 1990; Collins et al., 1995; Anandarajan et al., 2007; Rivard et al., 2003; Kim and Kross, 1998; Ahmed et al., 1999). Because banks are believed to want to lower regulatory (political) costs by avoiding violating capital requirements, discretionary loan loss provisions (a type of accrual) may be used for managing capital. Different versions of the Basel Accord has provided varying degrees of incentives to manage capital and varying degrees of trade-offs between capital management and earnings management (primarily income smoothing). In sum, findings on capital ratio management have been mixed and have varied over time and depending on the strength of the incentives created by the regulatory framework.

Whereas most of the discussion has been on opportunistic choices, accounting quality, and particularly disclosure quality, may also increase as a result of political (or legal) pressures. For example, the **litigation cost hypothesis** predicts that managers increase disclosures in the wake of controversial events or circumstances in order to avoid penalization. Large companies are typically more affected by these types of costs, which is why firm size is often used to proxy for the presence of potential political costs (e.g., Lang and Lundholm, 1993).[3]

The effect of litigation risk on accounting choices has been a prolific area of research, particularly in relation to US firms, which are said to operate in a litigious environment (see, for instance Chen et al., 2013; Donelson et al., 2012; Hanley and Hoberg, 2012; Rogers and Buskirk, 2009)).

8.2.4 Market forces

In this section, we discuss market (or asset pricing) incentives. Strong parallels may be drawn between this section and our discussion in Chapter 6, as we discussed determinants of disclosure. To avoid repetition, we now focus only on managerial (market) incentives rather than on firm-level (market) incentives. Recall our discussion in the beginning of this chapter concerning the role of market forces in disciplining managers. In essence, managers want to influence the price of the firm in order to strengthen their attractiveness in the labor market. Thus, asset pricing and labor market incentives go hand-in-hand, which is why they are discussed jointly below. Of course, managers may engage in legitimate strategic activities to raise stock price, but we focus on accounting choices to achieve this effect.

Evidence on the relationship between opportunistic accounting choices and executive turnover shows that the relationship is two-way: turnover may precede as well as follow accounting choices. In contrast to studies that fail to find evidence of increased turnover after discovered accounting irregularities (Beneish, 1999, see; Agrawal et al., 1999, see), Desai et al. (2006) find that firms that have announced earnings restatements are significantly more likely to see top management turnover. Displaced managers also face poorer future employment prospects, which indicates that there is indeed a penalty for accounting irregularities (earnings management or even fraud). If an executive may be replaced as a result of the board taking disciplinary action, managers should be more hesitant to make opportunistic accounting choices. According to Armstrong et al. (2010), however, more research in this area is needed. Meanwhile, accounting research has studied potential types of earnings management that is likely to *follow* executive turnover. The **big bath hypothesis** predicts that if firm performance is poor at the time a new CEO is appointed—and this poor performance was the reason for the appointment of a new manager or management team in the first place—the new CEO may think it advantageous to "take a big bath" to flush out, or wash away, losses feared to materialize soon enough anyway. This helps make the future earnings trajectory look brighter, which is good for the new CEO from a labor market perspective. Some accounting areas are particularly prone to opportunistic accounting choices and therefore subject to "big bath" behavior. AbuGhazaleh et al. (2011) consider goodwill write-offs according to IFRS 3 and examine managers' incentives to exercise discretion in impairment testing. The results

3 *Research note:* In practice, firm size is typically measured as the market value of equity (Lang and Lundholm, 1993) or the natural logarithm of the market value of equity (Leuz and Verrecchia, 2000), where market value is the adjusted share price times adjusted shares outstanding (Webb et al., 2008). The natural logarithm of total assets (Leuz and Schrand, 2009) is an alternative, non-market approach to measuring size, as is sales.

show that goodwill write-offs are associated with recent CEO change, income smoothing and "big bath" reporting behavior. Effective governance mechanisms (captured by the fraction of independent directors, the percentage of shares held by them and a concentrated ownership structure) help limit these behaviors. In a similar paper, Masters-Stout et al. (2008) examine the effect of CEO tenure on goodwill impairment decisions. It is hypothesized and found that CEOs will recognize this impairment in the early years of their tenure and blame the bad results on prior management's acquisition decisions.

While a manager may risk losing his or her job if accounting irregularities are detected, thus deterring him or her from making opportunistic accounting choices, the fear of losing one's job following poor firm performance, on the contrary, is a possible incentive to manage earnings. In some cases, firms have concrete targets to beat, in which case equity-market pressures produce incentives to manipulate earnings rather than to be transparent with regard to operations. Performance in relation to some benchmark (e.g., own targets, industry benchmarks or analysts' targets) is thus the determining factor here (see also Chapter 7, in which we introduce the idea that just meeting or beating targets may be an indicator of low earnings quality). It has been shown that managers who miss their earnings targets are at a greater risk of losing their bonus (Matsunaga and Park, 2001) and being released (Mergenthaler et al., 2012). Managers in firms that violate debt covenants are also at greater risk of losing their job according to Nini et al. (2012), which is consistent with violating firms having subsequent difficulties obtaining financing (Sufi, 2009; Roberts and Sufi, 2009).

The key point here is that meeting or beating targets constitutes a positive signal regarding a firm's current and future profitability outlook. In order to avoid missing analyst consensus forecast targets, managers may engage in *upwards* earnings management. An et al. (2014), who examine the association between earnings management and target beating, show that earnings management is indeed used for beating targets and that the market does not necessarily realize this (and therefore reacts positively to the earnings announcement).

8.3 The role of discretion

It is not realistic to expect to be able to fully eliminate earnings management in a firm. As we saw above, many incentives exist to make opportunistic accounting choices. Whenever there is room for managerial judgment and there are requirements that preparers of financial reports use their discretion in the valuation of assets and liabilities, there is also room for manipulation.

So, could one not simply allow less discretion and disallow accounting choices? For reasons discussed in Chapter 4 (where we compare principles-based and rules-based approaches to standard-setting), this introduces other problems. One is that a rigid accounting system that dictates every possible transaction becomes costly and unwieldy. It also threatens to encourage substitutes for accounting manipulation in the shape of business decisions that are detrimental to performance. For example, after the Enron debacle, the SEC speculated that a too strict rules-based system had encouraged loopholes and operating decisions that circumvented the intent of the standards even as the rules were followed (SEC, 2003). There is also evidence that the prevalence of *real* earnings management activities increased after the passage of the Sarbanes-Oxley Act (SOX), which was formed following Enron and several other accounting scandals and corporate governance failures (see Cohen et al., 2008). This suggests that firms are likely to have switched to manipulation of real activities, since they are harder to detect compared to accruals-based earnings management. Rules-based standards also risk reducing the ability of financial statements to faithfully represent underlying economics. By contrast, management may convey private information to investors through its estimates and judgments, which has positive implications for capital markets. This trade-off is one that many standard-setters (and investors) are willing to accept.

In Chapter 1, we mention that enforcement and monitoring are important determinants of accounting quality. More specifically, national and supranational enforcement as well as firm-level monitoring are important in counteracting the effect of managerial incentives, reducing earnings management, and bringing about the positive effects of allowing preparer discretion. Consequently, in the next chapter, we expound on the institutional environment (particularly the legal environment and enforcement) and firm-specific corporate governance practices.

8.4 Conclusions

The incentive problems that have received much attention are those that arise due to the separation of ownership and control. Assuming there is information asymmetry and misalignment of interests, the potential controversy relates to the idea that in maximizing the managers' utility, the owners' utility might not be maximized. The widely used agency model, of which Jensen is one of the founding fathers, analyzes incentive problems and suggests solutions for resolving them. The most recognized solution is to incentivize managers, primarily through contracts that tie the manager's pay to firm performance, thus aligning the interests of the agent (manager) and the principal (owner). What determines the efficiency of the contracts is the effectiveness of the performance measure in capturing managerial performance. In this chapter, we discussed the advantages and disadvantages of both accounting-based and market-based measures and the conditions under which one is favored above the other. The use of accounting in contracts or other control mechanisms constitutes the stewardship role of accounting. We also discussed different incentives to make accounting choices, which we classified as incentives arising from contractual arrangements, the political process and market forces. Accounting choices that do not result in faithfully represented and relevant financial statements lead to reduced quality. Note that due to non-zero transaction costs and compelling evidence against strong form efficient markets, shareholders and debtholders are not likely to see through these choices, which may result in a misallocation of resources.

In general, the quality of accounting comes into play in two ways where incentives and contracts are concerned:

1. The quality—and thus the usefulness—of accounting has implications for whether accounting numbers may serve as a basis for evaluating executives and thus constitute viable measures of performance in incentive plans (such as compensation contracts).

2. The quality of accounting is partially determined by executive incentives to make opportunistic accounting choices (that increase the benefits of the executives).

Ironically and somewhat paradoxically, then, the plans used for incentivizing executives to act in the shareholders' interest may likewise provide incentives to manipulate the accounts—since these are used as a basis of measurement in those plans.

If accounting is so important for contractual efficiency, one might ask why standard-setters and shareholders allow managers to exercise discretion and judgment. After all, opportunistic managers can misuse accruals to overestimate earnings and thus increase their compensation. Further, accounting choices may be made to avoid penalization from political and market forces. This leads us back to the rationales for principles-based accounting and the idea that only by allowing managers to convey their private information can faithful representation and relevance—and thus usefulness—be achieved. Nevertheless, in the presences of incentives, restrictions on accounting manipulations (and real decisions) are needed. This is where additional internal governance mechanisms and enforcement by external authorities come into the picture.

CHAPTER 9

Enforcement, monitoring and the institutional environment

Learning outcomes

Upon completion of this chapter, you will have gained insight into:

- Various enforcement and monitoring mechanisms, including the legal environment, country-level enforcement, and corporate governance.
- The effectiveness of enforcement and monitoring mechanisms in limiting managerial opportunism and enhancing the quality of financial statements.

SO FAR, WE HAVE CONSIDERED how managerial incentives affect financial reporting outcomes and, by extension, reporting quality. Depending on the institutional setting the firm operates in and the strength of various enforcement and monitoring mechanisms, the effects of incentives on accounting outcomes may vary. In this chapter, we explore some of these concepts further. By **enforcement**, we refer to the act of ensuring that rules, laws, standards or directives are adhered to or followed in the way intended. Meanwhile, **monitoring** in this context refers to the act of overseeing a firm's activities with the intention of detecting deficiencies in a timely manner, so that preventive or corrective measures can be introduced. The term **institutional environment** is used in a more general sense to indicate what type of setting firms operate in; some aspects to consider are whether tax authorities have a large influence on accounting outcomes, whether businesses tend to be predominantly family-owned rather than shares being widely held and to what extent shareholder rights are protected. Some institutional environments are more associated with greater enforcement and monitoring, as defined above, due to there being a greater commitment to corporate transparency in general. Such a commitment tends to coincide with widespread share ownership and longer capital market traditions. Anglo-American settings perhaps best exemplify this.

Enforcement and monitoring mechanisms relating to financial reporting may, in general, either be firm-specific or exist on a country level (see also Text Box 9.1). What characterizes

Text Box 9.1 **A few notes on terminology**

Enforcement and monitoring activities largely overlap and the distinction between the two should not be exaggerated. Having said that, the terms are used in the literature in slightly different ways. While *monitoring* most often refers to *internal control mechanisms* (i.e., firm-specific activities to reduce the incentive problem and ensure high-quality accounting), *enforcement* is typically set at the country level and is primarily concerned with regulatory *compliance*. Both monitoring and enforcement are *governance mechanisms* in a broad sense of the word. Even regulation and the institutional environment constitute governance mechanisms. For those who prefer a narrower definition of *corporate governance* and related mechanisms, the internal monitoring and control mechanisms are the primary focus.

country-level enforcement is that it is common to all firms operating within a given setting. Much of the relevant regulation of firms and financial reporting takes place in the financial market places and therefore applies to firms with traded securities on a country's main, regulated exchanges. Some institutions are government-funded while others are merely held accountable to government agencies. Finanstilsynet in Norway, the Financial Conduct Authority (FCA) in the UK and Finansinspektionen in Sweden are examples of such institutions. There is no true supranational enforcement agency in Europe, although some calls for this have been heard amidst complaints that harmonization of accounting or consistent application of IFRS cannot occur unless such an institution exists to ensure that national differences in interpretation are eliminated.

Meanwhile, when we speak of firm-specific monitoring mechanisms, we refer to those that may vary in quality and design between firms, even within a country. The most salient examples of these are the board of directors in a firm and the auditors' activities. Although national laws and acts dictate that firms must be audited by independent and external auditor and that they must have a corporate board representing the interests of investors, these bodies may hardly be classified as country-level enforcement. They are representatives of the private sector and chosen by the firm. As such, the work they carry out will vary by firm.

In the next sections, we consider research evidence on the effect of enforcement and monitoring on financial reporting. We consider how outcomes vary by country and firm and how observed differences point to variance in the monitoring effectiveness of country-level institutions, corporate boards and auditors.

9.1 The institutional environment

In this section, we primarily consider two aspects of the institutional environment: country-level enforcement and the legal environment. Although ownership structures partly depend on the institutional setting and traditions of a country, we treat ownership as firm-specific for the purpose of our discussion. Auditors, likewise, may be thought of as enforcers of regulation applied at the country-level; however, because audit quality varies by firm, we consider this a firm-specific enforcement/monitoring activity.

9.1.1 Country-level enforcement

Enforcement is often defined broadly as comprising certain procedures and mechanisms that ensure compliance with certain standards and security laws. Enforcement of accounting procedures involves examining the compliance of accounting information with a relevant accounting standard. What is most relevant to us is the accounting enforcement, which aims to ensure a consistent application of IFRS. Brown et al. (2014, p. 3) define accounting enforcement as:

> [t]he activities undertaken by independent bodies (monitoring, reviewing, educating and sanctioning) to promote firms' compliance with accounting standards in their statutory financial statements.

A slightly longer definition is provided by the European Securities and Markets Authority (ESMA):

> [E]nforcement of financial information is defined as examining the compliance of financial information with the relevant financial reporting framework, taking appropriate measures where infringements are discovered during the enforcement process in accordance with the rules applicable under the Transparency Directive and taking other measures relevant for the purpose of enforcement. Enforcement of financial information implies the examining of financial information to assess whether it is in accordance with the relevant financial reporting framework. In order for enforcement of financial information to be effective, enforcers should also take appropriate actions in accordance with these guidelines, where departures from the relevant financial reporting framework are detected, to ensure that, whenever necessary, the market participants are provided with accurate information compliant with the relevant financial reporting framework. Enforcers may also seek to encourage compliance by issuing alerts and other publications to assist issuers in preparing their financial statements in accordance with the relevant financial reporting framework. (ESMA, 2014, p. 42)

The idea that enforcement activities will cause the compliance of firms with existing rules and accounting standards to increase is based on the assumption that compliance leads to disclosures and earnings numbers that are of higher quality. In other words, with stricter enforcement, one expects the usefulness of financial reports to increase. The need for enforcement is primarily derived from the significant discretion given to managers in applying accounting standards. Interpretation and implementation guidance from external enforcers, along with continuous reviews and monitoring within firms, may help facilitate compliance. Note that as we treat firm-specific activities separately, the potentially important role of auditors as advisers and *enforcers* is discussed in the final section of the chapter.

The importance of country-level enforcement is becoming increasingly recognized. Studies investigating the effects of IFRS have concluded that while there are capital market benefits of adopting IFRS (such as increased liquidity), these benefits are only fully understood by also taking into account countries' legal and institutional settings and concurrent changes in accounting enforcement (see Text Box 9.2) (see, for example Christensen et al., 2013a; Leuz, 2010).

The belief that strong enforcement is important is not only held by the research community, but also by ESMA and its predecessor, the Committee of European Securities Regulators (CESR). Standards were issued by the CESR to foster enforcement of accounting standards as well as improve the coordination of enforcement activities across Europe. As of 2014, ESMA guidelines (ESMA, 2014) on enforcement are authoritative in the EU. They serve to:

> [e]stablish consistent, efficient and effective supervisory practices and to ensure the common, uniform and consistent application of Union law reinforcing a common approach, as noted in recital 16 of the IAS Regulation, to the enforcement of financial information under the Transparency Directive in view of achieving a proper and rigorous enforcement regime to underpin investors' confidence in financial markets and to avoid regulatory arbitrage. [SIC] (ESMA, 2014, p. 39)

With respect to the objective of enforcement of financial information, they clarify that it is

> to contribute to a consistent application of the relevant financial reporting framework and, thereby, to the transparency of financial information relevant to the decision making process of investors and other users of harmonised documents. Through enforcement of financial information, enforcers contribute to the protection of investors and the promotion of market confidence as well as to the avoidance of regulatory arbitrage. [...] In order for investors and other users of harmonised documents to be able to compare the financial information of different issuers, it is important that this information is based on a consistent application of the relevant financial reporting framework, in the sense that if facts and circumstances are similar, the recognition, presentation, measurement and/or disclosures will be similar to the extent required by that financial reporting framework. To ensure that enforcement of financial information throughout the EEA is carried out in a similar way, enforcers should share the same understanding of the principles as set out in these guidelines and react in a consistent manner if departures from the relevant financial reporting framework are detected. (ESMA, 2014, p. 41–42)

This may be compared in particular to the discussion in Part II of this book on the principles underlying the IASB's Conceptual Framework, harmonization of accounting and the qualitative characteristic known as comparability.

Whenever one studies country-level enforcement, an underlying accounting standard framework must be assumed or held constant. In other words, to speak of high or low enforcement without taking into account what is being enforced tends to render the analysis somewhat meaningless. Furthermore, the assumption should also be that what is being enforced is of high quality. What happens if we, for example, assume that IFRS is *not* of high quality? One could argue that *because* it is principles-based, not *despite* that it is principles-based, it is of lower quality. Enforcement would not help such a situation.

Text Box 9.2 **IFRS adoption and the enforcement effect on quality**

There are indications that the impact of IFRS on accounting quality is highly dependent on the extent to which the standards are actually enforced. For example, using a sample of over 6,000 observations of a little over one thousand EU firms between 1995 and 2006, Li (2010b) finds that (largely) voluntary IFRS adoption reduces the cost of equity capital through increased disclosures and greater information comparability, but only in countries with strong legal enforcement. That is, it is not enough to simply introduce high-quality standards, but compliance with these needs to be ensured through effective support mechanisms.

Some researchers will claim that accounting quality, in fact, is all about enforcement and very little about standards or regulation. Christensen et al. (2013a) look at IFRS adoption in the EU and conclude that apparent liquidity improvements of mandatory IFRS adoption are limited to countries where enforcement simultaneously underwent changes, and that liquidity improvements in fact also occurred in countries where enforcement changed but IFRS did *not* become mandatory. Whereas the implication of this is that IFRS itself had very little or nothing to do with said capital market effects, it may be noted that such conclusions have also been refuted. Enforcement may be required for the benefits of IFRS to materialize, but that does not mean IFRS does not also play a role in the improvements (Barth and Israeli, 2013).

Finally, an earlier study by Hodgdon et al. (2008) emphasizes the importance of taking compliance into account when studying the effects of IFRS. Even though firms claim full compliance and despite stricter regulation in the revised IAS 1, firms are not complying fully (see, for instance, Street and Gray, 2001, and Glaum and Street, 2003, in Hodgdon et al., 2008).

9.1.2 The legal environment

One aspect of the institutional environment often referred to in the accounting literature is the legal tradition, or legal "family," a country belongs to. As we saw in Chapter 4, a distinction is made between **code law** (or **civil law**) countries, including France, Germany and Scandinavia, and **common law** countries, which typically comprise Anglo-American countries. La Porta et al. (1998) classify many more countries based on this dichotomy and show that a greater extent of legal protection of investor rights, including voting rights and protection against expropriation by management, is a feature of common law countries. Furthermore, corporate financing and ownership structures are partly determined by these legal protections, which explains why ownership tends to be more dispersed in common law countries.

However, the question of interest is: what implications does this have for accounting outcomes and accounting quality? Whilst increased corporate transparency may encourage widespread ownership, widespread ownership also raises demands for transparency. In order to reduce information asymmetry and agency costs, firms with higher ownership dispersion must maintain a high quality in their disclosures and reported earnings. Furthermore, La Porta et al. (1998) also find that the quality of local accounting standards and law enforcement is associated with legal tradition (law enforcement covers the efficiency of the judicial system, rule or law, corruption, risk of governmental expropriation and the likelihood of contract repudiation by the government). Scandinavian countries are ranked the highest with respect to both of these factors, while countries with French civil law are ranked the lowest. Countries with German civil law are ranked second with respect to law enforcement and third with respect to accounting standards quality, while the reverse is true for common law countries. The above findings have been reiterated and relied upon in much accounting research and used for hypothesis development. Taken together, they point to an association between legal traditions and the institutional environment, the latter of which has been seen as having implications for accounting transparency, both via enforcement mechanisms and financing structures.

A much-cited paper by Ball et al. (2000) shows how the properties of accounting income vary depending on the institutional context in which the firm operates. In their study, a distinction is made between code law and common law countries and it is argued that in code law countries—characterized by a larger influence from institutions such as banks, labor unions and other business associations—the demand for highly transparent financial reporting and timely earnings is lower compared to common law settings. Specifically, the extent to which and the way in which information asymmetry is resolved varies between code and common law countries and this, in turn, affects the role of accounting information. In code law countries, shareholders often hold a large block of stock with a large number of voting rights. They also appoint their representatives to sit on the supervisory board and thus get access to *inside* information. By contrast, the lack of access to inside information in arm's-length equity markets in common law countries leads to a higher demand for high-quality public information. In another study, Ball et al. (2003) state that accounting standards are not the only determinant of income properties, but incentives should also be considered. Although this was referenced in the previous chapter, we reiterate it here since we want to emphasize that incentives may vary with the institutional setting. In general, the authors find that weak market forces and the existence of political costs reduce earnings quality as measured by the timeliness of reported earnings. They conclude that standards *per se* cannot ensure high earnings quality, an implication being that for IFRS to be successfully implemented worldwide and for harmonization to be achieved, reporting incentives must be addressed and proper enforcement ensured (see also Text Box 9.3).

Text Box 9.3 **More evidence on legal environment and accounting outcomes**

Studies that investigate the effect of enforcement or legal environment on accounting outcomes include those that have found that globalization interacts with the legal environment in determining disclosure outcomes (Webb et al., 2008), that banks' discretionary smoothing behavior decreases with stronger supervisory regimes (Bouvatier et al., 2014) and that earnings quality is higher for firms in countries with greater investor rights when (and only when) a firm has a Big Four auditor (Francis and Wang, 2008). Furthermore, earnings management decreases when investor protection is strong, as fewer opportunities to acquire private control benefits reduce incentives for manipulating earnings (Leuz et al., 2003).

Meanwhile, indications of improved accounting quality due to enforcement are also captured via analyst forecast accuracy and cost of the equity capital. For example, strong legal enforcement is found to be associated with higher forecast accuracy, consistent with "enforcement encourag[ing] managers to follow prescribed accounting rules, which, in turn, reduces analysts' uncertainty about future earnings" (Hope, 2003b, p. 235). This is in particular found to be true when there is a greater number of available choices of accounting methods (meaning more discretion is required). Another paper concludes that in countries with more extensive disclosure requirements, stronger securities regulation and stricter enforcement mechanisms, firms have a lower cost of equity capital. The importance of strong legal institutions does decrease, however, with more globally integrated capital markets (Hail and Leuz, 2006).

9.1.3 Criticism of the evidence

The above-cited studies have almost without exception relied on the division of countries into legal families based on La Porta et al. (1998), or some variation of the indices and measures provided by later, derivative studies (e.g., La Porta et al., 2002; La Porta et al., 2006). These studies have attracted many thousands of citations and are considered highly seminal and influential. However, flaws in the research design and the measures have not least been raised with respect to La Porta et al. (1998). This has been done both by legal scholars as well as by accounting researchers (Lindahl and Schadewitz, 2013). Some of these criticisms concern the fact that the distinction between legal families is rough and is becoming less relevant over time, and that differences *within* the families make the civil and common law groups and subgroups disconcertingly heterogeneous. In general, the main conclusion of La Porta et al. (1998)—that investor protection is greater in common law countries—is said to falter.

Moreover, even if one assumes that the classifications are correct, the appropriateness of drawing parallels to accounting quality is highly questionable (see also Text Box 9.4). Gross simplifications and poor theoretical motivations for why or how the law should affect accounting outcomes are pointed to as problematic. A large number of accounting studies refer to La Porta et al. (1998) without justifying why there should logically be a link between the chosen legal measures and accounting outcomes (Lindahl and Schadewitz, 2013). An interesting methodological fallacy in many of these studies is related to how the Germanic/French/Scandinavian legal categories in La Porta et al. (1998) were created. For a given measure of, for example, legal protection, a legal family will be awarded a score based on the scores of the countries belonging to that family. The index is equally weighted, so that the scores of Taiwan and South Korea (countries belonging to the Germanic group) contribute the same as Austria or Germany to the Germanic-origin average. If an accounting study uses this score based on a sample of European firms, clearly Taiwan's and South Korea's legal systems will have undue influence on the measures and consequently the results. Another methodological shortcoming is related to how enforcement is actually measured in La Porta et al. (1998) as well as in Kaufmann et al. (2007), another commonly cited study. Some of the components of these measures are unrelated to (or, at best, weakly correlated with) the enforcement of (financial) *reporting*. Examples include crime rates, price controls, the ease with which one may start a company, trade policy and the ability of citizens to participate in selecting their government. Similarly, the "rule of law" measure, which often makes up a subset of the legal environment, captures things such as kidnapping of foreigners, violent crime, and human trafficking (Lindahl and Schadewitz, 2013).

Text Box 9.4 **Examples of criticism**

In several discussion papers, the main conclusions of some influential "enforcement" papers have been challenged. Holthausen (2003) refers to the study by Ball et al. (2003) (see above) and their main conclusion that in addition to accounting standards, one should consider the effect of managerial incentives, the role of enforcement mechanisms, ownership structures and institutional settings on the quality of financial statements. As also emphasized by Holthausen (2003), while the results are interesting and point to the importance of considering the effect of country-specific institutions on the financial reporting process, there are problems with the interpretation of results. The main difficulty relates to the benchmarks used in this and many other studies. For instance, what is a good benchmark for defining high-quality financial reporting? Do we expect to have more conservatism in certain countries or do we believe that the extent of asymmetry between gains and losses should follow the same patterns observed in, for example, the US?

Barth and Israeli (2013) discuss the results of Christensen et al. (2013a) (see also Text Box 9.2) and argue that it is difficult to disentangle the effects of changes in accounting standards and changes in enforcement since they are very much intertwined. Methodological shortcomings imply that the conclusion that the capital market benefits from IFRS adoption is all about enforcement should be drawn with caution.

Prominent accounting researchers provide further cautionary notes on the interaction between accounting standards, enforcement and financial reporting outcomes (see, for instance, Holthausen, 2009; Pope and McLeay, 2011)) and advise future work to consider the importance of firm-level incentives and (internal) corporate governance mechanisms as well as enforcement for the financial reporting process. Looking only at one factor, or settling on *the most important determinant* of financial reporting quality, may lead to faulty conclusions and the belief that there is *one* optimal solution for all types of firms irrespective of institutional environment.

To summarize, it is not far-fetched that greater investor protection could lead to more dispersed ownership and consequently higher accounting quality. However, the direct link to legal families has been questioned and future research should be more careful in terms of making causal links between law and accounting quality. More clever research designs are here called for. Lindahl and Schadewitz (2013) draw attention to a study on success in the World Cup:

> Failure to consider alternative explanations invites unsupportable conclusions. West (2002) discovered that teams from countries of the French legal family had better success in the World Cup. He wrote: `Perhaps teams from countries with systems based on the French model (such as 1998 champions France and 2002 champion Brazil) perform well due to the remaining vestiges of the Napoleonic Code that somehow remove discretion from coaches and managers in the same manner that the civil law system curtails judicial activism. Or maybe—just maybe—some other forces are at work.' (p. 5)

The irony in this statement should be clear, as should the fact that correlation does not mean causality. There must be sound theoretical reasoning behind assumptions regarding links between the legal environment more generally and accounting quality.

The main takeaway here is that the issues raised above constitute a serious threat to the validity of what is likely a vast majority of studies linking accounting quality to legal enforcement. Even if the original constructs of legal environment and enforcement have been measured flawlessly, the automatic application of one set of measures in a different setting (relating to accounting outcomes) is inadvisable. To simply refer to a previous study using a given measure is not a good motivation for why a later study should also use it.

Ideally, one would like to measure enforcement *of accounting standards* more directly. An attempt at this has been made by Brown et al. (2014), who have constructed country-level enforcement indices based on a number of parameters explicitly related to, for example, the oversight of the accounting profession and the role of the accounting regulatory authority. They argue that particularly the role of audit and accounting enforcement—which vary depending on the institutional setting—is crucial for the application of, and compliance with, IFRS. Given that country differences have implications for the application of IFRS, enforcement promoting compliance may have a positive impact on the quality of financial reporting and thereby on capital markets.

9.2 Corporate governance

In the previous section, we discussed country-level enforcement and the legal environment, including shareholder protection. In focusing on *firm-specific* governance mechanisms and their interactions with each other, we now continue where we left off in Chapter 8. Governance mechanisms, such as monitoring by independent boards of directors and controlling shareholders, are expected to limit opportunistic behavior as well as enhance the transparency of the information environment.

Corporate governance, a term receiving increasing attention in business contexts, encompasses a combination of governance mechanisms aiming to reassure shareholders that their interests are protected. However, it is difficult to settle on a concise definition of corporate governance, given that firms' corporate governance may consist of a wide range of control mechanisms (Brickley and Zimmerman, 2010). Although some define the term more broadly than others, a commonly used definition of corporate governance (see Text Box 9.5) focuses on the separation between ownership and control and relates to the activities that are designed to reduce agency problems.

An extended focus on corporate governance is partly a result of regulatory pressures following several accounting scandals (Enron, Worldcom, etc.) at the beginning of the 2000s and the financial crisis of 2007–2008.

Following the EU calls in 2005 to improve corporate governance by including more non-executive or supervisory directors on the boards of listed companies (see Directive 2005/162/EC, EC,2005), EU member states have developed their own corporate governance codes. Accordingly, the first code of corporate governance was for instance introduced in Sweden in 2005 with the aim of improving the corporate governance of firms listed on the Swedish

Text Box 9.5 **Corporate governance definitions**

Cadbury (1992): "corporate governance is the system by which companies are directed and controlled. Boards of directors are responsible for the governance of their companies[. . .]" (Par. 2.5)

Shleifer and Vishny (1997):"corporate governance deals with the ways in which suppliers of finance to corporations assure themselves of getting a return on their investment." (p. 737)

Larcker et al. (2007): "corporate governance refers to the set of mechanisms that influence the decisions made by managers when there is separation of ownership and control." (p. 964)

Armstrong et al. (2010): "corporate governance [refers] to the subset of a firm's contracts that help align the actions and choices of managers with the interests of shareholders." (p. 181)

Brickley and Zimmerman (2010): "corporate governance is the system of laws, regulations, institutions, markets, contracts, and corporate policies and procedures (such as the internal control system, policy manuals, and budgets) that direct and influence the actions of the top-level decision makers in the corporation (shareholders, boards, and executives)." (p. 236)

securities market. In addition to this, the Swedish Companies Act (Aktiebolagslagen) is the main frame of reference for the Swedish corporate governance model and contains several requirements in relation to, for example, the formation of a company, company shares, a company's management, audits, mergers and acquisitions and the distribution of company profits. Meanwhile, US Congress passed the SOX Act in 2002 (which requires stronger internal control systems in firms) and created the Public Company Accounting Oversight Board (PCAOB). The PCAOB regulates the audit profession, which previously was not subject to federal regulation.

In Chapter 8, we went through the importance of efficient contracts, such as well-designed compensation plans that can align the interests of management and shareholders and reduce the problem of moral hazard. We also stated that high-quality accounting information is needed to enhance the efficiency of these contracts. If bonus plans are based on financial performance measures (e.g., accounting earnings), and these are subject to earnings management, they will become inefficient signals of managerial performance. Equity-based compensation plans, meanwhile, do not suffer from those exact problems. However, research indicates that disclosures may be manipulated either to avoid undervaluation in the market (an executive does not want an undervalued stock since it serves as a basis for his pay), or to actually encourage undervaluation (since an undervalued stock today means greater returns and thus higher pay tomorrow) (see more in, for instance, Healy and Palepu, 2001).

According to agency theory, incentive compensation systems are only one solution—and an imperfect one—to the agency problem. Even when compensation contracts are perceived as useful, their efficiency depends on to what extent *other* monitoring mechanisms are available to firms. This is considered the "complementary" governance role of monitoring mechanisms in firms. Furthermore, it is important to note that designing and enforcing certain governance mechanisms, such as incentive compensation contracts, is often costly, which may result in firms deciding to use alternative (less costly) governance mechanisms. This is known as the "substitute" role of monitoring mechanisms. An important point is that only focusing on one governance mechanism neglects the complementary or substitutive effects of other mechanisms, which generates an incomplete picture of the effectiveness of corporate governance. In response to this concern, several empirical papers looking at the effect of governance on accounting outcomes (such as disclosure quality) have constructed and used composite measures of corporate governance based on the aggregation of several governance proxies (see, for instance, García Osma and Guillamón, 2008; Ernstberger and Grüning, 2013). Although these scores or indices tend to cover several different aspects of corporate governance, constructing these indices and ranking firms based on these scores may be highly problematic. Indeed, Brickley and Zimmerman (2010, p. 241) view the idea that "a good governance index can be constructed" as a *myth* and argue that what is "good" or "bad" corporate governance is context- and firm-specific.

To summarize, the optimal combination of governance mechanisms in a firm depends on the unique situation of that firm. We continue this section with two important firm-specific governance mechanisms. First, we consider the extent to which agency problems depend on firms' ownership structures and how owners may contribute to efficient monitoring of financial reporting. Second, we discuss the prominent role of the board of directors in a governance context and how such a role has evolved over time.

9.2.1 Ownership structure

Ownership structure, which describes the distribution of control over a firm's equity, is important from a corporate governance perspective. In general, given that the separation of ownership and control is the very reason for information asymmetry and agency problems, it is unlikely that individual owners could successfully monitor firms' financial reporting process or managers' performance. Even if it were possible, they would likely not be willing to do so, due to the so-called *free rider problem*: if one shareholder makes an effort to provide monitoring and bears all the costs, other shareholders still enjoy the benefits of additional information or monitoring.

There is evidence, however, that certain ownership characteristics constitute governance mechanisms in their own right. One ownership feature that has been widely studied is **concentrated ownership** versus **dispersed ownership**. Firms with a concentrated ownership structure are those with an influential group of owners who are "controlling" or "active." In general, Porta et al. (1999) provide evidence that high ownership concentration is a common feature of ownership of large corporations worldwide. But who are these controlling and active owners? Although different definitions exist, **controlling owners** often refer to those holding a large percentage of a firm's capital. Jensen (1993, p. 867) defines **active owners** as "individuals or institutions that simultaneously hold large debt and/or equity positions in a company and actively participate in the firm's strategic direction." Given the presence of these owners—who have often invested a substantial portion of their wealth in the firm—it is not hard to believe that they have greater incentives to monitor and discipline managers.[1] This is why empirical research in this area has predicted and mostly found that the presence of controlling shareholders in firms diminishes the need for alternative costly governance mechanisms, such as performance-based compensation plans (e.g., Mehran, 1995; Ke et al., 1999; Frye, 2004).

However, similar to any other governance mechanisms, concentrated ownership is an imperfect mechanism and may even lead to new governance concerns. Firms with concentrated ownership may face another type of agency problem known as the **entrenchment problem**. This problem arises due to potential conflicts of interest between controlling shareholders and *other* (minority) shareholders. The primary source of these conflicts is that controlling shareholders exercise their power over management to pursue their own interests and desires. This may lead to a misallocation of corporate resources, with large, controlling shareholders expropriating assets at the expense of minority shareholders (Shleifer and Vishny, 1997; La Porta et al., 1999). In Europe, concentrated ownership is notably high and thus the extraction of private benefits by controlling shareholders has become a major concern (see Coffee, 2005). Renders and Gaeremynck (2012) argue that having conflicts of interest between large and small shareholders is associated with weaker corporate governance. In particular, one typically dominant type of shareholders in many parts of the world, **family owners**, has been the subject of much controversy. On the one hand, family owners have long-term goals and often recruit managers who are part of the family, indicating reduced or no classic agency conflicts between owners and managers. On the other hand, for the same reasons, they may have incentives and opportunities to expropriate other shareholders' wealth by only pursuing the interests of fellow family members. In particular, due to the potential altruism of family owners towards family-related CEOs or due to other private or *noneconomic* goals in family firms, corporate resources may not necessarily be used to enhance the performance of the firm (Michiels et al., 2013).

In other words, we have two sources of information asymmetry and conflicts of interest when considering the power of individual owners:

1. Principal-agent conflict: Between managers and shareholders.
2. Principal-principal conflict: Between large and small shareholders. With respect to the principal-principal conflict, there are two possible scenarios:
   a) The large owners are able to successfully monitor managers, protecting the interests of smaller shareholders while also protecting their own rights. This is known as the **monitoring incentive hypothesis**.
   b) The large (controlling) owners become "entrenched": instead of protecting the wider interests of (all) shareholders, they pursue their own interests. This is known as the **entrenchment hypothesis**.

In other words, while the monitoring incentives of controlling shareholders may mitigate the traditional agency problem induced by conflicts of interests between management and shareholders (Scenario (a)), the large influence of these owners over the decision-making of

1 The percentage of shares that should be held by an investor in order for that investor to be recognized as a large (controlling) shareholder is debatable and varies among countries. For example, while an investor holding (only) 5% of a firm's shares may be recognized as a large shareholder in the US, a common threshold in Sweden is 10% (see, for example, Swedish Corporate Governance Board, 2016).

management may lead to other types of problems (Scenario (b)). The question is which one of these scenarios has more validity: the monitoring incentive hypothesis or the entrenchment hypothesis? To answer this and similar questions, empirical research in accounting has looked at the effect of controlling shareholders on the quality of financial reporting.

Research on family owners and the quality of firms' financial reporting (e.g., Wang, 2006; Ali et al., 2007; Ghosh and Tang, 2015) has mostly found support for the monitoring incentive hypothesis, indicating that firms with family owners are less prone to accounting manipulation and thus exhibit superior reporting quality. Family owners, who often have long investment horizons and undiversified equity portfolios, are expected to have greater incentives to monitor the activities of managers. In addition, family owners are supplemented with superior knowledge of the business and the firm's operational activities, which enables them to effectively detect any opportunistic behavior in advance and discipline management in order to provide high-quality information. Another reason for better quality accounting information in family firms is that there is less earnings management motivated by compensation contracts. This is consistent with findings that firms with a higher percentage of shares held by large blockholders use relatively less performance-based compensation for managers (Mehran, 1995; Core et al., 1999). The reason is clear: monitoring problems are limited in firms with large blockholders and thus the need for other costly monitoring mechanisms, such as compensation contracts, is reduced (Yang, 2010).

Finally, due to the possible entrenchment problem, firms with controlling family owners may have higher-quality financial reporting due to the increased *demand* for transparency by outside shareholders, creditors and other users of financial statements (Wang, 2006). A general discussion on the relation between corporate governance and quality in accounting is provided in Text Box 9.6.

Text Box 9.6 **Corporate governance and accounting quality**

Mixed results with respect to the relationship between corporate governance and accounting quality bring us to the main challenge in corporate governance research: the **causality issue**. As mentioned in the main body of the text, research on family owners mostly points to a *positive* relationship between accounting quality and family ownership. However, it is not clear what causes this positive relationship. While this effect could very well be driven by the monitoring incentives of family owners, it can also be a result of a *demand* for enhanced transparency by smaller owners or outsiders due to concerns about possible entrenchment (see figure below). This problem is not unique to this relationship, but is also observed when studying the role of boards. While researchers have highlighted the causality issue and acknowledged limitations in current studies, a stronger theoretical framework is needed to explain such complex relationships within corporate governance.

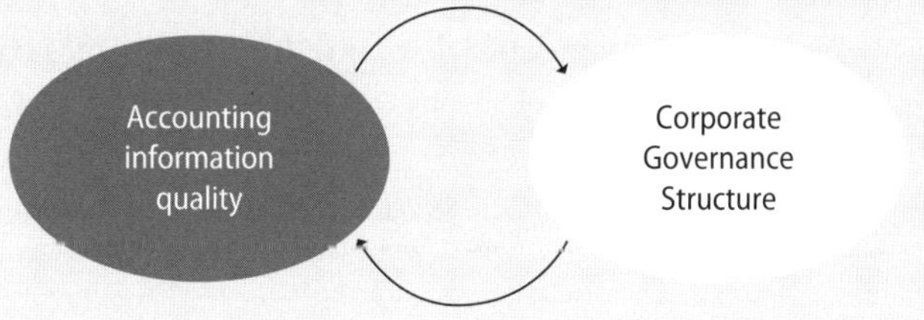

9.2.2 Board of directors

The board of directors, which represents a firm's shareholders, is another important (internal) governance mechanism (Fama and Jensen, 1983). The most widely recognized role of boards is to monitor and discipline management. This role is especially crucial in firms with dispersed ownership structure, given that direct monitoring is costly (or impossible) for small shareholders (see above). In addition to their monitoring role, boards also have an advisory role, as well as being responsible for hiring, firing, rewarding and assessing management and reviewing financial reports (Adams et al., 2010).[2]

These roles are largely interlinked. For example, monitoring, rewarding and assessing management go hand-in-hand. As we have already seen, boards provide managers with incentives to commit to transparent and high-quality financial information by linking their compensation to performance measures. Nagar et al. (2003) examine whether executives receiving equity-based compensation have more incentives to commit to higher-quality disclosures. Their findings support this prediction, suggesting that boards of directors use compensation plans that are linked to firm performance as a tool for enhancing the information environment. Furthermore, should management achieve poor performance or fail to provide reliable financial information, they face the risk of losing their job (see, for instance, Desai et al., 2006), and the discussion in Chapter 8). The role of hiring and firing management is thus a powerful governance tool.

The role of boards has been emphasized lately, with boards being blamed for failing in their governance and monitoring activities. Several changes in the corporate governance structures of firms have been introduced following new regulation (SOX in the US and Directive 2005/162/EC in Europe). Especially **board composition** has been subject to debate—and study in the literature. Two factors stand out here:

- Board independence
- Board diversity

The importance of having **independent directors** on the board, capable of challenging and monitoring the decision of management, has been emphasized. Independent directors are those who are neither managers nor enjoy close ties to management. Adams et al. (2010, p. 66) state that:

> With respect to monitoring the CEO, one imagines that directors who have close ties to the CEO (e.g., professionally, socially, or because the CEO has power over them) would find monitoring him more costly than directors with fewer ties.

Outside directors who are not employed by the firm (and have not been employed previously by the firm) are often considered independent and their presence is considered necessary for the monitoring performance of boards. However, one needs to remember that an outside

2 Due to this long list of responsibilities, boards are recommended to delegate tasks to certain committees inside the board of directors. For example, settling CEO compensation may require a special *compensation committee*, reviewing and overseeing financial reports and communicating with external auditors is believed to be best achieved in a separate *audit committee* and major board appointments are often carried out by a *nomination committee*.

(or non-executive) director may still have ties to the largest shareholder of the listed firm. A precise definition of independence, therefore, considers not only non-executive directors but also any representatives of the largest shareholders. Accordingly, most codes of corporate governance focus on both aspects of independence. For example, the Swedish corporate governance code (see, Swedish Corporate Governance Board, 2016) states that:

> In order to determine a board member's independence and integrity, the extent of the member's direct and indirect relationships with major shareholders is to be taken into consideration. A member of the board who is employed by or is a board member of a company which is a major shareholder is not to be regarded as independent. (Par. 4.5)

Following changes toward having more independent directors on the board and especially on the audit committee, several papers have examined the effect on financial reporting quality (e.g., Klein, 2002; Xie et al., 2003; Peasnell et al., 2005). This research argues that having more independent board members leads to improved earnings quality. In particular, an audit committee consisting of mostly independent directors is considered critical in reducing managerial incentives and preventing earnings management. Awarding a larger cash compensation to this group, however, is found to compromise their independence (Ye, 2010).

Although these results are interesting, one should note that the efficiency of an entirely independent board could be debated. The reason is that although independent directors may have stronger incentives to monitor management, they have limited access to information that may help them in their decision-making. In fact, information asymmetry between managers and independent directors may constitute a significant obstacle for boards in efficiently carrying out their responsibilities (Jensen, 1993). Conversely, directors who are themselves executives in a given firm and know the business (and/or management) very well, have greater access to information and are better able to influence, advise and monitor the CEO. Apart from board independence, recent literature has examined the effects of *diversity* of members on governance success in firms. Diversity can refer to national origin, gender, socioeconomic status, ethnicity, experience or education. Proponents of board diversity argue that this promotes greater insights into markets, employees and business and investment opportunities, while opponents of more diversified boards believe that dissimilarities on the board can lead to difficulties in communication and less agreement on firm goals. One of the most popular factors studied where diversity is concerned is *gender*. For example, there is evidence that in firms where the board consists of more females, the quality and informativeness of financial reports is higher (Gul et al., 2011). It is also argued that female directors provide better oversight over managers and, thus, by better monitoring of managers' reporting in more gender-diversified boards, the quality of earnings improves (Srinidhi et al., 2011). Improved board communication, greater effort and improved board attendance include some of the reasons raised by research in showing why a gender-diversified board exhibits better monitoring performance.

Having *employee representatives* on the board is common in many European countries and constitutes another aspect of diversity. Employee representatives are predicted to bring different perspectives to the board, affect decision-making in the boardroom and demand higher-quality communication. For example, there is evidence that firms with employee representatives on the board have higher-quality earnings (Overland and Samani, 2017). Furthermore, the participation of *foreign* board members has been investigated in research and it is found that foreign directors who usually have larger networks as well as more access to foreign markets can represent a significant contribution in terms of advising managers on strategical decisions, while at the same time causing monitoring deficiencies due to poor board meeting attendance (Masulis et al., 2012). Although this trade-off between *advising* versus *monitoring* can be problematic (whether it concerns foreign or other directors), one may argue that boards are shaped based on a combination of members with more or less ability to advise or monitor management and this mix contributes to the performance of the board as a whole.

9.3 Auditors

Because individual investors normally are unable to carry out any type of enforcement or monitoring themselves (except when individual investors are large shareholders), we have seen above that governments and states set up institutions that should serve shareholder interests—and those of the wider public. Investors also appoint representatives who sit on corporate boards with the aim of protecting their interests. **Auditors** constitute another monitoring mechanism. As financial intermediaries (along with, *inter alia*, analysts and rating institutes), their role is to improve communication and facilitate exchanges between the firm and its transacting parties. Research on intermediaries may focus on how effective auditors are at enhancing the credibility of financial statements, how effective financial analysts are as information intermediaries and how corporate disclosures affect analyst coverage of firms. As briefly touched upon in Chapter 6 in the context of analysts and disclosures, intermediaries may both *affect* and *be affected by* disclosures. Below, we go through evidence showing how auditors affect financial reporting outcomes and thus accounting quality. Considering the size and significance of the audit industry, it is perhaps no wonder that researchers have gone to such lengths to investigate the effectiveness of auditors in monitoring management and enforcing accounting regulation. The type of audit measures used may be categorized as follows:

- Audit effort (often in terms of billed hours or size of fees)
- Presence and quality of an audit committee on the board
- Quality of auditing standard
- Size of auditor
- Type (orientation) of auditor

First, as regards earnings quality, there is evidence that lower audit effort (as measured by fewer billed hours) is associated with comparatively larger positive abnormal accruals and a greater incidence of positive rather than negative abnormal accruals (Caramanis and Lennox, 2008). Similarly, lower audit committee independence is associated with higher abnormal accruals (Klein, 2002). Audit committees with higher pay—which is correlated with expertise—demand higher monitoring of the financial reporting process (Engel et al., 2010). This presumably has positive effects on outcomes.[3] Furthermore, findings on positive market implications are exemplified by Zhou (2007), who shows that higher auditing standard quality is associated with lower bid-ask spreads. This implies that equity capital markets perceive a lower information risk in these settings.

Another strand of research shows that large audit firms—commonly identified as belonging to the "Big *N*" (formerly "Big Six", now"Big Four", meaning KPMG, Deloitte, EY and PWC)—are associated with higher accounting quality in clients. This is mainly attributed to their greater level of expertise and access to specialists. However, evidence is mixed. Having a Big *N* auditor is found to constitute a constraint on earnings management (as captured by discretionary accruals) in US companies (Becker et al., 1998), but the effect of Big *N* firms on limiting earnings management is not found to be uniform across Europe—a stricter audit *environment* (according to the civil/common law distinction) does appear to be associated with higher accounting quality (Maijoor and Vanstraelen, 2006). Kim et al. (2003) find that having a Big *N* auditor is associated with reduced earnings management when managers have incentives to use income-*increasing* accruals. However, when there are incentives to instead use income-*decreasing* accruals, Big *N* auditors are actually less effective than their non-Big *N* counterparts at reducing opportunistic earnings management. This may be explained by what is commonly known as *auditor conservatism* and the preference of Big *N* auditors for income-decreasing accruals due to litigation concerns (smaller audit firms are believed to be less concerned with litigation risks or other reputation-threatening events (Francis and Wang, 2008)). The conservatism of Big *N* auditors has also been shown to influence the timeliness of firms' recognition of losses, consistent with them influencing reporting behavior (Chung et al., 2003).[4]

The results relating to the effect of large audit firms on disclosure quality are also rather mixed. While the use of large audit firms is associated with greater transparency in general—and especially in code law countries (a proxy for weaker legal environments, see comments above) (Han et al., 2012)—it is not found to be associated with lower bid-ask spreads (Muller and Riedl, 2002). In more general terms, Healy and Palepu (2001) show that evidence on the effectiveness with which these audit firms raise disclosure credibility suggests audit qualifications merely corroborate already known facts. Also, low usefulness of audits to capital markets may be caused by auditors' possibly lacking independence or their primary concern being legal liability rather than credibility.

In the debt market, having a Big *N* auditor has been shown to lead to lower required returns by investors on corporate bonds, and this is especially pronounced for firms whose instruments are below investment grade (Mansi et al., 2004). This is taken as evidence that investors ascribe an information as well as insurance role to audits. In other words, auditors act as information intermediaries as well as information insurers.

Finally, we also mention evidence on how auditor *orientation* affects the quality of reports. For example, Jamal and Hun-Tong (2010) show that principles-based standards may lead to

3 However, as we saw above, if their pay is *too* large, their independence may be compromised.
4 Timely loss recognition is commonly considered an earnings quality indicator (see Chapter 7)

less manipulation of the accounts and therefore higher reporting quality, but that this is conditional on a firm's type of auditor. More specifically, the auditor has to be principles-oriented as well, meaning that he or she focuses on the underlying substance of a transaction and the intent of the standards rather than on the letter of the rule.

Voluntary audits In most settings, listed firms or firms of a certain size are required to have audited financial statements. However, even firms that are not obliged to pay for audit services may decide to have an audit performed on their reports. Given that audits are costly to the firm, is there reason to believe that firms would like to have audits voluntarily (in accordance with signaling theory)? Given that information asymmetry is also costly to the firm, a cost-benefit analysis may very well show that having an external auditor give his or her opinion regarding the information provided by the firm may reduce information uncertainty in the capital market. If audits increase the reliability of the accounts and thus constitute credible *signals* (evidence of which can be found in the literature), managers themselves benefit from such audits. Certainly, this may at first sight only seem true in firms that perform well or do not engage in earnings management. However, since potential investors will be suspicious regarding the quality of the information in firms that decide *not* to have their accounts audited, any firm opting out of an audit may suffer a higher cost of capital or lower market liquidity.

Internal audits Proponents of *internal* audits consistently emphasize their potential role in limiting opportunistic earnings management and enhancing the quality of financial reports. Internal auditors may influence accounting outcomes through activities such as assisting external auditors in their audits of financial statements and by engaging in special consulting projects. Evidence on audit outcomes shows that external auditors rely on internal audits for financial statement audit assistance. In particular, it is argued that the joint presence of *competence* and *independence* is important in enhancing the effectiveness of financial reporting monitoring by internal auditors (Abbott et al., 2016). That is, in order to evaluate the internal audit quality, both the ability of auditors to detect accounting misstatement (i.e., competence) as well as their willingness to constrain potential opportunism of management in distorting the accounts (i.e., independence) should be considered.

9.4 Conclusions

Ensuring effective corporate governance is of interest to contracting parties in firms. Having confidence that the terms of contracts are adhered to and potential opportunism is alleviated enables more effective decision-making and thus better firm performance. Governance may be "top-down" through rules, laws, norms and external enforcers. Governance structures may also be firm-specific and "bottom-up." Given the assurance provided by governance structures, it is expected that both managers and owners have an interest in investing in additional internal control mechanisms. These include an effective (diverse and independent) board of directors and well-designed compensation plans that align the interests of managers and shareholders.

Although it is desirable to make a clear distinction between internal and external mechanisms that govern and protect firms and firm "behavior," successful governance is achieved through a "complex equilibrium process" (Jensen and Meckling, 1976, p. 311). No single governance mechanism can be considered perfect or complete. Instead, firms adopt several governance mechanisms to assure stakeholders that their interests are protected. The different mechanisms complement or substitute each other depending on the source and extent of agency problems, as well as the costs associated with these. For instance, in firms where owners can effectively control managers, there is less need for other costly mechanisms such as compensation plans. Accounting and governance are intertwined and interdependent. Accounting quality affects the structure and quality of governance, just as the structure and quality of governance affects accounting quality. The *stewardship role* of accounting is well-understood as the impact of accounting information on the efficiency of governance relationships. No matter which type and combination of governance mechanisms are used in firms, high-quality accounting information is demanded. Greater transparency and higher-quality earnings enable compensation committees to better evaluate managers' performance and design more efficient compensation contracts. Other governance mechanisms, such as auditors and other forms of enforcement of accounting standards, should be in place to ensure high-quality accounting. In shaping *and being shaped by* other governance mechanisms, accounting is considered one of the essential components of this *complex equilibrium process*.

Part V

Accounting quality and financial statement items

When talking about accounting quality, we argue in Part I that an objective function is necessary to distinguish "good" from "bad" accounting (i.e., to define accounting quality). An objective function, in turn, requires an intended financial statement user. We conclude that both research and many standard-setters define capital providers as the intended user. While Part II takes a standard-setter's perspective, Part III covers the views and operationalizations in research. The outcome of the financial reporting process—including the quality of financial statements—is largely determined by an interaction between accounting standards, managerial incentives and enforcement. While incentives and enforcement are covered in Part IV, we now return to the standard-setter's perspective—and the role of accounting standards in determining quality—by studying accounting policies and permissible choices related to individual financial statement items. In the current part of the book, we go through the remaining parts of the IASB's Conceptual Framework (see also Chapter 5), including definitions of financial statement items, measurement, entity issues and disclosure.

The question of how to design accounting standards in order to achieve the highest possible accounting quality is complex. A possible definition of quality is that financial statements provide a faithful representation of economic phenomena (cf. section 5.2), and accounting standards may be formulated based on such a definition. There are, however, many factors standard-setters must consider that complicate the design of standards. First, it is not clear which economic phenomena are relevant for users, as this requires knowledge of the decision-making processes of users. Second, economic phenomena are often not known until later periods, so financial statements must be based on assumptions and estimates that introduce (measurement) uncertainty. Third, standard-setters must consider additional factors that affect preparers, such as the legitimacy of standards, whether standards are understood by preparers, managerial incentives, enforcement and the cost of applying standards. Finally, an important consideration in the design of accounting standards is how much judgment should be required or allowed by management in the preparation of financial statements. Principles-based standards require more judgment, while rules-based standards require less. In section 4.5, we discuss principles versus rules in relation to entire regulatory frameworks (such as IFRS and US GAAP), but the dimension is also relevant for individual accounting items and areas. The reader of this book is likely to be a student with a working life that extends far into the future. During that time, current accounting standards will change substantially. The underlying issues faced by standard-setters, however, remain largely the same over time and thus we focus on such issues in this book. We refer to other books for a more detailed coverage of existing standards.

In Chapter 10, we provide a conceptual structure as a basis for analyzing and thinking about accounting standards. We cover both different types of economic phenomena (e.g., acquisition and consumption of assets as distinguished from provisioning for future transfers of resources) and choices standard-setters have (e.g. whether to require historical cost or fair value in the measurement of assets). Presenting overarching issues first makes it easier for the reader to discern similarities and differences between accounting areas. It helps prevent the reader from getting lost in all the detailed requirements in accounting standards. In subsequent chapters, we consider "unique" issues in relation to individual accounting items, as well as item-specific manifestations of the general issues.

In selecting issues and financial statement items to cover, we consider current and recent discussions and deliberations by standard-setters (primarily the IASB, but sometimes the FASB) as well as academicians (these discussions go hand-in-hand). Since 2005, much interest has been focused on the quality implications of IFRS following the endorsement of the standards by the EU in 2002 and deliberations to introduce them in the US. Research comparing IFRS with various local GAAP and US GAAP considers the effectiveness of different types of standards when it comes to conveying useful information to users. Such research, as well as studies of changes to standards **within** a given framework, are of potential interest to standard-setters as well as regulatory bodies because of what they reveal regarding what constitutes high-quality regulation and, in the end, high-quality accounting.

In general, research on financial statement items and specific accounting standards tends to be carried out at certain points in time, when the item is discussed or standard-setters issue new standards for the item. Research on share-based payment, for example, was primarily published in the period of 1995–2005. Just before 1995, the FASB issued an exposure draft requiring employee stock options to be recognized as expenses in the income statement. The exposure draft was not adopted, however, until 2005 when both the FASB and the IASB started to require the recognition of expenses. Recognition and impairment of goodwill has also been the subject of many studies following changes to standards for business combinations by the FASB in 2002 and the IASB in 2005. Fair value of financial instruments (and other items) has been studied extensively since the FASB started requiring fair value disclosures in the 1990s. In the early 1990s, several studies covered pension liabilities following a new standard in the area from the FASB (e.g., Amir, 1993).

These examples indicate that much of the research on individual financial statement items and accounting standards is based in the US and thus driven by activities by the FASB. With the ascendancy of the IASB after 2000, however, there is increasing research related to this standard-setter. Consistent with the main objectives of the IASB and FASB, the overwhelming majority of studies focus on the economic consequences of financial statements on capital markets and adopt an economic theory perspective. There is not much research done based on sociological theory nor from a critical or an interpretative perspective. The interest of, for example, constructivist researchers lies elsewhere. Research on specific items or standards that relate to standard-setters other than the FASB or IASB, is also largely absent from the most influential research outlets.

Today, almost all studies on individual items and standards are empirical. They either focus on accounting choices by preparers, and the incentives behind these choices, or on the (capital market) relevance of different accounting treatments. Specifically in relation to fair value, there is often an interest in the reliability of the measures. All of those empirical studies—though frequently without explicit theory references—are based on ideas of agency theory, information asymmetry and market efficiency. There are some studies on corporate governance that take a more explicit agency theory perspective. Examples include studies that examine CEO incentives and relate to share-based payment (Aboody et al., 2010; Nagar et al., 2003). In the area of leasing, studies that take a more finance-oriented perspective are common, as they study effects of lease accounting on firms' financing decisions. Financial statement presentation, such as studies on the effects of recognition of items in profit and loss versus OCI often focus on effects on the judgments of analysts and investors and relate to theories in behavioral economics. Disclosure studies, naturally, often relate to information asymmetry and the effect on the cost of capital. Finally, there is also research with a more conceptual interest, that focuses on the internal logic or theoretical foundation of different accounting treatments. The theory or logic used in such studies is often related to that of the FASB's or IASB's conceptual frameworks.

We divide Part V into six chapters, partly based on the structure of financial statements. Chapter 10—as mentioned—provides a general structure for some of the main issues discussed in relation to individual accounting items. The chapter also covers general measurement issues. Chapters 11 and 12 focus on the two sides of the balance sheet (i.e. the asset side and the liability and equity side). In the latter chapter, there is also reference to the statement of changes in equity. Chapter 13 covers the income statement (i.e. issues related to revenues and expenses). Issues specific to consolidated financial statements are discussed in a separate chapter (Chapter 14). We cover disclosure in the notes and provide an overview of financial statements in Chapter 15. This chapter also includes presentation issues.

We mention all accounting areas and financial statement items covered in IFRS, but some are selected for in-depth discussion. The selection of such areas is based on:

- The area is discussed in practice and in regulation
- There is more than a minimal amount of research done in the area
- The area involves issues that are especially interesting from a conceptual viewpoint and, as such, of pedagogical interest

Of course, in many cases the three areas overlap, meaning that if an area is discussed in regulation, there is also research in it and there are interesting conceptual issues. For each area selected, we identify the main issues, existing research in the area and relate to the current standard within IFRS that applies to the area. Note that some standards relate to several parts of the financial statements.

Some standards are excluded from the book as they have limited applicability in practice and do not add to the conceptual discussion. This applies, for example, to IFRS 14 and IAS 29.

Table V.1 lists the latest available IFRS for each accounting area. Whenever relevant, we also discuss previous standards.

Table V.1 Overview of standards in IFRS. The allocation of standards to chapters is based on the most important aspect (•), but the secondary aspects are also noted (o).

Standard within IFRS	Chapter 11 **Assets**	Chapter 12 **Liabilities and equity**	Chapter 13 **Income statement**	Chapter 14 **Group accounting**	Chapter 15 **Disclosure, etc.**
IFRS 1 First-time adoption of IFRS					•
IFRS 2 Share-based payment			•		
IFRS 3 Business combinations				•	
IFRS 5 Assets held for sale and discontinued operations	•				o
IFRS 6 Exploration for and evaluation of mineral assets	Not discussed in this textbook				
IFRS 7 Financial instruments: disclosures					•
IFRS 8 Operating segments					•
IFRS 9 Financial instruments	•	o			
IFRS 10 Consolidated financial statements				•	
IFRS 11 Joint operations				•	
IFRS 12 Disclosure of interests in other entities					•
IFRS 13 Fair value measurement	Discussed in Chapter 10				
IFRS 14 Regulatory deferral accounts	Not discussed in this textbook				
IFRS 15 Revenue from contracts with customers			•		
IFRS 16 Leases	•				
IFRS 17 Insurance contracts		•			
IAS 1 Presentation of financial statements					•
IAS 2 Inventories	•				
IAS 7 Statement of cash flows					•
IAS 8 Accounting policies, etc.					•
IAS 10 Events after the reporting period					•
IAS 12 Income taxes		o	•		
IAS 16 Property, plant & equipment	•				
IAS 19 Employee benefits		•			
IAS 20 Accounting for government grants	o		•		

Standard within IFRS	Chapter 11 **Assets**	Chapter 12 **Liabilities and equity**	Chapter 13 **Income statement**	Chapter 14 **Group accounting**	Chapter 15 **Disclosure, etc.**
IAS 21 The effects of changes in foreign exchange rates	o	o	•		
IAS 23 Borrowing costs	•				
IAS 24 Related party disclosures					•
IAS 26 Accounting and reporting by retirement benefit plans	Not discussed in this textbook				
IAS 27 Separate financial statements				•	
IAS 28 Investments in associates and joint ventures				•	
IAS 29 Financial reporting in hyperinflationary economies	Not discussed in this textbook				
IAS 32 Financial instruments: presentation			o		•
IAS 33 Earnings per share					•
IAS 34 Interim financial reporting					•
IAS 36 Impairment of assets	•				
IAS 37 Provisions, contingent liabilities, etc.		•			
IAS 38 Intangible assets	•				
IAS 40 Investment property	•				
IAS 41 Agriculture	•				

CHAPTER 10

Structure of accounting issues

Learning outcomes

Upon completion of this chapter, you will have gained insight into:

- Stylized situations for how accruals are used in the timing of revenues and expenses.
- Definitions of elements in financial statements.
- Different methods for measurement, with a special focus on fair value.

WHILE THERE SEEMS TO BE AN ALMOST ENDLESS number of technical issues in accounting that require thousands of pages of rules and prescriptions, in this chapter we argue that these can actually be condensed to a mere handful of issues. These relate to:

1. Definitions of items in the financial statements
2. Recognition and measurement: Four Stylized Accrual Situations (SAS)
3. Measurement bases
4. Disclosure

We begin this chapter by presenting definitions of financial statement items based on the IASB's Conceptual Framework for Financial Reporting, which was partially covered in Chapter 5. When considering the quality of financial statements, it is relevant to consider whether consistent definitions exist (in standards) and are met (in financial statements). The definitions are also necessary for the recognition and measurement of financial statement items.

With respect to the second item, rather than being overwhelmed by details, those who want to learn and understand accrual accounting may find it helpful to classify accruals into just four stylized situations. These situations are all related to the recognition and measurement of items. As we go through various issues relating to individual financial statement items in subsequent chapters, we note that many of these issues are in fact just a specific manifestation of one of the Stylized Accrual Situations (SAS).

In the final sections of this chapter, we present a discussion of possible measurement bases. Although the current chapter focuses on more general issues that transcend individual standards, we do include a reference to one particular standard, namely IFRS 13 *Fair Value Measurement*, since this is a general standard on measurement that applies to many individual financial statement items.

In sum, for any (potential) financial statement item, the main questions are whether it meets the definition of that item, whether it should be recognized, and how it should be measured (both initially and in future periods). A final question is how it should be disclosed, which is the focus of Chapter 15.

Finally, we want to highlight that some of these issues are theoretical or conceptual and thus the kind that researchers and standard-setters struggle with. For example, "what *is* an asset?" Or, "which underlying principle should govern whether there is an expense?" Or, "should an asset be measured based on its historical cost or fair value?" Other issues are practical, involve making potentially difficult judgments, and affect the preparers of financial statements. For example, "does this development project actually constitute an asset?" Or, "what is the actual expense relating to these stock options?" Or, "what is the purpose of owning this particular property?" Throughout these chapters, theoretical and practical issues intermingle; nevertheless, we emphasize that most of them can be related to the overarching issues mentioned above.

10.1 Definitions of financial statement elements

Although there is a strong link between the income statement and the balance sheet, the focus is often on one of the two statements. Over time, the IASB has increasingly moved towards a balance sheet focus (and with the implementation of IFRS 15 *Revenue from Contracts with Customers*, this move is basically complete, see Chapter 13). Consequently, in the definition of financial statement items, the IASB starts with the balance sheet.

In the balance sheet and income statement, there are five different types of elements: assets, liabilities and equity on the balance sheet and income and expenses in the income statement. The Conceptual Framework refers to "income" rather than "revenue," where income is a broader concept. The logic of definitions in the Conceptual Framework is that assets and liabilities are clearly defined and equity is defined as the residual of assets and liabilities. Meanwhile, income and expenses are defined in terms of changes of items on the balance sheet, which is congruent with a balance sheet focus.

The focus on the balance sheet does not mean that the income statement is unimportant. As argued in Chapter 7, earnings is an essential figure for investors. Rather, the IASB has concluded that it is easier to stringently define assets and liabilities compared to income and expense. Due to the strong link between the income statement and the balance sheet, asset and liability definitions and recognition criteria determine the level and timing of earnings.

Research also questions whether IFRS and the Conceptual Framework in fact have a full balance sheet approach. Penman (2007) and Barker and Teixeira (2017) point out that it is only when current values are used that there is a focus on the balance sheet. When historicalcost is used, which is the most common measurement basis, the focus is instead on the income statement. We return to different measurement bases in section 10.3.

10.1.1 Assets and liabilities

Definitions of assets and liabilities in the 2018 Conceptual Framework are:

> An asset is a present economic resource controlled by the entity as a result of past events. (Par. 4.3)
>
> An economic resource is a right that has the potential to produce economic benefits. (Par. 4.4)
>
> A liability is a present obligation of the entity to transfer an economic resource as a result of past events. (Par. 4.26)

These definitions contain two main components: 1.) **control** (or lack of control for liabilities) as a result of past events, and 2.) expected **future economic benefits** (or outflow of such benefits for liabilities). These definitions are more specific than what you would find in a regular dictionary, which may for example state that an asset is a "resource," something "useful" or "a valuable item." However, from a business perspective, the definitions are not particularly controversial.

An important change in the 2018 version compared to previous versions of the Conceptual Framework is that assets are defined as *rights*; that is, the right to use a specific asset, rather than defined as the asset *per se*. For financial and intangible assets, this does not constitute much of a change. For tangible assets, however, it does represent a different view. A machine, for example, is not an asset in itself. Instead, it is the right to use the machine that represents the asset of interest. This view by the IASB is already reflected in recent standards such as IFRS 15 *Revenue from Contracts with Customers* and IFRS 16 *Leases*.

Another change compared to previous versions of the Conceptual Framework is that the IASB has introduced a one-step process for the reporting of assets and liabilities. Previously, the definition of assets and liabilities was separated from **recognition criteria**. Consequently, it was possible to have assets and liabilities that met the definition, but not recognize them in the balance sheet, as they did not meet the recognition criteria. In the 2018 Conceptual Framework, the recognition criteria have been included in the definition, with reference to the qualitative characteristics of financial statements. The Conceptual Framework states the following, relating both to *relevance* and *faithful representation*

> [R]ecognition of a particular asset or liability and any resulting income, expenses or changes in equity may not always provide relevant information. That may be the case if, for example:
>
> (a) it is uncertain whether an asset or liability exists; or
>
> (b) an asset or liability exists, but the probability of an inflow or outflow of economic benefits is low. (Par. 5.12)

These criteria relate to relevance but are also an expression of the qualitative characteristic of faithful representation, since they are designed to ensure that items found on the balance sheet do in fact exist and that they are measured reliably. The Conceptual Framework explicitly states that faithful representation is to be interpreted as complete, neutral and free from error.

Given that managers are widely believed to be optimistically biased on average and that the recognition and measurement of many items are characterized by uncertainty, there is a tendency for regulators to attempt to counteract the potentially negative outcomes of this by imposing a level of conservatism on financial reports. Requiring information to be faithfully represented or reliable is reflective of this (notably, the neutrality and free-from-error criteria are also meant to deter undervaluation, and by no means should recognition of, for example, an asset be viewed as optional). As discussed in Chapter 5, however, the information provided also has to be relevant in the sense that there is a limit to the amount and level of certainty one can demand of preparers of financial reports. Demanding completely certain reports may result in no information being provided at all or in merely having after-the-fact cash flow reports. The value of cash is always certain because it is at face value,[1] but since most of the world's wealth is invested in non-cash assets,[2] obtaining approximations of those asset values is believed to be relevant—and therefore useful—to investors and creditors. In Chapters 1 and 3, we used the term "uncertainty" and concluded that some level of uncertainty is unavoidable in accounting.

Even if the main ideas remain, the 2018 Conceptual Framework results in some changes to the definitions of financial statement items (e.g., for assets). The new Conceptual Framework also includes a more comprehensive discussion of different concepts. The meaning of *control*—defined as the ability to determine how an asset is used and the right to receive economic benefits from the asset—is discussed at some length. An area that has been unclear within IFRS is the extent to which **executory contracts** meet the definition of assets and liabilities. In such contracts, none of the contracting parties have performed anything yet. For example, if firm A orders a product from firm B, does A's promise to pay B in the future represent a liability and does the confirmed order represent an asset (and revenue) for firm B? Executory contracts represent assets only if they are favorable and liabilities only if they are unfavorable. The Conceptual Framework states that if the net value of such a contract is zero, no asset and liability arises. In arms-length transactions, the assumption is that the value of incoming and outgoing resources is the same and executory contracts do not normally represent assets and liabilities.

10.1.2 Equity

The Conceptual Framework defines equity as the difference between assets and liabilities. In other words, once assets and liabilities have been defined and recognized in accordance with criteria, equity follows as a residual. Equity represents the claims of owners on the assets of the firms. Thus, it makes sense that what remains after all contractual and other obligations (i.e., liabilities) have been deducted is the claim. It also agrees with the legal rights of equity-holders. They have the right to receive the residual after the firm has paid all its creditors and other claimants. Equity-holders are sometimes referred to as "residual claimants."

In theory, liabilities are clearly defined. In practice, however, the distinction between liabilities and equity is not always clear, although it is a very important distinction for financial

1 It is true that this value can change rapidly in situations of hyperinflation, but the theoretical reasoning is unaltered by such scenarios.

2 www.worldwealthreport.com/reports/asset_allocation

statement users. It determines the level of debt to equity, which is a key measure of long-term financial stability. Increasingly, firms issue so-called "hybrid financial instruments" that have characteristics of both debt and equity.

Within IFRS, the distinction between debt and equity is covered in IAS 32 *Financial Instruments: Presentation*. IAS 32—consistent with general definitions—states that if there is a contractual obligation to make payments in the future, it is a liability. If there is no such obligation, but the holder of the instrument is a residual claimant, it is equity. In practice, however, there are instruments where this distinction is not apparent, as discussed further in section 12.5.

10.1.3 Income and expenses

As noted above, income and expense are defined in the Conceptual Framework based on assets and liabilities. More specifically, the definitions are:

> Income is increases in assets or decreases in liabilities that result in increases in equity, other than those relating to contributions from holders of equity claims. (Par. 4.68)
>
> Expenses are decreases in assets or increases in liabilities that result in decreases in equity, other than those relating to distributions to holders of equity claims. (Par. 4.69)

These definitions clearly show the strong link between the income statement and the balance sheet. The definitions are also consistent with the definition of equity. Net income—which is the difference between income and expense—is taken to equity. As equity is defined as the difference between assets and liabilities, net income (i.e., income after expenses) is defined in terms of changes to assets and liabilities. This corresponds with the idea that a balance sheet portrays the state of assets, liabilities and equity at a certain point in time, while the income statement is focused on changes of such items between two periods (changes between starting and ending balance sheets).

Note that the definition is also consistent with the notion that transactions with owners (equity participants) do not represent income and expense, and thus should not be reflected in the income statement.

The reader may wonder about the distinction between "income" and "revenue." This was discussed in the previous (2010) Conceptual Framework. Income is a broader concept that covers both revenue and gains. Revenue comes from ordinary activities in a firm, while gains arise from, for example, sale of long-term assets. IFRS 15 *Revenue from Contracts with Customers* only relates to revenue and not to gains. There is a similar distinction between expenses (from ordinary activities) and losses (e.g., from sale of long-term assets or from assets impaired). In the 2018 Conceptual Framework, the discussion regarding the distinction between income and revenue is removed. It was originally included to make it explicit that income includes gains and expenses include losses. Since this is now generally accepted, IASB now considers this discussion no longer necessary.

Income and expenses relate to another important concept in financial reporting: performance. Performance is a key measure of interest to investors. Earnings (such as net income) and cash flows are examples of alternative measures of performance. At the time of writing (August 2018), the IASB is discussing the presentation of performance as part of a project on primary financial statements.

We have now covered the broad definitions of financial statement items in the Conceptual Framework. In the next section we go through how the items appear in the income statement and balance sheet through accruals.

10.2 Four stylized accrual situations

We now turn to the four stylized accrual situations referred to at the outset of the chapter. The most basic issues in the production of financial statements have to do with *timing*. Firms have economic transactions and events, such as acquisitions and disposals (of both assets and liabilities) and changes in the value of a firm's assets and liabilities. The question is *when* these transactions and events are reflected in the financial statements (the focus here is on the income statement and the balance sheet). The timing issue lies at the heart of accrual accounting, as accruals assign transactions and events to the appropriate fiscal period. This use of accruals is a basic function of the financial reporting system (Dechow, 1994), see Figure 10.1.

Economic transactions and events should not be confused with cash transactions, as cash flows may occur in different periods. While cash flows mix investments and disinvestments with earnings-generating transactions such as sales, accruals are designed to shift cash flows over time to achieve better estimates of current performance. Over long time periods, however, the net result of economic transactions and events, cash flows and accounting earnings largely coincide (see below).

In structuring possible accruals, we note that the production of financial statements involve three basic types of "activities": *recognition* (and its counterpart *derecognition*),

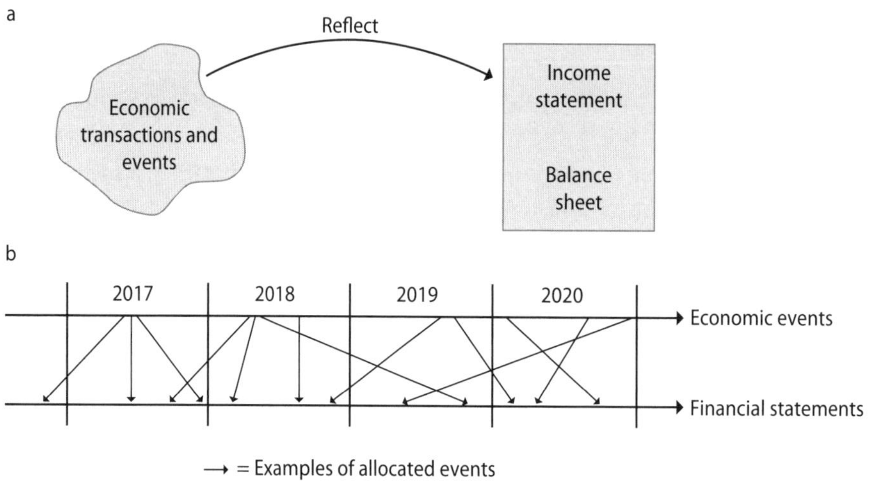

Figure 10.1 The financial reporting system: Accruals, transactions and events

measurement and *disclosure*. Recognition means inclusion in the income statement and/or balance sheet, while derecognition is removal from those financial statements. Measurement is the activity of assigning a monetary value to items in the income statement and/or balance sheet. Both recognition (derecognition) and measurement are thus focused on the income statement and the balance sheet. Disclosure, in standard-setter terminology, is the activity of providing additional information outside of those two financial statements—primarily in the notes.[3] As stated previously, whereas we focus on recognition and measurement here, disclosure is covered in Chapter 15.

The four stylized accrual situations are listed below.

1. **Acquisition of resource**: When a resource is acquired, it is always in the form of an exchange, as we assume that firms do not receive gifts (i.e., something in exchange for nothing). Consequently, the firm either gives up a resource (e.g., cash) or incurs a liability, which is accounted for with a credit entry. Based on the logic of double-entry bookkeeping, there must be a corresponding debit entry. This debit entry may either be in the form of an expense on the income statement or result in an asset on the balance sheet. So, the accounting issue in focus here is whether the resource acquired—in full or partly—meets the criteria for asset recognition. When resources are consumed, they are recognized as expenses. This could either happen immediately, or—if an asset is recognized—over time, as the asset is used. We thus distinguish between the choice of **capitalizing** the expenditure (i.e., recognizing it as an asset in the balance sheet) and **expensing** (i.e., recognizing it as an expense in the income statement). If an asset is recognized, the subsequent issue is over which time period and according to which logic the asset is consumed. The timing issue involved in the acquisition of resources is consequently when the resources are recognized as expenses on the income statement. See Figure 10.2 (a).

   If the acquisition is recognized as an asset, an accrual is made at the time of the acquisition. This accrual is reversed through the subsequent derecognition in the balance sheet (and simultaneous recognition in the income statement). Using the terminology of Dichev (2017), the matching of the accrual to an economic transaction is in this case done first, followed by the estimate of expenses. Consequently, the difficult judgments on measurement come in the subsequent estimates. In the initial matching, measurement is reasonably certain; however, judgment is required on the issue of recognition or not.

2. **Future outflows of resources**: Often firms may predict that outflows of resources will occur in future periods. An issue related to this is whether to recognize an expense when information about the future outflow is available or to wait until the actual outflows occur. If expenses are recognized early, a corresponding provision is included on the balance sheet. Note that there is asymmetry in this situation, as future

3 In other parts of the book, when focusing on research, we have adopted a broader definition of disclosure and taken it to mean any information provided by firms. In Part V, we discuss disclosure in a narrower, more technical, sense.

outflows of resources may be recognized, but not future inflows. This is related to the prudence principle, as discussed in section 5.3. There is an obvious timing issue in this case. See Figure 10.2 (b).

In this case, the accrual is made first (when the change in value is unrealized), and the matching to economic events, as well as the reversal of the accrual, occurs later when the change in value is realized. Consequently, judgment is often required when the accrual is made, while its reversal requires little judgment (Dichev, 2017).

3. **Changes in value of existing items**: When an item already recognized on the balance sheet—an asset or a liability—changes value, this may or may not be reflected on the balance sheet with a resulting gain or loss on the income statement. To be reflected means that the economic gain or loss is immediately recognized. If it is not reflected, the economic gain or loss will be recognized at a later time, usually when the asset or liability is disposed of or settled (i.e, when the gain or loss is realized). Note that this situation concerns non-systematic changes in value. Systematic changes are recognized through depreciation or amortization (cf. acquisitions of resources above). Clearly, there is a timing issue here. See Figure 10.2 (c).

   As in the previous case, in this accrual situation the accrual is made by making an estimate of future economic transactions, which often requires substantial judgment. Subsequently, the accrual is reversed through matching to economic transactions, which requires less judgment (Dichev, 2017).

4. **Revenue recognition**: The final stylized situation concerns when to recognize revenue. When resources—goods and services—are transferred to customers, it is not always obvious in which period revenue should be recognized. This could occur in an earlier period, in the same period or in a later period as the actual transfer takes place. See Figure 10.2 (d).

The stylized accrual situations are expressed in terms of recognition in the income statement and the balance sheet, but could also be seen as measurement. In SAS 1, the conversion of assets to expenses over time could be expressed as an issue of measurement of assets. SAS 2 could be seen as an issue of asset or liability measurement. SAS 3 relates to the measurement of liabilities. SAS 4 is most closely connected to the income statement, but just as in the discussion in section 13.1, it is possible to relate it to the measurement of assets and liabilities.

The close relationship between the income statement and the balance sheet is obvious in the stylized situations. In order to defer the recognition of expenses in the income statement from the acquisition of resources, an asset is recognized in the balance sheet. When changes in the values of assets and liabilities are recognized in the balance sheet, this has a direct effect on gains and losses in the income statement. When an expense is recognized in the income statement for future outflows of resources, a provision is required in the balance sheet. Finally, when revenue is recognized in the income statement before or after the actual transfer of resources to customers, a temporary asset or liability must be recognized in the balance sheet.

As we discuss in section 10.1, the focus can either be on the income statement or on the balance sheet. The point we want to make here is that regardless of which financial statement

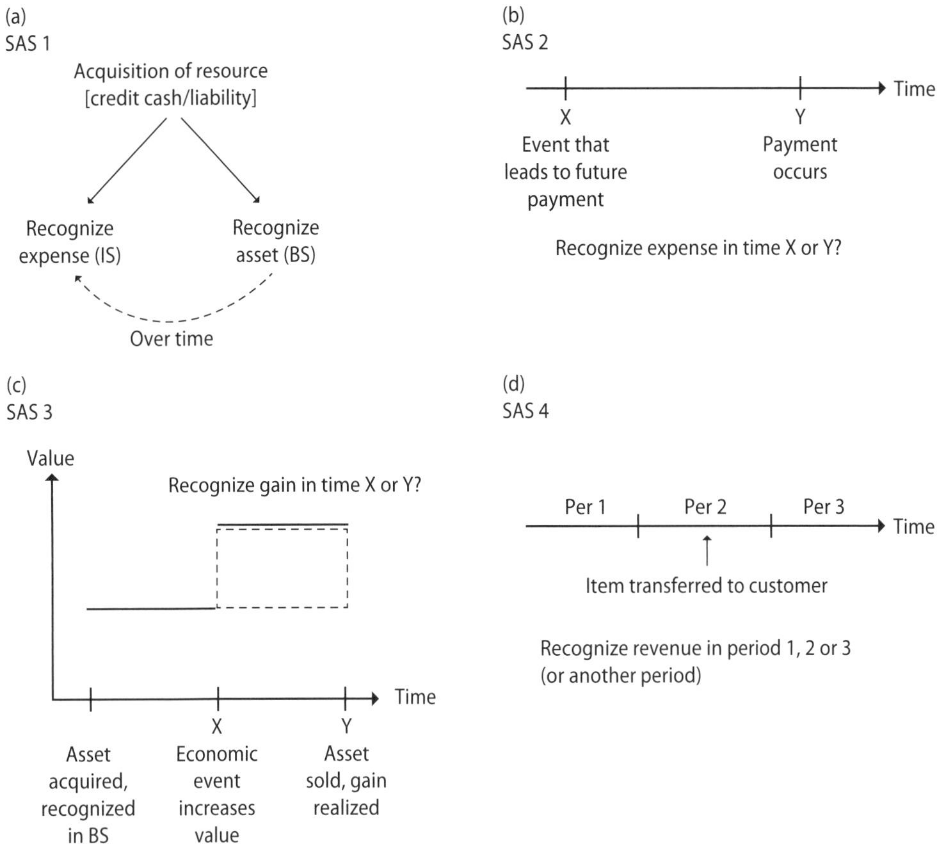

Figure 10.2 Stylized Accrual Situations (SAS)

is seen as primary or in focus, the two financial statements are linked. If an item is recognized in one of the two statements, it will have an effect on the other.

The stylized situations show how most accruals work. Common accruals include the relation between inventory and the cost of goods sold, as well as depreciation and amortization of fixed assets. Both of these relate to the acquisition of resources (SAS 1). Another important accrual is the recognition of provisions (SAS 2). The recognition of non-systematic value changes before realization—including impairment—is one type of accrual (SAS 3), as are accruals related to revenue recognition (SAS 4).

Although many accounting issues fit into one of the four stylized situations, there are some issues that are not meaningfully classifiable into any of them. Such issues include lease accounting as well as business combinations and consolidation. In those cases, additional issues arise, which we discuss in Chapters 11 and 14.

The focus on timing as the central issue suggests that what accountants actually do is to allocate transactions and events to the appropriate time periods. Accountants cannot "create" or "destroy" revenues and expenses, they can only move them between periods to provide more timely and relevant information. Long-term earnings are determined by economic transactions and events, suggesting that over long time periods, the total net effect of economic transactions and events converge with total accounting-based net income. As economic transactions and events at some point must result in cash flows, this also holds true for total cash flows. In other words, Σ (economic events and transactions) = Σ (net income) = Σ (cash flows) over long time periods.

With regard to all generalizations, however, there are some exceptions where the regularity does not hold. First, there is one group of economic transactions and cash flows that do not affect the income statement: transactions with owners, such as new stock issuance and payment of dividends. In an area such as share-based payment (see Chapter 13), the long-term relationship between economic transactions and earnings is actually affected by the requirements of the accounting standards. This is because one of the issues in that area is whether share-based payment should be recognized as an expense or whether it should be seen as an owner transaction. Second, whether or not the above regularity holds could depend on the earnings number selected. If net income is chosen, anything outside the income statement will be excluded from the regularity, primarily items in other comprehensive income (OCI). To include such items, we must focus on total comprehensive income.[4]

The issue of timing is linked to uncertainty (and subjectivity). It is often the case that the longer the time period between financial statement recognition and cash flows, the higher the level of uncertainty. This time period is referred to as **accrual duration** by Dichev (2017) and one example of this is pension accounting (see Chapter 12). Uncertainty is one potential cause of quality problems in accounting, as discussed in section 1.2.3. Each of the four accrual situations may be dealt with differently by standard-setters, leading to more or less uncertainty in financial statements. Specific standards and accounting items illustrate the four situations, as shown in the following chapters. We use the situations to obtain a structure in order to analyze and understand the effect of standards on accounting quality. It also provides a structure for understanding research on accruals, as research on specific financial statement items evaluates accounting standards with respect to the four accrual situations.

10.3 Bases for measurement

All items in the income statement and balance sheet are stated in monetary amounts. Consequently, all items recognized in those two financial statements must also be measured. In the current accounting system, measurement is **transaction-based**, but the transactions may vary in timing. The Conceptual Framework presents two measurement bases: historical cost and current value.

- **Historical cost** is the price paid for an asset on the date it is acquired, or the consideration accepted at the time of taking on a liability (i.e. measurement based on historical transactions).

4 This, however, creates additional difficulties, as some items in OCI have a very long-term nature and some are recycled—that is, recognized in the income statement when realized—while others are not. OCI includes items that relate to firm performance, but for various reasons are not relevant to include in the income statement nor reflect in net income. OCI is further discussed and explained in section 15.2.2.

- There are three different types of **current value**:
  - **Fair value** represents the market price of an item, and it can be estimated through current market price (i.e., measurement based on a hypothetical current transaction) or through discounted future cash flows (i.e., measurement based on a number of future transactions).
  - **Value in use** is based on discounted future cash flows (i.e., measurement based on a number of future transactions).
  - **Current cost** is the price in a hypothetical current transaction to acquire an asset or take on a liability.

As may be evident from the discussion, transactions can vary along two different dimensions: 1) the timing of the transaction, which can be in the past, present or future, and 2) whether the transaction reflects an entry price or an exit price. An **entry price** is the price paid by the firm for the acquisition of an asset, or the amount received for taking on a liability. An **exit price** is the price received upon disposal of an asset or the amount paid to settle a liability. In well-functioning markets, one would not expect much difference between entry and exit prices. However, in practice these prices can differ, due to the existence of various transaction costs. An overview of possible transaction-based measures is provided in Table 10.1.

The economic idea behind basing measurement on transactions is that transactions represent market prices and that such prices are relevant to include in financial statements. For market prices to be reflected, it is necessary that transactions occur between independent parties. If they do (and if some additional conditions are fulfilled, see below), the transaction price reflects fair value *at the time the transaction takes place.*

The idea that transactions represent market prices leads into an important distinction between **initial measurement** and **subsequent measurement**. Initial measurement occurs when an item is recognized in the financial statements. When, for example, an asset is acquired and recognized, it is measured based on an arms-length transaction. At that time, historical cost and fair value are the same, as the transaction just occurred. Later, at subsequent measurement, fair value may change and the two measures can therefore diverge. Consequently, the issue of whether to use historical cost or fair value is usually only relevant at subsequent measurements.

The difficulty with, and uncertainty in, measurement depends on the situation. Overall, current values are more difficult to estimate than historical cost, since historical cost is based

Table 10.1 Bases for measurement

	Direction of transaction	
Time dimension	**Entry price**	**Exit price**
Historical price	Historical cost	Never used
Current price	Current cost	Current market price (e.g., fair value)
Future price	Never used	Discounted cash flows (e.g., fair value or value in use)

on a transaction that has already occurred and is therefore objectively verifiable. There are, however, some possible difficulties with the determination of historical cost. Three examples are: 1) deciding what is included in historical cost when there are incidental costs (cf. PP&E and inventories in Chapter 11 in the acquisition, 2) assets acquired as a package where cost must be determined for individual items (cf. business combinations), and 3) exchange transactions that do not involve cash. Current values are often not objectively verifiable but have to be estimated, which creates uncertainty in such estimates.

Based on Table 10.2, we can discern an underlying logic in the use of different measurement models in IFRS. Historical cost is the default measurement model. Meanwhile, fair value is primarily used in two situations:

1. It is used for assets (and liabilities) where historical cost is not relevant, as the performance of the firm is evaluated based on changes in fair value. This applies to investment property (a special type of tangible asset) and biological assets (typically a type of inventory), and some financial instruments. Investment property refers to buildings held with the intention of earning rents or making gains from capital appreciation (i.e., buildings owned for own use are excluded). Fair values for investment properties are often subject to substantial changes over time. Biological assets, such as plants and livestock, often have a low value at recognition that *increases* greatly over time. In combination with long lives, historical cost is therefore frequently not a relevant measure for either of these types of assets. Fair values are also used for many financial assets in cases where the changes in value directly affect firms' cash flow.
2. It is used when the historical cost of a transaction must be estimated, because there is no cash transaction for the individual assets. This, for example, applies to assets and liabilities acquired in a business combination, used for share-based payment, and provisions.

We can relate measurement to the four stylized situations discussed above. SAS 1 relates to historical cost of assets, as it has to do with the acquisition of resources. SAS 2 is often characterized by high uncertainty as it is based on predictions of future events. Provisions (a type of liability) must, if recognized, be measured based on estimated future cash flows (i.e., fair values). SAS 3 has to do with subsequent measurement related to non-systematic changes in value. This includes impairment under either historical cost or fair value, systematic depreciation and amortization if historical cost is used, or even increases in current market values if fair values are used. SAS 4 is about revenue recognition, and revenue is normally measured at fair value at the time it is recognized. It is normally not problematic from a measurement perspective, as there is no subsequent, only initial, measurement (instead, difficulties associated with SAS 4 have to do with the timing of recognition).

Table 10.2 gives an overview of which different measurement bases are used for which items within IFRS.

Table 10.2 Measurement bases for different items within IFRS

		Current value	
Item	**Historical cost**	**Fair value**	**Other current value**
Property, plant and equipment	Default	Sometimes electable	Value in use in impairment
Investment property	Possible	Recommended	
Intangible assets	Default	Rarely electable	Value in use in impairment
Financial assets	Required for some assets	Required for most assets	
Inventory	Default	Impairment	
Biological assets		Required	
Financial liabilities	Required for most liabilities	Required for some liabilities	
Provisions			Special requirements
Pension liabilities			Special requirements
Deferred taxes			Special requirements
Share-based payment			Special requirements
Business combinations	Fair value used to determine historical cost		

10.3.1 The definition and measurement of fair value

Ever since the FASB started requiring fair value disclosures for some financial items in the 1990s, the use of fair value has been debated in both standard-setting and in research. In IFRS, fair value is required for some items, whereas historical cost is the most common measurement basis.

The issuance of IFRS 13 *Fair Value Measurement* in 2011, which was largely based on the FASB's Statement no. 157, partly represented a move toward greater convergence of accounting practices between the world's two largest standard-setters, and partially also represented a step closer to the realization of what has been termed the *fair value paradigm* (Hitz, 2007; Shortridge and Smith, 2009). The objective was the development of a consistent framework on fair value that would replace the piecemeal guidance dispersed throughout many IFRS. IFRS 13 is a pure measurement standard. It does not prescribe when fair value should be used (that is done in other standards). Instead, IFRS 13 determines *how* fair value should be measured when it is required in another standard. IFRS 13 *Fair Value Measurement* defines fair value as:

> The price that would be received to sell an asset or paid to transfer a liability in an orderly transaction between market participants at the measurement date. (IFRS 13, Appendix A)

A few aspects of fair value measurement are apparent from the definition. Fair value is defined as a market price. As such, no entity-specific considerations should be made in the estimation of fair value. Rather, one should attempt to determine what the price would be if a transaction occurred between market participants. This means that value in use—which is applied in impairment testing—differs from fair value (section 11.3). Meanwhile, the term "orderly transaction" suggests that the price should reflect normal market conditions and knowledgeable market participants. Fair value is not the price that would be received in, for example, a forced liquidation sale or in a transaction between parties unfamiliar with the market. By focusing on the price received, the IASB defines fair value as an exit price. The price of acquisition could potentially be different. Even if exit price seems clear, some questions arise (as discussed below).

Even if exit price is the preferred valuation technique, IFRS 13 recognizes that it is not always possible to obtain such a price, for example when no market prices are available. In some cases, a cost approach may be used instead, and in others an income approach is more applicable. The income approach is based on present value models.

Related to different valuation approaches is the fair value hierarchy that is defined in the standard. The hierarchy concerns the information (or input) used in the valuation techniques.

- **Level 1** inputs are quoted prices in active markets for identical assets and liabilities.
- **Level 2** inputs are observable market data not included in level 1.
- **Level 3** inputs are unobservable inputs.

It is called a hierarchy, as IFRS 13 requires that level 1 inputs be used if they are available. Level 3 inputs can only be used if level 1 and level 2 inputs are unavailable. It is also evident that level 1 inputs enable more objective measurement of fair value, while level 3 inputs require substantial judgment by preparers and therefore cause a high level of measurement uncertainty. Exit price valuation is easier when level 1 and level 2 inputs are available. Level 3 input is often used when fair value is estimated based on future discounted cash flows. As we shall see in the next section, research suggests that fair value measures based on level 1 inputs are in general more relevant for investors than those based on level 3 inputs. A term often used in research to relate to fair value is "mark-to-market" accounting. This would primarily relate to level 1 inputs. In the income approach with level 3 inputs, it is more correct to talk about "mark-to-model" (see, for instance, Meder et al., 2011), with the additional measurement uncertainty implied in that concept.

10.4 The fair value debate

The use of fair value in financial statements has led to a substantial discussion in research, both from theoretical (conceptual) and empirical points of view.

10.4.1 Theoretical (conceptual) views

Theoretically, researchers have pointed to inconsistencies in the definition of fair value and potential problems if entity-specific values are excluded. The definition of fair value is based on the assumption of market efficiency. This may be deduced from the Boards' justifications for fair value accounting—that fair value is timely in its incorporation of information concerning current market conditions as well as representative of collective market beliefs and actual market volatility (Milburn, 2008, see discussion in). The definition of fair value may be considered to function well under such an assumption. However, while accepting that an exit price is a reasonable benchmark for fair value where market prices are easily available, estimating fair value based on unobservable (level 3) inputs is potentially problematic. That level 3 inputs should represent an exit price from the perspective of a market participant is far from obvious, as the valuation techniques suggested are sometimes crude proxies for exit values. This is particularly troublesome for some assets, such as non-contractual assets with a high value in use (but a low realizable value). Clearly, there is significant reliance on the individual's judgments when making the estimates. Milburn (2008) uses the following excerpt from IFRS 13 as an example:

> If multiple valuation techniques are used to measure fair value, the results [...] shall be evaluated and weighted, as appropriate, considering the reasonableness of the range of values indicated by those results. A fair value measurement is the point within that range that is most representative of fair value in the circumstances (Par. 63).

Despite the arguments put forth in IFRS 13 Basis for Conclusions, that the different levels of inputs do not necessitate any distinctions between, or different labels for, different types of fair value, Milburn (2008) points out that:

> [T]he concept of fair value implicit in the provisions of SFAS No. 157 [and IFRS 13] might, taken as a whole, be considered to comprise a family of current value measurement bases ranging from reasonably efficient market values to current cost and present value bases that are significantly dependent on entity expectations—all described as 'fair value' (p. 312).

Practical difficulties may, in other words, obstruct *de facto* conceptual consistency.

Hitz (2007) expresses similar concerns when criticizing model-based fair value by adopting as a starting point the information aggregation hypothesis: the notion that "market price aggregates in an efficient and virtually unbiased manner the consensus expectations of investors in the market concerning the cash flow pattern of the asset or liability" (p. 328). This (along with the decision-usefulness paradigm) is a major driver of fair value accounting and may be considered acceptable if, and only if, there are functioning markets.

> [M]odel-based fair value cannot, by definition, represent an aggregate of expectations dispersed in the market place: since valuation rests on the information set of one person or one organization, this fair value loses its capacity to efficiently collect and aggregate consensus expectations about the cash flow profile of the relevant position. The paradigmatic information aggregation assumption falters—a result that substantially questions standard-setters' theoretical reasoning on the desirability of fair value measurement. Rather than market information, model-based fair value inevitably incorporates management's private information and assumptions, that is, elements of value in use. [...] Curiously, model-based fair value is capable of creating useful information in the strict, information content sense, when credible communication of private management information takes place. Empirical

> evidence suggests this is happening (Barth and Clinch, 1998; Beaver and Venkatachalam, 2003). Accordingly, fair value measurement on the marking-to-model level receives vindication only where the fair value definition is violated and elements of value in use are incorporated. Obviously, this observation refutes rather than confirms the theoretical basis of fair value measurement. (Hitz, 2007, pp.~343–344)

Whittington (2008a) brings up another view in a discussion on the relevance of market-based information devoid of entity-specific information. He emphasizes the need for entity-specific considerations in order for the information to be decision-useful; private information cannot and should not be ignored. If value in use is rejected on the basis that it is entity-specific and incorporates management skill, the relevance of exit prices may then also be questioned since share prices have been shown to reflect these entity-specific features (i.e., they are valued by investors) (see Barth and Landsman, 1995). Such an argument therefore seems inconsistent, and simply reflects a pragmatism that values market participants' estimates above management estimates.

The focus on market participants is consistent with the overall market orientation in IFRS 13 and the definition satisfactorily expands on the previously shorter definition, "knowledgeable, willing parties in an arm's length transaction." However, as Milburn (2008) points out, the focus on market participants instead of markets "seems in danger of confusing entity-specific (market participant) values with market value." Importantly, as Milburn (2008) also clarifies, the market is not a place where all market participants share the same view on the possible utility of an asset; rather, through interactions of actors with different expectations, a consensus might be reached. This means that if there is no active market, is it possible for an individual market participant (for example the firm preparing financial statements) to hypothetically estimate the price that would have been on an active market? This concern relates to the notion of the highest and best use of an asset, as suggested in IFRS 13. How do you, in practice, determine what is the highest and best use? If there is no active market and hypothetical prices must be sought for an asset that is currently not used to its full potential, how far do you go in a search for a "market value"? Can the intentions and objectives of only a few independent, knowledgeable, willing and able market participants serve to determine the highest and best use? The authors of this textbook have difficulties finding the answers to these questions. It is believed that where there are no observable inputs, estimating an exit price based on the highest and best use may in practice yield measurements that are unacceptably inaccurate, while still retaining the appearance of a market measure.

The research just presented was published as part of the discussion surrounding the IASB's work on IFRS 13. The severe financial crisis in 2007–2008 led to additional discussions among researchers whether fair value measurement in the financial statements of banks contributed to the severity of the crisis. The reasoning was that fair values on the balance sheet caused a "feedback loop." When asset prices in markets declined, this was reflected on the balance sheet in banks that measured assets and fair value. This, in turn, caused a deterioration in the financial position of banks, leading to even lower asset values, and so on. However, Laux and Leuz (2009) point out that this scenario was an unlikely contributor to the crisis.

In a kindred spirit to the IASB's view, Barlev and Haddad (2007) argue that fair value accounting (as opposed to historical cost accounting) may contribute to harmonization and comparability of international accounting, since for fair values the timing of measurements is "acceptable worldwide," purchasing power changes do not cause such severe distortions over time where fair value is reported, values are location-independent when based on international market prices and subjectivity is lessened since current prices are not entity-specific. A positive reinforcement cycle is made possible as an extended use of fair value in turn provides more globalized, harmonized capital markets, which in turn facilitate fair value accounting. Little reservation is exhibited with regard to the possibility of active markets being absent; potential reliability issues are believed to be dwarfed by the more serious problems caused by the local nature of historical cost accounting—both in time and geographically. The theoretical considerations in Hitz (2007) lead to a considerably different conclusion: that the fair value income concept is lacking in its very formulation or existence and that this is even more problematic for non-financial items in inactive or illiquid markets.

Overall, research raises doubts concerning the use of fair values in financial statements, especially when it is based on level 3 inputs in present value models. To some extent, the IASB has listened to the critique. While the board previously propagated an increased use of fair value, in the last few years it has moderated this approach. The current message from the IASB is that fair value should be used in situations where it is relevant, as noted in the Conceptual Framework. The Board also recognizes the issues involved in achieving a faithful representation of fair value in some situations.

10.4.2 Empirical (practical) views

The main practical concern with fair values as the basis for measurement is that they place too large a focus on the *expected future* cash flows associated with the asset or liability in question. In other words, the use of fair value in financial statements inserts predictions of future net cash flows (and earnings) into the financial statements, which can be contrasted with the use of verification-based, historical cost measures of assets and liabilities. Theoretically, if all assets and liabilities were measured at fair value, the equity on the balance sheet should equal capitalization on the stock market. The main problem with this is reduced reliability of financial statements due to measurement uncertainty related to fair values. The argument, then, is that fair values are more relevant. However, it is far from clear that investors should view fair values on the balance sheet as more relevant than historical costs. Historical cost reflects past actions by the firm management and this may constitute the best basis for investors' forecasts of future performance. Perhaps accountants should not participate in the forecasting activity. In the words of Penman (2012, page 8), "do not mix what you know with speculation." In order for financial statements to be useful "anchors" for investors, they should avoid reflecting current beliefs. Especially in corporate governance settings, it is possible that the performance of management is better assessed based on historical cost, since management cannot control changes in fair values (Shivakumar, 2013). In addition, historical cost is generally more enforceable as it has a higher level of verifiability (Watts, 2006).

When reviewing the evidence from empirical studies to assess the alleged merit of fair value accounting, one may conclude that, by and large, it is inconclusive; the picture is only less ambiguous when financial instruments are concerned. In the next few sections we look at some of the general value relevance studies carried out on fair value measurement, present some of the evidence on earnings management, and raise relevance and reliability concerns in relation to fair values.

Value relevance of fair values

Many of the early studies look at the value relevance of fair value disclosures under SFAS No. 107 Disclosures about Fair Value of Financial Instruments in order to find evidence that investors price fair value. One of these studies, carried out by Barth (1994), looks at investment securities in banks and the incremental value relevance of fair value disclosures as compared with historical costs. The author finds that fair values of this particular financial instrument can explain security prices, but that gains and losses in the studied securities are not value-relevant for fair value measurements, possibly as a result of the accumulation of estimation error (Penman, 2007). According to Eccher et al. (1996), fair value disclosures in commercial banks are associated with security prices, both alone and incrementally in order to benchmark book values. However, in the latter case, results are inconsistent over the studied period and, furthermore, any consistency observed only pertains to investment securities. Importantly, book values (based on historical cost) are more value-relevant on the whole compared to fair value disclosures (perhaps because the latter were not formally recognized, cf. Chapter 15). The results of Park et al. (1999) on fair value disclosures for investment securities and bank equity produce similar conclusions.

The regression model in Barth et al. (1996), which builds on other specifications and controls for certain variables, yields results that are more supportive of fair value disclosures, since in addition to investment securities, loans and long-term debt are shown to be value-relevant (deposits and off-balance sheet items are notably not). Raised reliability issues are thereby attenuated as far as loans are concerned.

This may be seen as a direct response to a study by Nelson (1996), which is contemporary with the study mentioned above. Her results offer a different picture. She also examines fair value disclosures under SFAS no. 107 and shows that fair values of investment securities in commercial banks have some incremental value relevance to book values, whereas fair value disclosures of most other financial instruments, such as loans, long-term debt, deposits and off-balance sheet items, are incapable of explaining security prices. However, another often cited study strengthens the support for fair value measurement by showing that off-balance sheet items, specifically bank derivatives, are indeed value-relevant as measured by the stock price association with fair value disclosures (Venkatachalam, 1996).

Furthermore, Hodder et al. (2006) look at volatility levels of different income measures in commercial banks and conclude that while the full-fair-value construct displays a much higher level of volatility compared to the other income measures, this volatility is representative of market-based risks and therefore has value relevance for investors. The results in So and Smith (2009) indicate that the placement of the fair value information matters; fair values of investment properties in the income statement are to a higher degree reflected in market returns than fair value changes in the revaluation reserve, which may be considered as confirmation of the importance and value relevance of the fair value measure. It is also a confirmation of the importance of the perceived reliability of the measure.

The support for fair value is extended further by Barth and Clinch (1998), who show that in an Australian setting, where such practices are permissible, revaluations of not only financial but also tangible and intangible assets are value-relevant. Meanwhile, Carroll et al. (2003) find that reliability issues when assets are measured at fair value in thin non-active markets are not as severe as feared: evidence from closed-end funds shows consistent value relevance even for such fair value estimates (based on the association between share prices and investment securities, as well as between stock returns and gains and losses in securities).

Reliability, earnings management and fair values

Although there is evidence that fair values of financial instruments in thin markets[5] as well as of non-financial assets are value relevant, this is enshrouded in substantial controversy. Doubts as to the existence and extent of value relevance of fair value arise when measurements rather become estimates. At the core of all this, we find a "reliability debate." Such a debate may be carried out on the basis of fair value measurements in general, but it is especially pertinent in relation to model-based measurements. That is, a direct implication of the findings below is that the merits of fair values for level 3 inputs should be questioned.

Whereas the exit price has verifiability merits when active markets exist, more or less severe estimation difficulties are expected when using level 2 and level 3 inputs for many non-financial assets in thin markets. The resulting measurement errors may be classified, as in Barth and Landsman (1995), as "unsystematic" in the sense that they are entirely random, or "systematic" to the extent that management's discretionary behavior biases estimates. The potential existence of unsystematic measurement errors was discussed above in the theoretical discussion; meanwhile, the empirical case for the latter scenario is inconclusive. For instance, whereas Beaver and Venkatachalam (2003) show that loan fair values contain measurement errors affecting their reliability, the discretionary components are still found to be value-relevant. Barth and Clinch (1998) further show that investors do not ostensibly distinguish between valuations made by independent appraisers as opposed to directors, meaning that potential manipulation of values by management is offset by the added benefits of private information. This is echoed by Aboody et al. (1999), who look at revaluation of fixed assets and future firm performance. Then again, the value relevance of asset revaluations is shown to be lower in firms with a high debt-to-equity ratio, suggesting that investors have reservations with regard to revaluations made by financially distressed firms.

The results in Dietrich et al. (2000), related to investment property estimates under fair value, are even less supportive of reliability claims for assets where fair value estimates are exposed to managerial discretion. Similarly, Nissim (2003) sets up proxies for management incentives and provides some evidence that banks manage the fair values of loans, a financial instrument for which market prices are frequently absent (cf. Barth et al., 1996; Nelson, 1996). Another related study looks at the recognition of acquired brands by UK firms measured at

5 Thin markets are characterized by lower liquidity and high price volatility.

fair value, where management is found to act on incentives related to the measurement of brand names (Muller, 1999).

One study on investment fund and real estate companies shows that for both industries, fair value accounting explains stock market returns better than historical costs (Danbolt and Rees, 2008). However, full-fair-value accounting is rejected based on their regression results displaying evidence of difficulties in determining non-financial asset fair values, as the explanatory power of fair value earnings in the real estate industry is considerably lower compared to the investment fund industry. An inference they draw from their results is the existence of earnings management in the real estate industry, where assets are deemed more difficult to estimate.

Relevance of fair values

Whereas most research has focused on the *reliability* of fair value measurements—and the resulting effect on *value* relevance— Barth et al. (2008a) focus on the relevance of measuring liabilities at fair value. A concern that has been raised related to the fair value measurement of liabilities is that a decline in credit rating will result in a gain and a resulting increase in equity. This effect is seen as counterintuitive, for example by the European Central Bank (ECB), and contrary to the interests of prudent bank regulators (in industries with regulated minimum capital requirements). Barth et al. (2008a), however, find that realized gains are superseded by larger losses realized in assets. The reason for a downgrade in ratings is that the firm is doing poorly, which is reflected in a decline in asset values. Thus, as long as both liabilities and assets are valued at fair value, the concern of, for example, the ECB does not appear to be applicable. This issue is further discussed in section 12.1.

Research suggests that fair value is appropriate for some items and not for others. This is an idea picked up in the IASB's Conceptual Framework. The IASB states that fair value is more relevant for items that will generate cash flows by being sold rather than used for production in combination with other assets. This suggests that management's intention for holding the item matters, which is for instance reflected in IFRS 9 *Financial Instruments*. The probability of realizing fair value changes in cash flows is higher for financial instruments and investment property than for most other assets and liabilities. The Conceptual Framework also states that fair value is more relevant for items that have high variability in values, where historical cost may not mean much. This is true for financial instruments, investment property and biological assets. Meanwhile, inventory meeting the criterion of realization through sales normally does not have a high variability in price due to its short-term nature. Therefore, inventory is measured at historical cost. The Conceptual Framework points out a constraint on the use of fair value. If there is high measurement uncertainty (so that it is difficult to achieve faithful representation), or if obtaining a fair value measure is very costly, fair value should not be used. Consequently, the use of fair value is a concrete example of a trade-off between relevance and faithful representation, which is discussed in general terms in Chapter 5.

10.5 Conclusions

When creating accounting standards, standard-setters are faced with a number of conceptual or theoretical issues that need to be solved in order for a coherent framework to emerge. Preparers, meanwhile, face practical issues when following the principles and rules set out in the standards. In order to simplify and clarify the types of issues standard-setters and preparers face, we classify them along a limited number of dimensions, and group them into broad categories. As the reader comes across item-specific issues in the remaining chapters of this part of the book, these should be more easily understood *at a conceptual level* when linked to the broader categories identified here. Table 10.3 summarizes the dimensions and categories.

Table 10.3 Summary of dimensions applied to accounting items in Chapters 11–15

Dimension	Categories within dimension
Stylized Accrual Situation	SAS 1: Acquisition of resource SAS 2: Prediction of future outflows of resources SAS 3: Unexpected changes in value SAS 4: Revenue recognition
Definitions of financial statement items	Assets Liabilities Equity Income Expenses

Measurement base	Historical cost
	Current value
	   Fair value
	   Value in use
	   Current cost

CHAPTER 11
Assets

Learning outcomes

Upon completion of this chapter, you will have gained insight into:

- Which accounting issues affect different types of assets, including why issues differ for different types of assets.
- How the measurement of assets relates to the structures presented in Chapter 10.
- The trade-offs made by standard-setters in regulating the accounting for assets and the effect of this on accounting quality.
- Item-specific research relating to accounting for assets.

FOLLOWING THE GENERAL OVERVIEW of accounting issues in Chapter 10, we now get to the subject of individual financial statement items, starting with assets in this chapter. While the income statement focuses on the value of what is being generated by the firm in the current period (flow measures), the balance sheet shows the value of the (net) assets available to capital providers to date (stock measures).

Assets can exist off or on the balance sheet, depending on whether they fulfill standard-setters' definitions. There are also several ways to acquire assets. Some assets are injected via transfers from creditors and investors and some are purchased. If the transactions are carried out at market value, there is no net increase in the firm's assets as a result of such transfers. In the first case, the asset increase is matched by the increase in equity or liabilities, and in the second case, some liquid financial asset is simply converted into a less liquid tangible or intangible asset (or sometimes another financial asset). Assets can also be generated internally, in which case this may be done at a profit or loss, thus increasing or decreasing the firm's net assets.

Of the four Stylized Accrual Situations (SAS) discussed in the previous chapter, the first and third relate to assets. When a resource is acquired, the associated expenditure can either be recorded as an expense or booked as an asset. In IFRS and US GAAP, this is not a matter of preference—if the definition of an asset is met, an asset *should* be recognized. There are three basic types of assets: tangible, intangible and financial. While investments in tangible and financial assets are nearly always recognized as assets on the balance sheet, this is not true for many intangible assets. The non-recognition of many intangible assets is one reason for observed accounting conservatism. In this chapter, (long-lived, fixed or non-current) tangible assets (property, plant and equipment) are covered separately from short-term (current) tangible assets (inventory). Financial assets—both current and fixed—are discussed together in one section.

Once an asset has been recognized on the balance sheet, the issue of subsequent measurement arises. An important issue for fixed tangible and intangible assets is depreciation and amortization.[1] For current assets, and for all financial assets (both fixed and current), this is not an issue, as such assets normally result in an expense upon derecognition. Apart from systematic depreciation and amortization, unexpected changes in value may occur. As pointed out in the third Stylized Accrual Situation, such changes in value can either be reflected immediately (while they are unrealized) or upon derecognition (when they are realized). In essence, two measurement models are possible: 1) historical cost and 2) fair value. With fair value measurement, all changes in value—both gains and losses—are recognized immediately. With historical cost, the main principle is that changes in value are not recognized until they are realized. In current accounting standards, however, there is asymmetry in this respect. Decreases in value (losses) are recognized immediately in the form of impairment, while increases in value (gains) are recognized when realized. This asymmetry is another reason for observed conservatism in the measurement of assets. In IFRS, impairment is covered in a separate standard, IAS 36 *Impairment of Assets*, which we discuss in section 11.3. However, this standard only applies to long-term tangible and intangible assets. Impairment of inventories and financial assets follow other methods and are covered in the applicable sections for those items.

The logic of different accounting treatments, and issues that exist for each item, are discussed below for each asset type.

11.1 Property, plant and equipment

Many argue that intangible assets are growing in importance as the economy moves from being manufacturing-based to being service-based. But even as the IT and service sectors grow, **tangible assets** remain an important cornerstone in many businesses. Figure 11.1 shows property, plant and equipment (PP&E) in proportion to total assets in all sectors on EU stock markets. Although the weighted average of the book value for the entire sample of firms is quite low (at 21%), some sectors clearly have large investments in property, plant and equipment. Notably, sectors that focus on raw materials and utilities come out on top of the list. For these types of firms, determining the value of their tangible assets involves many types of judgments that can have a large impact on the balance sheet and ultimately the income statement.

---

1 The term *depreciation* is used for tangible assets while *amortization* is used for intangible assets. Both terms refer to the gradual consumption of the asset over time and how it is systematically reflected in the financial statements.

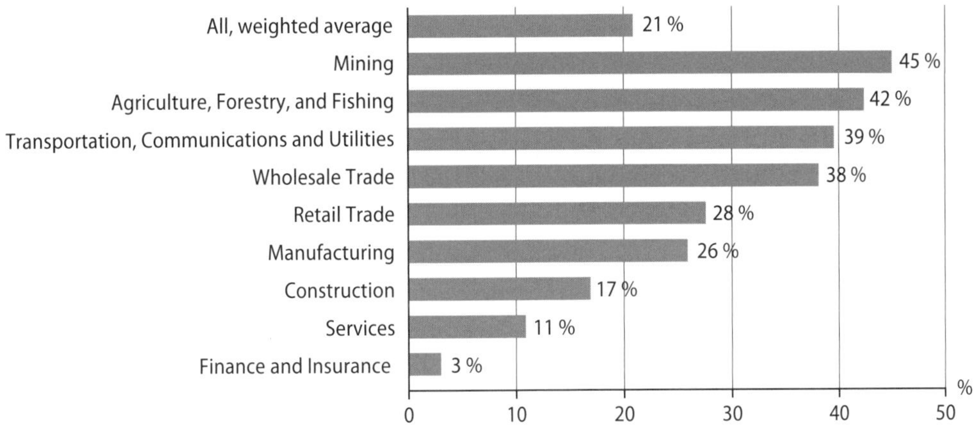

Figure 11.1 Proportion of property, plant and equipment in different industries on EU stock markets.
Source: Compustat Global

11.1.1 Definitions and summary of issues

Property, plant and equipment refers to the land, buildings and tools used in a firm's operations. Similar to inventories, the basic standards relating to PP&E have not changed much in the last few decades, and there has been limited discussion regarding those standards. What has been discussed, however, is the partial introduction of fair value in the measurement of such assets. This has also been subject to some research, as we discuss below.

The main accounting standard regulating the accounting for PP&E within IFRS is IAS 16 *Property, Plant and Equipment*. There are also some standards that provide guidance for specific situations relating to PP&E. For example, IAS 40 *Investment Property* is applicable to a particular subset of PP&E and impairment is covered in IAS 36 *Impairment*. If a firm decides to sell property, plant or equipment, IFRS 5 *Non-current Assets Held for Sale and Discontinued Operations* becomes applicable. IAS 36 is covered in a separate section in this chapter, as it applies to a broader set of assets than just PP&E, whereas IFRS 5 is covered in Text Box 11.1.

Compared to other accounting areas, the treatment of PP&E is frequently not considered all that complex, neither by firms nor standard-setting bodies. It is generally considered straightforward to determine whether an asset exists and whether it should be recognized. For example, the control criterion of the asset definition can often be established due to the nature of tangibles. However, knowing which costs should be included in the carrying amount at acquisition is one potential difficulty for firms.

Relating to SAS 1, investments in PP&E are usually recognized as assets on the balance sheet when acquired. An issue there is what to include in the cost of acquisition. Subsequently, PP&E is normally not derecognized through sales but through use (see also Text Box 11.1). To reflect the expense of using PP&E, depreciation is applied, involving judgments regarding the useful life of the asset and the method used. Depreciation is used for transferring the asset over time from the balance sheet to the income statement (via expenses).

After recognizing an asset on the balance sheet, the carrying amount in subsequent

Table 11.1 Summary of issues relating to PP&E

Generic issue	Specific issue: Choices and judgments	Comment
SAS 1 (Recognition at acquisition)	Capitalize or expense?	Capitalization most common
	Cost at acquisition?	Especially when produced in-house
	Depreciation (including method, useful life and residual value)?	
SAS 3 (Unexpected changes in value)	Measurement model (cost/revaluation)?	
	Impairment?	

periods can be determined in different ways. The two primary issues standard-setters as well as preparers should consider are which measurement model and which depreciation method to use. Finally, the depreciation schedule or useful life must be decided upon (see Table 11.1).

11.1.2 Cost at acquisition

With respect to SAS 1, the cost at acquisition must be determined. While the cost comprises the purchase price as well as any costs directly attributable to the delivery, assembly and installation of the asset, costs of opening a new facility or other getting-started or administrative costs are not to be included in the carrying value of the asset. According to IAS 16 (Par. 16(b)), costs that are involved in bringing the asset to "the location and condition necessary for it to be capable of operating in the manner intended by management" are included, but no subsequent costs (e.g., if a relocation or reorganization of operations takes place). Dismantling and restoration costs are included in the carrying amount as well, as these are inevitable aspects of acquiring or using any asset. Day-to-day servicing costs do not meet the recognition criterion, while some major replacement costs may very well do so. A previous version of the standard treated subsequent expenditures separately, but the IASB concluded that a separate recognition principle for subsequent expenditures led to inconsistencies and was less straightforward (IAS 16: BC5–BC12). The previous distinction between *maintaining* and *improving* an asset was also difficult to make in practice. Instead, the standard requires firms to treat any subsequent expenditures as it would initial expenditures, *derecognizing* replaced parts as needed. This is logically consistent with the use of *component depreciation* (see below). Furthermore, borrowing costs are included in the acquisition cost in accordance with IAS 23. This applies to assets involving a long construction process (e.g., buildings and bridges), where the cost of financing is incurred during the construction process.

While the ideas concerning which costs to recognize as part of the asset at acquisition may seem clear, in practice this involves substantial judgment. Measurement uncertainty is especially high for firms producing their own PP&E.

11.1.3 Measurement models

With respect to SAS 3, three possible **measurement models** for PP&E are the **cost model**, the **revaluation model** and the **fair value model**. An issue for preparers is which model to choose and, in the case of both the revaluation model and the fair value model, how to determine fair value.

The **cost model**, which is by far the most common, implies that the value is equal to its cost less any accumulated depreciation and impairment losses. The cost model is asymmetric in the sense that unrealized gains from increases in value are not recognized while losses are recognized through impairment. The **revaluation model**, meanwhile, requires systematic and periodic revaluations to fair value when there is a material difference between fair value and book value. The depreciation amount is adjusted based on the revalued amount. Although the revaluation model may seem more symmetric than then cost model, it is not entirely so. Gains are recognized on the balance sheet, but are taken through OCI and excluded from the income statement. Losses, on the other hand, are recognized in the income statement. Consequently, both measurement models reflect conservatism in accounting. With the **fair value model**, assets are measured at fair value at each balance sheet date and all gains and losses are recognized in the income statement (it is thus a symmetric model). No depreciation is carried out.

IAS 16 permits the cost model and the revaluation model. The two methods must be consistently applied to all assets within an asset "class." Examples of "classes" include land, aircraft and office equipment. This requirement is meant to prevent "cherry-picking"; that is, that managers select the revaluation model only for specific assets that increase in value, while not applying it to those that decrease in value.

IAS 40 *Investment Property* permits the cost model and the fair value model, but clearly expresses a preference for fair value. Fair value is relevant for investment properties, as it is likely that changes in fair value are used as an important performance indicator internally in the firm. Historical cost is typically of little relevance for buildings that are held for long periods of time, since the value can change substantially. Furthermore, the reliability criterion is usually fulfilled, as reliable fair value measurements are normally possible in a relatively active market for real estate.

As is always the case when historical cost and fair value measures are compared, even though the former may help ensure more *reliable* statements, the latter can increase the relevance of the information by letting managers use their discretion to reflect their private information. Hence, it is not particularly surprising that many local GAAP (typically used by small, unlisted firms) do not permit the revaluation model. Nor does US GAAP allow it due to a reluctance to introduce the subjectivity in measurement following from using the model.

Multiple research papers have been published aiming to address whether asset revaluations provide useful information to the market. This was of particular interest in the 1990s, when fair values and revaluation models were less prevalent or permitted by the FASB and the IASB. In particular, research was carried out on data from countries where local GAAP *did* permit more current value accounting. For example, in a large sample of UK firms, it was shown that upward revaluations of tangible fixed assets are associated with future changes in their operating cash flows, indicating that the revaluations *do* reflect underlying asset value changes (Aboody et al., 1999). The revaluations are also significantly and positively associated with annual stock returns. A weaker relationship for more leveraged firms indicates that such firms may be using their discretion opportunistically since they may have incentives for doing so.

Another study on Australian firms shows similar results, although revaluations of intangible assets were more consistently associated with price revisions in the market than revaluations of PP&E (Barth and Clinch, 1998). For example, revaluations of PP&E were indeed positively related to price changes in mining firms, but the association was not robust, and even negative, in other industries. Further, revaluations of property were only value relevant for non-bank financial firms. The authors consider their overall results as evidence that revaluations of non-financial assets *are* considered reliable by investors (or else the market would not respond to the revaluations).

Yet another study compares revaluations of PP&E before and after the adoption of IFRS and concludes that the greater the difference between IFRS and the prior local GAAP, the greater the increase in the association between revaluations and annual stock returns (Aharony et al., 2010). This implies that the market on average assigns a greater weight to revaluations made under IFRS than under local GAAP, indicating relatively higher reliability of the remeasurements under IFRS. Taken together, the above evidence points to the potential usefulness of market revaluations for the market, not least under a framework such as IFRS or UK or Australian GAAP. Some researchers will consequently vouch for the improved usefulness that would also benefit users of reports prepared under US GAAP if revaluation models were permitted for non-financial assets such as PP&E (Herrmann et al., 2006).

11.1.4 Depreciation method and useful life

Perhaps the main source of estimation uncertainty and thus the largest potential threat to the usefulness of information relating to PP&E is the determination of useful lives of such items. According to Runesson (2015), assessing and reassessing useful lives of tangible assets is considered by 30% of European firms to involve substantial judgment and be a major source of estimation uncertainty.

Outside accounting circles, one occasionally comes across the conception that depreciation is not a "real" expense. After all, it does not involve any movement in cash and must therefore be sort of fictitious, right? As any student in accounting will recognize, however, such a view is mistaken. Depreciation, being an accrual, is the process of allocating costs to appropriate periods. In the case of PP&E, the "appropriate" period is that in which the depreciated asset is used (consumed), normally in order to generate economic benefits. Receiving information on depreciation expenses is considered relevant for users since it smooths earnings and prevents unpleasant "surprises" in the form of sudden spikes in expenses at the time of large investments. Thereby, depreciation helps provide a more faithful representation of the economic performance of the firm.

There are several potential depreciation methods available to the firm: the **straight-line (uniform) method**, **accelerated methods**, **decelerated methods** or **methods based on**

actual physical usage (see Figure 11.2). The latter type differs from the rest in that it is not systematically related to the passage of *time*. From a standard-setter's as well as preparer's perspective, the most appropriate method is the one providing users with information that faithfully represents the use or consumption of the asset.

The straight-line method results in a constant depreciation charge over the useful life of the asset (provided that the useful life or residual value does not change). It is not only the most common method, but it has also become increasingly popular over the past two decades (Jackson et al., 2009). Given that the chosen depreciation method should "reflect the pattern in which the asset's future economic benefits are expected to be consumed by the entity" (IAS 16, paragraph 60), it may be worth questioning whether the use of a straight-line method is normally justifiable. After all, it is arbitrarily regular. It should be apparent that this is a typical case in which firms are forced to consider the trade-off between faithfully represented and relevant information, on the one hand, and the cost of estimating the inputs accurately, on the other. That is, non-straight-line measures could in theory be more relevant, but unless it is possible to accurately estimate the economic benefits in each period, faithful representation will not be achieved. The cost of making those estimates could also be prohibitive, which acts as a constraint on the achievement of relevant and faithfully represented information.

Because most assets generate the largest benefits in the early years, it is reasonable to let the allocation of depreciations reflect this fact. Accelerated methods involve taking greater charges in the beginning of the useful life. IAS 16 permits the accelerated method known as the **diminishing balance method** (*declining* balance method in US GAAP). One could, however, also consider other alternatives, such as the double-declining-balance method or sum-of-the years' digits method, which are permissible under US GAAP. Although we do not elaborate on these here, it is important to emphasize that standard-setters make choices concerning what goes into the standards.

Meanwhile, calculations of asset values employing an effective interest method—that is, a present value estimation of the gross income generated by the asset—constitute a *decelerated*

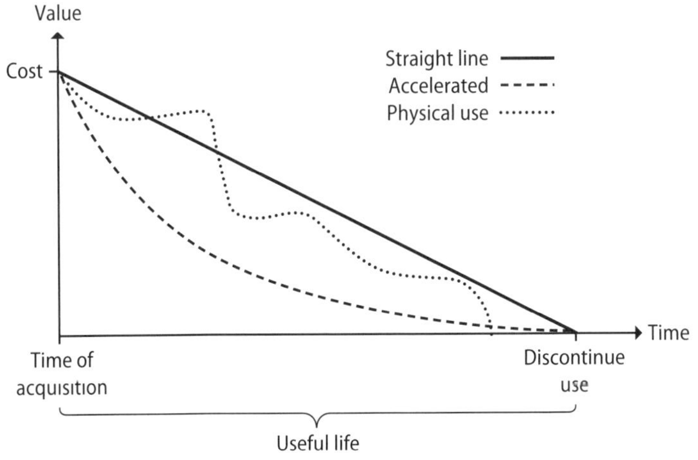

Figure 11.2
Different depreciation methods

method. Decelerated methods result in lower expenses initially and greater expenses in later periods. Although its role was much discussed in the earlier years of standard-setting, not least by researchers, the decelerated method is generally not permitted by either IFRS or US GAAP. A clear conservatism principle is reflected by the absence of this alternative. It is perhaps also difficult to find good examples of when such a depreciation pattern would reflect the actual use of a tangible asset. By contrast, the effective interest method often appears in the context of bond valuation (see section 11.6).

As for the **units of production method** under IAS 16, it is a method based on the actual physical usage of the asset. It seems reasonable that over its lifetime, an asset will be consumed more quickly when it is used more heavily, all else equal. Ideally, assigning the greatest expenses to those periods of heavy usage thus means that the units of production method performs better than other methods in terms of matching expenses to the consumption of the asset.

Although the depreciation method should *reflect* operations, a recent study shows that the opposite can also be true; that is, the depreciation method can have real effects *on* operations. For example, it is found that firms using accelerated depreciation have significantly higher levels of capital investments than firms using straight-line depreciation. The reasons for this are both managerial psychology and market incentives. Managers take less responsibility for assets that quickly disappear from the balance sheet, and financial statement users appear to share this view.

By their very nature, depreciation choices are always going to be subject to much judgment, and discretionary behavior may be exacerbated by the link between accounting and taxation. In some jurisdictions, there is a stronger link between the two, whilst the link is weaker in others. As shown in Chapter 4, particularly countries in the Continental group link financial reporting and taxation. A European study from 1996 put Germany, Sweden and Finland among those with a stronger link between accounting and taxation, while the UK, the Netherlands, Norway and Denmark were classified as having a weaker link (Hoogendoorn, 1996). The US likewise belongs to the latter group. Although there have been several decoupling movements in Sweden,[2] the link is still strong. If the link is weak, a firm's "book income" or "financial income" is not closely aligned with the taxable income and thus has little bearing on tax. This means there is less incentive for firms to make depreciation choices that will suppress earnings downwards and reduce taxes. On the other hand, because firms have a natural inclination toward optimism and a desire to please capital providers, a stronger link could counterbalance an otherwise strong incentive to manage earnings upwards.

The useful life of an asset is in IAS 16 defined in terms of the expected utility of the asset for the firm. A correct estimation of an asset's useful life, and consequently the depreciation schedule, is important for the same reasons as it is important to apply an appropriate depreciation method. The issue is mostly a practical one, as firms apply their judgment when determining the depreciation schedule.

Management is required to take into account the expected physical wear and tear of

2 An SOU (Statens offentliga utredningar, Swedish Government Official Reports) was launched in 2004 suggesting decoupling, but it did not result in any changes to the existing link between financial reporting and taxation.

the asset, the technical or commercial obsolescence of the item, as well as changing market conditions that may affect the demand for the output generated by the asset. According to IAS 16, the useful life of an asset may be shorter than its economic life, as firms may have policies to dispose of assets before their economic life is over. **Useful life** is the time period that the firm expects to use the asset. Still, the useful life should encompass the entire period during which it is *available* for use by the firm, regardless of whether it is actually being used or not. The opportunity cost of keeping the asset idle is thus thought to be captured. In determining the useful life of an asset, it is common for firms to benchmark against other firms in the industry. There is some soundness to this, but if the stated useful life of different items of PP&E does not reflect actual conditions within the firm, one achieves surface comparability rather than faithfully represented information.

It may be noted that the actual depreciable amount—what is to be depreciated over the asset's useful life—is reduced by the residual value of the asset. Both the useful life, the depreciation method and the residual value must be reviewed at each financial year-end, according to IAS 16. If the residual amount exceeds the carrying amount, the depreciation charge is zero until this ceases to be the case, but it may be pointed out that in practice, the residual value is often very small or immaterial.

The useful life of land deserves to be commented on separately. Unless one speaks of special-purpose sites, such as quarries, according to IAS 16 land is assumed to have an unlimited useful life. The view that land usually has an unlimited useful life is shared by practically all accounting frameworks and is considered uncontroversial.

Finally, we point out that IAS 16 requires *component depreciation*. That means that each material component follows a separate depreciation schedule. For example, an aircraft used for passenger transport may have a useful life of 25 years, while the engines need to be replaced after 7 years and the seats and interior only last for 3 years. Thus, the body of the aircraft is depreciated over 25 years, the engines over 7 years and the seats over 3 years. If estimates of useful lives are correct, component depreciation leads to lower volatility in depreciation expenses and higher faithful representation. The disadvantage is that it requires more effort on the part of preparers.

Research suggests a word of caution in relation to the relevance of depreciation. Although Barth et al. (2001b) show that depreciation adds information about future cash flows, Kang and Zhao (2010) suggest that this result is limited only to the real estate industry, and does not hold in other capital-intensive industries. Still, it is difficult to see any alternative treatment of PP&E than systematic depreciation. It seems reasonable to reflect the consumption of tangible assets over time in the financial statements. Even if depreciation *per se* is not value relevant, it could still provide important information about when the firm needs to invest in new assets. If a firm has PP&E that is fully depreciated, this indicates that investment in new PP&E is soon needed. A special case is PP&E held with the intention to sell, see Text Box 11.1.

Text Box 11.1 Assets held for sale

We have seen in a previous section of this chapter that the intended realization of an asset is important for determining which measurement model is relevant. Sometimes the intended use of long-term assets—both PP&E and intangible assets—changes. IFRS 5 *Non-Current Assets Held for Sale and Discontinued Operations* offers guidance for situations when a firm decides to realize its long-term asset through sales instead of own use.

Depreciation and amortization are used to reflect the consumption of the asset over time. When an asset is held for sale, this is no longer relevant. Consequently, IFRS 5 requires depreciation and amortization to cease when the decision to sell an asset is made.

Just as for other assets measured at historical cost, impairment is required if current value is below book value. However, value in use is no longer relevant, as the firm has already decided to sell the assets. Instead, only realizable value (fair value minus cost to sell) is used for determining the amount of impairment. This is similar to inventory, which is also held with the intention to sell.

There are two types of judgment preparers must exercise within the scope of IFRS 5 that can affect accounting quality. First, one must determine whether assets are held for sale or if they are held for continuing use. Second, in order to recognize impairment, net realizable value must be estimated.

IFRS 5 is broader than only covering assets held for sale. The standard also includes classification and disclosure requirements when entire operations are divested. This is called *discontinued operations*, as suggested in the title of the standard. Classification and disclosure issues are covered in chapter 15.

11.2 Intangible assets

Picture this scene: You take your Toyota to McDonald's, where you sit down to drink a Coke and work in Microsoft Office on your Apple computer, intermittently checking your Facebook messages on your Samsung cellphone or finding some interesting trivia or facts on Google, while also ordering goods, including a Disney movie, from Amazon. Chances are that the scenario just described is not only fully plausible, but that your familiarity with these brands and their logotypes helped make the picture you painted in your mind more vivid and detailed. The brands just mentioned were ranked by Forbes as being the top ten most valuable in the world in 2017 and perhaps for good reason.[3] In our information age, changing business models have made **intangible assets** (such as brand names) more prevalent than ever before and accounting for them in a satisfactory manner becomes all the more important.

11.2.1 Definitions and summary of issues

An asset, as we have seen above, is a resource controlled by an entity as a result of past events with the potential of producing economic benefits. Apart from meeting the general definition of an asset, IAS 38 *Intangible Assets* describes an **intangible asset** as an **identifiable** non-monetary asset lacking physical substance. Whereas identifiability was not clearly explained in earlier versions of IAS 38, the current standard defines identifiability as an asset being

3 http://www.forbes.com/powerful-brands/

separable, and thus capable of being transferred from an entity in some manner, or arising from **contractual** or other **legal rights** (regardless of the separability or transferability of those rights). For example, a brand name arises from legal rights and customer relations are separable, while a functioning organization or goodwill are not identifiable.

The accounting issues for intangible assets are similar to those of PP&E (see Table 11.2). However, in contrast to the case of tangible assets, determining whether there is an asset that should be recognized in the balance sheet can be difficult when it comes to intangible assets (cf. SAS 1). If recognized on the balance sheet, the next issue is how the intangible asset is transferred to the income statement over time as an expense. The idea of amortization for intangible assets is similar to depreciation for PP&E. However, some intangible assets are considered to have an *indefinite* useful life and are therefore not amortized. The non-recognition of many intangible assets, which may have substantial value, is an important reflection of general conservatism in financial accounting.

With respect to SAS 3, intangible assets are measured in accordance with the cost model. The revaluation model is possible, but its use is very restrictive, while the fair value model cannot be used for intangible assets. Just as for PP&E, impairment is required for intangible assets when the recoverable amount is below the book value (see section 11.3).

Table 11.2 Summary of issues relating to intangible assets

Generic issue	Specific issue: Choices and judgments	Comment
SAS 1 (Recognition at acquisition)	Capitalize or expense?	Often expensed, especially when internally developed
	Cost at acquisition (especially when internally developed)?	
	Finite or indefinite life?	
	Amortization (including useful life)?	
SAS 3 (Unexpected changes in value)	Measurement model?	Revaluation is applicable in limited situations
	Impairment?	

11.2.2 Recognition on the balance sheet

Intangible assets can be acquired in three separate ways: 1) separate external acquisition, 2) external acquisition as part of a business combination, and 3) generated internally. It may be noted that an intangible asset that has been acquired separately, rather than generated internally, is identifiable by definition (as it is, obviously, possible to transfer). In accounting for business combinations, there is also a general idea that all intangible assets should be recognized separately, even if this is not as self-evident as in a separate acquisition of a single asset. The US and Canadian standard-setters observed that intangible assets tended to be included in the goodwill amounts recognized in relation to acquisitions and that this reduced the usefulness of the accounts (see IAS 38: BC7). Just as standards in these countries were changed in 2001 to resolve this issue, the IASB—in developing IFRS 3 *Business Combinations* and revising IAS 38—decided to emphasize the identifiability criterion and make explicit its role in distinguishing other intangible assets from goodwill.

What about internally generated intangible assets? It is highly possible that the identifiability criterion does not cause difficulties and that determining whether an intangible asset exists is trivial even in this case. A brand, for example, is identifiable as it is possible to sell it or issue licenses to use it. Claiming that Apple has control over its brand in the form of legal rights is uncontroversial. Attempts to sell tablets or cellphones designed and labeled as iPads or iPhones, but without authorization, will inevitably lead to lawsuits for patent infringement, brand falsification and attempts to sell counterfeit goods. Having earned a net income of $48 billion in 2017, and with a market capitalization in early 2018 of almost $900 billion (both among the highest in the world), there is little doubt that "i"-products generate generous cash flows for Apple shareholders. Although its rivals can match Apple in terms of technical know-how, many will argue that, at least over the past decade, the firm has demonstrated exceptional market and customer knowledge. Nevertheless, as suggested in Text Box 11.2, recognition of the Apple brand on the balance sheet is not permissible under neither US GAAP nor IFRS.

Text Box 11.2 **Accounting for intangibles—quantum weirdness?**

The Economist - August 30, 2014

Accounting for brands

Untouchable intangibles

Sometimes you see brands on the balance-sheet, sometimes you don't.

Coca-Cola is worth $79.2 billion, according to Interbrand, a consultant. That does not seem excessive for the brand responsible for making Santa Claus look jolly. But neither that number nor anything close to it appears on the company's balance-sheet. "Trademarks with indefinite lives" (i.e., brands) are worth just $6.7 billion, say the company's accounts.

The reason is that both American and international accounting rules prohibit companies from recognising brands and many other "intangible" assets (such as customer lists) if they have created them themselves. Some marketers would like to change that. Roger Sinclair, who advises the MASB, an American body that sets marketing standards, points out that rules are inconsistent. The value of a brand—invisible when internally generated—is revealed when another company buys it.

That is because a different rule applies to acquisitions. In 2005 Procter & Gamble, a consumer goods company, paid $57 billion for the Gillette razor company. The brand alone, P&G reckonened, was worth $24 billion. Oddly, Gillette's value can now only go down. P&G must test it for "impairment" but cannot acknowledge any increase, though Interbrand says Gillette's value rose 1% last year.

Investors have a right to know how much brands are worth because so much of a firm's future depends on them, Mr Sinclair argues. The conflicting standards treat brands rather as if they were electrons that can be in two places at once.

Accountants seem content to live with such quantum weirdness. Brand values can "swing wildly", says Alan Teixeira of International Accounting Standards Board. Standard-setters worry that auditors would be quick to recognise rises but slow to acknowledge declines. Brands are unique, so it is hard to figure out what their market value is. "How do you separate a brand from customers that generate the sales or the know-how that enables the product to be made?" wonders Hilary Eastman of PWC, an accounting firm.

Then there are a few potential assets of the firm that are not considered assets at all from an accounting perspective. Most notably, staff and the training and education of staff fall into this category. Although possibly superfluous, explicit prohibitions to recognize such staff-related expenses are meant to bring clarity to the matter. The IASB argues that even though employees may possess unique skills and valuable know-how, it is not reasonable to consider the control criterion of the asset definition fulfilled. A slave-like relationship rather comes to mind when applying the idea of actual control over human resources!

For an asset to be recognized on the balance sheet, the firm in possession of the asset should be able to determine that recognition of the asset would result in relevant information and that the asset can be faithfully represented (measured reliably). The relevance criterion is not fulfilled if there is too much uncertainty regarding the probability and value of future economic benefits. The IASB argues that if a **separate acquisition** takes place of, for example, a brand, the purchase price should be a reasonable approximation of the expected future benefits and is usually easily determined. More specifically, the probability criterion is always considered fulfilled since the price indicates that there is a probability of future benefits (see IAS 38: BC27), while the reliability criterion is most often considered fulfilled, especially whenever the purchase price, representing the cost, is settled with monetary assets such as cash (see IAS 38: BC28). If an acquisition instead takes place as **part of a business combination**, both criteria are always considered to be met (see also Chapter 14). As above, the acquisition itself indicates a probability of future economic benefits. Although the estimates used for measuring an intangible asset's fair value may require a significant degree of judgment and may thus contain a considerable amount of uncertainty, the IASB believes that users would still benefit from the separate recognition of those intangible assets as opposed to recognizing the full amount as goodwill (see IAS 38: BC19B). The above is a clear example of when the relevance of the information is considered high enough to justify any measurement errors that could reduce the representational faithfulness of that information.

But how does one calculate the cost of **internally generated intangible assets**? In those cases, there is no apparent transaction on which to base the measurement. Research and development go through two phases: a research phase and a development phase. The IASB has determined *ex ante* that no intangible assets arising from research can be recognized. Even if it is possible to identify the costs associated with the research, the asset is believed to always fail the first recognition criterion; that is, future economic benefits cannot be determined with sufficient *probability*. By contrast, if an asset reaches the development phase, it is believed that future economic benefits may in some cases be shown to exist with sufficiently high probability. If the cost can also be measured *reliably*, recognition may occur. Internally generated brands fail on this point. Distinguishing the cost of developing the brand from other expenses relating to the business as a whole is considered impracticable. This explains the curious case of the missing Apple brand on the balance sheet. Internally generated goodwill must not be recognized for equivalent reasons (it also fails the identifiability criterion).

Could one instead consider allowing the fair value of the internally generated asset to be used as the carrying amount at the point of recognition, instead of the development cost? Some might argue this, not least because it could ensure that intangible assets are not excluded unnecessarily from the balance sheet. The IASB rejects such a proposition, however, primarily on the basis that such a treatment would be inconsistent with IAS 16 and that an active market would likely not exist anyway for what are inherently unique, internally generated assets (IAS 38: BCZ43-BCZ44). Serious reliability issues would follow.

The recognition of development expenses is not uncontroversial. Many regulatory frameworks, including many European local GAAP and US GAAP, do not allow the recognition of development costs at all.[4] It is true that it is difficult to fulfill the recognition criteria; nevertheless, the IASB argues that *ex ante* decisions to prevent recognition would be inappropriate since it is inconsistent with the purpose of financial reporting as stated in the Conceptual Framework. The reliability criterion refers to the fact that information should be faithfully represented. Financial reports should, however, also be relevant. As discussed previously, there is frequently a trade-off between faithful representation and relevance, and no less so with respect to intangible assets. Omitting large amounts of assets from the balance sheet may not be in the interest of users as it may reduce the relevance of the information (Srivastava, 2014; Lev and Zarowin, 1999), especially considering the significance of intangible assets to our economy (see IAS 38: BCZ39). It may also be disturbing in terms of comparability that theoretically similar or equivalent assets are treated differently depending on how they are obtained. A further threat to comparability, at least in theory, would be to allow a *choice* to capitalize development expenses (which, for example, is in the EU directive on accounting), even if Wyatt (2005) suggests that such treatment may lead to a good reflection of underlying economics. In IFRS, a firm *must* instead recognize assets arising from development if the recognition criteria are met. This is not to deny that this is a matter of subjective judgment and that different individuals make different assessments (cf. Prencipe et al., 2008). In fact, it constitutes a practical limitation to the achievement of comparability even when the standard-setter aims for a standard that is theoretically consistent with the Conceptual Framework.

11.2.3 Measurement models

Once an asset is recognized on the balance sheet, the question of subsequent measurement arises. Although the cost model and revaluation model are both available, as with tangible assets, only in rare circumstances does IAS 38 allow the revaluation model. The reason is that the revaluation model requires the fair value of the asset to be determined by reference to an active market, presumably as fair value estimates made on the basis of internal valuation models would not encourage faithfully represented information. Meanwhile, an active market does not exist for many intangible assets that are unique, such as brands, patents or music and film publishing rights. By contrast, transferable taxi or fishing licenses are provided by the standard as examples of intangibles with potentially active markets.

It may be noted that the revaluation model can also be applied to assets with an indefinite useful life (see below), although naturally without applying systematic amortization. Would it be "easier" or more consistent to simply assume that such intangible assets should not be carried at revalued amounts? The IASB is clear on this point, as it sees "no conceptual

4 An exception under US GAAP is software development.

justification for precluding some intangible assets from being carried at revalued amounts solely on the basis that there is no foreseeable limit to the period over which an entity expects to consume the future economic benefits embodied in those assets" (IAS 38: BC76).

What remains unclear in the standard is why there should be a choice between the two models in the first place. That there is a trade-off between relevance and faithful representation in both is perhaps clear, but the availability of choices always threatens to reduce comparability between firms. Of course, one could argue that if a firm has a business model that depends on the fair value of intangible assets (e.g., if the firm is a trader of licenses), it would be relevant to measure the assets at fair value. However, IAS 38 does not require the revaluation model in such cases, so there is still an issue with comparability.

11.2.4 Amortization method and useful life

Management also has to determine the useful life of each type of intangible asset in the firm as a basis for the amortization period. The judgment applied here can have a material impact on the balance sheet as well as the income statement, but requiring management to make estimates regarding the useful life is believed to increase the relevance of the financial accounts. The alternative, to impose a rule that, for example, all intangible assets should be amortized over five years, requires no estimates on behalf of management, but provides little useful information to investors. Once again, many local GAAP that prescribe the rules for small, unlisted firms take this approach. Although the current version of IAS 38 stipulates that the useful life should be estimated based on underlying economics, it is stated that it is unlikely that an intangible asset possesses a long useful life. This is meant to encourage a conservative estimate of how long it may be used. As for the pattern of amortization, the straight-line method is the most commonly used in practice. A method that results in a lower accumulated amortization amount than this method was previously expressed as being highly unlikely to be supported by the facts. However, because such a statement may discourage the use of, for example, a unit-of-production method, even when that method is more representationally faithful, that wording was removed from the standard. This is another example of when the standard-setter believes that the relevance of the information must be prioritized over its verifiability.

Unlike tangible assets (excluding land), intangible assets may also have a useful life that is not finite. Such is the case if there is no foreseeable limit to the period of time over which the asset may generate economic benefits for the firm. In the previous version of IAS 38, a maximum useful life of 20 years was assumed (but could be rebutted). This is more conservative than what is permitted by the IASB in the current standard, which permits assets to have an **indefinite** useful life. It is argued that there are cases where there is no foreseeable end to the cash flow streams associated with the asset, and to amortize that asset would fail to reflect the useful life and thus not provide representationally faithful information (IAS 38: BC61, BC63). This applies to goodwill and is often the case for brands. Even so, it is pointed out that although it may be difficult to accurately determine the useful life of an asset, this does not constitute a reason for regarding that useful life as indefinite (IAS 38: BC65). Intangible assets *are* different from tangible assets, the IASB argues, because the condition of being physical necessarily implies that tangible assets undergo deterioration or degeneration with time, which thus constitutes a limit to the expected utility one may derive from such assets.

11.3 Impairment of assets

So far we have discussed issues related to tangible as well as intangible assets, while deliberately ignoring one of the most important factors related to the measurement of these assets—and that is **impairment**. The recording of an impairment loss is commonly referred to as a write-down.[5] We first consider a layman definition of the term "impairment." It will typically say something to the effect of being "diminished," "weakened" or "damaged" (physically or mentally). In an accounting context, recording an impairment loss is the act of recognizing a non-cash expense as a result of an estimated reduction in the value of a non-current or current asset. The value of the asset is reduced correspondingly on the balance sheet. In general, for an asset to be considered impaired, it has to be overvalued in the books; that is, the book value exceeds some given benchmark value indicating its current value. Just like depreciation or amortization constitutes a "real" expense, so do impairment losses—despite there being no current cash flow effect from the actual impairment or write-down.

11.3.1 Definitions and summary of issues

Recognizing impairments follows logically from the asset definition in section 10.1, which says that an asset is a resource with a potential of providing future economic benefits. If, for some reason, the value of future economic benefits goes down, this decrease must be reflected in the financial statements. If this were not done, parts of the assets included on the balance sheet would not meet the definition of—or the recognition criteria pertaining to—assets. With respect to SAS 3, recording impairments reflects asymmetric accounting treatments, since write-downs represent the immediate recognition of unrealized losses, without a corresponding recognition of unrealized gains. In sum, the purpose of requiring impairments to be recognized is to avoid over-valuation in the financial statements (see Text Box 11.3).

The difficulty facing preparers is knowing when an impairment has occurred. The fact that this requires substantial judgment on behalf of preparers constitutes the first issue relating to impairments. We devote a considerable portion of this text to the discretionary nature of write-downs and its relative merits in relation to amortization when it comes to accounting for changes in the value of goodwill.

As part of a convergence project, the FASB and the IASB agreed in 2002 to eliminate major differences between the frameworks when it came to accounting for impairment. However, so far no further initiative is under way, which means that differences still persist. The different bases for write-downs are problematic since they cause a lack of comparability. This also highlights the choices of *standard-setters* in deciding on the appropriate accounting treatments.

---

5 Firms do not *impair* assets, although this usage of the word occurs quite frequently. Technically, an asset impairment can *lead* to a write-down.

Text Box 11.3 An impairment standard—a reflection of the conservatism principle

The main accounting principle governing write-downs is that of conservatism. The fact that no standard is dedicated to "appreciation of assets" is a telltale sign of the weight historically given to this principle. Such an apparent lack of neutrality, however, is not normally considered very controversial. Because of what may be referred to as "natural optimism" in managers, and because of the many incentives that exist for upward earnings management, write-down requirements are thought of as useful safety nets against over-valuation of assets. Although removed from the IASB's Conceptual Framework of 2010, and adjusted in the 2018 Conceptual Framework, the conservatism principle thus lives on in IAS 36 *Impairment of Assets*.

Table 11.3 Summary of issues relating to impairment

Generic issue	Specific issue: Choices and judgments
SAS 3 (Unexpected changes in value)	Impairment test needed?
	Write-down needed? Fair value and value in use? Discount rate?
	Value of goodwill? Cash-Generating Units? Fair value and value in use? Discount rate?

Note: With respect to all of the above items, standard-setters face choices and judgments with respect to how impairment tests should be carried out. This includes deciding on the definition of fair value, the definition of cash-generating unit or reporting unit, and whether discounted or undiscounted values should be used.

The standard we primarily refer to in this section is IAS 36 *Impairment of Assets*. For the sake of comparison, however, we also explain parts of ASC 360, which is the US GAAP equivalent of IAS 36. Impairment of inventory (treated in IAS 2 *Inventories*) and impairment of financial assets (regulated in IFRS 9 *Financial Instruments*) are discussed in the sections covering those particular asset types. For example, in section 11.6, we show that write-downs of financial assets—especially the reporting of credit losses—is highly discretionary.

11.3.2 Impairment tests

The first step in an impairment testing process is to determine whether an impairment has occurred, while the second step is to calculate the value of the impairment. IAS 36 requires that an impairment test be conducted when there are *indicators* that an impairment has occurred. Examples of such indicators are falling market values for the asset, physical damage, changing market conditions brought on by legal or technological changes related to the asset, as well as changes within the firm that can have an adverse effect on its ability to extract the full potential from the asset. Intangible assets with an indefinite useful life (i.e., that are not systematically amortized) are subject to impairment testing at least annually, even absent any indicators.

Impairment testing involves calculating the asset's *recoverable amount*, which represents the present value of future economic benefits the asset is expected to generate when realized. An asset can be realized in two alternative ways: 1) it is sold, or 2) it is used. If an impairment test shows that the recoverable amount is below the book value, an impairment is recognized corresponding to the difference between the two values. This results in a decrease in the value of the asset on the balance sheet and a corresponding expense on the income statement.

The recoverable amount is calculated based on the assumption that a firm will choose the realization that results in the highest benefit. That is, if it is more profitable to sell than to use the asset, the assumption is that the firm will sell it. If the reverse is true, the firm is expected to continue using the asset. Consequently, IAS 36 defines recoverable amount as the highest of the **realizable value** (fair value minus cost to sell) and the **value in use**. Value in use is calculated as the discounted value of future cash flows that the asset will generate. As many assets can only generate cash flows jointly with other assets, value in use must normally be estimated for **cash-generating units (CGU)** rather than for individual assets. It is important to point out that value in use is an entity-specific value (i.e., it shows the value of the asset to the firm). This should not be confused with fair value, which is a market value that is unaffected by firm-specific considerations. As value in use considers entity-specific value-drivers, it is often higher than fair value. The relevance of considering or ignoring entity-specific information is discussed, for example, by Whittington (2008a), see section 10.4.

The estimation of the recoverable amount requires substantial judgment. The estimation of fair value (especially in the absence of an active market) or the estimation of future cash flows and the discount factor when calculating value in use is potentially very subjective. Since the calculations are applied to non-liquid assets, for which market values are often unobtainable, impairment tests require significant judgment by management and involve much estimation uncertainty. Goodwill is an asset that is especially difficult to value, as we discuss below. There is no active market for such an asset and the related determination of CGU requires much judgment. It quickly becomes apparent that managerial choices related to impairment can have a significant effect on a firm's accounting quality.

Consistent with write-downs requiring substantial judgment, there is evidence in the literature that they are used in a discretionary manner to manage earnings. For example, after the implementation of SFAS No. 121 *Accounting for the Impairment of Long-Lived Assets* in the US in the 1990s, which allowed for more management estimates to be made when determining impairment losses, one study of US firms found that write-downs occurred disproportionately often in firms classified as having incentives to manage earnings (Riedl, 2004). "Big bath" reporting behavior—meaning excessive write-downs in certain situations—was also associated with upcoming restructuring events or executive turnover. Rather than write-offs reflecting actual impairment in asset values, they seem to be the product of strategic managerial choices (Elliott and Shaw, 1988).

As we saw above (in Chapter 7 on earnings quality), one may be interested in how a certain accounting policy affects earnings quality itself but also how it affects market outcomes. Either way, the assumption is that earnings quality ultimately has an impact on the market. Academic research studying impairments often consider the effect of impairments on either one of these: earnings quality or market outcomes. The market seems to place a lower value on earnings that contain impairments, and the more write-offs a given firm does, the less weight the market places on those earnings, apparently finding the earnings information less and less useful. One possible explanation for this is that impairments add noise to the financial reports and investors have trouble interpreting their implications for future earnings—thus making the value of the firm harder to estimate. If impairments are additionally used in a discretionary manner, which recurring write-offs may suggest, they are still less trustworthy (Elliott and Hanna, 1996). Whereas investors may discount the value of non-recurring items in general, either due to them being transitory or due to uncertainty regarding whether they indeed are permanent or transitory, there are indications that special items such as impairments can still be informative of future firm performance (Fairfield et al., 1996). The one thing that *is* certain when it comes to write-offs is that they are difficult for the user to evaluate, and thus potentially reduce the overall usefulness of the earnings number.

11.3.3 Goodwill impairment

Goodwill is the most controversial item on the balance sheet due to its subjective nature, not least when it comes to its role in impairment tests. Here we refer to the question posed in research: Should goodwill be amortized or subject to impairment tests only? Goodwill is only recognized when it is acquired in business combinations (never as internally generated). While business combinations are discussed in Chapter 14, the impairment of goodwill is covered here.

According to the now defunct standard IAS 22 *Business Combinations*, goodwill had to be amortized systemically over its estimated useful life. It was assumed that this useful life would not exceed twenty years, although this was rebuttable in individual cases. If a useful life longer than twenty years was adopted, the goodwill amount had to be tested for impairment at least annually (regardless of whether there was an indication of impairment). However, the IASB considered the most appropriate method of accounting for acquired goodwill after its initial recognition when it was developing IFRS 3 *Business Combinations*. Three approaches were considered: (1) straight-line amortization with an impairment test whenever there was an indication of the goodwill being impaired, (2) non-amortization with at least an annual impairment test, or (3) letting firms choose between the first two. There was wide agreement that the last approach would be inappropriate, as a choice between the two methods "impairs the usefulness of the information provided to users of financial statements because both comparability and reliability are diminished" (IAS 36: BC131C). There was, however, much support for the first (as summarized in IAS 36: BC131D):

> (a) [A]cquired goodwill is an asset that is consumed and replaced by internally generated goodwill. Therefore, amortisation ensures that the acquired goodwill is recognized in profit or loss and not internally generated goodwill is recognized as an asset in its place, consistently with the general prohibition in IAS 38 on the recognition of internally generated goodwill. (b) [C]onceptually, amortisation is a method of allocating the cost of acquired goodwill over the periods it is consumed, and is consistent with the approach taken to other

> intangible and tangible fixed assets that do not have indefinite useful lives. Indeed, entities are required to determine their depreciable amounts on a systematic basis over those useful lives. There is no conceptual reason for treating acquired goodwill differently. (c) [T]he useful life of acquired goodwill cannot be predicted with a satisfactory level of reliability, nor can the pattern in which that goodwill diminishes be known. However, systematic amortisation over an albeit arbitrary period provides an appropriate balance between conceptual soundness and operationality at an acceptable cost: it is the only practical solution to an intractable problem.

However, the Board finally opted for the second alternative. The most important arguments are concisely expressed in the Basis for Conclusions (IAS 36: BC131E,G):

> [In considering the arguments in favor of the first option], the Board agreed that achieving an acceptable level of reliability in the form of representational faithfulness while striking some balance with what is practicable was the primary challenge it faced in deliberating the subsequent accounting for goodwill. The Board observed that the useful life of acquired goodwill, and the pattern in which it diminishes generally are not possible to predict, yet its amortisation depends on such predictions. As a result, the amount amortised in any given period can be described as at best an arbitrary estimate of the consumption of acquired goodwill during that period. The Board acknowledged that if goodwill is an asset, in some sense it must be true that goodwill acquired in a business combination is being consumed and replaced by internally generated goodwill, provided than an entity is able to maintain the overall value of goodwill (by, for example, expending resources on advertising and customer service). However, consistently with the view it reached in developing [the Exposure Draft to IFRS 3], the Board remained doubtful about the usefulness of an amortisation charge that reflects the consumption of acquired goodwill, when the internally generated goodwill replacing it is not recognised. Therefore, the Board reaffirmed the conclusion it reached in developing [that Exposure Draft] that straight-line amortisation of goodwill over an arbitrary period fails to provide useful information. The Board noted that both anecdotal and research evidence supports this view. [...] The Board reaffirmed the view [...] that if a rigorous and operational impairment test could be devised, more useful information would be provided to users of an entity's financial statements under an approach in which goodwill is not amortised, but instead tested for impairment annual or more frequently if events or changes in circumstances indicate that the goodwill might be impaired. [...] The Board concluded that a sufficiently rigorous and operational impairment test could be devised.

The changes thus made to the accounting for goodwill meant that more room was given for judgment. More subjective impairment tests replaced systematic amortizations. Some may say that this is evidence of IFRS being principles-based, but it is worth remembering that the same change had occurred in US GAAP three years earlier through the publication of SFAS 142.

Sometimes large empirical studies can give statistical cues as to which accounting method or policy is preferable, in this particular case with respect to the alleged usefulness of impairments versus amortizations. For example, there is evidence that goodwill impairments are delayed in US firms (Hayn and Hughes, 2006). Whereas this may be attributed to management exploiting the discretion afforded by the impairment tests, various studies have been unable to definitely assign lack of impairments to managerial opportunism. That the frequency or likelihood of impairments is associated with factors other than economic ones could, as implied above, mean that there are incentives to make or delay impairments, but it could also be due to the difficulties in assessing the need for impairments, as well as a lack of standard enforcement or similar (Jarva, 2009; Jarva, 2014). The usefulness of impairment tests is highly dependent on the usefulness of fair value estimates. As we saw above, the "fair value debate" is propelled by two opposing views. Jarva (2009) summarizes these succinctly:

> Opponents of fair value accounting argue that allowing unverifiable estimates into accounting numbers can seriously compromise their usefulness and increase the likelihood of opportunistic disclosures. Proponents of fair value accounting believe that asset and liability measures that reflect current economic conditions and up-to-date expectations of the future will result in more useful information for making economic decisions. (p. 1060)

That is, on the one hand—consistent with the aim of SFAS 142—aspects of fair value accounting in goodwill impairment should lead managers to communicate their private information to investors. On the other hand, agency theory predicts that managers use the resulting discretion to promote their own agendas. One study testing these two competing hypotheses with respect to goodwill impairment was carried out by Ramanna and Watts (2012). Findings are consistent with the latter argument and that goodwill "non-impairment" is associated with CEO compensation, CEO reputation and debt-covenant violation concerns. Alternative explanations for why impairment is not carried out have also been provided. For example, there is evidence that hubristic executives recognize fewer goodwill impairments and that these are also delayed (Runesson and Samani, 2018). The explanation is that hubris, which is related to overconfidence and unrealistic views of one's own abilities, makes leaders unable to recognize deteriorating prospects for their own firms. The fair value estimates used in impairment tests will consequently be overstated. In such cases, amortizations may be a more reliable alternative when it comes to recognizing losses of asset values.

Given that public firms in the US and, for example, Sweden are all heavily influenced by the stock market and should have similar incentive structures, one might expect impairment frequencies to be similar in the two countries. In fact, impairments of goodwill should, if anything, be less frequent under US GAAP considering some of the differences between the standards (see below). However, a look at the population of firms with listed equity securities since 1990 reveals a stunning pattern in the growth of goodwill in the past few years, not least in Sweden (Hamberg et al., 2011). Descriptive statistics show that the average proportion of goodwill to total assets was around 1% in Sweden as well as in the US in the early 1990s. This number had increased to 20% in Sweden by 2014! The same development cannot be seen in the US, where goodwill instead peaked around 2000, presumably because of all the IT-related mergers and acquisitions at that time. What is the cause of the discrepancy between the two countries remains to be resolved, but it may be questioned whether there is sufficient monitoring of Swedish firms. There is no equivalent to the SEC in Sweden, although Finansinspektionen does oversee financial reporting. Overall, the level of enforcement from

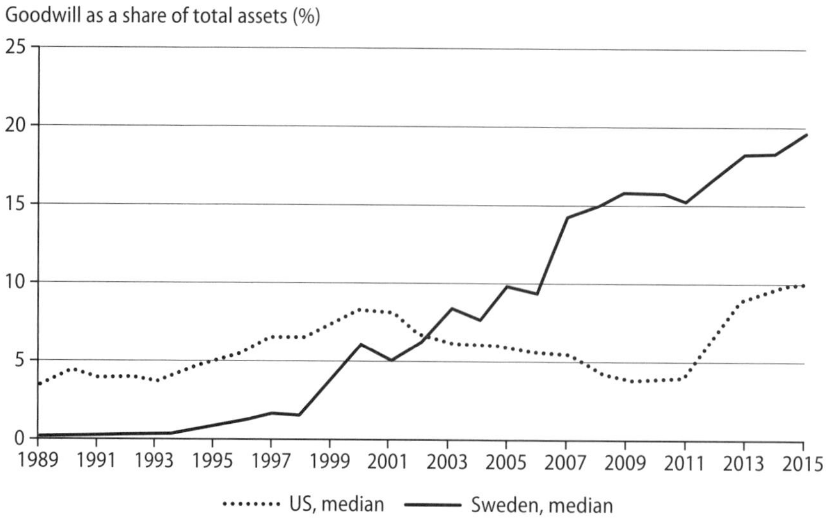

Figure 11.3 Goodwill development between 1989 and 2015. Source: Worldscope

authorities is substantially higher in the US than in Sweden and auditors are clearly unable to stem this increased flow of goodwill into firms (see Figure 11.3).

Research indicates that goodwill impairments are delayed by management (i.e., that they are taken later than they should (Li, 2013)). Hayn and Hughes (2006) estimate this delay to be on average 3–4 years. Ramanna and Watts (2012) suggest that the delay is explained by the unverifiable nature of goodwill impairment. Findings by Li et al. (2011) suggest that there is a real incentive for management to delay goodwill impairment, as investors react negatively to it. Petersen and Plenborg (2010) further point to the discretionary nature of goodwill, as they show that there is widespread non-compliance with IAS 36. Overall, research confirms that subjectivity and uncertainty in goodwill impairment is problematic and Bloom (2009) predicts its abandonment. The dilemma with the treatment of goodwill following a business combination is that several studies indicate that amortization of goodwill does not provide any relevant information either (see, for instance, Henning et al., 2000).

11.3.4 Impairment approaches under IFRS versus US GAAP

Recorded impairment losses can vary depending on how one calculates the benchmark value against which the carrying amount is compared. This causes a lack of comparability between firms using different frameworks. For example: under US GAAP, an asset is considered impaired if its carrying amount exceeds the asset's fair value (as defined under US GAAP); under IFRS, an asset is considered impaired if its carrying amount instead exceeds its recoverable amount.

The recoverable amount is indeed a type of current value, but it is not fair value (as defined in IFRS 13 or in US GAAP). As discussed above, it reflects the benefits a firm can derive from the asset either by selling it or by putting it to use in its operations; more formally, it is the *higher* of the asset's **fair value less costs to sell** and its **value in use**. IAS 36 defines value in use as the present value of the future cash flows expected to be generated from an asset or cash-generating unit. The value in use may exceed the fair value less costs to sell if the firm has a unique ability to put the asset to use—that is, if the asset can be used in a way that makes it more valuable to the firm than to the market (such as when the firm has created internal synergies or possesses special know-how).

In testing any non-current assets for impairment, under IFRS one uses a so-called one-step approach. This consists of comparing the carrying amount with the recoverable amount, where, as stated above, the recoverable amount is the higher of the value in use and the fair value less costs to sell. This is not the case under US GAAP. For non-current[6] assets with a *definite* useful life, a so-called **two-step approach** is employed, while a **one-step approach** is used for assets with an *indefinite* useful life (see special treatment of goodwill below):

- Two-step approach (US GAAP): For assets with a definite useful life, the carrying amount is first compared to the sum of all future *undiscounted* cash flows (step 1). Only if the carrying amount exceeds the undiscounted cash flow amount does the firm proceed to calculate the impairment loss (step 2). The loss is calculated as the difference between the carrying amount and the fair value. In case the carrying amount does *not* exceed the fair value, the loss will be zero after all.
- One-step approach (US GAAP): Equivalent to step 2 of the two-step approach. That is, the carrying amount is compared with the fair value and the loss calculated accordingly.

The above is illustrated in Figures 11.4 and 11.5.

Several differences between IFRS and US GAAP may be noted here, such as that "value in use" does not exist as a concept in US GAAP and undiscounted cash flows rather than discounted cash flows are used in the calculations under US GAAP. Because undiscounted cash flows are higher than discounted cash flows, chances are that an impairment becomes less likely under US GAAP than under IFRS, possibly leading to overstated earnings or delayed loss recognition. By contrast, overstating impairment losses could be the result under IFRS, given that the discounted cash flow is lower than the undiscounted amount and given that the choice of discount rate is a discretionary choice made by management. As for the value in use, it may be higher or lower than the fair value. It may be higher if the firm has a unique ability to employ the asset in the most profitable way. It may be lower if the asset is of little use to the firm as such, but control over a unique asset (such as a brand or a patent) is strategic in order to prevent competitors who value it much higher from profiting from it. In practice, value in use is typically higher than fair value.

The different ways of going about impairment tests means that a firm might have to carry out an impairment under one standard but not under the other.

6 "Long-lived" in US GAAP terminology.

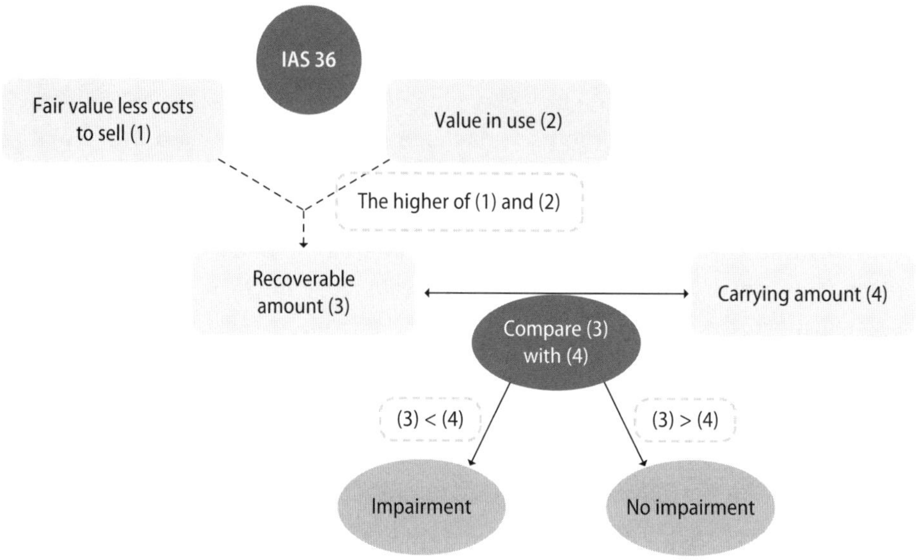

Figure 11.4 Impairment test under IAS 36, all assets

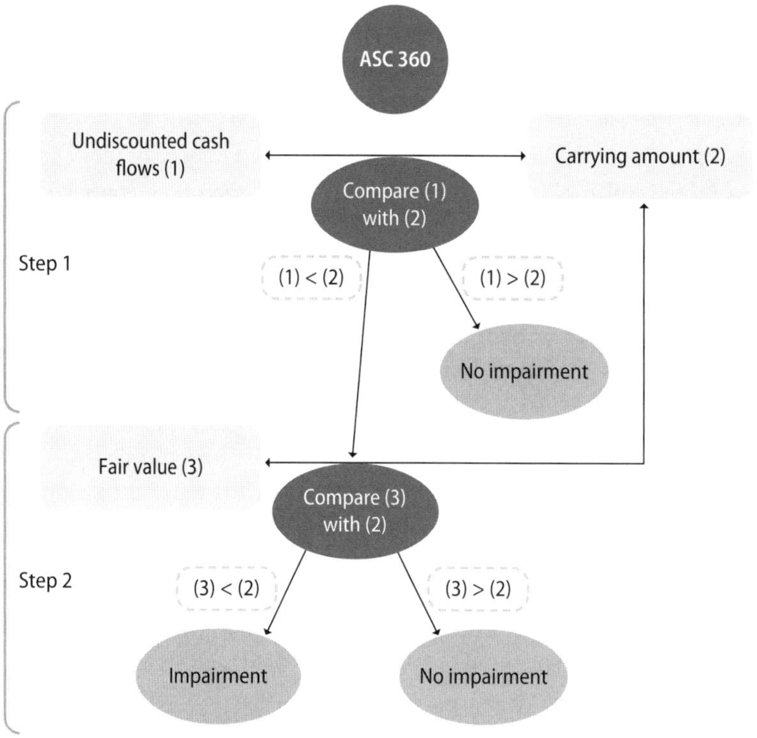

Figure 11.5 Impairment test under ASC 360, assets with definite useful lives

Example 11.1 **Impairment of asset**

Assume that a firm is to evaluate whether a non-current asset with a definite useful life needs to be impaired. The firm is very ambitious, which means that it has calculated all the amounts below:

- Carrying amount: TEUR 45
- Value in use: TEUR 40
- Fair value less costs to sell (IFRS): TEUR 37
- Recoverable amount (IFRS): TEUR 40
- Undiscounted cash flows: TEUR 50
- Fair value (US GAAP): TEUR 42

The firm will record an impairment loss under IFRS since the carrying amount exceeds the value in use as well as the fair value less costs to sell. However, since the carrying amount does not exceed the undiscounted cash flows, no impairment loss would occur under US GAAP. The effect of this difference is that impairments are less frequent in US GAAP. Meanwhile, once an impairment is recognized, it tends to be large, since the effect of discounting is reflected in the impairment amount.

Example 11.1 shows the potentially large variability in earnings if one allows for different methods. It is evidence that the notion of a "true" earnings number is problematic. Quality must rather be defined based on which approach provides the more useful information.

Meanwhile, when testing whether goodwill has been impaired, one looks at the **reporting unit** (RU) under US GAAP and the cash-generating unit (CGU) that the goodwill is associated with under IFRS. Under IFRS, if the recoverable amount of the CGU is deemed lower than the carrying amount, then an impairment loss is recorded. The loss is first assigned to the goodwill amount. If the loss exceeds the value of the goodwill, the remaining assets tied to the CGU are considered impaired. Under US GAAP, meanwhile, a two-step approach is applied that differs from the two-step approach described above. The carrying value of the RU is compared to its fair value (step 1). If the carrying amount exceeds the fair value, it is compared with the implied fair value of goodwill (step 2). If the implied fair value is higher than the carrying amount of the goodwill, then goodwill is impaired by that difference.

The differences above encourage earlier impairments under IFRS for at least three reasons: 1) reporting units are expected to be larger than cash-generating units, 2) the two-step approach reduces the likelihood of having to make an impairment, and 3) the impairment loss will not exceed the carrying value of goodwill under US GAAP, but can extend to other assets as well under IFRS. Interestingly, however, actual goodwill impairments have been larger under US GAAP during the past ten years, as was discussed in the previous section.

A study comparing US GAAP and IFRS indicates that impairments of non-current assets are more likely to be related to actual underlying economic factors under IFRS and are more likely to be driven by incentive structures under US GAAP (Gordon and Hsu, 2017). Pettersson (2015) studies shipping companies using IFRS in the EU in the years following the financial crisis. As prices in both markets for freights and ships declined, impairment testing became important. It turned out that many shipping companies had a strategy where they deferred impairment until later periods. When impairment was recognized, it was usually larger than underlying economics would suggest. In a sense, these IFRS firms—through the use of discretionary judgment—applied a method that resulted in similar results as US GAAP.

11.4 Inventories

Even though inventories constitute a relatively large balance sheet item in many firms, accounting for inventories has been relatively non-controversial for some time. It has not been discussed much in the last few decades and the standard-setters have not made substantial changes in this area. In IFRS, inventories are covered in IAS 2 *Inventories*, issued in its original form in 1975. There is also a specialized standard for inventories consisting of biological assets, IAS 41 *Agriculture*.

With respect to SAS 1, investments in inventories are nearly always recognized as assets. A common issue is how to measure finished goods at cost, especially for firms that produce their own inventory, and how to measure work-in-process. An important accounting issue is how the asset is transferred to the income statement and recognized as **cost of goods sold**. It is based on assumptions of how individual assets flow through the inventory. Like other assets, inventory also relates to Stylized Accruals Situation 3 and issues involve both whether to measure inventory at historical cost or at fair value, as well as—if the cost model is used—how to recognize impairment. Issues are summarized in Table 11.4.

A potential difficulty is knowing what to include in the investment as cost of acquisition, especially for finished goods produced by the firm itself. We discuss this issue in more detail in the section on property, plant and equipment (section 11.1). However, own production of inventory is much more common than own production of PP&E. Basically all manufacturing firms have some finished goods inventory that they themselves have produced. If the manufacturing has a material extension in time, there will also be work-in-process inventory

Table 11.4 Summary of issues relating to inventories

Generic issue	Specific issue: Choices and judgments	Comment
SAS 1 (Recognition at acquisition)	Capitalize or expense?	Capitalization most common
	Cost at acquisition Finished goods Work-in-progress	
	LIFO or FIFO?	Choice is applicable in US GAAP, not IFRS
SAS 3 (Unexpected changes in value)	Measurement model? (Cost/fair value)	
	Impairment?	Applicable if cost model is used

that must be measured, and this is subject to the same difficulties as the finished goods. In manufacturing firms, the models used for measuring both work-in-process and finished goods can have a large impact on the financial statements and therefore an impact on accounting quality.

The transfer of the asset to the income statement in the form of an expense occurs when inventory is sold (i.e., when it is realized). It is then included in cost of goods sold. An issue in the measurement of realized inventory is what assumption to make regarding which particular pieces of inventory are sold when there is a large number of similar items acquired at different times and at different prices. Based on IAS 2, the assumption can either be that the oldest items are sold first (first-in-first-out, FIFO) or that an average cost is used (average costing). In US GAAP, the alternative assumption of the newest items being sold first (last-in-first-out, LIFO) is also allowed. LIFO gives higher costs in times of inflation. The reason why LIFO exists in the US is not to increase accounting quality. Instead, it constitutes a tax benefit to companies when there is inflation. It is one of the very few areas in the US where there is a link between financial reporting and taxation, decided by the US Congress in 1939 (Davis, 1982).

Relating to Stylized Accrual Situation 3, inventories are measured at historical cost. Losses must be recognized if the net realizable value (fair value minus cost of sales) is below the historical cost. Write-downs of inventory is an area requiring some judgment and thus introduces uncertainty in the preparation of financial statements. As for long-term assets, it is asymmetrical and an example of conservatism in financial reporting.

Biological assets are measured at fair value in accordance with IAS 41. The reason is that historical cost is not particularly relevant. Biological assets are live animals and plants held as inventory. An important characteristic of such assets is that they "improve" over time (i.e., become more valuable). This is unlike other tangible assets, which are subject to wear and tear over time. For example, the cost of planting a tree is very small compared to the value of a fully grown tree. An additional reason for using fair value is that there are often active markets for harvested biological assets. When fair values are observable in active markets, the reliability of the measures is high.

Just as there has been limited standard-setting discussion on inventories, there is also limited research in the area. Most studies looking at inventories have a general financial statement analysis focus and only cover inventories as one accrual item among many. One study that does focus on inventories is Thomas and Zhang (2002). Sloan (1996) shows that investors do not consider the full information potential of earnings, in disagreement with EMH in the semi-strong form (see Chapters 3 and 7). Thomas and Zhang (2002) show that this effect is mostly driven by cost of goods sold through inventory accruals, thus pointing to the importance of inventory measurement for accounting quality.

11.5 Leases

All firms need and possess at least some assets. A startup firm may need cash in order to pay staff expenses, or it takes its cash and converts it into equipment used in its operations. More mature firms can have accumulated piles of cash (cf. Apple), intangible assets or tangible assets. Regardless of whether one speaks of tangible or intangible, current or non-current assets, prices may be high for these and require a high level of excess cash (e.g., real estate, vehicles, software licenses). When companies consider the initial cost of acquiring assets too high, an alternative way of obtaining those assets is via **lease contracts**. Indeed, leasing is a common way of obtaining the right to use and operate key assets in many industries, the airline and shipping industries being prominent examples of when leasing is prevalent. Sir David Tweedie, a former Chairman of the IASB, once said (15 August 2002):

> I can guarantee almost all of you here have never flown in a plane that has appeared in the airline's balance sheet. And the reason is they tend not to buy them, they lease them. And we all have leasing standards, and the great news is these leasing standards are perfectly harmonised world-wide. They are all absolutely useless. None of them work.

A firm's decision to lease or purchase an asset depends on various factors, such as available financing and tax benefits. Having an option to choose lease contracts especially for assets with a considerable price can be a great advantage for firms. One reason for leasing could be that it increases a firm's borrowing capacity. Schallheim et al. (2013) show that leases can both be used to replace other debt financing and increase the overall capacity of the firm to take on debt. However, this is not the only reason why lease contracts are so commonly used by firms. Leasing also provides companies, specifically the lessee, with the possibility to use an economic resource that does not appear in the financial statements. This *off*-balance sheet feature of leasing can be attractive, especially for firms seeking better-looking financial ratios and higher returns—the result of showing relatively lower amounts of assets and liabilities in the financial statements. Meanwhile, Altamuro et al. (2014) indicate that lending banks largely "see through" the off-balance sheet feature and consider all lease agreements in their credit assessments.

11.5.1 Definitions and summary of issues

A lease agreement is signed between a **lessor** and a **lessee**. The lessor owns the leased assets and the lease agreement transfers the right to use the asset for a specified time without a transfer of ownership. The main issue in the context of financial reporting is whether the asset should be recognized on the balance sheet of the lessee or the lessor. This is important since recognition on the balance sheet affects the income statement and has implications for firms' key financial ratios.

There are (at least) three different views that can be adopted regarding lease agreements:

1. A lease is a rental agreement
2. A lease is a rental agreement *or* a transfer of the underlying assets, depending on the conditions of the contract
3. Focus is placed on the transfer of **rights to use** the asset

If the lease agreement is seen as a rental, the asset is recognized by the lessor and the lessee only recognizes an expense for the rental. In the second case, the focus is on the asset *per se* and a distinction is made between leases that resemble a sale and those that are more like rentals. The former are called **finance leases** in IFRS (capital leases in US GAAP), while the latter are called **operating leases**. A finance lease resembles a sale in that, for example, the lease period is about the same as the economic life of the asset, the difference being that financing is provided through a lease agreement. The economic substance of the transaction resembles an installment purchase (i.e. payment is split into installments) and the lessee recognizes the asset on the balance sheet. An operating lease, meanwhile, is of shorter duration, so that the lessee only uses the asset for a part of its economic life. The lessor, not the lessee, recognizes the asset on the balance sheet. The third view is that the focus should be on the *right to use* the asset for a specific period of time rather than on the asset itself. So, even if the lease agreement only lasts for a limited part of the asset's economic life, the right to use the asset is still recognized as an asset by the lessee.

The view taken by standard-setters has shifted over time. For a long time, all lease agreements were considered rentals. When leases became more commonplace, however, both the FASB and the IASB adopted the second view. In IFRS this is reflected in IAS 17 *Leases*. In 2019, IAS 17 will be replaced by IFRS 16 *Leases*, which reflects the third view. Similar changes occur in US GAAP. We go through both IAS 17 and IFRS 16 below in order to contrast the views. When outlining the key features of each standard or view, we not only highlight the choices faced by regulators when creating standards, but also the choices and judgments preparers must make within the given context.

As stated previously, the main issue as regards lease accounting mostly relates to whether the lessor or the lessee should recognize the asset on the balance sheet. Once it is recognized, the asset is subject to issues similar to those for other assets. Fixed assets are subject to depreciation (amortization) and impairment may have to be considered. There are also measurement issues, such as whether historical cost or fair value should be used. We do not go through such issues here, as they are covered in other sections of this chapter. A summary of issues relating to accounting for leases is provided in Table 11.5.

An interesting note on lease accounting standards is that they represent "secondary" standards. The assets and liabilities involved are covered in other standards, which means that, in theory, lease standards may be viewed as superfluous. If a lessee leases an asset that meets the definition and recognition criteria of IAS 16 or IAS 38, the asset should be recognized. Note that the criteria in those standards do not include legal ownership as a prerequisite for recognition. The lease agreement also includes a financial asset with the lessor and a financial liability with the lessee. Both the financial asset and the liability meet the definitions and recognition criteria of IFRS 9 and should therefore be recognized. However, because of the special circumstances of lease agreements, they are treated in separate standards. Both the FASB and the IASB share the view that practice would not be consistent in the absence of such separate standards.

Finally, two important concepts in lease accounting are *comparability* and *conceptual consistency*. Standard-setters make choices regarding how to achieve conceptual consistency, as discussed below. The switch from IAS 17 to IFRS 16 involves a change in terms of which items are measured consistently and in terms of how comparability is achieved.

Table 11.5 Summary of issues relating to leases

Generic issue	Specific issue: Choices and judgments
Lessee perspective: Is there a lease contract?	If a lease contract: Value of asset? (See issues pertaining to PP&E and intangibles (SAS 1 and SAS 3)) Value of liability and associated interest expenses? If not a lease contract: Timing of recognition of expense?
Lessor perspective: Finance lease or operating lease?	If finance lease: Value of financial asset? Value of interest income? Revenue recognition from sale If operating lease: Value of asset? (See issues pertaining to PP&E and intangibles (SAS 1 and SAS 3)) Value of rental income?

Note: The distinction between a finance lease and operating lease has been important historically. For firms using IFRS, this binary distinction is removed for lessees with the issuance of IFRS 16.

11.5.2 Classification into operating and finance leases

As mentioned above, IAS 17 reflects the view that lease agreements are either operating or finance leases, depending on the economic substance of the agreement. The main difference between an operating lease and a finance lease is that under the former, the risks and rewards of ownership are not transferred to the lessee, whereas under the latter, the risks and rewards are substantially transferred from the lessor to the lessee.

Under a finance lease contract, the transfer of risks and rewards associated with the ownership of the asset makes it appropriate for the lessee to report this asset in its financial statements. Although legal ownership is not passed on from the lessor to the lessee, the economic substance of the transaction is such that the lessee should account for the contract as if it indeed did own the asset. The lessee also records a liability on the balance sheet that corresponds to the sum of future lease payments. The asset is depreciated over time and the liability is reduced over time based on lease payments made.

IAS 17 is consistent with a definition of assets based on a physical asset viewed as a whole. For example, a car could be an asset. If a firm leases a car, it either has or does not have risks and rewards of ownership of that particular car. Risks and rewards of ownership means that the lessee benefits if the car becomes more valuable and experiences a loss if the car becomes less valuable. This holds true if the lease agreement covers more or less the entire economic life of the car. Consequently, if risks and rewards of ownership are transferred to the lessee, it resembles a purchase of the car and is accounted for as a finance lease. If they are not transferred, the lease agreement resembles a rental agreement, accounted for as an operating lease. The focus on the asset as a whole differs from looking at assets as *rights* to use assets, which are divisible, see below.

In theory, the firm does not choose whether to account for a lease contract as a finance or operating lease. Rather, a finance lease exists if certain indicators exist, thereby obligating a firm to recognize an asset in its balance sheet. These indicators are not hard criteria; rather, paragraph 10 states that: "Whether a lease is a finance lease or an operating lease depends on the *substance of the transaction rather then the form of the contract*" (emphasis added). Five examples of situations that "individually or in combination would *normally* lead to a lease being classified as a finance lease" are then provided (again, emphasis added). These may be summarized as: 1) ownership will or is likely to be passed on to the lessee at the end of the contract period, or 2) the useful life of the asset does not significantly extend beyond the contract period, or the fair value of the asset for whatever other reason is equivalent to the present value of future lease payments.

Meanwhile, operating leases are all types of leases that may not be classified as finance leases. A lessee with an operating lease contract does not bear the risks of ownership associated with the asset, nor does it receive the benefits associated with the ownership of the leased asset. The underlying view, as noted above, is a focus on the individual asset *per se*.

IAS 17 covers accounting policies and disclosure requirements applicable to lessors as well as lessees. Table 11.6 provides a summary of how leases are treated in the financial statements of the lessee and the lessor. As shown, in the financial statements of the lessee, no balance sheet effect is recognized for the operating lease; instead, it is considered a rental expense in the income statement. The effects of the classification on the balance sheet and income statement are interesting as they show why an opportunistic firm management might have incentives to "choose" to classify leases as operating leases rather than as finance leases.

Since lessees do not show assets and liabilities for operating leases, such a classification improves the debt-to-equity ratio and the firm looks more financially stable. This is the reason why leasing is sometimes referred to as **off-balance sheet financing**. The lower level of assets and liabilities for operating leases also leads to improved return on assets and return on capital employed ratios. The effects on the income statement are less pronounced. For operating leases, there is a rental expense in operating items. For finance leases, there is depreciation in operating items as well as an interest expense in financial items. Even though there are different types of expenses for the two types of leases, the total expense for the

Table 11.6 Finance and operating leases in IAS 17

	Finance lease	Operating lease
Lessee:		
B/S:	Assets and liabilities	–
I/S:	Depreciation (operating expense) associated with the asset	Rental (operating) expense
	Interest (finance) expense associated with the liability)	
Lessor:		
B/S:	Lease receivable	Lease asset
I/S:	Interest (finance) income	Rental (operating) income

lessee is approximately the same in the two cases. Consequently, there is limited effect on net income from lease classification.

It is said that accounting should depict economic events and states. But what happens if accounting *creates* events and states? That is to say, what if accounting did not represent economic reality but instead influenced that reality? When it comes to lease contracts, this has been voiced as a real concern. The structuring of contracts in order to achieve a certain effect in the financial statements would seriously thwart the purpose of the standards and call into question the resultant quality of the financial accounts. More specifically, one would not achieve a faithful representation of the underlying economic transactions.

Of course, as discussed in Chapter 2, accounting choices do not matter if we maintain the assumption that markets are efficient and investors are able to "see through" the choices. Using several valuation models, including the discounted free cash flow and residual income models, Boatsman and Dong (2011) conclude that whether a lease contract is classified as an operating lease or a finance lease does not cause material changes for equity valuation purposes. Perhaps investors and analysts are not "fooled" by lease classifications, but merely encumbered by the extra cost of having to adjust their valuations to achieve cross-sectional comparability.

Either way, managers seem to think it worthwhile to recognize lease contracts as operating leases. As expected, research evidence shows that companies may strongly prefer operating leases over finance leases, since operating leases are kept off-balance sheet and thus result in better financial ratios, including greater returns on assets and lower debt-to-equity ratios (Duke et al., 2009; Lyon, 2010). In other words, operating leases represent a large off-balance sheet obligation that, if kept "hidden," makes the firm look better than it actually is. Using a large dataset of listed companies from 1980 to 2006, Cornaggia et al. (2013) show that the average of operating leases, when scaled by total debt, has increased significantly over the last few decades (see Figure 11.6).

Even when contracts are not deliberately adjusted in the above manner, the classification of a contract as an operating lease in order to avoid capitalization of the leased asset is still

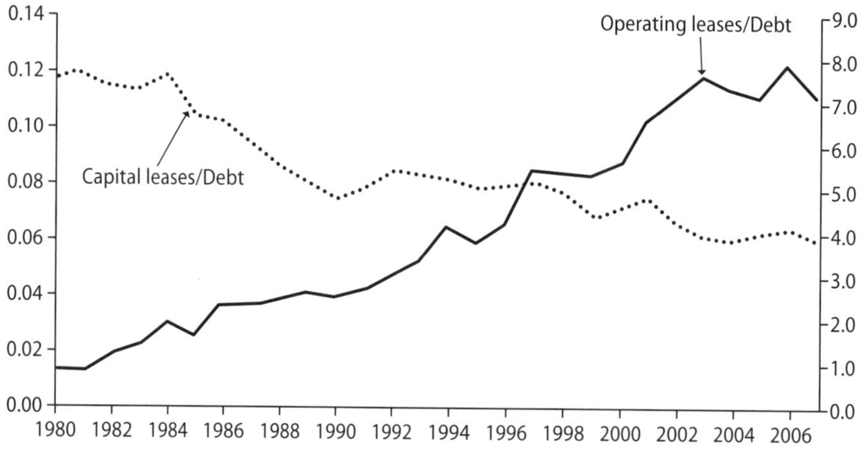

Figure 11.6 Average operating lease and finance lease as a percentage of total debt. The sample contains all listed firms merged in the CRSP-Compustat database from 1980 to 2006. Source: Cornaggia et al. (2013)

highly discretionary. The guidance provided on when to recognize a finance lease is not necessarily straightforward in practice and it involves judgments. A possible solution might appear to be to provide bright-line rules, specifying more concrete and definite criteria for when a finance lease is truly a finance lease. This was the situation under current US GAAP, which contained the following four criteria for when to classify a lease as a finance lease (*capital lease* in US GAAP terminology):

1. **Ownership:** The ownership of the asset is transfered from the lessor to the lessee at the end of the lease term.
2. **Bargain purchase option:** The lessee has the option of purchasing the leased asset at the end of the lease term at a price that is significantly lower than the expected fair value of the asset.
3. **The 75% lease term rule:** The lease term extends over at least 75% percent of the estimated useful life of the asset.
4. **The 90% minimum lease payment rule:** The present value of the minimum lease payments is greater than 90% of the fair value of the leased asset.

However, this approach has been considered inadequate both in the US and internationally (see Text Box 11.4). In fact, it is argued that having "bright-line" rules for lease capitalization results in misusing the standard (see Reither, 1998), causing a more principles-based approach to be taken under IFRS. Actually, lease accounting is one accounting area that has prompted the view that US GAAP is rules-based while IFRS is principles-based. This distinction is true regarding the classification of lease agreements.

Text Box 11.4 **The worst accounting standard?**

The results from a survey given to analysts, academics, regulators and public accountants at an AAA/FASB Financial Reporting Issues Conference showed that the lease standard (SFAS No. 13) was rated the *worst* accounting standard under US GAAP. A commentary article, "What Are the Best and the Worst Accounting Standards?" (Reither, 1998, p. 288) states the reasons why the accounting standard for leases was the main "loser":

> Respondents gave the following reasons for rating Statement No. 13 as one of the worst accounting standards:
>
> - Fails to achieve objectives because many obligations that, in substance, are capital, sales-type, or direct-financing leases are recognized as operating leases
> - Conceptually and operationally an accounting nightmare
> - Bright-line rules for lease capitalization result in abuse of standard
> - Complicated standard—which is evidenced by its many amendments and interpretations
> - Relies too heavily on disclosure to assess lease obligations
> - Does not significantly improve accounting for lease transactions.

However, IAS 17 has not escaped criticism either—far from it. The standard has come under fire both conceptually and operationally. Even assuming that the reporting firm has correctly determined whether or not the risks and rewards associated with the ownership of the asset have been transfered, one may question the validity of recognizing a finance lease from a theoretical standpoint. Returning again to the definition of an asset ("a resource controlled by the entity, as a result of past events, from which future economic benefits are expected to flow to the entity"), surely no asset exists if the control criterion is not fulfilled. However, the leased asset is expected to generate future economic benefits for the lessee *over a given time period*, which might suggest that this right to use the asset is an asset in itself that carries value and which should therefore be recorded on the balance sheet (Lyon, 2010). As is pointed out, "[m]aking a distinction between operating and finance leases could mean, for example, a business that leases an aircraft on an operating lease, and which relies for its business on that aircraft, could have a set of accounts that makes no reference to the aircraft. This, surely, means that the accounts fail to represent the whole story of the business" (Lyon, 2010, p. 329). The view expressed by Lyon (2010) is reflected in IFRS 16, see below.

The above reasoning is linked to concerns regarding *comparability* of financial statements across companies when a *binary* classification is applied. A binary classification results in large differences in financial statement outcomes depending on which of the two possible solutions is selected. The accounting treatment of leases under IAS 17 makes it highly likely that firms treat similar leasing transactions in different ways. Arbitrary classifications of leases are problematic due to the substantial effect of this on financial statements and financial ratios. The binary classification also gives very strong incentives for management to select the solution that fits their purposes. The incentives are made stronger by the fact that management is in an "either or" situation.

The logic and conceptual viewpoint adopted in IAS 17 is the same as in IAS 18 *Revenue*, a standard issued at about the same time as IAS 17. Both standards use the transfer of risk and rewards of the asset as a whole as a basis for the accounting treatment. In the case of IAS 17, this means that the lessee does not recognize the asset—nor the corresponding liability—when the risks and rewards are not transferred. This causes an inconsistency with IFRS 9 concerning financial instruments. The lessee has a contractual obligation to pay cash in the future, which meets the definition of a financial liability, regardless of whether leases are classified as operating or finance leases. Therefore, based on IAS 17 and IFRS 9, there are different treatments of financial liabilities within IFRS, which is problematic from a comparability perspective.

In summary, the uncertainty and lack of transparency associated with accounting for lease contracts has raised several criticisms against current accounting treatments. Considerable differences between the IASB and the FASB resulted in a joint project to improve lease accounting, with the IASB replacing IAS 17 *Leases* with a new standard. IFRS 16 *Leases* was released in January 2016 and is mandatory from January 2019. A similar standard will also be implemented in US GAAP. The conceptual changes, along with concerns raised in relation to IFRS 16, are discussed below.

11.5.3 Assets defined as rights

IFRS 16 takes a different conceptual approach compared to IAS 17, as it takes a full balance sheet view and is conceptually consistent with IFRS 9 and the new revenue recognition standard IFRS 15 (see Chapter 13). IFRS 16 defines assets as the *right* to use a resource, in agreement with the view taken in the Conceptual Framework. Since all lease agreements create a right to use a resource for lessees, it follows that all lease agreements should be recognized as assets (and corresponding liabilities) on the balance sheet. Using the terminology of IAS 17, all leases are classified as finance leases by lessees (even if that terminology is not used in IFRS 16). There are some exceptions, for example for short-term leases. Taking the example of a lease of a particular car (cf. above), IFRS 16 is no longer concerned with risks and rewards of ownership of the car. Instead, the focus is on the lessees' contractual *right* to use the car for a set period.

The issuance of the new standard was preceded by substantial debate. Comment letters to the ED revealed the concerns of respondents, not least with respect to the excessive costs of applying the standard, especially in SMEs, and the lack of consistency with existing GAAP (Barone et al., 2014). There were also concerns in the leasing industry that leases will become less popular, since IFRS 16 effectively removes the possibility for off-balance sheet financing by lessees. Given that the standard requires a lessee to recognize assets and liabilities for almost all leases in the financial statements, it will come as no surprise that one of the main concerns raised in response to the new standard is its effect on debt and profitability ratios. Research suggests that the airline industry, the shipping industry, as well as the retail and banking sectors, having relied particularly heavily on operating lease agreements, will be the most strongly affected by the new standard. For example, retailers often choose not to own real estate but lease properties, airlines lease their aircraft and shipping companies likewise lease their vessels. Nevertheless, empirical research also indicates that the major impact of this change will be on leverage ratio rather than profitability ratios (e.g., Economics, 2017; Grossmann and Grossmann, 2010).

Although the changes introduced in the final standard may have some potentially negative consequences for firms' financial ratios, the overall benefits have been determined to exceed the costs. First, the change in financial ratios may actually make financial statements better reflect underlying economics, as all lease agreements create financial liabilities for lessees (contractual future lease payments), and with the new standard such liabilities are reflected in the balance sheet. Second, IFRS 16 turns a binary classification of lease agreement into a judgment on a continuous scale (see Figure 11.7). A continuous outcome reduces the effect of managerial judgment on financial statement outcomes, while increasing faithful

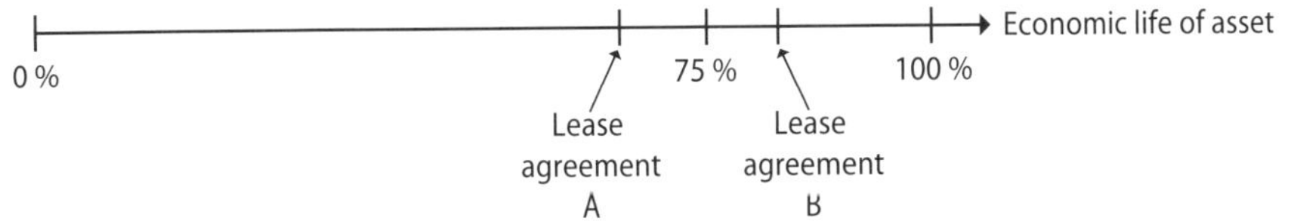

Figure 11.7 Binary and continuous classification of leases

representation and comparability. The difference in outcome between lease agreements A and B in Figure 11.7 becomes large with a binary classification, as A is an operating lease and B is a finance lease. With a continuous classification, the difference in outcome between the two situations is much smaller, as B results in an asset and a liability that is only 10–20% larger than A, but there is an asset and a liability in both cases.

Finally, an issue arising in the implementation of IFRS 16 for lessees is how to distinguish between the right to use an asset and a service contract. There is a general tendency that the service component in lease agreements is becoming more important. For example, a firm can either lease a copy machine or they can make an agreement with a copy machine supplier to pay for the service of making copies. In the former case, an asset and a liability are recognized in the lessee's balance sheet. In the latter case, only service fees are recognized, while nothing is shown on the balance sheet. So, the previous question of writing contracts in order to achieve off-balance sheet effects may still be open. As a result, IFRS 16 contains more guidance on what constitutes a lease agreement and what does not. A lease agreement gives the right to use a *specific asset* (e.g. a car) for a specified time. A service contract specifies the service to be provided (e.g. car transportation, without pointing to the use of a particular car). Accounting by lessors did not change in IFRS 16, see Text Box 11.5.

At this point, the reader may have noticed a lack of references to the four stylized accrual situations in this section. The reason is that accounting for lease agreements is one of the areas where these situations are less relevant, as pointed out in section 10.2. Lease assets and liabilities recognized by a lessee are simultaneously recognized on both sides of the balance at the inception of the lease, so a timing issue in relation to the income statement is not present. Of course, if an asset is recognized, it is depreciated (SAS 1) and subject to impairment (SAS 3) as other assets on the balance sheet. The point, however, is that the primary issue in leasing, whether or not to recognize the lease agreement on the balance sheet, is not meaningfully analyzed in terms of the four stylized accrual situations.

Text Box 11.5 **Lessor accounting**

We have not mentioned accounting by lessors in IFRS 16. They still follow the same logic as in IAS 17 and continue to classify lease agreements into operating and finance leases. The IASB made an attempt at aligning lessors' accounting with lessees' accounting, but it turned out to be difficult. Also, there was a general agreement that for lessors, lease accounting was not problematic. Therefore, the IASB decided not to make any changes to the reporting requirements for lessors.

11.6 Financial instruments

Financial instruments accounting is an area that has received substantial interest in the last few decades, and the discussion and standard-setting activity in the area increased after the 2007–2008 financial crisis. There are at least two reasons for this, as described below.

First, following worldwide deregulation of financial markets from the 1970s and onwards, the complexity of both financial instruments and markets have increased greatly. A pronounced globalization of markets has added to their complexity. This coincides with the increased size and economic importance of the markets. In other words, the underlying economics that financial instruments accounting is expected to reflect are increasingly complex. For example, many financial instruments are held by firms with the intention of benefiting from the instruments' changes in fair value. This suggests that fair value is the relevant measurement basis, which is not always easy to implement in practice. Furthermore, financial instruments are often used in hedging relationships, which are often quite complex.

Second, financial instruments are important in banks and insurance companies. Both banking and insurance are industries where governments and states have a substantial interest as guarantors of stability. Large banks and insurance companies with financial problems can threaten the stability of the entire financial system, so states are often involved in protecting stability. To the extent that financial reporting is a predictor of future stability, it has relevance for the supervision of banking and insurance. Consequently, states have an interest in how standards for financial instruments accounting are designed. This interest became especially evident after the 2007–2008 financial crisis.

The FASB started working on new accounting standards for financial instruments in the 1980s. Starting in the 1990s, disclosures of fair values for many financial instruments were required. Later, fair value requirements were extended to measurement and recognition on the balance sheet and income statement. The introduction of fair value resulted in a number of research studies on the relevance of such disclosures and measurement (see Chapter 10).

The IASB issued IAS 39 *Financial Instruments: Recognition and Measurement* in 1998. The standard required fair value measurement for many financial assets. It also covered impairment and hedge accounting. When the European Union introduced mandatory IFRS for all listed firms in 2005, IAS 39 was a controversial standard due to its effect on financial reporting in European banks. IAS 39 was not endorsed by the EU until November 2004, just one month before the introduction of IFRS in the EU.

The next big event to affect financial instruments accounting was the financial crisis of 2007–2008. Financial reporting was seen as a contributing factor to the crisis, as it laid bare some perceived weaknesses in financial reporting (see Text Box 11.6 for a summary of events and how these relate to financial reporting). A substantial part of the work of the IASB in the 10 years following the crisis has been focused on remedying those weaknesses, which may be summarized into three themes: *measurement*, *entity issues* and *disclosure*.

Text Box 11.6 **The 2007–2008 financial crisis and financial reporting**

The 2007–2008 financial crisis had several phases. It started with mortgages in the US and spread to banks in general in, for example, Europe. A few years later, there was a sovereign debt crisis affecting some countries in the euro area. We do not talk about the sovereign crisis here, as it is largely unrelated to financial reporting.

In the 1990s, banks in the US started giving mortgages to homeowners with low credit rating, so-called **subprime** mortgages. This was considered safe, as the home was a security for repayment of the mortgage, and prices of homes were rising. The mortgage banks often securitized the loans. The mortgages were packaged and transferred to a Special Purpose Entity (SPE). The SPE issued Mortgage-Backed Obligations (MBO) with the mortgages as security. The investors who bought the MBO supplied cash to the SPE and the cash was transferred to the bank (see figure below).

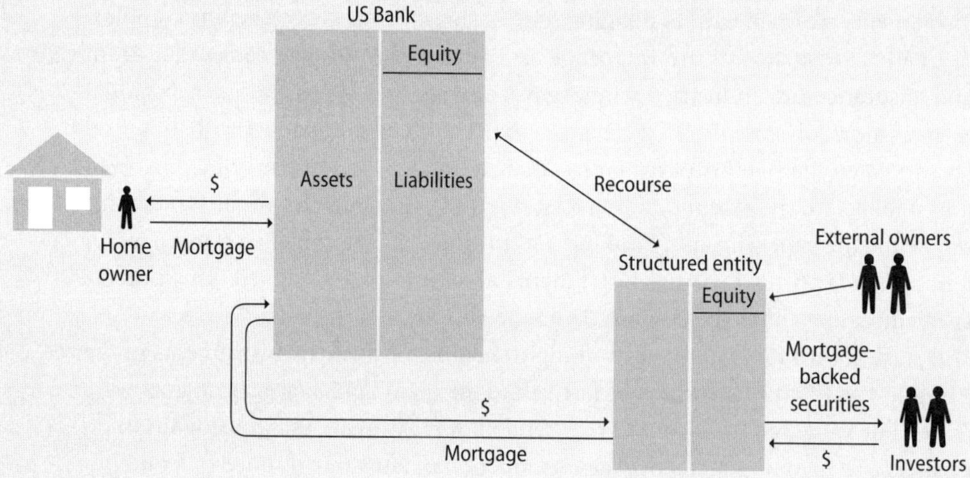

The home owner will not notice the transaction, as the original bank usually continues to manage transactions with the client. However, the mortgage has been removed from the bank's balance sheet and is replaced with cash. The SPE usually has recourse to the bank, meaning that if losses exceed a certain amount or percentage, the bank will repay the SPE and its investors.

In 2007, house prices started declining in many parts of the US and the default rate on subprime mortgages increased sharply. The recourse clauses in the agreements between banks and SPE started to be exercised, leading to large losses in many banks. These losses were unexpected, partly because the exposure to mortgage losses was not visible on the balance sheet of the banks. The mortgages (assets from the banks' perspective) were not included on the balance sheet, and there was scant or non-existent disclosure regarding the arrangements and the related risks.

Another consequence was that asset values on the MBO market declined sharply at the same time as the market activity decreased. As both banks outside the US and banks not in the mortgage business could be investors in MBOs, a general decline in trust in banks and financial markets followed; in other words, a full-fledged financial crisis erupted. In Europe, the situation deteriorated after the collapse of Lehman Brothers (a large US investment bank) in September 2008. In the fall of 2008, European banks were hit by the combined effect of declining values of many financial investments and increased credit losses among many of their clients.

Several weaknesses in financial reporting were identified following the crisis, including:

- **Derecognition** of, for example, financial assets transferred to SPEs with a recourse clause. Although the assets were derecognized, an exposure remained that resulted in losses during the financial crisis. There was no way for financial statement users to see the exposure, as there were no disclosures regarding derecognition and the continuing exposure.
- **Consolidation** of SPEs. This is related to derecognition, since assets transferred to consolidated SPEs remain in the consolidated financial statements. Since many SPEs were not consolidated, the assets and the related exposure were not visible in the consolidated financial statements.
- **Fair value measurement** did not work particularly well when markets became inactive. During the crisis, markets for some financial instruments—for example MBOs—became inactive, and it was difficult to measure these instruments at fair value.

In this section, we cover the first of these three themes, including fair value measurement and impairment of financial assets (see also Chapter 10 for a more extensive discussion on fair value). Entity issues (including consolidation of SPEs and derecognition of financial assets) and disclosures (e.g., regarding derecognized financial assets and continuing exposures) are covered in later chapters (Chapters 14 and 15).

The IASB's response to the financial crisis has resulted in a number of new and amended standards. IFRS 7 *Financial Instruments: Disclosure* was amended shortly after the crisis. A suite of standards relating to group accounting—IFRS 10 *Consolidation*, IFRS 11 *Joint Arrangements* and IFRS 12 *Disclosure of Interests in Other Entities*—became effective in 2013. IFRS 13 *Fair Value Measurement* also became effective that year. IFRS 9 *Financial Instruments* was implemented for fiscal year 2018. There have been similar developments and changes to US GAAP.

As the reader may already have figured out, financial instruments accounting is broad in scope. Apart from going through measurement of financial assets, we also consider hedge accounting. Financial liabilities are discussed in Chapter 12.

11.6.1 Definitions and summary of issues

Financial assets are defined as cash, contractual rights to receive cash (or other financial assets) in the future and equity instruments in other firms.

With respect to SAS 1, investments in financial assets are nearly always recognized as assets on the balance sheet. There is no systematic depreciation or amortization of financial assets over time, as such assets are not consumed over time.

The main issue relating to the measurement of financial assets is captured by the third Stylized Accrual Situation, namely when unrealized gains and losses should be recognized in financial statements. In IFRS, there are three measurement models used for financial assets:

1. Fair value through profit and loss (FVPL)
2. Fair value through other comprehensive income (FVOCI)
3. Historic (amortized) cost

In both fair value models, all unrealized gains and losses are immediately recognized on the balance sheet, but there is a difference regarding the recognition in the income statement. In FVPL there is immediate recognition of gains and losses in the income statement. For FVOCI, there are two possibilities. One method is that gains and losses are recognized in profit and loss (income statement) when they are realized (i.e., when the asset is derecognized). This is called **recycling** of OCI items. The other method is that the items are not recycled, meaning that the gains and losses recognized in OCI are never recognized in profit and loss. The presentation of OCI and recycling is discussed more in Chapter 15.

Using fair value is seen as *relevant* when either: 1) the changes in fair value are likely to be realized in the firm's cash flows, or 2) changes in value are used internally to assess performance, or a combination of the two. Meanwhile, fair value should only be used when *faithful representation* is obtainable. In other words, fair value should not be used when there is too much uncertainty in its measurement.

Impairment is only an issue for financial assets measured at amortized (historic) cost. When assets are measured at fair value, any changes in value are always reflected immediately in the fair value amount. Like other assets measured at historical cost, financial assets are subject to asymmetric measurement. That is, increases in value are not recognized until they are realized, while decreases in value are recognized immediately.

In hedge accounting, there is a departure from "normal" measurement principles in order to better reflect the underlying hedging relationship in financial statements. The main issue in hedge accounting is to determine when it is applicable. The main issues that apply to financial instruments are summarized in Table 11.7.

Table 11.7 Summary of issues relating to financial instruments

Generic issue	Specific issue: Choices and judgments
SAS 1 (Recognition at acquisition)	Derecognition (and related income statement effect)?
SAS 3 (Unexpected changes in value)	Measurement model? (Cost/Fair value) If fair value model: Fair value measurement
	Impairment? (Value of credit losses when measured at cost)
	Hedge accounting: measurement and specification of hedging relationships

11.6.2 Measurement

In the next subsection, we provide a few specific examples that may shed light on issues involved in the measurement of financial assets. This is followed by an overview of what IFRS says about measurement of financial assets and, primarily, the relevance criteria.

Examples of financial assets

As noted in previous sections, fair value is normally not used for PP&E and intangible assets. Since such assets are acquired for own use, it is unlikely that any fair value changes will be realized in cash flows. In addition, the firm's intention with the acquisition of such assets is not to benefit from changes in fair value. Both PP&E and intangible assets are also normally used in combination with other assets, so that the value in use can be substantially higher than the stand-alone fair value. For both types of assets, fair value is an option through the revaluation model. However, for intangible assets, this is highly restricted due to the difficulty of obtaining a faithful representation.

Financial assets differ from PP&E and intangibles in at least three respects: 1) fair value is more often relevant, 2) it is easier to obtain a reliable measure of fair value, and 3) financial assets are not used in combination with other assets, so their stand-alone fair value is a good reflection of the value to the firm. This has led to calls that all financial assets should be measured at fair value. The IASB, however, has settled for a model where—depending on circumstances—both fair value and historic (amortized) cost may be used.

Accounts receivables represent a common financial asset and one where fair value is likely to be *not* relevant. The intention of acquiring accounts receivable is to facilitate sales, not to benefit from changes in fair value.

Loans (non-standardized) and **bonds** (standardized) can have either fixed or variable interest rates. When the interest rate is variable, cash flows from the instrument vary with interest rate movements, but the value of the asset is largely stable. Therefore, for variable-interest instruments, there are basically no gains or losses from fair value changes. Fixed-interest instruments, however, have fixed cash flows and their value will differ when market interest rates change (we show how this works in Text Box 11.7). So, for fixed interest loans and bonds, there can be large changes in value and therefore large unrealized gains and losses.

A question is whether bonds (and non-standardized instruments) can be reliably measured at fair value and whether such measurement is relevant. These instruments can usually be measured without too much difficulty, so the measurement process does not preclude the use of fair value on the basis of low reliability. Meanwhile, the relevance of fair value depends on how the instrument is expected to be settled. For instruments that are held to maturity, no changes in fair value will be realized. Instead, the value of the instrument will converge to the nominal value by maturity. Only when instruments are sold before maturity will fair value changes affect cash flows. Therefore, it seems reasonable that it is only when fixed instruments may or are expected to be sold before maturity that fair value changes should be reflected in financial statements. In other words, for bondholders and holders of non-standardized fixed interest receivables, the relevance of fair value is related to the intent of holding the instruments. A pertinent question would, for example, be if the holder intends to hold the instruments to maturity. If the answer to that question is yes, fair value may not be relevant.

From the issuer's perspective, fair value is unlikely to be relevant. Bonds and other fixed interest debt are issued to finance operations, not to make gains on fair value changes (this is discussed further in relation to financial liabilities in Chapter 12).

Another type of financial instruments are **equity instruments** issued by another firm (equity instruments are not considered financial instruments from the issuing firm's perspective). Equity instruments do not revert to any nominal value over time. Instead, their current market value is—at least theoretically—the best estimate of their future value (cf. the efficient market hypothesis in Chapter 3). Therefore, changes in fair value are likely to be realized, at least in the long term, and fair value is likely to be relevant.

Text Box 11.7 **Fixed-interest financial instruments**

Bonds often have a fixed interest rate. There is a *nominal value* (sometimes called face value) of the bond, which represents the amount that will be paid to the bondholder on the maturity date (i.e., when the bond expires). Interest is calculated as a percentage of the nominal value. For example, a bond with a nominal value of €1,000,000 with a fixed interest of 5% pays €50,000 annually in interest. Let us assume that the bond has a term of 10 years. It is issued at the beginning of year 1 and maturity is at the end of year 10. Interest is paid annually at the end of each year. Then the total cash flows relating to this bond are as shown below:

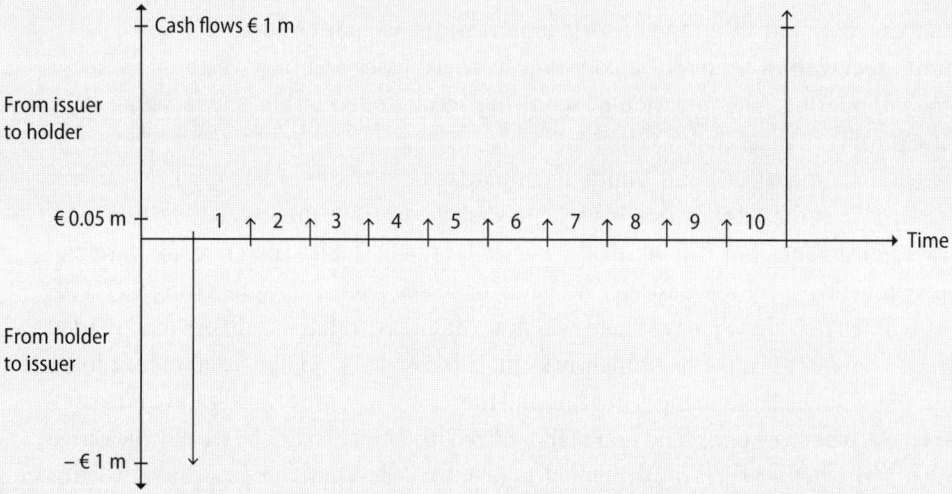

As seen in the figure, the cash flows for a bond are fixed, as the interest paid is based on a fixed rate. However, the interest rate used in the valuation of bonds will change over the term of the bond. There are two reasons for this: 1) risk-free market interest rates will vary, and 2) the risk premium on the specific bond changes if the credit standing of the issuer changes.

Bonds are valued based on discounted cash flow models, where the discount rate used is the current market rate, including the current risk premium. We may, for example, value the bond we used as an example at the end of year 6 (with four remaining years). We look at two situations, one where the market rate is 7% and one where it is 3%. The calculations are as follows:

$$\text{7\% interest:} \quad \text{Value} = \frac{50}{1.07} + \frac{50}{1.07^2} + \frac{50}{1.07^3} + \frac{1{,}050}{1.07^4} = 932$$

$$\text{3\% interest:} \quad \text{Value} = \frac{50}{1.03} + \frac{50}{1.03^2} + \frac{50}{1.03^3} + \frac{1{,}050}{1.03^4} = 1{,}074$$

As noted in the calculation, the current value (fair value, market value) of a bond exceeds the nominal value when the fixed interest rate is above the market rate, while the reverse is true when the fixed rate is below the market rate. At the time of acquisition of a bond, the difference between the fair value and the nominal value is either referred to as a *premium* (if the market value is higher) or a *discount* (if the market value is lower).

When bonds are initially issued, the fixed rate is often close to the market rate. Still, there could be differences—and resulting premiums or discounts—at that time too. There are even zero-interest bonds (often called zero-coupon bonds) with large discounts at issuance. However, if we look at a bond where fixed interest rate equals market rate at the time of issuance, the development of fair value over time could look like in the figure below. The scenario is based on market rates exceeding the fixed rate in early years, while the reverse is true in later years. At maturity, fair value and nominal value always converge.

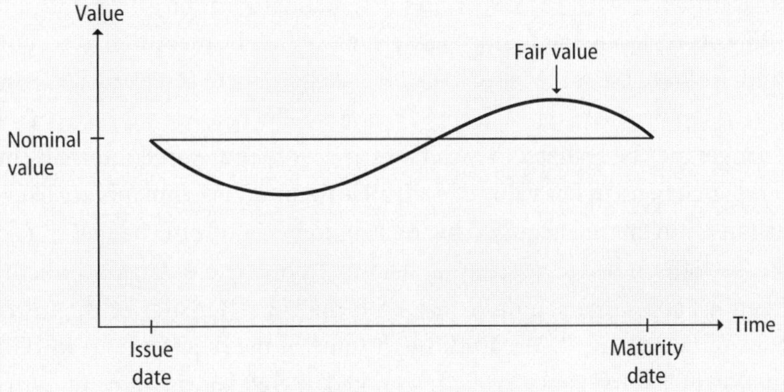

A difficulty with equity instruments is that measuring their fair value can introduce substantial measurement uncertainty. For listed instruments, it is easy to obtain a market value. Valuing unlisted equities, however, requires subjective forecasts of the future performance of the issuing firms, as well as a risk-adjusted discount rate. Consequently, it may be questionable whether a faithful representation can be obtained.

The last type of specific financial instruments we present here are **derivative financial instruments** ("derivatives"). Derivatives are defined in IFRS 9 as instruments where the value changes in response to an underlying variable (e.g., interest rate, exchange rate or stock price) require a "small" initial investment and are settled at a future date. We do not explain derivatives in detail in this book. Suffice it to mention that there are three basic types of derivatives. **Forward contracts** specify a price to be paid in a future transaction (e.g., for a currency, future currency exchange). **Options** give one party (the holder) the right but not the obligation to carry out a transaction with a fixed price in the future. The issuer of options have the obligation to carry out a transaction but no rights. The holder pays a fee to the issuer for taking on the obligation. Finally, **swaps** are contracts where cash flows from instruments are exchanged without any transfer of the underlying instrument. A swap could for example involve the swapping of variable and fixed interest rates.

Derivatives have properties that affect the risk level of firms. As such, derivatives are primarily used for either hedging (reduction of risk) or speculation (increasing risk). The desired effect on risk is achieved through changes in fair values of derivatives. Consequently, fair value changes are essential for firms and it is highly relevant to show these to external stakeholders. In addition, historical cost of derivatives is often small and the fair value fluctuations are large, thus rendering historical cost irrelevant.

To summarize the discussion on the relevance of specific types of financial instruments, we have mentioned accounts receivable, variable and fixed interest loans, equity instruments and derivatives.

Measurement of financial assets in IFRS

Both in accordance with IAS 39, IASB's first standard on measurement of financial assets, and IFRS 9, its replacement, financial assets may either be measured at cost or fair value. The two standards have the same basic logic for the choice between historical cost and fair value. Fair value is required when it is deemed relevant, which, as we suggested above, is when fair value changes may be realized in cash flows and/or they are used internally by management. For example, changes in fair value of derivative financial instruments are likely to be realized, and such instruments are acquired by the firm to benefit from changes in fair value (see, for example, section on hedge accounting below). In order to determine whether any of those two situations apply, the standards use both the characteristics of the instrument and the intentions of management. We go through some of the requirements in IFRS 9, where this combination of factors is very explicit. As noted, IAS 39 has the same underlying logic, but it is less obvious and more implicit.

The presumption in IFRS 9 is that all financial assets are measured at fair value, unless two conditions are met: 1) the asset pays only principal and interest, and 2) the asset is held within a business model where the firm collects only contractual cash flows.

The first condition is referred to as *solely payment of principal and interest* (SPPI). Note that "principal" corresponds to what we referred to as "nominal amount" above. This condition can only be met by loans and receivables (e.g., bonds and accounts receivables). Equity instruments and derivatives do not meet the SPPI criterion and must therefore be measured at fair value.

The second condition is used to evaluate the intention of management regarding loans and receivables. Collection of contractual cash flows means holding the assets to maturity and not selling them before that. This almost always applies to accounts receivables. It usually holds for non-standardized loans and may be true for bonds. As noted above, if assets are held to maturity, changes in fair value are not relevant and historical cost is used. On the other hand, if a firm holds bonds within a trading portfolio in which the assets are frequently traded, fair value is relevant. Then, the business model is not to collect only contractual cash flows, but also to collect cash flows from selling assets.

The presumption in IFRS 9 is that equity instruments can always be measured at fair value. IAS 39 included an exemption where historical cost could be used when the measurement of non-listed equity instruments was very difficult. This exemption has been removed in IFRS 9. IFRS 9 allows for the recognition of gains and losses from changes in the value of equity instruments in OCI instead of in profit and loss. Even though, as we suggest above, all fair value changes are expected to affect cash flows at some point, this may take a very long time for equity instruments. Therefore, recognition in OCI can be more relevant for such instruments.

As a final note on measurement of financial assets, we introduce the concept of **amortized cost**. So far we have used historical cost without further specification. For financial assets, historical cost is actually amortized cost. Amortized cost starts with the price of acquisition—just as historical cost—but over time it changes in a non-linear manner and reaches the nominal amount at maturity. This is shown in Figure 11.8.

Note that the issue of amortized cost differing from acquisition price is only an issue for fixed interest instruments. For variable interest instruments, there is no change in value over time, or at least it is very small.

When the IASB started working on IFRS 9 following the 2007–2008 financial crisis, they quickly developed new requirements for the measurement of financial assets. These were published already in 2009 and the idea was to move ahead quickly with the remaining parts of the standard. There were, however, two areas that proved very difficult and which delayed the publication—and implementation—of IFRS. They were impairment of financial assets and hedging, which we discuss next.

11.6.3 Impairment of financial assets

For financial assets measured at amortized cost, impairment must be considered. Financial assets differ from other assets in that only some decreases in value are recognized immediately. Only changes in value caused by an issuer's deterioration in credit quality are grounds for impairment. Decreases in value due to increases in general market interest rates (for fixed interest instruments, cf. above) are not recognized until they are realized. The reason is that in most cases, such decreases will not be realized before they are reversed. Recognizing them in the financial statements would therefore lead to unnecessary earnings volatility.

Both the assessment of whether there has been a deterioration of credit quality of the issuer and the estimation of the monetary effect of the deterioration require substantial judgment on the part of preparers. This often results in a high level of measurement uncertainty regarding impairment of financial assets. The standard-setter must make a trade-off between objectivity and subjectivity. Later recognition of impairment losses leads to less subjective

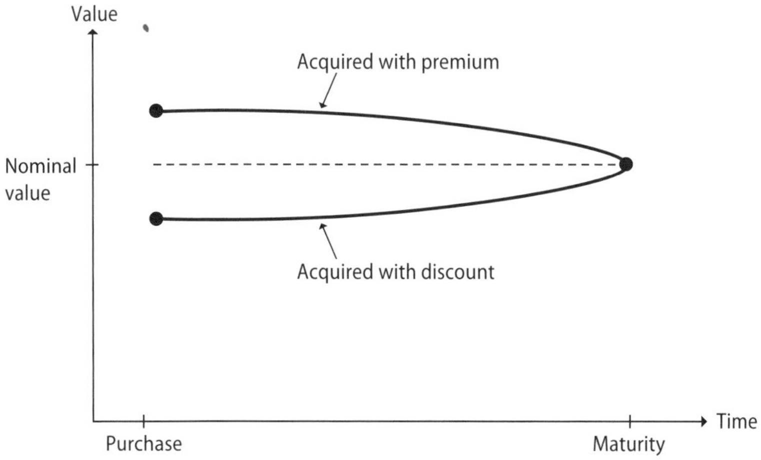

Figure 11.8
Amortized cost

estimates. On the other hand, the signal to financial statement users concerning impairment comes later, which normally renders it less relevant. Earlier recognition of impairment losses requires more subjective judgment, but earlier information may be more relevant. In a sense, it is the traditional trade-off between relevance and faithful representation. It can also be seen as a trade-off between principles-based and rules-based accounting standards.

IAS 39 required an **incurred loss model** for impairment. This model requires that a so-called objective event has happened with the issuer before impairment is recognized, which results in late (but more objective) impairment. IFRS 9 requires an **expected loss model**, which results in earlier recognition of impairment at the expense of objectivity.

A reason why impairment of financial assets was delayed in the work with IFRS 9 is the substantial interest that states have in this accounting issue. An important area where impairment of financial assets is applied is in accounting for credit losses in banks. Banking is an area where states have more supervision compared to in other industries due to the importance of banks in the functioning of financial and monetary systems. In addition, states often have explicit or implicit guarantees to support banks in financial difficulties. One of the most important causes of such difficulties is credit losses, so the signal provided by banks to states through credit loss accounting is very important.

Marton and Runesson (2017) study the effect on credit loss accounting in accordance with IAS 39 (representing the incurred loss model) and alternative local GAAP (representing more subjective expected loss models). They find that the ability of credit loss accounting to predict actual credit losses was lower with IAS 39 (i.e., the accounting quality is lower). The delayed signal concerning credit losses in accordance with IAS 39 may very well have exacerbated the 2007–2008 financial crisis, a view for example shared by FCAG (2009) and supported by Beatty and Liao (2011).

The IASB's change from the incurred loss model to the expected loss model may, therefore, constitute an improvement. A similar change is occurring in US GAAP. However, as pointed to by Marton and Runesson (2017), the more subjective nature of expected losses makes enforcement more important, especially when managerial incentives are high (cf. Beck and Narayanamoorthy, 2013; Kanagaretnam et al., 2004).

11.6.4 Hedge accounting

Hedging is a form of risk management. Normally, it involves reducing the exposure to a risk through the acquisition of an instrument (usually a derivative) with an opposite exposure. An example may help clarify. A firm using euro (EUR) as its currency has a receivable outstanding in US dollars (USD) (i.e., in a USD asset). The firm has an exposure to changes in the USD/EUR exchange rate (a currency risk). The EUR value of the loan increases if the USD/EUR rate increases and loses value if the USD/EUR rate decreases. The firm can neutralize this exposure by taking on a liability in USD at the same amount as the asset. Then, when the firm makes a loss on the asset it will make a corresponding gain on the liability, and vice versa. The net effect of exchange rate movements on profit and loss is zero. The same effect can be achieved through a forward contract (a derivative) for a future exchange of USD into EUR at a rate that is fixed in advance.

Hedging is a common way to manage and reduce exposure to different types of risks. The problem in accounting is that even though firms achieve good economic hedges, this is not always appropriately reflected in financial statements. An economic hedge is based on a negative covariation in fair values of the two sides of the arrangement (as in the case of the USD asset and liability). If one of the two sides is measured at fair value while the other is measured at historic (or amortized) cost, the hedge is poorly reflected in financial statements (see Example 11.2).

Example 11.2 **Hedge accounting**

At the beginning of Year 1, a company takes up a fixed-interest loan. As it is fixed interest, the loan is subject to variation in value if market interest rates fluctuate. Due to an increase in market rates during Year 1, the company makes a gain of €200,000. In Year 2, market rates are stable and so is the value of the loan. At the end of Year 2, the company pays back the loan, so the unrealized gain from Year 1 becomes realized.

The company has a hedging policy. In accordance with this policy, the company acquires an interest rate swap at the beginning of Year 1. The swap functions as a perfect hedge of the value of the changes in the value of the loans. Consequently, the company makes a loss of €200,000 on the swap in Year 1, and the value of the swap is stable in Year 2. At the end of Year 2, the company settles the swap.

Based on measurement rules in IFRS 9, the loan is measured at amortized cost, and gains and losses are only recognized when realized. Meanwhile, the swap—a derivative—is measured at fair value and all gains and losses are immediately recognized in profit and loss. Even though the company has a perfect hedge, reported earnings will fluctuate. In Year 1, the company recognizes a loss from the swap of €200,000. In Year 2, the company recognizes a gain from the loan of €200,000, as the gain is realized in that year. If hedge accounting had been used, both the loss and the gain would be recognized in Year 1, so that earnings would better reflect the fact that the company has a well-functioning hedge arrangement. The net effect on earnings would be zero, both in Year 1 and in Year 2.

In the example, a solution is to change the measurement policy of either the debt or the swap. And this is exactly what hedge accounting is about: a deviation from normal measurement principles so that both sides of the hedge arrangements are measured in the same way. Hedge accounting is voluntary, but if it was applied in the example, the debt would be measured at fair value through profit and loss (i.e., in the same way as the swap).

The difficulty from a standard setter's perspective with regulating hedge accounting is the trade-off between allowing firms to reflect their own unique hedging arrangement while preventing firms from using hedge accounting when economic hedging does not exist. If such prevention is not achieved, there is a risk of manipulation of financial statements through too much leeway in the measurement of financial instruments. If requirements are too strict, however, it may prevent firms from using effective hedging arrangements, making firms economically worse off. The background to the issue is the wide variety in actual hedging arrangements and derivatives used in such arrangements. Add to that the difficulty that standard-setting by nature provides *ex ante* regulation. In other words, the accounting standards must function and be applicable to hedging arrangements and derivative financial instruments that are developed after the standards are written.

The hedge accounting parts in IFRS 9 are more principles-based than in IAS 39. This makes it simpler for firms to apply hedge accounting in agreement with their own unique hedging arrangements. It does, however, introduce more subjectivity in the preparation of financial statements. This may give more room for managerial incentives in the preparation of financial statements.

There is also an issue that at the time of writing (August 2018) has not been settled in IFRS 9. It relates to *macro hedging* (sometimes referred to as portfolio hedging). Macro hedging is mostly used by banks. The balance sheets of banks primarily contain financial instruments on both the asset and the liability sides. Banks may use large parts of their balance sheets to manage certain exposures, for example interest rate risks, on a portfolio basis. This is macro hedging. This accounting issue relates to the stability of banks, where governments have a strong interest in maintaining stability. Because of government involvement, and the connection to political interests, this issue has been difficult to solve for the IASB.

We note that macro hedging was an issue already when the EU was about to adopt IAS 39 before 2005. The EU was not willing to accept the macro hedging rules in IAS 39 due to the possible effect of those rules on European banks. The solution was for the paragraphs on macro hedging to be deleted from the adopted version of IAS 39. This remained a difference between the IASB's version of IFRS and the EU's version of IFRS until the introduction of IFRS 9 in 2018.

An alternative to hedge accounting is to use the **fair value option (FVO)**. This was introduced by the IASB as a way to simplify for firms to achieve measurement mismatches, without having to use (rather complicated) hedge accounting. In short, the FVO allows firms to measure financial instruments at fair value, even when they should be measured at amortized cost. The FVO also turned out to be controversial at the introduction of IFRS in the EU before 2005. Again, the issue was related to banking. Regulators, including the European Central Bank, did not like the idea of allowing banks to measure their own fixed interest liabilities at fair value. So, the FVO was also removed from IAS 39 before adoption by the EU. The problem with fair value for liabilities, including the solution provided in IFRS 9, is discussed further in Chapter 12.

Research shows that hedging requirements in IFRS have been positive in the sense that they lead to an improved information environment (i.e., a reduced information asymmetry between firms and investors) (Panaretou et al., 2013). DeMarzo and Duffie (1995) point out, however, that full transparency does not lead to an optimal risk reduction strategy by the firm and that disclosures concerning hedging should be provided on an aggregate level. A real effect of hedge accounting seems to be a reduction in speculative hedging among firms that adopt hedge accounting (Melumad et al., 1999), which is seen as a positive effect.

11.7 Conclusions

Assets are the cornerstone of every business. Equity investors and creditors insert capital (assets) into the firm with the expectation that existing assets will help generate more assets (i.e., returns). Assets are also purchased and generated within the firm.

If the future cash flows associated with these assets are too uncertain, accounting standards will not permit capitalization of the expenditures (i.e., recognition on the balance sheet). Determining the probability and amount of future cash flows requires judgment and affects whether an asset is recognized, its value at the time of recognition, as well as its value in subsequent periods. Specifically, preparers must decide on appropriate measurement models and depreciation/amortization schedules. They also determine whether write-downs are needed (whether unexpected changes in value have taken place), which includes calculating fair values and discount rates. With respect to leases, the main question for firms using IFRS has been whether a lease agreement should be classified as a finance lease or an operating lease. Recent changes imply a removal of the binary distinction for lessees, making this issue less salient. Finally, accounting for financial assets is especially difficult in relation to unexpected changes in value (subsequent to recognition), as it involves estimating fair values and credit losses.

CHAPTER 12

Liabilities and equity

Learning outcomes

Upon completion of this chapter, you will have gained insight into:

- Which accounting issues affect different types of liabilities, including why issues differ for different types of liabilities.
- How the measurement of liabilities relates to the structures presented in Chapter 10.
- The trade-off made by standard-setters in regulating the accounting for liabilities and the effect of this on accounting quality.
- Item-specific research relating to accounting for liabilities.
- Issues relating to the presentation and classification of equity, including the distinction between liabilities and equity.

THE PREVIOUS CHAPTER FOCUSED ON ASSETS. In this chapter, we instead focus on the other side of the balance sheet, which contains liabilities and equity. As noted in Chapter 11, the balance sheet provides stock measures at a certain point in time. While assets are measured conservatively, liabilities are generally measured at approximately current value—which, of course, results in increased conservatism.

The measurement of liabilities involves different levels of uncertainty. Financial liabilities often have explicit contractual terms that directly specify future cash outflow. Provisions are a subset of liabilities that are uncertain in terms of timing or amount of future cash outflow, and where substantial judgment is often required in recognition and measurement. The liability side of the balance sheet also includes equity and this is discussed in this chapter. As equity is defined as the difference between assets and liabilities, there are no direct measurement issues for equity. Instead, issues concerning equity on the balance sheet mostly include the distinction between liabilities and equity, as well as presentation and classification issues.

Liabilities relate to the second and third Stylized Accrual Situations in section 10.2. The second situation is about the recognition of liabilities corresponding to future outflows of resources. For financial liabilities, this is mostly unproblematic, as the firm receives cash or another resource in exchange for taking on the liability. For provisions (non-financial liabilities), this is a much more difficult issue. A provision is recognized if the definition of a liability is met, including criteria related to the probability and reliable measurement of outflows of economic benefits. The decision whether to recognize a provision, and the measurement of it, often requires substantial judgment and involves a high level of uncertainty.

Once a liability is recognized, it can change value in subsequent periods (SAS 3). Overall, most liabilities are for different reasons measured at, or close to, fair value. Provisions (non-financial liabilities) are generally measured at current value (approximate fair value), meaning all changes in value, both realized and unrealized, are recognized immediately. Financial liabilities are normally measured at historical cost, but this is often close to fair value. For short-term liabilities, such as accounts payable, the time between recognition and derecognition is usually so short that any changes in value are immaterial. Long-term debt tends to have stable value over time so that historical cost approximates fair value. Fixed-interest liabilities are an exception, as discussed in section 12.1. An important reason for the use of historical cost is that both short- and long-term liabilities are usually taken on with no intention by management to realize changes in fair values. This, for example, applies to liabilities such as accounts payable and long-term debt. The former is taken on in order to generate sales, while the latter is taken on to finance operations. With regard to liabilities for which fair value changes are likely to be realized (such as derivative financial instruments), fair value measurement is generally applied.

12.1 Financial liabilities

Financial liabilities are contractual obligations to pay cash (or some other financial asset) in the future. They also include derivative financial instruments that currently have unfavorable conditions. Financial liabilities are found in basically all firms. The most common types are accounts payable and other short-term payables, as well as debt financing such as bank loans and issued bonds. In the last few decades, accounting for financial liabilities has not been discussed all that much with one exception: the measurement of own liabilities at fair value (see Text Box 12.1).

Financial liabilities are nearly always recognized on the balance sheet, so SAS 2 (regarding recognition and measurement of a liability corresponding to future outflows of resources) is not an important issue. There are clear and explicit contractual conditions forming the basis for recognition, so the existence of a liability is certain. Nor is measurement at the time of recognition difficult, as the firm normally receives cash (or another asset) representing the value of the liability at that time. The main issue instead relates to the third Stylized Accrual Situation; that is, whether or not unrealized changes in value should be recognized. In other words, the question is whether to use historic (amortized) cost or current value. These issues are summarized in Table 12.1.

The basic idea in IFRS 9 *Financial Instruments* (which is the same as IAS 39) is that fair value should be used when relevant. As for financial assets, these are presumed to be relevant when used internally for evaluating firm performance and/or when the changes in value are

Text Box 12.1 **Financial liabilities at fair value**

Before the introduction of IFRS in the EU, the IASB issued an amendment to IAS 39, in which preparers could designate any financial instruments as fair value through profit loss (the so-called *Fair Value Option* (FVO)). In other words, it allowed firms to voluntarily measure both financial assets and financial liabilities at fair value should they want to do so. The FVO for own debt was heavily criticized and was one reason for a delay in the European Commission adoption of IAS 39.

The FVO allowed firms to voluntarily measure any part of its own debt at fair value. As explained in section 11.6, the value of debt with fixed interest is inversely related to the level of interest rates. When interest rates rise, the value of debt decreases. A decrease in the value of a liability results in a gain in profit and loss. Interest rates of debt instruments depend on two factors: market interest rates and the credit quality of the issuer. If credit quality decreases—and risk increases—interest rates rise, which causes the value to go down. Consequently, the FVO would allow a firm to recognize *gains* following deteriorating conditions (i.e., when the firm is doing worse). This was criticized in Europe, especially in relation to banks. The European Central Bank found it "counterintuitive" that banks could make gains from a deterioration in their credit quality. A similar critique came from several European states.

The IASB argued that the decline in value of own debt, and the resulting gain, is nothing but a financial statement reflection of a real economic event. The fair value of debt does go down if credit quality decreases, so the gain is real. The IASB further argued that in practice, this will never be a problem, since a decline in credit quality is nearly always reflected in a decline in the value of assets, especially in banks. The decline in asset values, with a resulting loss, will supersede any gain from declines in debt values. However, the EU Commission did not adopt IAS 39 in its original form. Instead, the adopted version did not include the FVO. Subsequently, the IASB limited the use of the FVO and the Commission adopted the amended version.

In working on IFRS 9, the IASB decided to not change the measurement of financial liabilities, with one exception. For own debt measured at fair value through the use of the FVO, IFRS 9 requires that unrealized gains and losses are divided into two components. Gains and losses resulting from movements in market interest rates are taken to profit and loss, while gains and losses resulting from changes in own credit quality are taken to OCI. In IFRS 9, gains from deterioration in credit quality do not affect net income. In addition, the effect of credit quality changes is clearly shown in the financial statements. A possible interpretation of the thinking of the IASB is that the separation of fair value changes into two components combines two desirable effects. First, the full fair value changes are reflected in the balance sheet. Second, effects of changes in own credit standing do not affect net income. It is not clear whether the latter effect is considered relevant from the perspective of the IASB. In the Basis for Conclusion to IFRS 9, the IASB points to the concerns of, for example, regulators with regard to including it in net income. A possible interpretation is that the change has more to do with the politics of standard-setting rather than conceptual derivation from the principles in the Conceptual Framework.

Table 12.1 Summary of issues relating to financial liabilities

Generic issue	Specific issue: Choices and judgments	Comment
SAS 2 (Future outflow of resources)	Recognize a liability or not?	Almost always recognized
SAS 3 (Unexpected changes in value)	Amortized cost or fair value If fair value: Separate effect of own credit standing	

likely to be realized. IFRS 9 specifies that this is the case when financial liabilities are held for trading (as realization is likely) and for derivative financial instruments (because they are used internally based on fair value changes). In practice, the result is that most financial liabilities are carried at cost. In many cases, however, cost is close to fair value.

12.2 Provisions

Accounting for provisions entails making a large number of discretionary judgments and decisions that can potentially have substantial effects on a firm's balance sheet and income statement. Some provisions are made in a routine manner, such as those meant to cover future outflows of resources due to product warranties or sales returns (in firms that sell large amounts of similar products). Others require non-routine measurements that involve high estimation uncertainty, such as when a lawsuit has been filed against the firm or when a firm must undertake environmental remediation due to damages caused by its operations. In the extractive industry, firms that drill for oil or mine ore have a potentially large environmental impact on the environment. Making provisions for cleanup and site restoration costs becomes necessary. Decommissioning a nuclear facility likewise requires much work, effort and money before the contaminated site in question has been restored to its previous condition. Energy companies thus face similar future costs and are required to recognize environmental provisions that reflect this. However, since such activities are measured based on discounted present value and often take place far into the future, the choice of discount rate matters greatly for the outcome. Another example of provisions commonly made relate to restructuring reserves. If a firm is planning to perform restructuring activities, provisions are required to the extent that the firm has a legal or constructive obligation to go through with the plan. An obligation is considered to exist if there is an explicit plan for the restructuring and those affected by the plan have been notified. There is some evidence that firms use this form of provision opportunistically to improve future earnings (see, for instance, Moehrle, 2002) and additionally separate out the provision expenses from ordinary operations by labeling them extraordinary or as exceptional items.

12.2.1 Definitions and summary of issues

Within IFRS there is a general standard on provisions: IAS 37 *Provisions, Contingent Liabilities and Contingent Assets*. There are other standards covering certain types of provisions, such as IAS 19 *Employee Benefits* for pension liabilities, IAS 12 *Income Taxes* for deferred tax liabilities and IFRS 17 *Insurance Contracts* for insurance liabilities. The logic in IFRS is that a specialized standard takes precedence over a general standard in the particular cases where the specialized standard is applicable. Consequently, IAS 37 is not applicable to provisions where specialized standards exist. In this section, we relate to IAS 37, while we cover IAS 19 and IFRS 17 in separate sections below. IAS 12 primarily relates to the income statement and is therefore discussed in Chapter 13.

When a firm forecasts future outflows of resources, one question is whether these future outflows meet the definition of a liability (SAS 2). Another issue is related to measurement—

how to accurately estimate the size of the provision. Unlike financial liabilities, provisions are liabilities that are inherently uncertain, either with respect to *when* or *the amount in which* they will be settled, or both. Measurement uncertainty is thus not a reason *not* to recognize the provision. But why does IFRS (and most other accounting standards) require recognition of provisions? If there are future outflows of resources that the firm *cannot avoid*, this is important information for financial statement users. Both equity investors and creditors are interested in information concerning material liabilities. Standard-setters are thus willing to accept high uncertainty because of the potential relevance of the information.

Once a provision is recognized, the third Stylized Accrual Situation comes into play; that is, whether to show unrealized gains and losses due to changes in value. IAS 37 states that all changes in value should be recognized immediately to reflect the most up-to-date value of the provision. This is relevant as it relates to future payment (outflow of resources), so any changes in value are expected to be realized.

There are, in essence, two basic views on the purpose of provisions: a balance sheet view and an income statement view. Based on the balance sheet view—which is the one embraced in IAS 37—a provision is recognized as soon as a future outflow of resources cannot be avoided. Conceptually, this is a manifestation of conservatism, in that liabilities are recognized as soon as they are probable. Neutral accounting is to make the best possible estimate of expected future payments and, based on this estimate, recognize a provision early. The income statement view is that provisions are recognized to correctly measure all expenses required to generate certain revenues (cf. the matching principle). To the extent that obligating events take place, they do so within the course of a firm's revenue-generating operations. The fact that cash outflows may not occur until a much later date is no reason to neglect to recognize an expense in the current period, along with a provision. An example discussed below is the recognition of provisions for product warranties. The firm's obligation to provide a warranty is closely associated with the sale of the product and thus the expense for warranties should be recognized simultaneously with the revenue. In the case of product warranties, the balance sheet and income statement views give the same results in terms of the timing of provisions. There are other situations where it is more difficult to see a connection between provisions and revenues. Examples are provisions for lawsuits and restructuring provisions (discussed below). In such cases, the timing of provisions involves more uncertainty.

A summary of issues in accounting with regard to provisions is shown in Table 12.2.

Table 12.2 Summary of issues relating to provisions

Generic issue	Specific issue: Choices and judgments	Comment
SAS 2 (Future outflow of resources)	Recognize a liability or not? Legal or constructive obligation? Outflow of resources probable? Reliable estimate of value?	
SAS 3 (Unexpected changes in value)	Measurement model?	Current value is used in IFRS
	Amount of future outflows of resources?	
	Discount rate?	

12.2.2 Recognition on the balance sheet

Just as specified in the Conceptual Framework, IAS 37 defines liabilities as present obligations resulting from some past event and where it is expected that an outflow of resources is required to settle the obligation. The so-called obligating event can create a **legal** or **constructive obligation**, either of which the firm has little realistic chance of escaping. Legal obligations exist through a contract or a law, whereas constructive obligations arise when best practice, firm policies or firm actions create reasonable expectations that the firm will undertake the responsibilities associated with the obligation.

According to IAS 37, recognition of a provision should take place if an obligation as described above exists (but it is uncertain with respect to timing and amount) and it is probable that an outflow of resources will be required to settle the obligation. It should also be possible to make a reliable estimate, although the standard clarifies that this is nearly always the case. Provisions are inherently uncertain, but that is not an excuse for failing to recognize them.

The firm may predict future events that will cause significant costs to be incurred in coming periods. It is important to note, however, that if the firm can avoid these costs by changing its operations or future actions (however difficult or unattractive this notion may seem), there is no obligating past event and thus no present obligation. Following the same logic, future operating losses do not give rise to provisions either, however probable these are (see Example 12.1).

Example 12.1 **Recognition of a provision**

An airline has one airplane and in order to use the plane, the airline is legally required to perform a substantial overhaul and safety check every three years. The next overhaul is due in January of Year 2. The airline intends to perform the overhaul and continue its business. Should the airline recognize a provision for the overhaul in its financial statements at the end of Year 1? No, there should not be any provision. The airline has no present obligation to any external party and is therefore not required to carry out the overhaul. It can choose to sell the airplane or to discontinue its business.

A separate issue one might wonder about is how the expense for the overhaul should be recognized in the income statement. If there is no gradual buildup of a provision over three years (effectively allocating the expense evenly over the years), is there a large expense every three years (when the cost is taken) and no expense in the other years? No, that would lead to unnaturally high volatility in earnings and would not constitute a good reflection of underlying economics. In IFRS, the allocation of expense is done through component depreciation (see section 11.1). The cost of the overhaul is capitalized as an asset and then depreciated over three years.

As a separate question, the airline is currently not profitable, but intends to continue its business. Management has a plan to go through two loss-making years, after which they expect to start making profits. Should the airline set up a provision for the expected losses? No, since there is no obligation to any outside party. Management has the option to discontinue the business.

Contingent liabilities, meanwhile, exist if there are possible obligations due to past events but whose existence will only be confirmed by further events taking place—or not taking place—in the future. Contingent liabilities can also result when present obligations arising from past events may not be classified and recognized as provisions. This is the case when it is not possible to make a reliable estimate of the amount of the obligation or the probability of having to settle the obligation is too low.

By "probable," the standard implies "more likely than not." In other words, if there is more than a 50% chance of something occurring, then it is considered "probable." Hence, when a potential provision would be recognized, but if the probability of an outflow of resources is deemed to be 25%, the firm instead reports a contingent liability. Such a liability is not recognized on the balance sheet but is disclosed in the notes. Should the probability be so low that the chance of having to settle the obligation is considered "remote," then no such contingency is disclosed at all. A contingent liability could become a provision upon revision of the information available at the end of a new reporting period and, conversely, a provision could be derecognized or reversed if new estimates lead management to conclude that no provision exists. The amount could thus be eliminated completely or a contingent liability could be disclosed in its place. An overview of different levels of probability, and how they relate to recognition and disclosure, is provided in Figure 12.1.

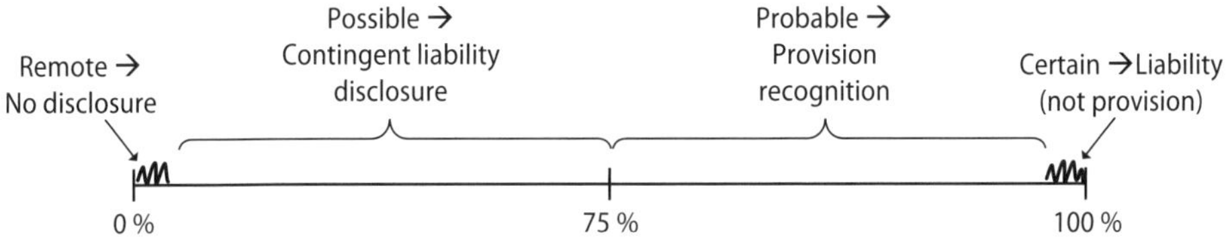

Figure 12.1 Level of probability of future outflow of resources

Interestingly, the non-recognition of contingent liabilities is not consistent with other parts of IFRS, such as IFRS 3 *Business Combinations*. In a business combination, some contingent liabilities in the acquired business are measured at fair value at the acquisition date. In 2005, the IASB made an attempt at reconciling such inconsistencies (see Text Box 12.2).

Text Box 12.2 **Non-financial liabilities**

The IASB issued an exposure draft for a new standard on non-financial liabilities, aimed at replacing IAS 37, as far back as in 2005. The project was initiated due to a desire to address inconsistencies with other standards (notably IFRS 3 *Business Combinations*), eliminate differences between IFRS and US GAAP, as well as to improve the measurement of non-financial liabilities. Due to the large number of comments received in response to the exposure draft, however, the project was delayed and a new and revised exposure draft came out in 2010. Hopes of issuing a new standard at the end of that year were similarly dashed due to new and widespread criticism of the proposals. As of August 2018, no new standard has been issued and the project is currently not on the IASB agenda. This, in itself, points to some of the difficulties associated with accounting for uncertain obligations.

The inconsistency noted between IFRS 3 and IAS 37 relates to the so-called 50% probability criterion for recognizing provisions under IAS 37. In theory, a binary criterion means that if there is a 49% probability that an outflow of resources will occur due to some obligating event, no provision should be recognized; instead, a contingent liability should be disclosed. If the probability is instead 51%, then the estimated amount should be recognized in its entirety. This may be contrasted with the recognition of liabilities under IFRS 3. The standard requires all liabilities to be recorded at their **expected values**. The expected value is an amount that reflects the probability distribution of all possible outcomes, which means that this is a continuous measure. In terms of expected value, there would be a small difference in the amount recognized between a probability of 49% and 51%.

Example of an expected value calculation: There are two possible outcomes—either the firm must pay MEUR 1 or nothing. The probability of having to pay MEUR 1 is estimated at 30%. Accordingly, the probability of not having to pay anything is 70%. The expected value of the provision is 30%*MEUR 1 + 30%*0; in other words, MEUR 0.3.

In the exposure drafts designed to lead up to a standard that would replace IAS 37, expected (present) values were introduced and meant to replace the probability criterion. However, this met with resistance. When undertaking a business combination (cf. IFRS 3), firms perform careful due diligence investigations and the calculation of all liabilities is done with great care, as management is keen on paying the right price for the target firm. By contrast, the requirement to value each potentially insignificant contingency on a continuous basis, as is the implication of the exposure drafts, would be too burdensome. Additionally, there is at least one theoretical objection to the use of expected values, and that is that the faithful representation and relevance of the amounts recognized would suffer. If there is a chance that a firm will have to make a large payment or, alternatively, no payment at all, one of those outcomes is the true outcome. It may then seem desirable to actually report one of those outcomes. Reporting an amount based on weighted probabilities would result in none of those possible outcomes being recognized; instead, what may be considered a fictitious amount would be recognized.

12.2.3 Measurement

Accounting for provisions is a highly interesting area of study for anyone wanting to problematize financial reporting. With provisions being innately uncertain, measurement is almost always going to cause practical difficulties for preparers. Below, we discuss some issues related to accounting for provisions in more detail by providing examples of specific types of provisions. In looking at these issues, we consider how different possible solutions will affect accounting quality.

Provisions based on statistical calculations and past experience

Some provisions are admittedly easy for management to account for. When Toyota sells cars, it knows beforehand that some cars will have faults and thus need adjusting, repairing or fixing in some ways. Based on past experience, firms must perform statistical calculations of these expected costs and make provisions for them when they record revenues from sales. Firms cover these costs by promising customers warranties, commonly lasting three, five or more years. They do so because it helps boost sales by reducing the customer's risks (and keeping some of the risks themselves). Either way, for a firm such as Toyota, which sells approximately 10 million vehicles annually, it is comparatively easy to make an estimate of the number of complaints that will follow the sale of vehicles in 2016 and make provisions accordingly. An illustrative example is shown in Text Box 12.3.

Text Box 12.3 **Extract from Toyota's 20-F Form, 2016, warranties**

Toyota generally warrants its products against certain manufacturing and other defects. Provisions for product warranties are provided for specific periods of time and/or usage of the product and vary depending upon the nature of the product, the geographic location of the sale and other factors. Toyota records a provision for estimated product warranty costs at the time the related sale is recognized based on estimates that Toyota will incur to repair or replace product parts that fail while under warranty. The amount of accrued estimated warranty costs is primarily based on historical experience as to product failures as well as current information on repair costs. The amount of warranty costs accrued also contains an estimate of warranty claim recoveries to be received from suppliers.

Provisions for lawsuits

What may be more difficult to foresee, however, are one-time events, including lawsuits filed against the firm, which obligate firms to take reputation-redeeming actions. For example, by early 2010, Toyota had been forced to recall some 9 million vehicles due to faulty accelerator pedals and problems with floor mats causing the foot pedal to get jammed. An illustrative example is shown in Text Box 12.4.

Text Box 12.4 **Extract from Toyota's 20-F Form, 2016, law suits**

From time-to-time, Toyota issues vehicle recalls and takes other safety measures including safety campaigns relating to its vehicles. Since 2009, Toyota issued safety campaigns related to the risk of floor mat entrapment of accelerator pedals and vehicle recalls related to slow-to-return or sticky accelerator pedals. In March 2014, Toyota entered into a Deferred Prosecution Agreement ("DPA") to resolve an investigation by the U.S. Attorney for the Southern District of New York ("SDNY") related to unintended acceleration in certain of its vehicles. The DPA provides for an independent monitor to review and assess policies and procedures relating to Toyota's safety communications process, its process for sharing vehicle accident information internally and its process for preparing and sharing certain technical reports.

In 2010, there was a recall related to the software program that controls the antilock braking system in certain models, including the Prius, which led to putative class action lawsuits on behalf of owners of recalled vehicles and owners of vehicles which were not recalled. The United States District Court for the Central District of California denied the plaintiffs' motions for class certification and granted summary judgment in Toyota's favor denying the plaintiffs' claims related to both the recalled vehicles and the non-recalled vehicles. Proceedings involving the recalled vehicles have concluded; the appeals of the granting of summary judgment and the denial of class certification of the claims for the non-recalled vehicles are still pending. [...]

Toyota has been named as a defendant in 33 economic loss class action lawsuits, which, together with similar lawsuits against Takata and other automakers, have been made part of a multi-district litigation proceeding in the United States District Court for the Southern District of Florida, arising out of allegations that airbag inflators manufactured by Takata are defective. These lawsuits are at an early stage. [...]

Beyond the amounts accrued with respect to all aforementioned matters, Toyota is unable to estimate a range of reasonably possible loss, if any, for the pending legal matters because (i) many of the proceedings are in evidence gathering stages, (ii) significant factual issues need to be resolved, (iii) the legal theory or nature of the claims is unclear, (iv) the outcome of future motions or appeals is unknown and/or (v) the outcomes of other matters of these types vary widely and do not appear sufficiently similar to offer meaningful guidance. Based upon information currently available to Toyota, however, Toyota believes that its losses from these matters, if any, beyond the amounts accrued, would not have a material adverse effect on Toyota's financial position, results of operations or cash flows.

Whenever a lawsuit is filed against a firm, there is a risk of future payments being required to settle the case. Sometimes these risks are deemed small, in which case a contingent liability may be disclosed, but sometimes a provision must be recognized. Because of the unique circumstances surrounding each legal proceeding, it is inherently difficult to determine possible future cash outflows, and even whether a contingent liability or provision should be reported. Statistical calculations based on past experience are commonly of little or no use. This means that management must use its judgment in making reliable estimates. If management has incentives to postpone expenses to later periods, by failing to recognize a provision in a timely manner, this may give them leeway to manage earnings and reduce the representational faithfulness of the accounts.

Decommissioning costs as provisions

A major issue that was discussed at the end of the 1990s and beginning of the 2000s was the accounting for decommissioning costs. Decommissioning is the act of dismantling and removing major facilities, such as nuclear power plants, at the end of their useful lives. This work typically involves cleanup and restoration of affected land to its former condition and taking potentially costly safety measures to ensure that the removal work proceeds without risks or damages to the surroundings. Essentially, no liabilities for decommissioning costs used to be recognized under US GAAP, but this changed with the introduction of SFAS 143 *Accounting for Asset Retirement Obligations* in 2001. A so-called **obligation approach** became mandatory. A similar treatment is suggested by the IASB in 2004 through IFRIC 1 "Changes in Existing Decommissioning, Restoration and Similar Liabilities." Several criticisms to the changes in the accounting treatment of decommissioning costs were put forward by interested parties in the US, as the uncertainty involved in the recognition of this obligation based on a present value model was considered (too) high (Enoch and

Pacter, 1995). However, proponents of the obligation approach believed that the nature of decommissioning costs imposes obligations to firms that should be satisfied in the future and which are compatible with FASB's liability definition. Regarding the uncertainty of this future obligation, it was pointed out that there are other accounting items (e.g., retirement obligations) that also use present value models and are based on uncertain assumptions. This should not prevent the liability from being recorded on-balance.

The increase in liabilities following the adoption of SFAS 143 substantially affects financial ratios and especially debt ratios in the electric utility industry (Boatsman et al., 2000). Schroeder et al. (2005) re-examine the sample of firms subject to change in the accounting of decommissioning cost in the study by Boatsman et al. (2000). The results indicate that although firms indeed were affected by the changes, the impact was often not "material" (in contrast to what Boatsman et al. (2000) predicted). Meanwhile, Khurana et al. (2001) assessed the effect of decommissioning costs being recognized as liabilities under the FASB's exposure draft (206-B, before the standard was issued) on the market and investigated whether these potential obligations were priced by investors. The authors found support for the effect of decommissioning obligations on the stock market; however, compared to the effect of other utility liabilities on the stock market, the effects of decommissioning obligations are smaller. The authors suggest that additional disclosures can benefit shareholders when assessing these obligations, especially given the inherent uncertainty in estimating the present value and future outcomes of these obligations. Furthermore, D'Souza et al. (2000) also find that equity values are negatively associated with the company's decommissioning costs, meaning that investors value the liability. One may then reflect upon the fact that there was actually no need to change the standard from an efficiency perspective, since investors were able to value already available information. However, given that financial statements should provide a faithful representation, one could argue that the liabilities in question should be reported as just that: liabilities. Recall the definition of relevance: information should be provided based on whether it is *capable* of influencing investor decisions, not based on whether it actually brings about changes in investor behavior. If information is provided elsewhere, by the entity or otherwise, this does not render the information irrelevant. For example Li and McConomy (1999) show that disclosures of provisions relating to future removal and site restoration costs are value-relevant. In terms of the quality and the extent of environmental disclosure, the authors argue that "only about half of the discussions were comprehensive enough for the reader to understand the underlying issues" (referring to a study by PwC, 1995).

As discussed in the section on employee benefits, some liabilities relating to such benefits were considered value-relevant. That is, investors found the information about these to be useful and, perhaps not surprisingly in retrospect, considered them to have implications for the value of the firm. These findings contributed to the development of the US standards and IFRS for employee benefit accounting and the increased requirements to recognize the liabilities on the balance sheet.

Discount rate

Estimating discount rates is not only potentially difficult but choices and judgments regarding discount rates can have a large effect on the value of a provision—especially where long-term provisions are concerned. The effect of using different discount rates is shown in Example 12.2. Not only does the discount rate affect total expenses in different periods. In addition, to the extent that the interest expense on the discounted amounts is classified as financial rather than operating, this could cause additional incentives for a high discount rate for firms focusing on EBIT (Earnings Before Interest & Taxes, a type of operating income). Note also that with a high discount rate, provisions for things such as land rehabilitation and other restoration work may occur so far into the future that the recorded provision is immaterial.

Example 12.2 **Discount rates**

Below, two different scenarios are presented to illustrate the effect of discount rates.

Scenario A: Assuming a lower discount rate

Nominal provision	15,550
Settlement date	Year 4
Discount rate	5%

	Year 1	Year 2	Year 3	Year 4	Total
Discounted provision amount	13,433 $=15{,}550/1.05^3$	14,104 $=15{,}550/1.05^2$	14,810 $=15{,}550/1.05^1$	15,550 $=15{,}550/1.05^0$	
Operating expenses	13,433	0	0	0	**13,433**
Financial expenses (interest)	0	672	705	740	**2,117**
Total expenses	**13,433**	**672**	**705**	**740**	**15,550**
Provision	13,433	14,104	14,810		
Cash (settlement of provision)				−15,550	

The operating expense in Year 1 represents the provision made after taking into account necessary discounting. The financial expense in Year 2 represents the difference between the discounted provision amount in Year 1 and Year 2. Due to a lower effect of the discount factor as one approaches the settlement date, the provision amount to be recognized is 14,104. Since 13,433 has already been recognized, the extra expense is the difference between the two amounts. This is often considered a financial expense (even if that is not required in IFRS).

Scenario B: Assuming a higher discount rate

Nominal provision	15,550
Settlement date	Year 4
Discount rate	10%

	Year 1	Year 2	Year 3	Year 4	Total
Discounted provision amount	11,683 =15,550/1.1^3	12,851 =15,550/1.1^2	14,136 =15,550/1.1^1	15,550 =15,550/1.1^0	
Operating expenses	11,683	0	0	0	**11,683**
Financial expenses (interest)	0	1,168	1,285	1,414	**3,867**
Total expenses	**11,683**	**1,168**	**1,285**	**1,414**	**15,550**
Provision	11,683	12,851	14,136		
Cash (settlement of provision)				-15,550	

A higher discount rate leads to a smaller expense in Year 1. In addition, it shifts expenses from EBIT (through lower operating expenses) to net financial expenses (if interest is classified as a financial expense).

The present value calculations require a good deal of judgment and the references to the discount rate in IAS 37 have been considered vague compared to, for example, IAS 19 *Employee Benefits*. This has led firms to choose their discount rates in what is considered an arbitrary manner. Requirements that the discount rate should reflect "current market assessments of the time value of money and the risks specific to the liability" (IAS 37, Par. 47) may not be considered specific enough. Also, although some firms voluntarily disclose the discount rate, there are no formal disclosure requirements with respect to the discount rate. This makes it even more difficult for users to determine whether the amount of the provision is realistic.

In their annual review of the energy market, the consulting firm Capgemini pointed out that common practices must be enforced when it comes to the reporting for nuclear decommissioning costs. Lack of comparability between entities prompted the following statement, as reported by the news agency Reuters:[1]

> Europe needs banking-industry style regulation to bring more transparency to the costs of nuclear reactors. [...] Establishing what methodology is used to estimate the overall cost is essential, but it is never explained in annual reports, with each player relying on the estimates of their own experts in that area. [...] For obvious reasons to do with transparency, it is urgent that a process be instituted at European level [...] similar to the international regulatory framework for banks (Basel III) following the financial crisis that affected most European countries.

It was pointed out that "[n]uclear operators like France's EDF, Germany's E.ON and RWE and Sweden's Vattenfall all use different discount and inflation rates to calculate the present value of long-term liabilities and the parameters for these calculations are left to individual companies to decide." Another audit and consultancy firm, KPMG, has raised concerns regarding the variation in disclosures of discount rates in the oil and gas industry. Discount rates were found not to be disclosed in the majority of firms, and when they were disclosed, firms tended not to reveal the underlying assumptions (KPMG, 2008). The overall accounting quality effect is

1 http://www.reuters.com/article/nuclear-decommissioning-idUSL8N12X22J20151102

that comparability between firms suffers as a result of the above deficiencies, especially since both cases refer to long-term liabilities, where the value is heavily affected by the discount rate.

The IASB has initiated a discount rate project to review and seek solutions to issues such as these. One has sought to understand why the choices firms make look the way they do, as well as the impact of potential reporting inconsistencies on stakeholders. Particularly IAS 37 has come under scrutiny in this context. The IASB (2015) has acknowledged that:

> [s]ome investors consider IAS 37 measurement less reliable because [in] the companies there is no disclosure of how [the discount rate] is calculated and the measurements do not seem to move with the market as much as those in IAS 19 even though those measurements are meant to be based on a market-based rate.

The final result of this project, as well as the work with IAS 37, still (as of August 2018) remains to be seen.

12.2.4 Provisions and incentives

As is evident from the previous sections, there is substantial managerial judgment involved in accounting for provisions. While such judgment can help management provide important private information to investors, it can potentially also be used to manage earnings in accordance with managerial incentives and to the detriment of investors.

There are at least two different reasons managers may not want to be neutral in their estimates (Nelson et al., 2002). First, management could want to recognize expenses early. This is the case when it is especially beneficial to show a clear positive trend. If the firm has been performing badly, either due to strategic mishaps or due to industry-wide shocks (such as caused by a global recession), it may be seen as better to report large losses as soon as possible since these can be "camouflaged" against the larger amounts of losses already recognized. In this case, one speaks of firms building "cookie jar reserves." In some scenarios, especially when the firm has suffered from poor performance, CEO turnover can create additional incentives for early recognition of losses. When a new CEO takes office, it may be seen as advantageous to recognize losses that can be blamed on the previous management. Having made provisions in a perhaps discretionary manner by exaggerating beliefs concerning future cash outflows, a positive development in earnings can be reported over the following years. In these cases, one speaks of management taking a "big bath." In the extreme scenario, no provision was actually needed, and it becomes necessary to reverse the provision—which increases earnings—in future periods.

Second, management could have incentives to hide liabilities. That is, even if the recognition of a provision is warranted, management uses its discretion to avoid recognition, for example in order to improve the debt-to-equity ratio of the firm. Cohen et al. (2011) show that this is the case for warranty reserves, for example. This is one form of "off-balance sheet liabilities" we mention in relation to lease accounting in Chapter 11.

There are multiple ways of managing earnings via provisions. One is through the *timing* of expenses (see above), another is through the estimate of the discount rate. In accordance with IAS 37, the measurement of provisions should consider the time value of money; that is, discounting should be applied. The use of different discount rates can be a subtle form of earnings management that is hard to detect. The potential effect of the discount rate is especially pronounced for long-term provisions, such as provisions for land rehabilitation (see above) or employee benefits (see below).

Provisions for restructuring have been identified in the literature as a type of provision that is particularly subject to high preparer judgment and therefore could be used to manage earnings (Moehrle, 2002). Due to the high level of uncertainty both in timing of recognition and in measurement, IAS 37 contains specific paragraphs regarding restructuring. As noted above, restructuring provisions are not recognized until a firm has decided to restructure and this has been communicated so as to create a legal or constructive obligation to carry out the restructuring. A similar issue with high uncertainty and the resulting risk of incentives-driven reporting led the FASB and the IASB to remove restructuring provisions in business combinations (see Chapter 14). Below is an example illustrating the effect of restructuring provisions on financial statements.

In order to understand managerial incentives, let us consider a numerical example in order to understand the mechanics of provisions and their effect on the balance sheet and income statement (see Example 12.3, where discounting is ignored).

Example 12.3 **Restructuring provisions**

A firm considers carrying out a restructuring in Year 2. In Year 1, a constructive obligation exists, so that a provision for restructuring may be set up. Now, consider three scenarios:

1. no provision is made
2. a neutral provision is made
3. an excessive provision is made

Assume that in the third scenario, the excessive provision is such that it has to be partially reversed.

The following effects on the balance sheet and income statement then follow (amounts are in MEUR, and income taxes and discounting are ignored):

		Scenario 1			Scenario 2			Scenario 3		
Year 1	BS:	*no effect*			Liability (provision) account		100	Liability (provision) account		200
	IS:	*no effect*			Expense account	100		Expense account	200	
Year 2	BS:	Asset (bank) account		100	Liability (provision) account	100		Liability (provision) account	200	
					Asset (bank) account		100	Asset (bank) account		100
	IS:	Expense account	100					Expense account		100

Scenario 2:
A provision of 100 is recognized in year 1. A credit entry is made in a liability account and a debit entry is made in an expense account.

In year 2, the provision is derecognized. A debit entry is made in the liability account and a credit entry is made in an asset account (e.g., a bank account).

Scenario 3:
A provision of 200 is recognized in year 1. A credit entry is made in a liability account and a debit entry is made in an expense account.

In year 2, the provision is derecognized. A debit entry is made in the liability account, but instead of only crediting an asset account, a part of the expense recorded in year 1 must be reversed. This requires a credit entry in an expense account (i.e., an income).

The effect on net income is thus:

	Scenario 1	Scenario 2	Scenario 3
Information from the income statement:			
Year 1			
Net income before provision	500	500	500
Restructuring expense (related to provision)	0	-100	-200
Net income	500	400	300
Year 2			
Net income before restructuring expense	500	500	500
Restructuring expense	–100	0	100
Net income	400	500	600
Information from the cash flow statement			
(relating to restructuring charges in Year 2):	–100	–100	–100

Consequently, the effect of a provision is to bring forward expenses and decrease earnings in the period when it is recognized. This enables a firm (perhaps a newly appointed CEO) to show comparatively higher earnings in future periods, and possibly also a growth trend—especially when provisions are excessive. Note that accruals cannot create or destroy earnings; they can only move earnings between periods. Over long time periods, Σ(Earnings) = Σ(Cash flows).

12.3 Employee benefits

Employees are often said to be one of a firm's most valuable assets, especially in today's knowledge-intense businesses, whose success depends on know-how, specialized skills and individual expertise for the development of patentable ideas and high-tech products. Although employees cannot be recognized as assets to the firm, the services they render can have considerable value that shows up in revenue streams. However, employees also incur costs for firms. These take on many different forms, such as salaries and pension benefits. Whereas some benefits paid to employees are easy to calculate and report, others depend on events that have not yet occurred at the balance sheet date, causing difficult estimates to be made and provisions for future payments to be recorded. As with all provisions, there is uncertainty with respect to the settlement date as well as the amount of the provision, which is why employee benefits can be such a difficult accounting area for firms. Forty percent of European firms have been found to disclose employee benefits as an especially problematic accounting area that requires much judgment and causes particular estimation difficulties (Runesson, 2015). Seventeen percent of US firms disclose that pensions and other post-retirement benefits represent critical accounting policies (Levine and Smith, 2011).

Employee benefits include all considerations received by employees in return for services provided to the employer. Employee benefits are regulated in IAS 19 *Employee Benefits* with some exceptions, such as employee benefits in the form of share-based payments. These are deemed to require separate treatment due to the particular complexities arising in those situations (see section 13.2).

12.3.1 Definitions and summary of issues

Employee benefits are divided into four categories in IAS 19: **short-term benefits**, **post-employment benefits**, **other long-term benefits** and **termination benefits**. Short-term benefits refer to the payment of salary, short-term bonuses, social security contributions and granting of annual leave, such as vacation and other paid absences. These cause payments in the current period, the recording of an expense and possibly a current liability in the form of an accrued expense to the extent that all payments are not made immediately and some are settled after the end of the reporting period. Meanwhile, post-employment benefits and other long-term benefits refer, *inter alia*, to health care benefits in countries where these are handled by the private sector, post-employment life insurance, pensions, other potential benefits that are paid after one's employment (excluding termination benefits) and long-service leave. Finally, termination benefits may become relevant in cases where a firm must end the employment of an employee or employees prematurely (before the normal retirement date) or provide benefits as part of a redundancy scheme. Different difficulty levels with respect to accounting treatment are associated with different employee benefit types. The most difficult are generally the post-employment benefits, which are in focus in this section.

When it comes to post-employment benefits, one must distinguish between **defined benefit plans** and **defined contribution plans**. In the case of the former, the firm guarantees that a certain amount be paid to the employee at the settlement date. In the case of the latter, the firm only promises to make an agreed-upon fixed payment during the employee's active work period, without being the guarantor of the final pension amount. Consequently, in defined benefit plans, the firm has a commitment to a future payment and must recognize a provision for this commitment. Accounting for defined contribution plans is much easier, as it only involves short-term payments to separate entities (e.g., a trust or insurance company).

In practice, employers are increasingly unwilling to enter into defined benefit agreements, and thus the popularity of such schemes is decreasing. However, due to their prevalence in the past, managers, accountants and auditors will continue having to handle the difficulties associated with these for a long time.

Defined benefit plans are often funded, meaning that regular payments are made to a fund to ensure future payments related to the benefit. Such a fund constitutes the so-called **plan assets**. Plan assets are typically held by a legally separate entity. Either way, assets are protected from outside claims in the event of bankruptcy. The net pension obligation (i.e., what is recorded on the balance sheet) is equal to the present value of the defined benefit obligation less the fair value of plan assets. Whether there is a liability (SAS 2) and how changes in its value is accounted for (SAS 3) become relevant to consider. A summary of issues relating to pensions and other post-employment benefits is provided in Table 12.3.

Table 12.3 Summary of issues relating to pensions and other post-employment benefits

Generic issue	Specific issue: Choices and judgments	Comment
SAS 2 (Future outflow of resources)	Recognize a liability or not? Value of defined benefit obligation (based on actuarial assumptions)	Recognition if defined benefit plan
	Fair value of plan assets	
SAS 3 (Unexpected changes in value)	Measurement model?	Current value is used in IFRS
	Actuarial gains and losses?	Based on actuarial assumptions, including the discount rate

12.3.2 Recognition and measurement

An objective of accounting for defined benefit plans is to recognize expenses in the period when resources are consumed rather than when payments are made (this represents an income statement view). For example, a 35-year-old employee works in 2018. In exchange for this, in addition to salary and other current benefits, she will receive pension payments starting in 2050 and expecting to continue until 2070. The firm consumes resources (the employee's services) during 2018, even if part of the payment for those services occurs in 2050–2070. This is shown in Figure 12.2.

Accounting for defined benefit plans involve the second and third Stylized Accruals Situations. When payment for a service is deferred (such as for pension benefits), IAS 19 requires that the firm recognizes a liability (a provision) for the future outflow of resources

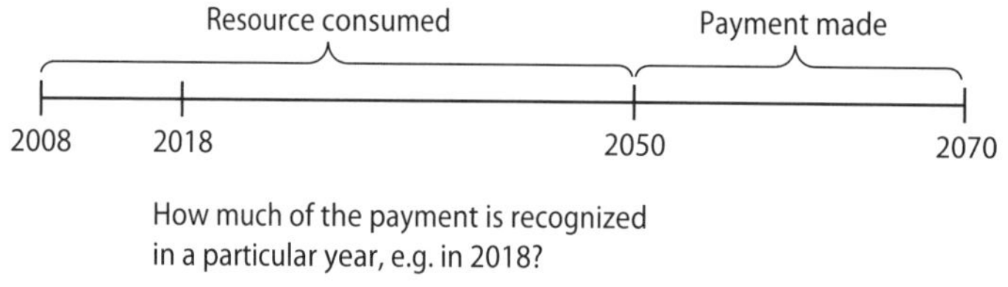

Figure 12.2 Accounting for defined benefit plans

(this represents a balance sheet view). Under a defined benefit plan, the employee works and in exchange obtains (in addition to salary and other compensation) the right to future pension payments. The pension payments represent the future cash outflows for the firm. If the firm cannot avoid these cash outflows, they represent a liability and must be recognized on the balance sheet. Discounted cash flow valuation is applied due to the long-term nature of the liabilities. Additionally, because of the measurement uncertainty involved, the liabilities are classified as provisions. Essentially all changes in value are immediately recognized, although several special rules apply depending on the reason for the change in value.

The measurement uncertainty associated with post-employment liabilities is caused by the fact that there are many factors that may affect the timing and size of the future payments. The resulting complexity of the accounting area is explicitly stated by the IAS 19 in the following terms:

> Accounting for defined benefit plans is complex because actuarial assumptions are required to measure the obligation and the expense and there is a possibility of actuarial gains and losses. Moreover, the obligations are measured on a discounted basis because they may be settled many years after the employees render the related service. (Par. 48)

Actuarial assumptions, mentioned in paragraph 48, are required for estimating the present value of the obligation as well as for determining the fair value of the associated assets. Actuarial assumptions can be demographic and include assumptions regarding the life expectancy of employees, their health and gender, as well as the time they are expected to remain in the firm (which in turn depends on health, gender, staff turnover, retirement age and firm and country age structures). Actuarial assumptions can also be of a financial kind and cover estimations of final and average salaries (which are a function of the inflation rate in the economy, the time the employee stays in the firm, promotions, the labor market) as well as the discount rate, which depends on market conditions. All of these estimates are actuarial assumptions, which affect the measurement of the defined benefit obligation. Which particular variables affect future payments depend on the specifics of the contract between the firm and the employee. However, an example of a contractual agreement could be as shown in Example 12.4.

Example 12.4 **Employee pensions**

The employee receives a pension of 1.5% of the final salary for each year of service at the firm. The pension is paid from the year the employee turns 65 until the employee dies. The pension is indexed with the inflation rate. In order to estimate the future cash outflow, the firm must estimate the following variables: 1) the number of years the employee will work at the firm; 2) the salary increase until the person turns 65; 3) the inflation rate after the person turns 65; and 4) the life expectancy, including the probability that the person dies before 65. In order to discount the estimated future cash flows, a discount rate must be applied.

In the following sections, we focus on the effect of actuarial assumptions on the balance sheet and income statement, as well as the implications of these judgments on accounting quality. More specifically, we consider the choice of discount rate and the presentation of gains and losses due to changes in actuarial assumptions.

So far, we have discussed the measurement of the provision amount and thus the effect on the balance sheet.[2] However, as noted above, an important objective with post-employment accounting is to obtain faithfully represented and relevant earnings in the income statement. More specifically, a net expense is recorded that corresponds to changes in the value of the net pension liability (i.e., after taking fair value changes in plan assets into account). There are three main components of the net expense:

1. The **current service cost**, which is the increase in the pension liability caused by the employee's services in the current period. In Figure 12.2, this is the additional pension benefits earned by the employee in 2018.
2. The **interest cost**, which is simply the increase in the pension liability caused by the time of payment drawing closer. The future payment is closer at the end of 2018 than at the beginning of 2018, so the *present value* of the obligation increases.
3. The **return on plan assets**, which is an income, not an expense, meaning it reduces the net expense in profit and loss.

The estimates of all three components are based on actuarial assumptions. As such, they involve a substantial level of uncertainty and are subject to managerial discretion in the preparation of financial statements.

12.3.3 Discount rate

Actuarial assumptions concern the future and involve considerable measurement uncertainty. Because they are also potentially material, they can have large effects on the balance sheet and income statement. One of the assumptions that has been researched and discussed the most is the discount rate. The discount rate affects the present value of the defined benefit obligation, the current service cost (i.e., the increase in said obligation as a result of employees rendering services in the current period) as well as the net interest cost (i.e., the interest cost on the obligation as well as the interest income on plan assets). Note that a low discount rate increases the size of the obligation.

The choice of discount rate can be controversial. The standard stipulates that a market-based approach to measurement is required. More specifically, IAS 19 (Par. 78) states that "[t]he rate used to discount post-employment benefit obligations [...] shall be determined by reference to market yields at the end of the reporting period on high quality corporate bonds. In countries where there is no deep market in such bonds, the market yields (at the end of the reporting period) on government bonds shall be used." However, the interval within which the discount rate may vary can be significant (see Text Box 12.5).

2 Most firms have plan assets to cover at least part of the future payments. These plan assets are measured at fair value. The actual liability (provision) recognized on the balance sheet is the net of the defined benefit obligation and the plan assets. Sometimes the net is an asset, even if that is not particularity common in practice.

Text Box 12.5 **Discount rates in a sample of European firms**

A quick look at the choice of discount rates in a sample of 979 European firms at the end of 2014* reveals that the size of the discount rate is positively correlated with the size of the defined benefit obligation as a proportion of total assets. The rank correlation is at 30% and is statistically significant at the 0.1% level, indicating a large certainty that the correlation is not random. Of course, other factors may play a role in explaining this relationship, but caution may be advised when evaluating the objectivity with which firms choose their discount rate. The authors' mini-study suggests that there is a possibility that firms with large obligations have incentives to choose high discount rates in order to limit the effect of the obligation on the balance sheet. Also considering that the defined benefit obligation used in the study is post-discounting, the amount prior to discounting would be even larger in firms with high obligations.

* The sample consists of all firms in the EU that have been listed on a regulated stock market since 2007, have defined benefit obligations and have data available in Thomson Reuters Datastream.

Not only does the discount rate involve much subjectivity and cause estimation difficulties in practice. Theoretically, the soundness of the requirements for the discount rate may also be questioned; however, they stand up quite well to criticism and alternatives. For example, some comment letters were received as IAS 19 was being developed, in which it was suggested that the discount rate should reflect the entity's own credit rating (IAS 19: BC31). The problem with this approach, however, is that a poorly performing firm with a low credit rating would recognize a smaller liability (cf. the discussion on fair value of own liabilities in section 12.1). It was further proposed that the return rate on plan assets linked to the plan should be used in order to determine the discount rate (IAS 19: BC27). However, it is hardly reasonable that riskier assets with higher expected returns should be allowed to reduce the value of the obligation, which would be the case if higher returns from riskier assets would increase the estimated discount rate. The expected returns, furthermore, are not considered satisfyingly objective. (In fact, this has caused amendments to IAS 19, in which it is now required that the expected return on plan assets instead be based on the discount rate, potentially leaving less room for firms to estimate the fair value of plan assets in an opportunistic manner.) Consequently, the IASB decided that the discount rate should "reflect the time value of money but should not attempt to capture those risks" associated with the defined benefit obligation (IAS 19: BC31). Following the financial crisis in 2007–2008, interest rates on financial markets changed substantially. This led to a discussion in Sweden, see Text Box 12.6.

Text Box 12.6 **Discussion of discount rate in Sweden**

In Sweden, the discount rate for pension liabilities came to be debated after the financial crisis of 2007–2008. As the economy went into a downward spiral, corporate bond rates went up. Simultaneously, government bond yields in most countries went down, as such bonds were comparably safe. The difference between the yields from corporate bonds and government bonds therefore increased. Swedish firms, which generally must use the yields on government bonds due to there being no deep and liquid market for corporate bonds in the Swedish currency, did not look favorably upon this development. Many found it "unfair" that their obligations should increase as a result of decreasing yields, whereas their European counterparts saw the opposite effect (as there were deep and liquid markets for corporate bonds in, for instance, EUR and GBP). Subsequently, there was an attempt to convince the IASB to have the standard changed. It was proposed that firms should be able to make their own estimations of what corporate bond yields would have been had a market existed. An Exposure Draft was issued in 2009, but the project was discontinued. The IASB argued that too much uncertainty was involved in such an approach and that a lack of objectivity would be detrimental to the quality of the estimates. Interestingly, Swedish firms found a workaround to this problem in that they started using yields from mortgage bonds, the assumption being that these are equivalent to corporate bonds. Being higher than government yields, firms could keep their discount rate figures up. An investigation into firms on the Swedish stock market also shows that firms kept the 2007 rate in 2008. Auditors consequently seemed to accept the explanation that the interest rate change was *temporary*. However, the standard clearly stipulates that "financial assumptions shall be based on market expectations, at the end of the reporting period, for the period over which the obligations are to be settled."

To avoid recognizing changes simply because they are temporary may be thought of as highly questionable. However, the relevance of reporting changes in assumptions relating to an obligation that is not to be settled for many years may likewise be questioned. A solution is to recognize large fluctuations caused by changes in actuarial assumptions (such as discount rates) in OCI rather than in the income statement. This is also what the current version of IAS 19 requires, see section 12.3.4.

Overall, the market-based approach, in which the discount rate reflects the time value of money, but not the investment risk nor the entity's own credit risk, is believed to yield faithfully represented and unbiased estimates. Nevertheless, the discount rate chosen can cause comparability to suffer to the extent that different bond yields are used as the reference rate, whether voluntarily or by necessity.

12.3.4 Recognition versus disclosure: The case of actuarial gains and losses

When actuarial assumptions change, the size of the defined benefit obligation changes and this results in **actuarial gains and losses**. More specifically, if a changed assumption makes the defined benefit obligation increase, an actuarial loss occurs, while if the change makes the defined benefit obligation decrease, an actuarial gain occurs. Examples of such items include gains from a higher discount rate and losses from higher expected salary increases to employees.

Prior to January 2013, IAS 19 permitted three alternative ways of accounting for these gains and losses. They could be recognized directly in net income, in other comprehensive income (thus affecting comprehensive income and equity but not net income) or recognition could be partially avoided using an off-balance-sheet method called the "corridor method/approach." With respect to the latter, the previous IAS 19 required that:

> 92. In measuring its defined benefit liability [...] an entity shall [...] recognize a portion [...] of its actuarial gains and losses as income or expense if the net cumulative unrecognized actuarial gains and losses at the end of the previous reporting period exceeded the greater of:
>
> (a) 10% of the present value of the defined benefit obligation at that date (before deducting plan assets); and
>
> (b) 10% of the fair value of any plan assets at that date.

The "corridor" amount refers to that which is less than the 10% limit and did not have to be recognized. Even the amount that was to be recognized could, moreover, be deferred to future periods. In other words:

> 93. The portion of actuarial gains and losses to be recognized for each defined benefit plan is the excess determined in accordance with paragraph 92, divided by the expected average remaining working lives of the employees participating in that plan. However, an entity may adopt any systematic method that results in faster recognition of actuarial gains and losses, provided that the same basis is applied to both gains and losses and the basis is applied consistently from period to period. An entity may apply such systematic methods to actuarial gains and losses even if they are within the limits specified in paragraph 92.

The sum of a firm's *accumulated unrecognized* actuarial gain or loss is made up of the amounts specified under the above two paragraphs. They were not recognized on the balance sheet, but they were disclosed in the notes.

The amendment to the standard that became effective in 2013 eliminated "corridor" accounting as well as the option to record the gains and losses in net income. One could say that two extreme options were eliminated in favor of having all firms record all actuarial gains and losses in other comprehensive income (OCI) as they were incurred.[3] This caused a transitional effect as firms restated their equity to reflect changes in accounting methods, and previously unrecognized gains and losses that had been accumulated had to be recognized. For the firms that recognized gains and losses in net income, there was obviously no net effect on equity, but only a shift between net income and other comprehensive income.

This change was primarily motivated by the IASB in terms of increased *comparability*. That is, the IASB feared that the old rules meant that firms with the same underlying economics presented gains and losses in different ways. Rather than allowing many different options, a single method is now permitted. Could one argue that flexibility has now been reduced too much, preventing firms from representing their underlying economics in a faithful manner? This is highly unlikely, as it implies that the different methods were more or less appropriate in different firms, depending on their circumstances, and that the different methods truly did reflect different underlying economics. Instead, what is more likely is that different methods were chosen opportunistically, depending on a firm's financial position, or at best randomly. Having *one* permitted method removes such arbitrariness. However, why was the

3 It may be observed that these gains and losses are referred to as "remeasurements" in the updated standard.

OCI method opted for, while the others were dropped? In what way is this method better than the others? In the Basis for Conclusions to IAS 19, the IASB argues that:

- having off-balance sheet items reduces transparency; it produces an artificial smoothing effect on income and is associated with a lack of matching between income and expenses;
- meanwhile, recording all gains and losses in net income causes volatility in net income (that is, the other extreme opposite of smoothing) that is unnecessary and undesirable, given that the provision is settled far into the future and any remeasurements may fail to materialize in the end. What thus appears to be a faithful representation of matters in net income, might not actually be a very accurate representation anyway.

A pragmatic approach, one could say, is to keep the changes in the actuarial assumptions clearly visible, but not to let them affect net income—that is, in OCI. The decision to place them in other comprehensive income is also consistent with the classification of similar transactions in OCI, such as currency translation gains and losses (over which the firm has little or no influence and which are not expected to be realized in the foreseeable future). One could also assume that *understandability* increases with this increased transparency and elimination of methods. A recent study indicates that investors have trouble valuing gains and losses, or find them less reliable, when they are partially hidden using the "corridor" (Runesson, 2015).

A large debate in the accounting literature is related to whether *recognition* of financial statement items has different implications than mere *disclosure*. When speaking of implications, this refers to the faithful representation and relevance of the items, as well as their perceived usefulness for users. Studies on employee benefits in a US setting show that market participants value recognized items more than disclosed items, even though results are weak (Davis-Friday et al., 1999; Amir, 1993). Employee benefits is an example of an accounting area where the broader issue of recognition versus disclosure has been studied. A more general discussion is provided in Chapter 15.

12.4 Insurance contracts

Insurance is an industry where accounting for provisions is a central issue. The liability side of the balance sheet in insurance companies is mostly insurance contracts, which from the point of view of insurance companies are provisions. The business model of insurance companies is to accept cash in advance in return for potential future payments. The future payments are based on uncertain future events. For example, a car insurance will lead to payment if there is a car accident, while a home insurance will pay out if there is a fire, theft, etc. Life insurance is usually paid out upon the death of the insured. Life insurance companies also often have pension plans, which involve issues similar to the ones described in section 12.3. What is common to all insurance contracts is that the future payment is characterized by uncertainty and that the value of future payments must be estimated. The insurance contracts create an uncertain future payment, which meets the definition of a provision. From an accounting point of view, accounting for insurance contracts is a specialized form of accounting for provisions.

In the time period from the receipt of cash to the payment of cash, the insurance company holds investment assets, usually financial instruments and sometimes real estate. The time period from receipt to payment can be short (e.g., for property insurance such as car and home insurance) or long (e.g., for life and pension insurance). Largely, the balance sheet of an insurance company looks like the one in Figure 12.3.

States have an interest in insurance companies through explicit or implicit guarantees to keep the companies stable. In that sense, insurance companies are similar to banks (see section 11.6) and are subject to more regulation than most other firms. The reason for the interest of states is both consumer protection and to maintain the stability of the financial system. Insurance companies have many customers relying on their financial stability. These customers are rarely able to assess the financial status of the company on their own. To protect customers, most countries regulate insurance companies (e.g., by means of solvency requirements). Meanwhile, the calculation of solvency depends on the measurement of provisions in insurance contracts. Many countries require a conservative measure of insurance contracts (as they are liabilities, this means that they have a high value) in order to protect customers. A conservative measure of insurance contracts limits the risk of bankruptcy, thereby reducing the exposure of states.

The combination of inherent uncertainty and state involvement has made it difficult for standard-setters to set standards for insurance contracts. The asset side of the balance sheet of an insurance company following IFRS is largely measured at fair value. Many financial assets are measured at fair value in accordance with IFRS 9, and investment property in accordance with IAS 41. The measurement of insurance contracts, however, has been discussed for some time. In 2004, the IASB issued IFRS 4 *Insurance Contracts*. IFRS 4 permits insurance companies to keep their local conservative accounting policies and thus has a limited effect on harmonization.

IFRS 4 was seen as a temporary standard and the IASB soon started working on its replacement. A new standard, IFRS 17 *Insurance Contracts*, was issued in May 2017 and is mandatory from 2021. IFRS 17 is much stricter than IFRS 4. In general, it requires that

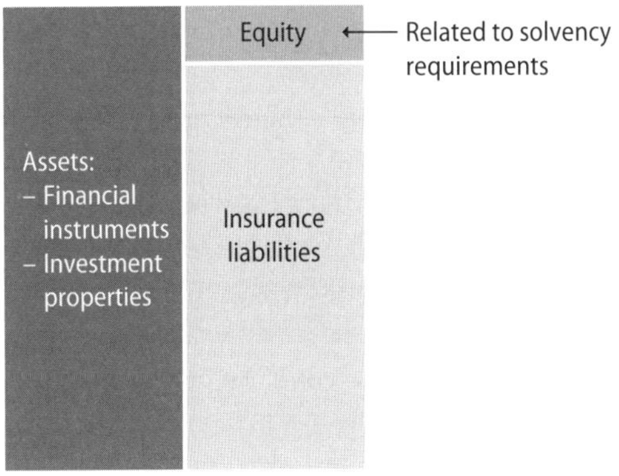

Figure 12.3 Insurance company balance sheet

insurance contracts are measured at current value. Insurance companies from which regulators require more conservative measures will have to provide two sets of financial statements, one for investors (in accordance with IFRS) and one for regulatory authorities (with more conservatism).

IFRS 17 relates to some interesting issues for the entire package of standards within IFRS with regard to conceptual consistency across standards and the scope of standards. With respect to conceptual consistency, in accordance with IFRS 17, revenue is recognized as it is earned through performance of insurance services. Currently, some insurance companies using IFRS 4 recognize revenue as insurance premiums are received. The method for revenue recognition in IFRS 17 is harmonized with IFRS 15 *Revenue from Contracts with Customers* (discussed in more detail in Chapter 13) and this leads to a higher level of conceptual consistency for revenue recognition. The scope of standards is based on definitions. For example, accounting for insurance contracts is based on IFRS 17 (or IFRS 4), while accounting for derivatives is based on IFRS 9. However, the distinction between insurance contracts and derivatives is not always obvious, as discussed in Text Box 12.7. In standard-setting, it is important to clearly define which standard is applicable to an economic phenomenon, otherwise standards could be selected opportunistically. In other words, if standards have different requirements, managers could select the one that best fit their incentives rather than the one resulting in more relevant financial statements. In addition, even in the absence of incentives, managers could randomly choose different standards for similar economic phenomena, which would hinder comparability between financial statements from different firms. The solution, of course, is more principles-based standard-setting.

Text Box 12.7 **The distinction between insurance contracts and derivatives**

The definition of *insurance contracts* in IFRS 17 (shown above) highlights insurance risk related to uncertain future events. Meanwhile, IFRS 9 defines a *derivative* as a contract that changes in value in response to an "underlying" and is settled in the future. It may not be immediately apparent, but the definition of derivatives actually encompasses insurance contracts. For example, if we look at car insurance, the underlying could be the cost of a car crash, which is settled in the future. In order to avoid the problem of two standards (IFRS 9 and IFRS 17) applying to the same contract, the IASB added a limitation in the definition of derivatives in IFRS 9. It states that if the underlying is a non-financial variable (such as a car crash), the variable cannot be specific to a party to the contract. A car crash clearly *is* specific to the policyholder and thus car insurance is excluded. The price of oil (also non-financial) is not specific to contracting parties, so a future contract to purchase oil at a fixed price is a derivative.

So, what about a contract where cash is paid based on weather conditions? For example, if the holder of a contract receives cash if there is a certain amount of rain during a specific week, is that an insurance contract or a derivative? That depends on the conditions. If it pays a fixed amount (e.g. €1,000) if there is more than 20 mm of rain, then it is a derivative, as the weather is not specific to the holder of the contract. However, if the contract indemnifies the holder for losses resulting from rain (or lack of sunshine), then it is an insurance contract, as the losses are specific to the contract holder. An example would be a farmer who insures the effect of rain on a crop.

There is limited research on accounting issues in the insurance industry. Petroni (1992) shows that insurance companies tend to understate the value of insurance contracts when they are in a weaker financial situation or when they are subject to regulatory pressure. Anthony and Petroni (1997) use the fact that there is publicly available data on the predictive ability of the measurement of insurance contracts in the US. In other words, the quality of accounting for insurance contracts is directly observable. Anthony and Petroni (1997) show that investors use this information by relying less on financial statements from insurance companies with a history of poor quality financial statements.

12.5 Equity

We have now covered central issues related to assets in Chapter 11 and liabilities in this chapter. The only remaining item on the balance sheet is (shareholders') equity. Equity is defined as the difference between assets and liabilities; that is, it is a residual item (see definition in section 10.1). As such, there are no specific measurement issues related to equity. Instead, the value of equity on the balance sheet is determined through the measurement of assets and liabilities.

The nature of equity is to represent the owners' interest in the firm. The owners are different from other stakeholders of the firm in that they are the decision-makers. For example, the owners appoint the board of directors, which in turn appoints the firm's management. The owners are also *residual claimants* of the resources (assets) of the firm. In times of financial difficulties (e.g., bankruptcy), the other stakeholders get paid before the owners. On the other hand, the owners have no upside limit to the potential cash flows from the firm.

Not only are owners distinct in economic and legal terms, but in financial reporting, the interest of owners is treated differently from that of other stakeholders. In the definitions of income and expenses, transactions with owners are excluded (see section 10.1). The effect is that net income (or comprehensive income) represents the total contribution to owners. In standard-setting, owners' required return is not considered an expense that is deducted from net income, as, for example, it is for debt holders (in the form of interest expense). Studies sometimes use models that include an expense based on expected return to shareholders, so-called **residual income models**. For example, the Ohlson (1995) model discussed in Chapter 7 is such a model. In practice, consulting firms provide similar models; the most well-known is **Economic Value-Added** (EVA) promoted by Stern Value Management in New York.

The two main financial reporting issues related to equity are:

1. the distinction between liabilities and equity
2. classification of equity into different items

We cover these issues in separate sections below.

12.5.1 Distinction between liabilities and equity

The main distinguishing feature between liabilities and equity relate to the obligation for future outflows of resources. For liabilities, there is a contractual, legal or constructive obligation to deliver resources (such as cash) to external parties. Equity represents the owners' interest in the firm and any payment to the owners is discretionary. The owners themselves decide whether cash should stay in the firm or whether it should be paid out to them.

A reason why the distinction between liabilities and equity is important is that the proportion of debt in relation to equity (the debt-to-equity ratio) is a measure of the financial risk of a firm. The debt-to-equity ratio is often used in the analysis of firms (e.g., by banks and other debtors). A high level of equity is seen as less risky, precisely because equity does not entail any contractual (or other) obligations for future cash outflows. Thus, in valuing a company, and when considering its risk exposure, this distinction becomes relevant. The distinction is especially important since it is binary. There is no continuous classification between liabilities and equity. Research suggests that accounting standards on the distinction between liabilities and equity can have real effects on firms' financing decisions (see, for instance, Levi and Segal, 2015; De Jong et al., 2006).

While the distinction between equity and liabilities is clear on a conceptual level, in practice there are many technical issues. There are instruments issued by firms that have characteristics of both liability and equity, and sometimes instruments must be separated into different components of liability and equity. Often, the measurement of each of these components requires substantial judgment. Examples of instruments where the classification is unclear include preference shares and bonds that are convertible into equity.

Within IFRS, the technical issues related to the distinction between liabilities and equity are covered in IAS 32 *Financial Instruments: Presentation*. Currently (August 2018), the IASB has a research project aimed at improving the requirements in IAS 32. A discussion paper on the issue was published in 2018. Current ideas by the IASB is that even if the classification in the balance sheet is binary, additional nuances regarding some instruments can be provided through disclosure in the notes.

12.5.2 Classification and presentation of equity

Although there are no direct measurement issues related to equity, the classification and resulting presentation of different components of equity is an issue. Here, one could adopt both an economic and a legalistic viewpoint.

In economic terms, equity consists of two main components: capital contributed by owners and accumulated earnings from operations. Normally, the two components are separated in the presentation of equity. Often, issued shares have a par (nominal) value and the capital contributed by owners can thus be divided into share capital (equal to the par value) and additional paid-in capital. Accumulated earnings from operations of the firm represent income earned that has not been distributed to owners.

IFRS generally does not prescribe exact structures for the financial statements. However, IAS 1 *Presentation of Financial Statements* requires the presentation of a *Statement of Changes in Equity*, where accumulated net income (called retained earnings) and accumulated other comprehensive income (OCI, called reserves) must be separated.[4] Since IFRS makes a distinction between profit and loss, on the one hand, and OCI, on the other (see Chapter 13), the total accumulated earnings of the firm are divided into two components.

Both profit and loss and OCI affect the size of equity, so they both affect the balance sheet in similar ways. In terms of the performance of the firm, however, inclusion in profit and loss, and in OCI, give different signals. Within IFRS, items in OCI are often those that affect the wealth of owners but for some reason add unwanted volatility to the performance measure, or those that are not expected to be realized in the foreseeable future (such as actuarial gains and losses on pension liabilities, but also currency translation adjustments). The conceptual reasoning behind the distinction between profit and loss and OCI is further discussed in Chapter 15. Here, we simply acknowledge that the distinction does affect the presentation of equity.

The presentation of equity is also affected by legal requirements in many jurisdictions. For example, in Sweden, the Companies Act ("Aktiebolagslagen") requires a distinction between restricted and unrestricted equity. The distinction is important, as only unrestricted equity may be given out as dividends and other distributions to owners. Restricted equity cannot be distributed. Although this legal distinction does not affect consolidated financial statements, all individual financial statements by Swedish companies must make this distinction. Many countries have similar special requirements for the presentation of equity.

12.6 Conclusions

To finance operations, a firm needs funds. These can be provided through a number of sources, including shareholders, banks, bondholders and suppliers. Whereas shareholders supply risk capital through equity financing, banks and bondholders give loans and charge fixed interest on those loans. In some cases, the distinction between equity and liabilities is not clear and require judgment—the classification depending on the terms with which capital is provided.

Other liabilities arise in the course of a firm's operations. For example, suppliers provide operating loans by allowing generous payment terms (interest is charged implicitly through higher prices), and employees render services but are partly paid in much later periods (after retirement), meaning the firm has an obligation toward those employees. Warranties and unforeseen events that lead to lawsuits or environmental clean-up constitute other potential obligations to customers and the public that will lead to future cash flows and must therefore be recognized as provisions in the meantime.

Depending on the type of liability, preparers of financial statements face different accounting issues. The main question is, should an expense be recorded in the current period, along with a provision, or should the expense be recognized in later periods, in association with the outflow of cash? In other words, *is* there a liability? Having determined this, estimating the probable future outflows of resources and estimating a suitable discount rate require difficult judgments on behalf of management. Measurement errors as well as incentives to shift income between periods using provisions, can have detrimental effects on the quality of the financial statements.

4 OCI items used to be classified as "dirty surplus items" because they represented changes to equity that did not pass through a statement of performance (such as the income statement).

CHAPTER 13

Profit and loss

Learning outcomes

Upon completion of this chapter, you will have gained insight into:

- Which accounting issues affect items in profit and loss (i.e., revenues and expenses).
- How the measurement of revenues and expenses relates to the structures presented in Chapter 10.
- The trade-offs made by standard-setters in regulating revenues and expenses, and the effect of this on accounting quality.
- Item-specific research related to revenues and expenses.

AFTER HAVING GONE THROUGH BOTH SIDES of the balance sheet in Chapters 11 and 12, in this chapter we focus on the income statement (statement of profit and loss). Unlike the balance sheet, which shows assets and liabilities at a certain point in time (assets and liabilities are so-called *stock variables*), the income statement depicts events over a time period (revenues and expenses are *flow variables*). The bottom line of the income statement is net income (earnings) for the period, which is a measure of firm *performance*.

As we saw in Chapter 10, the IASB bases its definitions of financial statement items on the balance sheet. Even the conceptual foundation for revenue recognition (an income statement item) is based on assets and liabilities (see IFRS 15 *Revenue from Contracts with Customers*). Meanwhile, from a user perspective, it is likely that earnings (and the income statement in general) are more important than balance sheet items. Consequently, there is a significant amount of research focused on earnings quality (see Chapter 7). This is not necessarily contradictory, however, as the balance sheet and income statement are closely linked.

Out of the four Stylized Accrual Situations (see Chapter 10), the fourth directly concerns the income statement, as it has to do with the timing of recognized revenue in the income statement. Note, meanwhile, that the other three stylized situations relate indirectly to the income statement. When acquired resources are not recognized as assets, they are immediately expensed in the income statement. If they are recognized as assets, they will be expensed in subsequent periods (SAS 1). Provisions on the balance sheet for future outflows of resources result in the immediate recognition of expenses in the income statement and no or reduced expenses in future periods (SAS 2). Changes in the value of assets and liabilities will result in gains and losses on the income statement if they are recognized even if they are unrealized. If they are not recognized until they are realized, gains and losses will be included in the income statement in later periods (SAS 3). In summary, while the chosen accounting treatment in situation 4 affects the timing of revenue, the accounting treatment in SAS 1–3 affects the timing of expenses (and gains in SAS 3).

As a consequence of the link between the balance sheet and the income statement, many items on the income statement are covered in Chapters 11 and 12. This includes, for example, depreciation and amortization of fixed assets, expenses for employee benefits such as pensions and effects of fair value measurement of financial instruments. In this chapter, we focus on items where the income statement is the primary focus; in other words, accounting standards where the objective is to obtain an appropriate measure of revenues or expenses. Such standards cover revenue recognition (for revenues), income taxes, expenses for share-based payment, government grants and foreign currency (for expenses).

In IFRS, a distinction is made between items included in profit and loss (income statement) and other comprehensive income (OCI). Net income (the bottom line number of the income statement) and total comprehensive income (a broader bottom line number that also includes OCI) are alternative measures of firm performance. In this book, we treat the distinction between profit and loss, on the on hand, and OCI, on the other, as a presentation issue. Currently, there is a broader discussion on how best to measure firm performance, where the usefulness of alternative income measures such as EBIT (earnings before interest and taxes) is debated. We return to presentation issues as well as the performance measure debate in Chapter 15.

13.1 Revenue recognition

The importance of revenue in companies is indisputable (see, for instance, Ertimur et al., 2003; Wagenhofer, 2014). Revenues are key building blocks for firm valuation and affect key performance ratios. In profitability analyses, revenues are used as a basis for calculating fundamental ratios such as profit margins and earnings per share. Revenues are primary drivers of firm performance and without revenues from customers, firms cannot generate value. For most firms, revenues represent the largest individual line item in the financial statements. Revenue recognition often requires preparer judgment. Increasingly complex business models, for example in high-tech industries, explain why the accounting treatment of revenue constitutes a challenge for many firms.

Regulatory bodies, practitioners and researchers have long been concerned with revenue recognition. After the "IT bubble" and multiple accounting scandals at the beginning of the 2000s, the importance of reliable revenue recognition ended up in the center of the attention of the IASB and the FASB. The standard-setters commenced a joint project in 2002 to develop a comprehensive accounting standard for revenue recognition, which was also partly motivated by the main aim of harmonization between these two standard-setting bodies. However, the main reason for a radical change in the revenue recognition standard within the joint project was that accounting standards on revenue recognition did not match the needs of firms with new business models and more complex customer contracts. The multitude of accounting scandals in the early 2000s was seen as evidence of poorly working standards (see Text Box 13.1).

Text Box 13.1 **Revenue, fraud and accounting scandals**

Misstatement of revenue is known to be a common way to commit fraud and therefore trigger accounting scandals. Indeed, given the wide-ranging discretion and room for judgment given to managers, the choice of accounting methods for revenue recognition is likely to be motivated by managerial incentives. For example, there is evidence that firms carrying out initial public offerings (IPOs) attempt to advance the recognition of revenues and thereby show more positive earnings (and future prospects).

During the build-up of the "IT bubble" in the late 1990s, many IT (and other high-tech) firms were evaluated based on revenue growth and not on profit growth. This gave management in such firms strong incentives to overstate revenue in order to drive up stock prices, especially when management had stock options. The most well-known accounting scandal at the time was Enron. Ball (2009, p.299) states that:

> Between 1995 and 2000, reported revenues grew from \$9.2 billion to \$100.8 billion: a tenfold increase in five years. However, reported profits did not even double over the period, and consequently the net profit margin on sales fell by 2000 (using reported numbers) to less than 1%. We now know that even that slim margin actually was not earned, because reported profits that year were overstated.

Enron was not an isolated case. There were many cases of erroneous revenue recognition noted by enforcement agencies in both the US and Europe. Beasley et al. (2000) examine the documented fraudulent financial reporting in the Securities and Exchange Commission's Accounting and Auditing Enforcement Releases over the period 1987–1997 for several industries. The results of this study show that *improper revenue recognition* is the main issue for 76% of firms in the technology sector. The second and the third leading factors allowing opportunities for fraud in these firms are also related to revenue; that is, *recording fictitious revenues* in 40% of the cases and *recording revenues prematurely* in 48% of the cases. In another study, Graham et al. (2005) ask 401 financial executives: "Near the end of the quarter, it looks like your company might come in below the desired earnings target. Within what is permitted by GAAP, which of the following choices might your company make?" Responses show that around 40% of executives agree that early discretionary revenue recognition is what they do in order to reach the benchmark.

These accounting scandals were not only worrisome *per se*, they also pointed to a more general concern regarding the quality of revenues in financial statements, as well as the value relevance and information usefulness of reported revenues under existing accounting standards. Bias in reported revenues may result both from the underlying uncertainty associated with the estimation of revenues (not least due to the complexity of underlying transactions) and from firm-specific incentives to manage earnings. Levine and Smith (2011) show that 55% of US firms disclose revenue recognition as a critical accounting policy (i.e., an area firms consider to be characterized by measurement uncertainty).

13.1.1 Definitions and summary of issues

The IASB and the FASB launched a joint project to develop a comprehensive standard for revenue recognition in 2002. The main objectives of this joint collaboration were to clarify the principles for revenue recognition under US GAAP and IFRS, enhance the comparability of revenue recognition practices, and improve disclosure requirements to ensure the provision of useful information to users of financial statements. It was a long and arduous process, with revised exposure drafts being necessary, as well as deferrals of the effective date for the new revenue standard. IFRS 15 *Revenue from Contracts with Customers* came into effect in 2018. The IFRS and US GAAP standards are not identical, but share the same conceptual views on revenue recognition.

The perceived problems with pre-existing standards differed between IFRS and US GAAP. In IFRS, there was a general standard for revenue recognition (IAS 18 *Revenue*) that was principles-based but did not provide adequate guidance. Consequently, the practice of revenue recognition could differ, even for firms with similar transactions. IAS 18 made a distinction between revenue from sale of goods and revenue from rendering of services. Sale of goods occurs at a point in time and the primary notion in IAS 18 was that revenue should be recognized when risks and rewards of ownership were transferred to the customer. Services are rendered over a period of time and IAS 18 stated that revenue should be recognized based on the stage of completion of the service. In US GAAP, there were several standards covering revenue recognition, including some industry-specific standards. This was perceived as overly rules-based and not leading to harmonization across industries. Actually, the difference between IFRS and US GAAP in revenue recognition was one reason behind the debate regarding principles-based versus rules-based standards, where IFRS was considered principles-based and US GAAP rules-based (see Chapter 4).

Principles-based standards work better when underlying principles are explicit. While IAS 18 was conceptually focused on the transfer of risks and rewards of ownership to the customer (a transaction-focused view), IFRS 15 adopts a balance sheet view—consistent with the Conceptual Framework—and the definition of income in IFRS 15 is expressed so as to mirror that of the CF (cf. Chapter 10):

> Increases in economic economic benefits during the accounting period in the form of inflows or enhancements of assets or decreases of liabilities that result in an increase in equity, other than those relating to contributions from equity participants. (IFRS 15, Appendix A)

In addition, IFRS 15 defines revenue as a subset of income, referring to it as "income arising in the course of an entity's ordinary activities." (IFRS 15, Appendix A)

As seen in the definitions, income is defined based on changes in assets and liabilities. Expressed differently, the balance sheet items are independent while the income statement items are dependent.

With the issuance of IFRS 15, the IASB essentially completed its work to base all standards on a balance sheet approach. Both the IASB and FASB claim that the asset-liability approach provides a more objective picture—especially for revenue recognition—compared to the alternative revenue-expense approach based on matching principles (in which expenses are matched to revenues).[1] The competing argument—that the matching principle enhances the quality of earnings (see Dichev et al., 2013)—has not convinced standard-setters. Still, even IFRS 15 retains some aspects that resemble an income statement approach (Marton and Wagenhofer, 2010; Wagenhofer, 2014). For example, the transaction price is allocated based on stand-alone transaction prices, instead of measurement of performance obligations. Also, service transactions are recognized over time. Whereas the above discussion reflects a conceptual issue relating to revenues, we discuss practical issues below.

IFRS 15 takes a five-step approach to revenue recognition. There is no clear distinction between sale of goods and rendering of services, as there was in IAS 18. Instead, all revenue recognition is based on the same method, on the same underlying principle. The five steps are:

1. Identify the *contract* with a customer.
2. Identify *performance obligations* in the contract.
3. Determine the *transaction price*.
4. *Allocate* the transaction price to performance obligations.
5. Recognize revenue as performance obligations are *satisfied*.

These steps all require choices and judgments to be made in varying degrees depending on the type of firm and transaction. The main accounting issue for revenues is the *timing* of revenue recognition (i.e., SAS 4, see Table 13.1), which is captured by the final step in the process described above. In particular, accounting difficulties arise when transactions are spread over several reporting periods and when several transactions are combined into one. In the next section, we consider this process in greater depth.

Table 13.1 Summary of issues relating to revenues

Generic issue	Specific issue: Choices and judgments	Comment
SAS 4 (Revenue recognition)	Performance obligation satisfied?	Recognize revenue based on allocated transaction price

13.1.2 Choices, judgments and the five-step approach to revenue recognition

Difficulties with revenue recognition—and the possibility for managerial opportunism—vary greatly by situation. Revenue recognition can be simple, for example in many retail situations. The retailer delivers goods to the customer, is paid at the same time and thus recognizes revenue at that time.

1 Although the matching principle was not explicit in IAS 18, it was easily detected, for example in the recognition criteria for revenues, which state that revenue shall not be recognized until "the costs incurred or to be incurred in respect of the transaction can be measured reliably" (Par. 14(e)).

However, other situations are more complex and require preparer judgment. Often, difficulties stem from transactions that combine several components, when delivery occurs over an extended period of time, or when the customer has a right to return purchased products. Transactions containing several components include, for example, cellphone operators selling a combination of phones and phone services and IT consultants providing both hardware and consulting services in a package. Issues in such situations include both allocation of revenue to the good and service, respectively, and the *timing* of revenue recognition. Delivery over long time periods includes both long-term construction contracts and service contracts. Customers' right to product returns requires the selling firm to estimate the probability of a return when accounting for revenue.

The basis for revenue recognition in accordance with IFRS 15 is the **contract** between the reporting firm and the customer. A basic assumption is that arms-length transactions—such as sales from a firm to its customers—represent an exchange of equal value (Figure 13.2). The contract gives rise to both assets and liabilities that, based on the assumption, have equal value. The assets are the future payments that will be received from the customer. The liabilities are the **performance obligations**—that is, the obligations to deliver goods or services in the future. Note that at the time the contract is entered into, no assets or liabilities are recognized on the balance sheet, but such recognition follows from the recognition of revenue in step 5. Initially, the assets and liabilities represent conceptual structures that make the two sides in a sales transaction explicit, and help preparers identify events that form the basis for revenue recognition. Another aspect of the emphasis on contracts in IFRS 15 is the focus on firms' specific economic situations. A contract must be analyzed in detail in order for revenue recognition to be performed correctly.

A contract includes one or several performance obligations. Each **distinct** performance obligation should be identified separately, where "distinct" may be interpreted as possible to sell separately. An example (noted above) is telecommunication firms that combine sales of phones with phone services. It is clear that these can be sold separately, so they represent distinct performance obligations. This second step in IFRS 15 was introduced as a response to the problem of disentangling complex contracts into separate performance obligations. Even if IFRS 15 always requires separation into distinct performance obligations, it only becomes an issue if the goods and services are delivered at different points in time. In the case of telecommunications, for example, a phone is sold at a certain point in time, while phone services are provided in future periods. If, on the other hand, a TV set is sold with a toaster as an extra perk, revenue recognition is unaffected by the identification of the two performance obligations (delivery of TV set and delivery of toaster), as they are delivered simultaneously.

To be able to recognize revenue based on performance obligations, it is also necessary to measure them. As noted, the two sides in a transaction between a firm and its customers are assumed to have equal value. If a customer pays in cash or other monetary assets, it is easy to measure the value of payments to the firm. The total transaction price is assumed to equal the total value of all performance obligations. For example, a telecommunications firm may charge SEK 12,000 for a phone and two years of telecommunication services. IFRS 15 requires that the transaction price is allocated to the performance obligations identified. The basic idea is that the allocation should be based on the stand-alone prices that would be paid in the market for each of the performance obligations. For example, the price of a phone may be SEK 5,000 and the price of two years' worth of services may be SEK 7,000 (which, combined, add up to a total transaction price of SEK 12,000).

The final step in the process is the actual recognition of revenue over time, based on when the performance obligations are satisfied. For the sale of goods, this is often at *one* point in time, when the goods are transferred to the customer. Services, on the other hand, may be delivered over a period of time. Continuing with the telecommunications example, revenue from the sale of a phone is recognized as the phone is physically transferred to the customer, while revenue for telecommunication services is recognized over the contractual period (e.g., 24 months). When revenue is recognized over time, a question arising is how to allocate the revenue to different periods. The answer is that it will depend on the contract. Revenue from phone services may be recognized on a linear basis (i.e., with the same amount each month). A long-term construction contract, on the other hand, should probably be recognized based on the proportion of the construction carried out each time period. IFRS 15 was issued about the same time as IFRS 16, and the two standards are related, see Text Box 13.2.

Text Box 13.2 **Revenues and leases**

There is a scope issue with respect to IFRS 15 and IFRS 16 *Leases* (see section 11.5), in that there is a potential for overlap between the two standards where some economic phenomena may relate to both standards. A lease agreement conveys the right to *use* an asset for a specified time period. Sometimes, judgment is required to determine whether a contract relates to the use of an asset or if it is a service contract. For example, a firm providing copying services to other firms may either lease specific copy machines or provide the service to enable copying in the customers' offices. In the first case, it is a lease agreement, while the latter may be sale of services. In a lease agreement, IFRS 16 is applicable, while IFRS 15 is applied to sale of services. Depending on the classification, different rules thus apply, which ultimately has implications on accounting quality.

High measurement uncertainty—as we may have here—can be mitigated through disclosures regarding the judgments made (see more in Chapter 15). IFRS 15 has substantial disclosure requirements, including for disclosures regarding judgments.

In sum, IFRS 15 provides a structure for how to think about the timing of revenue recognition. It allows firms to adapt their revenue recognition to their own particular contractual circumstances. However, this requires substantial judgment from preparers. In the trade-off between principles and rules, the IASB clearly opts for principles in this case. As of yet, there is no research available to suggest whether IFRS 15 leads to higher or lower accounting quality. This remains to be seen.

13.2 Share-based payment

Imagine that you have finally completed your education and that you are ready to deal with the challenges of the job market. We assume that all of you have high goals and that you want to go for top jobs in accounting, auditing and finance. Although it may take some years, you are offered a managerial position in a high-tech company. However, you have only been given this position on one condition: you will receive only a minimum salary and instead accept payments based on the stock market performance of the firm. In your contract, you are offered a generous **share-based compensation**—provided that the firm performs well. To some, this will sound risky; to others, exciting. For firms that are short on cash but have a potentially bright future (such as start-ups and research and development firms), such solutions may be all but necessary.

Indeed, share-based compensation is a type of compensation plan that has become increasingly popular in many parts of the world. The reason is not only that this type of compensation is useful in firms with cash constraints, but also that it is considered an important tool in resolving conflicts of interests between managers and shareholders. As we saw in earlier chapters, the idea is that well-designed compensation contracts can be potentially useful mechanisms for aligning the interests of managers with those of shareholders. This is because by using share-based compensation, managerial benefits depend on the performance of the firm's shares and thus on shareholder value.

Common types of share-based compensation plans are stock options and restricted stocks. In **stock option** plans, managers (and other employees) are granted options allowing them to acquire shares in the company in the future. Such plans entail a cost for participants in the plan that is equal to the exercise price of the acquired options. The grant of restricted shares, on the other hand, is without initial costs to participants. **Restricted stock** is usually contingent on a certain amount of time elapsing, or a certain performance target being achieved, before the stock can be traded. The board of directors considers and defines specific performance measures as well as the conditions of long-term incentive plans that the managers are required to fulfill. Share-based compensation plans often cover a time span of three to ten years. A long-term element (i.e., longer than one year) implies that there are issues related to accruals in financial statements. An example of share-based compensation is shown in Text Box 13.3.

Text Box 13.3 **Share-based compensation in Volvo: Extract from the annual report of 2016**

The Volvo Group also has share-based incentive programs for the years 2011–2013 and for the years 2014–2016 (terminated one year in advance), including both a cash-settled and an equity-settled part. The fair value of the equity-settled payments is determined at the grant date, recognized as an expense during the vesting period and offset in equity. The fair value is based on the share price reduced by dividends connected with the share during the vesting period.

» particular financial year amounts to at least 10 percent, a number of performance shares. Maximum allotment of performance shares corresponds to seven shares for the CEO, six shares for other members of group management, and five shares for other participants in the program for each invested share, subject to ROE reaching 25 percent. ROE for 2011 was 23.1%, which means that number of performance shares reached about 90 percent of the maximum grant. Allotment of shares will be made through Volvo owned, earlier re-purchased, Volvo shares. Participants in certain countries will be offered a cash-based version of the incentive program. For participants in these countries, no investment is required by the participant and the program does not comprise an element of matching shares. Allotment of shares in this version is replaced by a cash allotment at the end of the vesting period. Other program conditions are similar between programs.

Long term incentive program (share settled plan version)	Vesting year	Shares granted conditional under the plan but not yet alloted (in thousand shares) Beginning of the year	Granted 2011	Cancelled/ forfeited 2011	Allotments during 2011	End of the year	Cost 2011 (SEK M)1
Year 2011 Incentive program	2014/2015	**0**	**2,488**	**(11)**	(1)	**2,476**	69.8

1 The fair value of the payments is determined based on the share price at the grant date reduced by the discounted value of expected dividends connected with the share during the vesting period. The cost for the program is recognized over the vesting period. The cost includes social security cost.

The cost for the cash-based version of the incentive program amounted to SEK 4 million including social security cost during 2011.

A number of program participants that are leaving the company has been determined to be "good leavers" and are therefore entitled to accumulated allotment of shares. During 2011, 929 shares have been alloted to participants, and an additional 203,520 shares will be alloted to participants when the employees leave the company.

The total cost for the 2011 incentive program over the period 2011 to 2014 is estimated to SEK 273 million including social security cost. Actual cost will be impacted by changes in the share price.

We can see that the total value of share-based compensation is small in relation to the overall operation of Volvo Group. The cost in 2016 is SEK 106.8 million, while net income in that year was SEK 13.2 billion. Still, information concerning share-based compensation could be important from a corporate governance perspective.
Source: Volvo's Annual Report 2016, p. 154.

Long-term share-based incentive program (equity-settled version)	Vesting year	Shares granted conditional under the plan but not yet allotted (in thousand shares) Beginning of the year	Adjustment	Cancelled/ forfeited 2016	Allotments during 2016	End of year	Cost 2016 (SEK M)1
Year 2011 incentive program	2014/2015	**3**	–	–	–3	–	–
Year 2012 incentive program	2015/2016	**313**	–	–	–313	–	0.8
Year 2013 incentive program	2016/2017	**395**	–	–3	–271	**121**	10.2
Year 2014 incentive program	2017/2018	**446**	–	–6	–68	**372**	15.5
Year 2015 incentive program	2018/2019	**1,543**	170	–14	–69	**1,630**	80.4
Total		**2,699**	**170**	**–22**	**–725**	**2,122**	**106.8**

1 The fair value of the payments is determined based on the share price at the grant date reduced by the discounted value of expected dividends connected with the share during the vesting period. The cost for the program is recognized over the vesting period. The cost includes social security cost.

Share-based compensation became increasingly popular in the 1990s, while there were still no requirements for recognizing such compensation as an expense in financial statements. Employees and managers in many firms, particularly in the US, were awarded large numbers of shares and options as part of their compensation packages. Figure 13.1 shows the compensation data for executives in the US S&P 500 Firms, including both non-equity-

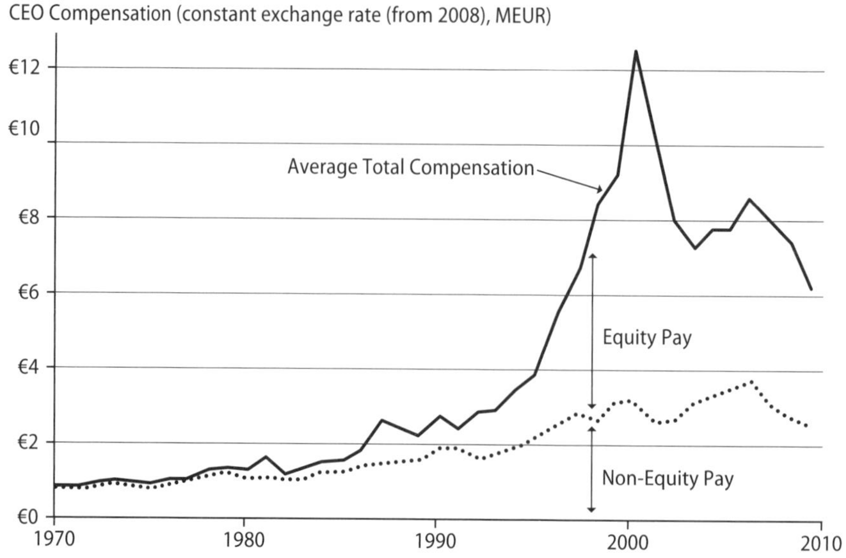

Figure 13.1 Average equity and non-equity compensation for CEOs in US S&P 500 firms, 1970–2009. Source: Conyon et al. (2011)

based pay (i.e., salary and bonus) and equity-based pay (i.e., restricted stocks and stock options). As one can see in Figure 13.1, executive pay has evolved considerably over time. However, a striking increase in executive compensation occurred at the beginning of the 1990s and was mostly attributable to the considerable increase in share-based compensation. The fact that firms did not have to recognize an accounting cost for granting stock options to executives raised the popularity of share-based compensation during this period. In other settings, including Europe, share-based compensation is less common than in the US. In fact, while share-based pay has been part of compensation plans for CEOs for more than half a century in the US, providing executives with share-based compensation is a more recent practice in other countries. For example, it was not until the end of the 1990s that share-based compensation became common across Europe.

13.2.1 Definitions and summary of issues

So far, we have used the term share-based *compensation*, which is recipient-based terminology. From the firm's point of view, the accounting area in question may also be referred to as **share-based payment**, in which case it covers compensation to employees (primarily executives), but also payments made to other parties using the firm's own shares. IFRS 2 *Share-Based Payment* defines share-based payment as a transaction in which a firm receives or acquires goods and services in exchange for its equity instruments (**equity-settled payment**) or by incurring liabilities based on the price of the equity instruments (**cash-settled payment**).[2]

2 Although hybrids of these exist (equity-settled payment with cash alternatives), we do not consider such arrangements further.

Equity-settled payment refers to when employees receive equity instruments, such as shares or stock options, in exchange for their services in firms. Meanwhile, cash-settled payment refers to when the payment to employees is carried out in cash, but the amount is *derived* from the firm's stock price or the value of some other equity instruments.

An idea in IFRS 2—and in IFRS in general—is that since the two sides in a transaction have equal value, measurement should be based on the component that is more easily measured. Normally, when an entity obtains a good or service from a non-employee/someone outside the firm, it is considered possible to reliably measure the fair value of the goods or services *directly*. However, because employees often carry out multiple services, it is considered difficult to distinguish which service is rendered in exchange for the granted stock or shares. Accordingly, in IFRS 2 the fair value of the service must be measured *indirectly* through reference to the fair value of the equity instruments granted. The main issue relating to this accounting area is therefore related to the measurement of stock-based compensation to employees—both upon recognition and in later periods. A summary of issues in accounting in relation to share-based payment is shown in Table 13.2. Note that there is no reference to the Stylized Accrual Situations in the table. They are not helpful here, as the main issue concerns whether to reflect the transaction in financial statements *at all*.

Table 13.2 Summary of issues relating to share-based payment

Generic issue	Specific issue: Choices and judgments	Comment
Recognition or disclosure		If not recognized, treat as owner transaction
Measurement	Value of transaction? Allocation of value to periods?	

Before getting into the other issues, we begin by discussing the rationale for recognizing share-based compensation as an expense in the financial statements. Any requirements for recognizing these expenses were previously absent both in US GAAP and IFRS. Following a long and arduous standard-setting process, requirements for recognition of share-based payment have been introduced. Although these changes now seem dated, the conceptual discussion behind these changes is of general interest to us as we discuss accounting quality.

13.2.2 Recognition versus disclosure: The case of share-based payment

Recognition versus disclosure is a general issue discussed in more depth in Chapter 15. Share-based payment is one example of an area where this general issue has been applicable in the last few decades. It cuts to the core of what an expense is.

In 1992, the FASB launched an initiative to recognize an expense for payments to employees in the form of stock or stock options and issued a formal proposal on this matter in 1993. The proposal, however, created a large debate as to whether an expense should be recognized in the financial statements for these kinds of transactions. In particular, much of the criticism was put forward by high-tech companies, accountants and compensation consultants. The opponents believed that granting shares and options to executives (and other employees) did not constitute a cost to the company.

In March 1994, the FASB held public hearings on the issue. In the aftermath of the overwhelmingly negative response, the FASB announced that it was delaying the proposed accounting change by at least a year, and in December it dropped the proposal. The FASB was subject to very strong political pressure. Some members of Congress, as well as the White House, argued that expense recognition would hurt the high-tech industry and therefore US competitiveness. Even President Clinton participated in the debate in 1993, expressing that "it would be unfortunate if FASB's proposal inadvertently undermined the competitiveness of some of America's most promising high-tech companies" (Wall Street Journal, 1993). It is likely that the FASB faced a choice between withdrawing its proposal or else being effectively closed down. Meanwhile, research indicated that recognition of expenses for share-based payment was not negative from a stock market perspective (Dechow et al., 1996).

In 2001, one of the worst accounting scandals in recent US history, the Enron case, was exposed. This was followed by other scandals, including Worldcom. Following these scandals, the focus shifted from high-tech firms to executive compensation. Many argued that the scandals happened because of strong managerial incentives connected to excessive share-based compensation. Although legal restrictions on the compensation *per se* were not proposed, there was now strong political pressure to recognize the expense of the compensation in financial statements. In addition, the bursting of the IT stock market bubble in 2000 shifted the political focus away from high-tech firms. Consequently, the previous proposal from the FASB was slightly adjusted and came into effect in 2005.

Meanwhile, in July 2001, the IASB added a project on share-based payment to its agenda. The Board received both positive and negative comments on a discussion paper for accounting for share-based payments. At the beginning of 2004, the IASB issued IFRS 2, which covers recognition and measurement of share-based payments. In the Basis for Conclusions (IFRS 2: BC6), the standard-setter adopts a user perspective when it states that:

> Users of financial statements and other commentators are calling for improvements in the accounting treatment of share-based payment. [...] In particular, the omission of expenses arising from share-based payment transactions with employees has been highlighted by investors, other users of financial statements and other commentators as causing economic distortions and corporate governance concerns.

As we see here, the recognition of share-based payment as an expense has been the subject of controversy. The main conceptual argument against seeing it as an expense is that it constitutes an *owner transaction*. Remember that the definition of an expense in the Conceptual Framework excludes transactions with owners. Since employees receive equity instruments in share-based compensation plans, they become owners of the firm. Another (perhaps less convincing) argument is that since no cash payments are involved, no expense should be recognized. Actually, when employees exercise options, the firm *receives* cash!

The belief, however, that share-based payments *do not constitute an expense* has been declared misguided and erroneous for primarily two reasons. First, there is an "opportunity" or economic cost of granting equity instruments to employees. This follows from the fact that the company could have received a higher amount had it instead issued the shares or options in an open market. Employees would not be interested in share-based compensation if they did not receive a discount on shares or options, which suggests that it would be possible for the firm to receive more if shares were issued to other parties. Second, given that a company has to buy the existing shares from shareholders or issue new shares in order to complete the transaction with the managers and employees, there will be a **dilutive effect** on the capital structure of the firm and a corresponding decrease in *existing* shareholders' value when the shares are given or the options are exercised. In order to get a better understanding of this, let us assume that an employee has been granted shares in the firm, resulting in an increase in the number of shares. This implies that the pre-existing shareholders now own a smaller percentage of company shares, which in turn means less value for previously issued shares. That is, granting shares and options can have direct effects on investors since the issuance of options by firms and the subsequent exercise of stock options by employees leads to an outflow of future cash flows to the new shareholders. From an investor perspective, the dilutive effect on shareholder value is a real cost, which calls for recognition in the financial statements.

Finally, the IASB argues that a firm's consumption of resources (e.g., services from employees) should be recognized as an expense by stating:

> Some argue that because share-based payments do not require the entity to sacrifice any cash or other assets, there is no cost to the entity, and therefore no expense should be recognised. The board regards this argument as unsound, because it overlooks that:
> (a) every time an entity receives resources as consideration for the issue of equity instruments, there is no outflow of cash or other assets, and on every other occasion the resources received as consideration for the issue of equity instruments are recognized in the financial statements; and
> (b) the expense arises from the consumption of those resources, not from an outflow of assets. (IFRS 2: BC40–44)

Expensing thus promotes comparability between firms. Let us assume that we have two firms (A and B). Firm A pays cash salary to its employees, while firm B pays employees with share-based compensation. The firms are identical in all other respects. To achieve comparability in the measurement of the performance (earnings) of firms A and B, the consumption of employee services must be recognized in both firms.

Before the introduction of IFRS 2 and the corresponding US GAAP standard (SFAS 123R), the accounting requirements for share-based payment were limited to disclosure of these transactions or voluntary income statement recognition. As mentioned before, in the wake of accounting scandals and more active investors, the mandatory recognition of share-based payment as an expense in income statements was introduced in 2005. The question then is why disclosure of information on share-based payment was not enough? In other words, is there any improvement in information usefulness relating to share-based payment following the recognition in income statements?

In the accounting literature, some studies have tried to answer the above questions by explicitly examining the evolution of share-based payment from disclosure to recognition.

For instance, Frederickson et al. (2006) predict and find that mandated income statement recognition, as required under SFAS 123R, leads to higher user assessments of reliability compared to either voluntary income statement recognition or note disclosure of options, which were allowed under SFAS 123.

However, this does not imply that disclosure of share-based payment is not important. Instead, the complexity in the measurement of these transactions requires a high level of transparency. Choudhary (2011) investigates the reliability of inputs to the fair value of executive share options and compares firms that only recognize fair value in the income statement with firms that also disclose information regarding estimates of fair value. Findings show that firms that recognize the fair value but do not provide adequate disclosure are more likely to underestimate the fair value by reducing their estimates of stock price volatility. The broader issue of recognition versus disclosure, where share-based payment is one example, is discussed further in Chapter 15.

13.2.3 Measurement

Once standard-setters conclude that share-based compensation represents an expense, questions arise as to *how to measure* the expense and *when* it should be recognized. We begin with the issue of measurement. A basic assumption in accounting is that in arm's-length transactions between knowledgeable parties, the value of that which is received equals the value of that which is given up (see Figure 13.2). Since cash is often involved in transactions, they are easily measured. It is, for example, possible to measure the value of employee services through the salary paid to employees. The issue with non-cash transactions is that both sides of the transaction can be difficult to measure.

In accordance with IFRS 2, equity instruments should be measured at fair value. For actively traded, listed shares, this is simple, since the fair value can be observed in the stock market. For non-listed shares, this is much more difficult, as fair value measures are based on level 3 inputs (cf. Chapter 10). When it comes to stock option plans, the fair value is estimated using different option valuation techniques, such as the Black-Scholes model. Often, employee stock options are not standardized and therefore not traded in markets, which means that firms must choose a valuation model in order to determine the fair value of the stock options. We do not go through these models, but as pointed out in IFRS 2, all option valuation models consider the following factors (Par. B6):

- Exercise price
- Life of option
- Current share price
- Risk-free interest rate
- Expected volatility of share price
- Expected dividends on share

While most of these factors are observable in the option contract or in the market, the expected volatility and dividends must be estimated. The fact that the expected volatility can

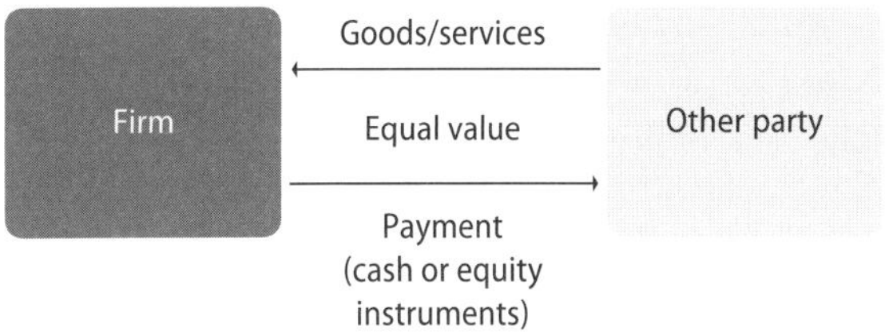

Figure 13.2
Value of two sides of a transaction

have a substantial effect on the option value and is highly dependent on preparer judgment creates uncertainty in the measurement.

The total fair value of an option plan forms the basis for the expense to be recognized in financial statements. Once the value is determined, the next step is to allocate the expense to different periods. In order to facilitate an understanding of the issues, an overview of a typical employee stock option is provided in Figure 13.3. Stock options give the holder the right, but not the obligation, to purchase shares at a price that is fixed in advance. The **grant date** is the day when the options are granted to the employee (i.e., when the employer and the employee agree on the option contract). Most compensation plans (but not all) require that the employees work for a certain period before they obtain the right to receive the options, called the **vesting period**. The **vesting date** is the date when employees have completed the vesting period. The **exercise date** is when the options are used to buy shares (or expire).

The objective of IFRS 2 is to correctly reflect the consumption of resources (employee services) paid for by stock options. The best measure of the value of employee services is provided on the grant date, as this is the day when the employer and the employee agree on the contractual terms. In other words, this is the date when—in a contract between the employer and the employee—the value of the services to be provided in exchange for equity instruments is determined. Consequently, the value of the equity instruments at that date represents the best estimate of the value of the service rendered and there is no need to adjust this afterwards (i.e., the value of the service does not change just because the instrument changes its value due to market movements). Once the total value of the transaction is determined, the next question is *when* to recognize the expense. Based on IFRS 2, the expense is allocated over the vesting period. The idea is that services paid for through equity-based compensation are provided and consumed during the vesting period. This is logical, as the employee agreed to work during the vesting period in exchange for the options. Measuring the options on the grant date, and then allocating the expense over the vesting period, reflects the objective in IFRS 2 in terms of correctly reflecting the consumption of resources in the income statement.

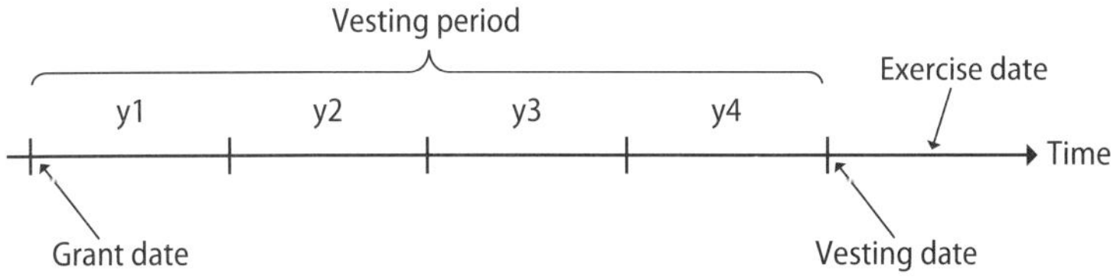

Figure 13.3
Timing of employee stock options

The **exercise price** is the fixed price at which shares can be bought in the future. The holder will exercise the option (i.e., purchase shares) if the market price of shares is above the exercise prices on the exercise date. If the market price is below the exercise price at the exercise date, the option will expire without being used, thus rendering the options worthless at that time. Such situations do not affect the expense recognized in accordance with IFRS 2, based on the logic described above.

Meanwhile, accounting for share-based payment is complicated by the fact that there are two types of payment, equity-settled and cash-settled. In equity-settled payments, the options can be used to buy shares on the exercise date. In cash-settled payments, the options give the right to receive cash based on the stock price on the exercise date, but not the right to buy shares. For example, if a cash-settled scheme has an "exercise price" of 100, employees would get 10 if the stock price on the exercise date is 110, 20 if the price is 120 and 0 if the price is 90. While the wealth effects of cash-settled payments for the employee is similar to that of equity-settled payment, the accounting implications are different.

Cash-settled payments involve a potential future payment of cash and the firm recognizes a liability for the estimated future payment. The liability is updated on each balance sheet date based on the current fair value of the options. The idea that the fair value on the grant date should not be subsequently adjusted is not valid with regard to cash-settled compensation. Instead, the firm must adjust the value based on all available information in order to obtain the best current estimate of the future payment. If this was not done, the firm would risk getting a very large gain or loss on the exercise date, when the actual payment occurs. The difference with equity-settled options is that they do not involve any payment from the firm to the option-holder. Instead, if exercised, equity-based options result in a payment (the exercise price) from the holder to the firm in exchange for shares.

To summarize, the objective of IFRS 2 is to correctly reflect resources consumed in the income statement, specifically services from employees. The objective is met through measuring the value of equity-settled stock options on the grant date (i.e., the date when the firm and the employee agree on the terms of the option contract). The measurement is not subsequently adjusted for changes in fair value of the option. It is then recognized over the vesting period (i.e. the period when the employee grants services to the firm). Since cash-settled options involve a future payment in cash, subsequent adjustments to fair value are necessary in order to avoid large gains and losses in the final period

IFRS 2 increases comparability between firms that pay salary to their employees and firms that use share-based renumeration to employees, which is arguably positive for accounting quality. A negative aspect is that the standard introduces substantial measurement uncertainty, as the measurement of non-standardized options is very subjective.

Apart from providing measures of resources paid for by equity instruments, an objective with IFRS 2 is to provide information regarding share-based compensation to top executives, as this may have implications for corporate governance (see Text Box 13.4).

Text Box 13.4 Research on the effects of share-based payment

The idea with share-based compensation to executives is to align the interests of owners and managers. However, as evidenced by the accounting scandals at the beginning of the 21st century, such compensation may also induce managers to opportunistically manage earnings and reporting in general to their own benefit. Research has provided some evidence on opportunistic behavior of managers maximizing their stock option compensation. For example, Aboody and Kasznik (2000) investigate whether CEOs manage the timing of bad or good news around stock option awards. Their findings suggest that managers indeed do opportunistically delay good news and reveal bad news in order to reduce the exercise price of options at the grant date and thereby boost the time value of their options in the future. Further evidence of earnings manipulation by managers with large share-based compensation is provided by Bergstresser and Philippon (2006) and Cheng and Warfield (2005). Such opportunistic behavior is clearly detrimental to financial reporting quality and may have a subsequent negative impact on firm valuation and the relevance of accounting information.

Research referred to above suggests the importance of providing information regarding share-based compensation in financial statements. Even if the amounts of compensation are often immaterial (cf. Text Box 13.3), the potential effect on corporate governance and managerial behavior make the compensations plans material for stock market investors. In an attempt to improve the transparency of incentive plans in public firms and to mitigate the potential conflicts of interest between shareholders and executives, legislators have adopted a wide range of governance regulations regarding the disclosure of remuneration of executives in listed firms, particularly with regard to equity incentive plans.

13.3 Other profit and loss items

In this final section, we raise three additional accounting areas that have been considered problematic and where accounting issues may be identified: government grants, foreign currencies and income taxes. The issues are further identified in each respective section, but in summary the main issues are:

- **Government grants:** How does a firm account for the fact that it receives resources without any corresponding consideration?
- **Foreign currency:** When firms have items and transactions in foreign currency changes in currency rates will result in gains and losses. When are such gains and losses recognized?
- **Income taxes:** How does a firm account for income taxes when financial reporting and taxation are based on different regulations?

13.3.1 Government grants

As shown in Figure 13.2, a basic assumption in accounting is that the external transactions of firms involve an exchange of items with equal value. Government grants represent an unusual type of transactions, as this basic assumption does not hold. Instead, firms receive resources from a government without giving up anything of equal value.

Accounting for government grants has not been discussed all that much in the last few years, and as such it is relatively uncontroversial. Still, we mention government grants briefly here in order to point out how such an unusual transaction may be reflected in financial statements. There are two views on how to recognize a government grant:

1. It is seen as income and should therefore be reported in the income statement.
2. It is seen as financing and should not be recognized in the income statement.

In IFRS, government grants are covered in IAS 20 *Accounting for Government Grants and Disclosure of Government Assistance.* IAS 20 takes the income view and makes a distinction between grants received to cover costs and those received to support the acquisition of assets. In the former case, the grants are recognized as income in the same period as the expenses covered by the grant are recognized. For grants received to acquire long-term assets, firms have a choice under IFRS. They can either be presented as deferred income (a liability) or as a reduction in the asset value. In the first case, the liability is recognized as income over time as the asset is depreciated. In the second case, the depreciation expense is reduced. Consequently, the net effect in the income statement is the same in the two cases, but the choice is potentially negative in terms of comparability. The effect of the government grant will appear in different items in the income statement depending on the firm's choice of method.

13.3.2 Foreign currency

Firms can have assets, liabilities, transactions and operations in currencies other than their reporting currency (called *foreign currency*). As currency exchange rates fluctuate, and assets and liabilities change value in the reporting currency, gains and losses ensue. Foreign currencies are relevant both to the income statement and the balance sheet. We have chosen to include this discussion in this chapter, as we focus on gains and losses. The central issue with foreign currencies from the preparer's point of view is which rate to use in subsequent measurement; in other words, this relates to SAS 3. The possible choices are to use historic or current exchange rates (i.e. it resembles the more general choice between historical cost and fair value). An overview of these issues is provided in Table 13.3.

In today's world of free and liquid currency markets, it may be difficult to imagine a world with fixed exchange rates. However, following World War II, the Bretton Woods agreement established more or less fixed exchange rates among developed economies. It was not until the termination of the agreement in the early 1970s that currencies became an important issue in accounting. Within Europe and the EU, there have been several attempts at minimizing currency movements, culminating in the introduction of the euro in 1999. While this has lessened the importance of currency issues inside the euro area, the issue remains on a global level.

In accounting, foreign currency has not been the subject of much discussion in the last few decades, with the exception of some technical details related to hedge accounting. Following the collapse of the Bretton Woods agreement, and the resulting increase in currency rate fluctuation, foreign currency translation was discussed in the 1970s and 1980s.

Table 13.3 Summary of issues relating to foreign currencies

Generic issue	Specific issue: Choices and judgments
SAS 3 (Unexpected changes in value)	For individual assets and liabilities (foreign currency transactions: Use current or historical rates? If current rates: Recognize gains/losses in profit and loss or OCI? Distinguish between different types of assets and liabilities (e.g., monetary and non-monetary)
	Foreign operations in group accounting (foreign currency translation): Use current or historical rates for each line item in financial statements? If current rates: Recognize gains/losses in profit and loss or OCI? Distinguish between different types of operations (e.g., independent and integrated)

Frequently, a distinction is made between issues involving **foreign currency transactions** and **foreign currency translation**. The former has to do with exchange rates for individual transactions and items, while the latter is about how to translate financial statements of foreign operations in the consolidated financial statements. In IFRS, foreign currencies are covered in IAS 21 *The Effects of Changes in Foreign Exchange Rates*. Regarding foreign currency transactions, IAS 21 requires that:

- Transactions are measured at the current exchange rate when the transaction is recognized in financial statements.
- Monetary items on the balance sheet are translated at the current exchange rate on the balance sheet date.
- Non-monetary items measured at historical cost are translated at the historic exchange rate.
- Non-monetary items measured at fair value are translated at the exchange rate on the date of the measurement.

Monetary items are those where the value is directly expressed in monetary terms, such as euro, US dollar or British pound. This includes liquid assets, receivables and payables. It makes sense to translate them at current exchange rates, since they are directly transferable into the home country currency. Non-monetary items, for example inventory and intangible assets, are translated at the exchange rate at the date when they were last measured. For items measured at historical cost, historical exchange rates are used. For items measured at fair value, the exchange rate at the measurement date (usually the balance sheet date) is used. The idea is obviously that the exchange rate at the measurement date provides the best reflection of the value of assets and liabilities in the home country currency. It should be noted that it is quite unusual that an exchange rate is needed in the measurement of non-monetary items. If, for example, a Swedish firm buys a machine from Germany, the machine is measured in Swedish krona at the time it is acquired, using the EUR/SEK exchange rate at the time. Subsequently, the machine is measured in Swedish krona on the balance sheet and the depreciation amount is recognized in Swedish krona in the income statement. It is only if the machine for some reason continues to be measured in euro that an exchange rate must be used. This could be the case if the Swedish firm has a branch in Germany where the machine is used and the German branch prepares financial statements in euro.

Foreign currency translation relates to group accounting and consolidation (see Chapter 14). When a group has subsidiaries that use a currency other than the currency used in the consolidated financial statements, the balance sheet and income statement of the subsidiary must be translated to the group's currency before consolidation can begin. Historically, two methods have been used: the **current method** and the **monetary/non-monetary method**. The current method implies that both assets and liabilities in the foreign subsidiary are translated at the current exchange rate (i.e., at the rate on the balance sheet date). The monetary/non-monetary method implies that monetary items are translated at the current rate and non-monetary items at the historic rate. As the reader notices, the latter method is the one used for foreign currency transactions. There is also a difference between the two methods regarding recognition of gains and losses. While gains and losses are recognized in profit and loss in the monetary/non-monetary method, they are recognized in other comprehensive income in the current method.

The items on the balance sheet that are translated using current exchange rates are exposed to currency fluctuations. As they are translated with updated rates, gains and losses may result in relation to those items. The items translated at historic rates do not give rise to foreign currency gains and losses, as they have constant rates. The two translation methods result in different net exposures, as shown in Figure 13.4.

What gives rise to foreign currency gains and losses is the net exposure. If there are both assets and liabilities in a foreign currency, gains and losses cancel out. Figure 13.4 highlights

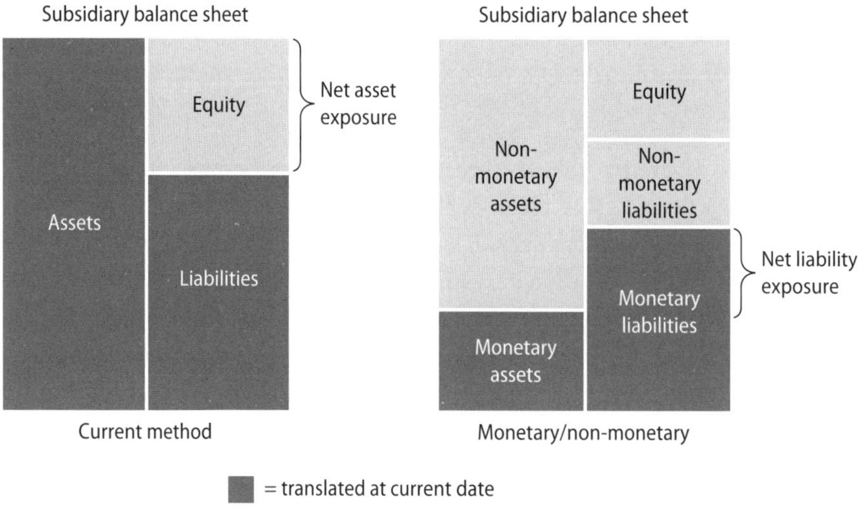

Figure 13.4 Foreign currency exposure

the net exposures. In most firms, assets are larger than liabilities (as equity is normally positive), meaning that the current method usually implies a net asset exposure. This means that when foreign currencies become more expensive, the firm has gains, and when foreign currencies become less expensive, the firm has losses. Meanwhile, most firms have more monetary liabilities than monetary assets. Therefore, the monetary/non-monetary method usually implies a net liability exposure. Therefore, the firm has losses when foreign currencies become more expensive and gains when they become less expensive.

In the 1970s and 1980s, there was a discussion regarding which method should be used. Generally, firms wanted the current method when their own currency declined and the monetary/non-monetary method when their own currency rose. In other words, firms wanted currency gains rather than losses.

Subsequently, both the IASB and the FASB settled on standards where both the current method and the monetary/non-monetary method may be used, depending on the relationship between the parent company and the foreign operation. In short, more independent operations are translated using the current method, while more integrated operations are translated using the monetary/non-monetary method. The distinction between independent and integrated operations is a matter of judgment, which can cause measurement uncertainty, especially as the financial statement effects of the two methods differ substantially. In practice, however, the current method dominates. As the method moves foreign currency gains and losses to OCI, this solution appears to be acceptable to preparers, as they do not have to show large gains and losses in the income statement.

The current standards relating to accounting for foreign currency in IFRS and US GAAP do not require much judgment on behalf of preparers. Still, there are potentially large effects on financial statements when currencies fluctuate, so the relevance of financial statements might be affected.

13.3.3 Income taxes

IFRS is based on the notion of a separation between financial reporting and taxation. As such, it may be surprising that there is an accounting standard on taxes (IAS 12 *Income Taxes*). However, the standard covers the recognition and measurement of the tax expense in the income statement and it has no relation to the calculation of taxable income.

The tax expense in the income statement has two components: *current tax* and *deferred tax*. Current tax represents the tax payable to tax authorities for the period. It is determined by the tax authorities and therefore does not represent a measurement issue in accounting. Deferred tax, however, is an accounting adjustment intended to provide a better reflection of the tax expense in relation to accounting income and it involves several measurement issues. These are summarized in Table 13.4.

The use of deferred income taxes is an interesting example of the trade-off between relevance and reliability. A relevant measure of deferred tax liability should probably consider both the probability of payment and the effect of discounting. However, IAS 12 is based on the idea that this would lead to too much measurement uncertainty. It is difficult to estimate which proportion of deferred taxes is likely to be paid. Discounting would require estimates of timing

Table 13.4 Summary of issues relating to income taxes

Generic issue	Specific issue: Choices and judgments
SAS 2 (Future outflow of resources)	Recognize a deferred tax liability? Adjust for probability of payment? Apply discounting? Which tax rate to use?
SAS 3 (Unexpected changes in value)	Update for changes in value or wait until realized?

of future taxes, which in many cases is very uncertain. The result is that the deferred tax liability is overstated in the balance sheet, which is confirmed by research (see, for instance, Amir et al., 1997; Laux, 2013). On the other hand, Gordon and Joos (2004) show that in the UK before IFRS, where managers only recognized the tax liabilities assumed to be paid, this discretion was used opportunistically. Consequently, the reduced discretion in IAS 12 also has benefits.

The reason for having a standard on income taxes is to attempt to estimate a "correct" tax expense in the income statement. Still, IAS 12 clearly takes a balance sheet approach. Changes in deferred tax liabilities drive deferred tax expenses and revenues in the income statement. Consequently, the overstatement of deferred tax liabilities affects the items on the income statement. It is perhaps not surprising that the focus in company valuation is often on an income statement number where income taxes are excluded, such as EBIT (Earnings Before Interest and Taxes), see chapter 15. Financial analysts often adjust the reported income statement in their valuation models by calculating their own estimated tax expense (or using taxes payable).

13.4 Conclusions

Profit and loss, which make up net income or the "bottom-line", are the main indicators of a firm's ability to create value and thus the focus of shareholders. Whereas some important accruals affecting the income statement, such as depreciation and impairment, were discussed in previous chapters in relation to assets and liabilities, two items that *directly* affect the income statement are revenue recognition and share-based payments.

The main issue concerning revenues is the timing of revenue recognition. The question is "When has the firm fulfilled its performance obligation?" or in accordance with some accounting frameworks, "When has the firm transferred key risks associated with the sale of goods or services to the buyer?" This is certainly a practical issue, but it has also represented a theoretically difficult issue. Recently, standard-setters have spent considerable effort attempting to make the criteria for revenue recognition more conceptually consistent. For example, rather than basing the definition of revenues on whether there has been a gross inflow of economic benefits, the definition in IFRS is now (conceptually) based on whether there have been changes in assets and liabilities (a balance sheet approach).

Share-based payment is also an accounting area that has been debated—the question being whether share-based compensation should be considered an expense at all from the perspective of the firm. The IASB and the FASB have arrived at the conclusion that it should, which has generated a number of new practical issues relating to the measurement of these expenses.

CHAPTER 14

Group accounting

Learning outcomes

Upon completion of this chapter, you will have gained insight into:

- Accounting issues related to group accounting, including scope of the entity and business combinations.
- The debate on group accounting in the last few decades, the main issues in the debate and the implications for accounting quality.
- Conceptual perspectives on group accounting —the owner perspective and the entity perspective and how these views are implemented into accounting policies.
- Item-specific research related to group accounting.

SO FAR WE HAVE FOCUSED on measurement (and to some extent recognition) of items in the incomes statement and the balance sheet. In this chapter, we shift our focus to another dimension: the **entity** represented in the financial statements. When financial statements are prepared for a single legal entity (such as a corporation), the entity is often well-defined. Difficulties involving the entity are instead associated with *group accounting* and the preparation of consolidated financial statements for groups of legal entities. The issues we identify may be classified into one of the following three categories: scope of consolidation, measurement in business combinations, and perspectives on group accounting.

Group accounting refers to the preparation of **consolidated financial statements** that show the combined activities of the companies in the group. In essence, a group consist of a **parent company** and *subsidiaries* over which the parent company has *control* (see Figure 14.1). The idea of group accounting is that parent company investors are not only interested in the parent company, but also in other entities controlled by the parent company. The **scope of the entity** (or the scope of consolidation) refers to the boundaries of the firm—and what should consequently be included in the consolidated financial statements. The significance of scope becomes apparent as we consider the main idea behind consolidated financial statements: to only show transactions and balances with parties that are *external to*

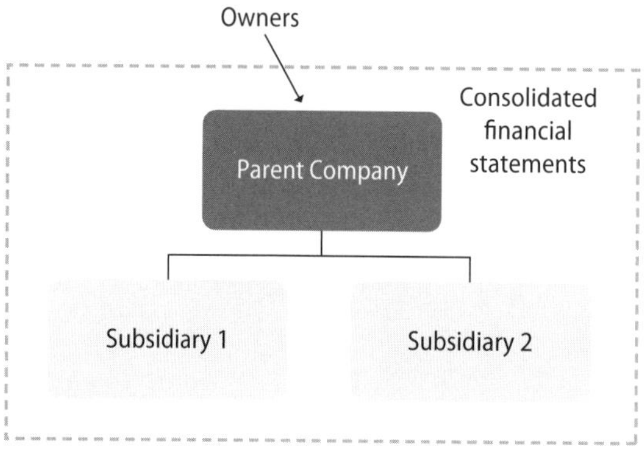

Figure 14.1
Group accounting

the group. Although some transactions and balances are external from the perspective of the parent company or the individual company, they may be internal from the perspective of the group—and should be eliminated.

With respect to business combinations (i.e, the forming of new groups through acquisitions of subsidiaries), these have been subject to much debate over the last few decades. Fundamental changes with regard to how business combinations are accounted for were introduced in the early 2000s in US GAAP and IFRS. In particular, we highlight issues associated with the accounting for goodwill and restructuring provisions. Additional changes—affecting, for example, stepwise acquisitions and disposals of subsidiaries—were introduced in 2008. The issues related to business combinations are essentially measurement issues, allowing us to refer to the stylized accrual situations (specifically SAS 1–3).[1]

Whereas issues concerning the determination of scope and the measurement of assets and liabilities in business combinations are of a practical kind (affecting preparers), an issue for standard-setters is which overarching perspective to take on group accounting. Depending on the chosen perspective, there will be different effects on the consolidated financial statements. This is because the definition of scope as well as measurement are dependent on the perspective. There are two main perspectives that may be applied to group accounting: the **owner perspective** and the **entity perspective**, each constituting a distinct conceptual view.

As shown in Figure 14.2, the owner perspective takes the perspective of the owners of the parent company, while the entity perspective takes the perspective of the consolidated entity itself. The difference between the two perspectives appears when the subsidiaries are not wholly owned. Then, there is a non-controlling interest in the subsidiaries (i.e. there are owners other than the owners of the parent company involved in the group). From the owner perspective, non-controlling interests are not considered owners. From the entity perspective, even non-controlling interests are considered owners. Over the last two decades, the IASB has increasingly moved from an owner to an entity perspective. This has an effect on, for example, the calculation of goodwill and other asset values in business combinations, the

1 Although there are issues unique to group accounting, the issues discussed in previous chapters are applicable to consolidated as well as individual financial statements (i.e., issues concerning the four Stylized Accrual Situations, the definitions of financial statement elements and the possible measurement bases).

measurement and presentation of non-controlling interest as well as stepwise acquisitions and disposals. We go through all these situations, including the effects of owner and entity perspectives, in the different sections below. As should be clear from the descriptions of the perspectives, the entity perspective does not mean that the IASB ignores owners as important users of financial statements. Instead, it means that when consolidated financial statements are produced, both controlling and non-controlling interests in subsidiaries are treated as owners.

Issues related to group accounting are summarized in Table 14.1.

Table 14.1 Summary of issues related to group accounting

Generic issue	Specific issue
Consolidation	Scope of the entity Structured entities Extent of control (incl. non-controlling interest) Elimination of internal transactions and balances
	Associates and joint arrangements Equity method or proportional consolidation?
Business combinations	Measurement of consideration (purchase price)
	Measurement of assets and liabilities in acquired entity Proportion applicable to non-controlling interest Restructuring provisions
	Treatment of goodwill
	Stepwise acquisitions

Note: the entity and owner perspectives affect the listed issues in different ways. Whereas most of these issues are practical (affecting preparers), whether to adopt and entity or owner perspective is a conceptual issue (affecting standard-setters).

There are several standards within IFRS that concern entity issues. IFRS 10 *Consolidation* covers the scope of the entity, the preparation of consolidated financial statements, as well as stepwise acquisitions and disposals. IAS 28 *Investments in Associates and Joint Ventures* and IFRS 11 *Joint Arrangements* cover accounting for associates and other joint arrangements, while IFRS 3 *Business Combinations* concerns acquisitions of subsidiaries. IAS 27 *Separate*

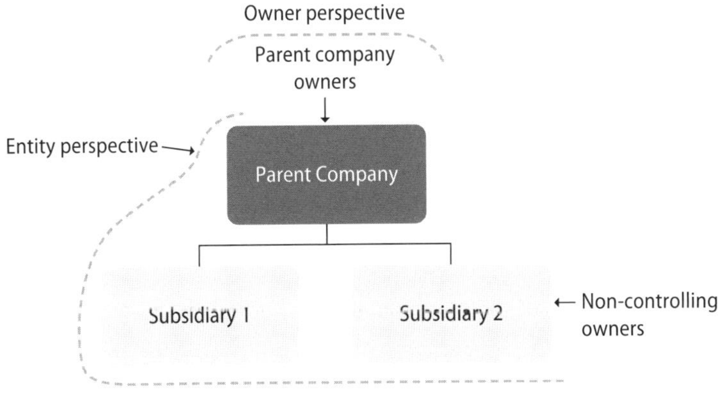

Figure 14.2
Perspectives on group accounting

Financial Statements sets requirements for parent companies' separate financial statements. Finally, IFRS 12 *Disclosure of Interest in Other Entities* regulates disclosures. Many of the recent IFRS—such as IFRS 9 *Financial Instruments*, IFRS 13 *Fair Value Measurement*, and a suite of standards related to consolidation (IFRS 10, IFRS 11 and IFRS 12)—have been issued in response to financial reporting problems noted in relation to the 2007–2008 financial crisis.

14.1 Consolidation

The consolidated income statement gives the parent company investors an overview of all the assets controlled—directly and indirectly—by the parent company, as well as all the liabilities (claims) against those assets. The income statement shows the revenues and expenses, and therefore the net income, that the owners of the parent company benefit from. The consolidated group of legal entities constitutes the **reporting entity** (see Text Box 14.1).

A basic idea regarding the financial statements of a reporting entity is that only external balances and transactions are reflected. Therefore, any balance or transaction between legal entities within the group must be *eliminated* in the preparation of consolidated financial statements. In practice, it is common that each legal entity prepares its own financial statements, the statements are then combined, and eliminations of internal balances and transactions are made afterwards (see Figure 14.3).

Text Box 14.1 Distinction between consolidated group and parent company

Volvo Group, the Swedish truck manufacturer, is an example of a consolidated reporting entity. The parent company, Volvo AB, has corporate functions and its main activity is ownership of its large subsidiaries. In 2016, Volvo AB had just over 300 employees and sales of SEK 625 million. Meanwhile, the group had around 95,000 employees and sales of over SEK 300 billion. The shareholders of Volvo AB are primarily interested in the activities of the subsidiaries and they use the consolidated financial statements—not the parent company financial statement—for making investment decisions.

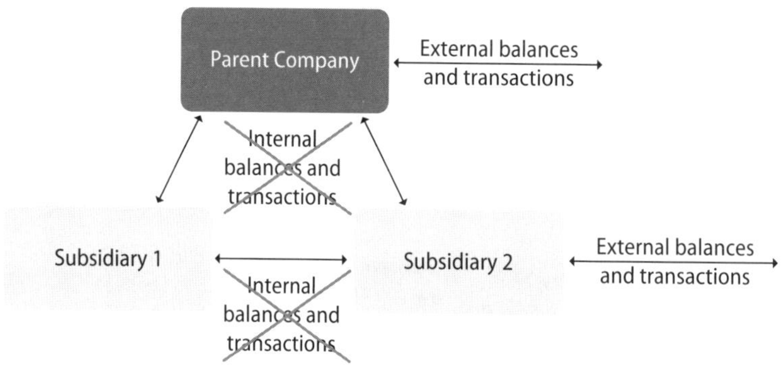

Figure 14.3
Consolidation

An internal balance that always needs to be eliminated is the parent company's ownership in the subsidiaries. Other common internal balances are receivables and payables, as well as loans and debt. Common internal transactions are sales of goods and services, interest revenue and expense and dividends from subsidiaries to the parent company. The elimination of internal balances and transactions are meant to reflect the situation as it would have been had the group been a single entity. In such a case, the internal balances and transactions would not have been recognized in financial statements. For example, the sale of goods from a subsidiary to the parent company is—from the group's perspective—merely a transfer of goods within the entity. As such, it does not generate any consolidated revenue or expense.

One could argue for the elimination of internal balances and transactions based on financial reporting conventions. There are, however, also arguments that such eliminations avoid problems of both *adverse selection* and *moral hazard*. Example 14.1 helps clarify this.

Example 14.1 **Effect of intra-group transactions**

Firm A owns 100% of Firm B. Firm A has an old car with a recorded value of EUR 1,000. The management of A wants to report higher earnings, so they decide to sell the car to B for EUR 11,000. As B is controlled by A, B has no choice but to accept the price of EUR 11,000, even if it seems very high. A reports a realized gain of EUR 10,000. In consolidated financial statements, this gain is eliminated, but without such an elimination A would overstate net income.

An example of adverse selection is when investors buy shares in A based on the overstated net income, while an example of moral hazard is when owners of a parent company distribute the profit from an asset sale as dividends, leaving debtholders with potential default.

14.1.1 Scope of the entity

In order to know which transactions and conditions should be eliminated, the scope of the (reporting) entity needs to be determined. This is essential in the preparation of consolidated financial statements, since only external transactions and balances should be reflected in these. If the scope of the entity is incorrectly defined, the financial statements will not provide a faithful representation of the underlying economics—what the parent company investors actually invest in and what accounting-based return they obtain from this investment. For example, if the parent company has transactions with companies over which it has control but are not identified as being a part of the group, it is possible for the parent company to overstate earnings. There are several famous examples of this (see Text Box 14.2), such as Prosolvia in Sweden and Enron in the US. In both cases, investors bought shares based on non-relevant information. The earnings had been overstated due to a failure to eliminate internal transactions.

Even if there have been some accounting scandals related to consolidation (based on the issue of scope), regulatory requirements regarding the elimination of internal balances and

Text Box 14.2 **Group accounting gone wrong—A tale of two failed companies**

Prosolvia in Sweden and Enron in the US constitute two examples of where scope of each respective entity was not appropriately defined. This prevented internal transactions from being eliminated and resulted in overstated earnings.

Prosolvia In the second half of the 1990s, investments in IT startups were very popular. The Swedish company Prosolvia developed software for interactive simulation. In 1997, it was listed on the Stockholm Stock Exchange and it reached a top market capitalization of SEK 4.7 billion. Considering that Prosolvia had limited sales and net income, this could be seen as a high value. As the market value was driven by future growth prospects, Prosolvia's management had strong incentives to show growth in sales and net income.

Prosolvia had subsidiaries where the parent company owned 50.5%. As the other owners had an option to buy 1% of the subsidiaries (which would lower Prosolvia's share to 49.5%), these subsidiaries were not consolidated. Consequently, sales to the subsidiaries were external transactions and thus included in Prosolvia's consolidated income statement.

In 1998, Prosolvia's consolidated financial statements were questioned, which later led to the company going bankrupt. Several court cases followed, which were not completed until 2013, when the accounting firm PwC agreed to pay 742 million SEK in a settlement with Prosolvia's creditors. This is the highest amount of damages ever paid in Sweden for accounting misconduct.

Enron The energy trading firm Enron was one of the fastest-growing large companies in the US during the second half of the 1990s. At the time, investors in high-growth firms were more interested in growth than in net income. Growth is measured in sales, so Enron's management had strong incentives to report higher growth. Partially, they achieved this by setting up unconsolidated structured entities. Transactions between the consolidated entity and the structured entities were conducted with the sole purpose of increasing sales.

In 2000, the last year for which Enron produced annual financial statements, Enron was the fourth largest listed company in the US based on sales. Meanwhile, its actual operations (measured for example by number of employees) was substantially smaller (Ball, 2009). In the fall of 2001, investors started suspecting that something was wrong in Enron's financial statements. Several financial reporting issues were discovered, of which overstated sales was one. In December 2001, Enron ceased operations.

Enron became the largest accounting scandal in the US in the last few decades and it had a significant impact. The US Congress passed the Sarbanes-Oxley Act in 2002, which strengthened the regulation of both the audit profession and corporate internal control systems. Arthur Andersen, the audit firm involved with Enron, was dissolved. As a result, the Big Five global accounting firms became the Big Four.

transactions have been uncontroversial and stable for a long time. The lack of controversy is reflected in IFRS 10. Even if the entire standard spans almost 60 pages, the elimination requirements are summarized in one sentence in an appendix. IFRS 10, paragraph B86(c) states that consolidated financial statements: "eliminate in full intragroup assets and liabilities, equity, income, expenses and cash flows relating to transactions between entities of the group." There is not much uncertainty on how to eliminate internal balances and transactions. Instead, the uncertainty relates to the issue of scope, which determines which balances and transactions are seen as internal.

14.1.2 Control

The concept of control is central in relation to the discussion regarding consolidation and scope. The underlying idea behind including a subsidiary is to show those assets over which the parent company (and its owners) has control (consistent with this idea, a subsidiary is defined as an entity over which the parent company has control).

As noted in Chapter 10, the definition of assets in the Conceptual Framework includes the term *control*. An entity has control of an economic resource if it has "the present ability to direct the use of the economic resource and obtain the economic benefits that may flow from it" (Par. 4.20). IFRS 10 mirrors this definition and has the following definition of control of an *investee* (subsidiary):

> An investor controls an investee when the investor is exposed, or has the rights, to variable returns from its involvement with the investee and has the ability to affect those returns through its power over the investee. (IFRS 10, Appendix A)

This definition combines two aspects: exposure to returns from the other entity and the power to manage (direct the activities of) the other entity. Control is frequently based on ownership, but the definition is not limited to this. There could be other circumstances forming the basis for control. In many cases, it is easy to establish control. For example, when a parent company owns 100% of the shares in another entity, it is usually unproblematic to establish control. Situations in which there is more uncertainty whether the investor has control include:

- There is an agreement regarding who has control that is not only based on ownership.
- The investor holds less than 50% of the shares in the investee, but some of the other investors do not participate in decision-making. This could lead to a situation of *de facto* control.
- There are potential shares—for example options—that are exercisable. The holder of the options could convert them into shares if important decisions are to be taken and thereby have *de facto* control over the investee. This setting has some similarities to the Prosolvia case, where Prosolvia argued that it had an existing agreement to transfer some of the shares.
- The investee is a structured entity where ownership and control are not necessarily aligned.

Over time, IFRS have moved toward an increased focus on actual control, rather than on legal ownership. This leads to more preparer judgment in determining the scope of the entity and possibly more uncertainty in financial statements. The focus on actual control is reflected in the Conceptual Framework published in 2018. It has a section on "reporting entity," where consolidated financial statements are defined as comprising resources (assets) and claims against resources (liabilities) that are both directly and indirectly controlled. The parent company has **direct control** over its own assets and liabilities and **indirect control** over assets and liabilities in subsidiaries.

There are cases where the parent company has control, but no interest in exercising this control. IFRS 10 identifies *investment entities* as such a case. An investment entity is a firm providing investment management services to outside investors with the objective of obtaining returns from capital appreciation and/or dividends, and it evaluates the performance of investments based on fair value. In accordance with IFRS 10, investment entities are not allowed to consolidate subsidiaries, but must instead measure them at fair value. The IASB argues that such accounting treatment results in more relevant financial statements for investment entities. It does, however, add uncertainty in the preparation of financial statements, as judgment is sometimes required to determine whether or not a firm is an investment entity.

An area of consolidation that has been subject to changes over the last few decades is that of **non-controlling interest** (NCI). This is sometimes referred to as **minority interest**. The background is that when the parent company has control of a subsidiary, it also has indirect control of the subsidiary's assets. Consequently, 100% of the subsidiary's assets, liabilities, revenues and expenses are included in consolidated financial statements. Meanwhile, the parent company can obtain control even with less than 100% ownership in the subsidiary. Normally, control is obtained when the parent owns more than 50%. In structured entities, the parent company may even have control with zero ownership (cf. section 14.1.3). Consequently, consolidated subsidiaries can have other owners apart from the parent company and the owners of the parent company. The interests of these other owners (NCI) need to be reflected in the consolidated financial statements (see Figure 14.4). NCI is shown separately on the balance sheet. As stated in the beginning of this chapter, there are (at least) two possible views that can be taken with regard to NCI. One view is that it is not equity, as it does not belong to the owners of the parent company. According to this perspective, it is a type of liability, as it involves rights to claimants outside the parent company owners. This is consistent with the *owner perspective*. Another possible view is that NCI is equity, as there are no contractual payments associated with NCI. As such, it helps stabilize the group during periods of poor performance. This view is consistent with the *entity perspective*. The treatment of NCI in the income statement corresponds to the balance sheet treatment. If NCI is not seen as equity, it is not included in net income, while it is included if it is considered equity.

The accounting treatment of NCI has changed over time, as the entity perspective has replaced the owner perspective. Today, IFRS takes a full entity perspective, so NCI is included in both equity on the balance sheet and in net income in the income statement. From the group's perspective, this provides a more faithful representation of the size of equity that may be used as a "cushion" during bad times. As such, the entity perspective is more relevant for the analysis of financial stability of the group. On the other hand, it is slightly more difficult for the parent company owners to discern their interest in subsidiaries, even if that information is still available in the form of disclosures.

There are possible alternative methods of consolidation. In *proportional consolidation*, the percentage of ownership is reflected in the amounts of assets (and liabilities, revenues and expenses) recognized in consolidated financial statements. The view in IFRS, and basically all other accounting regulatory frameworks, is that with parent company control follows full indirect control of 100% of assets (liabilities, revenues and expenses), so proportional consolidation is not relevant. Instead, 100% of assets, etc. are included in consolidated financial statements.

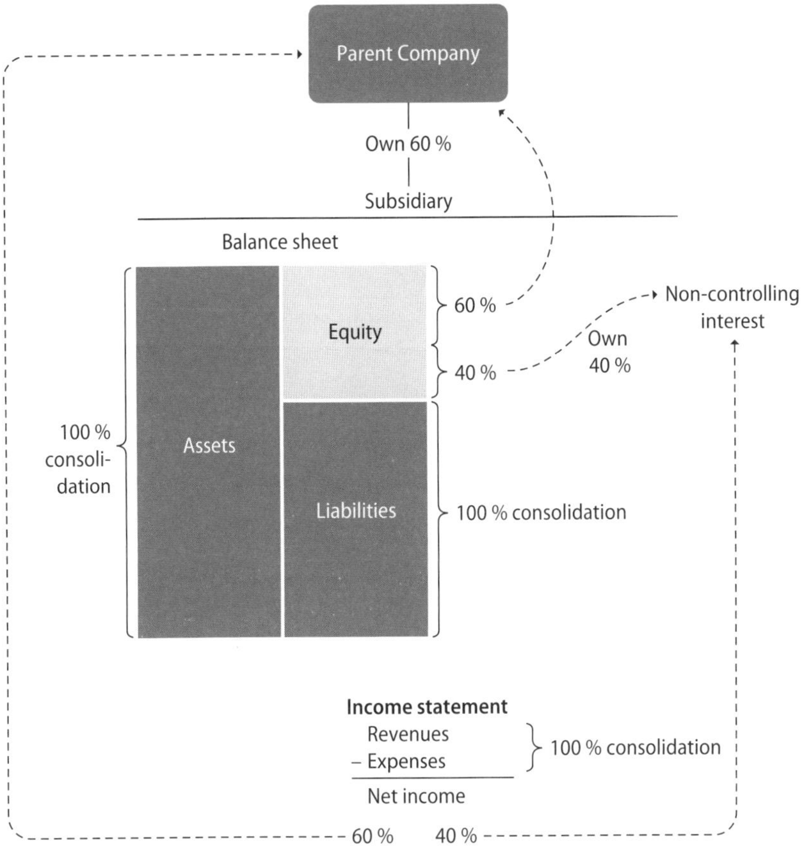

Figure 14.4 Non-controlling interests

14.1.3 Derecognition and structured entities

The scope of financial statements was discussed following the 2007–2008 financial crisis, especially in relation to so-called **structured entities** (SE).[2] These are legal entities where "normal" scope requirements are difficult to apply. During the financial crisis, the issue mostly revolved around derecognition of financial assets in connection with SE.[3] The issue relating to the reporting entity is that if structured entities are unconsolidated, assets transferred to such entities are derecognized in the consolidated financial statements. As a consequence, the exposure to credit risk in the assets is not apparent in the financial statements.

Following the financial crisis, the IASB has issued and amended several standards in order to remedy the situation. Disclosure requirements for transferred assets with continuing involvement were strengthened through an amendment to IFRS 7 *Financial Instruments: Disclosures*. The IASB issued IFRS 12 *Disclosure of Interests in Other Entities*, which requires disclosures of risks related to both consolidated and unconsolidated structured entities. The

2 Previously, structured entities were known as special purpose entities (SPE).

3 Although the issue of derecognition is not only part of group accounting, we include it in this chapter since it is closely related to the scope of the financial reporting entity (see also discussion in section 11.6).

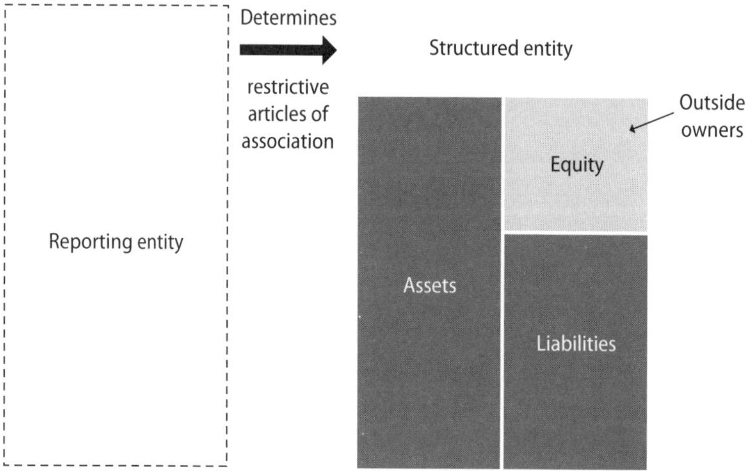

Figure 14.5 Structured entity

IASB also issued IFRS 10 to clarify scope requirements of group accounting in relation to structured entities.

A structured entity is defined in IFRS 12 as "[a]n entity has been designed so that voting rights or similar rights are not the dominant factor in deciding who controls the entity" (IFRS 12, Appendix A). In other words, control cannot be established through ownership. Structured entities are often set up to handle a very specific type of transaction. Examples of such transactions include acquiring mortgage loans and issuing collaterized debt obligations (recall the run-up to the financial crisis) and constructing and managing natural gas pipelines. Structured entities often have very restrictive articles of association, sometimes referred to as being managed on "autopilot." As such, the creator of the structured entity may have *de facto* substantive control, even if there are other investors who later take over the administrative control. Also, structured entities are normally set up in the interests of the organization taking the initiative to create the entity. Motivations for structured entities include a separation of certain activities so as to not expose the rest of the organization to unnecessary risks. Figure 14.5 provides an overview of the setup for a structured entity. Of course, if the structured entity is consolidated, any asset transferred to the entity remains in the consolidated balance sheet and no derecognition occurs. Both the FASB and the IASB strengthened scope requirements for structured entities after the financial crisis so that structured entities are more likely to be consolidated than before.

14.1.4 Associates and joint arrangements

Having discussed scope and control, we now consider different forms that the relationship between an investor and an investee may take. Two extreme cases are:

- The investor has full (100%) control of the investee, in which case the investee is a subsidiary.
- The investor has no or very limited influence, such as when an investor buys shares in a firm, but the holdings are so small that the investor has no real influence.

Between these two extreme cases, there are intermediate levels of control and influence:

- *Significant influence*: IAS 28 defines significant influence as "the power to participate in the financial and operating policy decisions of the investee but [...] not control" (Par. 3). Investees in which the investor has significant influence are called **associates**.
- *Joint control*: This implies that two or more investors have joint control over an investee. IAS 28 and IFRS 11 define this as having shared control, which requires unanimous consent for important decisions concerning the investee. An investment over which multiple parties have joint control is called a **joint arrangement**.

The presence of significant influence may be difficult to determine. A guideline traditionally used is that the investor has significant influence if it has 20% or more of the voting power in the investee. As more than 50% of the voting power corresponds to control, significant influence is normally present when voting power is in the 20–50% range. A typical situation of common control would be when two investors each have 50% of the voting power.

There are different possible accounting methods that *could* be used for associates and joint arrangements, including full consolidation, **proportional consolidation**, the **equity method**, fair value or historical cost. Full consolidation is rarely seen as relevant, as the investor does not have control of individual assets, liabilities, revenue, or expenses in the investee. Fair value or historical cost is likewise not particularly relevant in most cases, unless the firm is an investment entity (see section 14.1.2) that does not have any influence or does not exercise any control over the investee.

Instead, with respect to associates, the most common accounting method is the equity method, and it is also the method currently required in IFRS. The equity method is sometimes referred to as "one-line consolidation." In accordance with this method, the investor recognizes its share in the investee's equity as an asset in its balance sheet and its share in the investee's net income as revenue in the income statement. In other words, the investee is reflected in one line on the balance sheet and one line in the income statement (hence the term "one-line consolidation"). The effect on consolidated equity and net income is the same regardless of whether full consolidation or the equity method is applied. The difference is that the equity method implies that the assets, liabilities, revenues and expenses of the associate are not included in consolidated financial statements. This is logical, as the associate has no indirect control of the assets, liabilities, etc.

With respect to joint arrangements, it should first be pointed out that this is a relatively new term; these used to be referred to as **joint ventures**. Historically, the equity method has been used for joint ventures, with proportional consolidation as a voluntary alternative. The logic behind the equity method is that there is no (indirect) control of assets, liabilities, etc., as control of the investee is joint with one or more other entities. When applying proportional consolidation, a proportion of assets, liabilities, revenues and expenses are recognized in the consolidated financial statements. The proportion recognized corresponds to the ownership percentage. For example, if the investor (parent company) controls 50% of the investee (joint venture), 50% of the investee's assets (liabilities, revenues, expenses) are recognized. The logic behind proportional consolidation is that the investor has some control over the assets, liabilties, etc. (even if that control shared with another party).

The reader may be forgiven for not clearly seeing which choice—the equity method or proportional consolidation—-is more logical for joint arrangements. The IASB recognized this lack of clear logic and issued IFRS 11 *Joint Arrangements* in 2011. IFRS 11 makes a distinction between two types of joint arrangements:

- Joint venture
- Joint operation

In a joint venture, the investors have an interest in the equity of the joint arrangement; that is, the joint venture is a separate legal entity where the investors are residual claimants in the form of owners. In a joint operation, the investors have a direct interest in the *individual assets* of the joint arrangement (see Figure 14.6).

For a joint venture, it is logical to use the equity method, as the criteria for full consolidation are not met. For joint operations, the investors recognize their respective interests in the individual assets, liabilities, revenues, and expenses of the investee. Thus, joint operations are accounted for using a method that may resemble proportional consolidation. This means that in IFRS 11, the joint arrangement is accounted for in a way that is much more dependent on the actual contractual terms of the arrangement. This also means that IFRS 11 contributes to more relevant consolidated financial statements compared to a situation in which the equity method is always applied. However, this comes at a cost, as the preparation of financial statements becomes more complex and involves more judgment and uncertainty.

With respect to the owner versus entity perspective, this has no bearing on the accounting for associates and joint arrangements. However, as noted earlier, the two perspectives result in differences in consolidated financial statements when a non-controlling interest (NCI) is present in the reporting entity's financial statements. In other words, the perspective matters when the reporting entity has control over a subsidiary and there are other owners with

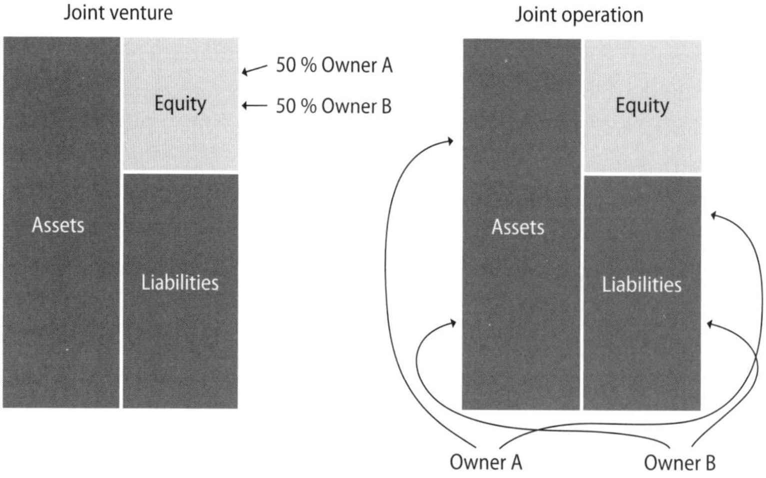

Figure 14.6 Two types of joint arrangements

less ability to control the subsidiary. By contrast, in cases where the investee is an associate or joint arrangement, the reporting entity does not have control[4], or has the same level of control as the other owners, and the perspectives are not applicable.

14.2 Business combinations

The term *business combinations* encompasses transactions where legal entities are combined into groups. This may take place either through a legal entity acquiring another entity or through a merger between two entities. In practice, the activities leading to business combinations are often referred to as **mergers and acquisitions (M&A)**. Business combinations can take many different forms. Examples include one company (parent) acquiring another company (subsidiary), thereby creating a group. It may also be an existing group of companies where the parent (or one of the subsidiaries) acquires a company or a group of companies, which leads to an expansion of the pre-existing group. A merger is a transaction where two more or less equal companies or groups decide to merge in order to form a larger group.

To facilitate the understanding of accounting for business combinations, we begin with an overview of IFRS 3. There are four steps one should go through in accordance with the standard.

- **Determine who the acquirer is**: In IFRS 3, no transaction is seen as a merger. Instead, one of the transacting parties is always seen as the acquirer and the other as the acquiree, and a business combination occurs when an acquirer obtains *control* of an acquiree.
- **Determine the transaction price** (i.e., what the acquirer pays for the acquiree): This could be easy if the transaction is based on a payment of liquid assets. However, this is often more difficult if payment is made in shares, especially if they are unlisted. Another challenge is if part of the payment is in the form of a contingent consideration, meaning the payment depends on future events. For example, it is common that additional payment is made if the acquiree meets certain profitability thresholds during a certain time period after the transaction. All components of the payment are measured at fair value. A contingent consideration requires estimating the probability of payment, which can be quite difficult and involve substantial measurement uncertainty.
- **Allocate the transaction price to assets (including goodwill) and liabilities**: The assumption in IFRS 3 is that there is an arms-length transaction and that both sides of the transaction have equal value. Therefore, the price represents the value of the acquiree on the transaction date. Meanwhile, as previously noted, consolidated financial statements should reflect the group as one single entity. From the group's perspective, the acquisition does not involve an entity, but instead a package of assets and liabilities. Logically, the assets and liabilities are measured at fair value on the date

4 In fact, the reporting entity may be an NCI if the associate is a subsidiary in another reporting entity.

of the transaction. If the transaction price exceeds the net of assets and liabilities, the excess is recognized as goodwill.

- **Determine the subsequent measurement of assets and liabilities in the acquiree**: In general, normal IFRS measurement methods are used, with some exceptions. For example, contingent liabilities are measured at fair value on the date of the transaction and are thus recognized. Unlike the normal method in IAS 37 (see Chapter 12), contingent liabilities acquired through a business combination continue to be recognized. If this special rule did not apply, all contingent liabilities would just be derecognized when the first consolidated balance sheet was issued after the business combination.

Following this overview of the process for accounting for business combinations, we now go through some different issues. Accounting for business combinations has for a long time been one of the most controversial areas. Traditionally, there has been a distinction between acquisitions and mergers, which creates uncertainty in how to determine what is an acquisition, and what is a merger. However, in practice most business combinations are acquisitions, and the most contentious issue has been the accounting treatment of *goodwill*. Whereas goodwill—-the most controversial item on the asset side of the balance sheet—is discussed in section 14.2.1, restructuring provisions—the most controversial item on the liability side of the balance sheet—is discussed in section 14.2.2.

14.2.1 Goodwill accounting

Goodwill is a summary term for non-identifiable intangible assets. These are assets that can have an economic value, but that do not meet the accounting definition of a reportable asset. Examples include a functioning organization, employee knowledge and so-called "synergy effects"[5]. In an acquisition, the payment the investor (parent) makes in order to acquire the investee (subsidiary) must be allocated to something in the consolidated financial statements. This is described in Example 14.2.

In subsequent consolidated balance sheets, something needs to be done with the goodwill. There are three main alternatives:

- Immediate elimination against equity. This reduces consolidated equity.
- Amortization over the expected useful life. In practice, the allowable useful life has historically varied between 5 and 40 years.
- Goodwill is measured at historical cost with no amortization. Instead, periodic impairment testing is performed.

5 Synergy effects represent cost savings that may be obtained through economies of scale when smaller entities are combined into larger ones

Example 14.2 **Allocation of transaction price**

Company A acquires company B for TEUR 1,000. On the date of the acquisition, company B has the following balance sheet:

Subsidiary balance sheet

TEUR	
Non-current assets	1,200
Current assets	750
Total assets	1,950
Equity	500
Liabilities	1,450
Total equity & liab.	1,950

Company A pays TEUR 500 more than the book value of company B. Let us assume that this amount represents non-identifiable assets, such as a functioning organization and well-educated staff. Hence, the TEUR 500 surplus represents goodwill.

In the parent company, the transaction results in an asset on the balance sheet—shares in subsidiaries—measured at TEUR 1,000 (i.e. at historical cost). In the preparation of a consolidated balance sheet, this item is considered an internal balance and must therefore be eliminated. The elimination of the parent company's asset is done through a credit of TEUR 1,000. To maintain the balance equation (assets = liabilities + equity), a debit of TEUR 1,000 must be recorded. TEUR 500 is debited against the subsidiary's equity and TEUR 500 is debited to goodwill (see worksheet below).

Consolidation work sheet for balance sheet

TEUR	Parent	Subsid.	Elim.	Consol.
Shares in subsidiary	1,000		-1,000	0
Non-current assets	3,400	1,200		4,600
Goodwill			500	500
Current assets	2,100	750		2,850
Total assets	6,500	1,950	-500	7,950
Equity	3150	500	-500	3,150
Liabilities	3,350	1,450		4,800
Total equity & liab.	6,500	1,950	-500	7,950

In the consolidated balance sheet, both the parent company's asset shares in subsidiaries and the subsidiary's equity are removed. Further, a goodwill asset of TEUR 500 is included.

All three alternatives are problematic, but in different ways. Immediate elimination against consolidated equity can result in negative equity if the entity includes business combinations with large goodwill amounts, and firms normally want to avoid reporting negative equity. Amortization of goodwill over time may seem like a reasonable alternative. However, an amortization period must be determined and goodwill has no apparent useful life. In addition, research has shown that goodwill amortization has little relevance for financial statement users (Henning et al., 2000). Replacing amortization with more systematic impairment tests has the disadvantage of impairment testing by default being based on judgment and thus involving substantial uncertainty (see discussion concerning goodwill in Chapter 11).

One reason why accounting for business combinations has been so controversial is that it is commonly believed to affect real firm behavior through managerial incentives. The incentives come from different effects on earnings after the transaction. The three methods of accounting for goodwill differ in terms of impact on earnings, since they differ as to how goodwill is recognized as an expense. When goodwill is eliminated immediately, there is never any expense from goodwill, so earnings after the transaction are high. Also, return on equity can be even higher, as the numerator (earnings) is high while the denominator (equity) is low. Amortization results in systematic recognition of expenses and lower earnings. This effect becomes stronger the shorter the amortization period. If there is no amortization, there are no systematic expenses and, consequently, higher earnings. Instead, the expenses become concentrated in a few periods, when impairment is recognized.

In general, CEOs of acquiring firms want to report high earnings after the acquisition in order to show financial statement users that the decision to acquire an entity was the right one (resulting in high post-acquisition earnings). Consequently, management prefers not to carry out any amortization and if amortization is carried out, a longer time period is preferred. These incentives have driven the debate on goodwill accounting (see Text Box 14.3).

Currently, the measurement of goodwill at historical cost, with no amortization but annual impairment testing, is the global standard (and the requirements in IFRS 3, see Text Box 14.3). However, this has been debated for both conceptual and practical reasons. Both the FASB and the IASB argued that no amortization and impairment provides more relevant information compared to systematic amortization. There is a possible deterioration in relevance in the few cases in which a true economic merger takes place and *pooling* (see Text Box 14.3) would be appropriate (leading to no goodwill being recognized), but this must be weighed against the reduced room for incentives in acquisition cases.

Standard-setters argue that goodwill has no apparent decline in value over time, which is why there is weak conceptual motivation for amortization. Instead, a decline in value through impairment only makes sense when an economic decline has occurred. An argument against this view is that it mixes acquired and internally generated goodwill. When goodwill is acquired, it has a value that is equal to cost. Over time, it retains this value only if the firm makes reinvestments in the business. So, over time, acquired goodwill is replaced by internally generated goodwill. Amortization reflects the decline in value of the acquired portion of goodwill, while internally generated goodwill is not recognized. This is consistent with the general view in IAS 38 *Intangible Assets*. It is, of course, possible to argue that as long as goodwill is maintained at a certain level, it is relevant to show the unamortized value

Text Box 14.3 **Accounting for goodwill**

In the 1980s there was a high activity in mergers and acquisition. At the time, the UK allowed firms to eliminate goodwill against equity, the US required amortization with a maximum amortization period of 40 years, while Sweden required amortization over no more than 10 years. US firms argued that UK firms had an advantage in business combinations and that UK firms could pay higher prices as they did not recognize any goodwill-related expenses following acquisitions. In Sweden, the argument was that Swedish firms had a competitive disadvantage in business combinations compared to US firms, as the shorter Swedish amortization period resulted in lower earnings. By the 1990s, some Swedish firms started using 40-year amortization for acquisitions in the US, arguing that such a long period better reflected the economic environment in the US.

In the second half of the 1990s, the merger and acquisition activity was once again high in both Europe and in the US, coinciding with the growth of IT firms. Many of the transactions involved high tech companies with substantial goodwill amounts. At the time, mergers could be accounted for using the *pooling* method, which resulted in no goodwill being recognized. For acquisitions, the *purchase* method was required, where goodwill is reported (and amortized). The high goodwill amounts gave firms a very strong incentive to classify transactions as mergers rather than acquisitions. Even though true mergers are rare in practice, at the time, 30–40% of business combinations by US firms applied the pooling method.

The FASB saw this as a problem and decided that only the purchase method should be allowed in US GAAP. The argument was that almost all business combinations are acquisitions and that even in cases with characteristics of a merger, it is possible to identify an acquirer. Meanwhile, goodwill should not be amortized but tested for impairment annually. This accounting treatment became mandatory in US GAAP in 2001 and 2002. With the aim of achieving harmonization between IFRS and US GAAP, the IASB promulgated similar requirements with the issuance of IFRS 3, which became mandatory in 2005.

on the balance sheet. Whether it leads to a faithful representation (in the sense that financial statements show what they purport to reflect) of goodwill depends on what users expect. If users expect to see only acquired goodwill in the balance sheet, it would make sense to amortize it over time.

A common belief was that the FASB had a weak conceptual basis for the new way of accounting for business combinations. They proposed it as a concession to preparers, to make them accept the removal of the pooling method. The new method has the same effect as pooling in that no expenses are recognized for goodwill (as long as there is no impairment). The IASB followed the FASB since there at the time was a strong desire to achieve convergence between IFRS and US GAAP, following the Norwalk Agreement signed in 2002 (see Chapter 4).

A more practice-oriented argument against IFRS 3 is that it creates a very high level of uncertainty. It is claimed to be unenforceable and to leave substantial discretion with preparers (Jarva, 2009). One could certainly argue that the removal of a possible accounting method (pooling) leads to reduced opportunities for discretionary choices. However, the impairment test of goodwill is highly judgment-based and research has shown that management has substantial discretion over when to recognize an impairment (Hayn and Hughes, 2006).

Delayed impairment, for instace, can lead to high goodwill amounts on the balance sheet and reduce the relevance of the financial statements (cf. Figure 11.3 in Chapter 11).

Another feature of IFRS 3 is that it strengthened the requirements to measure identifiable assets (including intangible assets) at fair value at the time of acquisition. If this is done correctly, goodwill should be smaller. For example, it used to be common that goodwill contained both brand names and customer relations. IFRS 3 requires that such assets be identified separately from goodwill, which should reduce the goodwill amount. However, it appears as if in practice, the recognition of identifiable assets varies substantially (Rehnberg, 2012) and the identification seems to be affected by managerial incentives (Shalev et al., 2013). Some firms seem to apply IFRS 3 as intended, while others do not. There is an incentive to allocate as much as possible to goodwill, since goodwill is not amortized while most identifiable assets are. Post-acquisition earnings are therefore higher if a larger portion of the purchase price is allocated to goodwill.

In summary, there are two separate instances of high uncertainty in IFRS 3: 1) in the recognition of identifiable assets, and 2) in the impairment testing of goodwill. Due to the criticism of IFRS 3, and the uncertainty it creates in financial statements, the IASB currently has a research project looking into whether the standard should be revised.

Apart from goodwill, there are some additional issues that arise in business combinations, which we mention briefly here. These include common control transactions, restructuring provisions, non-controlling interest and stepwise acquisitions and disposals.

14.2.2 Restructuring provisions

One area where managerial discretion decreased with the introduction of IFRS 3 is that which relates to restructuring provisions. Earlier, it was common to set up restructuring provisions as part of a business combination. The idea is that acquirers often make plans for a restructuring to integrate the acquiree into the group, and a provision may be recognized to be used against future restructuring costs. This adds an additional liability and in order for the consolidated balance sheet to balance, a corresponding asset must be recognized. Since goodwill is measured as a residual, goodwill will increase in order to balance the provision.

The problem with restructuring provisions in business combinations is that there are strong managerial incentives to overstate them. When the provisions are derecognized in subsequent periods, expenses are reduced, leading to higher net income. This was previously balanced against higher goodwill amortization (as the initial goodwill amount was higher). However, restructuring provisions were removed in the first few years, while goodwill was amortized over long time periods, so the positive effects of provisions dominated negative goodwill effects. This provided strong incentives, as the first few years after a business combination are the most important in the assessment of its success and, consequently, the assessment of management.

The incentive to overstate restructuring provisions became even stronger when goodwill amortizations ceased. In the 2000s, both the FASB and the IASB disallowed the use of such provisions in business combinations. The conceptual argument is that the business combination is not an obligating event, and hence no restructuring provisions can be recognized as part of the transaction. Provisions can be recognized after the transaction, but then they result in expenses (and lower earnings) in the consolidated financial statements, thus reducing the incentive for such subsequent recognition. Note that restructuring provisions in situations other than business combinations are allowed, as discussed in Chapter 12.

14.2.3 Non-controlling interest

As noted in section 14.1.2, control may be obtained with less than 100% ownership, resulting in non-controlling interest (NCI). The acquiree as well as the NCI may be measured in two different ways in a business combination, depending on the adopted perspective:

- According to the owner perspective (where the focus is on the owners of the parent company), only the *parent* company has made a transaction that warrants remeasurement of the acquiree's assets and liabilities. In that case, only the proportion acquired by the parent company is remeasured at fair value and the proportion owned by the NCI is measured at the acquiree's (subsidiary's) reported value.
- According to the entity perspective (where the focus is on the group itself and different owner groups are seen as more or less equal) the transaction resulting in a business combination is a good basis for the *group's* (entity's) remeasurement of the acquiree's assets and liabilities. Then, 100% of the subsidiary is remeasured at fair value.

Example 14.3 shows the distinction between the two perspectives.

Example 14.3 **Owner and entity perspectives in business combinations**

Firm A acquires 60% of Firm B for TEUR 1500. At the time of acquisition, Firm B has the following balance sheet.

TEUR	
Real estate	2,000
Other non-current assets	800
Current assets	350
Total assets	3,150
Equity	1,750
Liabilities	1,400
Total equity & liab.	3,150

The due diligence of Firm B shows that the fair value of the real estate is TEUR 2,750. For all other assets and liabilities, fair values agree with reported values. The following measures of the real estate of Firm B will be included in the consolidated balance sheet immediately following the acquisition in accordance with the owner and the entity perspective (deferred taxes are ignored).

Owner perspective: Only the proportion of real estate acquired by the parent company is remeasured at fair value. The full difference between fair value and reported value is TEUR 750. Sixty percent of TEUR 750 is TEUR 450. Consequently, real estate is measured at TEUR 2,450 in the consolidated balance sheet.

Entity perspective: Here the full fair value is recognized, even if 40% is attributable to non-controlling interest. Consequently, the real estate is measured at TEUR 2,750 in the consolidated balance sheet.

IFRS 3 adopts an entity perspective, so 100% of acquirees' assets and liabilities are measured at fair value on the date of the transaction. Goodwill, however, is an exception. IFRS 3 gives firms a choice, where they may either recognize only the parent company's share of goodwill or the full goodwill amount. The reason for this choice is that full goodwill could be difficult to measure. It is not always the case that the value of the NCI's share of goodwill is proportional to the value of the parent company's share. Often, the parent company's share is proportionally more valuable, since it includes a **control premium**. Investors see a value in having control of a firm that goes beyond the proportional value of the future cash flows of the firm.

14.2.4 Stepwise acquisition and disposal

Related to the issue of NCI is stepwise acquisition. A stepwise acquisition is when different parts of a subsidiary are acquired at different points in time. There are two different ways of accounting for stepwise acquisitions. One approach is to account for each transaction separately and then add them up. This is consistent with remeasurement of a proportion of the acquiree's assets and liabilities. For example, a firm acquires 60% of another firm in year 1 and 20% in year 3. In accordance with separate accounting for each transaction, 60% of assets and liabilities are remeasured at fair value in year 1 and 20% are remeasured in year 3. As a consequence, the subsidiary's assets and liabilities have three values: the fair value in year 1, the fair value in year 3 and the subsidiary's own historical cost (the remaining 20%). This accounting treatment is consistent with the owner perspective.

Another approach is to focus on when control is obtained and remeasure 100% of assets and liabilities at that time (cf. the entity perspective in the example in the previous section). Using the current example, that would mean that 100% of assets and liabilities are remeasured in year 1. There is no additional remeasurement in year 3 and there is no proportion of assets and liabilities measured at the subsidiary's historical cost. This accounting treatment is consistent with the entity perspective and it is required in accordance with IFRS 3. Based on this perspective, the acquisition of 20% in year 3 is a transaction between different owner groups and it does not result in any changes to asset and liability values. Instead, it is treated as changes in the equity portion of the balance sheet. An overview of the different transactions is provided in Figure 14.7.

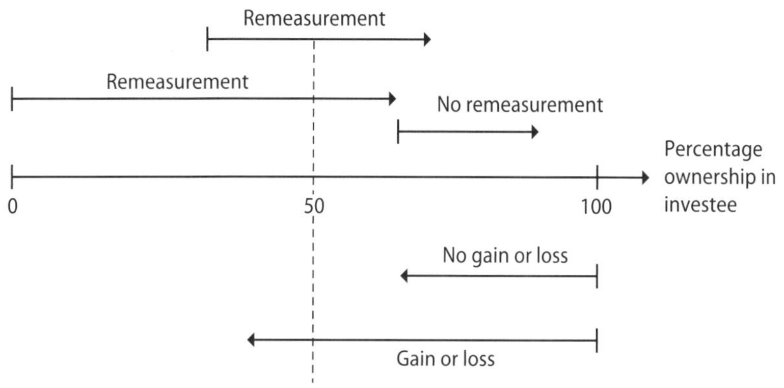

Figure 14.7 Stepwise acquisition and disposal

Two analogous views exist with respect to stepwise disposals. One view is that each disposal is seen as a separate transaction, where gains or losses applicable to parent company owners accrue separately in each transaction. The other view is that when control is lost, the group may have gains or losses, but there are no effects before that.

IFRS 3 adopts a clear entity perspective, and gain and loss of control—rather than individual transactions—are seen as crucial events (resulting in the recognition of gains and losses in the consolidated income statement). Note that a gain or loss of control may even occur without any transaction taking place. It may be the result of agreements between different owners, statements by regulators or courts, or other types of events such as bankruptcy or political developments. In accordance with IFRS 3, assets and liabilities are remeasured when control is obtained and gains and losses are recognized when control is lost, regardless of the cause.

14.2.5 Common control transactions

Finally, we bring up one more issue related to business combinations, and that is common control transactions. A **common control transaction** is one that takes place between two companies that are under common control (see Figure 14.8). The owner of the transacting companies may "move" or shift the ownership of a subsidiary for taxation purposes. That

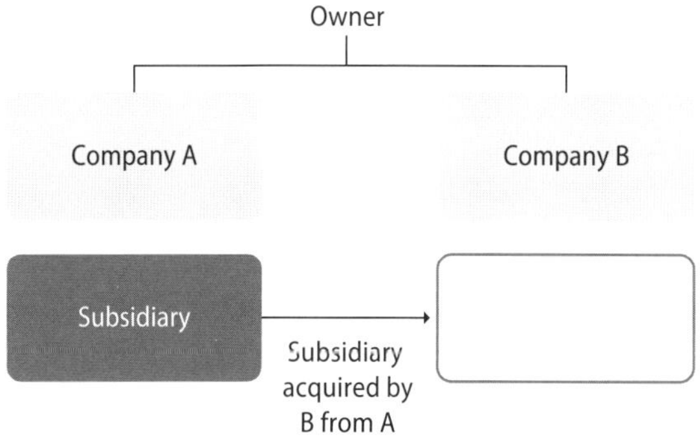

Figure 14.8 Common control transaction

is, reducing taxes may be more important than paying the fair value for the entity. As noted above, an assumption in IFRS 3 is that the transaction price represents the fair value of the business acquired. This assumption is reasonable if there is an arm's-length transaction between two independent parties. In a common control transaction, this assumption does not hold.

The scope of IFRS 3 excludes common control transactions. As the basic assumption concerning the value of the transaction does not hold, the application of IFRS 3 to such transactions does not make sense. Currently, there is no IFRS that applies to common control transactions, so it is one of a few areas not regulated in IFRS. However, the IASB is currently (August 2018) in the early stages of a project to develop standards in this area.

14.3 Conclusions

Group accounting and the preparation of consolidated financial statements introduces several difficulties for firms, not least of which is determining the scope of consolidation. If internal balances are not eliminated, the financial statements will not faithfully represent underlying economics. Depending also on the amount of control exercised over the investee (e.g., whether there is 100% control, significant influence, joint control, or no control), there are different considerations to be made. In theory, there are primarily five different ways of including an investment or the conditions and transactions of an investee in the financial statements: full consolidation, proportional consolidation, the equity method, fair value or historical cost.

Issues in the context of business combinations are primarily related to goodwill accounting, restructuring provisions, non-controlling interests and stepwise acquisitions. The two perspectives lead to different accounting treatments for business combinations when there is less than 100% ownership in a subsidiary (see Table 14.2).

Table 14.2 Owner perspective and entity perspective

Situation	Owner perspective	Entity perspective
NCI in consolidation	Equity and net income do not include NCI	Equity and net income include NCI
Remeasurement of assets and liabilities in business combinations	Only parent's share is remeasured	100% of assets and liabilities are remeasured
Stepwise acquisitions and disposals	Each transaction is accounted for separately	Gain and loss of control are the key events resulting in remeasurement

CHAPTER 15

Presentation format and disclosure

Learning outcomes

Upon completion of this chapter, you will have gained insight into:

- Presentation issues that affect the income statement and the balance sheet, and what is known regarding the effect of presentation issues on users.
- Time series properties of financial statements when accounting policies or estimates change.
- Issues related to disclosures in financial statements, including motivations for disclosures, regulation of disclosures, and their usefulness.
- Research on presentation format and disclosure in financial statements.

IN THIS CHAPTER, WE GO BEYOND measurement in the income statement and the balance sheet (including measurement in group accounts) and start discussing broader communicative aspects of financial statements. Here we cover presentation format, time series aspects of financial statements, and disclosure.

In Chapter 10, we mentioned the three "activities" of financial statement preparation: recognition, measurement and disclosure. In the previous chapters in Part V, we mostly focus on measurement, with some discussion of recognition (and derecognition). Presentation format is related to recognition in that all recognized items must be classified into one or several specific line items on the income statement and/or balance sheet. Disclosure is related to recognition and measurement in several ways. First, with regard to economic events and transactions that do not meet the criteria for recognition, disclosure is an alternative. Second, disclosures often relate to and provide additional information regarding recognized items. Third, disclosure may be used as a way of compensating high measurement uncertainty in recognized items.

In economic research on information asymmetry and the efficient market hypothesis (see Chapters 2 and 3), access to information is often seen as binary. In other words, a piece of information is either (publicly) known or not known. This view is also reflected in much of disclosure research (Chapter 6). An effect of such a view is that the mode of presentation of an information item does not affect the user of the information. Modes of presentation include whether information is provided in the primary financial statements or in the notes (i.e., whether or not an item is recognized) or if it is for instance presented in profit and loss or in OCI. More recently, behavioral economists have attempted to model the communicative aspects of information in the financial statements, thus going beyond the simplistic assumption that the *how*—not just the *what*—matters when it comes to corporate information. There is also a growing body of empirical literature looking at the effects of such aspects.

Currently, standard-setters such as the IASB are discussing how to improve the communicative aspect of financial statements. This includes both financial statement presentation and disclosures. In a Discussion Paper on principles of disclosures (DP/2017/1), the IASB suggests that principles of effective communication mean that the information should be (paragraph 2.6):

- Entity-specific
- Described in a simple and direct way
- Organized to highlight important matters
- Linked to other information in the financial statements
- Not duplicated
- Comparable
- Provided in an appropriate format

The current overall standard in the area of presentation format and disclosure is IAS 1 *Presentation of Financial Statements*. Time series properties are primarily covered in IAS 8 *Accounting Policies, Changes in Accounting Estimates and Errors* for firms using IFRS, and in IFRS 1 *First-Time Adoption of International Financial Reporting Standards* for firms adopting IFRS. Disclosure requirements—and rules for what to include in OCI—are spread over a large number of standards. We mention some of these standards in the different sections below.

15.1 Definitions and summary of issues

Before we discuss substantial presentation and disclosure issues, we provide an overview of financial statements and other types of information in annual reports. As noted in Chapter 1, the information environment includes a broad set of information concerning firms. Information provided by firms may be both regulated and non-regulated. In this chapter, we focus on regulated information, as this is defined in accounting standards.

Comprehensive regulated accounting information is often found in *annual reports*, with a shorter version in *interim reports* (e.g., quarterly). Regulated information is also found in *prospectuses* firms publish before they issue shares (e.g., initial public offerings, IPO). In some countries—and for some industries—there is additional regulated information that must be submitted to authorities. In the US, all listed firms must submit financial information to the SEC. They must submit a so-called 10-K annually (which is an annual report, with some additional information) and a 10-Q quarterly (similar to a quarterly report, with additional information). In research, these documents are beneficial, both because they are made public by the SEC and because they have a somewhat standardized structure. In banking and insurance, all firms must submit substantial amounts of disclosures to authorities, but the public availability of these disclosures varies. In many European countries, including Sweden, all limited liability companies must submit annual reports to authorities and these reports are public. This facilitates research on non-public entities in countries such as Sweden.

The regulated parts of reports are often referred to as **financial statements**. IAS 1 defines the following five financial statements:

- **Statement of financial position**. In this book, we often refer to this statement as the *balance sheet*. In US GAAP, both terms are used.
- **Statement of profit or loss and other comprehensive income**. US GAAP uses the term income statement. In contrast, we usually use the term *income statement* to refer to the profit and loss section, which shows net income, and the acronym OCI to refer to the rest of the statement. Together, net income and other comprehensive income (OCI), make up (total) **comprehensive income (CI)**.
- **Statement of changes in equity**. In US GAAP this is called *statement of changes in stockholders' equity*.
- **Statement of cash flows**.
- **Notes**. These are alternatively referred to as supplementary notes, or footnote disclosures under US GAAP. They constitute additional quantitative and qualitative information and may contain both regulated (mandatory) and unregulated (voluntary) disclosures.

In addition to the five financial statements, most accounting reports contain additional information, both mandatory and voluntary. Many firms provide a CEO letter to shareholders and most listed firms have a *management discussion and analysis* (MD&A). An MD&A is not required in IFRS, but it is for instance required for Swedish firms in accordance with company law. Company law in many countries also requires additional information (e.g., concerning corporate governance or sustainability), at least for the largest firms. Such additional information is discussed further in section 6.2.

The first four financial statements listed above are often referred to as **primary financial statements** to distinguish them from the notes. As noted above, the term "disclosure" is used with different meanings in different contexts. In research it is used in a broad sense to include all information provided to financial statement users, even, for example, earnings. In regulation, disclosure is used to refer to information provided outside the primary financial statements (i.e., in the notes).

With respect to presentation format and disclosure, we identify a number of issues and present them in Table 15.1. Most of these issues are conceptual, and are therefore issues that standard-setters face (not preparers).

The five financial statements are discussed in different sections in this chapter. Sections 15.2 and 15.3 relate to primary financial statements, while notes are covered in section 15.4.

Table 15.1 Summary of issues relating to presentation format and disclosure

Generic issue	Specific issue: Choices and judgments
Presentation	Format of balance sheet? Show operating and financing items? Show current and non-current items?
	Format of income statement? Show operating and financing items? Non-GAAP measures? OCI and extraordinary items?
	Format of cash flow statement? Show operating and financing items?
Time-series aspects	Reflect changes in accounting policies and estimates? Retrospective or prospective application?
	Reflect changes due to discontinued operations?
	Interim reporting? How much information to provide? How manage interaction effects between interim and annual statements?
	Reflect information after the accounting period?
Mandatory disclosure	Mandatory or voluntary?
	Over-regulation, information overload, materiality and boilerplate disclosures
	Disclosure or recognition?

15.2 Financial statement format

Issues related to the format of primary financial statements include classification and which items are shown separately. In this area, a standard-setter must balance two different considerations regarding the level of standardization. A low level of standardization allows firms to properly reflect their own specific situation. A high level of standardization, on the other hand, facilitates users' comparisons between different firms. The trade-off is similar to the general distinction between principles-based and rules-based accounting standards (cf. section 4.5). IFRS—in line with being a principles-based framework—has a relatively low level of standardization regarding financial statement format.

Below we go through some formatting issues related to the primary financial statements. The IASB currently (August 2018) has an ongoing project on primary financial statements, so their format may change in the future.

15.2.1 Balance sheet and statement of changes in equity

The balance sheet includes three types of items: assets, liabilities and equity. Currently, the dominating format is to show assets on one side and liabilities and equity on the other side. The two sides always balance. The conceptual logic of this format is that assets used for production are shown on one side, and claims from capital providers (both lenders and owners) are shown on the other side. An alternative format is to show assets minus liabilities and have equity as the residual. Such a format takes a clearer owner perspective, with equity as the "bottom line." Accordingly, the balance sheet has a format resembling the income statement format (where the owners' interest in earnings, net income, is shown as the bottom line). Another alternative is a combination of the former two, consisting in separating assets and liabilities that pertain to operating and financing activities, and netting the assets and liabilities for each type. On one side of the balance sheet, one shows net operating assets (operating assets–operating liabilities). On the other side, one shows equity and net financial liabilities (financial liabilities—financial assets). The purpose of this is to highlight the business on the one hand (the operating activities) and the financing activities on the other. When doing a fundamental analysis of a firm and its financial statements (cf. Chapter 3), analysts can benefit from such a classification and therefore carry out a reformulation of GAAP statements prepared according to the first alternative described here. The three formats are presented in Figure 15.1.

Another format difference is whether assets (liabilities) are shown in descending or increasing order of liquidity. In the EU, increasing order of liquidity tends to be used, since this is required in the directive on accounting. US firms normally use a descending order of liquidity. IFRS is silent on which format to be used, so all formats mentioned here may be used within IFRS.

Some of the format issues mentioned so far are pure presentation issues and may not be particularly important or problematic for users. More substantive classification issues, however, include the distinction between:

- current and non-current items
- liabilities and equity
- operating and financing items

Current and non-current items

A **current asset** is expected to be consumed or derecognized within a production cycle (such as inventory), while a **non-current asset** is used over several cycles (such as property, plant and equipment and intangible assets). For a financial statement user, it is important to

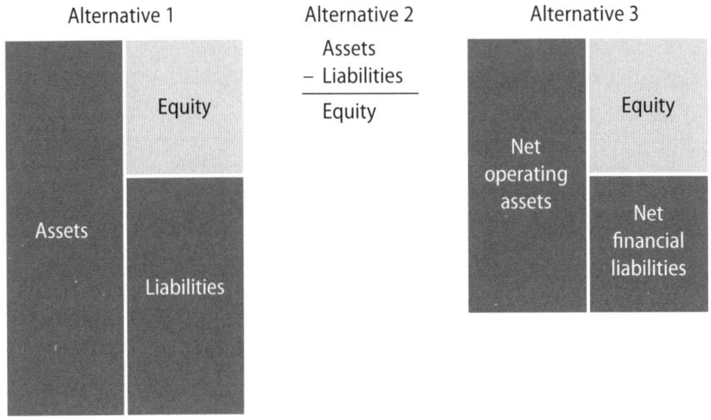

Figure 15.1
Balance sheet presentation formats

distinguish between current and non-current assets in order to gauge the value creation and capital requirements of a firm.

Perhaps even more important are distinctions between different types of financing (i.e., between both current and non-current liabilities) and between liabilities and equity. **Current liabilities** must be paid within one year, while **non-current liabilities** are paid beyond one year. It is important to know which liabilities will be paid soon, since if there are too many such liabilities, the firm could face liquidity problems. In most cases, it is easy for preparers to distinguish between current and non-current liabilities, based on the contractual terms for the liabilities. In some cases, however, the distinction requires judgment. For example, if a firm has a non-current loan from a bank where the bank can require early repayment if certain conditions are met. If the probability is high that those conditions will occur, the liability may be classified as current. Another situation is if a firm has a current liability, but has an agreement to extend the term of the liability. Hence, it could be seen as non-current.

Liabilities and equity

The distinction between liabilities and equity is important as it relates to the communicated risk level of the firm. This is discussed further in section 12.5. There are also presentation issues with regard to equity. Changes in equity may occur through transactions with owners or through effects of operations, and this distinction is normally reflected in financial statements. There is an assumption that it is important for owners to see the distinction between the capital they put into the firm and the return this capital has generated. In IFRS, there is an additional distinction for equity from operations between equity earned through profit and loss (shown in retained earnings) and equity earned through OCI (shown in reserves).

Regardless of whether equity earned from operations is shown in retained earnings or in reserves, equity forms a link between the balance sheet and the income statement. To summarize the effects on equity, IFRS requires that all changes over a period are summarized in a separate statement of changes in equity. In other regulatory frameworks, information concerning changes in equity can be presented in the notes. An example of a balance sheet and a statement of changes in equity from an IFRS firm (the German company Siemens) is provided in Figure 15.2.

Figure 15.2 Example: balance sheet and statement of changes in equity

B.3 Consolidated Statements of Financial Position

(in millions of €)	Note	2017	September 30, 2018
Assets			
Cash and cash equivalents		8,375	10,604
Available-for-sale financial assets		1,242	1,293
Trade and other receivables	8	17,160	16,287
Other current financial assets	9	7,664	6,800
Inventories	10	19,942	18,160
Current income tax assets		1,098	790
Other current assets		1,467	1,204
Assets classified as held for disposal	3,22	1,482	190
Total current assets		58,429	55,329
Goodwill	11	27,906	24,159
Other intangible assets	12	10,926	7,747
Property, plant and equipment	12	10,977	10,157
Investments accounted for using the equity method	4	2,727	3,012
Other financial assets	13	19,044	20,610
Deferred tax assets	7	2,297	3,431
Other assets		1,498	1,779
Total non-current assets		75,375	70,388
Total assets		133,804	125,717
Liabilities and equity			
Short-term debt and current maturities of long-term debt	15	5,447	6,206
Trade payables		9,755	8,048
Other current financial liabilities		1,444	1,933
Current provisions	17	4,247	4,166
Current income tax liabilities		2,355	2,085
Other current liabilities	14	20,049	20,437
Liabilities associated with assets classified as held for disposal	3	97	40
Total current liabilities		43,394	42,916
Long-term debt	15	26,777	24,761
Provisions for pensions and similar obligations	16	9,582	13,695
Deferred tax liabilities	7	1,599	829
Provisions	17	4,579	5,087
Other financial liabilities		902	1,142
Other liabilities		2,445	2,471
Total non-current liabilities		45,884	47,986
Total liabilities		89,278	90,901
Equity	18		
Issued capital		2,550	2,550
Capital reserve		6,368	5,890
Retained earnings		35,696	27,454
Other components of equity		1,671	1,921
Treasury shares, at cost		(3,196)	(3,605)
Total equity attributable to shareholders of Siemens AG		43,089	34,211
Non-controlling interests		1,438	605
Total equity		44,527	34,816
Total liabilities and equity		133,804	125,717

B.5 Consolidated Statements of Changes in Equity

(in millions of €)	Issued capital	Capital reserve	Retained earnings	Currency translation differences	Available-for-sale financial assets	Derivative financial instruments	Treasury shares at cost	Total equity attributable to shareholders of Siemens AG	Non-controlling interests	Total equity
Balance as of October 1, 2015	2,643	5,733	30,157	1,794	726	(357)	(6,218)	34,474	581	35,066
Net income	-		5,450	-	-	-	-	5,450	134	5,584
Other comprehensive income, net of income taxes	-		(1,637)	(985)	434	208	-	(2,879)	-	(2,879)
Dividends	-		(2,627)	-	-	-	-	(2,827)	(239)	(3,066)
Share-based payment	-	158	(67)	-	-	-	-	91	-	91
Purchase of treasury shares	-		-	-	-	-	(446)	(446)	-	(446)
Re-issuance of treasury shares	-	(1)	-	-	-	-	391	390	-	390
Cancellation of treasury shares	(93)		(2,573)	-	-	-	2,668	-	-	-
Transactions with non-controlling interests	-		(42)	-	-	-	-	(42)	92	51
Other changes in equity	-		-	-	-	-	-	-	37	36
Balance as of September 30, 2016	2,550	5,890	27,454	909	1,160	(148)	(3,605)	34,211	605	34,816
Balance as of October 1, 2016	**2,550**	**5,890**	**27,454**	**909**	**1,160**	**(148)**	**(3,605)**	**34,211**	**605**	**34,816**
Net income	-	-	**6,046**	-	-	-	-	**6,046**	**133**	**6,179**
Other comprehensive income, net of income taxes	-	-	**2,737**	**(1,084)**	**685**	**149**	-	**2,487**	**(78)**	**2,409**
Dividends	-	-	**(2,914)**	-	-	-	-	**(2,914)**	**(184)**	**(3,098)**
Share-based payment	-	**279**	**(86)**	-	-	-	-	**193**	-	**193**
Purchase of treasury shares	-	-	-	-	-	-	**(934)**	**(934)**	-	**(934)**
Re-issuance of treasury shares	-	**199**	-	-	-	-	**1,342**	**1,541**	-	**1,541**
Changes in equity resulting from major portfolio transactions	-	-	**2,473**	-	-	-	-	**2,473**	**919**	**3,393**
Other transactions with non-controlling interests	-	-	**(11)**	-	-	-	-	**(11)**	**(8)**	**(20)**
Other changes in equity	-	-	**(3)**	-	-	-	-	**(3)**	**51**	**48**
Balance as of September 30, 2017	**2,550**	**6,368**	**35,696**	**(175)**	**1,845**	**1**	**(3,196)**	**43,089**	**1,438**	**44,527**

For equity investors, knowing which items are considered operating and which are considered financing may be considered important. This is because a firm's operations are the source of its value and value creation. However, balance sheets prepared according to IFRS, US GAAP or other local GAAP, provide scant information with respect to this classification (although the notes may help).[1]

15.2.2 Income statement

There are several classification and format issues related to the income statement. These include presentation of summary amounts and OCI, but also classification of temporary items. The income statement is the primary statement for providing a measure of the performance of firms (additional measures of performance are provided by the statement of cash flows, see below). Different measures of performance can be generated from the income statement, depending on which items of revenue and expense are included in the measures.

IFRS does not prescribe any particular income statement format. It only specifies what has to be included in profit and loss and what is included in OCI. In practice, however, it is common that the income statement has three main summary amounts: operating income, income after financial items (or income before tax) and net income. Consequently, items on the income statement are divided into operating items, financial items and tax. Operating income is used when the focus is on the operations *per se*, without taking into consideration how they are financed. Operating income is available to all capital providers, both lenders and owners. Net income, on the other hand, represents earnings available to owners, so this is an important performance measure in relation to equity investors. Often, income before tax is used by investors instead of net income, as the tax amount is perceived as very volatile (cf. section 13.3.3). Fairfield et al. (1996) show that the disaggregation of earnings into three performance measures is useful, as it improves the forecasting ability of the income statement.

Non-GAAP measures

Other frequently used measures of performance that are not always directly available in the income statement are **earnings before interest and taxes (EBIT)** and **earnings before interest, taxes, depreciation and amortization (EBITDA)**. EBIT is meant to represent operating income, while EBITDA is operating income adjusted for depreciation and amortization. Consequently, EBITDA is close to operating cash flows. Research suggests that the alternative performance measures are important to investors (Marques, 2010) and that their importance has grown over time (Bradshaw and Sloan, 2002), especially in service and high-tech industries (Bhattacharya et al., 2003). As part of its project to develop primary financial statements, the IASB will also discuss performance measures. So far, EBIT

1 Meanwhile, the income statement and cash flow statements provide some indications of which income and cash flows pertain to which activity, although the classification choices are largely discretionary and the presentation is weakly regulated (see below).

(and EBITDA) measures have been unregulated and are therefore commonly referred to as **non-GAAP measures** of performance. Since they are unregulated, there are multiple interpretations regarding what they should include, and standard-setters fear that this opens up for opportunistic classifications of revenues and expenses. The same item may be classified as financing in one firm and operating in another, reducing comparability between firms. At the time of writing (August, 2018), we do not know which conclusions the IASB will draw from the current discussion.

Other comprehensive income

There are some items that meet the definitions of recognizable revenues and expenses but are not considered relevant in the income statement. In IFRS and US GAAP, such items are included in OCI. Net income plus OCI gives an additional measure of performance: *comprehensive income*. It represents the total effect on equity for the period coming from firm operations (and not from transactions with owners). One type of item included in OCI are gains and losses that are temporary and therefore have a reasonable probability of reversal before they are realized. Examples in IFRS include currency translation gains on foreign subsidiaries and actuarial gains and losses on pension liabilities.

Another type of item included in OCI are those representing gains and losses in the balance sheet, but which are not considered relevant measures of firm performance. An example includes gains and losses on derivative financial instruments used in hedging arrangements. Note that OCI opens up for discretionary behavior to the extent that unrealized losses are recognized as OCI, while realized gains are shown in net income. In the long run, the losses will have to be recognized, but in the short run, earnings can be managed in this manner. An example of an income statement and a statement of comprehensive income from an IFRS firm (Siemens) is shown in Figure 15.3.

OCI is a concept that has appeared in US GAAP and IFRS in the last few decades. Previously—and this is still the case in many local GAAP (e.g., in the EU Directive on Accounting)—items in OCI were recognized directly in equity, and there was no explicit measure of comprehensive income. In research, the term *clean surplus* has been used to describe the situation when no items are taken directly to equity and all effects on equity from operations are reflected in net income. For example, this is an important assumption in the modeling by Ohlson (1995). If there are items taken directly to equity, or which go through OCI, this is called *dirty surplus*.

The standard-setter perspective seems to be that items included in OCI are not relevant for users in gauging firm performance. Accordingly, comprehensive income should be less useful than net income. There are several studies on the relative usefulness of different earnings numbers. These studies were primarily carried out when the FASB issued new OCI requirements in the 1990s and when the IASB did the same in the 2000s. Dhaliwal et al. (1999) show that net income is more useful than comprehensive income in predicting future cash flows and stock returns. Meanwhile, there are suggestions in the literature that OCI can provide information that is useful in addition to net income, both for professional analysts (Hirst and Hopkins, 1998) and for non-professional investors (Maines and McDaniel, 2000).

B.1 Consolidated Statements of Income

(in millions of €, per share amounts in €)	Note	2017	Fiscal year 2016
Revenue		83,049	79,644
Cost of sales		(58,021)	(55,826)
Gross profit		25,029	23,819
Research and development expenses		(5,164)	(4,732)
Selling and general administrative expenses		(12,225)	(11,669)
Other operating income	5	647	328
Other operating expenses	6	(595)	(427)
Income (loss) from investments accounted for using the equity method, net	4	43	134
Interest income		1,487	1,314
Interest expenses		(1,051)	(989)
Other financial income (expenses), net		135	(373)
Income from continuing operations before income taxes		8,306	7,404
Income tax expenses	7	(2,180)	(2,008)
Income from continuing operations		6,126	5,396
Income from discontinued operations, net of income taxes		53	188
Net income		6,179	5,584
Attributable to:			
Non-controlling interests		133	134
Shareholders of Siemens AG		6,046	5,450
Basic earnings per share	27		
Income from continuing operations		7.38	6.51
Income from discontinued operations		0.07	0.23
Net income		7.44	6.74
Diluted earnings per share	27		
Income from continuing operations		7.23	6.42
Income from discontinued operations		0.06	0.23
Net income		7.29	6.65

B.2 Consolidated Statements of Comprehensive Income

(in millions of €£)	Note	2017	Fiscal year 2016
Net income		6,179	5,584
Remeasurements of defined benefit plans	16	2,734	(2,636)
therein: Income tax effects		(1,070)	1,065
Items that will not be reclassified to profit or loss		2,735	(2,636)
Currency translation differences		(1,118)	(796)
Available-for-sale financial assets	22	687	436
therein: Income tax effects		(7)	4
Derivative financial instruments	22, 23	136	256
therein: Income tax effects		(63)	(89)
Income (loss) from investments accounted for using the equity method, net		(30)	(141)
Items that may be reclassified subsequently to profit or loss		(326)	(244)
Other comprehensive income, net of income taxes		2,400	(2,879)
Total comprehensive income		8,588	2,705
Attributable to			
Non-controlling interests		55	134
Shareholders of Siemens AG		8,533	2,571

Figure 15.3 Example: income statement and statement of comprehensive income

In both cases, the positive effect is more pronounced when OCI is included in primary financial statements than if it is included in the notes (cf. Mitra and Hossain, 2009). Biddle and Choi (2006) show that OCI is not useful for corporate governance (e.g., for executive compensation). This is logical, as OCI contains items that are less affected by management's efforts compared to items in the income statement.

Extraordinary items

Another classification and format issue in the income statement is whether temporary items and effects should be shown separately. Investors primarily use financial statements to predict the future performance of the firm. Prediction—and confirmation of past predictions—is used to define relevance, for example in the IASB's Conceptual Framework. Consequently, the time series properties of measures such as earnings are important. In other words, the relation between current and future earnings matter. Temporary items and effects make prediction more difficult, as such items are not expected to continue in the future. Therefore, it is beneficial for investors if management separates temporary items and effects. This, however, requires judgment. An example of a temporary item is gains or losses on sales of real estate. If the firm rarely sells real estate, it is correctly classified as temporary. If such sales are common, it may not be temporary. Judgment is required in order to determine whether it represents temporary or ordinary activities.

Management is most suitable to determine whether or not an item is temporary. However, managerial choices may also be affected by incentives. Previously, both US GAAP and IFRS included items called **extraordinary activities**, which were supposed to capture temporary items not part of ordinary activities. Such items were later disallowed, as they tended to be very asymmetric in practice. Losses were often included in extraordinary items, but not gains. As investors tend to disregard extraordinary items in their valuation models, the asymmetry made firm performance look better than it really was.

15.2.3 Statement of cash flows

A few years after the FASB, the IASB issued IAS 7 *Statement of Cash Flows*, which is very similar to the FASB standard. The FASB approach to the statement of cash flows is now a *de facto* global standard. Figure 15.4 shows a statement of cash flows from an IFRS firm (Siemens).

Information concerning cash flows may be important for several reasons. First, they present an alternative measure of performance that some argue is more useful than earnings.[2] Second, earnings include accruals, which are based on judgment and are thus more affected by incentives compared to cash flows.[3] Third, cash flows can provide information concerning the liquidity situation of the firm.

---

2 Research indicates that overall, earnings are more value relevant than cash flows (see, for instance, Barth et al., 2001b). Still, in some industries and some cases, cash flows may be more relevant. Also, even if earnings are more relevant, cash flows may provide additional relevant information (Ohlson and Aier, 2009).

3 Even if cash flows are considered objective, there could be so-called *real earnings management*, discussed in Chapter 8 and by Ewert and Wagenhofer (2005).

B.4 Consolidated Statements of Cash Flows

(in millions of €)	2017	Fiscal year 2016
Cash flows from operating activities		
Net income	6,179	5,584
Adjustments to reconcile net income to cash flows from operating activities—continuing operations		
Income from discontinued operations, net of income taxes	(53)	(188)
Amortization, depreciation and impairments	3,211	2,764
Income tax expenses	2,180	2,008
Interest (income) expenses, net	(436)	(325)
(Income) loss related to investing activities	(329)	(373)
Other non-cash (income) expenses	552	400
Change in operating net working capital		
Inventories	(1,250)	(1,009)
Trade and other receivables	148	(579)
Trade payables	306	327
Billings in excess of costs and estimated earnings on uncompleted contracts and related advances	(799)	20
Additions to assets leased to other in operating leases	(482)	(484)
Change in other assets and liabilities	(1,719)	(281)
Income taxes paid	(2,039)	(1,738)
Dividends received	381	302
Interest received	1,375	1,219
Cash flows from operating activities—continuing operations	7,225	7,668
Cash flows from operating activities—discontinued operations	(50)	(57)
Cash flows from operating activities—continuing and discontinued operations	7,176	7,611
Cash flows from investing activities		
Additions to intangible assets and property, plant and equipment	(2,406)	(2,135)
Acquisitions of businesses, net of cash acquired	(4,385)	(922)
Purchase of investments	(500)	(271)
Purchase of current available-for-sale financial assets	(882)	(1,139)
Change in receivables from financing activities	(685)	(1,356)
Disposal of investments, intangibles and property, plant and equipment	542	377
Disposal of businesses, net of cash disposed	(69)	9
Disposal of current available-for-sale financial assets	931	1,031
Cash flows from investing activities—continuing operations	(7,456)	(4,406)
Cash flows from investing activities—discontinued operations	(1)	262
Cash flows from investing activities—continuing and discontinued operations	(7,457)	(4,144)
Cash flows from financing activities		
Purchase of treasury shares	(931)	(463)
Re-issuance of treasury shares and other transactions with owners	1,123	(13)
Issuance of long-term debt	6,958	5,300
Repayment of long-term debt (including current maturities of long-term debt)	(4,868)	(2,253)
Change in long-term debt and other financing activities	260	(1,408)
Interest paid	(1,000)	(809)
Dividends paid to shareholders of Siemens AG	(2,914)	(2,827)
Dividends attributable to non-controlling interests	(187)	(236)
Cash flows from financing activities—continuing operations	(1,560)	(2,710)
Cash flows from financing operations—discontinued operations	-	-
Cash flows from financing activities—continuing and discontinued operations	(1,560)	(2,170)
Effect of changes in exchange rates on cash and cash equivalents	(387)	(98)
Change in cash and cash equivalents	(2,228)	660
Cash and cash equivalents at beginning of period	10,618	9,958
Cash and cash equivalent at end of period	6,389	10,618
loss: Cash and cash equivalents of assets classified as held for disposal and discontinued operations at end of period	15	13
Cash and cash equivalents at end of period (Consolidated Statements of Financial Position)	8,375	10,604

Figure 15.4 Example: statement of cash flows

There are three main issues that standard-setters need to tackle in relation to the statement of cash flows: the definition of cash (funds), the format of the statement, and the starting point of the statement. In the 1980s, the FASB developed a new standard for the statement of cash flows, in dialogue with financial analyst organizations. The new standard determined that the statement should reflect cash flows and not other funds. Previously, it was common to focus on **working capital** (current assets minus current liabilities) instead of cash. From an analysis perspective, information regarding cash flows is more useful than information regarding changes in working capital. Further, the FASB decided that the statement of cash flows should be divided into three sections: operating activities, investing activities and financing activities, in order to enable users to distinguish between cash generated through operations, cash used for investing and cash obtained through financing. The starting point of the statement could either be gross cash flows (representing the **direct method**) or an earnings number that is subsequently adjusted (representing the **indirect method**). Even if the FASB preferred the direct method, many preparers claimed that it was difficult to apply. The FASB allowed both methods and the indirect method dominates in practice. Some argue that the indirect method does not provide a proper statement of cash flows, as it only shows accounting earnings with adjustments. In other words, reported cash flows are not actual, objective cash flows, but the residual from a calculation of income less accruals (which are subject to judgment). Orpurt and Zang (2009) suggest that the direct method is more useful for investors than the indirect method.

An item considered important in company valuation is **free cash flow**. It represents the cash flow available to capital providers after the reinvestments of cash that are "necessary" in order to maintain operations. However, the free cash flow is not apparent from the statement of cash flows, so firms must provide additional information to enable users to obtain information about it. Possibly, free cash flow can be estimated from the statement of cash flows as the net of cash from operating and investing activities, but the financial statement user does not know whether or not all use of cash in those sections, especially investing, is necessary. Investing activities, as defined in GAAP statements, mix operating and financing activities (that is, investments in operating assets and investments in financial assets).

15.3 Time series aspects

In this section, we cover issues relating to changes in recognition or measurement that could limit the usefulness of primary financial statements. As noted, investors benefit when historic earnings may be used as a basis for forecasting future earnings. This requires consistency in the measurement of earnings. The issues discussed here relate primarily to measurement in the income statement, but they are covered in this chapter since they have important implications for the presentation.

The issues in question include changes in accounting policies and estimates, as well as errors in prior periods, which are covered in IAS 8 *Accounting Policies, Changes in Accounting Estimates and Errors* and IFRS 1 *First-Time Adoption of International Financial Reporting Standards*. A separate issue related to timing is what to do with information obtained after the reporting period, covered in IAS 10 *Events after the Reporting Period*. Yet another timing-related issue concerns interim reporting and is covered in IAS 34 *Interim Financial Reporting*. Finally, time-series disruptions caused by discontinued operations are relevant to consider in order to achieve comparability over time (the structure of reporting entities are covered in IFRS 5 *Non-Current Assets Held for Sale and Discontinued Operations*).

15.3.1 Changes in accounting policies and estimates

Changes in policies or estimates usually cause a disruption in the earnings stream at the time the change is made. A policy change can refer to a change initiated by a standard-setter (due to the replacement or removal of a policy) or a change voluntary made by the firm. A change in estimates refers to a situation where the underlying economics have changed (requiring a revised estimate) but the policy is constant.

Figure 15.5 shows the effect of such a change, where a new policy/estimate leads to a higher level of earnings compared to the previous policy/estimate. There are two main ways in which the change can be reflected in financial statements: **retrospective application** and **prospective application**. Retrospective application means preparing financial statements as if the new policy/estimate had always been applied. It usually also involves presenting comparative information concerning prior periods in accordance with the new policy/estimate. Prospective application means applying the new policy/estimate only on transactions occurring after the change and no previous transactions are remeasured with the new policy/estimate. The effect, as shown in Figure 15.5, is a gradual shift to the earnings stream as measured using the new policy/estimate.

From a user perspective, retrospective application is likely to be more useful for changes in accounting policies, as it provides a historic time series of earnings as a basis for predicting

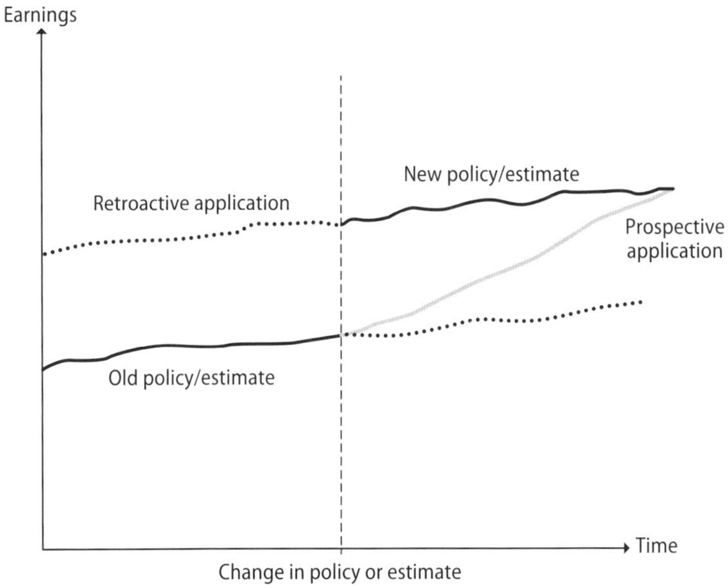

Figure 15.5 New policies and estimates

future earnings (which will be based on the new policy). Consequently, both IAS 8 (for firms using IFRS) and IFRS 1 (for firms switching to IFRS) require retrospective application for changes in policies. Sometimes, however, retrospective application is difficult as firms do not have enough information. Another difficulty is to avoid *hindsight*; that is, to avoid using subsequent information when making estimates regarding economic phenomena. Retrospective application requires that estimates in prior periods be reconstructed based on the information available at the original date. It may be very difficult to ignore information that was received later showing that the estimate was wrong. For example, assume that a new accounting policy—introduced in Year 5—requires that real estate be measured at fair value. A firm applies this retrospectively and an estimate of the fair value of the firm made in Year 3 would have resulted in a value of €15 million. However, there was a real estate crash in Year 4, so the value of the building declined to €5 million. Can the firm ignore the real estate crash in making the retrospective application in Year 5?

As a consequence, both IAS 8 and IFRS 1 allow prospective application when retrospective application is too difficult. It is less obvious which method leads to more useful information when it comes to changes in estimates. A possible argument is that retrospective application is more useful, for the same reason as for a change in accounting policy. IAS 8, however, requires prospective application for changes in estimates. A motivation is that a new estimate relates to changes in the underlying economics and that it would be illogical to apply estimates regarding a new situation retrospectively to the pre-existing economic situation.

Once the financial statements for an accounting period are published, they are not subsequently changed or amended. Therefore, a question arises as to what to do if an *error* relating to prior periods is discovered. IAS 8 requires retrospective adjustment for errors, applied to financial statements (including comparative information) in the period when the error is discovered.

15.3.2 Information after the accounting period

A fundamental aspect of financial statements is that they are prepared for limited periods of, for example, one year or a quarter of a year. In the preparation of financial statements, one issue is how long one should wait to gather information. Early issuance of financial statements makes them more useful by the qualitative characteristic of timeliness being met (cf. the Conceptual Framework). The trade-off is that the longer one waits, the more certain the information becomes. An extreme example is the estimation of useful life of a non-current asset to be applied to depreciation. Useful life is based on an estimate and a prediction of the future use of the asset. If one waited until the useful life ended, there would be complete certainty in the estimate. The problem is that this would take so long (several years) that the financial statements would no longer be relevant.

The IASB's Conceptual Framework points out that timeliness is an important qualitative characteristic. Over the last few decades, the time to issuance of financial statements has tended to shrink. Some firms issue statements as early as a week after the end of the period and in most countries all listed firms provide financial statements within two months of the end of the period.

Still, the issue remains concerning how information obtained between the end of the period and the issuance of financial statements should be treated. IAS 10 prescribes that if the information pertains to the reporting period, it should be considered when financial statements are prepared. If the information pertains to the subsequent period, it should not be considered for primary financial statements. This is based on the idea that the balance sheet should reflect economic conditions on the balance sheet date, not subsequent events. Disclosure in the notes may be warranted if a post-period event is very important to the firm. In practice, judgment is required to determine whether information pertains to the current or subsequent period. For example, a firm with a calender year-end suspects that inventory may be impaired at year-end. In February, the inventory is sold at a loss, below historic cost. The question is whether the decline in value occurred before or after year-end. If it occurred before year-end, the firm should recognize an impairment. If it occurred after year-end, no impairment should be recognized, but disclosure may be warranted if the loss is material (and the loss recognized in the subsequent period). The difficulty in distinguishing between what happened before and after year-end leads to uncertainty in financial statements and thus a possible reduction in quality.

15.3.3 Interim financial statements

There is a long history in accounting of focusing on annual financial statements. The annual report is seen as the primary document issued by firms. IFRS requirements apply to annual financial statements, and in most countries, both listed and unlisted firms provide such statements. However, on most stock markets in the world, listed firms must also provide interim financial statements. This is a requirement by regulators or stock markets, it is not an IFRS (or US GAAP) requirement. There has been some criticism of quarterly financial statements; for example, that they induce too much short-term focus, as management strives to meet market demands in each quarter instead of investing for the long term. They are also unregulated and unaudited, allowing firms to make more discretionary choices and focus on non-GAAP measures.

Although IFRS is silent on whether or not quarterly (or other interim) financial statements should be provided, *if* an IFRS firm issues interim financial statements, IAS 34 must be followed. The basic idea in this standard is that the same accounting policies are followed in interim and annual financial statements. Therefore, the income statement and balance sheet are basically the same in annual and interim reports (i.e., they are based on the same accounting policies and thus have the similar quality and uncertainty). However, interim financial statements are more summarized and contain much less information (in the notes) than annual financial statements. An assumption in IAS 34 is that users of interim financial statements have access to the more expansive disclosures in the annual financial statements. Therefore, the focus in IAS 34 is on disclosures helping users understand what has happened since the last annual statements.

IAS 34 states that the fact that interim financial statements are issued should not have any impact on annual earnings. This gave rise to an interesting conceptual issue resulting in the issuance of IFRIC 10 *Interim Financial Reporting and Impairment*. IAS 38 *Intangible Assets* states that goodwill impairment should be recognized if the recoverable amount is below the carrying amount on the balance sheet date (e.g., for an interim report). Meanwhile, goodwill impairment cannot be reversed. In a situation where the recoverable amount of goodwill is below the carrying amount in, for example, the second quarter, only to rebound in the fourth quarter, the issuance of a second quarter report does affect the measurement of goodwill in the annual report if IAS 38 is followed. However, based on IAS 34, this should not happen. So, there is a conflict between two standards and both cannot be followed simultaneously. In response, the IASB issued IFRIC 10 saying that IAS 38 should be followed, thus creating an exception to the general principle in IAS 34. In the example, impairment should be recognized in the second quarter, with no reversal in the fourth quarter.

15.3.4 Discontinued operations

Finally, an issue relating to the time-series aspect of financial statements is the presentation of income when operations have been discontinued. When a firm has decided to sell or close down parts of the operation, it is helpful for users to see historic information without the discontinued operations. This is shown in Figure 15.6. The solid lines show actual earnings, and there is a "break" in the earnings stream at the time of disposal of operations. Consequently, IFRS 5 requires separate presentation of discontinued operations in the income statement. The separate presentation helps users predict future performance for the remaining (continuing) operations.

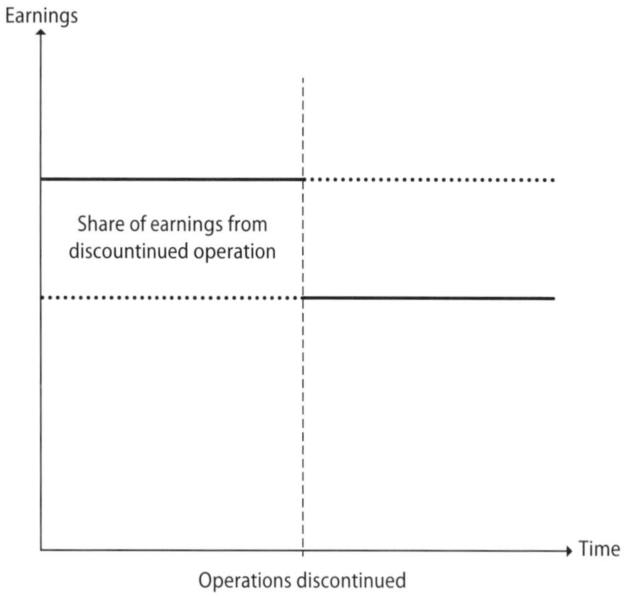

Figure 15.6
Discontinued operations

15.4 Mandatory disclosure

Previously, we discussed ways in which increased disclosure is considered beneficial to both preparers and users. From a user perspective, high-quality information is needed for improved decision-making, and from the preparer perspective, disclosure is needed to improve firm transparency and mitigate adverse selection arising from information asymmetries. Due to potential market failures (see Chapter 4), leaving the provision of information to the free market can be suboptimal, meaning that mandatory disclosures are necessary. This appears to be the view of multiples governing bodies, as we have seen increased disclosure requirements of accounting and corporate governance practices (not least following the accounting scandals and financial crises in the early 2000s).

As argued in Chapter 4, accounting may be viewed as a *public good* that would be underproduced if the decision to disclose was left entirely to preparers. That is, there are positive externalities associated with accounting information, with benefits extending beyond the firm to outside stakeholders. In this situation, it becomes necessary to perform cost-benefit analyses and consider the type of externalities that exist, as the introduction of mandatory disclosures in cases where voluntary disclosures would suffice is inefficient and costly from a societal perspective. Standard-setting resources would, in other words, be wasted (Dye, 1990).

Furthermore, another type of market failure is the existence of asymmetric information. This becomes, or at least remains, a problem due to the *incentive problem*; managers may desire to hide information from outside stakeholders so as to be able to maximize their own benefits. Mandated disclosure may facilitate the monitoring of management by the board of directors. In fact, it is unlikely that board members, especially independent directors with more to gain from successful monitoring, would be willing to rely on voluntary disclosures made by managers. Instead, they are expected to require public (mandatory) disclosures that are typically audited and carry higher credibility compared to voluntary disclosures.

Empirically, mandatory disclosures have been shown to serve as an important mechanism to ensure a *commitment* to providing credible information that voluntary disclosures cannot fully substitute (Cheng et al., 2013). It has been observed that even when holding the disclosed information constant, market illiquidity has gone up for a sample of firms subject to deregulation of disclosure. That is, when the disclosure of a set of information items became voluntary rather than mandatory, adverse market effects were found even for firms that voluntarily disclosed the information. This points to the existence of a "commitment effect."

There is also reason to believe that mandatory and voluntary disclosures interact with one another in complex ways. Depending on the mandatory disclosure environment (taking into account things such as the scope of the requirements and the level of discretion required), voluntary disclosure outcomes will vary (Einhorn, 2007). One implication of this is that "the value of mandatory disclosure requirements cannot be properly assessed without an understanding of what, if any, voluntary disclosures might be made in addition to the mandatory disclosures."

In this section, we discuss mandatory disclosures in the notes. As noted, in research the term *disclosure* is used in a broad sense to cover any information item communicated from the firm to users. As such, earnings, for example, represents a disclosure item in research. Here, we exclude all items included in primary financial statements from the term disclosures. In addition, we only focus on mandatory disclosures, as our focus is on disclosures in relation to standard-setting.

Disclosures in the notes have been the subject of much discussion among standard-setters in the last few years. Both the IASB and the FASB have launched projects as a result of this discussion. The IASB calls it the "Disclosure Initiative" and we cover it in further detail in section 15.4.1. There is a large number of specific disclosure requirements in IFRS. In section 15.4.2, we discuss a selection of these requirements from a conceptual perspective. One way of testing whether communicative aspects matter to financial statement users is to compare market responses to items recognized in primary financial statements with items disclosed in the notes. Such comparisons are covered in section 15.4.3.

15.4.1 The Disclosure Initiative

Although some useful information will be provided voluntarily by firms (arguably driven by the positive capital market effects of disclosure, see section 6.3.1), corporate disclosures have increasingly become subject to mandatory requirements. The introduction of mandatory disclosures should be preceded by careful cost-benefit analyses. These are not easy to carry out in practice, but should attempt to evaluate the extent of proprietary costs imposed on firms following mandatory requirements, as well as determine any potential underproduction of information that could result in positive externalities (see Chapter 4 and Leuz and Wysocki (2016)). As part of such an analysis, one must not forget the adverse outcome of *too much* information. More specifically, **over-regulation** has been a concern of late. This discussion points to the need to regulate with care. To slim down regulation could potentially lead to more effective regulation. Principles-based disclosure requirements—requiring the firm to use its judgment in determining materiality thresholds and what information to provide based on firm-specific conditions—are believed to be part of the solution.

As we saw in Chapter 4, the US FASB was created in 1973. At the time, accounting standard-setting was seen as *ad hoc* and lacking a conceptual foundation. An important reason for the creation of the FASB was to achieve more coherent standard-setting. During the 1970s, the FASB created a *Conceptual Framework* to serve as a basis for the development of new standards. This framework was an important inspiration for the Conceptual Framework published by the IASC (the predecessor organization of the IASB) in 1989. For several decades, the conceptual frameworks have provided a foundation for the development of standards for recognition (derecognition) and measurement in the primary financial statements. The frameworks do not, however, include principles of disclosures.

The lack of principles of disclosures was pointed out as a problem by Schipper (2007). In the early 2010s, several problems with disclosures were identified by standard-setters and the usefulness of disclosures in their current state was questioned. In order to remedy these problems, several standard-setters launched different activities. EFRAG[4] in cooperation with

4 European Financial Reporting Advisory Group (EFRAG) is a private organization that supports the adoption and implementation of IFRS in the European Union.

the French and British standard-setters issued the report *Towards a Disclosure Framework for the Notes* (commented in Barker et al. (2013)). The IASB initiated a projected termed the "Disclosure Initiative." As part of the initiative, the IASB has included a chapter on disclosure in its 2018 Conceptual Framework and issued a discussion paper on *Principles of Disclosures*. In addition, the IASB is updating some individual standards, see below.

Problems identified

From a communication perspective, three main problems with disclosures in practice were identified:

- There is a lack of relevant information.
- There is too much irrelevant information.
- The notes are not organized well enough to constitute effective communication.

There are extensive disclosure requirements and financial statements have become longer following the introduction of IFRS in the EU. Still, users experience a lack of relevant information. Instead, too much in disclosures is irrelevant. Many firms provide standardized disclosures that provide too little firm-specific information. For example, disclosures concerning accounting policies include too much text copied directly from standards instead of discussing accounting policies that are specific to the disclosing firm. A term often used is that there is too much "cookie cutter" disclosure (an example of this is shown in section 6.4.2). The importance of accounting policy disclosures is pointed out by Hope (2003a).

With regard to extensive disclosures, it is important to organize them so as to allow users to find the information they are interested in. The third problem identified suggests that this is often not the case. Instead, the multitude of disclosures hides the relevant and important information. The issue can be described as a trade-off between quantity and quality of disclosures.

While the issue of too much disclosures is identified as a problem in practice, Barker et al. (2013) point out that research has not identified such a problem. Instead, research shows capital market benefits of additional disclosures. This may be a weakness in current research methods, but the fact remains that we currently do not have a strong evidence-based foundation for making statements concerning disclosure problems. Instead, current standard-setting activities are based on comments obtained from practice. An additional issue pointed out by Bischof et al. (2014) is that there is substantial variety in which disclosures are viewed as relevant by users. Just because disclosures are currently not relevant does not mean that they do not have the potential of being relevant. In support of standard-setters' view of too much disclosure as problematic, Hoitash and Hoitash (2018) show that there is a negative association between the number of disclosure items and disclosure quality.

Suggested purpose and solutions to problems

Before going through standard-setters' suggested solutions to the disclosure problem, we provide an overview of the suggested purposes of the notes. Schipper (2007) identifies implied purposes of notes by systematically going through actual disclosure requirements in two standards in US GAAP. She finds three main purposes:

- Disaggregation of amounts included in the primary financial statements. The income statement and balance sheet are highly summarized and additional detail regarding the line items included there can be provided in the notes.
- Provide information regarding measurement uncertainty of items in primary financial statements. Included here are disclosures regarding measurement uncertainty for specific items. Such disclosures could provide more detailed information on how the estimate was made, including underlying assumptions. This gives the user of financial statements the ability to identify the existence of uncertainty, get an idea of the effect of uncertainty and gauge the reasonableness of the estimate.
- Give information regarding effects of alternative accounting treatments. For example, notes could provide information concerning items not recognized in the primary financial statements.

Schipper (2007) uses a fully inductive approach to identify the purpose of the notes. In its Discussion Paper on principles of disclosures, the IASB uses a combination of deductive approach and empirical observation of practice (inductive) in order to identify a similar set of purposes. The IASB groups the purposes into two main areas, as follows:

- Information concerning items in the primary financial statements
- Disaggregation of items
- Description of the nature of items
- Information regarding measurement methods and issues (including uncertainties)
- Additional information regarding the firm
- Information regarding unrecognized items
- Information regarding the firm's exposure to risks

An item of particular interest in this textbook—which relates directly to accounting quality—is information concerning measurement uncertainty. It may even be the case that disclosures can partially mitigate negative effects of measurement uncertainty, so that higher uncertainty is acceptable if high quality disclosures are provided. Landsman (2007), for example, suggests that disclosure of valuation assumptions and inputs may provide a (partial) remedy for the reliability issue and adverse selection facing fair values, especially for level 3 inputs (cf. also Blacconiere et al., 2011). A word of caution is provided by Hammersley et al. (2008) and Beneish et al. (2008), who suggest that investors' perception of risk may *increase* with additional disclosures, at least when information is provided regarding internal control weaknesses and when the disclosures provided are vague.

The challenge facing standard-setters is how to write standards that support the achievement of suggested purposes of disclosures, while overcoming the problems listed in the previous section. A suggestion is to make disclosure requirements more principles-based and less rules-based. The idea—as in measurement—is that principles-based standards allow management to provide private and entity-specific information tailored to the particular situation of the reporting firm (Schipper, 2003). In order for principles-based disclosure standards to work in practice, standard-setters have identified two necessary conditions:

1. that coherent high-level principles of disclosure are developed
2. that firms receive additional guidance on how to apply materiality

Principles-based standards work best when based on consistent high-level principles, as this helps preparers interpret and understand the standards. To achieve this objective, high-level principles must be explicit (written down) and well-defined both to enable standard-setters to base different standards on consistent principles and to allow preparers to benefit from knowledge of the principles.

With respect to preparers' application of **materiality**, this is essential in order to overcome problems with both too much disclosure and too little relevant information. Limiting disclosures to information that is relevant would reduce the length of notes, especially removing standardized and "cookie cutter" disclosures (also referred to as **boilerplate disclosures** in the academic literature). Material information tends to be entity-specific and is by definition relevant (as it can affect user decisions). In practice, however, the problem is that it is difficult to determine what is relevant to users (cf. Liu and Mittelstaedt, 2002). IASB has responded to the challenge by making amendments to IAS 1, for example by explicitly stating that disclosures required in IFRS do not have to be provided if the information is immaterial. In addition, the Board issued a so-called *Materiality Practice Statement* in order to guide preparers.

A problem, as pointed out by Barker et al. (2013), is that the application of materiality in the preparation of financial statements has been required in IFRS for a long time, suggesting that any improvement based on materiality will not occur automatically. It could be supported through enforcement of auditors or authorities. However, Barker et al. (2013) point out that enforcement of principles-based disclosure standards risks being very difficult.

15.4.2 Specific disclosure requirements

There are a number of disclosure requirements in IFRS, but these are not well-organized in current standards. In most cases, disclosure requirements are listed at the end of each standard, following requirements for recognition and measurement (e.g., in IFRS 13 *Fair Value Measurement* and IFRS 16 *Leases*). In other cases, disclosure requirements related to an accounting area are assembled in a separate standard (e.g., in IFRS 7 *Financial Instruments: Disclosures* and IFRS 12 *Disclosure of Interests in Other Entities*). Finally, requirements on specific disclosure issues unrelated to any particular measurement issue are provided in separate standards (e.g., IFRS 8 *Operating Segments* and IAS 33 *Earnings per Share*). While the latter type of disclosure requirements are naturally provided in separate standards, the reason for having a separate standard for disclosures relating to measurement issues is much less clear. As part of the work with a Discussion Paper on principles of disclosures, the IASB is considering how best to organize disclosure requirements in IFRS. One radical idea is to include all disclosure requirements in *one* (very large) standard.

We do not in this section provide a comprehensive overview of all disclosure requirements in IFRS. Instead, we go through some examples that are of interest as they highlight different issues in financial reporting. These include disclosures related to measurement uncertainty and risk, responses to the 2007–2008 financial crisis, shareholder-oriented disclosures such as disclosures concerning operating segments and earnings per share.

Disclosures of measurement uncertainty and risk

We noted above that disclosures regarding measurement uncertainty may partially offset negative effects of such uncertainty in primary financial statements. There are many disclosure requirements relating to uncertainty and we provide some examples here. IAS 1 *Presentation of Financial Statements* requires disclosure regarding major sources of estimation uncertainty. IAS 19 *Employee Benefits* includes requirements for disclosures concerning assumptions used in the estimation of pension liabilities, as well as a sensitivity analysis relating to those assumptions. IFRS 13 requires substantially more disclosure regarding items measured based on level 3 inputs (with high uncertainty) compared to those measured based on level 1 inputs (with low uncertainty) (see Chapter 10). IAS 36 requires disclosure concerning impairment, especially for firms that have goodwill.

A different type of measurement uncertainty comes from violation of the arms-length assumption in transactions. In such cases, actual transaction prices may not be an appropriate reflection of fair value. Consequently, IAS 24 *Related Party Disclosures* requires information concerning transactions with related parties.

Operational risk is a related, but somewhat different, issue and it is also important that users receive information on this matter. For example, IFRS 7 includes substantial disclosure requirements relating to risks from financial instruments, which policies for financial risk management are in place and how firms manage their financial risks. Financial risks are defined in IFRS 7 to include credit risk (the risk that the firm will not get paid for loans and receivables), liquidity risk (the risk that the firm will not be able to pay its debtors) and different market risks (e.g., risks related to fluctuations in currency markets, interest rate markets and other markets). IFRS 7 also requires a sensitivity analysis relating to those risks. Under US GAAP, firms must also make such risk factor disclosures, and research has investigated whether they are considered useful by the market. Contrary to the notion that they reduce investors' risk perception, Kravet and Muslu (2013) find that they seem to draw attention to previously unknown risks (see discussion in section 6.1.3). This is evidenced by more dispersed earnings forecasts, greater stock volatility and increased trading volume around the SEC filings of firms that increase their risk disclosures.

Disclosures in response to the 2007–2008 financial crisis

As noted in Chapter 11, the 2007–2008 financial crisis resulted in some financial reporting changes. The crisis started in the US when collateralized mortgage obligations (MBO) were derecognized even with a remaining exposure. Transactions involved unconsolidated **structured entities**. As a result, disclosure requirements in IFRS 7 on derecognized financial assets was strengthened. Bischof (2009) shows that disclosure quality did increase in European banks following the IFRS 7 changes, especially regarding credit risk. In addition, IFRS 12 was issued and it requires substantial amounts of disclosure regarding both consolidated and unconsolidated structured entities, as well as transactions with such entities.

Segment disclosures and disclosures of EPS

In accordance with the Conceptual Framework, an important objective of financial statements is to enable users to make forecasts about firms. In large firms, with business segments with different growth rates, profitability and investments needs, forecasting for the whole firm can be difficult. Therefore, IFRS 8 requires separate disclosures regarding different operating segments of the firm. IFRS 8 has a so-called "management approach," which means that the identification of segments is based on how internal reporting to the corporate level is carried out. The management approach leaves more discretion with managers in identifying operating segments compared to previous standards (André et al., 2016). A question is which incentives affect the identification of segments by managers, specifically the question on how many segments to disclose. As financial statements are publicly available to competitors, there is an incentive to try to conceal profitable segments (Hayes and Lundholm, 1996). In relation to financial statement users, there are incentives to conceal segments that do not perform well (Berger and Hann, 2007). Still, even with the incentives, the number of reportable segments increased with the introduction of the management approach (Botosan and Stanford, 2005; Nichols et al., 2012). Ettredge et al. (2005) conclude that the new disclosure requirements increased the predictability of earnings, which suggests that IFRS 8 (and the corresponding US GAAP standards) met their objectives.

Finally, IAS 33 requires disclosures regarding **earnings per share** (EPS), which may be viewed as information facilitating the analysis of the firm from a shareholder perspective. A particularly important requirement is that firms must provide information regarding **diluted EPS**. Such EPS shows how current shareholders are potentially affected by equity instruments that are issued and can be converted into shares in the future. For example, if there are many outstanding employee stock options, diluted EPS will decrease. In other words, if all the outstanding options are executed and used for issuance of new shares, the proportion of earnings that goes to existing shareholders goes down.

To summarize, mandatory disclosure requirements are initiated as a response to specific user needs. High judgment in the preparation of primary financial statements can allow management to provide private information, and disclosures can mitigate the negative effect of the resulting measurement uncertainty. Specific events, such as financial crises, can drive new disclosure requirements. User needs, for example the use of financial statements for forecasting, may be supported by more granular disclosures. Even if the IASB to date does not have high-level principles as a basis for disclosure requirements, it is still possible to inductively identify motivations for existing disclosure requirements, as we have done in this section.

15.4.3 Disclosure versus recognition

An issue related to disclosures, which we noted above, is to what extent the mode of presentation affects the interpretation of information. In economic theory, mode of presentation is generally not modeled. Instead, the provision of information is seen as binary: a piece of information is either publicly available or not. However, as discussed in Chapter 3, behavioral economics has started looking into effects of users' limited attention and processing costs with regard to disclosures (see, for instance, Hirshleifer and Teoh, 2003).

An issue that has received some attention in accounting research is whether users react differently to information if it is included in the primary financial statements or if it is included in the notes. Of course, the very term "primary financial statements" indicates a higher level of importance in comparison with the notes. It is also an assumption in practice that items in the primary financial statements are more important and are consequently afforded more attention by users. For example, when employee stock options were discussed in the US in the 1990s, recognition of an expense in the income statement met with heavy resistance (see section 13.2). Disclosure of the same amount in the notes, however, met with no resistance.

Research has primarily focused on two areas where items were first disclosed in the notes and subsequently recognized in the balance sheet, which gives an opportunity to study effects of the change. The areas are accounting for post-employment benefits (see section 12.3), share-based payment (see section 13.2), and OCI. Research generally confirms the view in practice that information in primary financial statements has a higher level of importance compared to information in the notes. Maines and McDaniel (2000) show that non-professional investors only react to OCI information when presented in primary financial statements (in US GAAP, firms can choose whether to present OCI in primary financial statements or in the notes). According to Harper et al. (1987) both sophisticated and unsophisticated users react more to pension items when presented in the balance sheet rather than in the notes, and these findings are supported by both Mitra and Hossain (2009) and Davis-Friday et al. (1999). Imhoff et al. (1993) indicate that the relative use of recognized and disclosed items vary by users. They show that investors adjust for information regarding leases provided in notes, but that executive compensation committees do not make such adjustments. Choudhary (2011) shows that different user treatment of recognized and disclosed information is reflected in preparer choices, as there are stronger incentives for managers to manipulate recognized than disclosed information.

A word of caution is provided by Barth et al. (2003). They point out that the relation between recognized and disclosed information may not be as simple as suggested in research and in practice. Typically, whether an amount is reliable helps determine whether it is recognized. However, an unreliable amount can still be value-relevant when recognized, while some recognized, reliable amounts are *not* value-relevant. A conclusion from Barth et al. (2003) is that reliability cannot serve as the only basis for recognition (instead of disclosure in the notes)—one must also take into account relevance. It should be pointed out that one of the difficulties facing researchers comparing recognized and disclosed items, is that the act of recognizing an item can *make* it more reliable. This is because management increases their estimation efforts since recognized items are more strictly audited.

Differences in the use of information presented in different ways in financial statements relate to behavioral aspects of users. In a related study, Kennedy et al. (1998) look at accounting for contingent liabilities. They consider cognitive mechanisms and users' judgments and decisions in relation to uncertain items (in this case, contingent environmental liabilities). They highlight how investors anchor or fixate on available information when trying to estimate undisclosed parameters (and ultimately liability values). Essentially, preparers can provide information regarding expected minimum or maximum values, best estimates or ranges. Using an experimental design (on financial managers, bankers and MBA students), users had to make judgments with regard to investment risk and make decisions concerning the value of the contingency. The study finds that maximum parameter disclosures lead users to perceive higher firm risk and pay a greater sum to settle the environmental liability. Users would also invest less in such a firm. A firm would therefore be better off disclosing a minimum parameter estimate, since users fixate on this and narrow their perception of the firm's exposure to loss. This in spite of the fact that a minimum parameter disclosure might actually reflect greater uncertainty regarding the upper end of the distribution of possible losses. While ranges or best estimates make users perceive management as more credible, credibility and risk perceptions cannot explain the settlement and investment decisions. This has implications for standard-setters in that it shows that the way in which an estimate is disclosed can affect investors.

15.4.4 A note on research on mandatory disclosures

Although we refer to research in previous sections, in this section we summarize some observations relating to research on mandatory disclosures. A broader discussion on disclosure research is provided in Chapter 6. Much of the research on disclosures has focused on effects of disclosures, for example in reducing information asymmetry and thereby estimation uncertainty and cost of capital. As noted in Chapter 6, voluntary disclosures are more useful in the study of the effects of disclosures, as they exhibit more variability than mandatory disclosures. Most of the research on mandatory disclosures has studied a different question: how well accounting standards are implemented. This is often studied through a disclosure index based on the explicit requirements in the standard. A typical example is Glaum et al. (2013), who study which factors determine how well some IFRS disclosure requirements are implemented in the EU, and Verriest et al. (2013) who look at the effect of corporate governance on firms' disclosure choices.

Given the lower variability of mandatory disclosures, it is difficult to study the effects of these unless one has access to very large samples, and few such studies have been carried out (Leuz and Wysocki, 2016). To date, most disclosure index studies have been based on hand-collected material from the notes, which limits the sample size. A recent example of one of the few studies on the effects of mandatory disclosures is Mazzi et al. (2017), who find a reduction in cost of capital with more disclosures, but only when enforcement is strong. More powerful machine-based textual analysis tools could very well allow more large-sample studies of text-based disclosures in the notes in the future (see Chapter 16). This would be important also for research on voluntary disclosures, as in order to understand determinants and consequences of disclosures, one must understand the interaction between voluntary and mandatory disclosures (Einhorn, 2007).

15.5 Conclusions

It is now widely accepted that the format of corporate disclosures is important for their usefulness. In other words, the *how*—not just the *what*—of disclosure matters.[5] Standard-setters therefore face questions related to the presentation format of financial statements (including the level of aggregation of line items) as well as the classification of different items into current- and non-current, operating and financing, and ordinary and extraordinary/unusual.

When estimates or policies change, or the structure of a reporting entity changes, this affects the amounts on the financial statements. In order to achieve comparability over time, standard-setters must consider how best to achieve it. Issues include deciding how to present such changes and how firms should present comparative information.

Furthermore, one major issue facing standard-setters (*ex ante*) as well as preparers (*ex post*) is whether an item should be recognized in the *primary* financial statements or merely disclosed in the notes. Any decision should take into consideration both the reliability and relevance of the item. Finally, standard-setters must decide on which disclosures should be mandatory as opposed to voluntary, and how these mandatory disclosures should be regulated. The IASB has identified a number of problems with current disclosure requirements and highlighted weaknesses in current disclosure practices. In essence, firm communication has been criticized by academics and standard-setters as being ineffective and containing too much irrelevant information and too little relevant information. To some extent, this can be attributed to over-regulation, a part of which is the result of specific disclosure requirements appearing in response to current events.

5 This is in contrast to the neoclassical economic view that markets are efficient and that investors have unlimited information processing capacity.

CHAPTER 16

Concluding remarks

MANY ACADEMIC DISCIPLINES are concerned with finding methods or making discoveries that can improve people's lives. Improvement can be in the form of better medicines, technological advances that simplify daily tasks, or, in economics, a higher economic standard of living. Growth in economic output, full employment or sustainable development can be means to that end. But what makes accounting important or able to bring about such desirable improvements? In this book, we hope to have provided some of the proposed answers—along with some of the caveats, or difficulties, associated with the quest for *high-quality accounting*.

Decision-usefulness It is clear that financial reports can be used by a wide range of individuals, including a firm's employees, suppliers and competitors, as well as politicians, activists and other interested parties in society. Although it is thus possible to draw up various potential uses of accounting, the main objectives of financial reports can be derived from the role that investors and creditors have played throughout history as well as in shaping current standard setting. More specifically, investors and creditors require information about firms in order to make investment and lending decisions. The extent to which information is decision-useful is thus an indicator of its quality. Investors will find information useful if it helps predict future firm performance and is capable of informing the decisions to buy, hold or sell shares. In addition, information is useful if it helps investors evaluate past performance and monitor management, or helps creditors determine the liquidity and default risk associated with making loans to the firm.

Capital markets The underlying premise of this discussion is that there is information uncertainty in a capital market setting. Information uncertainty can be decomposed into two parts: measurement uncertainty and information asymmetry. More specifically,

- Management may not have knowledge about the true earnings number because of *measurement (estimation) uncertainty*. That is, the underlying economic conditions and transactions (events and states), or their value implications are unknown—even to the firm. An interpretation of this is that the *precision* of the information is low.
- Management *does* have knowledge about underlying economic events and states, but does not disclose them or the potential estimation difficulties associated with them, causing *information asymmetry*.

The first type of uncertainty is partly innate to a given condition or transaction, and thus to the associated accounting item on the balance sheet or income statement. But it is also affected by accounting procedures and methods. For example, we may identify some items as being subject to greater measurement uncertainty, and this is more salient when accounting standards allow more discretion.[1] Whereas measurement uncertainty affects both investors and managers, the second type of uncertainty (information asymmetry) constitutes an extra source of uncertainty mainly for investors.

The above discussion relates directly to quality in that quality (usefulness) may be evaluated in primarily two different ways: 1) in terms of how well the financial statements reflect that which they purport to reflect—and this is affected by estimation uncertainty, and 2) in terms of how well the information is communicated to users—and this is related to information asymmetry. In standard-setting terminology, the first point is related to the *faithful representation* (or reliability) of underlying economic transactions and conditions, while the second point is related to the *relevance* of financial reporting to users.

High-quality accounting (essentially, faithfully represented and relevant financial reports) enhances the communication between entrepreneurs and financiers, working like lubrication in the economic system and helping to direct capital to where the highest returns can be made. In the best of worlds, reduced information asymmetry and uncertainty between management and capital providers improves resource allocation and increases economic efficiency. Assuming there are economic trickle-down effects when capital is efficiently allocated, accounting is also able to promote economic growth on a larger scale and increase the overall wealth in the economy (i.e., there are wider macroeconomic effects of accounting). The welfare of society, rather than that of certain individuals, thus becomes the wider target of analysis.

1 Of course, assuming there is a "true", underlying reality that accounting is meant to portray, measurement uncertainty is exogenous to (unaffected by) the choice of method. In other words, whether or not we recognize the need for managerial judgment has no bearing on the amount of actual uncertainty that exists in a reported number. This discussion is rather philosophical and we do not explore this idea further here.

16.1 Key findings and conclusions

In this book, we have attempted to take a holistic approach to accounting theory and empirical research. Instead of describing each adopted theory in detail, we position them in the broader (empirical) literature on determinants of accounting, and the effects of accounting in capital markets. Although we do not always make explicit references to actual theories, a substantial volume of research has been done that touches upon the core concepts and ideas in the field of financial accounting. This means that there is considerable knowledge available regarding the reasons for why accounting standards are designed the way they are, explanations for various managerial choices and discretionary judgments, as well as the effects that different accounting standards and accounting choices have on financial statements and their quality.

We recognize that theories can be positive (descriptive) or normative (prescriptive). Economic theories borrowed from finance and economics are largely positive, while accounting-specific conceptualizations, such as provided by regulators, are normative. Although the global standard-setters have not developed a complete or coherent framework that can be classified as a comprehensive accounting theory, they make attempts to create theoretical and logical structures for financial reporting. There is an objective function—that accounting should be useful—and concrete ideas for how this objective should be fulfilled. These include the primary qualitative characteristics of relevance and faithful representation, as well as other qualitative characteristics (e.g., understandability and timeliness) and principles that are implied rather than explicit (e.g. substance over form and matching). Behind the framework is the technique of double-entry bookkeeping. In this context, a principles-based approach is often compared to a rules-based approach to regulation. The question is whether principles—which have a higher level of abstraction—are better or worse than explicit, bright-line rules when it comes to achieving the stated objective. The development of standards shows that a certain level of rules are believed to be necessary.

In developing standards, regulators benefit from empirical input provided by research, and more specifically, positive theories. For example, the extent to which markets are efficient, or the existence of information asymmetry, can help explain the usefulness of accounting information. They predict management's behavior and accounting choices, as well as investors' ability to process the information as well as see through accounting choices. Agency theory further predicts that managers have incentives to disclose in certain ways. Potential opportunism impacts on capital providers' decision-making, and creates demands for regulation, monitoring and enforcement. Further incentives are generated by a desire to legitimize operations, resulting in increased transparency or, conversely, impression management.

We think of useful disclosures as being informative, non-opportunistic and non-biased. Meanwhile, biased disclosures—due to (intentional) opportunism or unintentional errors—will be less informative and thus less useful. Because of the sustained belief that informative disclosures carry benefits for firms as well as capital providers—that is, they have positive capital market effects—much research has been carried out on disclosure quality. There is a large number of studies that have sought to show what the effects of disclosure are, including consequences for liquidity, price volatility, cost of capital and analyst accuracy. Inherent in this literature is the continuous discussion of what disclosure quality actually *is*. Quantity-based measures using check-lists were used in earlier studies, but in recent years, concerns about information overload has shifted the focus to how disclosures are written and presented. This is considered especially pertinent given the existence of information-processing costs and theories in behavioral economics that point to investors' limited attention.

One specific line item that has been singled out from firms' disclosure package is *earnings*. Earnings quality is considered to be important for investors and has been examined in relation to its determinants and its consequences. Determinants refer to factors identified in the accounting choice literature, including contract-based incentives, while consequences refer to various capital market effects—both the usefulness of earnings for stewardship purposes and evaluating managerial performance, and their usefulness for security valuation (an analysis of determinants and consequences can, of course, be applied to disclosures other than earnings). Different measures of earnings quality, such as income smoothing, the value relevance of earnings, and the quality of the accruals, have been employed and scrutinized.

As we looked at individual line items in the balance sheet and further up the income statement (Part V), we indirectly considered earnings quality and accruals quality. Earnings are made up of many small items, and these are affected by choices that affect the income statement directly as well as indirectly via the balance sheet. Several of the items have been subject to substantial discussion in standard-setting. Examples of particularly controversial items include goodwill, financial instruments, share-based compensation, and the definition of subsidiaries.

16.2 Key articles

In this book, we have provided over five hundred references to academic articles published in the field of accounting. Our focus has been on *paradigmatic* research, or what is sometimes referred to as "mainstream" accounting research. Because the purpose of our literature has been to give an overview of the subject to those who are not yet initiated in the research literature, we make no claims of being comprehensive. We have inevitably missed important papers and topics. However, we have tried to give a fair description of the work, as a whole, that has had considerable influence on the direction accounting research has taken over the past few decades, while simultaneously linking this to practice and regulation, and issues raised by standard-setters.

Some streams of research, particularly the growing literature pertaining to sustainability reporting, has been almost completely neglected. This does not mean it is not relevant. We think that in the future, this research will have growing influence on the field as a whole. However, this research is currently not considered core, as both researchers and standard-setters to date have focused on economic reporting aspects. Further, it is not our area of expertise and we leave it to scholars who are more knowledgeable in this area to cover such topics.

We have carried out a simple bibliometric analysis and present the results in this section. Table 16.1 shows the 25 most cited papers in the top 26 journals in the subject of accounting.

Citation statistics are obtained from Web of Science (WoS)[2] (an online, scientific citation indexing service). Top journals are identified using the Chartered Association of Business Schools' Academic Journal Guide (AJG, described further in the next section). You will recognize a large number of the article titles from this book, consistent with our perception that they are "core" papers in the field. We have classified them roughly according to their most central topic—topics you should also be able to recognize from this book (see the Category column). As you can see, a large majority of the papers are about earnings quality, earnings management, market responses, and the cost of capital. There is a small number of studies that treat one particular topic we have *not* discussed in this book—and that is the prediction of financial distress in firms. Notably, the studies shown in the table are all somewhat dated, and the list is biased toward older studies since it takes time for citations to accumulate. It is therefore possible to weight the citations depending on the age of the article. There are several possible algorithms one can apply for this purpose, but we have opted for a simple calculation that takes the average number of citations per year since its publication. The results are shown in Table 16.2 and reveal that accounting researchers have recently taken increased interest in international accounting issues (which coincides with the adoption of IFRS in a number of countries), and research design or methods-related issues. The latter is consistent with increasing pressure to produce not only theoretically well-anchored but econometrically sound work. Among the 100 top citations, there are (still) only five papers that have to do with sustainability or environmental disclosures. One of them appears on the time-adjusted Top 25 list.

Of the top five articles in Table 16.1, four are related to earnings quality, and are discussed in Chapter 7. More specifically, Jones (1991); Dechow et al. (1995); Kothari et al. (2005) relate to abnormal accruals, while (Ball and Brown, 1968) is an early version of value relevance research. This is an indication of the importance given to earnings in financial accounting research. Table 16.2 gives a similar picture, with four out of the top five articles focusing on abnormal accruals (Kothari et al., 2005; Dechow et al., 1995; Dechow and Dichev, 2002; Jones, 1991).

---

2 It is fully possible to use other citation tools, the most well-known of which perhaps is Google Scholar. Google Scholar is extremely useful for a number of tasks (especially for finding individual papers), but its larger number of reported citations also means it is noisier; it captures citations from a number of less desirable sources. Even though the WoS citation number is smaller, it is more likely that citations are relevant. Although one cannot compare the number of citations between WoS and, for example, Google Scholar, comparisons made within each database will yield unbiased results.

Table 16.1 Top 25 cited articles in accounting journals

No. Cit.	Authors	Title	Category	Journal	Year
1501	Jones, J	Earnings management during import relief investigations	EQ	JAR	1991
1409	Dechow, P; Sloan, R; Sweeney, A	Detecting earnings management	EQ	TAR	1995
1217	Ball, R; Brown, P	Empirical evaluation of accounting income numbers	MR	JAR	1968
1211	Ohlson, J	Financial ratios and the probabilistic prediction of bankruptcy	F	JAR	1980
1179	Kothari, SP; Leone, A; Wasley, C	Performance matched discretionary accrual measures	EQ	JAE	2005
1167	Graham, J; Harvey, C; Rajgopal, S	The economic implications of corporate financial reporting	EQ	JAE	2005
1075	Sloan, R	Do stock prices fully reflect information in accruals and cash flows about future earnings?	MR	TAR	1996
996	Healy, P	The effect of bonus schemes on accounting decisions	AC	JAE	1985
983	Klein, A	Audit committee, board of director characteristics, and earnings management	EQ	JAE	2002
948	Dechow, P; Dichev, I	The quality of accruals and earnings: the role of accrual estimation errors	EQ	TAR	2002
940	Botosan, C	Disclosure level and the cost of equity capital	MR	TAR	1997
927	Beasley, M	An empirical analysis of the relation between the board of director composition and financial statement fraud	EQ	TAR	1996
914	Ball, R; Kothari, SP; Robin, A	The effect of international institutional factors on properties of accounting earnings	I	JAE	2000
871	Basu, S	The conservatism principle and the asymmetric timeliness of earnings	EQ	JAE	1997
849	Burgstahler, D; Dichev, I	Earnings management to avoid earnings decreases and losses	EQ	JAE	1997
832	Beaver, W	Financial ratios as predictors of failure	F	JAR	1966
767	Lang, M; Lundholm, R	Corporate disclosure policy and analyst behavior	MR	TAR	1996
738	Verrecchia, R	Discretionary disclosure	MR	JAE	1983
729	Bushee, B	The influence of institutional investors on myopic R	D investment behavior	AC	TAR
716	Lang, M; Lundholm, R	Cross-sectional determinants of analyst ratings of corporate disclosures	MR	JAR	1993

No. Cit.	Authors	Title	Category	Journal	Year
679	Leuz, C; Verrecchia, R	The economic consequences of increased disclosure	MR	JAR	2000
673	Francis, J; Lafond, R; Olsson, P; Schipper, K	The market pricing of accruals quality	MR	JAE	2005
656	Zmijewski, M	Methodological issues related to the estimation of financial distress prediction models	F	JAR	1984
655	Defond, M; Jiambalvo, J	Debt covenant violation and manipulation of accruals	EQ	JAE	1994
633	Dechow, P	Accounting earnings and cash flows as measures of firm performance - the role of accounting accruals	EQ	JAE	1994

Notes: Two papers have been dropped from the list because they are deemed to belong to management accounting: "The new public management in the 1980s—Variations on a theme" by Christopher Hood (1995), and "Management control systems design within its organizational context: Findings from contingency-based research and directions for the future" by Robert Chenhall (2003), both published in *Accounting, Organizations and Society.* Another paper has been dropped from the list because it is a review paper: "Information asymmetry, corporate disclosure, and the capital markets: A review of the empirical disclosure literature" by Paul Healy and Krishna Palepu (2001). The categories that the papers have been assigned to are not mutually exclusive, and some papers could easily be assigned to multiple categories. However crude the labels are, we still believe they give an idea of what the focus in the literature is. Categories—EQ: Earnings quality (including earnings management); MR: Market responses (including cost of capital and analyst behavior); F: (predicting) Failure, bankruptcy and financial distress in firms; AC: Accounting choice (including earnings management); I: Institutional factors affecting accounting. Journal abbreviations—TAR: *The Accounting Review*; JAE: *Journal of Accounting & Economics*; JAR: *Journal of Accounting Research.*

Table 16.2 Top 25 cited articles in accounting journals—Time-adjusted

Authors	Title	Category	Journal	Year
Kothari, SP; Leone, A; Wasley, C	Performance matched discretionary accrual measures	EQ	JAE	2005
Klein, A	Audit committee, board of director characteristics, and earnings management	EQ	JAE	2002
Dechow, P; Sloan, R; Sweeney, A	Detecting earnings management	EQ	TAR	1995
Dechow, P; Dichev, I	The quality of accruals and earnings: the role of accrual estimation errors	EQ	TAR	2002
Jones, J	Earnings management during import relief investigations	EQ	JAR	1991
Barth, M; Landsman, W; Lang, M	International accounting standards and accounting quality	I	JAR	2008
Francis, J; Lafond, R; Olsson, P; Schipper, K	The market pricing of accruals quality	MR	JAE	2005
Ball, R; Kothari, SP; Robin, A	The effect of international institutional factors on properties of accounting earnings	I	JAE	2000
Larcker, D; Rusticus, T	On the use of instrumental variables in accounting research	M	JAE	2010

Authors	Title	Category	Journal	Year
Dhaliwal, D; Li, O; Tsang, A; Yang, Y	Voluntary nonfinancial disclosure and the cost of equity capital: the initiation of corporate social responsibility reporting	MR	TAR	2011
Sloan, R	Do stock prices fully reflect information in accruals and cash flows about future earnings?	MR	TAR	1996
Roychowdhury, S	Earnings management through real activities manipulation	EQ	JAE	2006
Cohen, D; Dey, A; Lys, T	Real and accrual-based earnings management in the pre- and post-Sarbanes-Oxley periods	EQ	TAR	2008
Daske, H; Hail, L; Leuz, C; Verdi, R	Mandatory IFRS reporting around the world: early evidence on the economic consequences	I	JAR	2008
Botosan, C	Disclosure level and the cost of equity capital	MR	TAR	1997
Clarkson, P; Li, Y; Richardson, G; Vasvari, F	Revisiting the relation between environmental performance and environmental disclosure: an empirical analysis	E	AOS	2008
Gow, I; Ormazabal, G; Taylor, D	Correcting for cross-sectional and time-series dependence in accounting research	M	TAR	2010
Ball, R; Shivakumar, L	Earnings quality in UK private firms: comparative loss recognition timeliness	EQ	JAE	2005
Lambert, R; Leuz, C; Verrecchia, R	Accounting information, disclosure, and the cost of capital	MR	JAR	2007
Beasley, M	An empirical analysis of the relation between the board of director composition and financial statement fraud	EQ	TAR	1996
Basu, S	The conservatism principle and the asymmetric timeliness of earnings	EQ	JAE	1997
Burgstahler, D; Dichev, I	Earnings management to avoid earnings decreases and losses	EQ	JAE	1997
Francis, J; Lafond, R; Olsson, Pm; Schipper, K	Costs of equity and earnings attributes	MR	TAR	2004
Lennox, C; Francis, J; Wang, Z	Selection models in accounting research	M	TAR	2012
Ball, R; Robin, A; Wu, J	Incentives versus standards: properties of accounting income in four East Asian countries	I	JAE	2003

Notes: One paper has been dropped from the list because it is deemed to belong to management accounting: "The new public management in the 1980s—Variations on a theme" by Christopher Hood (1995), published in *Accounting, Organizations and Society*. Three other papers have been dropped from the list because they are review papers. The categories that the papers have been assigned to are not mutually exclusive, and some papers could easily be assigned to multiple categories. However crude the labels are, we still believe they give an idea of what the focus in the literature is. Categories—EQ: Earnings quality (including earnings management); MR: Market responses (including cost of capital and analyst behavior); F: (Predicting) failure, bankruptcy and financial distress in firms; AC: Accounting choice (including earnings management); I: Institutional factors affecting accounting; E: Non-financial/sustainability/environmental disclosures; M: Methods-based paper. Journal abbreviations—AOS: *Accounting, Organizations & Society*; TAR: *The Accounting Review*; JAE: *Journal of Accounting & Economics*; JAR: *Journal of Accounting Research*. Citations per year range between 91 (max.) and 38 (min.).

A simple content analysis of the titles of the 100 top-cited articles reveals the frequency with which each word appears. Table 16.3 lists all words that occur at least five times, and shows that disclosure, earnings (including earnings management), quality, value relevance, cost of capital, and auditing are central topics in the literature.

Table 16.3 Frequency of words in the titles of the 100 top-cited articles

Count	Word	Comment
32	earnings	
21	accounting	
14	disclosure	
12	corporate	
11	management	(eight of which refer to earnings management)
11	financial	
11	empirical	
9	performance	
8	relevance	(five of which refer to value relevance)
8	quality	
8	information	
8	capital	
7	equity	
7	cost	(all of which refer to cost of capital)
7	analysis	
7	accruals	
6	value	(five of which refer to value relevance)
6	research	
6	environmental	
6	auditor	
5	theory	
5	stock	(three of which refer to stock prices, and two of which refer to stock options)
5	reporting	
5	evidence	
5	audit	

Note: the following words have been omitted from the analysis: the, and, in, on, for, an, to, do

16.3 Research outlets and focus

As shown in the previous section, the most cited articles come from a limited number of journals, so called "A-journals", or "AJG 4 'star' journals". In general, there is a large concentration of literature in a select few journals, and scholars compete to appear in these prestigious outlets. In fact, from the 100 most cited articles, 45 appear in *Journal of Accounting & Economic* (JAE), 26 in *Journal of Accounting Research* (JAR), 21 in *The Accounting Review* (TAR), and 8 in *Accounting, Organizations and Society* (AOS).

Different rating systems exist, but we present here the top journals as specified by the AJG in 2018.[3] A journal that is considered to be of acceptable quality will be rated—where 1 marks the lowest rating and 4 marks the highest rating—while those journals that are considered to be of lower academic quality are unrated. A total of 88 accounting journals were included in the most recent guide, six of which are rated a 4, twenty-one a 3, thirty-four a 2, and twenty-seven a 1. We show the journals that have been rated a 4, a 3 or a 2 in Table 16.4.

Table 16.4 List of accounting journals with a top rating according to the AJG 2018 (by the Chartered Association of Business Schools)

AJG 4-rating	**AJG 2-rating**
Accounting Review*	Accounting and Finance
Accounting, Organizations and Society*	Accounting and the Public Interest
Journal of Accounting and Economics*	Accounting in Europe
Journal of Accounting Research*	Accounting Research Journal
Contemporary Accounting Research	Accounting, Economics and Law—A Convivium
Review of Accounting Studies	Advances in Accounting
	Advances in Accounting Behavioral Research
	Advances in Management Accounting
AJG 3-rating	Advances in Taxation
Abacus	Asia-Pacific Journal of Accounting and Economics
Accounting and Business Research	Asian Review of Accounting
Accounting Forum	Australian Accounting Review
Accounting Horizons	China Journal of Accounting Research
Accounting, Auditing and Accountability Journal	Current Issues in Auditing
Auditing: A Journal of Practice and Theory	International Journal of Accounting and Information Management
Behavioral Research in Accounting	International Journal of Accounting, Auditing and Performance Evaluation

3 The AJG was previously known, and is frequently referred to, as the ABS ranking system.

AJG 3-rating	AJG 2-rating
British Accounting Review	International Journal of Accounting Information Systems
British Tax Review	International Journal of Auditing
Critical Perspectives on Accounting	International Journal of Disclosure and Governance
European Accounting Review	International Journal of Managerial and Financial Accounting
Financial Accountability and Management	Journal of Accounting and Organizational Change
Foundations and Trends in Accounting	Journal of Accounting in Emerging Economies
International Journal of Accounting	Journal of Applied Accounting Research
Journal of Accounting and Public Policy	Journal of Contemporary Accounting and Economics
Journal of Accounting Literature	Journal of International Accounting Research
Journal of Accounting, Auditing and Finance	Journal of International Financial Management and Accounting
Journal of Business Finance and Accounting	Journal of Management Accounting Research
Journal of International Accounting, Auditing and Taxation	Journal of Management Control
Journal of the American Taxation Association	Journal of Public Budgeting, Accounting and Financial Management
Management Accounting Research	Journal of Tax Administration
	Managerial Auditing Journal
	Qualitative Research in Accounting and Management
	Research in Accounting Regulation
	Sustainability Accounting, Management and Policy Journal

Note: *marks the absolute top journals, so called "star" journals. Within each category journals are in alphabetical order.

Journal ratings in general are based on their impact factor and number of citations, metrics which are believed to be associated with the perceived quality and scientific integrity of a given journal. AJG ratings are somewhat different, in that they are qualitative as opposed to just quantitative, informed by subject experts in the academic community.

Different journals do not only have different ratings, but they also differ with respect to focus and style. Depending on the topic investigated and which research design is employed, a researcher will consider different potential outlets. Some journals are more open to studies on regulation, others to social responsibility and accountability issues, and yet others to "mainstream" capital market studies. Some are more open to normative debates, while others only accept empirical research. All major (AJG 4-rated) academic journals, except

Accounting, Organizations and Society, are clearly positioned within an economics-based and empirical[4] research paradigm.

With respect to the "AJG 4 'star' " journals, these are largely dominated by scholars from US universities, and three of the top four journals are US-based: *The Accounting Review* was founded by the American Accounting Association, its first issue dating back to 1926; *Journal of Accounting Research* was created by the University of Chicago Booth School of Business[5], in collaboration with the London School of Economics, in 1963; and *Journal of Accounting & Economics* was founded by Ross Watts and Jerold Zimmerman at the University of Rochester in 1979. Today, all of these represent the positive research tradition. Meanwhile, *Accounting, Organizations and Society*, which was established by Anthony Hopwood in 1975, originates in Britain. Although it does publish empirical studies, it is more methodologically diverse.

The creation and development of these journals largely reflect the shift from normative to positive research described in Chapter 2. In the twenty years between 1945 and 1965, TAR had a large focus on normative research, and included work by practitioners and educators (Dyckman and Zeff, 1984). The wish for a competitive outlet with a different focus led to the launch of JAR. Initially, although JAR encouraged empirical research, normative papers actually outnumbered empirical papers. However, over the next ten years of the journal's existence, JAR shifted its focus solely to empirical papers that were largely rooted in the disciplines of economics and finance. Incidentally, the same shift came about in TAR.

Between 1986 and 2005, virtually all (99%) of articles published in TAR were statistical or contained "complex mathematical equations" (Heck and Jensen, 2007). Normative, historical, practice-oriented and case-based studies were nowhere to be seen.[6] The same trend could be seen in the other top journals as well. One might claim this was partly a bottom-up movement—the bulk of submitted papers were simply changing in character. Researchers may thus simply have been more interested in statistical methods, as data availability increased. At least according to Hopwood (2007, p. 1366), the change was "largely a revolution from below". Consistent with Kuhn's view of scientific revolutions, older generations are seldom the cause of revolutions. Edwards et al. (2013) lists Ray Ball, William Beaver, Philip Brown, Joel Demski and Ross Watts as examples of the type of pioneering, new generation of researchers that instigated the "revolution". However, in many ways, it was also a top-down movement. Top schools incorporated publications in top journals into their promotion requirements, making it essential for researchers to conform to the demands of journal editors. Some editors were clearly pro-empirical work, one individual explaining the rejection of a paper by a renowned normative researcher as a result of "[a] lack of harmony between the paper and the changing state-of-the-art (#9738)" (Edwards et al., 2013). Normative research was simply not in vogue.

---

4 We partly use the term "empirical" in a broad sense here (cf. positive). It encompasses both analytical research used to generate economics-based, positive theory and empirical research that uses statistics to test theory.

5 COMPUSTAT and CRSP, the most important sources of accounting and pricing data today, were created by the University of Chicago in 1962 and 1960, respectively, unequivocally contributing to the development described in this section.

6 Interestingly, in 2005, TAR was pronounced too narrow in scope by then-president of the AAA, Judy Rayburn (Heck and Jensen, 2007).

This does not mean that all journals that today are empirical, were at all times receptive of the new type of research. The study by Ball and Brown (1968) was famously rejected by TAR for not being an "accounting manuscript".

Whether the changes here were driven by top-down or bottom-up influences, some academics point to the existence of (local) elite groups that dominate top journals (see, e.g. Lee, 1995; Lukka and Kasanen, 1996) and make a convincing argument that it is this *academic elite* who decide on what is to be considered legitimate knowledge, and what is deserving of being published (Lee, 1999; Edwards et al., 2013). Edwards et al. (2013) note that:

> The academic accounting community therefore exists within a defined social space ... [N] ormative theorists [failed] to maintain their elite status within the field of academe. Instead, their social space was successfully overrun by empiricists-cum-positivists who, in contrast, have protected and substantially maintained their position in the social order through to the present day ... (p. 368)

We do not mean to cast a dark shadow over the research presented in this book with such critical assessments of the research landscape. We wish to acknowledge, however, that we fall short of presenting a comprehensive picture of all accounting research, having focused on one paradigm only. Admittedly, a book of this kind must always be limited in scope, and therefore, almost inevitably, "biased". In all fairness, more weight could be placed on other types of research or other views on accounting than those reflected here. We, ourselves, are thus swept up by the efforts and accomplishment of the established elite! Having said this, we hope to have provided a sufficiently accurate picture of *mainstream* research in accounting, the nature of the reigning paradigm and the theories contained within, and finally, a better understanding of how research and standard-setting interact.

In the two final sections of the book, further criticism of empirical work is briefly presented, followed by a brief commentary on research in the immediate future.

16.3.1 Criticism of the current state of affairs

One major problem, highlighted as early as in 1975 by Chambers and in 1983 by Zeff, and reiterated by James Ohlson in 2015, is that "the practising and academic arms of the profession are at an intellectual arm's length" (see letter to Sterling by Chambers in Edwards et al., 2013). That is, there is little connection between practice and academia. Researchers are disconnected from the "real world", presenting hypotheses that are divorced from reality (Ohlson, 2015). It is like the issues raised are living their own life. Zeff calls them "contrived"—essentially an excuse to try out some new research design—while Kaplan questions the *external* validity of much empirical research (see citations in Edwards et al., 2013).[7]

Ohlson (2015) launches a near full-on attack on empirical research, presenting four major

---

7 While "internal" validity is the notion that one successfully measures that which one purports to measure, external validity has more to do with the relevance of the measurements. Research that applies rigorous methods and carefully motivated choices of variables could exhibit high internal validity, but if the underlying constructs that the variables are meant to capture are of little interest, external validity will suffer.

concerns about the current state-of-affairs. Being in the "empirical camp" himself, it is not the methods themselves Ohlson (2015) criticizes, but rather the mindless—or opportunistic—application of them. First, he points to the lack of realism in research questions (see above), with earnings management being his primary example of where research seems to have been divorced from reality (admittedly, the critique could have been developed more thoroughly here). The world is complex, but accounting researchers have oversimplified their explanations, even when the underlying phenomena are far from intuitive or straightforward. This leads to his second point—results are "too clean". How come the evidence presented is so often unambiguous, given the underlying complexities, and given that the explanatory variable studied is typically added to a large number of variables already examined in the literature? There is apparently no end to the amount of variables that can be used to explain a single phenomenon. Third, given the number of variables, researchers should be more concerned with the goodness-of-fit of their models. To have statistically significant variable coefficients is not very impressive when the number of observations is in the tens of thousands. Instead, researchers should be more concerned with whether the additional variable actually increases the explanatory power of the model (one such measure—though criticized for reasons we do not go through here—is a regression model's *R*-squared). All too frequently, no discussion is dedicated to such concepts, the predicted reason being that findings would disappoint the researcher; while statistically significant, the new variable is likely to have low or no *economic* significance. Finally, on a more technical note, the scaling of variables is often inappropriate and can lead to spurious results. The sum of all of these problems, is irrelevant research that, additionally, too often rejects a true null hypothesis of *no association*.[8] Dyckman and Zeff (2014) as well as Dyckman and Zeff (2015) raise similar issues, with respect to inappropriate significance tests and a failure of many studies to address the economic significance of their work.

It behooves researchers (including current students and soon-to-be researchers) to think about the implications and relevance of their work. We must determine (maybe even agree on?) the objective(s) of accounting, and then proceed in a similar fashion with respect to the objective of our research. Only then can we, feasibly, do meaningful research and make worthwhile accomplishments.

16.4 Future challenges and research

With 20/20 hindsight, the rejection of the seminal paper by Ball and Brown (1968) may elicit a smile or two (see above). However, it is wise to consider Hopwood's (2007) observation (p. 1367):

> There were then, there have been in the intervening period, and there are now people who think that they know what accounting—and auditing for that matter—is. How wrong these people are. They are the ones who list the attributes of the status quo, seemingly wanting to confine the new to being within the boundaries of the old. They have no conception that

8 This is what may be referred to as a Type I error. A Type II error occurs when one fails to reject a null hypothesis when it is *not true*. See similar comment on accruals quality models in Chapter 7.

> accounting and accounting research have repeatedly changed across time, and when things change they become what they were not, at least in part. Accounting has been a craft that has had no essence. It has changed significantly across time, adopting new forms, methods, and roles. Likewise for accounting research.

Perhaps accounting research has matured, and what we see today is the future of accounting research. Or, what we think of as core research today might not at all be considered relevant a hundred years from now.

Worryingly, as pointed out by Hopwood (2007) and others, accounting academics have become increasingly conservative and rigid, afraid to try out new things, and narrow in their focus. They hide within the confines of the safe paradigmatic walls they have built. One reason for this effective insulation, and that research is divorced from practice, may very well be that academics simply have decreasing professional experience outside of the business school (Hopwood, 2007).

To be innovative and not conformist, academics must look outside of academia, and understand the social and economic context in which businesses operate and accounting serves. This does not mean they should get caught in the political winds that blow through the halls of our schools and universities. Quite the opposite. Long-term trends and technical developments could, however, provide a framework for a new set of questions, even if the current research paradigm persists. The past few decades have witnessed a rise in research on sustainability and corporate social responsibility. The novelty of this area around the end of the second decade of the 21st century is perhaps doubtful, but it is far from a mature or saturated field. As accounting for social and environmental matters becomes increasingly regulated, we are likely to see more research in this area. Rather than being peripheral, it may become commonplace or mainstream.

In these final paragraphs, we conclude that—although a "buzz word"—*digitization* is likely to have an increasing impact on accounting research. It has already started to influence how research is carried out; in other words, more heavily computerized research methods are being employed in the context of data collection as well as data analysis (not least text analysis). IT-based solutions and algorithms allow researchers to process data in novel ways. However, the importance of digitization is perhaps even greater when it comes to its influence on the underlying objects of researchers; in other words, its influence on businesses, accountants, the actual systems for financial reporting used in firms, and the shape of the financial statements themselves.

Closely tied to digitization is the concept of *Big Data*. Depending on the size of the storage and the processing capabilities, what is considered "big" will vary (Vasarhelyi et al., 2015), but what is certain is that Big Data is changing how businesses and organizations operate. The amount of data produced around the world is increasing daily. Businesses and organizations are realizing that in order to stay competitive, the available information must be harvested and used.

Accounting is information, and more information—as a result of Big Data—may drastically change the way we think about accounting. We might experience a paradigm shift (Vasarhelyi et al., 2015). Once upon a time, financial reporting consisted of yearly accounts showing summaries of a few key line items. Eventually, capital providers would eagerly await the quarterly rather than annual update. Over the past few decades, ever since the IT revolution, information has been delivered to users in real time. The focus, however, has remained on summary measures, because information processing abilities have not caught up with information availability. Until recently, that is. Access, and the ability to process, large quantities of (largely unstructured) information is pointing to a possible future where summary measures are less important. So-called **Business Intelligence** systems (Chen et al., 2012; Watson and Wixom, 2007) enable storage (warehousing) and analysis of complex data sets using combinations of deep machine learning, statistics and other tools. Depending on the users' needs, they themselves can extract the underlying, raw data necessary for analysis. Some have even voiced the coming "death" of the annual report. Warren Jr et al. (2015, p. 397) declare that:

> The rising importance of Big Data will significantly impact accounting. This will be reflected in how data are accumulated and recorded, how management uses data to attain organizational goals, and how reporting elements are processed and assembled.

Warren Jr et al. (2015) propose a number of ways in which accounting can be affected by Big Data. For example, by using the large amounts of data generated inside firms, new corporate governance mechanisms may appear, and it is possible that there will be changes in the way boards carry out monitoring or managerial performance evaluations. Meanwhile, the declining value relevance of financial statements, possibly due to increasing levels of off-balance sheet items, such as intangibles (Srivastava, 2014; Collins et al., 1997), is believed to threaten their usefulness. This trend could be countered if asset values could be analyzed using data-mining algorithms. Another accounting area that is fraught with challenges is fair value accounting. Warren Jr et al. (2015) explain how estimations of fair value, especially when level 3 inputs are used, could be improved using Big Data-techniques. Finally, depreciation and amortization schedules are often based on straight-line methods that poorly reflect the actual use of assets. This could be remedied with up-to-date, detailed information about how assets are actually used.

There are other lines of technical development that might have a large impact on the practice of accounting in the future, and thus indirectly affect accounting research. Accounting is a way to instill trust between independent parties involved in economic transactions. In 14th century Venice, double-entry bookkeeping helped instill trust between capital providers and captains responsible for trade voyages at sea. In the 21st century, *blockchain* may be a technique to instill trust in various situations. To date, it is difficult to forecast the effect of blockchain on accounting, but there is a potentially substantial impact.

So what can we learn from financial accounting research? It is complex, the evidence provided is often mixed, and there are many factors that affect the quality of financial statements. Even if critics such as Ohlson (2015) point to weaknesses in many individual studies in financial accounting, there is still substantial accumulated knowledge within the research presented in this book. There is compelling evidence in a number of areas, and some conclusions can safely be drawn. For example:

- Accounting is useful for capital providers as it alters the level of information uncertainty in the market.
- Managerial incentives affect accounting quality.
- Standards—and compliance with them—affect accounting quality.
- Regulated (mandatory) as well as unregulated (voluntary) disclosures can affect information asymmetry and the cost of capital.
- Accounting has an important role in many corporate governance settings.

Research has also provided many insights regarding how to operationalize and think about concepts such as relevance and faithful representation (i.e., how to measure accounting quality as defined by standard-setters). The increasing knowledge coincides with an increased interest by standard-setters to be informed by research in the standard-setting process (i.e. evidence-based standard-setting).

Finally, we hope this book has been able to guide and point the reader to important developments in the field, as well as generated interest in a comparatively young and constantly evolving academic discipline. Anyone interested in accounting research—and in developing accounting theory— should find plenty of opportunities for future contributions.

BIBLIOGRAPHY

Abbott, L.J., Daugherty, B., Parker, S., and Peters, G.F. (2016). Internal audit quality and financial reporting quality: The joint importance of independence and competence. *Journal of Accounting Research*, 54 (1): 3–40.

Aboody, D., Barth, M.E., and Kasznik, R. (1999). Revaluations of fixed assets and future firm performance: Evidence from the UK. *Journal of Accounting and Economics*, 26 (1-3): 149–178.

Aboody, D., Johnson, N.B., and Kasznik, R. (2010). Employee stock options and future firm performance: Evidence from option repricings. *Journal of Accounting and Economics*, 50 (1): 74–92.

Aboody, D. and Kasznik, R. (2000). CEO stock option awards and the timing of corporate voluntary disclosures. *Journal of Accounting and Economics*, 29 (1): 73–100.

Abraham, S. and Shrives, P.J. (2014). Improving the relevance of risk factor disclosure in corporate annual reports. *British Accounting Review*, 46 (1): 91–107.

AbuGhazaleh, N.M., Al-Hares, O.M., and Roberts, C. (2011). Accounting discretion in goodwill impairments: UK evidence. *Journal of International Financial Management & Accounting*, 22 (3): 165–204.

Achleitner, A.K., Günther, N., Kaserer, C., and Siciliano, G. (2014). Real earnings management and accrual-based earnings management in family firms. *European Accounting Review*, 23 (3): 431–461.

Adams, R., Hermalin, B., and Weisbach, M. (2010). The role of boards of directors in corporate governance: A conceptual framework & survey. *Journal of Economic Literature*, 48 (1): 58–107.

Agoglia, C.P., Doupnik, T.S., and Tsakumis, G.T. (2011). Principles-based versus rules-based accounting standards: The influence of standard precision and audit committee strength on financial reporting decisions. *Accounting Review*, 86 (3): 747–767.

Agrawal, A., Jaffe, J.F., and Karpoff, J.M. (1999). Management turnover and governance changes following the revelation of fraud. *The Journal of Law and Economics*, 42 (S1): 309–342.

Aharony, J., Barniv, R., and Falk, H. (2010). The impact of mandatory IFRS adoption on equity valuation of accounting numbers for security investors in the EU. *European Accounting Review*, 19 (3): 535–578.

Ahmed, A.S., Neel, M., and Wang, D. (2013). Does mandatory adoption of IFRS improve accounting quality? Preliminary evidence. *Contemporary Accounting Research*, 30 (4): 1344–1372.

Ahmed, A.S., Takeda, C., and Thomas, S. (1999). Bank loan loss provisions: A reexamination of capital management, earnings management and signaling effects. *Journal of Accounting and Economics*, 28 (1): 1–25.

Akerlof, G.A. (1970). The market for "lemons": Quality uncertainty and the market mechanism. *Quarterly Journal of Economics*, 84 (3): 488–500.

Al-Tuwaijri, S.A., Christensen, T.E., and II, K.H. (2004). The relations among environmental disclosure, environmental performance, and economic performance: A simultaneous equations approach. *Accounting, Organizations and Society*, 29 (5-6): 447–471.

Ali, A., Chen, T., and Radhakrishnan, S. (2007). Corporate disclosures by family firms. *Journal of Accounting and Economics*, 44 (1): 238–286.

Altamuro, J., Johnston, R., Pandit, S.S., and Zhang, H.H. (2014). Operating leases and credit assessments. *Contemporary Accounting Research*, 31 (2): 551–580

Amernic, J. and Craig, R. (2011). Detecting linguistic traces of destructive narcissism at-a-distance in a CEO's letter to shareholders. *Journal of Business Ethics*, 101 (4): 563–575.

Amernic, J.H. and Craig, R.J. (2007). Guidelines for CEO-speak: Editing the language of corporate leadership. *Strategy & Leadership*, 35 (3): 25–31.

Amihud, Y. and Mendelson, H. (1986). Asset pricing and the bid-ask spread. *Journal of Financial Economics*, 17 (2): 223–249.

Amir, E. (1993). The market valuation of accounting information: The case of postretirement benefits other than pensions. *Accounting Review*, 68 (4): 703–724.

Amir, E., Kirschenheiter, M., and Willard, K. (1997). The valuation of deferred taxes. *Contemporary Accounting Research*, 14 (4): 597–622.

An, H., Lee, Y.W., and Zhang, T. (2014). Do corporations manage earnings to meet/exceed analyst forecasts? Evidence from pension plan assumption changes. *Review of Accounting Studies*, 19 (2): 698–735.

Anandarajan, A., Hasan, I., and McCarthy, C. (2007). Use of loan loss provisions for capital, earnings management and signalling by Australian banks. *Accounting & Finance*, 47 (3): 357–379.

André, P., Filip, A., and Moldovan, R. (2016). Segment disclosure quantity and quality under IFRS 8: Determinants and the effect on financial analysts' earnings forecast errors. *The International Journal of Accounting*, 51 (4): 443–461.

Anthony, J.H. and Petroni, K.R. (1997). Accounting estimation disclosures and firm valuation in the property-casualty insurance industry. *Journal of Accounting, Auditing & Finance*, 12 (3): 257–281.

Armstrong, C.S., Guay, W.R., and Weber, J.P. (2010). The role of information and financial reporting in corporate governance and debt contracting. *Journal of Accounting and Economics*, 50 (2): 179–234.

Baber, W.R., Janakiraman, S.N., and Kang, S.H. (1996). Investment opportunities and the structure of executive compensation. *Journal of Accounting and Economics*, 21: 297–318.

Ball, R. (2009). The global financial crisis and the efficient market hypothesis: What have we learned? *Journal of Applied Corporate Finance*, 21 (4): 8–16.

Ball, R. and Brown, P. (1968). An empirical evaluation of accounting income numbers. *Journal of Accounting Research*, 6 (2): 159–178.

Ball, R. and Foster, G. (1982). Corporate financial reporting: A methodological review of empirical research. *Journal of Accounting Research*, 20: 161–234.

Ball, R., Kothari, S.P., and Robin, A. (2000). The effect of international institutional factors on properties of accounting earnings. *Journal of Accounting and Economics*, 29 (1): 1–51.

Ball, R., Robin, A., and Wu, J.S. (2003). Incentives versus standards: Properties of accounting income in four East Asian countries. *Journal of Accounting and Economics*, 36 (1-3): 235–270.

Balsam, S., Haw, I.M., and Lilien, S.B. (1995). Mandated accounting changes and managerial discretion. *Journal of accounting and economics*, 20 (1): 3–29.

Banghøj, J., Marton, J., Plenborg, T., and Runesson, E. (2018). Contractual implications of financial reporting enforcement and IFRS adoption.

Barbu, E.M., Dumontier, P., Feleaga, N., and Feleaga, L. (2014). Mandatory environmental disclosures by companies complying with IASs/IFRSs: The cases of France, Germany, and the UK. *International Journal of Accounting*, 49 (2): 231–247.

Barker, R., Barone, E., Birt, J., Gaeremynck, A., McGeachin, A., Marton, J., and Moldovan, R. (2013). Response of the EAA FRSC to the EFRAG Discussion Paper: Towards a disclosure framework for the notes. *Accounting in Europe*, 10 (1-2): 1–26.

Barker, R. and Teixeira, A. (2017). Gaps in the IFRS conceptual framework. Working paper.

Barlev, B. and Haddad, J.R. (2003). Fair value accounting and the management of the firm. *Critical Perspectives on Accounting*, 14 (4): 383–415.

— (2007). Harmonization, comparability, and fair value accounting. *Journal of Accounting, Auditing & Finance*, 22 (3): 493–509.

Barone, E., Birt, J., and Moya, S. (2014). Lease accounting: A review of recent literature. *Accounting in Europe*, 11 (1): 35–54.
Barron, O.E., Kile, C.O., and O'Keefe, T.B. (1999). MD&A quality as measured by the SEC and analysts' earnings forecasts. *Contemporary Accounting Research*, 16 (1): 75–109.
Barry, C.B. and Brown, S.J. (1985). Differential information and security market equilibrium. *Journal of Financial and Quantitative Analysis*, 20 (4): 407–422.
Barth, M. and Israeli, D. (2013). Disentangling mandatory IFRS reporting and changes in enforcement. *Journal of Accounting and Economics*, 56 (2-3, Supplement 1): 178–188.
Barth, M.E. (1994). Fair value accounting: Evidence from investment securities and the market valuation of banks. *Accounting Review*, 69 (1): 1–25.
Barth, M.E., Beaver, W.H., Hand, J.R.M., and Landsman, W.R. (1999). Accruals, cash flows, and equity values. *Review of Accounting Studies*, 4: 205–229.
Barth, M.E., Beaver, W.H., and Landsman, W.R. (1992). The market valuation implications of net periodic pension cost components. *Journal of Accounting and Economics*, 15 (1): 27–62.
— (1996). Value-relevance of banks' fair value disclosures under SFAS No. 107. *Accounting Review*, 71 (4): 513–537.
— (2001a). The relevance of the value relevance literature for financial accounting standard setting: Another view. *Journal of Accounting and Economics*, 31 (1-3): 77–104.
Barth, M.E. and Clinch, G. (1998). Revalued financial, tangible, and intangible assets: Associations with share prices and non-market-based value estimates. *Journal of Accounting Research*, 36 (3): 199–233.
Barth, M.E., Clinch, G., and Shibano, T. (2003). Market effects of recognition and disclosure. *Journal of Accounting Research*, 41 (4): 581–609.
Barth, M.E., Cram, D.P., and Nelson, K.K. (2001b). Accruals and the prediction of future cash flows. *The Accounting Review*, 76 (1): 27–58.
Barth, M.E., Hodder, L.D., and Stubben, S.R. (2008a). Fair value accounting for liabilities and own credit risk. *Accounting Review*, 83 (3): 629–664.
Barth, M.E. and Landsman, W.R. (1995). Fundamental issues related to using fair value accounting for financial reporting. *Accounting Horizons*, 9 (4): 97–107.
Barth, M.E., Landsman, W.R., and Lang, M.H. (2008b). International accounting standards and accounting quality. *Journal of Accounting Research*, 46 (3): 467–498.
Barth, M.E., McNichols, M.F., and Wilson, G.P. (1997). Factors influencing firms' disclosures about environmental liabilities. *Review of Accounting Studies*, 2 (1): 35–64.
Bartov, E., Gul, F.A., and Tsui, J.S. (2000a). Discretionary-accruals models and audit qualifications. *Journal of Accounting and Economics*, 30 (3): 421–452.
Bartov, E., Radhakrishnan, S., and Krinsky, I. (2000b). Investor sophistication and patterns in stock returns after earnings announcements. *Accounting Review*, 75 (1): 43–63.
Basu, S. (1997). The conservatism principle and the asymmetric timeliness of earnings. *Journal of Accounting and Economics*, 24 (1): 3–37.
Basu, S. and Waymire, G.B. (2006). Recordkeeping and human evolution. *Accounting Horizons*, 20 (3): 201–229.
Battalio, R.H. and Mendenhall, R.R. (2005). Earnings expectations, investor trade size, and anomalous returns around earnings announcements. *Journal of Financial Economics*, 77 (2): 289–319.
Beasley, M.S., Carcello, J.V., Hermanson, D.R., and Lapides, P.D. (2000). Fraudulent financial reporting: Consideration of industry traits and corporate governance mechanisms. *Accounting Horizons*, 14 (4): 441–454.
Beatty, A. and Liao, S. (2011). Do delays in expected loss recognition affect banks' willingness to lend? *Journal of Accounting and Economics*, 52 (1): 1–20.
Beaver, W. and Venkatachalam, M. (2003). Differential pricing of components of bank loan fair values. *Journal of Accounting, Auditing & Finance*, 18 (1): 41–68.

Beaver, W.H. (1968). The information content of annual earnings announcements. *Journal of accounting research*, 6: 67–92.

Beaver, W.H. and Demski, J.S. (1974). The nature of financial accounting objectives: A summary and synthesis. *Journal of Accounting Research*, 12 (3): 170–187.

Beck, P.J. and Narayanamoorthy, G.S. (2013). Did the SEC impact banks' loan loss reserves policies and their informativeness? *Journal of Accounting and Economics*, 56: 42–65.

Becker, C.L., Defond, M.L., Jiambalvo, J., and Subramanyam, K. (1998). The effect of audit quality on earnings management. *Contemporary Accounting Research*, 15 (1): 1–24.

Beelitz, A. and Merkl-Davies, D.M. (2012). Using discourse to restore organisational legitimacy: 'CEO-speak' after an incident in a german nuclear power plant. *Journal of Business Ethics*, 108 (1): 101–120.

Beneish, M.D. (1999). Incentives and penalties related to earnings overstatements that violate GAAP. *The Accounting Review*, 74 (4): 425–457.

Beneish, M.D., Billings, M.B., and Hodder, L.D. (2008). Internal control weaknesses and information uncertainty. *Accounting Review*, 83 (3): 665–703.

Bennett, B., Bradbury, M., and Prangnell, H. (2006). Rules, principles and judgments in accounting standards. *Abacus*, 42 (2): 189–204.

Benston, G.J., Bromwich, M., and Wagenhofer, A. (2006). Principles- versus rules-based accounting standards: The FASB's standard setting strategy. *Abacus*, 42 (2): 165–188.

Berger, P. and Luckmann, T. (1966). The social construction of knowledge: A treatise in the sociology of knowledge. *NY: Doubleday.*

Berger, P.G. and Hann, R.N. (2007). Segment profitability and the proprietary and agency costs of disclosure. *The Accounting Review*, 82 (4): 869–906.

Bergstresser, D. and Philippon, T. (2006). CEO incentives and earnings management. *Journal of Financial Economics*, 80 (3): 511–529.

Berle, A.A. and Means, G.G.C. (1932). The modern corporation and private property. Transaction Publishers.

Bernard, V.L. and Thomas, J.K. (1989). Post-earnings-announcement drift: delayed price response or risk premium? *Journal of Accounting research*, 27 (Supplement): 1–36.

— (1990). Evidence that stock prices do not fully reflect the implications of current earnings for future earnings. *Journal of Accounting and Economics*, 13 (4): 305–340.

Bettman, J.R. and Weitz, B.A. (1983). Attributions in the board room: Causal reasoning in corporate annual reports. *Administrative Science Quarterly*, 28 (2): 165–183.

Bhattacharya, N., Black, E.L., Christensen, T.E., and Larson, C.R. (2003). Assessing the relative informativeness and permanence of pro forma earnings and GAAP operating earnings. *Journal of Accounting and Economics*, 36 (1-3): 285–319.

Bhattacharya, N., Desai, H., and Venkataraman, K. (2013). Does earnings quality affect information asymmetry? evidence from trading costs. *Contemporary Accounting Research*, 30 (2): 482–516.

Bhojraj, S., Hribar, P., Picconi, M., and McInnis, J. (2009). Making sense of cents: An examination of firms that marginally miss or beat analyst forecasts. *Journal of Finance*, 64 (5): 2361–2388.

Biddle, G.C. and Choi, J.H. (2006). Is comprehensive income useful? *Journal of Contemporary Accounting & Economics*, 2 (1): 1–32.

Bischof, J. (2009). The effects of IFRS 7 adoption on bank disclosure in Europe. *Accounting in Europe*, 6 (2): 167–194.

Bischof, J., Daske, H., and Sextroh, C. (2014). Fair value-related information in analysts' decision processes: Evidence from the financial crisis. *Journal of Business Finance & Accounting*, 41 (3-4): 363–400.

Blacconiere, W.G., Frederickson, J., Johnson, M., and Lewis, M.F. (2011). Are voluntary disclosures that disavow the reliability of mandated fair value information informative or opportunistic? *Journal of Accounting and Economics*, 52 (2-3): 235–251.

Bloom, M. (2009). Accounting for goodwill. *Abacus*, 45 (3): 379–389.
Bloomfield, R.J. (2002). The "incomplete revelation hypothesis" and financial reporting. *Accounting Horizons*, 16 (3): 233–243.
Boatsman, J. and Dong, X. (2011). Equity value implications of lease accounting. *Accounting Horizons*, 25 (1): 1–16.
Boatsman, J.R., Khurana, I.K., and Loudder, M.L. (2000). The economic implications of proposed changes in the accounting for nuclear decommissioning costs. *Accounting Horizons*, 14 (2): 211–233.
Boschen, J.F., Duru, A., Gordon, L.A., and Smith, K.J. (2003). Accounting and stock price performance in dynamic CEO compensation arrangements. *Accounting Review*, 78 (1): 143–168.
Botosan, C.A. (1997). Disclosure level and the cost of equity capital. *Accounting Review*, 72 (3): 323–349.
Botosan, C.A. and Plumlee, M.A. (2002). A re-examination of disclosure level and the expected cost of equity capital. *Journal of Accounting Research*, 40 (1): 21–40.
Botosan, C.A. and Stanford, M. (2005). Managers' motives to withhold segment disclosures and the effect of SFAS No. 131 on analysts' information environment. *The Accounting Review*, 80 (3): 751–772.
Bouvatier, V., Lepetit, L., and Strobel, F. (2014). Bank income smoothing, ownership concentration and the regulatory environment. *Journal of Banking & Finance*, 41: 253–270.
Bradshaw, M.T. and Sloan, R.G. (2002). GAAP versus the street: An empirical assessment of two alternative definitions of earnings. *Journal of Accounting Research*, 40 (1): 41–66.
Brammer, S. and Pavelin, S. (2008). Factors influencing the quality of corporate environmental disclosure. *Business Strategy and the Environment*, 17 (2): 120–136.
Brennan, M.J. (1994). Incentives, rationality, and society. *Journal of Applied Corporate Finance*, 7 (2): 31–39.
Brenner, M. (1979). The sensitivity of the efficient market hypothesis to alternative specifications of the market model. *The Journal of Finance*, 34 (4): 915–929.
Brickley, J.A. and Zimmerman, J.L. (2010). Corporate governance myths: comments on Armstrong, Guay, and Weber. *Journal of Accounting and Economics*, 50 (2): 235–245.
Brown, P., Preiato, J., and Tarca, A. (2014). Measuring country differences in enforcement of accounting standards: An audit and enforcement proxy. *Journal of Business Finance & Accounting*, 41 (1-2): 1–52.
Brown, S., Lo, K., and Lys, T. (1999). Use of *R2* in accounting research: Measuring changes in value relevance over the last four decades. *Journal of Accounting and Economics*, 28 (2): 83–115.
Brown, S.V. and Tucker, J.W. (2011). Large-sample evidence on firms' year-over-year MD&A modifications. *Journal of Accounting Research*, 49 (2): 309–346.
Bushee, B.J. and Leuz, C. (2005). Economic consequences of SEC disclosure regulation: Evidence from the OTC bulletin board. *Journal of Accounting and Economics*, 39 (2): 233–264.
Bushman, R., Chen, Q., Engel, E., and Smith, A. (2004). Financial accounting information, organizational complexity and corporate governance systems. *Journal of Accounting and Economics*, 37 (2): 167–201.
Bushman, R.M. and Smith, A.J. (2001). Financial accounting information and corporate governance. *Journal of Accounting and Economics*, 32 (1): 237–333.
Bushman, R.M. and Williams, C.D. (2012). Accounting discretion, loan loss provisioning, and discipline of banks' risk-taking. *Journal of Accounting and Economics*, 54 (1): 1–18.
Butler, M., Leone, A.J., and Willenborg, M. (2004). An empirical analysis of auditor reporting and its association with abnormal accruals. *Journal of Accounting and Economics*, 37 (2): 139–165.
Cadbury, A. (1992). Cadbury report: The financial aspects of corporate governance. *Tech reprt, HMG, London*.
Callao, S. and Jarne, J.I. (2010). Have IFRS affected earnings management in the European Union? *Accounting in Europe*, 7 (2): 159–189.
Callen, J.L., Hope, O.K., and Segal, D. (2005). Domestic and foreign earnings, stock return variability, and the impact of investor sophistication. *Journal of Accounting Research*, 43 (3): 377–412.

Campbell, J., Chen, H., Dhaliwal, D., Lu, H.M., and Steele, L. (2014). The information content of mandatory risk factor disclosures in corporate filings. *Review of Accounting Studies*, 19 (1): 396–455.

Capkun, V., Jeny-Cazavan, A., Jeanjean, T., and Weiss, L.A. (2008). Earnings management and value relevance during the mandatory transition from local GAAPs to IFRS in Europe. Working paper. Available at: https://papers.ssrn.com/sol3/papers.cfm?abstract_id=1125716.

Caramanis, C. and Lennox, C. (2008). Audit effort and earnings management. *Journal of Accounting and Economics*, 45 (1): 116–138.

Carrington, T., Catasús, B., Eklöv Alander, G., Johed, G., Lundqvist, P., Marton, J., and Runesson, E. (2015). IFRS—Dilemman och utmaningar. Lund: Studentlitteratur. ISBN: 978-91-44-10997-8.

Carroll, T.J., Linsmeier, T.J., and Petroni, K.R. (2003). The reliability of fair value versus historical cost information: Evidence from closed-end mutual funds. *Journal of Accounting, Auditing & Finance*, 18 (1): 1–23.

Chambers, R.J. (1993). Positive accounting theory and the PA cult. *Abacus*, 29 (1): 1–26.

Chatfield, M. and Vangermeersch, R. (2014). The History of Accounting (RLE Accounting): An International Encylopedia. Routledge Library Editions: Accounting. Taylor & Francis.

Chatterjee, A. and Hambrick, D.C. (2007). It's all about me: Narcissistic chief executive officers and their effects on company strategy and performance. *Administrative Science Quarterly*, 52 (3): 351–386.

Chen, C., Xiumin, M., and Xin, W. (2013). Insider trading, litigation concerns, and auditor going-concern opinions. *Accounting Review*, 88 (2): 365–393.

Chen, H., Chiang, R.H., and Storey, V.C. (2012). Business intelligence and analytics: from big data to big impact. *MIS quarterly*: 1165–1188.

Chen, H., Tang, Q., Jiang, Y., and Lin, Z. (2010). The role of international financial reporting standards in accounting quality: Evidence from the European Union. *Journal of International Financial Management & Accounting*, 21 (3): 220–278.

Cheng, E.C. and Courtenay, S.M. (2006). Board composition, regulatory regime and voluntary disclosure. *International Journal of Accounting*, 41: 262–289.

Cheng, L., Liao, S., and Zhang, H. (2013). The commitment effect versus information effect of disclosure-evidence from smaller reporting companies. *Accounting Review*, 88 (4): 1239–1263.

Cheng, Q. and Warfield, T.D. (2005). Equity incentives and earnings management. *The Accounting Review*, 80 (2): 441–476.

Cho, C.H. and Patten, D.M. (2007). The role of environmental disclosures as tools of legitimacy: A research note. *Accounting, Organizations and Society*, 32 (7-8): 639–647.

Cho, C.H., Roberts, R.W., and Patten, D.M. (2010). The language of US corporate environmental disclosure. *Accounting, Organizations and Society*, 35 (4): 431–443.

Choi, B., Collins, D.W., and Johnson, W.B. (1997). Valuation implications of reliability differences: The case of nonpension postretirement obligations. *Accounting Review*, 72 (3): 351–383.

Choudhary, P. (2011). Evidence on differences between recognition and disclosure: A comparison of inputs to estimate fair values of employee stock options. *Journal of Accounting and Economics*, 51 (1): 77–94.

Christensen, H.B., Hail, L., and Leuz, C. (2013a). Mandatory IFRS reporting and changes in enforcement. *Journal of Accounting and Economics*, 56 (2-3): 147–177.

Christensen, P.O., de la Rosa, L.E., and Feltham, G.A. (2010). Information and the cost of capital: An ex ante perspective. *Accounting Review*, 85 (3): 817–848.

Christensen, P.O., Frimor, H., and Sabac, F. (2013b). The stewardship role of analyst forecasts, and discretionary versus non-discretionary accruals. *European Accounting Review*, 22 (2): 257–296.

Chung, R., Firth, M., and Kim, J.B. (2003). Auditor conservatism and reported earnings. *Accounting and Business Research*, 33 (1): 19–32.

Clapham, S.E. and Schwenk, C.R. (1991). Self-serving attributions, managerial cognition, and company performance. *Strategic Management Journal*, 12 (3): 219–229.

Clarkson, P.M., Kao, J.L., and Richardson, G.D. (1994). The voluntary inclusion of forecasts in the MD&A section of annual reports. *Contemporary Accounting Research*, 11 (1): 423–450.
— (1999). Evidence that management discussion and analysis (MD&A) is a part of a firm's overall disclosure package. *Contemporary Accounting Research*, 16 (1): 111–134.
Clarkson, P.M., Li, Y., Richardson, G.D., and Vasvari, F.P. (2008). Revisiting the relation between environmental performance and environmental disclosure: An empirical analysis. *Accounting, Organizations and Society*, 33 (4-5): 303–327.
Clatworthy, M.A. and Jones, M.J. (2006). Differential patterns of textual characteristics and company performance in the chairman's statement. *Accounting, Auditing & Accountability Journal*, 19 (4): 493–511.
Coase, R.H. (1937). The nature of the firm. *Economica*, 4 (16): 386–405.
Coffee, J.C. (2005). A theory of corporate scandals: Why the USA and Europe differ. *Oxford Review of Economic Policy*, 21 (2): 198–211.
Cohen, D., Darrough, M.N., Huang, R., and Zach, T. (2011). Warranty reserve: Contingent liability, information signal, or earnings management tool? *The Accounting Review*, 86 (2): 569–604.
Cohen, D.A., Dey, A., and Lys, T.Z. (2008). Real and accrual-based earnings management in the pre-and post-Sarbanes-Oxley periods. *The Accounting Review*, 83 (3): 757–787.
Cohen, D.A. and Zarowin, P. (2010). Accrual-based and real earnings management activities around seasoned equity offerings. *Journal of Accounting & Economics*, 50 (1): 2–19.
Coller, M. and Yohn, T.L. (1997). Management forecasts and information asymmetry: An examination of bid-ask spreads. *Journal of Accounting Research*, 35 (2): 181–191.
Collins, D.W., Maydew, E.L., and Weiss, I.S. (1997). Changes in the value-relevance of earnings and book values over the past forty years. *Journal of Accounting and Economics*, 24 (1): 39–67.
Collins, J.H., Shackelford, D.A., and Wahlen, J.M. (1995). Bank differences in the coordination of regulatory capital, earnings, and taxes. *Journal of Accounting Research*, 33 (2): 263–291.
Conyon, M., Fernandes, N., Ferreira, M., Matos, P., and Murphy, K. (2011). The executive compensation controversy: A transatlantic analysis. Working paper. Available at: https://digitalcommons.ilr.cornell.edu/ics/5/.
Core, J.E., Guay, W.R., and Verdi, R. (2008). Is accruals quality a priced risk factor? *Journal of Accounting and Economics*, 46 (1): 2–22.
Core, J.E., Holthausen, R.W., and Larcker, D.F. (1999). Corporate governance, chief executive officer compensation, and firm performance. *Journal of Financial Economics*, 51 (3): 371–406.
Cormier, D., Demaria, S., Lapointe-Antunes, P., and Teller, R. (2009). First-time adoption of IFRS, managerial incentives, and value-relevance: Some French evidence. *Journal of International Accounting Research*, 8 (2): 1–22.
Cormier, D. and Magnan, M. (1999). Corporate environmental disclosure strategies: determinants, costs and benefits. *Journal of Accounting, Auditing & Finance*, 14 (4): 429–451.
Cornaggia, K.J., Franzen, L.A., and Simin, T.T. (2013). Bringing leased assets onto the balance sheet. *Journal of Corporate Finance*, 22: 345–360.
Courtis, J.K. (1986). An investigation into annual report readability and corporate risk-return relationships. *Accounting and Business Research*, 16 (64): 285–294.
— (1995). Readability of annual reports: Western versus Asian evidence. *Accounting, Auditing & Accountability Journal*, 8 (2): 4–17.
Daley, L.A. and Vigeland, R.L. (1983). The effects of debt covenants and political costs on the choice of accounting methods: The case of accounting for R&D costs. *Journal of Accounting and Economics*, 5: 195–211.
Danbolt, J. and Rees, W. (2008). An experiment in fair value accounting: UK investment vehicles. *European Accounting Review*, 17 (2): 271–303.
Darrough, M.N. and Stoughton, N.M. (1990). Financial disclosure policy in an entry game. *Journal of Accounting and Economics*, 12 (1-3): 219–243.

Daske, H. and Gebhardt, G. (2006). International financial reporting standards and experts' perceptions of disclosure quality. *Abacus*, 42 (3/4): 461–498.

Daske, H., Hail, L., Leuz, C., and Verdi, R. (2008). Mandatory IFRS reporting around the world: Early evidence on the economic consequences. *Journal of Accounting Research*, 46 (5): 1085–1142.

Davis, H.Z. (1982). History of LIFO. *Accounting Historians Journal*, 9 (1): 1–23.

Davis-Friday, P.Y., Folami, L.B., Liu, C.S., and Mittelstaedt, H.F. (1999). The value relevance of financial statement recognition vs. disclosure: Evidence from SFAS No. 106. *Accounting Review*, 74 (4): 403–423.

Day, R.G. (2000). UK accounting regulation: An historical perspective. Working Paper, Available at: eprints.bournemouth.ac.uk/3074/1/296.pdf.

De Franco, G., Kothari, S., and Verdi, R. (2011). The benefits of financial statement comparability. *Journal of Accounting Research*, 49 (4): 895–931.

De Jong, A., Rosellón, M., and Verwijmeren, P. (2006). The economic consequences of IFRS: The impact of IAS 32 on preference shares in the Netherlands. *Accounting in Europe*, 3 (1): 169–185.

De Villiers, C. and Van Staden, C.J. (2006). Can less environmental disclosure have a legitimizing effect? Evidence from Africa. *Accounting, Organizations and Society*, 31 (8): 763–781.

Dechow, P., Ge, W., and Schrand, C. (2010). Understanding earnings quality: A review of the proxies, their determinants and their consequences. *Journal of Accounting and Economics*, 50 (2-3): 344–401.

Dechow, P.M. (1994). Accounting earnings and cash flows as measures of firm performance: The role of accounting accruals. *Journal of Accounting and Economics*, 18 (1): 3–42.

Dechow, P.M. and Dichev, I.D. (2002). The quality of accruals and earnings: The role of accrual estimation errors. *Accounting Review*, 77 (Supplement 1): 35–59.

Dechow, P.M., Hutton, A.P., and Sloan, R.G. (1996). Economic consequences of accounting for stock-based compensation. *Journal of Accounting Research*, 34 (Supplement): 1–20.

Dechow, P.M., Richardson, S.A., and Tuna, I. (2003). Why are earnings kinky? An examination of the earnings management explanation. *Review of Accounting Studies*, 8 (2–3): 355–384.

Dechow, P.M., Sloan, R.G., and Sweeney, A.P. (1995). Detecting earnings management. *Accounting Review*, 70 (2): 193–225.

Deegan, C. and Rankin, M. (1996). Do Australian companies report environmental news objectively? An analysis of environmental disclosures by firms prosecuted successfully by the Environmental Protection Authority. *Accounting, Auditing & Accountability Journal*, 9 (2): 50–67.

Deegan, C., Rankin, M., and Tobin, J. (2002). An examination of the corporate social and environmental disclosures of BHP from 1983–1997: A test of legitimacy theory. *Accounting, Auditing & Accountability Journal*, 15 (3): 312–343.

DeFond, M.L. and Jiambalvo, J. (1994). Debt covenant violation and manipulation of accruals. *Journal of Accounting and Economics*, 17 (1): 145–176.

DellaVigna, S. and Pollet, J.M. (2009). Investor inattention and Friday earnings announcements. *The Journal of Finance*, 64 (2): 709–749.

DeMarzo, P. and Duffie, D. (1995). Corporate incentives for hedging and hedge accounting. *Review of Financial Studies*, 8 (3): 743–771.

Demsetz, H. and Lehn, K. (1985). The structure of corporate ownership: Causes and consequences. *Journal of Political Economy*, 93 (6): 1155–1177.

Demski, J.S. (2007). Is accounting an academic discipline? *Accounting Horizons*, 21 (2): 153–157.

Desai, H., Hogan, C.E., and Wilkins, M.S. (2006). The reputational penalty for aggressive accounting: Earnings restatements and management turnover. *The Accounting Review*, 81 (1): 83–112.

Detzen, D. and Zülch, H. (2012). Executive compensation and goodwill recognition under IFRS: Evidence from European mergers. *Journal of International Accounting, Auditing & Taxation*, 21 (2): 106–126.

Devine, C.T. (1960). Research methodology and accounting theory formation. *The Accounting Review*, 35 (3): 387–399.

Dhaliwal, D., Subramanyam, K., and Trezevant, R. (1999). Is comprehensive income superior to net income as a measure of firm performance? *Journal of Accounting and Economics*, 26 (1): 43–67.

Diamond, D.W. and Verrecchia, R.E. (1991). Disclosure, liquidity, and the cost of capital. *Journal of Finance*, 46 (4): 1325–1359.

Dichev, I.D. (2017). Accrual duration. Working paper. Available at: https://ssrn.com/abstract= 3043973.

Dichev, I.D., Graham, J.R., Harvey, C.R., and Rajgopal, S. (2013). Earnings quality: Evidence from the field. *Journal of Accounting and Economics*, 56 (2): 1–33.

Dietrich, R.J., Harris, M.S., and Muller, K.A. (2000). The reliability of investment property fair value estimates. *Journal of Accounting and Economics*, 30 (2): 125–158.

DiMaggio, P.J. and Powell, W.W. (1983). The iron cage revisited: Institutional isomorphism and collective rationality in organizational fields. *American Sociological Review*, 48 (2): 147–160.

Donelson, D.C., McInnis, J.M., Mergenthaler., R.D., and Yong, Y. (2012). The timeliness of bad earnings news and litigation risk. *Accounting Review*, 87 (6): 1967–1991.

Doyle, J.T., Ge, W., and McVay, S. (2007). Accruals quality and internal control over financial reporting. *The Accounting Review*, 82 (5): 1141–1170.

D'Souza, J., Jacob, J., and Soderstrom, N.S. (2000). Nuclear decommissioning costs: The impact of recoverability risk on valuation. *Journal of Accounting and Economics*, 29 (2): 207–230.

Duke, J.C., Hsieh, S.J., and Su, Y. (2009). Operating and synthetic leases: Exploiting financial benefits in the post-Enron era. *Advances in Accounting*, 25 (1): 28–39.

Duru, A. and Reeb, D.M. (2002). International diversification and analysts' forecast accuracy and bias. *The Accounting Review*, 77 (2): 415–433.

Dyckman, T.R. and Zeff, S.A. (1984). Two decades of the Journal of Accounting Research. *Journal of Accounting Research*, 22 (1): 225–297.

— (2014). Some methodological deficiencies in empirical research articles in accounting. *Accounting Horizons*, 28 (3): 695–712.

— (2015). Accounting research: Past, present, and future. *Abacus*, 51 (4): 511–524.

Dye, R.A. (1985). Disclosure of nonproprietary information. *Journal of Accounting Research*, 23 (1): 123–145.

— (1990). Mandatory versus voluntary disclosures: The cases of financial and real externalities. *The Accounting Review*, 65 (1): 1–24.

Dye, R.A. and Verrecchia, R.E. (1995). Discretion vs. uniformity: Choices among GAAP. *The Accounting Review*, 70 (3): 389–415.

Easley, D. and O'Hara, M. (2004). Information and the cost of capital. *Journal of Finance*, 59 (4): 1553–1583.

Easton, P.D. and Harris, T.S. (1991). Earnings as an explanatory variable for returns. *Journal of Accounting Research*, 29 (1): 19–36.

Easton, P.D., Harris, T.S., and Ohlson, J.A. (1992). Aggregate accounting earnings can explain most of security returns: The case of long return intervals. *Journal of Accounting and Economics*, 15 (2): 119–142.

EC (2005). Recommendation (2005/162/EC), on the role of non-executive or supervisory directors of listed companies and on the committees of the (supervisory) board. European Commission.

Eccher, E.A., Ramesh, K., and Thiagarajan, R.S. (1996). Fair value disclosures by bank holding companies. *Journal of Accounting and Economics*, 22: 79–117.

Economics, E. (2017). Ex ante impact assesment of IFRS 16.

Edwards, J.R., Dean, G., Clarke, F., and Wolnizer, P. (2013). Accounting academic elites: The tale of ARIA. *Accounting, Organizations and Society*, 38 (5): 365–381.

Edwards, J.R. and Walker, S.P. (2007). Accountants in late 19th century Britain: A spatial, demographic and occupational profile. *Accounting and Business Research*, 37 (1): 63–89.

Einhorn, E. (2007). Voluntary disclosure under uncertainty about the reporting objective. *Journal of Accounting and Economics*, 43 (2–3): 245–274.

Elliott, J.A. and Hanna, J.D. (1996). Repeated accounting write-offs and the information content of earnings. *Journal of Accounting Research*, 34: 135–155.

Elliott, J.A. and Shaw, W.H. (1988). Write-offs as accounting procedures to manage perceptions. *Journal of Accounting Research*, 26: 91–119.

Engel, E., Hayes, R.M., and Wang, X. (2010). Audit committee compensation and the demand for monitoring of the financial reporting process. *Journal of Accounting and Economics*, 49 (1-2): 136–154.

Enoch, R. and Pacter, P. (1995). FASB's nuclear decommissioning costs project may well have broad implications. *Journal of Corporate Accounting & Finance*, 6 (3): 95–108.

Ernstberger, J. and Grüning, M. (2013). How do firm-and country-level governance mechanisms affect firms' disclosure? *Journal of Accounting and Public Policy*, 32 (3): 50–67.

Ertimur, Y., Livnat, J., and Martikainen, M. (2003). Differential market reactions to revenue and expense surprises. *Review of Accounting Studies*, 8 (2): 185–211.

ESMA (2014). ESMA/2014/807 Final report - ESMA guidelines on enforcement of financial information. European Securities and Markets Authority, Brussels.

Ettredge, M.L., Kwon, S.Y., Smith, D.B., and Zarowin, P.A. (2005). The impact of SFAS No. 131 business segment data on the market's ability to anticipate future earnings. *The Accounting Review*, 80 (3): 773–804.

Ewert, R. and Wagenhofer, A. (2005). Economic effects of tightening accounting standards to restrict earnings management. *Accounting Review*, 80 (4): 1101–1124.

Fairfield, P.M., Sweeney, R.J., and Yohn, T.L. (1996). Accounting classification and the predictive content of earnings. *Accounting Review*, 71 (3): pp. 337–355.

Fama, E.F. (1970). Efficient capital markets: A review of theory and empirical work. *Journal of Finance*, 25 (2): 383–417.

— (1980). Agency problems and the theory of the firm. *Journal of Political Economy*, 88 (2): 288–307.

Fama, E.F., Fisher, L., Jensen, M.C., and Roll, R. (1969). The adjustment of stock prices to new information. *International economic review*, 10 (1): 1–21.

Fama, E.F. and French, K.R. (1992). The cross-section of expected stock returns. *Journal of Finance*, 47 (2): 427–465.

Fama, E.F. and Jensen, M.C. (1983). Separation of ownership and control. *Journal of Law and Economics*, 26 (2): 301–326.

FCAG (2009). Report of the Financial Crisis Advisory Group.

Fekrat, M.A., Inclan, C., and Petroni, D. (1996). Corporate environmental disclosures: Competitive disclosure hypothesis using 1991 annual report data. *The International Journal of Accounting*, 31 (2): 175–195.

Feldman, R., Govindaraj, S., Livnat, J., and Segal, B. (2010). Management's tone change, post earnings announcement drift and accruals. *Review of Accounting Studies*, 15 (4): 915–953.

Feltham, G.A. and Ohlson, J.A. (1995). Valuation and clean surplus accounting for operating and financial activities. *Contemporary Accounting Research*, 11 (2): 689–731.

Fields, T.D., Lys, T.Z., and Vincent, L. (2001). Empirical research on accounting choice. *Journal of Accounting and Economics*, 31 (1): 255–307.

Filzen, J.J. and Peterson, K. (2015). Financial statement complexity and meeting analysts' expectations. *Contemporary Accounting Research*, 32: 1560–1594.

Fisher, S.A. and Hu, M.Y. (1988). Does the CEO's letter to the shareholders have predictive value. *Business Forum*, 14 (1): 22.

Flower, J., ed. (1994). The regulation of financial reporting in the Nordic countries. Stockholm: CE Fritzes AB.

Flyvbjerg, B. (2001). Making Social Science Matter. Cambridge: Cambridge University Press.

Fonseca, A.R. and González, F. (2008). Cross-country determinants of bank income smoothing by managing loan-loss provisions. *Journal of Banking & Finance*, 32 (2): 217–228.

Foster, G., Olsen, C., and Shevlin, T. (1984). Earnings releases, anomalies, and the behavior of security returns. *Accounting Review*, 59 (4): 574–603.

Francis, J., LaFond, R., Olsson, P.M., and Schipper, K. (2005). The market pricing of accruals quality. *Journal of Accounting and Economics*, 39 (2): 295–327.

Francis, J., Nanda, D., and Olsson, P. (2008). Voluntary disclosure, earnings quality and cost of capital. *Journal of Accounting Research*, 46 (1): 53–99.

Francis, J.R. and Wang, D. (2008). The joint effect of investor protection and Big 4 audits on earnings quality around the world. *Contemporary Accounting Research*, 25 (1): 157–191.

Franz, D.R., Hassabelnaby, H.R., and Lobo, G.J. (2014). Impact of proximity to debt covenant violation on earnings management. *Review of Accounting Studies*, 19 (1): 473–505.

Frederickson, J.R., Hodge, F.D., and Pratt, J.H. (2006). The evolution of stock option accounting: Disclosure, voluntary recognition, mandated recognition, and management disavowals. *The Accounting Review*, 81 (5): 1073–1093.

Freedman, M. and Patten, D.M. (2004). Evidence on the pernicious effect of financial report environmental disclosure. *Accounting Forum*, 28 (1): 27–41.

Freedman, M. and Wasley, C. (1990). The association between environmental performance and environmental disclosure in annual reports and 10Ks. *Advances in Public Interest Accounting*, 3 (2): 183–193.

Freeman, R.N., Ohlson, J.A., and Penman, S.H. (1982). Book rate-of-return and prediction of earnings changes: An empirical investigation. *Journal of Accounting Research*, 20 (2): 639–653.

Friedman, M. (1953). The methodology of positive economics. *Essays in positive economics*, 3 (3).

Frost, G.R. (2007). The introduction of mandatory environmental reporting guidelines: Australian evidence. *Abacus*, 43 (2): 190–216.

Frye, M.B. (2004). Equity-based compensation for employees: Firm performance and determinants. *Journal of Financial Research*, 27 (1): 31–54.

García Osma, B. and Guillamón, E. (2008). Corporate governance and impression management in annual results press releases. *Accounting, Organizations and Society*, 36 (4): 187–208.

Gebhardt, G. and Novotny-Farkas, Z. (2011). Mandatory IFRS adoption and accounting quality of European banks. *Journal of Business Finance & Accounting*, 38 (3-4): 289–333.

Geijsbeek, J.B., Manzoni (16th cent), D., Mainardi (17th cent), M., Christoffels (16th cent), J.Y., Stevin (1548-1620), S., Dafforne, R., Pacioli (ca. 1445-1517), L., and Pietra (16th cent), A. (1914). Ancient double-entry bookkeeping : Lucas Pacioli's treatise (A.D. 1494 - the earliest known writer on bookkeeping). Denver, Colorado: John B. Geijsbeek.

Gelb, D.S. (2000). Corporate signaling with dividends, stock repurchases, and accounting disclosures: An empirical study. *Journal of Accounting, Auditing & Finance*, 15 (2): 99–120.

Geppert, J. and Lawrence, J.E. (2008). Predicting firm reputation through content analysis of shareholders' letter. *Corporate Reputation Review*, 11 (4): 285–307.

Ghosh, A. and Tang, C.Y. (2015). Assessing financial reporting quality of family firms: The auditors' perspective. *Journal of Accounting and Economics*, 60 (1): 95–116.

Glaum, M., Schmidt, P., Street, D.L., and Vogel, S. (2013). Compliance with IFRS 3- and IAS 36-required disclosures across 17 European countries: Company- and country-level determinants. *Accounting and Business Research*, 43 (3): 163–204.

Glosten, L.R. and Milgrom, P.R. (1985). Bid, ask and transaction prices in a specialist market with heterogeneously informed traders. *Journal of Financial Economics*, 14 (1): 71–100.

Glover, J.C. (2012). Disclosure and incentives. *Accounting Horizons*, 26 (2): 371–380.

Goergen, M. and Renneboog, L. (2011). Managerial compensation. *Journal of Corporate Finance*, 17 (4): 1068–1077.

Goodwin, J., Ahmed, K., and Heaney, R. (2008). The effects of international financial reporting standards on the accounts and accounting quality of australian firms: A retrospective study. *Journal of Contemporary Accounting & Economics*, 4 (2): 89–119.

Gordon, E., Ma, X., and Runesson, E. (2017). Information uncertainty and critical accounting policies and estimates. Working paper.

Gordon, E.A. and Hsu, H.T. (2017). Tangible long-lived asset impairments and future operating cash flows under US GAAP and IFRS. *The Accounting Review*, 93 (1): 187–211.

Gordon, E.A. and Joos, P.R. (2004). Unrecognized deferred taxes: Evidence from the U.K. *The Accounting Review*, 79 (1): 97–124.

Gordon, I. and Gallery, N. (2012). Assessing financial reporting comparability across institutional settings: The case of pension accounting. *British Accounting Review*, 44 (1): 11–20.

Graham, B. (1976). A conversation with Benjamin Graham. *Financial Analysts Journal*, 32 (5): 20–23.

Graham, J.R., Harvey, C.R., and Rajgopal, S. (2005). The economic implications of corporate financial reporting. *Journal of Accounting and Economics*, 40: 3–73.

Grossman, S.J. and Stiglitz, J.E. (1980). On the impossibility of informationally efficient markets. *The American Economic Review*, 70 (3): 393–408.

Grossmann, A. and Grossmann, S. (2010). Capitalizing lease payments: Potential effects of the FASB/IASB plan. *CPA Journal*, 80: 6–11.

Gul, F.A., Srinidhi, B., and Ng, A.C. (2011). Does board gender diversity improve the informativeness of stock prices? *Journal of Accounting and Economics*, 51 (3): 314–338.

Guthrie, J. and Parker, L.D. (1989). Corporate social reporting: A rebuttal of legitimacy theory. *Accounting and Business Research*, 19 (76): 343–352.

Hail, L. and Leuz, C. (2006). International differences in the cost of equity capital: Do legal institutions and securities regulation matter? *Journal of Accounting Research*, 44 (3): 485–531.

Hall, B.J. and Liebman, J.B. (1998). Are CEOs really paid like bureaucrats? *Quarterly Journal of Economics*, 113 (3): 653–691.

Hamberg, M., Paananen, M., and Novak, J. (2011). The adoption of IFRS 3: The effects of managerial discretion and stock market reactions. *European Accounting Review*, 20 (2): 263–288.

Hammersley, J., Myers, L., and Shakespeare, C. (2008). Market reactions to the disclosure of internal control weaknesses and to the characteristics of those weaknesses under section 302 of the Sarbanes Oxley Act of 2002. *Review of Accounting Studies*, 13 (1): 141–165.

Han, S., Kang, T., and Yoo, Y.K. (2012). Governance role of auditors and legal environment: Evidence from corporate disclosure transparency. *European Accounting Review*, 21 (1): 29–50.

Handa, P. and Linn, S.C. (1993). Arbitrage pricing with estimation risk. *Journal of Financial and Quantitative Analysis*, 28 (1): 81–100.

Hanley, K.W. and Hoberg, G. (2012). Litigation risk, strategic disclosure and the underpricing of initial public offerings. *Journal of Financial Economics*, 103 (2): 235–254.

Harper, R.M., Mister, W.G., and Strawser, J.R. (1987). The impact of new pension disclosure rules on perceptions of debt. *Journal of Accounting Research*, 25 (2): 327–330.

Harris, R. (1994). The bubble act: Its passage and its effects on business organization. *Journal of Economic History*, 54 (3): pp. 610–627.

Harris, T.S., Lang, M.H., and Möller, H.P. (1994). The value relevance of German accounting measures: An empirical analysis. *Journal of Accounting Research*, 22 (2): 187–209.

Hayes, R.M. and Lundholm, R. (1996). Segment reporting to the capital market in the presence of a competitor. *Journal of Accounting Research*, 34 (2): 261–279.

Hayn, C. and Hughes, P.J. (2006). Leading indicators of goodwill impairment. *Journal of Accounting, Auditing & Finance*, 21 (3): 223–265.

Healy, P.M. (1985). The effect of bonus schemes on accounting decisions. *Journal of Accounting and Economics*, 7: 85–107.

Healy, P.M. and Palepu, K.G. (2001). Information asymmetry, corporate disclosure, and the capital markets: A review of the empirical disclosure literature. *Journal of Accounting and Economics*, 31 (1-3): 405–440.

Healy, P.M. and Wahlen, J.M. (1999). A review of the earnings management literature and its implications for standard setting. *Accounting Horizons*, 13 (4): 365–383.

Heck, J.L. and Jensen, R.E. (2007). An analysis of the evolution of research contributions by The Accounting Review, 1926–2005. *Accounting Historians Journal*, 34 (2): 109–141.

Heninger, W.G. (2001). The association between auditor litigation and abnormal accruals. *Accounting Review*, 76 (1): 111–126.

Henning, S.L., Lewis, B.L., and Shaw, W.H. (2000). Valuation of the components of purchased goodwill. *Journal of Accounting Research*, 38 (2): 375–386.

Herrmann, D., Saudagaran, S.M., and Thomas, W.B. (2006). The quality of fair value measures for property, plant, and equipment. *Accounting Forum*, 30 (1): 43–59.

Hirshleifer, D., Hou, K., and Teoh, S.H. (2012). The accrual anomaly: Risk or mispricing? *Management Science*, 58 (2): 320–335.

Hirshleifer, D. and Teoh, S.H. (2003). Limited attention, information disclosure, and financial reporting. *Journal of Accounting and Economics*, 36 (1): 337–386.

Hirst, D.E. and Hopkins, P.E. (1998). Comprehensive income reporting and analysts' valuation judgments. *Journal of Accounting Research*, 36 (Supplement): 47–75.

Hitz, J.M. (2007). The decision usefulness of fair value accounting—A theoretical perspective. *European Accounting Review*, 16 (2): 323–362.

Hodder, L.D., Hopkins, P.E., and Wahlen, J.M. (2006). Risk-relevance of fair-value income measures for commercial banks. *The Accounting Review*, 81 (2): 337–375.

Hodgdon, C., Tondkar, R.H., Harless, D.W., and Adhikari, A. (2008). Compliance with IFRS disclosure requirements and individual analysts' forecast errors. *Journal of International Accounting, Auditing and Taxation*, 17 (1): 1–13.

Hoitash, R. and Hoitash, U. (2018). Measuring accounting reporting complexity with XBRL. *The Accounting Review*, 93 (1): 259–287.

Holmström, B. (1979). Moral hazard and observability. *Bell Journal of Economics*, 10 (1): 74–91.

— (1999). Managerial incentive problems: A dynamic perspective. *Review of Economic Studies*, 66 (1): 169–182.

Holthausen, R.W. (2003). Testing the relative power of accounting standards versus incentives and other institutional features to influence the outcome of financial reporting in an international setting. *Journal of Accounting and Economics*, 36 (1-3): 271–283.

— (2009). Accounting standards, financial reporting outcomes, and enforcement. *Journal of Accounting Research*, 47 (2): 447–458.

Holthausen, R.W. and Leftwich, R.W. (1983). The economic consequences of accounting choice implications of costly contracting and monitoring. *Journal of Accounting and Economics*, 5: 77–117.

Holthausen, R.W. and Watts, R.L. (2001). The relevance of the value relevance literature for financial accounting standard setting. *Journal of Accounting and Economics*, 31 (1): 3–75.

Hoogendoorn, M.N. (1996). Accounting and taxation in Europe: A comparative overview. *European Accounting Review*, 5 (sup1): 783–794.

Hooghiemstra, R. (2010). Letters to the shareholders: A content analysis comparison of letters written by CEOs in the United States and Japan. *International Journal of Accounting*, 45 (3): 275–300.

Hope, O.K. (2003a). Accounting policy disclosures and analysts' forecasts. *Contemporary Accounting Research*, 20 (2): 295–321.

— (2003b). Disclosure practices, enforcement of accounting standards, and analysts' forecast accuracy: An international study. *Journal of Accounting Research*, 41 (2): 235–272.

Hope, O.K., Hu, D., and Lu, H. (2016). The benefits of specific risk-factor disclosures. *Review of Accounting Studies*, 21 (4): 1005–1045.

Hoppit, J. (2002). The myths of the South Sea Bubble. *Transactions of the Royal Historical Society (Sixth Series)*, 12: 141–165.

Hopwood, A.G. (2007). Whither accounting research? *The Accounting Review*, 82 (5): 1365–1374.

Horton, J., Serafeim, G., and Serafeim, I. (2013). Does mandatory IFRS adoption improve the information environment? *Contemporary Accounting Research*, 30 (1): 388–423.

Huang, A.H., Zang, A.Y., and Rong, Z. (2014). Evidence on the information content of text in analyst reports. *Accounting Review*, 89 (6): 2151–2180.

Hughes, J.S., Liu, J., and Liu, J. (2007). Information asymmetry, diversification, and cost of capital. *Accounting Review*, 82 (3): 705–729.

Hung, M. (2001). Accounting standards and value relevance of financial statements: An international analysis. *Journal of Accounting and Economics*, 30: 401–420.

Hyland, K. (1998). Exploring corporate rhetoric: Metadiscourse in the CEO's letter. *Journal of Business Communication*, 35 (2): 224–245.

IASB (2015). Staff Paper: Prseent value measurement—discount rates research. Agenda ref 17C. International Accounting Standards Board, London.

Imhoff, E., Lipe, R., and Wright, D. (1993). The effects of recognition versus disclosure on shareholder risk and executive compensation. *Journal of Accounting, Auditing & Finance*, 8 (4): 335–368.

In-Mu, H., Ho, S.S., Bingbing, H., and Woody, W. (2010). Analysts' forecast properties, concentrated ownership and legal institutions. *Journal of Accounting, Auditing & Finance*, 25 (2): 235–259.

Ingram, R.W. and Frazier, K.B. (1980). Environmental performance and corporate disclosure. *Journal of Accounting Research*, 18 (2): 614–622.

Jackson, S.B., (Kelvin) Liu, X., and Cecchini, M. (2009). Economic consequences of firms' depreciation method choice: Evidence from capital investments. *Journal of Accounting and Economics*, 48 (1): 54–68.

Jacob, J. and Jorgensen, B.N. (2007). Earnings management and accounting income aggregation. *Journal of Accounting and Economics*, 43 (2–3): 369–390.

Jamal, K. and Hun-Tong, T. (2010). Joint effects of principles-based versus rules-based standards and auditor type in constraining financial managers' aggressive reporting. *Accounting Review*, 85 (4): 1325–1346.

Jarva, H. (2009). Do firms manage fair value estimates? An examination of SFAS 142 goodwill impairments. *Journal of Business Finance & Accounting*, 36 (9–10): 1059–1086.

— (2014). Economic consequences of SFAS 142 goodwill write-offs. *Accounting & Finance*, 54 (1): 211–235.

Jeanjean, T. and Stolowy, H. (2008). Do accounting standards matter? An exploratory analysis of earnings management before and after IFRS adoption. *Journal of Accounting and Public Policy*, 27 (6): 480–494.

Jegadeesh, N. and Titman, S. (1993). Returns to buying winners and selling losers: Implications for stock market efficiency. *The Journal of Finance*, 48 (1): 65–91.

Jensen, M.C. (1993). The modern industrial revolution, exit, and the failure of internal control systems. *Journal of Finance*, 48 (3): 831–880.

— (1994). Self-interest, altruism, incentives, and agency theory. *Journal of Applied Corporate Finance*, 7 (2): 40–45.

Jensen, M.C. and Meckling, W.H. (1976). Theory of the firm: Managerial behavior, agency costs and ownership structure. *Journal of financial economics*, 3 (4): 305–360.

Jensen, M.C. and Murphy, K.J. (1990). Performance pay and top-management incentives. JSTOR.

Jha, A. (2013). Earnings management around debt-covenant violations—an empirical investigation using a large sample of quarterly data. *Journal of Accounting, Auditing & Finance*, 28 (4): 369–396.

Jiang, H., Habib, A., and Hu, B. (2011). Ownership concentration, voluntary disclosures and information asymmetry in New Zealand. *British Accounting Review*, 43 (1): 39–53.

Jones, J.J. (1991). Earnings management during import relief investigations. *Journal of Accounting Research*, 29 (2): 193–228.

Kahneman, D. and Tversky, A. (1973). On the psychology of prediction. *Psychological Review*, 80 (4): 237–251.

— (1979). Prospect theory: An analysis of decision under risk. *Econometrica*, 47 (2): 263–291.

Kanagaretnam, K., Lobo, G.J., and Yang, D.H. (2004). Joint tests of signaling and income smoothing through bank loan loss provisions. *Contemporary Accounting Research*, 21 (4): 843–884.

Kang, J.K. et al. (1997). Why is there a home bias? An analysis of foreign portfolio equity ownership in Japan. *Journal of Financial Economics*, 46 (1): 3–28.

Kang, S. and Zhao, Y. (2010). Information content and value relevance of depreciation: A cross-industry analysis. *The Accounting Review*, 85 (1): 227–260.

Kang, T., Krishnan, G.V., Wolfe, M.C., and Yi, H.S. (2012). The impact of eliminating the 20-F reconciliation requirement for IFRS filers on earnings persistence and information uncertainty. *Accounting Horizons*, 26 (4): 741–765.

Kaufmann, D., Kraay, A., and Mastruzzi, M. (2007). Governance matters VI: Aggregate and individual governance indicators. *Working Paper*, July 2007.

Ke, B., Petroni, K., and Safieddine, A. (1999). Ownership concentration and sensitivity of executive pay to accounting performance measures: Evidence from publicly and privately-held insurance companies. *Journal of Accounting and Economics*, 28 (2): 185–209.

Ke, D., Ng, L., and Wang, Q. (2010). Home bias in foreign investment decisions. *Journal of International Business Studies*, 41 (6): 960–979.

Kennedy, J., Mitchell, T., and Sefcik, S.E. (1998). Disclosure of contingent environmental liabilities: Some unintended consequences? *Journal of Accounting Research*, 36 (2): 257–277.

Khurana, I.K., Pettway, R.H., and Raman, K. (2001). The liability equivalence of unfunded nuclear decommissioning costs. *Journal of Accounting and Public Policy*, 20 (2): 155–185.

Kim, J.B., Chung, R., and Firth, M. (2003). Auditor conservatism, asymmetric monitoring, and earnings management. *Contemporary Accounting Research*, 20 (2): 323–359.

Kim, M.S. and Kross, W. (1998). The impact of the 1989 change in bank capital standards on loan loss provisions and loan write-offs. *Journal of Accounting and Economics*, 25 (1): 69–99.

Kim, O. and Verrecchia, R.E. (1994). Market liquidity and volume around earnings announcements. *Journal of Accounting and Economics*, 17 (1–2): 41–67.

Kim, Y. and Park, M.S. (2009). Market uncertainty and disclosure of internal control deficiencies under the Sarbanes-Oxley Act. *Journal of Accounting and Public Policy*, 28 (5): 419–445.

Kirk, M.P. and Vincent, J.D. (2014). Professional investor relations within the firm. *The Accounting Review*, 89 (4): 1421–1452.

Klein, A. (2002). Audit committee, board of director characteristics, and earnings management. *Journal of Accounting and Economics*, 33 (3): 375–400.

Kothari, S. (2001). Capital markets research in accounting. *Journal of Accounting and Economics*, 31 (1): 105–231.

Kothari, S., Xu, L., and Short, J.E. (2009). The effect of disclosures by management, analysts, and business press on cost of capital, return volatility, and analyst forecasts. A study using content analysis. *Accounting Review*, 84 (5): 1639–1670.

Kothari, S.P., Leone, A.J., and Wasley, C.E. (2005). Performance matched discretionary accrual measures. *Journal of Accounting and Economics*, 39 (1): 163–197.

KPMG (2008). The application of IFRS: Oil and Gas. KPMG.

Kravet, T. and Muslu, V. (2013). Textual risk disclosures and investors' risk perceptions. *Review of Accounting Studies*, 18 (4): 1088–1122.

Kvaal, E. and Nobes, C. (2012). IFRS policy changes and the continuation of national patterns of IFRS practice. *European Accounting Review*, 21 (2): 343–371.

La Porta, R., Lopez-de Silanes, F., and Shleifer, A. (1999). Corporate ownership around the world. *Journal of Finance*, 54 (2): 471–517.

— (2006). What works in securities laws? *Journal of Finance*, 61 (1): 1–32.

La Porta, R., Lopez-de Silanes, F., Shleifer, A., and Vishny, R. (2002). Investor protection and corporate valuation. *Journal of Finance*, 57 (3): 1147–1170.

— (1998). Law and finance. *Journal of Political Economy*, 106 (6): 1113–1155.

Labelle, R. (1990). Bond covenants and changes in accounting policy: Canadian evidence. *Contemporary Accounting Research*, 6 (2): 677–698.

Laeven, L. and Majnoni, G. (2003). Loan loss provisioning and economic slowdowns: Too much, too late? *Journal of Financial Intermediation*, 12 (2): 178–197. Special Issue for the Federal Reserve Bank of Boston.

Laksmana, I., Tietz, W., and Yang, Y.W. (2012). Compensation discussion and analysis (CD&A): Readability and management obfuscation. *Journal of Accounting & Public Policy*, 31 (2): 185–203.

Lambert, R., Leuz, C., and Verrecchia, R.E. (2007). Accounting information, disclosure, and the cost of capital. *Journal of Accounting Research*, 45 (2): 385–420.

Lambert, R.A. (2001). Contracting theory and accounting. *Journal of Accounting and Economics*, 32 (1-3): 3–87.

Lambert, R.A. and Larcker, D.F. (1987). An analysis of the use of accounting and market measures of performance in executive compensation contracts. *Journal of Accounting research*, 25: 85–125.

Landsman, W.R. (2007). Is fair value accounting information relevant and reliable? Evidence from capital market research. *Accounting and Business Research*, 37: 19–30.

Landsman, W.R., Maydew, E.L., and Thornock, J.R. (2012). The information content of annual earnings announcements and mandatory adoption of IFRS. *Journal of Accounting and Economics*, 53 (1): 34–54.

Lang, M. and Lundholm, R. (1993). Cross-sectional determinants of analyst ratings of corporate disclosures. *Journal of Accounting Research*, 31 (2): 246–271.

Lang, M. and Stice-Lawrence, L. (2015). Textual analysis and international financial reporting: Large sample evidence. *Journal of Accounting and Economics*, 60 (2): 110–135.

Lang, M.H. and Lundholm, R.J. (1996). Corporate disclosure policy and analyst behavior. *Accounting Review*, 71 (4): 467–492.

Lapointe-Antunes, P., Cormier, D., Magnan, M., and Gay-Angers, S. (2006). On the relationship between voluntary disclosure, earnings smoothing and the value-relevance of earnings: The case of Switzerland. *European Accounting Review*, 15 (4): 465–505.

Larcker, D.F., Richardson, S.A., and Tuna, I. (2007). Corporate governance, accounting outcomes, and organizational performance. *Accounting Review*, 82 (4): 963–1008.

Laux, C. and Leuz, C. (2009). The crisis of fair-value accounting: Making sense of the recent debate. *Accounting, Organizations and Society*, 34 (6-7): 826–834.

Laux, R.C. (2013). The association between deferred tax assets and liabilities and future tax payments. *The Accounting Review*, 88 (4): 1357–1383.

Lee, T. (1995). Shaping the US academic accounting research profession: The american accounting association and the social construction of a professional elite. *Critical Perspectives on Accounting*, 6 (3): 241–261.

— (1999). Anatomy of a professional elite: The executive commitee of the American Accounting Association 1916-1996. *Critical Perspectives on Accounting*, 10 (2): 247–264.

Lehavy, R., Li, F., and Merkley, K. (2011). The effect of annual report readability on analyst following and the properties of their earnings forecasts. *Accounting Review*, 86 (3): 1087–1115.

Leuz, C. (2010). Different approaches to corporate reporting regulation: How jurisdictions differ and why. *Accounting and Business Research*, 40 (3): 229–256.

Leuz, C., Nanda, D., and Wysocki., P. (2003). Earnings management and investor protection: An international comparison. *Journal of Financial Economics*, 69 (3): 505–527.

Leuz, C. and Schrand, C. (2009). Disclosure and the cost of capital: Evidence from firms' responses to the Enron shock. Working paper. Available at: http://www.nber.org/papers/w14897.

Leuz, C. and Verrecchia, R.E. (2000). The economic consequences of increased disclosure. *Journal of Accounting Research*, 38 (Supplement: Studies on accounting information and the economics of the firm): 91–124.

Leuz, C. and Wysocki, P.D. (2016). The economics of disclosure and financial reporting regulation: Evidence and suggestions for future research. *Journal of Accounting Research*, 54 (2): 525–622.

Lev, B. and Zarowin, P. (1999). The boundaries of financial reporting and how to extend them. *Journal of Accounting Research*, 37 (2): 353–385.

Levi, S. and Segal, B. (2015). The impact of debt-equity reporting classifications on the firm's decision to issue hybrid securities. *European Accounting Review*, 24 (4): 801–822.

Levine, C.B. and Smith, M.J. (2011). Critical accounting policy disclosures. *Journal of Accounting, Auditing & Finance*, 26 (1): 39–76.

Li, F. (2008). Annual report readability, current earnings, and earnings persistence. *Journal of Accounting and Economics*, 45 (2–3): 221–247.

— (2010a). The information content of forward-looking statements in corporate filings—A naïve Bayesian machine learning approach. *Journal of Accounting Research*, 48 (5): 1049–1102.

Li, J. (2013). Accounting conservatism and debt contracts: Efficient liquidation and covenant renegotiation. *Contemporary Accounting Research*, 30 (3): 1082–1098.

Li, S. (2010b). Does mandatory adoption of international financial reporting standards in the European Union reduce the cost of equity capital? *Accounting Review*, 85 (2): 607–636.

Li, Y. and McConomy, B.J. (1999). An empirical examination of factors affecting the timing of environmental accounting standard adoption and the impact on corporate valuation. *Journal of Accounting, Auditing & Finance*, 14 (3): 279–313.

Li, Z., Shroff, P., Venkataraman, R., and Zhang, I. (2011). Causes and consequences of goodwill impairment losses. *Review of Accounting Studies*, 16 (4): 745–778.

Lindahl, F. and Schadewitz, H. (2013). Are legal families related to financial reporting quality? *Abacus*, 49 (2): 242–267.

Lindblom, C. (1983). The concept of organizational legitimacy and its implications for corporate social responsibility disclosure. *American Accounting Association Public Interest Section*: 220–221.

Liu, C.C. and Ryan, S.G. (2006). Income smoothing over the business cycle: Changes in banks' coordinated management of provisions for loan losses and loan charge-offs from the pre-1990 bust to the 1990s boom. *Accounting Review*, 81 (2): 421–441.

Liu, C.S. and Mittelstaedt, H.F. (2002). Materiality judgments and disclosure of retiree health care costs under SFAS No. 81. *Review of Accounting Studies*, 7: 405–434.

Lo, A.W. (2004). The adaptive markets hypothesis: Market efficiency from an evolutionary perspective. Journal of Portfolio Management, 30(5): 15-29.

— (2005). Reconciling efficient markets with behavioral finance: The adaptive markets hypothesis. Working paper. Available at: https://papers.ssrn.com/sol3/papers.cfm?abstract_id=1702447.

Loughran, T. and McDonald, B. (2016). Textual analysis in accounting and finance: A survey. *Journal of Accounting Research*, 54 (4): 1187–1230.

Lukka, K. and Kasanen, E. (1996). Is accounting a global or a local discipline? Evidence from major research journals. *Accounting, Organizations and Society*, 21 (7 8): 755–773.

Lundholm, R.J. and Myers, L.A. (2002). Bringing the future forward: The effect of disclosure on the returns-earnings relation. *Journal of Accounting Research*, 40 (3): 809–839.

Lundholm, R.J., Rogo, R., and Zhang, J.L. (2014). Restoring the tower of babel: How foreign firms communicate with U.S. investors. *Accounting Review*, 89 (4): 1453–1485.

Luo, S., Courtenay, S.M., and Hossain, M. (2006). The effect of voluntary disclosure, ownership structure and proprietary cost on the return-future earnings relation. *Pacific-Basin Finance Journal*, 14 (5): 501–521.

Lyon, J. (2010). Accounting for leases: Telling it how it is. *Journal of Property Investment & Finance*, 28 (5): 328–332.

Maijoor, S.J. and Vanstraelen, A. (2006). Earnings management within Europe: The effects of member state audit environment, audit firm quality and international capital markets. *Accounting and Business Research*, 36 (1): 33–52.

Maines, L.A. and McDaniel, L.S. (2000). Effects of comprehensive-income characteristics on nonprofessional investors' judgments: The role of financial-statement presentation format. *Accounting Review*, 75 (2): 179–207.

Mansi, S.A., Maxell, W.F., and Miller, D.P. (2004). Does auditor quality and tenure matter to investors? Evidence from the bond market. *Journal of Accounting Research*, 42 (4): 755–793.

Marques, A. (2010). Disclosure strategies among S&P 500 firms: Evidence on the disclosure of non-GAAP financial measures and financial statements in earnings press releases. *The British Accounting Review*, 42 (2): 119–131.

Marton, J. and Runesson, E. (2017). The predictive ability of loan loss provisions in banks—Effects of accounting standards, enforcement and incentives. *The British Accounting Review*, 49 (2): 162–180.

Marton, J. and Wagenhofer, A. (2010). Comment on the IASB discussion paper 'preliminary views on revenue recognition in contracts with customers'. *Accounting in Europe*, 7 (1): 3–13.

Masters-Stout, B., Costigan, M.L., and Lovata, L.M. (2008). Goodwill impairments and chief executive officer tenure. *Critical Perspectives on Accounting*, 19 (8): 1370–1383.

Masulis, R.W., Wang, C., and Xie, F. (2012). Globalizing the boardroom—The effects of foreign directors on corporate governance and firm performance. *Journal of Accounting and Economics*, 53 (3): 527–554.

Matsunaga, S.R. and Park, C.W. (2001). The effect of missing a quarterly earnings benchmark on the CEO's annual bonus. *The Accounting Review*, 76 (3): 313–332.

Mazzi, F., André, P., Dionysiou, D., and Tsalavoutas, I. (2017). Compliance with goodwill-related mandatory disclosure requirements and the cost of equity capital. *Accounting and Business Research*, 47 (3): 268–312.

McConnell, D., Haslem, J.A., and Gibson, V.R. (1986). The President's Letter to stockholders: A new look. *Financial Analysts Journal*, 42 (5): 66–70.

McNichols, M.F. (2002). Discussion of the quality of accruals and earnings: The role of accrual estimation errors. *Accounting Review*, 77 (Supplement): 61–69.

Meder, A., Schwartz, S.T., Spires, E.E., and Young, R.A. (2011). Structured finance and mark-to-model accounting: A few simple illustrations. *Accounting Horizons*, 25 (3): 559–576.

Mehran, H. (1995). Executive compensation structure, ownership, and firm performance. *Journal of Financial Economics*, 38: 163–184.

Melumad, N.D., Weyns, G., and Ziv, A. (1999). Comparing alternative hedge accounting standards: Shareholders' perspective. *Review of Accounting Studies*, 4 (3): 265–292.

Mergenthaler, R., Rajgopal, S., and Srinivasan, S. (2012). CEO and CFO career penalties to missing quarterly analysts forecasts. Working paper. Available at: https://papers.ssrn.com/sol3/ papers.cfm?abstract_id=1152421.

Merkley, K.J. (2014). Narrative disclosure and earnings performance: Evidence from R&D disclosures. *Accounting Review*, 89 (2): 725–757.

Meyer, J.W. and Rowan, B. (1977). Institutionalized organizations: Formal structure as myth and ceremony. *American Journal of Sociology*, 83 (2): 340–363.

Michiels, A., Voordeckers, W., Lybaert, N., and Steijvers, T. (2013). CEO compensation in private family firms pay-for-performance and the moderating role of ownership and management. *Family Business Review*, 26 (2): 140–160.

Milburn, J.A. (2008). The relationship between fair value, market value, and efficient markets. *Accounting Perspectives*, 7 (4): 293–316.

Miller, M.H. and Modigliani, F. (1961). Dividend policy, growth, and the valuation of shares. *The Journal of Business*, 34 (4): 411–433.

Mitra, S. and Hossain, M. (2009). Value-relevance of pension transition adjustments and other comprehensive income components in the adoption year of SFAS No. 158. *Review of Quantitative Finance and Accounting*, 33 (3): 279–301.

Modigliani, F. and Miller, M.H. (1958). The cost of capital, corporation finance and the theory of investment. *American Economic Review*, 48 (3): 261–297.

Moehrle, S.R. (2002). Do firms use restructuring charge reversals to meet earnings targets? *The Accounting Review*, 77 (2): 397–413.

Moses, O.D. (1987). Income smoothing and incentives: Empirical tests using accounting changes. *Accounting Review*: 358–377.

Moyer, S.E. (1990). Capital adequacy ratio regulations and accounting choices in commercial banks. *Journal of Accounting and Economics*, 13 (2): 123–154.

Muller, I.K.A. (1999). An examination of the voluntary recognition of acquired brand names in the United Kingdom. *Journal of Accounting and Economics*, 26 (1-3): 179–191.

Muller, I.K.A. and Riedl, E.J. (2002). External monitoring of property appraisal estimates and information asymmetry. *Journal of Accounting Research*, 40 (3): 865–881.

Murray, A., Sinclair, D., Power, D., and Gray, R. (2006). Do financial markets care about social and environmental disclosure? Further evidence and exploration from the UK. *Accounting, Auditing & Accountability Journal*, 19 (2): 228–255.

Muslu, V., Radhakrishnan, S., Subramanyam, K.R., and Lim, D. (2015). Forward-looking MD&A disclosures and the information environment. *Management Science*, 61 (5): 931–948.

Nagar, V., Nanda, D., and Wysocki, P. (2003). Discretionary disclosure and stock-based incentives. *Journal of Accounting and Economics*, 34 (1-3): 283–309.

Nelson, K. (1996). Fair value accounting for commercial banks: An empirical analysis of SFAS No. 107. *Accounting Review*, 71 (2): 161–182.

Nelson, M.W. (2003). Behavioral evidence on the effects of principles- and rules-based standards. *Accounting Horizons*, 17 (1): 91–104.

Nelson, M.W., Elliott, J.A., and Tarpley, R.L. (2002). Evidence from auditors about managers' and auditors' earnings management decisions. *The Accounting Review*, 77 (s-1): 175–202.

Nichols, N.B., Street, D.L., and Cereola, S.J. (2012). An analysis of the impact of adopting IFRS 8 on the segment disclosures of European blue chip companies. *Journal of International Accounting, Auditing and Taxation*, 21 (2): 79–105.

Nini, G., Smith, D.C., and Sufi, A. (2012). Creditor control rights, corporate governance, and firm value. *The Review of Financial Studies*, 25 (6): 1713–1761.

Nissim, D. (2003). Reliability of banks' fair value disclosure for loans. *Review of Quantitative Finance & Accounting*, 20: 355–384.

Nissim, D. and Penman, S.H. (2001). Ratio analysis and equity valuation: From research to practice. *Review of Accounting Studies*, 6 (1): 109–154.

Nobes, C. (1992). International classification of financial reporting. 2nd edition. Routledge.

— (2013). The continued survival of international differences under IFRS. *Accounting and Business Research*, 43 (2): 83–111.

Ohlson, J.A. (1995). Earnings, book values, and dividends in equity valuation. *Contemporary Accounting Research*, 11 (2): 661–687.

— (2015). Accounting research and common sense. *Abacus*, 51 (4): 525–535.

Ohlson, J.A. and Aier, J.K. (2009). On the analysis of firms' cash flows. *Contemporary Accounting Research*, 26 (4): 1091–1114.

Ohlson, J.A. and Penman, S.H. (1992). Disaggregated accounting data as explanatory variables for returns. *Journal of Accounting, Auditing & Finance*, 7 (4): 553–573.

Ohlson, J.A. and Shroff, P.K. (1992). Changes versus levels in earnings as explanatory variables for returns: Some theoretical considerations. *Journal of Accounting Research*, 30 (2): 210–226.

Orpurt, S.F. and Zang, Y. (2009). Do direct cash flow disclosures help predict future operating cash flows and earnings? *The Accounting Review*, 84 (3): 893–935.

Ou, J.A. and Penman, S.H. (1989). Financial statement analysis and the prediction of stock returns. *Journal of Accounting and Economics*, 11 (4): 295–329.

Overland, C. and Samani, N. (2017). The sheep watching the shepherd: The monitoring of financial reporting and employee representatives. Working Paper. Available at: https://papers.ssrn.com/sol3/papers.cfm?abstract_id=2832770.

Ozkan, N., Singer, Z., and You, H. (2012). Mandatory IFRS adoption and the contractual usefulness of accounting information in executive compensation. *Journal of Accounting Research*, 50 (4): 1077–1107.

Paananen, M. and Lin, H. (2009). The development of accounting quality of IAS and IFRS over time: The case of Germany. *Journal of International Accounting Research*, 8 (1): 31–55.

Panaretou, A., Shackleton, M.B., and Taylor, P.A. (2013). Corporate risk management and hedge accounting. *Contemporary Accounting Research*, 30 (1): 116–139.

Park, M.S., Taewoo Park, M.S., and Ro, B.T. (1999). Fair value disclosures for investment securities and bank equity: Evidence SFAS No. 115. *Journal of Accounting, Auditing & Finance*, 14 (3): 347–370.

Patten, D.M. (2002). The relation between environmental performance and environmental disclosure: a research note. *Accounting, Organizations and Society*, 27 (8): 763–773.

Peasnell, K.V., Pope, P., and Young, S. (2000). Accrual management to meet earnings targets: UK evidence pre- and post-Cadbury. *British Accounting Review*, 32 (4): 415–445.

— (2005). Board monitoring and earnings management: Do outside directors influence abnormal accruals? *Journal of Business Finance & Accounting*, 32 (7-8): 1311–1346.

Peltzman, S. (1976). Toward a more general theory of regulation. *The Journal of Law and Economics*, 19 (2): 211–240.

Penman, S.H. (2007). Financial reporting quality: Is fair value a plus or a minus? *Accounting and Business Research*, 37 (supplement 1): 33–43.

— (2010). Financial Statement Analysis and Security Valuation. 4th edition. McGraw Hill Higher Education.

— (2012). Financial Statement Analysis and Security Valuation. 5th edition. McGraw Hill Higher Education.

Penman, S.H. and Sougiannis, T. (1998). A comparison of dividend, cash flow, and earnings approaches to equity valuation. *Contemporary Accounting Research*, 15 (3): 343–383.

Perez, D., Salas-Fumas, V., and Saurina, J. (2008). Earnings and capital management in alternative loan loss provision regulatory regimes. *European Accounting Review*, 17 (3): 423–445.

Perry, T. and Zenner, M. (2001). Pay for performance? Government regulation and the structure of compensation contracts. *Journal of Financial Economics*, 62 (3): 453–488.

Peters, G. and Romi, A. (2013). Discretionary compliance with mandatory environmental disclosures: Evidence from SEC filings. *Journal of Accounting and Public Policy*, 32 (4): 213–236.

Peters, R.M. and Emery, D.R. (1978). The role of negative numbers in the development of double entry bookkeeping. *Journal of Accounting Research*, 16 (2): 424–426.

Petersen, C. and Plenborg, T. (2010). How do firms implement impairment tests of goodwill? *Abacus*, 46 (4): 419–446.

Petroni, K.R. (1992). Optimistic reporting in the property-casualty insurance industry. *Journal of Accounting and Economics*, 15 (4): 485–508.

Pettersson, A.K. (2015). Nedskrivning av fartyg—En studie av hur IAS 36 har tillämpats i Europeiska rederier. Göteborg: BAS Publishing.

Pope, P.F. and McLeay, S.J. (2011). The European IFRS experiment: Objectives, research challenges and some early evidence. *Accounting and Business Research*, 41 (3): 233–266.

Popper, K.R. (1959). The Logic of Scientific Discovery. Eleventh edition. London: Hutchinson.

Powell, W. (1961). Report on the accounting research activities of the American Institute of Certified Public Accountants. *Accounting Review*, 36 (1): 26–31.

Prasad, A. and Mir, R. (2002). Digging deep for meaning: A critical hermeneutic analysis of CEO letters to shareholders in the oil industry. *Journal of Business Communication*, 39 (1): 92–116.

Prencipe, A., Markarian, G., and Pozza, L. (2008). Earnings management in family firms: Evidence from R&D cost capitalization in Italy. *Family Business Review*, 21 (1): 71–88.

PWC (2010). IFRS news—Emerging issues and practical guidance. PricewaterhouseCoopers.
Ramanna, K. and Watts, R. (2012). Evidence on the use of unverifiable estimates in required goodwill impairment. *Review of Accounting Studies*, 17 (4): 749–780.
Ravenscroft, S. and Williams, P.F. (2009). Making imaginary worlds real: The case of expensing employee stock options. *Accounting, Organizations and Society*, 34 (6–7): 770–786.
Rehnberg, P. (2012). Redovisning av immateriella tillgångar i samband med förvärvskalkylering - principbaserade redovisningsregler och relevans (Reporting intangible assets in business combinations - principles-based accounting standards and relevance). Göteborg: BAS Publishing.
Reither, C.L. (1998). What are the best and the worst accounting standards? *Accounting Horizons*, 12 (3): 283–292.
Renders, A. and Gaeremynck, A. (2012). Corporate governance, principal-principal agency conflicts, and firm value in European listed companies. *Corporate Governance: An International Review*, 20 (2): 125–143.
Richardson, S., Tuna, I., and Wysocki, P. (2010). Accounting anomalies and fundamental analysis: A review of recent research advances. *Journal of Accounting and Economics*, 50 (2-3): 410–454.
Riedl, E.I. (2004). An examination of long-lived asset impairments. *Accounting Review*, 79 (3): 823–852.
Rivard, R.J., Bland, E., and Hatfield Morris, G.B. (2003). Income smoothing behavior of U.S. banks under revised international capital requirements. *International Advances in Economic Research*, 9 (4): 288–294.
Roberts, M.R. and Sufi, A. (2009). Renegotiation of financial contracts: Evidence from private credit agreements. *Journal of Financial Economics*, 93 (2): 159–184.
Rogers, J.L. and Van Buskirk, A. (2009). Shareholder litigation and changes in disclosure behavior. *Journal of Accounting and Economics*, 47 (1–2): 136–156.
Roychowdhury, S. (2006). Earnings management through real activities manipulation. *Journal of Accounting and Economics*, 42 (3): 335–370.
Runesson, E. (2015). Disclosures and judgment in financial reporting: Essays on accounting quality under International Financial Accounting Standards. PhD thesis at the University of Gothenburg. Göteborg: BAS Publishing. ISBN: 978-91-7246-335-6.
Runesson, E. and Samani, N. (2018). Goodwill or "No-will": A study of CEO hubris. Working Paper.
Ryan, B., Scapens, R.W., and Theobald, M. (2002). Research method and methodology in finance and accounting. London: Thomson.
Salancik, G.R. and Meindl, J.R. (1984). Corporate attributions as strategic illusions of management control. *Administrative Science Quarterly*, 29 (2): 238–254.
Schallheim, J., Wells, K., and Whitby, R.J. (2013). Do leases expand debt capacity? *Journal of Corporate Finance*, 23: 368–381.
Schipper, K. (2003). Principles-based accounting standards. *Accounting Horizons*, 17 (1): 61–72.
— (2007). Required disclosures in financial reports. *Accounting Review*, 82 (2): 301–326.
Schroeder, R., Sevin, S., and Yarbrough, K. (2005). Reporting effects of SFAS 143 on nuclear decommissioning costs. *International Advances in Economic Research*, 11 (4): 449–458.
Searle, J.R. (1995). The Construction of Social Reality. London: Penguin Books Ltd.
SEC (2003). Study Pursuant to Section 108(d) of the Sarbanes-Oxley Act of 2002 on the Adoption by the United States Financial Reporting System of a Principles-Based Accounting System. Securities and Exchange Commission, Washington, D.C. Available at: http://www.sec.gov/news/studies/principles-basedstand.htm.
Segars, A.H. and Kohut, G.F. (2001). Strategic communication through the World Wide Web: An empirical model of effecitiveness in the CEO's letter to shareholders. *Journal of Management Studies*, 38 (4): 535–556.
Sengupta, P. (1998). Corporate disclosure quality and the cost of debt. *Accounting Review*, 73 (4): 459–474.
Shalev, R., Zhang, I.X., and Zhang, Y. (2013). CEO compensation and fair value accounting: Evidence from purchase price allocation. *Journal of Accounting Research*, 51 (4): 819–854.

Sharpe, W.F. (1991). The arithmetic of active management. *Financial Analysts Journal*, 47 (1): 7–9.
Shivakumar, L. (2006). Accruals, cash flows and the post-earnings-announcement drift. *Journal of Business Finance & Accounting*, 33 (1-2): 1–25.
— (2013). The role of financial reporting in debt contracting and in stewardship. *Accounting and Business Research*, 43 (4): 362–383.
Shleifer, A. and Vishny, R.W. (1997). A survey of corporate governance. *Journal of Finance*, 52 (2): 737–783.
Shortridge, R.T. and Smith, P.A. (2009). Understanding the changes in accounting thought. *Research in Accounting Regulation*, 21 (1): 11–18.
Simnett, R., Vanstraelen, A., and Chua, W.F. (2009). Assurance on sustainability reports: An international comparison. *The Accounting Review*, 84 (3): 937–967.
Simon, H.A. (1955). A behavioral model of rational choice. *The Quarterly Journal of Economics*, 69 (1): 99–118.
Sloan, R.G. (1996). Do stock prices fully reflect information in accruals and cash flows about future earnings. *The Accounting Review*, 71 (3): 289–315.
Smith Jr, C.W. and Watts, R.L. (1992). The investment opportunity set and corporate financing, dividend, and compensation policies. *Journal of Financial Economics*, 32 (3): 263–292.
So, S. and Smith, M. (2009). Value-relevance of presenting changes in fair value of investment properties in the income statement: Evidence from Hong Kong. *Accounting and Business Research*, 39 (2): 103–118.
Spence, M. (1973). Job market signaling. *The Quarterly Journal of Economics*, 87 (3): 355–374.
Srinidhi, B., Gul, F.A., and Tsui, J. (2011). Female directors and earnings quality. *Contemporary Accounting Research*, 28 (5): 1610–1644.
Srivastava, A. (2014). Why have measures of earnings quality changed over time? *Journal of Accounting and Economics*, 57 (2): 196–217.
Sterling, R.R. (1990). Positive accounting: An assessment. *Abacus*, 26 (2): 97–135.
Stevens, W.P. (1984). Market reaction to corporate environmental performance. *Advances in Accounting*, 1: 41–61.
Stigler, G.J. (1971). The theory of economic regulation. *Bell Journal of Economics and Management Science*, 2 (1): 3–21.
Suchman, M.C. (1995). Managing legitimacy: Strategic and institutional approaches. *The Academy of Management Review*, 20 (3): 571–610.
Sufi, A. (2009). Bank lines of credit in corporate finance: An empirical analysis. *The Review of Financial Studies*, 22 (3): 1057–1088.
Swales Jr., G.S. (1988). Another look at the President's Letter to stockholders. *Financial Analysts Journal*, 44 (2): 71.
Swedish Corporate Governance Board (2016). The Swedish Corporate Governance Code.
Tan, H., Wang, S., and Welker, M. (2011). Analyst following and forecast accuracy after mandated IFRS adoptions. *Journal of Accounting Research*, 49 (5): 1307–1357.
Tan, H.Y., Ying Wang, E., and Zhou, B. (2014). When the use of positive language backfires: The joint effect of tone, readability, and investor sophistication on earnings judgments. *Journal of Accounting Research*, 52 (1): 273–302.
Tengblad, S. and Ohlsson, C. (2010). The framing of corporate social responsibility and the globalization of national business systems: A longitudinal case study. *Journal of Business Ethics*, 93 (4): 653–669.
Thomas, J.K. and Zhang, H. (2002). Inventory changes and future returns. *Review of Accounting Studies*, 7 (2): 163–187.
Thomas, W.B. (1999). A test of the market's mispricing of domestic and foreign earnings. *Journal of Accounting and Economics*, 28 (3): 243–267.
Tversky, A. and Kahneman, D. (1974). Judgment under uncertainty: Heuristics and biases. *Science*, 185 (4157): 1124–1131.

— (1992). Advances in prospect theory: Cumulative representation of uncertainty. *Journal of Risk and uncertainty*, 5 (4): 297–323.
Twedt, B. and Rees, L. (2012). Reading between the lines: An empirical examination of qualitative attributes of financial analysts' reports. *Journal of Accounting & Public Policy*, 31 (1): 1–21.
van Tendeloo, B. and Vanstraelen, A. (2005). Earnings management under German GAAP versus IFRS. *European Accounting Review*, 14 (1): 155–180.
Vasarhelyi, M.A., Kogan, A., and Tuttle, B.M. (2015). Big Data in accounting: An overview. *Accounting Horizons*, 29 (2): 381–396.
Venkatachalam, M. (1996). Value-relevance of banks' derivatives disclosures. *Journal of Accounting and Economics*, 22 (1-3): 327–355.
Verrecchia, R.E. (1983). Discretionary disclosure. *Journal of Accounting and Economics*, 5 (Supplement C): 179–194.
— (2001). Essays on disclosure. *Journal of Accounting and Economics*, 32 (1): 97–180.
Verriest, A., Gaeremynck, A., and Thornton, D. (2013). The impact of corporate governance on IFRS adoption choices. *European Accounting Review*, 22 (1): 39–77.
Voulgaris, G., Stathopoulos, K., and Walker, M. (2014). IFRS and the use of accounting-based performance measures in executive pay. *The International Journal of Accounting*, 49 (4): 479–514.
Wagenhofer, A. (2014). The role of revenue recognition in performance reporting. *Accounting and Business Research*, 44 (4): 349–379.
Walden, W. and Schwartz, B. (1997). Environmental disclosures and public policy pressure. *Journal of Accounting and Public Policy*, 16 (2): 125–154.
Walker, S. and Lee, T., eds. (1999). Studies in Early Professionalism: Scottish Chartered Accountants, 1853-1918. New works in accounting history. Garland.
Wall, L.D. and Koch, T.W. (2000). Bank loan loss accounting: A review of theoretical and empirical evidence. *Federal Reserve Bank of Atlanta Economic Review*, Second Quarter.
Wang, D. (2006). Founding family ownership and earnings quality. *Journal of Accounting Research*, 44 (3): 619–656.
Warren Jr, J.D., Moffitt, K.C., and Byrnes, P. (2015). How Big Data will change accounting. *Accounting Horizons*, 29 (2): 397–407.
Watson, H.J. and Wixom, B.H. (2007). The current state of business intelligence. *Computer*, 40 (9): 96–99.
Watts, R.L. (1992). Accounting choice theory and market-based research in accounting. *The British Accounting Review*, 24 (3): 235–267.
— (2003). Conservatism in accounting part I: Explanations and implications. *Accounting Horizons*, 17 (3): 207–221.
— (2006). What has the invisible hand achieved? *Accounting and Business Research*, 36 (sup1): 51–61.
Watts, R.L. and Zimmerman, J.L. (1978). Towards a positive theory of the determination of accounting standards. *The Accounting Review*, 53 (1): 112.
— (1979). The demand for and supply of accounting theories: The market for excuses. *The Accounting Review*, 54 (2): 273–305.
— (1986). Positive Accounting Theory. Englewood Cliffs, NJ: Prentice-Hall.
— (1990). Positive accounting theory: A ten year perspective. *The Accounting Review*, 65 (1) : 131–156.
Webb, K.A., Cahan, S.F., and Sun, J. (2008). The effect of globalization and legal environment on voluntary disclosure. *International Journal of Accounting*, 43 (3): 219–245.
Weber, J. (2010). Assessing the 'tone at the top': The moral reasoning of CEOs in the automobile industry. *Journal of Business Ethics*, 92 (2): 167–182.
Whittington, G. (2008a). Fair value and the IASB/FASB conceptual framework project: An alternative view. *Abacus*, 44 (2): 139–168.
—(2008b). Harmonisation or discord? the critical role of the IASB conceptual framework review. *Journal of Accounting and Public Policy*, 27 (6): 495–502.

Williamson, O.E. (1979). Transaction-cost economics: the governance of contractual relations. *The Journal of Law and Economics*, 22 (2): 233–261.
Wiseman, J. (1982). An evaluation of environmental disclosures made in corporate annual reports. *Accounting, Organizations and Society*, 7 (1): 53–63.
Wu, J.S. and Zhang, I.X. (2009). The voluntary adoption of internationally recognized accounting standards and firm internal performance evaluation. *Accounting Review*, 84 (4): 1281–1309.
Wyatt, A. (2005). Accounting recognition of intangible assets: Theory and evidence on economic determinants. *The Accounting Review*, 80 (3): 967–1003.
Xie, B., Davidson III, W.N., and DaDalt, P.J. (2003). Earnings management and corporate governance: The role of the board and the audit committee. *Journal of Corporate Finance*, 9 (3): 295–316.
Xie, H. (2001). The mispricing of abnormal accruals. *The Accounting Review*, 76 (3): 357–373.
Yang, M.L. (2010). The impact of controlling families and family CEOs on earnings management. *Family Business Review*, 23 (3): 266–279.
Ye, K. (2010). Independent director cash compensation and earnings management. *Journal of Accounting and Public Policy*, 33 (4): 391–400.
Zachary, M.A., McKenny, A., Short, J.C., and Payne, G.T. (2011). Family business and market orientation: Construct validation and comparative analysis. *Family Business Review*, 24 (3): 233–251.
Zeff, S.A. (1984). Some junctures in the evolution of the process of establishing accounting principles in the U.S.A.: 1917–1972. *The Accounting Review*, 59 (3): 447.
— (1989). Recent trends in accounting education and research in the USA: Some implications for UK academics. *The British Accounting Review*, 21 (2): 159–176.
Zhou, H. (2007). Auditing standards, increased accounting disclosure, and information asymmetry: Evidence from an emerging market. *Journal of Accounting and Public Policy*, 26 (5): 584–620.
Zimmerman, J.L. (2015). The role of accounting in the twenty-first century firm. *Accounting and Business Research*, 45 (4): 1–25.
Zucker, L.G. (1987). Institutional theories of organization. *Annual Review of Sociology*, 13 (1): 443–464.

INDEX